A Destiny of Undying Greatness:

Kiffin Rockwell and the Boys Who Remembered Lafayette

Mark M. Trapp

www.undyinggreatness.com

System D Publishing Company

Chicago, 2019

ISBN: 978-1-7331712-2-9

For Stinky ... my favorite pilot

Kiffin killed this morning aerial battle in Alsace.

-Lieutenant William Thaw, telegram dated September 23, 1916[1]

O white clouds floating above my head
Sail on, sail on, sail over the sea,
Til you find the place where my boy lies dead,
And kiss him and bathe him with tears for me.

"After the Wreck," by James Chester Rockwell, 1888[2]

Table of Contents

Part Four – Lafayette, we are here!

Afterword

The Boys Who Remembered Lafayette

Author's Note

Acknowledgements

Deeds are the only medium through which we may become noble.

- *James Chester Rockwell, 1885*[3]

Introduction

Not terribly far from the Swiss border, in a beautiful little village in France, two flags – the tricolour of France and the stars and stripes of the United States of America – fly over a single grave. Marked by a simple cross exactly like those that surround it, the grave is the final resting place of a boy named Kiffin. How and more importantly *why* this American son came to lie in French soil, under the flags of two proud nations, is a tale worth telling.

* * * * *

Although few remember it now, the name Kiffin Yates Rockwell was once recognized around the world. At his passing one hundred years ago, Kiffin was a celebrity, a war hero, his name known throughout America and Europe. He evoked the distinctly American spirit, and his death helped propel his home country into World War I on the side of its long-time friend and ally France.

Kiffin was an aviator, a fighter pilot; one of the first Americans to earn the title. An early biographer and member of his aviation unit called Kiffin a "born soldier," and he was.[4] Soldiering was in Kiffin's blood – he descended from a long line of soldiers and preachers, men of principle and purpose, men of deeds and action, men whom others chose to follow. Both of his grandfathers and a step-grandfather fought in the Civil War, and young Kiffin heard plenty about military life. His mother's father, Enoch Shaw Ayres, never tired of recounting the battles in which he had participated, glorifying the role of the citizen soldier. Raised on tales of combat and gallantry, it was only natural for Kiffin to seek to prove himself when war struck the European continent.

In fact, the Great War presented the soldierly stage on which Kiffin had yearned to step much of his young life. Even as his own country proved unwilling to enter the fray, Kiffin immediately and eagerly sided with France, and was perhaps the very first American volunteer. Before becoming a *chasse* (pursuit) pilot, Kiffin enlisted in the French Foreign Legion, and received wounds taking the German trenches on the front lines in Western France. After recovering from his injury, Kiffin was granted a transfer into the French aviation service.

While France permitted Americans to serve in the Foreign Legion, it initially resisted accepting Americans into aviation. There was no shortage of French young men seeking out this exciting work and, at least at the outset of the war, neither France nor the other involved nations realized the important role aviation would play in the conflict.

It didn't take long, however, for the French government to recognize three things: first, the war would not end quickly; second, aviation would be an important part of the war, and modern warfare generally; and third, having Americans voluntarily flying for France in a close-run war would likely create a wonderful propaganda opportunity. Perhaps, thought the French, they could use American volunteers to influence the as-yet sleeping United States to wake up, and enter the fray. Soon enough, at least partially to maximize the press coverage, France even created a special all-American unit, the *Escadrille Américaine* – the American Squadron. This allowed the French to broadcast America's participation, and build support for her further involvement, while also filling a void for an American public half-shamed by its own country's failure to take an active and official role in the astonishingly bloody struggle. Kiffin was among the initial aviators assigned to the newly-formed unit.

Boosted by Kiffin's quick and decisive victory in his first encounter with a German plane, the squadron was an immediate sensation. As volunteer soldiers flying for France, Kiffin and his comrades soon captured the world's imagination dogfighting above the skies of Europe. Their deeds flashed from the front to Paris, and from there popped up in headlines across America. The romantic idea of pilots as knights-errant, and the gallant nature of early aerial combat, seemed ready-made for an American public eager for news of the war to end all wars, especially with their own country sitting on the sidelines.

The *escadrille* came along at a time when both aeroplanes and movies were establishing themselves in the public consciousness. Recognizing this, the French government hastily filmed propaganda footage of the pilots at the front and, working with an American film company, quickly released a movie showcasing the daring young aviators. The film was a hit in both Paris and in America, raising both awareness and much-needed funds for the war effort. The newsreel footage and press accounts combined to make household names of the swashbuckling flyboys, especially Kiffin, who won the squadron's first victory just after the filming took place.

But Kiffin's appeal was personal, as well. Although he did not make friends easily, Kiffin evoked strong feelings in and demonstrated great loyalty to those he made. A fellow pilot said Kiffin was "hard to know at first but once your friend he would stick all the way through."[5] A friend who fought beside him in both the trenches and the skies wrote that Kiffin "was one of the noblest and most courageous men I have met in my life."[6] After his death, another soldier said plaintively: "it ain't every day you meet fellows like Kiffin."[7]

Kiffin's fame lived on after the war. His name and the names of the other brave pilots of the *Lafayette Escadrille*, as the squadron eventually became known following a diplomatic tiff with Germany, were prominently featured on a beautiful and impressive war memorial in Paris. Later they appeared on bubble-gum cards and cigar rings and were featured in dime magazines and comic book strips, their deeds glorified (and sometimes exaggerated) beyond all proportion.[8] One anecdote had Kiffin knocking out a German pilot mid-flight before commandeering his plane and returning to France with both the subdued aviator and the plane.[9] Another dubbed Kiffin the "four-shot fighter," commemorating his feat of killing two German sky-fighters and bringing down his first plane with just four bullets, after which he (supposedly) modestly joked that the other pilots in his outfit "wouldn't have wasted the other three shots like I did."[10] Whether true or not, these stories paid tribute to the accomplishments of the best America had to offer. Sadly, today they evoke a different time and place – an America eager and willing to celebrate its heroes and ideals.[11]

* * * * *

Although Kiffin called himself a "dreamer," and was rather a wanderer, he had a strong personality and an uncompromising moral core. While not arrogant, Kiffin could show flashes of pride, and had a huge independent streak. He was once accurately described as "uncommon in his ability to know what it was he wanted."[12] Unquestionably, Kiffin felt that making his own decisions – and reaping the reward or suffering the consequences – was a significant part of becoming a man. In a letter telling his mother of his decision to make for France, Kiffin bluntly stated, "I must and will live my life as I think best even though I am often mistaken."[13]

Until the outbreak of the war, Kiffin's restlessness and lack of focus detracted somewhat from his evident talents. While intelligent and capable, before he turned nineteen, Kiffin had left two colleges and one prep school without graduating and had also resigned a coveted appointment to the Naval Academy. While he always displayed great potential and had achieved limited success in a few jobs and other endeavors, Kiffin's heart never seemed to be in it. In fact, it almost began to appear as if the right opportunity to match Kiffin's big dreams might never come along. As his older brother Paul wrote, Kiffin seemed merely to be "unconsciously marking time," and "usually had a far-away, dreamy look in his eyes[.]"[14]

The Great War changed all that. Its eruption offered the ultimate opportunity for Kiffin, as it provided the perfect proving ground for a would-be soldier. Based on his admiration for the actions of the Marquis de Lafayette during the American Revolution, Kiffin felt duty bound to take up arms in defense of France when she was threatened. Of course, he also wanted to live the soldier's life, to see war, and more than anything to prove himself.

Kiffin's wartime letters reveal a principled yet imperfect idealist. He did not like anything he perceived as unjust and refused to choose sides based on expediency or self-interest. While slow to anger, Kiffin would take offense when he felt he was being cheated and bristled if not given proper recognition for his work. Even so, Kiffin shunned the limelight and sought to avoid publicity, despite the numerous and easy opportunities he had to engage in self-promotion. And though, unlike many of his comrades, Kiffin was not independently wealthy, he shared what he had with those who had less.

If conduct in war is the truest measure of a man, during his two years in France, first in the dirt and then in the clouds, Kiffin's measure was taken and not found wanting. When he became part of the *Escadrille Américaine*, a tumbler fell into place, and unlocked the door to Kiffin's soul. His commanding officer called Kiffin a "born fighter."[15] A fellow pilot described him as "a man all the way through," while another would later write that men like Kiffin "are rare and unmistakable when met; they stand a little aloof from the rest of the world and radiate a sense of great things – an atmosphere which shames the cynic and stills the voice of the doubter."[16] Not long after Kiffin's death, one writer suggested there was "something dashing, brilliant, about him," something "that evoked applause."[17]

In this respect, Kiffin was like a number of the Americans who volunteered for France. They too, were idealistic and did not want to miss this chance to prove their mettle and take a stand for liberty and civilization. John Jay Chapman, the grandson of John Jay, the first Chief Justice of the Supreme Court, and father of Kiffin's best friend and fellow American pilot Victor Chapman, wrote "the more we find out about these boys the more we see that in each of them there was a soul's history that led up to this especial consummation."[18] In the crucible of war, Kiffin found companions whose ideals and conduct equaled his own, and among such men he rose to the full measure of his potential.

* * * * *

Kiffin had tremendous strength of will, and a genuine greatness of soul. He was the real deal. What you saw was what you got. Kiffin's war-time decisions were based on principle, rather than expedience, and often made without regard to his own comfort, self-interest or even life. In short, Kiffin's soul was the soul of a man, and his deeds the deeds of a man. Men like Kiffin are uncommon in any age, but in the century since his death, such men have become increasingly rare, and today are virtually unknown.

But even one hundred years ago, Kiffin stood apart. Unlike most Americans of the time, Kiffin was not in any sense "neutral" – in the war, or in life.[19] Kiffin understood the simple truth that some things are worth fighting for; indeed, there are some things for which one must fight. Because of this, in taking up for France, Kiffin did not consider himself a volunteer. Rather, he felt he was merely doing his duty, paying his debt, and even amidst the grime and sludge of the trenches, Kiffin always believed he was serving a higher purpose. As his beloved brother wrote, Kiffin had "a spirit which could rise high above the grim horror and miserable sordidness of war and see all the glory and wonder of it."[20]

One Legionnaire described Kiffin as "a real American."[21] This was a good description, for on some elemental level, Kiffin understood the old scriptural injunction that Lincoln forged into America's creed – that right makes might. Kiffin saw clearly the far-reaching consequences of the awful conflagration into which he had thrown himself, and sensed that if France were defeated, liberty itself could be extinguished. So in that great conflict, whether obligated or not, Kiffin would be found on the battlefield.[22] Ultimately, Kiffin's commitment to live like a man caused him to die like one.

* * * * *

To the reader, a gentle (if obvious) reminder: everyone in this book lived in a different time, with different views, customs and mores. From our perch in the present, it is all too easy to pass judgment on and fault prior generations for views we no longer share. But as the latest entries on the family pedigree charts of mankind, we would do well to remember that every prior generation once held the same spot, and somehow made mistakes or held beliefs we now find so easy to criticize.

We must also not forget that Kiffin knew no more about his future than we do about ours.[23] That is, just as our certainty as to yesterday does not carry over to tomorrow, neither did his. Kiffin was a man, a real live human being, faced with real choices, the outcome of which could not be known with certainty. And for the last two years of his life, Kiffin made his decisions in the midst of a great war, and the split-second world of the fighter pilot. Under such trying settings, allowances could be made for occasionally living in the moment or believing morals a luxury. However, from all that appears, Kiffin does not seem to have lowered his standards to match his circumstances.

Of course, Kiffin was not perfect, and this book is not a hagiography. Nor is one necessary – Kiffin's life and deeds stand on their own. But just like anyone else, Kiffin had shortcomings and made his share of mistakes. Resisting any preconceived notions of his greatness helps us properly value Kiffin's decisions and story.

In any event, one can best appreciate Kiffin without encircling him with a historical halo or presuming him to be some sort of superhero or action figure. While fate presented a unique stage onto which Kiffin stepped, and the Great War provided a vehicle through which his character was tested, refined and ultimately proved, the outcome was not foreordained, and Kiffin still had to choose, and ultimately to act. Combat, both on the ground and in the air, offered the grand test Kiffin had been seeking – an opportunity to measure up to his own standards.

And measure up he did. When his chance to prove himself came, Kiffin was ready, and seized it. He didn't wait for someone else to step up, or for a consensus to form – he acted. Throughout his enlistment, Kiffin never pretended to be something he wasn't, and although presented with many opportunities, he never backed out and never backed down. And when things got tough, he did not let up. Even after the world realized the hostilities would not be bound by age-old assumptions about human conflict, and that the weaponry now available to mankind allowed for mechanized murder on a scale never imagined, Kiffin didn't flinch, but rather determined to do all he could to stay in the fight and stand fast by his commitment. So whatever else is said about him, it must always be remembered that Kiffin's involvement in the defining issue of his time was a direct result of his own voluntary choice, one made so early and by so few American boys that this fact alone marks him as distinctly different.[24]

And let there be no mistake – Kiffin's decision to go to war came with no guarantees. The carnage of World War I is almost beyond comprehension. In just the week before Kiffin enlisted in the Legion, the French army lost forty thousand men, twenty-seven thousand of whom were killed on a single day, the 22nd of August.[25] By the end of 1914 – just five months of fighting – France had suffered more than three hundred thousand casualties.

When Kiffin left America for the war, the lights of freedom were going out, not just in Europe, but all over the world. Like most Americans, Kiffin sensed this, but unlike most Americans, Kiffin chose to stand, to act, to rush towards the call of war and the sound of the guns. And although he would go down fighting, Kiffin blazed a trail for other would-be heroes to follow. Indeed, against all odds, Kiffin charted a course for an entire hesitant nation.

* * * * *

Men like Kiffin should live forever. By that I mean *Kiffin Rockwell* is a name we should remember and honor, and his deeds are deeds we should remember and honor. This book is an effort to capture some of Kiffin's greatness and revive our admiration for men willing to offer their lives to defend an ideal. It is a tribute to that full measure of manhood, that sense of right and wrong, of good and evil, of *principle* that Kiffin and others like him possessed and exemplified. It is an attempt to keep faith with Kiffin and the other "boys who remembered Lafayette."

Hopefully, it will stand as a small memorial to Kiffin's life and death and help us better appreciate the truth spoken by Kiffin's father when but a lad of seventeen – that "deeds never die."

Come with me. Turn the pages of history and relive Kiffin's life. Come back to a time when men stood as men, when war raged across continents, and a boy named Kiffin became a hero worthy of our remembrance. A hero worthy of two flags.

Prelude ~ War

August 2, 1914.

Iron, fire and death would soon flash through Europe. The powder keg that was the Old World was about to blow sky high, and once it did things would never be the same.

The chain of events set in motion just over a month prior when Serbian nationalist and Black Hand member Gavrilo Princip gunned down Archduke Franz Ferdinand and his wife in the streets of Sarajevo was now sparking declarations of war across Europe and would soon threaten peace around the world. As one historian noted, that incident "was the small stone that, loosened, brings the avalanche."[1]

In Paris, crowds thronged the streets, ignited by the posting of official yellow placards announcing the mobilization of France's forces. Filled with fervor and excitement, patriotic citizens spilled out of cafés, banding together in cheering bunches. Cabs went to the highest bidder as flag-waving processions numbering in the thousands swept the boulevards of the old city, all singing the Marseillaise and crying "On to Berlin!"[2] As everyone always knew it would, war had returned to the Continent.

* * * * *

An ocean away, on a hot Sunday afternoon in their small Atlanta apartment on West Peachtree Street, brothers Paul and Kiffin Rockwell were sharing a mid-day meal with friends.[3] The ever-restless Kiffin had for the past few months been employed as an "ad man" for one of the largest advertising houses in the South. His brother Paul, who had hopes of becoming a writer, worked as a reporter for *The Atlanta Constitution*. Paul and Kiffin knew and were friendly with reporters from one of the *Constitution's* primary rivals, *The Atlanta Journal*. Atlanta's two leading daily newspapers vied for readership and supremacy across the South – the *Constitution* billed itself as "The Standard Southern Newspaper," while the *Journal* boasted "The Journal Covers Dixie

Like the Dew."

But on this particular Sunday, the *Journal* was covering more than Dixie. It was covering rapidly-moving world events that most people in Atlanta – or America for that matter – could hardly believe. The European crisis had developed with startling rapidity, and now seemed poised to ensnare the entire continent. In large bold type, the *Journal's* front-page headline proclaimed the impending peril: "Germany Declares War and Then Invades Luxemburg." Below that, in smaller lettering: "England Says She Is Under No Obligation to Aid France."[4] The *Journal* informed its readers, correctly as it turned out, that actual warfare was both certain and imminent:

Now the die is cast, and Europe is to be plunged into a general war, which has been the apprehension of European statesmen for generations. It is now only a question of how soon a state of actual war will exist between Germany and France.[5]

Not to be outdone, the front page of the *Constitution* further confirmed the grim reality. Its headlines read: "Europe Is Plunged Into Bloody Welter By Kaiser's War Order Against Russia," and "France Mobilizes Her Army."[6]

In the Rockwells' apartment, more talking was going on than eating. Kiffin and Paul read the latest news with an ominous sense of fear, tinged with excitement. This was the darkest prospect to face Europe in decades, perhaps a century. Even so, the boys could perceive the hinges of history swinging open, and the discussion among the brothers and their guests turned swiftly to the coming war.[7]

Kiffin felt the looming conflict would inevitably draw in the entire world and, not wanting to wait, was particularly intent on joining the French forces.[8] A few years younger than Paul, Kiffin tended to see things in black and white, and raged against Germany's shocking conduct. Kiffin felt an obligation to defend France and, as he saw it, humanity. From their boyhood, both he and Paul had admired the historic friendship between the Marquis de Lafayette and George Washington and cherished the help Lafayette had given America in its time of greatest need. Now, Kiffin meant to make good on his portion of America's debt.[9] Paul was also game. Both boys, you see, had been raised with strong principles, and backbones.

But even as Kiffin and Paul spoke of "how interesting it would be to go over and fight for France," their companions merely "agreed mildly that it would be a great thing to fight against the Germans, and turned the conversation to the hands they had held in their last poker game."[10]

This was not surprising. Beginning then, and for some time after, "neutrality" was a word on the lips of many Americans. The national economy was doing well and promised to do even better in a war in which the country could maintain business ties with both sides. Given this fact, few wished to engage militarily in what most saw as a local dispute between feuding European nations thousands of miles from American shores.

In fact, even as it noted the inevitability of war, the *Journal* also reported that the United States intended to follow a policy of "hands off."[11] Kiffin, however, was not a "hands off" kind of guy. Paul later wrote of that Sunday:

After lunch, Kiffin called me aside and very seriously told me that he had been thinking a great deal during the past several days about the coming war, and that if I really wanted to go to France and join the French forces, his mind was fully made up to go.[12]

On Monday morning, the news reached Atlanta that Germany had violated the neutrality of Belgium.[13] The brothers had heard enough – they quickly prepared a letter to the French Consulate in New Orleans, offering their services to the French government.

The Tuesday evening edition of the *Journal* carried the news that the Rockwells had offered their services to the French and, if accepted, "would shoulder arms in defense of France."[14] It further reported the young brothers "did not offer their services on impulse," but had "determined to fight under the Tri-Color in the present great war which threatens to engulf all Europe," and hoped the French government would accept their offer.[15] Interestingly, in the very same edition, the paper's front page informed readers that President Woodrow Wilson had officially issued a proclamation of neutrality that prohibited Americans from "[e]nlisting or entering into the service of either of the said belligerents" as a soldier or sailor.[16]

But President Wilson's proclamation did not deter the Rockwells. The day after their offer was reported in the *Journal*, and before they had even heard back from the French Consulate, the two brothers learned of an American-flagged ocean liner leaving in two days for England from New York.

After securing their places on board the ship, Paul and Kiffin hurriedly settled their affairs and packed their bags, then quickly embarked on a train to New York. On Thursday, August 7, 1914, the idealistic brothers were at sea, steaming for Europe, and war.[17]

Part One – A Boy Named Kiffin

"A child's real education comes from the feelings and attitude of the family in which he grows up.... It was but natural that I should hear much talk of war and glory among close relatives whose minds were ever filled with memories and regrets..."

- Gilbert du Motier, Marquis de Lafayette[1]

"Kiffin was my only brother and truest friend."

- Paul Rockwell to John Jay Chapman, October 5, 1916.[2]

Chapter One

Tout homme a deux pays, le sien et puis la France.

Every man has two countries – his own and France.

Often attributed to Thomas Jefferson, the saying actually traces back to an 1875 play written by French poet and dramatist Henri de Bornier. In de Bornier's play *La Fille de Roland*, Charlemagne utters the line "*Tout homme a deux pays, le sien et puis la France.*"[3]

Whatever its exact provenance, the phrase perfectly suits Kiffin Yates Rockwell. For although he was the quintessential American, Kiffin's story begins and ends in France. On both the paternal and maternal sides, Kiffin's early ancestry traces back to France, and it is a historical fact that he gave his life fighting for that country and its people. But Kiffin's choice to fight for France revealed more than just old blood ties. It reflected the strong principles on which he was raised, principles which led him instinctively to side with the weak over the strong, the victim over the aggressor and liberty over tyranny. For Kiffin, his choice to volunteer for France when its fate – and the world's – hung in the balance, was easy. It was simply a choice of right over wrong.

Glimpses into Kiffin's ancestry provide more than a simple genealogy, for in his ancestors we see the traits exemplified by Kiffin, and in Kiffin we see the culmination of the highest ideals of his forebears. Daniel Webster once said "[w]e are true to ourselves only when we act with becoming pride for the blood we inherit, and which we are to transmit to those who shall fill our places."[4] This thought may help us better understand Kiffin's actions, for he was never more true to himself or his ancestry than when he stepped forward to defend France. Indeed, Kiffin's stand was just another link in a family chain forged by a lineage chock full of soldiers and preachers, men who ordered their lives around principles of right and wrong. Kiffin's brother Paul once said, "if you know the past of a people, you can pretty well foresee their future," a statement that would prove accurate for he and his little brother.[5]

Kiffin descended from a long line of prominent and principled men and intelligent and virtuous women. Strong Norman blood coursed through Kiffin's veins, and a love of liberty – coupled with an awareness of its fragile and fleeting nature – was taught from his youth. Throughout the family's history, the Rockwells displayed a willingness to leave their homes or even their native land for a cause or an ideal. Kiffin was raised to believe that, like his ancestors, he had a role to play in the affairs of men, and longed to prove himself a worthy inheritor of a family name burnished by his predecessors' many illustrious deeds.

Of his remote ancestors, little is known; happily, a good deal more is known of Kiffin's immediate predecessors. But let's begin at the beginning.

* * * * *

Not far from the Normandy beaches stormed by the Allies in World War II lies the French city of Caen. Kiffin's earliest known ancestor, Bertrand de Rocheville, held feudal rights and powers near this place and the surrounding territory. From the de Rochevilles sprang the family name of Rockwell, hence the Rockwell name is of Norman origin.[6] The Rockwell coat of arms derives to this time, as does the family motto, rendered in French: *Tout pour mon Dieu, et mon roi* – all for my God and my king.[7]

In the twelfth century, the Empress Matilda, grand-daughter of William the Conqueror, crossed from Normandy into England to secure the throne of England. Kiffin's ancestor Sir Ralph de Rocheville accompanied Matilda, and aided her in her struggles against her cousin, King Stephen of England. Eventually, in 1154, Matilda's eldest son succeeded to the English throne as Henry II, who as king rewarded the Baron de Rocheville with three "knight's fees" of land in the County of York.[8] The Rockwells descended from this line, and in the course of time, the name *de Rocheville* became anglicized to Rockwell.[9]

* * * * *

The family's American history begins in Somerset County, England, where in 1591 William Rockwell was born. Strongly Puritan, the people of Somerset had become increasingly dissatisfied with the limited extent of the English Reformation, and with the Church of England's tolerance of practices associated with the Roman Catholic Church.

When Charles I ascended to the throne in 1625, William Rockwell and his new bride Susanna Chapin, together with others in their congregation seeking greater strictness of life and simplicity of worship, began to lay plans to emigrate to North America.[10] A few years later, on March 20, 1630, with their four-year old daughter (who would celebrate her fifth birthday mid-ocean) and two-year old son, the Rockwells set sail on the *Mary and John*, seeking "an asylum where they might be beyond the interference and annoyance of those who would restrict that liberty wherewith Christ has made us free."[11]

Seventy days later, at the end of May, 1630, the ship and its 140 passengers dropped anchor in Massachusetts Bay. This marked the arrival of the Rockwells in America. To solemnize their first Sabbath in the new world, William and his young family, along with the other new settlers, sang a portion of the 90th Psalm.[12] That scripture ends:

Let thy work appear unto thy servants, and thy glory unto their children. And let the beauty of the Lord our God be upon us: and establish thou the work of our hands upon us; yea, the work of our hands establish thou it.[13]

With this injunction still ringing in their ears, William and the other colonizers set to work, clearing the land, planting crops and building log cabins. The industrious settlers soon incorporated the town of Dorchester and organized a church, choosing William Rockwell as one of the two deacons.[14] In this capacity, William signed the town's first land grants and was himself granted a half acre of ground on which to build a place to live. In one of his first acts as owner, William had the Rockwell family coat of arms painted on the panels of their new home.[15]

While the town prospered, and soon contained more than two hundred snug houses, over time, dissensions arose, mostly concerning the form of worship and other theological quarrels. Many colonists, including a good number of those in Dorchester, determined to remove to the settlements in Connecticut. Although still a deacon, William was among those who felt the clergy was wielding too much temporal power, so in 1637 he moved with his wife and now four children (two more having been born in the interim) to Windsor, where his name is carved on a monument recognizing the founders of that town.[16] At Windsor, the Rockwells welcomed a fifth child, and enjoyed the first Thanksgiving Day celebrated in Connecticut.[17] A few years later, "worn out by the trials of two migrations and the efforts of helping found two new settlements," Deacon William Rockwell died on May 15, 1640.[18] From Windsor, the descendants of William and Susanna Rockwell would spread forth across America.

Looking back over the generations, soldiering stands out as a dominant trait among the Rockwell men.[19] For example, William's eldest son, John Rockwell, was mustered out and fought with a Windsor-based troop of Dragoons in the Indian hostilities preceding King Phillip's War. John's son Joseph moved to Middletown, Connecticut, "where for years he was captain commanding the Middletown troops, serving in Queen Anne's War and other French and Indian troubles."[20] Later descendants of William and Susanna fought in the Revolutionary War and for both the North and the South during the Civil War.[21] Generations later, Paul Rockwell would reflect that "there have been soldiers in my family, in every war, as far back as I can trace."[22] For the Rockwells, "Soldiering was a family art and patriotism a family passion."[23]

But soldiering was not the only, or perhaps even the most notable characteristic of the Rockwells. Religious traditions ran equally strong in the family, and Deacon William Rockwell was not Kiffin's only religious progenitor. In fact, the entire line of Rockwells held ardent Christian beliefs, and a "surprisingly large number" became preachers of the gospel.[24]

A few of their stories demonstrate that Kiffin's life and character were consistent with the military and religious traditions of his forefathers. As one author aptly put it, speaking of the brothers Paul and Kiffin: "The guide rails of their ancestry were straight and clear and led to the highest ideals of modern civilization."[25]

* * * * *

Noadiah Rockwell, from Middletown, Connecticut, was Kiffin's great-great grandfather. While still a teenager he volunteered to fight against the British in the fight for American independence, enlisting with the cavalry and serving throughout the entire harsh war.[26] His daughter Sarah later recalled the many nights the family spent "sitting around the fireside" listening to their father "relate the trials and suffering of the Revolutionary War..."[27]

Noadiah married Alice Hall, a deeply religious woman who "ardently loved" her Savior.[28] The couple's youngest son was Kiffin's paternal great-grandfather, Chester Rockwell. Born in 1802, Chester was responsible for relocating his branch of the Rockwell family tree to the South. Family lore had it that when visiting North Carolina from Middletown, one of the large landowners in the area asked Chester why he did not settle in the state to which he responded, "I will, if your daughter will marry me."[29]

She would, and he did. Thus did Chester marry one Anne Smith, the daughter of Major Samuel White Smith of the Revolutionary War, and the grand-daughter of Captain James Council. Council had been a distinguished leader and one of the delegates to the Fourth Provincial Congress of North Carolina, which on April 12, 1776 adopted the so-called "Halifax Resolves," the first official action in which one of the American colonies authorized its delegates to the Continental Congress to vote for independence from England.[30]

Following his marriage, Chester became the proprietor of a large cotton and tobacco plantation in Columbus County, North Carolina. Situated in the southeast corner of the state near the South Carolina border, Chester's estate encompassed much of the present-day town of Chadbourn, extending almost to the courthouse in Whiteville.[31] Chester and Anne had five children together in slightly less than 12 years of marriage before she died in 1842. Chester subsequently remarried and had two more children.

Chester prospered as a planter, and eventually became one of the richest men in his part of North Carolina.[32] He was known in the community as a generous man, intensely devoted to his family. A devout Christian, Chester donated the land on which the first Presbyterian church in Whiteville was erected.[33]

When the Civil War broke out, Chester was too old to enlist, but was "heart and soul" with his adopted state of North Carolina. Although a transplant to the South, Chester used his fortune and influence to aid the Confederacy, for which all his sons enlisted and fought. However, like many others in the South, Chester's "wealth was swept away by the War, and when the struggle came to an end in 1865, all that was left to him was his land."[34]

* * * * *

Chester Rockwell's oldest son Henry Clay Rockwell was Kiffin's paternal grandfather. Henry worked as a laborer on his father's cotton farm until in 1860 he married Sarah Jane Powell, the great grand-daughter of Captain Absalom Powell, who had served as a captain in the Revolutionary War, and later served two terms in the North Carolina legislature.[35] Sarah Jane, always called Sallie J. by her family and friends, was one of the "belles" of Eastern Carolina, and was known as "an unusually beautiful girl, with wavy chestnut hair, an oval face with cheeks delicately tinted with rose, chestnut brown eyes, gracious, red lips, and gentle poise."[36] As a child, Sallie J.'s grandson Paul Rockwell often heard older people speak of what a charming bride she had been. Like many of the

Rockwell wives, however, Sallie J. was not merely beautiful – she was also well educated. In fact, she was a college graduate, quite an unusual accomplishment before (and for many years after) the Civil War.[37]

Eleven months into their marriage, and just days after the shelling of Fort Sumter ushered in the Civil War, Henry and his young wife had their first child, a boy they named William. While to this point North Carolina had resisted secession, the firing on Fort Sumter compelled President Lincoln to requisition troops, and in response, on May 20, 1861, North Carolina finally and reluctantly seceded from the Union, realizing that "the only alternative was that of fighting against the South."[38]

Of course, being a Rockwell, Henry soon volunteered to fight, leaving behind his cotton farm, as well as his wife and infant son. Commissioned as an officer, Henry was rapidly promoted to Captain in Company H of the 51st North Carolina infantry regiment, in which he would serve throughout the conflict.[39]

A few of Henry's experiences in the Civil War were preserved in letters he wrote home and were surely known by Kiffin. Through these letters, Kiffin learned something of the hardships and difficulties of war. For example, while defending Charleston Harbor in the summer and fall of 1863, Henry told his father "we live pretty hard," and described an extended struggle without much movement:

We have had quite a long siege here. I think the Enemy have thrown five hundred thousand shot and shell at our Works since the siege commenced. We hold the same ground now that we did when I came here nearly two months since.[40]

In 1864, as part of General Clingman's brigade, Henry helped lead the 51st regiment in defense of Richmond and was then sent to Cold Harbor to help fortify the Confederate positions. At Cold Harbor, in one of the bloodiest and most lopsided battles of the war, Henry and his men helped repulse the hopeless frontal assaults Ulysses S. Grant launched against General Lee and his armies. General Grant later wrote that he "always regretted that the last assault at Cold Harbor was ever made," as "no advantage whatever was gained to compensate for the heavy loss we sustained."[41]

In a letter to his sister, Henry hoped the summer of 1864 would be "the last summer we will have to stay away from friends and the comforts of home."[42] After several years of fighting, and the loss of both of his brothers, Henry had also developed strong thoughts on the seemingly endless war. Noting the desolation of thousands of homes and the loss of thousands of brave sons, Henry lamented that "we have been made to feel sorely and suffer for our sins," and trusted that "surely the time is not far distant when peace will once more visit our bleeding Country."[43]

Although Henry had given much, and longed for the day when he would "be restored to the bosom of my own dear little Family," he believed that perhaps God willed the war to continue:

If it is the will of an all Merciful Creator we will have that long wished and prayed for time soon, but it may be that we are not prepared for it. It may be that we have not atoned sufficient for our sins.[44]

Nevertheless, displaying a trait common in the Rockwells, Henry was committed to stand by his decision. Having made up his mind to fight, he stayed with his regiment, and declared: "May our cause progress & may the Yankees be brot [sic] back from the error of their ways and allow us to depart in peace is my fervent prayer."[45]

After Cold Harbor, the 51st regiment suffered through several dreary, starved months in the trenches at Petersburg, Virginia before being detached to defend Wilmington, North Carolina. As the North's grip tightened, the regiment's remaining men joined with other scattered Confederate forces under General Joseph E. Johnston in the spring of 1865. When the war drew to a close, Henry finally made his way home to Whiteville, North Carolina, and "began the struggle to restore his fortune and help upbuild his ruined state."[46]

* * * * *

In the following years, Henry rose to prominence among the people of Columbus County, described by one publication of the time as "plain, intelligent, hard-working and thoroughly Democratic. And they were Democratic even in old times, and believe in the old-fashioned, honest doctrines of Andrew Jackson, Tho[mas] Jefferson and old Father Ritchie of the Richmond *Enquirer*."[47] Henry certainly fit that mold.

Like his father Chester, Henry was known as a generous and loyal friend. Thoroughly benevolent and charitable, he gave away "most of what the Yankees left him to disabled Confederate soldiers and to widows and orphans of the war."[48] For many years afterward, the residents of Whiteville and Columbus County remembered Henry's kindness and generosity to the less fortunate.[49]

H.C., as Henry was known in the community, knew how to run a farm and at one point owned at least 2,600 acres. Cotton was increasingly becoming a primary cash crop in Columbus County, and a few years after the war ended, Henry received an award from the local agricultural association for the largest cotton crop on one acre of land.[50] The county had fertile soil, and many crops could be grown quite easily. One visitor remarked that "as to rice and sweet potatoes, there is no end; they seem to grow without effort, and are easily cultivated."[51]

Henry also became an active businessman and built a reputation as one of the leading citizens of the region. He started a general store in Whiteville, selling staples, dry goods, hats, shoes, saddles, plows and a variety of other wares useful in a small farming community.[52] In addition, with two partners he opened the Whiteville Wine Company.[53] The company bottled annually 6,000 gallons of wine, and also made and sold by the barrel a very fine grape brandy.[54]

At that time, distilling turpentine from the sap of long-leaf pine trees was a big business; indeed, probably as a result of this industry, North Carolina would become known as the "tar heel" state. Turpentine was used in many industrial and naval products of the day, and the commercial demand for turpentine products provided an occupation for many residents. In addition, the *Wilmington, Columbia and Augusta Railroad* which passed through Columbus County allowed the distillers there to ship large quantities of so-called "naval stores" to ports such as Wilmington.[55] Henry participated in the turpentine industry and helped form and was elected the first president of the Turpentine Distillers Association of North Carolina, South Carolina, and Georgia.[56]

The Rockwells also re-started their family, which to that point included only William, who was four years old when the war ended. About ten months after General Lee surrendered at Appomattox Court House, Henry and Sallie J. were blessed with a little girl, Lucy Syrena. Two years later, on January 21, 1868, the Rockwells had another boy. Taking his first name from Sallie's father, and his middle name from Henry's father, who had passed on only a few months before, the couple christened their new son James Chester Rockwell.

J.C., as he was often called, was Kiffin's father.

Chapter Two

A noble youth, with a wide horizon of beautiful promise.

Although Kiffin never knew his father, who died just before Kiffin's first birthday, it is undeniable that James Chester Rockwell had a significant influence in Kiffin's life. Indeed, in some respects, Kiffin's life parallels his father's.

For example, both Kiffin and J.C. were primarily raised by single mothers following the deaths of their fathers and spent substantial portions of their youths living with their maternal grandfathers. Kiffin's mother would inculcate in Kiffin and his brother the same qualities she had loved in their father. Thus, Kiffin had a serious independent streak, much like his father who while still quite young struck out on his own seeking to "fight his own battles," as James Chester later put it. Similarly, both Kiffin and his father pursued other enterprises or drifted for a period of time before finding their true calling.

Both were mature beyond their years and perceived as older than they actually were, allowing them to command the respect of men much older than themselves. Both were leaders with an ability to quickly grasp the nature of a thing, and a desire to count. Both had a strong sense of justice, a sound moral compass, and a commitment to do right. While both had an easy manner around others, neither made friends easily. Neither was brash or boastful, so when they spoke, men listened. Both aspired to recognition. Both displayed strong loyalty and could be counted on to stand by their decisions, even when difficult.

Both had a natural intelligence, but Kiffin's curiosity about the world sometimes led him to impetuous acts, while J.C. was more serious and contemplative. Similarly, while both loved to be outdoors in nature, Kiffin seems to have been more of a sportsman, whereas his father was more of a book learner. This may help explain why Kiffin became a soldier while J.C. became a poet preacher. It seems, however, that each of them found his true vocation based on the same desire – to accomplish the most good he could.

Kiffin's father bequeathed to Kiffin courage and conviction and, like other Rockwells, the courage of his convictions. Kiffin also inherited his father's pleasing appearance and height (J.C. stood six feet two inches).[1] One friend described Kiffin's father as "physically and intellectually precocious," and other terms that also fit Kiffin: "mild and benevolent in aspect and manner, but underneath this benign exterior was strength and determination without limit."[2]

Kiffin seems not to have suffered from his father's sometimes weak constitution that would plague Kiffin's older brother Paul. Thus, physically, Kiffin was a Rockwell: tall, firm and resolute. While Kiffin certainly got the Rockwell genes, he also seems to have inherited his father's sense of purpose. In the end, that may have influenced Kiffin as much as any other factor. For this reason, a full discussion of J.C. Rockwell's life provides a better understanding of how and why Kiffin became who he became.

* * * * *

Several events would have a profound impact on young J.C. Rockwell. To begin with, born less than three years after the South's surrender at Appomattox, J.C. grew up in a South devastated by the war and facing huge economic challenges and cultural adjustments. The difficult years of Reconstruction would get even harder for his family when J.C.'s father died suddenly just after J.C.'s sixth birthday. This was surely the hardest challenge J.C. faced in his youth, and it would change the course of his life. In a brief autobiographical sketch, the first event J.C. mentioned after his own birth was his father's death: "I was born in Whiteville, North Carolina on January 21st, 1868. My father died while I was quite young...."[3]

J.C.'s father Henry Rockwell was known as a man of uncommon generosity, "ever ready to aid and succor the needs of the unfortunate and distressed," and one whose purse was "ever open to the widow and orphan."[4] Although Henry was successful in farming and business, he was perhaps too generous with his abundance. When he died unexpectedly, Henry left "what should have been a very comfortable fortune, large land holdings ... and money advanced to various War comrades and 'in laws.'"[5] Unfortunately, "a good deal of the money due the estate never was paid, and most of the land was badly sold, due to the sad conditions in the South during and following the Reconstruction period."[6]

Henry's untimely death surely placed significant financial stress on his widow, who now faced the prospect of raising alone their five surviving children

– William 13, Lucy 8, J.C. 6, Robert 2, and Henry Clay, Jr., who was not yet even one year old.[7] Although Sallie J. received some help from her father, it was in her family's interest for her to remarry.

Accordingly, two and a half years after the death of her beloved Henry, Sallie J. wed again, this time to her cousin John Willis Council. Unfortunately, according to Sallie's grandson, J.W. Council lived only a few years, and managed the remaining estate badly.[8]

The family suffered other tragedies as well. The year after Sallie remarried, J.C.'s youngest brother, four-year-old Henry Clay Rockwell, Jr., died. Less than two years later, J.C.'s older sister Lucy also died. This left three boys from Sallie's original marriage to Henry Rockwell, along with two half-siblings – John and Lillie Council, born in 1877 and 1879, respectively.

While the reason is not entirely clear from the historical record, at some point Sallie moved the family into the home of James Calvin Powell, J.C.'s maternal grandfather.[9] Described as "a big, rambling, *ante bellum* plantation house," his homestead still bore "scars from the bullets with which the Northerners riddled it."[10] J.C. had always been a hard worker, which came in handy on his grandfather's farm, where J.C. and his younger brother Robert helped with the farmwork. Their older brother William had gone to live with their uncle Alexander F. Powell, a successful Whiteville merchant who ran Powell & Co., a general store located in the train depot. He also ran a cotton gin and press.[11]

Although in his youth J.C. suffered his share of hard times, there were many bright spots, especially in his education. In his early years in Whiteville, which at the time had a population of about five hundred, J.C. was educated by private teachers. When he was about twelve years old, his older brother William arranged for J.C. to come and live with him in Laurinburg, North Carolina and to take classes under the tutelage of W.G. Quackenbush, a noted Eastern Carolina educator of the day and principal of the Laurinburg academy.[12]

While at the academy, J.C. proved to be "an accomplished student and an inveterate reader," and began to write essays and poetry.[13] He rapidly built a reputation as a brilliant scholar, even learning some Hebrew, Greek, Latin and German.[14] J.C. spent several years in Laurinburg before circumstances forced his return to Whiteville. Always grateful for William's efforts on his behalf, later in life J.C. fondly recalled that "thanks to the loving kindness and self-sacrificing spirit of my eldest brother, I enjoyed very good educational advantages until I reached the fifteenth year of my age.... Since that time, I have fought my own battles and pursued my studies privately."[15]

Around the time J.C. turned fifteen, the economic clouds again darkened for the Rockwell family and, no longer able to stay with his brother in Laurinburg, J.C. returned to live with his grandfather. He became a clerk in a general store (probably Powell & Co., owned by his uncle), and tried to help out as best he could. However, not long after J.C. returned to Whiteville, the noteholder foreclosed on the family's remaining land from the estate of their father.[16]

During this time of economic hardship, J.C. continued to work, and to write. His writing showed much promise, and over the next few years, many newspapers published his poetry. Among his first published poems was a clever little rhyme suggesting that noble deeds come about not by thinking, but by doing. He called it "Weeds":

Sometimes we grasp a growing notion,
Of doing noble deeds;
But ere we put it into motion,
Our thoughts have gone to weeds.[17]

At sixteen, J.C. was already trusted enough by the community to teach a term in one of the local schools, while on the strength of his essays and poetry his reputation continued to grow. By the time he reached the age of seventeen, J.C.'s work was regularly published in papers around the state. Although he was still young, with his height, demeanor, intelligence and bearing, others already saw J.C. as a "mature man in stature and intellect."[18]

After closing his term as a teacher, J.C. decided to strike out on his own, and "undertook the editorship of a small literary publication whose aims were high but whose finances were low."[19] He began work as editor of the *The Belles Lettres*, a paper in Reidsville, North Carolina that was, as its masthead indicated, "Devoted to Polite Literature: Ancient, Modern and Current."[20] The owner and founder of the publication later remembered J.C. as a "noble youth," with a "wide horizon of beautiful promise."[21] After only a short while as editor, hoping to rekindle the market in North Carolina for high-minded literature, the ambitious youngster purchased the paper and moved it from Reidsville to Raleigh.[22]

* * * * *

If you have not yet formed an impression of James Chester Rockwell, imagine a boy who at seventeen acquires a newspaper and relocates it to a new, large city to write, publish and distribute all on his own. That was young J.C. Rockwell – intelligent, independent, strong-willed and, like many generations of Rockwells before him, a firm believer in action.

J.C.'s youth, passion and confidence were on full display in one of his first editorials as owner of the paper. Titled "False destiny," it began with the simple yet bold statement: "Every man should make his own destiny."[23] J.C. did not intend this declaration as literary fluff, for it was surely a sentiment in which he believed, and he put it forth in earnest. The conviction that a man could and should *make his own destiny* was a defining characteristic of the Rockwells, and J.C. was no exception. Still, being of a poetic mind, he could not avoid altogether the use of flowery language to make his point:

O man, be up and doing. Laugh down the foolish idea that you are but a helpless reed in the hands of a fickle destiny. Scorn the thought that you cannot do noble things, simply because fate says you must not. Be true to yourself and to humanity, and you make for yourself a destiny of undying greatness and grandeur![24]

These lines could serve as a nice script for anyone looking to live a life worthy of recognition or emulation, and surely were well received by the paper's few subscribers. Upon reviewing his first edition from Raleigh, another North Carolina publication declared J.C. "a young man of genius and literary talent," and predicted for him "a brilliant and successful career in the field of letters and journalism."[25]

J.C. threw himself into his new venture, recruited several promising writers to contribute to his fledgling publication, and began publishing twice a month. However, it was a time of scarcity in a South still recovering from the effects of the Civil War. Most folks in North Carolina barely had two nickels to rub together, let alone an extra dollar to subscribe to what aspired to be a pure literary journal. Struggling to overcome a lack of money and subscribers, J.C. soldiered on. Although the reality of his situation was nearly overwhelming, in a letter to his mother J.C. displayed the familiar Rockwell resolve:

I must tell you that the way at present is not very bright, although something seems to whisper to me always that success will come at last. I can see no way to success but nevertheless I feel confident I will succeed. I have never before found anything to cling to when everything seemed hopeless, but now, notwithstanding the way is dark, I do not care to leave it. I cannot bear the thought of failing, of having to give up. While I might find an easier way to support myself than this is, still I had rather toil day and night, and go through untold trouble, than to give it up and seek some easier path. I have found my sphere, and I am going to stay in it.[26]

Unfortunately, despite J.C.'s best efforts, the financial prospects of the publication did not improve. After just a few months in Raleigh the "enterprise proved a losing venture," and "followed in the wake of all its luckless predecessors in the South."[27] But even in defeat, J.C. showed a remarkable sense of grace, and humor. In his last edition, in an article headlined "Dead!" he wrote: "*The Belles-Lettres* is dead. After a brief struggle with that fatal disease – adversity, it has passed away. We desire to return thanks to its few – alas, how few – friends who have given it encouragement."[28] To ensure that none of his subscribers would lose out, in his final act as owner, J.C. transferred the paper's subscription list to another periodical.[29]

Following this setback, J.C. left Raleigh and returned to teaching, just across the border in Little River, South Carolina. Undaunted by his publishing failure, J.C. continued writing, and papers throughout the South published his poems, stories and sketches. As his reputation as a poet and teacher continued to grow, soon enough J.C. again seemed on the cusp of success and recognition. However, events were about to set his life on a different course.

* * * * *

"Up to this date," J.C. later recalled, "I had made no profession of religion. In fact, I had drifted away into utter scepticism." While proud of his own character and abilities, and aspiring to a lofty standard of living, J.C. admitted that "over my soul hung the gloom of unbelief."[30] But in his eighteenth year, "there came an awakening, and henceforth the current of my life was never to flow in the olden channel again."[31] Like many of the significant changes in J.C.'s life, this one was brought about by a death in his family.

On March 12, 1886, J.C.'s older and favorite brother William died at the age of 25. Willie had always supported and encouraged J.C. in his education and writing efforts, and his death hit J.C. very hard. The young man's spirits took a turn for the worse and his health, never very robust, began to decline.[32] "Hearts and Faces," a poem written by J.C. the month after William's death, shows his melancholy state of mind:

Because you cannot see my heart,
And read the story written there,
You deem that I am one whose life,
Has never felt the touch of care.

It may be best, O blinded eyes –
The lines of grief you cannot trace:
You cannot look within and see
The hidden heart behind the face.

The heart may break – the face must smile,
Thus let the story pass along:
Your heart's your own – your face is not,
The sigh is yours, but not the song.[33]

As his health and spirits faltered, J.C. finished out his teaching term, and later that summer went to convalesce in Old Fort, a small town tucked in the lush green mountains of western North Carolina.[34] Old Fort had gained a reputation as a healthy mountain resort, good for both body and soul, and J.C. would spend the rest of the summer season there.[35]

Looking too tall and far too bony, J.C. appeared in Old Fort in early August, hoping to reinvigorate his fading health and flagging strength. In the bracing mountain climate, his condition quickly improved: he gained eight pounds within his first ten days and reported that he felt "like a new man."[36]

Still looking for something to soothe his aching heart, J.C. began attending services at the local Baptist church, which had recently hired Claudius M. Murchison, a young preacher engaged in his first pastorate. Although the Rockwells were Presbyterian and J.C. had attended church throughout his childhood, to that point in his life, J.C. viewed religion more as a family tradition than a deeply held personal belief. But the death of his older brother caused J.C. to ponder questions of life and death, and to reflect on issues of eternal significance, and a few of his poems had taken on a more religious tone.[37]

As he was new in town, J.C. also paid many social visits to the home of Pastor Murchison and continued attending services at his church. One day near the end of the summer, J.C. accompanied him on a visit to the home of a minister of another denomination who had fallen ill, a Mr. Settlemyre of Old Fort. The young man listened intently, sometimes with tears streaming down his face, as the two preachers conversed about baptism and the Lord's Supper. At the end of their conversation, Mr. Settlemyre asked to join Pastor Murchison's congregation.

On their way home, Pastor Murchison and J.C. walked in silence for several minutes before the pastor suggested that perhaps J.C. had not enjoyed the visit as much as he would have enjoyed spending time with the other young people in the resort town. According to Murchison's later recollection, J.C. replied:

Mr. Murchison, I have never enjoyed anything so much in my life as this conversation ... and your interpretation of those scriptures[.] I think that I am converted, but not a member of any church. My people are not Baptists. I have been just where Mr. Settlemyre was until now relative to those things you have been discussing. I am now satisfied. I will return home and do my duty soon. I thank you very much indeed. I am glad that Providence sent me to Old Fort to recuperate. I am stronger physically and spiritually for the coming.[38]

Shortly thereafter, a noticeably recovered J.C. returned to his hometown of Whiteville. His spiritual conversion was sincere and, as promised, he "did his duty" – J.C. was baptized in October 1886, by Reverend A.W. Price.[39] A few weeks later, Pastor Murchison was pleased to receive a letter from J.C. informing him that his young friend had joined himself to the Baptist church.[40]

* * * * *

Although a brand-new convert and just eighteen years of age, J.C. "was immediately licensed to preach" and "entered straightway into an active work of the ministry."[41] He preached his first sermon in the Spring Branch church in Horry County, South Carolina on Sunday, November 14, 1886.[42] His theme that day was following Christ, and he ended his sermon:

Come and follow Jesus; and when the shadows of the long night are gathering around you, and when the sunlight of earth forever fades from your vision; and when the pale and shadowy boatman comes to ferry you across the fathomless stream of death; and when you launch out upon the waves of its desolate waters, the blessed morning of eternity will dawn for you, and Jesus will stand upon the shore to welcome you into his eternal home.[43]

J.C. had already gained a reputation as a "young gentleman of pronounced poetical talent," and his new calling provided a vocation into which he could channel his literary gifts.[44] Within a few months, he was preaching at many of the country churches scattered throughout Columbus County.[45] Places with names like Porter Swamp, Fair Bluff, Boyce Chapel and Lake Waccamaw.[46]

Now a poet preacher, J.C. was happy to be home in Whiteville, and able to spend time with his mother, as her health was precarious. Sallie's life had not been easy – after thirteen years of marriage her husband had died and, counting William's death less than a year before, four of her six children from that union had also died. In addition, she was still raising J.C.'s younger brother Robert, as well as two children from her marriage to J.W. Council: John and Lillie, now aged nine and seven. Through it all, she steadfastly nurtured and supported her precocious son James Chester, always encouraging him to become the person she knew he could be. One of her son's first published poems he titled "Mother," which begins with this verse:

Dear friend, so true, I cling to you –
You will forsake me never;
Though others harm, and fears alarm,
You shield your child forever.[47]

History does not reveal the cause or exact timing, but in the latter part of her life, Sallie's health failed completely. She became an invalid and lived with her brother Alexander F. Powell until her death a few years later.[48] This may have occurred around the time J.C. returned home in late 1886, as at that time J.C. decided to publish a narrative poem he had written when seventeen, which he dedicated to his mother.

Titled *Chrystella: The Echo of a Dream*, it was the longest poem he had ever written, and according to one observer, "contained passages of real poetry, and gave promise of future excellence."[49] Just before his nineteenth birthday, J.C. printed the poem in pamphlet form and offered it for sale at five copies for a dollar. At the beginning of the pamphlet, he included the following tribute:

At the feet of my mother I lay this little volume as a token of loving regard from an affectionate heart, – trusting that in the years that are to come, I may be permitted to produce something more worthy the son of such a true and noble woman.[50]

Soon another true and noble woman would take her place at the side of James Chester Rockwell.

Chapter Three

Many daughters have done virtuously, but thou excellest them all.[1]

Even had she not been the mother of Paul and Kiffin Rockwell, Loula Ayres Rockwell would have been counted a remarkable woman. Always "reputed to be a very intellectual lady," Loula earned a four-year degree at a time when few women graduated from high school, much less college.[2] Suddenly widowed two days before her twenty-seventh birthday, and left on her own to raise three very young children, for nearly ten years she taught in the local schools in Newport, Tennessee, and "was later credited with providing the impetus that led to the development of Newport's public school system."[3] She helped organize the newly-constructed Newport Academy for its opening in 1898, eventually becoming the school's first (and for the next 100 years, only) female principal.[4]

When Kiffin was ten years old, to better provide for her growing children, Loula determined to change her profession and at age 37 enrolled in America's first osteopathic medical school. Upon graduation, she moved with her family to Asheville, North Carolina, where she became that state's first female osteopathic physician. Loula would go on to practice medicine in North Carolina for more than fifty years.[5]

Despite her impressive professional and personal accomplishments, Loula's three children stand as the greatest testament to her character and nobility. Even in her immensely difficult circumstances, Loula raised her young ones well, and maintained the finest traditions of both the Rockwell and Ayres families. Of her two sons, the oldest served France in three wars, and became a famous writer and intellectual, while the youngest became a war hero and the primary subject of this book.

Loula's only daughter also distinguished herself. Agnes Rockwell graduated from Wellesley College then, like her mother, married a preacher. She had three children before tragically dying at the age of thirty-five in the act of bringing her fourth child into the world. At her funeral, in words which could as easily have been said of her mother, the eulogist summed up Agnes' spirit and drive:

"No whining, no shirking, no evasion, she faced life with a smile and met it with a valor worthy of the best traditions of all womanhood."[6]

Kiffin sprang from the union of James Chester Rockwell and Loula Ayres and embodied the best qualities of those two stalwart families. Indeed, a look at Kiffin's maternal ancestry reveals many of the same virtues found in his paternal genealogy – bravery, independence and a people unafraid to stand for their principles. Like the Rockwells, the Ayres were "noted for their definite and deep-seated convictions," as well as the "courage with which they defended them."[7] It is hardly surprising then, that just like the Rockwell branch, the Ayres branch of Kiffin's lineal tree was planted thick with soldiers, and full of religion.

* * * * *

The Ayres family was "Southern," with a capital S, thank you. Loula's father Enoch Shaw Ayres was an imposing figure who fought on the side of the South for all four years of the War Between the States and was with General Joseph E. Johnston near Bennett Farm in Durham County, North Carolina when he belatedly surrendered what remained of the Confederate armies in late April 1865. Refusing to take the oath of allegiance, Enoch mounted his horse and rode home to "Beechwood," his large cotton plantation where, Loula said, he "remained until the end of his days what some call an 'unreconstructed Rebel.'"[8]

Enoch Shaw Ayres was born, reared, married and died in Marion County, South Carolina, the son of a converted Baptist preacher. The conversion story of his father, William Ayres is quite remarkable:

William Ayres was ... considered by many of his neighbors as an ungodly man. He had the finest scuppernong vineyard for miles around and made his own wine which was famed among his friends. He enjoyed dancing, played "the instrument of the devil," the fiddle, and was not in regular attendance at church[.] One can readily imagine the impression he made in the Baptist stronghold of Marion District, South Carolina!

One evening in 1834, William Ayres, now almost in middle age, rode on horseback with a party of friends to a dance in Horry County, where the gaiety did not break up until a late hour. Returning home about dawn, the group was crossing the Mill Branch Swamp, which lay between the old Daniel and Ayres plantations. Suddenly, to the surprise of his companions, William Ayres dismounted and knelt at the foot of a huge pine near the road. He prayed aloud as his friends recounted afterwards, and asking forgiveness for his sins, vowed he would begin preaching the gospel as soon as he could be ordained. The following Sunday he appeared at the Bear Swamp Baptist Church, to what must have been the vast astonishment of most of those present, and shortly thereafter was licensed to preach.[9]

William served as an itinerant missionary, a peripatetic preacher who on horseback traveled to the numerous country churches (many of which he helped establish) that dotted both sides of the North and South Carolina border. In fact, during his twenty-seven years as a missionary, the reverend was said to have "traveled 2,350 days, baptized fifteen hundred persons, and preached over twenty-five hundred sermons."[10] William was frequently away from home for weeks at a time – his wife sometimes said that she "saw less of her husband after he became a good Christian than before."[11] On one occasion when Reverend Ayres had been gone several weeks, it was mistakenly reported throughout the countryside that he had been accidentally killed, and his family went into mourning. Sometime later people were amazed to see the preacher ride into his home village and told him he was supposed to be dead. "Yes, I've heard that story several times lately," he replied, "but I knew it was a lie the first time I heard it."[12]

William was much beloved by his congregation at Bear Swamp where, when not traveling the countryside, he served as pastor for much of the time from 1841 until his death in 1863.[13] It was said that he had particular powers of "describing the sinner's mind and purposes, so as to bring him suddenly under conviction and repentance[.]"[14] Reverend Ayres "stood well among his clerical brethren, and was dearly beloved by the laity of his church...."[15] A fellow minister asserted that he "underwent more trials and persecutions, raised more churches, endured more fatigue, and made more sacrifices than any five men in our midst."[16] Following his death in 1863, the *Biblical Recorder* remembered Reverend Ayres as "a son of thunder who wielded the sword of the spirit to the downfall of Satan's kingdom wherever he went."[17]

Enoch was born the year after his father's spiritual awakening, kneeling by that big old pine tree. The pine by which Enoch's father (Kiffin's great grandfather) prayed "stood for many years and was pointed out to more than one of his descendants," but eventually was cut down after the first World War when the road through the Mill Branch Swamp was widened.[18]

One of ten children, Enoch was still young when his father became the pastor at Bear Swamp Baptist Church and served as a missionary for the Cape

Fear Association. Because their father was often traveling, Enoch and his older brother Tommy learned early on to work the family's huge plantation, and when he was old enough, Enoch helped Tommy manage the whole estate. The brothers would later become successful farmers in their own right.

Enoch was twenty-five years old when Abraham Lincoln was elected president. The next month South Carolina became the first state to secede, and in April 1861 open war broke out between the North and South following the attack at Fort Sumter. Enoch was one of the first volunteers to enlist in the 8th South Carolina Regiment, in which he served as sergeant during the four-year conflict.[19] Darius Dwight Ayres, Enoch's youngest brother, also enlisted, as did his uncle John Ayres, who had been living in Mississippi for a number of years.[20] Enoch's nephews, William and Joseph Ayres, ages 16 and 15, also signed up, and when they told their father – Enoch's 37 year-old brother Tommy – he said "if you boys are going to the war, I must go along too, to look after you."[21] All told, six men comprising three generations of the Ayres family marched off to fight the yankees. Only two of them would return – Enoch and Tommy.[22]

Although Enoch would survive the war, it certainly did not leave him or his family unscathed. His youngest brother died in battle in 1862.[23] In early 1863, Enoch's Uncle John (Jack) Ayres was granted leave and went to visit his brother the Reverend William Ayres. Unfortunately, unbeknownst to Jack, he had been exposed to smallpox in his army camp, and shortly after arriving at William's home, he died from the virus. Thereafter, Enoch's father, mother and little sister all died from the epidemic. Knowing nothing of these deaths, Enoch received his only leave during the war, and in February of 1863 arrived home just in time to see the funeral procession for his mother.[24] Having lost so much during the conflict, one source later declared that Enoch "never forgave the 'damn yankees.'"[25]

* * * * *

After the war, Enoch and Tommy returned home, divided their father's plantation and resumed farming. About six months later, in December 1865, Enoch married Samantha Tyler, whose ancestors included President John Tyler. On her mother's side, Samantha's ancestry traced back to French Huguenots, and her grandmother left France to escape the Reign of Terror.[26] Almost exactly nine months after their wedding, on September 16, 1866, Enoch and Samantha – Enoch always called her "Mantha" – welcomed their first child, a daughter they named Loula. Loula was the oldest of nine children, each spaced about two years apart.

Later in her life, Loula would note that "from babyhood I had lived in stirring and perilous times."[27] The Reconstruction period in South Carolina certainly saw plenty of social, political and economic turmoil. Large portions of the state lay in ruins, and the devastation was immense. Of course, for former slaves it was a new day and a time of great hope. These changing fortunes led to tension and conflict as the parties struggled for control over local government and social institutions. Northern "carpetbaggers" and Southern "scalawags" used the Republican party as a vehicle to push further reforms as a part of Reconstruction, fiercely resisted by the old school white Democrats. While the Ayres were able to keep their farms, many landowners saw their taxes greatly increased and some had their lands confiscated for non-payment.

This was a huge deal, for in the rural South, land was everything. This was certainly true in Marion County, which is generally level, with good soil and climate; its fertile lands led to plentiful harvests. Many crops grew profitably there, including vegetables of all kinds, and most or all of the cereals, such as corn, wheat, rye, oats, rice and barley. Of course, the primary crops were cotton and tobacco.[28] Rice had also been a big cash crop before the war, but became much less profitable afterwards, so thereafter only cotton and tobacco were cultivated on the Ayres plantation.[29]

Enoch became a very successful farmer, known for running his farm "better than anybody else in the community."[30] The large quantities of cotton and tobacco grown on their farm served to keep Loula's family fairly well off during her youth. Enoch was a well-respected man, and many people in the community looked to him to arbitrate their differences. Often encouraged to run for office, he "steadfastly refused."[31] Loula's Uncle Tommy also did well for himself and was elected and served a term or two as county commissioner.[32]

Not much is known of Loula's youth. Many former slaves were sharecroppers on the Ayres' land, and Loula and her younger brothers adored and followed around Henry, the "big, faithful" overseer of their plantation. She also had fond memories of "Aunt Barb," a black cook for the family who also helped look after the young children.[33] Between Aunt Barb and her mother, Loula surely learned all the useful skills taught to young girls in those days, such as cooking, cleaning, sewing and so forth. However, as Enoch had quite progressive views on schooling, Loula also received more formal education under private instructors.[34]

Loula later went to high school at the Ashpole Institute, a private boarding school established in 1878 by the Cape Fear Baptist Association.[35] Although the school was across the border in North Carolina, it drew pupils from both states. During the week, Loula and other students boarded with Stinceon Ivey, the pastor who founded the school.

By her teen years, Loula had grown to be a very tall and very pretty girl. She may have been as tall as five foot nine or ten inches, unusually tall for a girl back then. Loula had long, black hair, blue eyes, a pretty oval face, and dark complexion. Her appearance reflected her French ancestry, and her manners her fine upbringing.

Loula was not only talented, educated, and attractive, she was also very devout in her Baptist faith. Her deeply religious father Enoch ensured the family's regular attendance at the Bear Swamp Baptist Church near their home, where his own father had served as pastor for so many years.[36]

When Loula was seven years old, Enoch was appointed a deacon at Bear Swamp, and later started one of the first and best Sunday Schools on either side of the state line.[37] Enoch was a far more constant presence than the circuit-riding preachers attached to the little country church, and was such an upright and commanding figure that many in the Bear Swamp congregation referred to him as "the pope."[38] Loula's mother was also quite pious, and a fervent believer in prayer. From her early girlhood, Mantha was known as a fiercely religious Baptist, and kept a strong and clear memory until she died at age 86.[39] Like her mother, Loula would maintain her faith throughout her life, even in trying times.

When she finished high school, Loula enrolled in the Chowan Baptist Female Institute, a four-year women's college in Murfreesboro, North Carolina, more than two hundred miles from home. At Chowan, in addition to her other courses, Loula took mathematics, French and even Latin, and continued to excel academically. In fact, at its commencement ceremony following her third year, the school awarded two medals, one for the highest average in general scholarship and the other for the highest mark in Latin. Loula was awarded both, to loud applause.[40]

Loula set a great example for her younger siblings, all or nearly all of whom would go on to attend college. Not quite twenty years old when she received her diploma in June 1886, Loula surely saw a bright future for herself, even in a world dominated by men. While traditional in her views, Loula never felt held back by her sex. Indeed, as shown by the subsequent course of her life, success came naturally to Loula, and she was completely unconstrained by any old-fashioned notions about a woman's "proper place." Instead, Loula did what she needed to do to provide for her children, both in the home and outside of it, and never once thought to pat herself on the back for succeeding in so-called "male" professions. Fittingly, she titled her senior essay at Chowan "The Unwritten History of Woman."[41]

* * * * *

While one source suggests the Rockwell and Ayres families knew one another before Loula and J.C. became acquainted, it is at least as likely that they did not.[42] But whether they knew one another previously or not, fate was about to intertwine the paths of college graduate Loula Ayres and the newly-converted preacher J.C. Rockwell.

J.C. had spent the late summer of 1886 in Old Fort, before returning home to Whiteville, getting baptized and embarking on his preaching career. Many country churches in that time and place considered themselves lucky if they could arrange for an actual preacher every other week; most had a licensed preacher only once a month or even less often. Although not yet fully licensed, J.C. quickly built a reputation as a hard-working, dedicated man of God, preaching at as many of the churches in his area as he could. Just a few months after his conversion, the *Biblical Recorder* noted the young preacher was "succeeding well with his churches," and declared him "full of zeal for the Master." J.C. was quoted as saying "I do not want to go to heaven empty-handed. I do not wish to go into the presence of my dear Lord without laying trophies at his feet."[43]

Following her graduation from Chowan that same summer, Loula returned to her family's plantation in Marion County. On Sundays, Loula and the family surely took up their usual pew at Bear Swamp Baptist Church near the Ayres' home, where her father was still superintendent over the Sabbath School he had started.

By early 1887, J.C. was called to preside over four little congregations, including Fair Bluff, North Carolina, only seven miles from Bear Swamp. He also began teaching again, taking charge of 45 pupils at a grammar school there, the Fair Bluff Academy.[44] At some point he started preaching intermittently in at least one church in Marion County, not far from the Ayres' plantation.[45] It is possible that J.C. even spoke at Bear Swamp. Given their proximity, whether J.C. and Loula knew one another previously or not, it is likely that their romance began to blossom around this time.[46]

A poem written by J.C. a few months later provides some support for this assertion. In May of 1887, the *Wilmington Morning Star* published a poem written by the fledgling preacher that suggests a blooming romance, and has the feel of young love:

"You are my Queen," the lover said,
In tender accents, low and sweet;
And then he bowed his manly head,
And knelt down gently at her feet.

"Rise up, my King," I heard her say,
"And reign forever in my heart;
It is not meet that you should play,
The fawning courtier's humble part."

And hand in hand, across the years,
They journeyed on through changeless spring;
And love was never lost in tears –
She was his Queen, and he her King.[47]

Perhaps Loula came to hear J.C. preach one Sunday that summer at a church not far from the Ayres' homestead. One older minister who heard the sermon that day recorded:

And of Rockwell, what shall I say? Not yet 21 [in fact, he was only 19], *has been preaching but a little over six months, is over six feet high, and as awkward as he is long, he is the best preacher for his experience I ever heard. He is naturally a poet, and much of his preaching is couched in poetic expressions, yet he is by no means fanciful, or given to sky-scraping oratory. I should pronounce him the Talmage of the Cape Fear.*[48]

As he was courting Loula, J.C. surely became known to Enoch Ayres that summer. In addition, J.C. was called to teach at a three-day "Sunday School Institute" just across the state line from Bear Swamp. Given his position as leader of the Sabbath School at Bear Swamp, Enoch likely would have attended both the institute and the discussion led by J.C. on the "Qualifications and

Deportment of Sunday School Workers."[49] Perhaps Enoch was also assessing this particular young man's qualifications and deportment!

If so, it is a safe bet that the youthful preacher, recently proclaimed "a well-known writer of verse and a successful teacher" by one area newspaper, made a favorable impression on Enoch.[50] Being a religious man and the son of a Baptist minister himself, Enoch surely would have been pleased to see his oldest daughter, intelligent and strong, married to a pastor and poet, similarly intelligent and with a bloodline like the Rockwells. The scriptural phrase is "equally yoked." At any rate, it is apparent that J.C. must have begun courting Loula around this time.

While wooing Loula, J.C. continued preaching and, drawing upon his own personal experiences, quickly built a reputation for stirring oratory. In one of his early sermons, J.C. likened Jesus' raising of Lazarus to circumstances in his own life, and how he had found his calling as a preacher poet. He said:

There has been a time in my life when I have seen the fairest and dearest hopes of my heart lying crushed and bleeding at my feet; I have seen the grandest aspirations of an aspiring mind consigned to graves so deep that I felt in my heart that no Gabriel's horn could ever resurrect them from what I thought to be an eternal death; I have stood over the graves of those fond hopes and cherished aspirations, and have wept aloud in the piercing anguish of my soul, and no comforting balm was poured upon my bleeding heart[.]

But lo' down from the far off heights of the Celestial City there came a sweet and loving voice which said: "Patience, patience, and all will be well."

And so I waited, sorrowing, but trusting in that divine assurance.

And by and by the morning began to break; the shadows fled from the presence of the coming day, and behold the Master revealed before me in all of his tender compassion and pitying love. And I heard him say in the sweetest voice that the ear of man has ever heard, "I am the resurrection and the Life: he that believeth in me, though he were dead, yet shall he live. And whosoever liveth and believeth in me shall never die."

And then it seemed to me that the angels came, and rolled the stones away from the sepulcher of those dead hopes of mine, and at the Master's command they came back to life again, not the vain, worldly hopes and aspirations that I had buried with so many heart-pangs and tears, but now purified and made resplendent and glorious with the golden promise of the future.[51]

On September 29, 1887, J.C. was "fully set apart to the work of the gospel ministry" in his hometown of Whiteville.[52] The *State Chronicle* in Raleigh noted his ordination and declared Reverend Rockwell "the youngest ordained minister in the state – perhaps in the world."[53]

* * * * *

As he grew into and began to feel more settled in his chosen vocation, J.C.'s thoughts began to turn to marriage. At the end of 1887, he wrote Loula the following letter:

My dear Friend:

You will remember that you gave me permission to call and see you at your home during the holidays, - so you may expect me Friday evening next. I will go to Nichols on the train, and drive out from there.

I will wait until I see you before I attempt to express my thanks for your kind remembrance of me.

Yours faithfully,

James C. Rockwell[54]

The young pair must have had a good visit, and James Chester must have asked Enoch for Loula's hand, because they were married two months later, on "leap day," February 29, 1888. The wedding ceremony took place at the Ayres' residence in Marion County. One paper took notice of the new "power couple," stating:

Mr. Rockwell is the youngest Baptist preacher in North Carolina and has decided talent as a poet. The Chronicle rejoices with him in winning as his bride so charming a young woman as Miss Ayres, and extends its heartfelt good wishes.[55]

Hand in hand, the Reverend and Mrs. James Chester Rockwell embarked on their new life together. James had just turned twenty. Loula was twenty-one.

Chapter Four

All well, doing well, and well pleased.

The newlyweds lived in Fair Bluff, where James Chester continued teaching at the academy and preaching to his small stable of country churches.[1] He was also able to take advantage of a timely opportunity to fill the pulpit of Antioch Baptist Church in Marion. Having preached there a few times dating back to the previous summer, J.C. was able to add Antioch to his circuit when the regular pastor removed to Durham.[2] His reputation as a preacher of the gospel continued to grow, and soon the leading Baptist publication of the day was calling him "the Poet Laureate of the Baptists of North Carolina."[3]

The couple spent spring and summer together before deciding that J.C. would further his preaching career by attending the Southern Baptist Theological Seminary in Louisville that fall.[4] Complicating this decision was the fact that by the time J.C. left for the seminary Loula was around five months pregnant.[5] She stayed behind at her father's farm while James Chester went to school in Kentucky more than 600 miles away. The young bride and her new husband would never be further apart than at this time.

At the seminary, J.C. focused on his studies, mainly the New Testament and English Theology, and continued writing poems. Early in his second semester, he and Loula's first son was born on February 3, 1889, at Loula's father's plantation.[6] The new parents named their son after Southern poet, editor and literary critic Paul Hamilton Hayne, who years before had befriended J.C. and encouraged his literary pursuits.[7] Loula's surname made a nice middle name; hence, they named their first child Paul Ayres Rockwell.

* * * * *

Unfortunately, not long after Paul's birth, J.C again took ill, and was unable to complete his studies at the seminary. Believed to have malaria and ordered to the mountains, that spring J.C. returned to the rolling hills and green timberlands of western North Carolina.

Covered with thick forests, dotted with lakes and shot through with rivers and streams, J.C. always felt better in his "mountain home." With his usual lyrical flair, J.C. described his feelings towards the area:

Nature is fond of beauty and grandeur, and here she has exerted her powers to the utmost in producing scenery picturesque and sublime beyond description. I sigh for the pen of a poet that I might write in glowing words the praises due to God's beautiful and magnetic handiwork so generously displayed in the Land of the Sky.[8]

Around April of 1889, the new father arrived in Waynesville, North Carolina, "broken in health and almost broken in spirit."[9] Soon enough, he found his condition "improving rapidly under the influence of the delightful mountain climate and the delicious water and pure air."[10] As he expected to spend the entire summer in Waynesville, J.C. promised to lecture for the church there.[11] Even in western North Carolina, the young preacher's growing reputation preceded him – the *Biblical Recorder* noted the "very accomplished young minister" stood "deservedly high with his brethren of the east," while another paper also reported J.C.'s move and asserted "the Waynesville people are to be congratulated."[12]

Preaching every Sabbath in Waynesville that summer, Reverend Rockwell found his congregations "usually large, intelligent and attentive."[13] But however large and attentive the congregations, J.C. was hardly getting rich passing the collection plate – on a typical Sunday he collected about five or six dollars in donations.[14] Still, his congregants found him worthy of their attention. In August, the local paper reported:

At the Baptist Church Sunday, we listened to one of the most powerful sermons we have heard in many days. It was delivered by Rev. J.C. Rockwell, pastor of that church, who is certainly one of the finest clergymen in this part of the state. His delivery as an orator is good and his voice commends him to the pulpit of the worthy Divine. Almost everyone in the congregation seemed spellbound.[15]

Fully restored, by the end of the summer J.C. began contemplating evangelistic work. He aimed to tramp across the mountains of western North Carolina, visiting the Baptists "at their fireside and in their churches."[16] In October he made his way to Asheville, where he spoke on both days of the convention of the Western North Carolina Baptists.[17] J.C. must have tramped his way right across the Smoky Mountains, because later that fall in Morristown,

Tennessee he accepted his first full-time pastorate, beginning his work on December 1, 1889.[18] The *Biblical Recorder* lamented the young preacher's parting: "Bro. Rockwell is one of our promising young pastors and will, we hope, be kindly treated by our Tennessee brethren."[19] But North Carolina's loss was Tennessee's gain – a Baptist publication there noted that although J.C. Rockwell was very young, he was also "a poet and an orator," and would be "heartily welcomed among us."[20]

* * * * *

As Reverend Rockwell settled in at the First Baptist church in Morristown, he was joined by Loula and his infant son. It is unknown whether Loula had accompanied her husband to Waynesville, but the existing evidence suggests she stayed at her parent's farm with newborn Paul until J.C. landed his first full-time ministry.[21] Perhaps much like her grandmother, Loula saw more of her husband before he became a preacher than after. No doubt J.C. was pleased to have his family with him as he embarked on his first pastorate.

The Rockwells set about establishing themselves in their new community. With a population of about two thousand people, Morristown was a growing commercial center and the county seat of Hamblen County. Situated in the foothills of the Smoky Mountains, the climate and elevation were to J.C.'s liking, and there was plenty to keep him busy.

J.C. was welcomed by his congregation and threw himself into his pastoral work. Only a few weeks into his new office, he wrote a short, positive message to the *Asheville Baptist*: "All well, doing well, and well pleased."[22] This was surely a happy time for the family. Although only twenty-one years old, J.C. held a prominent position in the community, and with a beautiful wife and young son, he had much to be grateful for. The couple would soon learn that Loula was expecting their second child, bringing even more joy into their lives.

At Morristown, J.C. began to come into his own as a preacher. His sermonizing had a redemptive quality to it – he saw repentance as a vehicle for individual growth, and God's mercy as a wonderful blessing. One of his favorite sayings was "No man ever progressed to greatness and goodness but through great mistakes."[23] He once wrote "You cannot always judge a man's past by his present life – nor his future life by his present. The best of men have their bitter memories."[24] Traditional in his gospel views, J.C. disagreed with those who said Christian teachings were no longer practical, and needed to adapt to remain relevant. To the contrary, Reverend Rockwell preached "Christianity is not a failure. A new gospel is not needed. But a more earnest and complete obedience to the teachings of the old gospel is an absolute necessity."[25] His sermons relied heavily upon the scriptures, particularly the New Testament, and he once said, "There is nothing better than taking up the life of Christ and studying it in chronological order."[26] He also loved church music, and carefully selected the hymns to accompany his sermons.

Fully engaged in his work as a minister, and helping with his young son and pregnant wife, J.C. no longer had time to write poems or essays for other publications. That summer the *Biblical Recorder* noted that although he still loved his North Carolina brethren, the hard-working preacher was "too busy to write much for this paper."[27] Instead, using his literary skills, he put out his own little publication by the name of the *Pastoral Visitor.*[28] Reverend Rockwell sent the bulletin to the members of his congregation for, as he put it: "The pastor delights in visiting, but finds it impossible to visit as often as he desires; he, therefore, sends out the *Pastoral Visitor.*"[29] He also began holding morning and evening services on Sundays, preaching at 10:30 a.m. and again at 7:30 p.m.[30] A visitor who spent a few days in Morristown that summer reported the following about their eager new shepherd:

[T]here is not a member in all the church that is not delighted with the administration of the pastor, and ready to sustain him in every good word and work. He is only twenty-two years of age, yet he has the maturity and wisdom rarely found below forty, is an able and eloquent preacher, and what is equally important a successful pastor.[31]

* * * * *

To appear a little older and better look the part, J.C decided to grow a beard. It must have worked; a friend of his later recalled that once it had grown in, J.C. "looked somewhat like my conception of one of the twelve apostles."[32]

Another item occupying the reverend's time was his service in the broader Baptist community. As a result of his excellent work in Morristown, Rockwell was quickly recognized as a leading voice among the pastors in Eastern Tennessee. In August of 1890, a regional Baptist association selected him to preach the introductory sermon at their convention near Morristown. His sermon so "captivated the audience," he was appointed to preach again the following day.[33] At the convention, he also served as Chairman of the Committee of Foreign Missions and gave a well-received speech on that subject.[34]

A few weeks after the convention, the Rockwells welcomed their second child, a daughter they named Agnes. Perhaps in recognition of his hard work and growing family, the church increased Rockwell's salary.[35] In the short time the reverend had served in Morristown, his congregation had grown to "almost idolize him," finding him to be "an earnest, faithful Christian gentleman of sterling worth – gold within and gold without."[36] And for J.C., all was going well – he was "succeeding finely in his work," and was again in good health.[37]

However, his unceasing labors and many responsibilities eventually took their toll. Near the end of February, almost fifteen months into his service at Morristown, *The Baptist and Reflector* reported:

Brother Rockwell, the most lovable and eloquent young pastor at Morristown, is off to the mountains of North Carolina for a month's rest. Overwork has utterly prostrated his nervous system. We join his people in prayer for his speedy recovery. He is loved very greatly by everybody who knows him.[38]

The next month his condition had improved enough for J.C. to return to his post in Morristown.[39] Unfortunately, he immediately suffered a relapse, and felt compelled to resign his pastorate. Initially, the church rejected his notice, but when Reverend Rockwell insisted, his congregation relented.[40] And so, with the best wishes of his church, and leaving his family behind in Morristown, the young pastor once again returned to the mountains of western North Carolina.

* * * * *

Seeking "rest and relief from the pressure of pastoral duties," J.C. planned to spend the summer months in the highlands of North Carolina recuperating, hunting and fishing. He hoped that once his health was restored, he could again engage in evangelistic work.[41]

After recovering over the summer, that fall J.C. trekked through western North Carolina and eastern Tennessee, visiting the local churches and several Baptist associations.[42] Then, in late 1891, Reverend Rockwell secured another regular position, this time in Newport, Tennessee.[43]

In Newport, J.C. was again reunited full-time with Loula and his two small children. The first resident pastor of the First Baptist Church in Newport, he was perhaps enticed back into resident pastorhood by the church's agreement to build a parsonage for he and his family to live in.[44] J.C. himself drew up the plans, and oversaw the building of it on Woodlawn Avenue, overlooking the town.[45]

Kiffin was born in this parsonage.

Chapter Five

It is deeds, not years, that make life long.

Although Paul Rockwell was not yet four years old when his little brother was born, Kiffin's birth stuck in Paul's young mind:

I well remember the first time I saw Kiffin. I was about four years old, and my sister and I had been sent to spend the night with some little friends. When we returned home in the morning, our father took us by the hand and led us into our mother's bedroom to see 'the present Dr. Snoddy had brought during the night.' As I looked at the tiny red mite my feelings were of pride and pleasure that I had a brother.[1]

1892 was the centennial year of the Baptist foreign missions, and just a month before Kiffin's birth on September 20, his father had agreed to help with the centennial movement taking place in Tennessee.[2] Reverend Rockwell always had a strong missionary focus; indeed, while serving as head of a committee on foreign missions two years earlier, he had suggested the need to send foreign missionaries "both for the heathen's sake and for our own sake."[3] Loula, too, was missionary minded. As a young girl at Bear Swamp, she had donated small amounts to assist in foreign missions, and after her marriage wholeheartedly supported her husband's evangelizing efforts. Thus, "full of missionary zeal and lofty poetic idealism," when their second son was born, Loula and J.C. "christened the baby after two great Baptist missionaries" using the last names of William Kiffin and Matthew Yates as his first and middle names, respectively.[4] This choice of names says a lot about Kiffin Yates Rockwell's parents, and of their priorities and outlook.

William Kiffin was a worthy namesake. Born in London in 1616, William was orphaned at the age of nine, both his parents having died from the plague. Although he was covered with sores, and "nothing but death was looked for" by those around him, the young lad was spared and lived a long life devoted to God's work. J.C. surely saw similarities between himself and William, who in his youth had also been converted by a powerful minister and went on to lead his own congregation.

William engaged extensively in mercantile pursuits, and over time built up quite a fortune. One anecdote relates how King Charles II, always in want of money, once asked William for a loan of forty thousand pounds. William "replied that he had not then so large a sum at his command, but that, if his Majesty would accept ten thousand pounds as a gift, he was heartily welcome. The King took the money, and William, as he was accustomed to say, saved thirty thousand pounds by his liberality; for Charles would have forgotten to pay the debt."[5]

Known for his integrity and honesty, William served for six decades as pastor of a congregation in Devonshire. In his memoirs, he wrote: "unless God has some work for me to do in the world, for his service and glory, I see nothing else to make life desirable."[6] As shown by their decision to name their son after such a man as William Kiffin, above all, J.C. and Loula admired dedication to an ideal.

Matthew Yates was a Baptist foreign missionary who served many decades in China; he died less than three weeks after J.C. and Loula were married. In fact, the church in Bear Swamp held a memorial service in Yates' honor, raising $13.50 to send to China.[7] Converted while a young farmboy, Yates eventually became the first North Carolinian to serve a mission in a foreign land. Like Reverend Rockwell, Yates was very tall (about six feet two) and concerned for the souls of others. He was also a man of duty – following his baptism, his regular prayer throughout his life became: "Lord, what wilt thou have me do? Show me my duty and grant me grace and courage to do it."[8]

The lives and ideals of these two foreign missionaries embodied many of the hopes and dreams the Rockwells had for their newest son. One could even argue that Kiffin's exemplary service in France many years later was a mission (of sorts) in a foreign land, and that Kiffin had followed in the paths of his namesakes after all.

* * * * *

Kiffin's birthplace was a beautiful little town situated along the Pigeon River in the foothills of the Great Smoky Mountains. At that time, Newport numbered less than a thousand people, but was experiencing significant growth as the county seat of Cocke County. Push and progress seemed to be everywhere, and although largely a frontier town, the community would nearly double its size in the decade following Kiffin's birth.

Southern Appalachia still had its share of roughhewn characters, however, and Newport was no exception. Paul remembered "a few families of education and culture" in Newport, but "in the main, the population was rough, ignorant and lawless."[9] When one afternoon Reverend Rockwell attempted to break up a brawl in front of his home involving several drunken men from two enemy mountain clans, some of the men "struck him and threatened to kill him" before his efforts to make peace succeeded.[10] A few days later, they returned with a supply of chickens and eggs, a goodwill offering to the peacemaking pastor.[11]

In such a place, J.C. felt more keenly his desire to improve the minds and living conditions of his fellow men through religion and education. In one of his pastoral notebooks, he left this fragment: "O how hard it is for man to realize that they are wretches without the grace of God."[12] He also once stated "there would be better times ahead for us all if people could only be persuaded to get a little more knowledge into their heads, and a great deal more religion into their hearts."[13]

Accordingly, as he had in Morristown, Reverend Rockwell offered to his congregation and the public the many volumes in his private collection as "The James C. Rockwell Free Library of Christian Literature."[14] It was at the time one of the largest private libraries in Eastern Tennessee, and included many reference and theological works, sets of poetry and classical novels. Folks came from far and wide to browse and borrow books.[15] A very young Paul remembered his father spending "much time in his generously stocked library."[16]

Probably due to his fragile health, J.C. Rockwell was contracted to preach only two Sundays a month in Newport.[17] He spent the rest of his time visiting members, performing service and continuing his activity in the Baptist associations.[18] Loula helped by teaching in the Sunday school.

Reverend Rockwell was by now a prominent man, prominent enough that early in his tenure at Newport he was invited to give the commencement address at Carson-Newman College in Jefferson City.[19] He chose for his topic something he knew a little about: "Poets and Poetry of the South." One account said the speech was "the finest literary address ever delivered in this place."[20]

While not politically ambitious, J.C. was a firm believer in and lover of his country. Just a few weeks after Kiffin's birth, J.C. was invited to speak at the Tennessee State Baptist Convention. Combining his love for missionary work with his firm patriotism, Reverend Rockwell was quoted as saying: "I love my native land, and especially this sunny Southland. All the problems which vex our country are to receive their solution through the gospel of Jesus Christ. That is what this nation needs." He lamented the fact that instead of greeting immigrants to this country "with an open Bible, we do it with an uncorked bottle."[21] As to be expected from a man of the cloth, Reverend Rockwell's patriotism had a religious tint to it; he held it "the inalienable prerogative of every free citizen of a free Republic to ... guard with jealous devotion the ark of covenant bequeathed to all succeeding generations' posterity by the Founders of the Nation."[22]

Over time, J.C. again settled into his preaching duties. On the first Sunday in December 1892, he delivered two "delightful and edifying" sermons, and the *Baptist & Reflector* reported that "his health, once very precarious, has greatly improved and he is able to preach every Sunday."[23] Thus, the paper declared that "any church in reach of him would do itself great good to secure his services" on his two vacant Sundays.[24] Some of the area congregations must have taken up the offer, as thereafter Pastor Rockwell spoke in several churches throughout Eastern Tennessee.[25]

He also began to adjust to his growing family. From all that appears, J.C. was a good father, and cared deeply for his three young children. He often joked that "babies and books were all that preachers had in this world."[26] On a more serious note, he said that "Children are never young enough to be treated with neglect and inconsideration."[27] Paul's early memories of his father were of a "gentle, kindly-faced, handsome man[.]"[28] While Kiffin had no memories of his father, he was certainly told plenty about him.

Reverend Rockwell advised his congregation: "Do not fancy that children are destitute of mental faculties. Remember that the children of today will be the men and women of tomorrow."[29] Because of this, he felt strongly that ministers of the gospel needed to understand "the art of dealing wisely with the children in their congregations," and jotted down some informal rules for clergymen that he surely followed himself, both as a preacher and in his role as a father: "Have the welfare of the children at heart. Converse with the children. Preach to the children. Do not slight them."[30]

Always fond of seeing friends, J.C. spent much time visiting members of his congregation in their homes, and he and Loula would occasionally call on their many friends in Morristown, only twenty miles north of Newport. Rockwell was also popular with his fellow ministers, many of whom came to see "the cultivated and laborious pastor at Newport" and enjoy the hospitality of "Sister Rockwell's dining room."[31] In February 1893, a little over a year into J.C.'s pastorship in Newport, one minister visited the newly-built "elegant parsonage," and reported: "Pastor Rockwell has aroused the saints of this place.... His people love him. He feeds and leads." The visitor proclaimed J.C. and his "noble wife" the "delight of the Newport saints."[32]

Rockwell spent the spring and summer of 1893 serving in Newport and the surrounding areas, preaching sermons as far away as Jonesborough, Tennessee.[33] In July, he joyfully reported baptizing four people into his congregation, and declared "the Baptist cause is moving forward" in Newport.[34] That same month, he taught at the Eastern Tennessee Baptist Sunday School convention in Johnson City.[35]

* * * * *

Sadly, after preaching a sermon at Carson Springs on August 13, Reverend Rockwell suddenly fell ill.[36] This was to be his last sermon.

He had caught a strain of typhoid going around the area, and for several weeks fought a burning fever. Even in his weakened state, Reverend Rockwell continued to visit the members of his church. One member of his congregation later wrote that when the ailing pastor came to visit her family shortly before his death, her husband had loaded him into their carriage and taken him out to the Springs, "but he continued to grow weaker and passed away a week later."[37]

Reverend Rockwell was "dearly beloved by his congregation," and his death was deeply mourned in Newport.[38] Hundreds of people from all over Eastern Tennessee and Western North Carolina attended his funeral, held at his old church in Morristown.[39] He was laid to rest in the Emma Jarnigan Cemetery.[40] The minister who conducted his funeral eulogized his friend:

Rockwell was more than an ordinary man. He possessed some of those rare qualities which genius alone can show. He was a close thinker, an orator, a poet, a really great preacher.... He was modest, but as bold as a lion in defense of the truth. He was fearless in dealing with sin and felt intensely the weight of his mission. He was so sweet spirited and pure that he was loved by all who knew him best.[41]

Many newspapers took note of Reverend Rockwell's passing. *The Biblical Recorder* said "[t]he death of no other man has ever cast such gloom over this community. The people, without regard to denomination, loved him, and he died without an enemy."[42] The *Baptist and Reflector* remembered him as "one of the best men and finest preachers we had in the state."[43] *The Henderson Gold Leaf* said Rockwell "possessed true poetic genius and sang in a higher key than many whose years and fame were greater than his."[44] Speaking of his death, the *Biblical Recorder* asserted that "the example of his life is left to speak for his silent voice," and declared:

J.C. Rockwell was no ordinary man. While he was greatly beloved as a Christian minister, and admired as a young man of brilliant promise, it was only those with whom he was intimately associated that recognized his real strength and ability. He undoubtedly possessed many of the elements of true greatness. Born in 1868, he was less than twenty-six years old at the time of his death. Yet we can truly say that his life was not short, for it is deeds, not years, that make life long.[45]

The death of her beloved husband James C. Rockwell left Loula a widow just two days before her 27th birthday, with sole responsibility for the care of their three young children. Paul was only four, and Agnes three. Kiffin, the youngest, was just a few days short of his first birthday.

Chapter Six

That fearless boy...

Young and all alone, Loula had to pick up the pieces following her husband's unexpected death. Two qualities she had in abundance – determination and intelligence – helped her make it through. Looking back on her life shortly after World War I began, Loula wrote: "Twenty-seven years ago I was married to a brilliant young minister. Six years later he succumbed to typhoid fever, leaving me with three babies – two boys and one girl. My means enabled me to buy ... a small cottage but nothing more. By my own efforts, first as teacher, later as [an] osteopathic physician I have raised and educated these three delicate children."[1]

James Chester's death must have been a hard blow, and Loula needed some time to regain her footing. She also required help with the children, especially baby Kiffin. Following her husband's funeral, the family gathered their things and traveled to Loula's father's cotton plantation for an extended stay. Paul later wrote that "With our mother, we three children spent the following winter at our maternal grandparents' place in South Carolina."[2]

Kiffin was the youngest grandchild, and quickly became his grandmother's favorite. In fact, until the Rockwells moved to Asheville when Kiffin was thirteen, his grandmother "insisted on his spending at least half his time with her."[3] But it wasn't just his grandmother who was drawn to Kiffin – as a young infant in tragic circumstances, all the women of the neighborhood looked after him. Indeed, one woman remembered that Loula, "as well as every neighbor, worshiped him."[4] During his youth, Kiffin would spend much time among these neighbors, often staying the summer in Tennessee, and the winter in South Carolina.[5]

Once she was ready, Loula and her three children returned to Newport. As her late husband surely would have wanted, Loula raised her young ones in a home of Christian culture, with a heavy emphasis on education and religion. She later stated that "[w]hen my husband died ... my life became theirs."[6]

Loula taught her three children to work and worked hard herself, putting her education to good use. After turning down a position at Carson-Newman College because its distance from Newport would have meant giving up the personal care of her children, Loula began teaching in Newport's public school system, where the local school was within close walking distance of her home.[7] In addition, she once again took a leading role in the Sunday School in the First Baptist church where her husband had formerly been pastor.[8]

Loula personally supervised the early education of her children; Paul recalled plenty of "reading, writing and arithmetic," along with "a good deal of history."[9] Due to their French ancestry, Paul "learned as soon as I could read to be grateful to France and to Lafayette and his French comrades."[10] Like her husband, Loula was patriotic, and as a result, the boys were also steeped in admiration for General Washington and his role in America's struggle for independence.[11]

Paul, Agnes and Kiffin also spent a good deal of time in South Carolina, where they attended "a little school on their grandfather's place," and had "their early education supervised by their mother."[12] Kiffin spent more time on the Ayres' farm than did Agnes or Paul, and attended the old Hillsboro School in Marion County.[13] Paul remembered going to school "some in Marion County, and some in east Tennessee."[14]

* * * * *

Both Rockwell boys loved wildlife and all things of the natural world, and whether in the mountains of Tennessee or at their grandfather's place in South Carolina were "much out of doors."[15] In Newport, Paul and Kiffin ran together in the hills and splashed through the creeks near their home. Paul loved his little brother, and the death of their father strengthened his instincts to protect Kiffin. Although Paul was a few years older, the boys' developed a strong brotherly bond, and he always felt compelled to look after and watch over Kiffin. He never was able to see him suffer – even as a little boy, Paul "would weep bitterly" when Kiffin was punished for some mischief.[16]

And Kiffin was often in need of protection. Tennessee had been the last state to secede and, both before and during the Civil War, the eastern portion of the state was profoundly divided. According to Paul's view of things, "the lowest class of East Tennessee mountaineers turned traitor" and "sided with the North."[17] A generation later, the young Rockwell boys' favorite pastime was refighting the battles of that conflict with and against the other boys of Newport – "the descendants of Confederate veterans on one side and sons and grandsons of bushwhackers on the other."[18] In these scraps, as they would throughout their lives, the boys stood up for one another, and in fights large and small, Kiffin learned not to back down.

His determination was on full display as a youth riding Shetland ponies owned by a neighbor. Kiffin and Paul would gather with other Newport boys on Jones Hill, where Kiffin enjoyed riding Dandy Jim, an obstreperous Shetland pony that, when tickled in the flanks, "would start a hump-backed, stiff-legged lunging and plunging act that wouldn't quit until his tongue lolled out." Kiffin's boyhood friend recalled: "But that fearless boy – puffing and sweating too from all of that rough riding – would be on Old Dandy's back when the jumping stopped."[19] No other boys, not even those several years older, could stay on the bucking pony.[20]

The same boyhood chum remembered another incident when Kiffin, not yet ten years old, mounted their horse, "Kentucky Chief." The large horse suddenly bolted, with Kiffin attached, making straight for the barn and the low entrance to its stable:

I thought surely that Kiffin would be well bashed when the horse reached that spot. But he wasn't hurt. At the opportune split second that boy simply reached up and caught hold of a piece of convenient timber, and just let Old Chief spurt on into the stable. Boy, that gave us a fright, but it didn't seem even to shock Kiffin.[21]

Kiffin loved the mountains of Tennessee, but felt equally at home among the creeks, swamps and cypress trees surrounding his Grandfather Ayres' plantation in South Carolina. That "region abounded in virgin stands of timber" with plentiful wildlife, and Kiffin spent most of his time there out in the open.[22] In addition to reinforcing their horseback riding skills, their grandfather taught Kiffin and Paul to "fish and hunt, and to love the wild animals and birds, and everything pertaining to outdoor life."[23] Paul was more of a reader and collector, while Kiffin was the better fisherman and marksman.[24]

Both boys learned to handle guns at an early age. Honing their skills sniping bullfrogs with air-rifles,[25] the pair "spent many hours in the woods and swamps shooting bobwhites, hawks, rabbits, squirrels," and other abundant wildlife.[26] But a good many of the animals they encountered ended up as pets, including dogs, opossums, raccoons, and even a pair of ducks named Jack and

Jill, "who followed after them quacking[.]"[27]

Taught by their grandfather to hook and land trout, bass and redbreast sunfish, the boys considered it a "great delight" when he would take them on one of his fishing excursions to the Lumber River, not far from the plantation.[28] They also became good swimmers, but had to be alert around the river, as it was home to alligators.[29] The outdoor living at his grandfather's estate did much to mold Kiffin's character.

Although Kiffin was not overly fond of schoolwork (or, as Paul diplomatically put it: "for his books he did not especially care"), he liked to read on his own, and "fairly reveled in" the historical adventure books by G.A. Henty.[30] Henty's books extolling the deeds of gallant heroes were very popular in the late nineteenth century, and tailor-made for Kiffin, with stories full of courage, integrity, virtue, and patriotism. Kiffin also enjoyed the books of Thomas Mayne Reid, a novelist especially popular with adventure-minded young boys, including a young Theodore Roosevelt.[31] Reid dedicated Roosevelt's favorite story, *The Boy Hunters*, to "the boy readers of England and America," hoping to benefit them "by begetting a fondness for books – the antidotes of ignorance, of idleness, and vice."[32]

* * * * *

Kiffin was raised by a single mother, but – at least in South Carolina – he had several strong male role models. Perhaps the most lasting male influence on young Kiffin was his grandfather, Enoch Shaw Ayres. Kiffin "imbibed much of his martial spirit and sense of devotion to a cause" from this strong Confederate veteran.[33] Remembered as "a tall, bearded man who loved his friends and knew how to hate his enemies thoroughly and picturesquely," he had "the kindest heart in the world."[34] From his grandfather, Kiffin learned to enjoy the outdoor life, as well as hunting, fishing, horseback riding, and shooting. Enoch taught Kiffin the skills of a soldier and instilled in him a hardheaded strength of will – there was no quit in young Kiffin, who seemed raised to take a stand.

Kiffin's and Paul's great-uncle Thomas Ayres (Enoch's brother, Loula's uncle), another Confederate veteran, lived not far from Enoch's farm and also spent much time with the boys in their youth. Among other things, the boys learned courage and bravery from these two men. Many years later, a neighbor who knew the Ayres well averred that "[t]he Rockwell boys came of a fearless family of people."[35]

The Civil War and its aftermath strongly impacted both the Ayres and Rockwell families. In addition to both their grandfathers, and a step-grandfather, Paul and Kiffin had six great uncles and many cousins who fought in the Confederate army, several of whom were killed or wounded.[36] Paul later said: "You grow up with that. My family on both sides suffered a great deal from the war, and had a good many members of the family killed and others wounded, and lost a good deal of possessions."[37] Enoch's own losses – he lost his father, mother, brother and little sister, as well as an uncle and at least two nephews during the war – strongly colored his views: although known as a genial host, to the end of his days he "never allowed a 'damnedyankee' to come on his place."[38]

* * * * *

As the Rockwell boys, especially Kiffin, spent much of their youth on their grandfather's farm, Enoch's many stories about his time as a soldier during the Civil War left a lasting impression on them. Paul later wrote:

From his grandfather Kiffin heard stories of war, in camp and in battle. The little boy would listen for hours to his grandfather, his great-uncle Tommy, and other elderly men of the neighborhood recounting their battles, their marches, their sufferings from hunger and cold, and their disappointment and grief over the "Lost Cause," and their struggles after.[39]

Kiffin greatly admired his grandfather and gained from Enoch's example a desire to *achieve... to be... to do*. Kiffin wanted to accomplish something great, something important – not for recognition, but simply because of its greatness and importance. As he listened to his grandfather, Kiffin gleaned that "a man's real worth could only be determined on the battlefield."[40]

Enoch had plenty of war tales to tell, and not just his own. Both of Enoch's grandfathers fought in the Revolutionary War and, as his example would be to Paul and Kiffin, their example had been a significant influence on Enoch in his youth. Indeed, Enoch's middle name – Shaw, his mother's maiden name – was a constant reminder to Enoch of his maternal grandfather, Lieutenant Daniel Shaw, who fought in the Revolutionary War. After three years fighting, Shaw was taken prisoner by the British at the surrender of Charleston, May 12, 1780, and spent more than a year on a prison ship.[41] Eventually released as part of a prisoner exchange, Shaw immediately rejoined the fight, and was subsequently wounded in battle. After recovering, Shaw served the remainder of the war with his regiment.[42] Enoch often spoke of how as a boy he remembered Daniel Shaw's sword being proudly displayed at his grandfather's house.[43]

At a young age, Enoch's paternal grandfather Darius Ayres volunteered from his native state of Maryland to fight for independence from Britain in the Revolutionary War. After the war, Darius lived for several years in North Carolina, then settled in Marion toward the end of the 18th century.[44] Late in his life, "he became a member of the Baptist church in which relation he sustained, during the remainder of his life, a respectable and irreproachable standing."[45] It was said his Christian example "exerted a benign influence and gave the most unquestionable proof that he was indeed a child of God."[46] When he died, he gathered all his children (and probably his grandchildren, including Enoch, then almost five years old) around him, "telling them not to grieve for him, but to prepare to meet him, that he was going to rest."[47]

The boys also heard many times of Enoch's own experiences fighting all four years of the Civil War. Following Abraham Lincoln's election, South Carolina quickly seceded and called for the raising and arming of ten regiments. As more Southern states seceded, and war appeared imminent, Enoch was one of the first to volunteer to fight for the Confederacy.

Enoch's older brother Thomas and younger brother Darius Dwight also enlisted. Enoch and Dwight's regiment, the Eighth South Carolina, fought in many important battles of the War. Sent to Virginia at the outset of the conflict, the Eighth fought at First Manassas, arriving in time to reinforce the army's left flank. Entering the field of battle, Enoch and the other soldiers "charged the federals, recaptured the plateau, and drove the enemy back across Bull Run in great disorder."[48]

Thereafter, Enoch fought with the Eighth Regiment in all its engagements – Second Manassas, Sharpsburg, Fredericksburg, Chickamauga and many others. As part of "Kershaw's Brigade," the Eighth earned a reputation as one of the hardest fighting regiments in the Confederate army. A monument at Gettysburg commemorates the valorous part the brigade played in fighting near the Peach Orchard and the Wheatfield. Never absent from duty unless wounded, Enoch fought all the way through to Bentonville, the last major skirmish of the war.[49]

Enoch's younger brother Darius Dwight (likely named after his grandfather), barely 21 years old, died defending Richmond in May of 1862.[50] Enoch fought on, and "always remembered" the terrible winter of 1862-63, when he did picket duty on the Rappahannock River, along the banks of which the two armies "lay watching, with their camp fires in sight of each other."[51] Another memory was vividly impressed on Enoch's mind when, while fighting at Chancellorsville in May 1863, he "heard the volley fired which mortally wounded the noble Stonewall Jackson[.]"[52] Paul remembered that Enoch "never could speak in unbroken tones" of Stonewall's death.[53]

Enoch's older brother Tommy signed up "to look after" his two oldest sons William and Joseph (Enoch's nephews) who had already enlisted.[54] Fighting alongside his two boys at Port Walthall Junction, near Petersburg, Virginia, in early May, 1864, Tommy and the rest of the soldiers in Company L, 21st Regiment, of the South Carolina volunteers helped fight off five Yankee brigades.[55] Paul described the battle:

Thomas W. Ayres fell, wounded in the head, and near him went down his son Joseph, mortally struck in the abdomen. His other son, William, also fell, with a bullet hole through his chest. Joseph Ayres was buried on the battlefield. Thomas and William were taken at night to a hospital in Petersburg, where William died on May 30, 1864.[56]

Thomas recovered and fought the remainder of the war. He lived until 1908, when Kiffin was sixteen. His last words before he died were: "I am going back to Virginia to see my two boys."[57]

* * * * *

After the war, Enoch rode home "to live and die an unreconstructed Confederate."[58] His and Tommy's war stories inspired young Kiffin, who desired "to shine upon the battlefield for a worthy purpose."[59] Of course, other aspects of the cause for which he fought were less worthy of emulation.

Like everyone else, Enoch was at least to some degree a product of his time and place, and from the Southern perspective, the period of Reconstruction proved very harsh. This was especially true in Marion County, and for the Ayres family. Looking back many years later, Loula still remembered the turbulent times of her youth:

I heard increasing talk about trouble with Negroes, carpetbaggers, scalawags. (The last two terms had to be explained to me, as they were new to our language.) My father and mother and guests discussed, at table and elsewhere, instances of property owners who could not pay the exorbitant taxes and were being sold out, and of young men – usually former soldiers we all knew – who had got into trouble with the occupying military and had left for the West (most of them to never return home). There were stories of shootings and murders and riots at Charleston and in various other parts of the state. Marion County was one of those most continuously occupied by Yankee troops – they were not withdrawn from the county seat at Marion until after the elections of 1876.[60]

Enoch took a great interest in politics and was frequently called on to serve as a delegate from Marion County to the Democratic State conventions.[61] And although he would never run for office, Enoch "always was consulted by candidates about political conditions in our section of the state."[62] In the hard-fought election of 1876, increasing resentment against the corrupt Northerners who had come to oversee the state led to the so-called "Straight Out" Democrats refusing all compromise with the white Republican carpetbaggers, instead resolving to "regain control of their native soil or die."[63] Like many staunch Southern Democrats of the era, Enoch was a participant in Klan-related activities, at least during that election campaign of 1876 – sixteen years before Kiffin's birth.[64] As Loula remembered, that election "was to be all or nothing for the white Democrats."[65] Although the election outcome was contested, after newly-elected President Rutherford B. Hayes ordered the federal troops to leave the state, the Democrat gubernatorial candidate Wade Hampton became sole governor, effectively ending Reconstruction in South Carolina.

Given the time and place of large portions of their upbringing – South Carolina in the generation immediately following the Civil War and bitter Reconstruction – one can safely assume Kiffin and Paul were not unfamiliar with the biases of many white Southerners towards blacks. Indeed, as one author has stated, "[i]n many ways they inherited these prejudices during the months they spent sitting in the presence of the grandfather they adored," and surely the boys heard former slaves referred to in derogatory terms.[66] However, "[t]o what extent Kiffin internalized such talk is difficult to say, since he did not specifically address the issue in the letters of his that survive."[67]

In any event, by the time he enlisted and fought in World War I, there is no evidence that Kiffin felt as strongly about race relations as did many other Southerners of the time. Indeed, some evidence suggests he did not.[68] Even though many aspects of the cause for which he fought were not admirable, Enoch was a great example of commitment to a cause. The cause in which Kiffin enlisted had no such moral baggage.

* * * * *

There was at least one wholly positive aspect of Enoch's influence – he lived his faith. One of his contemporaries praised Enoch's sterling reputation, saying that "like Washington," Enoch "was never known to tell a lie, nor do a dishonorable or dishonest act."[69] Enoch's faith-filled example proved to be a strong reinforcement of Kiffin's religious upbringing.

In the Ayres' household, this was manifest in daily prayer and regular church attendance. While at his grandfather's place, Kiffin surely learned to pray – his grandmother "was a firm believer in the power of prayer," and every night Enoch "called everyone in his house together, read a chapter of the Bible, and offered up a prayer."[70] Naturally, the family went to church at Bear Swamp, where Enoch's father had served as pastor, and where over the years Enoch himself functioned as superintendent of the Sunday school, as deacon, and in numerous other leadership roles.

Perhaps it was when Loula brought her children home to South Carolina following the death of her husband that one of the Ayres' neighbors remembered seeing young Kiffin at Bear Swamp:

I first saw Kiffin in an old country church ... he was sitting in the old pine bench pew with his expressive curly head resting on his mother's shoulder while he ... slept and dreamed.[71]

Chapter Seven

By 1914, we understood him.

Back in Newport, to help meet the family's needs Loula taught school and took in boarders. A teacher staying with the Rockwells, Mary Jane Adaline Susong, was the younger sister of Jacob Andrew Susong, a prominent banker in Newport. Jacob Susong married Loula's younger sister Mary Irene Ayres, giving the Rockwells another important family connection.

Originally, the school where Loula taught held its classes at the local Masonic Lodge. But as Newport continued to grow the need for a permanent school became apparent and Loula, who had already established herself as a strong educator, "aided in organizing the Graded School system of Newport."[1] In 1898, construction was completed on a hand-molded brick building situated on five acres atop a hill overlooking the town. The Newport Academy officially opened that year, and Loula continued to teach there. The school's original structure "remains the oldest continually used elementary building in the state of Tennessee."[2]

Paul and Agnes attended school at the new building, where Kiffin would join them a few years later. Loula continued to teach, and eventually became the first female principal of the academy, which for many years provided both elementary and secondary education to Newport's young people.[3] According to its catalog from the time she was principal, the little school's most important duty was "the fixing of correct principles of character and conduct."[4]

* * * * *

While Paul loved nature and the outdoors, his "indoor" habits of reading and collecting may have been prompted by the fact that he was not as healthy and strong as Kiffin.[5] Paul inherited his father's susceptibility to lung problems and was not overly vigorous as a child. During his youth in Newport, Paul seemed to catch every childhood ailment that passed around and had pneumonia almost every winter.[6] In one particularly alarming episode, Paul suffered a hemorrhage of the lungs.[7] The doctors in the area all predicted Paul would die of consumption before he turned fourteen.[8]

Paul's frailty continued into his teen years, and eventually Loula placed him under the care of an osteopathic physician who visited Newport once a week from Knoxville.[9] Osteopathy was a new branch of science, and many claims were made on its behalf. For example, one article in a leading Southern newspaper around this time recounted how, "as if by a miracle," a New Jersey man "almost totally blind for nearly ten years" had recovered his sight under the care of a young osteopath.[10] While no such miraculous results occurred for Paul, the treatment did prove beneficial, and over time Loula became convinced of the merits of the nascent and promising new discipline.[11]

With the zeal of a new convert, just after Paul's fifteenth birthday Loula resigned her position as principal at the Newport Academy to train as an osteopath. This drastic change allowed Loula to kill two birds with one stone – as she put it, she chose to attend osteopathic school "for the purpose of studying the science and also to place Paul under the care of the founder of osteopathy."[12] Other developments helped make Loula's decision to pursue a new profession a particularly timely and fortuitous one for the Rockwell family.

At that time, the medical establishment firmly opposed osteopathy and sought to prohibit what it viewed as encroachment on the proper practice of medicine. But in late 1902, probably after Paul was already under the care of the traveling osteopath, a decision from the Supreme Court of North Carolina eased the path for the practice of osteopathy in that state. The case, *State v. McKnight*, involved an osteopath indicted for practicing medicine without a proper medical license.[13] The court ruled for the osteopath, noting that his treatment of patients "did not consist in the administration of drugs or medicines, but in manipulation, kneading, flexing and rubbing the body of his patients, and in the application of hot and cold baths, and in prescribing rules for diet and exercise[.]" Holding that a medical license was not required to engage in such activities, the court joked:

We only know that the practice of osteopathy is not the "practice of medicine or surgery," as commonly understood, and therefore it is not necessary to have a license from the Board of Medical Examiners before practicing it. If it is a fraud and imposition, and injury results, the osteopath is liable both civilly and criminally. Certainly "baths and diet" could be advantageously prescribed to many people, and rubbing is well enough if the patient is not rubbed the wrong way.[14]

Following the *McKnight* decision, the North Carolina legislature took another shot at regulating osteopaths as practicing medicine, but in *State v. Biggs* the Supreme Court of North Carolina also found this statute infirm.[15] Perhaps these rulings helped spur Loula's original decision to become an osteopath – the *Biggs* decision issued on December 18, 1903, and Loula Rockwell left for osteopathic school just over two months later, in February 1904.

* * * * *

Whatever her reasoning, Loula's decision opened up not only the probability of a substantial increase in income, but also a return to western North Carolina, which her husband had so loved and with which Loula was already very familiar. Given her favorable experience with Paul's treatment, the opportunity to better provide for her family, and the fact that North Carolina was now wide open to the practice of osteopathy, Loula's decision to embark on a second career path made sense. For all these reasons, at the age of thirty-seven, and with Paul – but not Agnes and Kiffin – in tow, Loula took the train to Kirksville, Missouri to enroll at the American School of Osteopathy.

Loula arrived in Kirksville, settled her living arrangements, and placed Paul in school. During his time in Missouri, Paul attended Kirksville High School, graduating with the Class of 1906.[16] He also received further osteopathic care and grew healthier and stronger.

And so it was that on February 23, 1904, a 37-year old widow of a Baptist preacher matriculated at the American School of Osteopathy, established twelve years earlier by the founder of osteopathic medicine, frontier physician Andrew Taylor Still.[17] Loula's year of entrance was the last in which the school would award a doctor of osteopathy degree after only two years of study; beginning the next year, the degree program lengthened to three years.[18] The substantial savings – annual tuition was $325, quite a sum in those days – were surely not the only benefit for Loula, who wished to reunite with her family as soon as she could. Loula saw an opportunity to quickly earn her doctoral degree and establish a practice in the state of North Carolina – at the time she began her schooling, that state had only two practicing osteopaths.[19]

As one would expect from a former teacher and principal, Loula took her studies very seriously, and performed well in her classes – in four terms over two years, she received no grade of less than ninety percent.[20] In addition, during her first two terms, she did not miss a single day of class, and only two days in her entire two years.[21]

Agnes and Kiffin, ages 13 and 11, spent those two years living with the Ayres in South Carolina.[22] Without his mother and older brother around, Kiffin increasingly learned to rely on and take care of himself. Having no father, and under circumstances that necessitated his mother's absence, independence learned from his youth came to be one of Kiffin's defining characteristics.

While at medical school, Loula surely missed Kiffin. A familiar poem published around the time was later found with some of her materials at the school, copied in Loula's hand on the back of what was probably part of a photo frame. Titled "To My Son," the poem reads:

Do you know that your soul is of my soul such part,
That you seem to be fibre and core of my heart,
None other can pain me as you, dear, can do
None other can please me or praise me as you

Remember the world will be quick with its blame
To shadow or stain ever darker your name
"like mother like son" is a saying so true
The world will judge largely of "Mother" by you

It's yours then the task, if task it shall be
To force the proud world to do homage to me
I'm sure it will say when its verdict you've won
"she reaped as she sowed," Lo! This is her Son.[23]

While Loula did not write this poem, and it is unclear if it was meant for Kiffin or Paul, it well encapsulates Loula's feelings towards her boys – unbreakable love, motherly pride, and an unwavering belief that they were meant for greatness.

Loula's two years in medical school passed quickly, and she received her Doctor of Osteopathy degree on January 25, 1906.[24] The *Journal of Osteopathy* published a grainy photo of Loula in her gown, mortarboard and tassel.[25] In the picture, those accoutrements of graduation frame a face not quite sad, but with the corners of the mouth turned down, clear eyes firmly fixed. Their mother's look of rigid determination was surely one with which her children were familiar.

The graduation ceremony that day was well attended, overflowing the halls, porch and even the windows of the building where it was held. Many people were turned away.[26] It is unknown if Agnes, Kiffin and the Ayres were able to attend, but it is not likely.

Loula must have missed her family too much during her two years away to agree fully with the statement made by the class representative to the people of Kirksville in his graduation speech that "although we may stray far, far away, and our roads lie in many different climes, the memory of our stay with you will always be a bright place in our lives."[27] For Loula, although she enjoyed the intellectual rigor and challenge of medical school, the two years she spent apart from her full family were a trial through which it was necessary to pass, rather than a period she was likely to remember as a bright place in her life. As the graduation ceremony came to a close, Loula's thoughts were surely elsewhere as she anxiously awaited the coming reunion with all of her children.

Now a doctor, Loula set her sights to the east, and the Land of the Sky.

* * * * *

Given her husband's love for western North Carolina, perhaps it was inevitable that Loula would one day take her family to the mountains there. Although born and raised along the southern border of North Carolina, before his death Reverend Rockwell had always felt most at peace among the mountainous western region of the Old North state and had once written "the sun does not shine upon a fairer region than our own mountain country of Western North Carolina."[28]

Thus, it is not surprising that immediately after her graduation from osteopathic school, Loula relocated her entire family – Paul, Agnes and Kiffin – to Asheville, North Carolina. This move must have been in the works for some time, as Dr. William Banks Meacham was already running ads in that city's local papers announcing his association with the new graduate Dr. Loula Rockwell.[29] As it turns out, Loula was likely the first female osteopath in North Carolina.[30]

The timing was ideal for Loula to establish a practice in Asheville. Indeed, for many reasons, as the *Journal of Osteopathy* noted not long after the Rockwells moved there, North Carolina seemed "an exceptionally good field for the right kind of practitioner who is seeking a location."[31] First, Asheville's cool mountain air and mild climate (one commentator aptly described it as "mountain country with a Southern exposure") attracted many health seekers, leading to the establishment of retreats and sanitariums for the treatment of tuberculosis and other respiratory diseases.[32]

The city's beautiful natural setting also attracted numerous visitors. This led to the development of many hotels and boarding houses, as well as several luxury inns and resorts, solidifying Asheville's reputation as a cosmopolitan tourist destination. The Biltmore House, still the largest private home in America, had been completed in 1895, and construction began on a majestic mountain lodge, the Grove Park Inn, several years after the Rockwells arrived. The city's well-known status as a health retreat and tourist destination fueled tremendous growth – between 1910 and 1920, Asheville's population ballooned from eighteen thousand to more than twenty-eight thousand.

Combined with the city's climate, reputation as a health retreat and unprecedented growth, the state's favorable treatment of osteopaths made Asheville a logical choice for Loula to settle her family. Loula also hoped her children would benefit from Asheville's more favorable educational opportunities – as Paul later recollected, compared to their prior locations, Asheville was larger, a better place to live and most importantly for Loula, "better for growing children[.]"[33]

* * * * *

The family settled in at 84 Church Street and began attending services at the First Baptist Church. Loula threw herself into her new practice with Dr. Meacham. In addition, as she always encouraged the boys to work, Paul – now seventeen years old and a high school graduate – began looking for a job. He eventually got on with a southern railway surveying corps in Tennessee, South and North Carolina.[34] The year after the Rockwells arrived in Asheville, Kiffin started as a clerk at J.S. Coleman Lumber Co., manufacturers and dealers in hardwood and poplar lumber.[35]

Although Kiffin was just thirteen when his family moved to Asheville, he had already grown quite tall. Almost too tall, in fact – he looked gangly, and had not quite grown into his big ears. Having bounced between Newport and Marion for most of his life, Kiffin did not have any friends with whom he was particularly close. But with his easy-going nature, he fit in well and was soon running with the society set in Asheville. Always polite and well-mannered, Kiffin was rather strait-laced, and respected even by those who did not know him well. Perhaps this was why his family took to calling him "Senator Smoot," after the Mormon senator from Utah whose name was much in the news around that time.

During the summer of the Rockwell's first year in Asheville, a committee of the United States Senate voted seven to five to deny Senator-elect Reed Smoot his seat in that body. The majority asserted that Smoot's calling as an apostle in the Church of Jesus Christ of Latter-day Saints conflicted with his role as a senator and, more spuriously, that the church was still encouraging polygamy. However, as noted in the committee's minority report, Smoot's character was "according to all the witnesses, irreproachable," and all who testified conceded that Smoot "led and is leading an upright life, entirely free from immoral practices of any kind."[36] Although the background behind Kiffin's nickname is unknown, one can easily imagine Kiffin admiring a man such as Senator Smoot, and attempting to pattern his conduct after him.[37] And like the senator whose spotless integrity reminded others of teenaged Kiffin, throughout Kiffin's life even those who may not have taken any particular liking to him respected Kiffin's character.[38]

During the Rockwell's first year in Asheville, one of the most remarkable events in Asheville's history occurred. On a cold night in November 1906, a rifle-toting black man supposedly named Will Harris rampaged through town, killing five people, both white and black, including two police officers.[39] The man, whose true identity remains unknown to this day, was hunted down and killed by a posse.[40] The incident left quite a mark on those who remembered it. Thomas Wolfe, who went on to literary fame, was a young boy in Asheville at the time and later dramatized the incident in a short story.[41] Wolfe, from whom Paul used to buy the Saturday Evening Post, was most famous for his book fictionalizing his youth in Asheville, *Look Homeward, Angel*.[42]

Although much younger, for some time Thomas Wolfe attended the same school as Kiffin, Asheville's Orange Street School. At the time, both the grade school and the Asheville High School met there.[43] Kiffin probably attended there through the eighth or ninth grade. Thereafter, the city purchased the old Asheville Female College building at Oak and College streets where it relocated Asheville High School. Kiffin finished the tenth grade (and his schooling) there.[44]

Smart and athletic, Kiffin was popular with his fellow students, and became friends with Asheville local Fagg Malloy, as well as the brothers Lawrence and Richard Loughran. Strengthened by his job working for the lumber company over the summer, Kiffin played football, and was one of the better players on the team.[45] Kiffin was also well liked by the faculty, even though, as one teacher remembered, his mind was often "in the far blue."[46] Kiffin, she explained, was "not in the least" rude or boisterous, and "always a perfect gentlemen, always smiling." However, she and the other teachers "simply could not interest him in books."[47]

Although only a teenager, Kiffin made a deep and lasting impression on his teachers. Kiffin was a favorite pupil of his English teacher, Mrs. Mary Walden Williamson, who remembered adolescent Kiffin as a "handsome, intelligent, chivalrous boy of fifteen, immaculate in person as in honor, impatient of the tedium of school routine, restive, though ever-courteous under restraint; with serious, deep-set, gray-blue eyes, aglow with enthusiasm over tales of daring adventure; breaking rarely into surprising light of merriment."[48]

Others also remembered Kiffin's eyes. One teacher who taught Kiffin as a freshman later recalled "[h]e had the most beautiful eyes I ever saw. I taught hundreds of pupils during ten years or so, but remember the eyes of none but Kiffin Rockwell. They were perfect in shape, large, sparkling, with long black lashes."[49] Asked if she remembered Kiffin Rockwell, a third teacher responded, "Oh yes, I taught him algebra. I can see him standing at the board, and I can see those *eyes*; they were *so* blue... yes, his name was Kiffin."[50]

* * * * *

By the summer of 1907, Paul had ended his work with the surveying company and decided to travel a bit before entering college. Always a fan of history, he went to the Jamestown Exposition in Norfolk, celebrating the three hundred-year anniversary of the settlement at Jamestown. The event showcased many interesting attractions: there was a wild-west show, a recreation of the recent San Francisco earthquake, and a huge scale model of the Panama Canal. But for Paul, probably the most interesting thing was the recreation of the Battle of Hampton Roads, the first battle between ironclad ships, which took place during the Civil War in March 1862. Paul spent a few weeks at the exposition before traveling on to see New York.

Unfortunately, Paul did not fare so well in the big city – after loaning all his money to a so-called friend, who promptly vanished, he had to accept a job as a ticket-taker at Luna Park at Coney Island to earn some cash, something he later remembered as "the most amusing experience of his life."[51] The other employees – mostly theatre workers from New York City – were all much amused by the "green" Southerner, and encouraged him to return home and go to college.[52] That he did – in the fall of 1907, Paul enrolled in Wake Forest University, founded in 1834 by the Baptists and at the time an all-male school.

Not much is known about Paul's first year at Wake Forest except the following story. Although officially prohibited by the school, hazing of freshman was a time-honored ritual. Early in his first year, Paul was caught out of his room after hours and ended up in a scuffle with some upperclassmen intent on "blacking" him – that is, smearing a concoction of lamp-oil and boot-black over his hair and scalp. Paul successfully kept the mess out of his hair but ruined a new suit in the process.[53]

When he returned to the Wake Forest campus for his sophomore year, Paul assumed it was now his turn to haze and joined in with an older group of students calling themselves the Night Hawks, known for their "practice of swooping, without warning or mercy, on freshmen found too late or too far from the nest."[54] Apparently one of the group's "blacking" victims complained, and the faculty, intent on putting an end to hazing, voted to expel Paul and an accomplice. Paul later recalled that the university president "offered him the gentlemen's alternative of voluntary retreat," and so "like Lee," Paul "decided to make his last stand in Virginia," and transferred to Washington and Lee University in Lexington.[55]

In the meantime, Loula was building up her practice with Dr. Meacham. In October of 1907, she attended the fourth annual meeting of the North Carolina Osteopathic Society at the Hotel Selwyn in Charlotte.[56] She presented a talk on "Chronic Gonorrhea in Women," and was elected to the Board of Trustees for the fledgling organization.[57] Already much loved by her patients, Loula was gaining recognition as a skilled osteopath, becoming known for combining "gentleness and understanding to such a high degree that her patients became her friends and they leaned on her for strength and wisdom."[58]

* * * * *

While Paul was dodging boot-black at Wake Forest, Kiffin was attending high school in Asheville. But even at the young age of fifteen, Kiffin was restless and ready to seek his fortune. Around this time, probably in the fall of 1907 or spring of 1908, Kiffin did something unheard of, but in retrospect, perhaps not so surprising – he ran away. It was no stunt; Kiffin got as far as Knoxville, more than one hundred miles distant. When he returned – unwillingly – "[t]he whole school was excited, and Kiffin was a hero...."[59]

No one knew why Kiffin ran off. Perhaps Kiffin himself did not yet know what he was looking for. But he was looking. As one of Kiffin's teachers wistfully remembered: "That is all I knew about Kiffin until 1914: those glorious, expressive eyes, and that he ran away. By 1914, we understood him."[60]

Chapter Eight

He is so anxious for the military school...

Kiffin did not return to Asheville High School in the fall of 1908. Having completed the tenth grade (at the time, generally all that was expected), he longed to get on with his life, but was unsure of what to do. He may have returned to work, perhaps at the lumber company, but whatever he was doing, he was still seeking his fortune. Kiffin remembered a family friend from their time in Newport who spoke enthusiastically of his alma mater, the Virginia Military Institute, and began to think more seriously about pursuing a military career.[1]

When Paul "retreated" from Wake Forest to Washington and Lee, Kiffin saw his chance. Located in Lexington, Virginia, W&L is just a short walk from the Virginia Military Institute. Over Christmas break, Paul spoke admiringly of the sharp-dressed VMI cadets he saw around town, increasing Kiffin's desire to attend. By the time Paul went back to Lexington, Kiffin was clamoring to go with him. As she didn't quite know what else to do with Kiffin, Loula requested a catalog from VMI.

When the catalog arrived, Kiffin eagerly read how cadets at VMI were "trained to habits of neatness, system, order, [and] punctuality," and how they would "acquire a sense of personal obligation and responsibility."[2] The military school's goal was "to cultivate discretion, tact, [and] judgment," and to inculcate "the power to command others and to control one's self" – in short, to make boys into men, and men into leaders.[3] That settled it – Kiffin wanted to go to VMI.

Loula felt VMI was a good choice for Kiffin. After reviewing the second term curriculum, the former school teacher felt comfortable with her son's ability to keep up with the work, although she harbored a doubt or two about geometry. Moreover, although just sixteen, Kiffin was already as tall and strong as most boys several years older, so Loula was confident he could handle the physical side of the VMI environment. Finally, and maybe most importantly for Loula, Kiffin would be very near his brother.[4]

Thus, in late January 1909, Loula sent Kiffin off to Lexington. Her plan was that he would interview for admission, and, if admitted, stay and begin school. If not, he could visit Paul and return home. The day before Kiffin left, Loula wrote the following letter to one of VMI's professors:

I thank you for the catalogue and kind letter. My son, Kiffin Rockwell, will leave here tomorrow and in company with his brother from Washington and Lee will probably call upon you Saturday.

He has had two years in German and two in Latin and I think will have no trouble with any of your work unless it be Geometry. He had plane geometry last year but I did not think his work was at all thorough. The fact that he was out of school all fall will not make it any easier for him now. However, he thinks he can by hard work keep up with even that branch. If he cannot, I'd be glad for him to take both Latin and German and have only Algebra this spring and take the work in Geometry next fall. If necessary, I'd give him some private work in that during the summer. I wish him to pay special attention to History and English this term.

If after consulting the boy, you think he cannot well enter the fourth class, he can simply make his brother a little visit and return home. But as he is so anxious for the military school and is growing so tall, with inclination to stoop, I prefer entering him now if possible.[5]

* * * * *

Kiffin arrived at VMI on Saturday, January 30, two days after the start of the second term. He must have convinced the administration he was ready to enter the "fourth class" (as first-year cadets are known), because on February 1, 1909, Kiffin signed VMI's register, making the matriculation promise "to discharge all my duties as cadet with regularity and fidelity."[6] Kiffin couldn't wait to begin the physically and intellectually demanding life of a cadet, and as he looked around VMI, he felt sure he was where he was meant to be.

The parade ground, the barracks, the library, the mess hall – everything about the place conveyed the military spirit Kiffin was seeking. Assigned as a private in Company D, Kiffin immediately learned he was nothing but a "rat" – the term applied to new cadets by the upperclassmen. From the moment he stepped on post, Kiffin learned to stand at attention – if nothing else, VMI would cure him of his inclination to stoop!

Already a full term behind his classmates, Kiffin was also among the youngest members of the fourth class, just a few months beyond his sixteenth birthday. Not only was he one of the youngest cadets, but only one boy entered the fourth class later than Kiffin and stayed, so Kiffin was also the "new kid" for the remainder of the semester. The hazing was rather severe at that time, and Kiffin must have had it particularly bad, as even those classmates who had already completed their first term surely lorded their meager superiority over Kiffin.[7]

Paul confirmed that the "rats" were "beaten regularly and religiously with bed-slats, tin dippers, flats of bayonets, broomsticks, or anything else that came to hand of the masterful third-classmen." He observed Kiffin's stripes and bruises when Kiffin would visit him for lunch on Saturdays. Incensed, Paul "would fairly froth at the mouth with rage and indignation," but Kiffin laughed it off, saying "that the best way to make men of the 'rats' was to haze them."[8]

Saturdays were about the only free time Kiffin had. In addition to his classwork (Algebra, Geometry, German, English and History), there was endless drilling and marching, as a section, company, and battalion. The cadets kept a regular schedule. On most days, they had bayonet, first aid or signal drill; on other days, it was target practice. Fourth class cadets also had compulsory daily training in the gymnasium on the ground floor of Stonewall Jackson Memorial Hall.[9] And of course, Kiffin went to church each Sunday. As stated in the official VMI register:

Cadets are required to attend church on Sundays. Those who are members of the church have the privilege of attending the morning services of the church to which they belong; other cadets are marched to the different churches of the town in rotation.[10]

Not only was Kiffin's schedule filled with all the duties and routines of a first-year cadet but, in preparation for the upcoming inaugural parade in Washington, D.C. of newly-elected President Taft, the whole corps had willingly undertaken *extra* drilling. The exciting news had been confirmed just as Kiffin arrived on post and the whole place was buzzing with anticipation.[11] It was the first time the school would march in the parade, and with just over a month to prepare, each cadet hoped to acquit himself well and so did not mind the additional work.

Kiffin settled in to his classes and quickly got up to speed on the drills. Despite the strict discipline and ritual hazing he endured, Kiffin very much enjoyed the atmosphere at VMI. He met and became friends with Stanty

Boykin, Jon Dalton and some of the other North Carolina boys. During their sporadic free time, they would saunter into Lexington for some shoe polish or stationary, or maybe grab a fountain soda at McCrum Drug Co. The cadets could also purchase their blouses, trousers, belts, collars, cuffs, notebooks, pens and ink on account with VMI.[12]

On February 22, in honor of Washington's Birthday, the boys enjoyed a break from classes and a dance sponsored by the assistant professors. Fortuitously for the cadets, many of the female visitors who had come to Lexington for a dance at W&L the night before stayed over for this one. Noting the "many attractive girls present," the post's student-run newspaper *The Cadet* gushed that "a better time for a dance could not have been chosen."[13]

As the trip to Washington, D.C. drew closer the cadets focused on the inaugural parade. School pride and spirit ran strong at VMI, and everyone wanted their visit to the capital to reflect well upon the institute. *The Cadet* reminded everyone to be on their best behavior, as "[i]t would spoil the success of a showing however good, were we to conduct ourselves when out of restraint any way except that becoming gentlemen."[14]

* * * * *

The morning of March 3, the full battalion marched through Lexington and boarded a special seven-car train provided by the C&O Railroad for the trip to the nation's capital. The boys enjoyed the train's roomy coaches, and the three huge ham sandwiches they were each served about one o'clock. Despite this ample lunch, the cadets cleaned out a fried chicken vendor when the train stopped in the Gordonsville station.[15] The train pulled into D.C. about four o'clock that afternoon, and the cadets marched through falling snow to their quarters at the New Masonic Temple.[16]

The poor weather forced the cancellation of a few planned ceremonies outside, so after a speech in the auditorium at which some gathered alumni presented to the corps a silk flag, the cadets were dismissed with permission to spend the evening in the city.[17] Some spent the night with relatives, while others attended various parties. Kiffin may have gone with a few others to see the famous actress Florence Rockwell in *The Merry Widow* at the New National theatre.[18]

Dawn on March 4 ushered in "a most unpropitious day for an inauguration."[19] At reveille, the cadets "were much disappointed to find snow still falling and streets, to all appearances, as wet as ever."[20] Unfortunately, conditions didn't get much better before the parade – their orders required the cadets to be in position at 2:10 p.m., but they were instead forced to wait in the inclement weather for nearly two hours. When they finally took their place behind the Stonewall Brigade Band it was almost four o'clock, and the cadets were wet to the knees and nearly frozen. Still, they maintained their spirit and step as at last they swung into the procession.

In a few places along the parade route, the cold cadets marched through slushy snow and water nearly a foot deep. But even in such adverse conditions, they "splashed along with lines as perfect and heads as erect as if we had been on dry ground," and when the marchers passed by President Taft, "every man was in perfect step, every piece was carried in precisely the correct position, and every platoon held a perfect line."[21] At least one D.C. paper concurred with this self-assessment. *The Washington Herald* reported that as the VMI corps passed the reviewing stand, a smile lighted up President Taft's features and he "seemed especially pleased at the quick stride and perfect alignment shown by the boys from the Virginia school."[22]

When the event ended, the cadets again had time on their own, which some used to attend the inaugural balls and festivities, while others went to the theatre. Their adventure over, the next day the cadets boarded their train back to Lexington, where late in the evening they marched through the crowds lining the streets to welcome them home.[23] Kiffin had a great time, and his participation in such an important event made Loula immensely proud.[24]

While in Washington, a private talk with an Army general impelled the upper-classmen to address the brutal physical hazing which was hurting the school's reputation in the outside world.[25] And so, shortly after their return to Lexington, the first- and second-class cadets gathered together and voted to abolish the hazing of the "rats," at least insofar as it involved any physical contact. Thereafter, hazing was to consist of ostracism only. However, the third class – the class most responsible for the rats' treatment – refused to accede to this vote. Still, the first and second classes had effectively set a new tone.[26]

The big parade and extra drilling behind them, and now largely free from physical hazing, Kiffin and the other rats buckled down to their schoolwork. Kiffin's life consisted of study, drill, and an occasional jaunt into Lexington with fellow cadets. On weekends, he might attend a lecture or dance, and always visited Paul. He took his studies seriously, and performed well in his classes, although he had a hard time with Geometry. In one of those funny quirks of history, Kiffin's best subject was German.

Soon enough, the term had flown by. With finals approaching, the cadets were given a break from academic work. In late May the entire corps spent a full week in a military-style encampment outside of Lexington, trading their barracks and cots for cramped tents with hard boards for floors. Unfortunately, rain and unpleasant weather marred nearly every day of the event. Although the conditions cleared enough one day to allow the cadets to pull off their planned military exercises, including a full regimental review and parade, the rest of the time they had to amuse themselves with other pursuits – one cadet suffered a broken collarbone engaging in "blanket tossing." When the appreciative campers returned to post and the relative comfort of the barracks, *The Cadet* reported that although "the experience was in some respects an unpleasant one, it was valuable in that it gave the men a taste of campaign life under the least ideal conditions."[27]

Kiffin would later learn that conditions could be far worse.

* * * * *

After his exams concluded on June 19, Kiffin returned home to Asheville.[28] Paul had already returned from his first year at Washington and Lee, and Agnes was back from Wellesley, so the whole family enjoyed some time together.

Kiffin's grades at VMI reflected a solid performance. Loula's intuition was right, and Kiffin struggled a bit in Geometry, which brought down his score in mathematics. But he excelled in everything else, and at the end of his term, Kiffin ranked forty-second out of the one hundred and twenty remaining cadets in the Fourth Class (one hundred and sixty-six had enrolled at one point or another throughout the year). And were it not for his mathematics score, Kiffin would have shown much higher – he ranked 26th in history, 23rd in English, and 9th in German. Showing how seriously he took the military aspect of his schooling, Kiffin accumulated only 18 demerits the entire semester.[29]

Paul and Agnes would return to their respective schools in September. However, Kiffin's fine performance at VMI and his growing family connections helped him secure an appointment to the Naval Academy, so rather than heading back to VMI, he decided to get ready for the entrance exams by attending a preparatory school.[30] So around the time Agnes left for Wellesley and Paul returned to Washington and Lee, Kiffin headed to the Werntz

Academy in Annapolis.[31]

* * * * *

The U.S. Naval Academy Preparatory School was at the time one of two preparatory schools in Annapolis. Founded and run by Robert L. "Bobby" Werntz, a Naval Academy graduate of 1884, the school – informally known as Werntz Academy or, less formally still, "Bobby's War College" – offered no academic credit. It had no library, dormitory, or dining hall and very few textbooks. Its sole aim was to prepare candidates for the Naval Academy's entrance examinations given annually in April. Thus, in a single large room furnished only with student desks and a blackboard, for eight hours a day, five days a week, the hopeful candidates studied and crammed, relying mostly on copies of examinations from prior years.[32]

The atmosphere at Werntz was nothing like VMI, with its beautiful parade grounds, military discipline and honor code. As Kiffin contemplated his decision to try for the Naval Academy, several things caused him to have second thoughts. Primarily due to the boys he was thrown in with, Kiffin quickly determined that he did not care for the school. Many of his fellow students were at Werntz only due to family pressure or other external considerations, and by and large his future class- and ship-mates did not have the same focus and discipline to which Kiffin had become accustomed at VMI. That is, judged against Kiffin's standards, the boys at Werntz did not measure up.[33]

In reaching this judgment, Kiffin was not being snobbish; he was simply refusing to compromise or water down his own standards. In any event, Kiffin's higher ideals were far more conducive to military life. In fact, in a report to the Secretary of the Navy the next year, the Superintendent of the Naval Academy confirmed Kiffin's poor impression of the environment at Werntz. The report claimed that the preparatory schools in Annapolis "exercise[d] little or no disciplinary restraint upon the attending candidates," and that this lack of discipline led the candidates to "acquire habits and associations which are in most cases wholly undesirable, and which cling to them throughout their course at the Academy, and frequently afterwards."[34]

From reviewing the exams of prior years, Kiffin also recognized that the test's focus would likely be his poorest subject: mathematics. Even worse, the exam was timed, making it really "more of a test of speed than of knowledge, particularly in mathematical subjects."[35] The year before Kiffin came to

Annapolis, only 96 of 233 candidates had passed.[36] While Kiffin probably would have done just fine (as his performance at VMI attests), the exam's emphasis on his toughest subject was perhaps another reason for Kiffin to reconsider.

This was especially true since even if he took and passed the entrance exam, Kiffin was not guaranteed a place at the Naval Academy. Significantly, Kiffin had been given a so-called "alternate" appointment. This meant that if the "principal" appointee also took and passed the exam he, rather than Kiffin, would obtain the spot in the class.[37] If that happened, Kiffin would need to secure an appointment through other means, which was hardly a sure thing.[38]

These issues were weighing on Kiffin's mind when he visited Paul at W&L a few weeks after starting at Werntz. The year prior, Paul had been elected an officer in his fraternity, Sigma Phi Epsilon. Shortly after the school year began, Kiffin returned to Lexington for a brief visit, during which Paul's fraternity held an initiation for new members and admitted Kiffin as a "special" member.[39] Kiffin already knew several of his fraternity brothers from his regular visits with Paul during his previous year at VMI, and another student from Asheville, Richard Loughran, was also pledging the fraternity.[40] Richard played left end on the football team, and was a popular man on campus. He and the other "brothers" made Kiffin feel quite at home, both in the fraternity and at W&L. Kiffin began to think he might be better off at W&L, where at least he would control his own destiny.

Nonetheless, Kiffin returned to Annapolis and continued preparing for the Naval Academy's entrance exam. However, the more he thought about it, the more he felt he should leave Werntz, where he "did not admire" the boys, and go to Washington and Lee, where he did. In addition, from speaking with his classmates, Kiffin "got the impression that it would be many a day before the United States Navy would see action," and "began to fear that in the Navy he would be doomed to an inactive life."[41]

As the negatives accumulated, Kiffin no longer saw much point in hanging around at Werntz, and so made his decision – he would transfer to Washington and Lee. Now he and Paul had only to convince their mother to let Kiffin resign his appointment and again switch schools. But of course, Loula readily consented – she was happy to have both her boys at W&L, and told Kiffin she "only wanted him to do that which would make him the most happy and the most useful in life[.]"[42] And so, on November 23, 1909, Kiffin returned to Lexington and matriculated at W&L, pledging his word and honor that he would "faithfully obey all laws, rules and regulations of Washington and Lee University so long as I continue a student of the same."[43] He was still just seventeen.

* * * * *

The week before Kiffin entered W&L, President Taft – in whose inaugural parade Kiffin had marched eight months earlier – issued a proclamation officially appointing Thursday, November 25 "a day of general thanksgiving." Noting that they had been "highly blessed" during the past year, and had "lived in quietness, undisturbed by wars or rumors of wars," President Taft called upon the American people to lay aside their usual vocations on that day and "repair to their churches and unite in appropriate services of praise and thanks to Almighty God."[44]

Chapter Nine

I have always been a great roamer...

Founded in 1749, and nestled among the Blue Ridge Mountains in Lexington, Virginia, Washington and Lee University is named for two of America's most famous generals and influential men: George Washington and Robert E. Lee. The school was a perfect fit for Paul, who admired these two generals "above all other Americans and men in history[.]"[1] Thus, after he beat his gentlemanly retreat from Wake Forest, Paul enrolled at W&L, attracted "by its glorious traditions, so closely bound up with the history of the South."[2]

W&L is the ninth oldest institution of higher learning in America, and was called Liberty Hall Academy until 1796, when President Washington gave the school its first major endowment.[3] Washington's timely gift of one hundred shares of stock in the James River Canal Company essentially saved the institution, after which the grateful trustees renamed it in his honor.

Following the Civil War, for five years Robert E. Lee served as president of the school, now called Washington College. Under Lee's steady stewardship, the college broadened its curricula, and began offering degrees in business, engineering and journalism, setting it apart from many liberal arts institutions of the time. Lee emphasized high standards of conduct and self-control, as best reflected in his reply to a new student who asked him for a copy of the school's rules: "Young gentleman, we have no printed rules. We have but one rule here, and it is that every student must be a gentleman."[4] Following Lee's death in 1870, in honor of his service, the school was renamed Washington and Lee University.

W&L sits on a beautiful campus, centered around the Colonnade, a row of five connected buildings made of red brick, the three tallest fronted by striking white pillars. Sitting atop the middle building is an eight-foot statue of George Washington, called *Old George*. The statue was placed on the building in 1844, in remembrance of President Washington's gift. Directly opposite the Colonnade, General Lee and many members of his family are buried in Lee

Memorial Chapel, and his horse Traveller is interred on the side of the chapel. According to Paul, General Lee "seemed ever present" on campus.[5]

Both brothers surely admired the school's high ideals. The moral examples of General Washington and General Lee formed the standard of conduct for generations of future students, and every young man was expected to comport himself so as to comply with Lee's singular rule – to be a gentleman. For Kiffin, this expectation represented a welcome change from the atmosphere at Werntz.

Kiffin was also excited to be back in Lexington, not much more than a stone's throw from his old stomping grounds at VMI. Tall and straight, like the pillars on the colonnade, Kiffin was now nearly six feet tall, and struck most people as being older than he was. While very mature for his age and accustomed to socializing with older boys, Kiffin had completed only one semester of college and academically was still just a freshman.

When Kiffin arrived, Paul was in his third year of college and second year at W&L, preparing for a career in diplomatic service.[6] In his time on campus, Paul had formed many friendships and taken a leadership role in several organizations. For example, he served as president of the North Carolina club, which Kiffin also joined, doubtless appreciative of the club's motto *Esse quam Videri* – to be, rather than to seem.[7] Paul also filled the office of historian for the Sigma Phi Epsilon fraternity into which Kiffin had recently been initiated. Kiffin would likewise become active in the fraternity, and even attended the organization's conclave in Washington, D.C. near the end of his first school year at W&L.[8] As he had in high school and at VMI, Kiffin again took up German, while Paul opted for French. Both boys studied politics and history; Paul later remembered history being the only subject in which Kiffin had any real interest.[9]

Kiffin at seventeen was strikingly handsome, and his good looks and charisma made him a popular man on campus, especially with the numerous girls who visited for the many dances and balls. He was also a good student, "bright enough not to have to grind in order to learn his lessons," and so "had plenty of time to mix with the other students."[10] Kiffin had time enough to try out for the track team but, like many others, apparently did not make the cut.[11]

Although there is no proof of it, at the beginning of his second year at W&L, Kiffin probably played a role in the decision by the sophomore class to abolish the physical hazing of freshmen. The hazing had apparently gotten a bit out of hand: at the very least, it involved the "over generous use of the paddle," and some freshmen had even been forced to fight their way through a gauntlet down Main Street.[12] It is not a huge stretch to believe that Kiffin's rough experience as a VMI rat influenced his class's decision to abandon such harsh behavior. The school newspaper credited the action, stating "It is to be hoped that future sophomore classes will make no backward steps toward this form of barbarism."[13]

* * * * *

Paul and Kiffin's time at W&L would overlap for less than a single academic year. Late in the spring of 1910, Paul left the university to take a job as the advertising manager for the Piedmont Directory Company. In this position, Paul traveled throughout the South establishing and printing directories for more than fifty cities, while living with his mother in Asheville.[14] Loula's practice with Dr. Meacham was thriving, and in July 1910 they relocated to the newly-completed Legal Building on the south side of Pack Square.[15]

Pack Square was the geographic and social center of Asheville, and during breaks from school Kiffin enjoyed "passing a line" there with his pals. While the Rockwells were not wealthy, Loula's practice was flourishing and the family was solidly upper middle class. Accordingly, Paul, Agnes and Kiffin were friends and contemporaries of the sons and daughters of prominent Asheville families, and both at school and at home, Kiffin and Paul hobnobbed with the monied set. This included Richard and Lawrence Loughran, who were also W&L men. Their father Frank owned the fancy Swannanoa Hotel just off the square, and the hotel's large ballroom was the site of many dances and other social gatherings.[16] Paul and Kiffin, along with the Loughran brothers, organized the Asheville alumni chapter of Sigma Phi Epsilon there in 1911.[17] During Kiffin's time at W&L, the Loughran family made headlines when Frank became the first Asheville motorist to make a round trip to New York by auto; on the return trip, he dropped off his son Lawrence at W&L.[18]

Judged by how often he was mentioned in the society pages, Kiffin seems to have spent most of the summer after his first year at W&L attending dinners, concerts, dances and parties hosted by his upper-crust Asheville friends.[19] For example, with his friends Fagg Malloy and Richard Loughran, Kiffin and three young society ladies (appropriately chaperoned, of course) saw the operetta *Cinderella* at the Auditorium in downtown Asheville.[20] On another occasion, Kiffin and the rest of the high society crowd took a specially-hired cable car to a dance they got up at the casino at Overlook Park, a retreat located on Sunset Mountain near the Grove Park Inn. One local paper reported that Kiffin and the other young people enjoyed the orchestra so much they "remained on the mountain until late in the evening."[21] Kiffin also spent many afternoons and evenings playing cards and attending various social gatherings.

Paul eventually left the directory business, and relocated to Washington, D.C., still thinking he might enter the consular or diplomatic service.[22] However, soon enough he realized that with the Republican Party in power, a young and unknown Southern Democrat such as himself had little hope of an appointment. After briefly considering law school at W&L, Paul instead took up newspaper work in Atlanta, Georgia.[23]

As for Kiffin, as much as he enjoyed his time at W&L, he "usually had a far-away, dreamy look in his eyes, and often seemed to be living in another world from that surrounding him." Many years later, Paul realized that all along Kiffin had only been "unconsciously marking time," while seeking an opportunity to match his dreams.[24] Thus, during his second year at W&L, Kiffin again left college, this time to try his hand at business.

Loula was probably not thrilled with Kiffin's decision but continued to support her son. Realizing he "was still young and restless and undecided [as to] what course of study he wished to pursue," she told Kiffin he "needed to learn the worth of a dollar." Hence, Kiffin agreed to work, and Loula agreed to help him return to college once he "had fully chosen his life's work."[25] But Kiffin never would return to school.

Instead, with three other young men, Kiffin organized an outfit they called "The Southern Press Bureau," and began traveling around the country promoting special advertising editions of newspapers.[26] This venture meshed well with Kiffin's desire to see and experience other places, and he spent the summer of 1911 in Indiana and Michigan drumming up business.[27] Thereafter, Kiffin never seemed to stay too long in one place. Indeed, staying put did not seem to be in his nature. Kiffin himself would later admit "I have always been a great roamer and to have to stay in the same place is my greatest trial."[28]

* * * * *

In pursuit of his business, over the next several years Kiffin roamed far and wide. He loved the freedom of being on his own, making his own way, and did not mind hard work. In fact, he viewed one's willingness and ability to work hard as a measure of manhood, and toil as a stepping stone to independence.

Accordingly, Kiffin *wanted* to labor, to strive, to sweat, to hustle, to travel, to live on his own, and to take care of himself – in short, Kiffin wanted to be a man. As he grew older, Kiffin stayed away from home for longer and longer periods of time, his work and insatiable wanderlust combining to keep him on the move.

And so Kiffin traveled, from city to city and state to state, with occasional visits back home to Asheville. Before he was twenty years old, Kiffin had already journeyed over a large part of the United States and must have been one of the most well-traveled teenagers of the era. It seems that deep down, Kiffin was still driven by the same headlong spirit that at fifteen had caused him to run away. More than anything else, Kiffin was seeking his purpose and place in life.

His travels also began to broaden his perspective. Kiffin was a born-and-bred Southern boy, and that identity would always be at his core, but as he spent more time away from home, he began to feel that many folks in the South were "old-fashioned" and "set in their ways."[29] He even began thinking of settling elsewhere, perhaps out West. One day, Loula received a postcard from Montana. The front showed a photograph of Kiffin and two friends, along with a bull terrier he had purchased on his travels. In the photo, Kiffin exudes optimism and confidence, the hint of a smile seen more in his eyes than his mouth. In a scrapbook she kept, Loula's hand-written caption states that Kiffin was "out West getting out advertising editions of paper."[30] Thereafter, Kiffin toured the Pacific Coast, and then found his way up into western Canada.[31]

Kiffin eventually alighted in San Francisco, which suited him well. He liked the city greatly and, according to Paul, "came very near stopping there." Several years later, after the pair had traveled to France for the war, Kiffin told Paul that "life in San Francisco was more nearly like that of France than any other place he knew in America[.]"[32] Although he considered starting a paper or magazine, Kiffin took a job as a salesman for the Advance Publicity Co.[33] While in the city, Kiffin lived on Eddy Street, within walking distance of the company's offices on Market Street and not far from San Francisco Bay.[34]

Over time, the pull of family overcame Kiffin's desire to roam, and in late 1913, he left San Francisco and returned to Asheville to spend Christmas with Loula.[35] Having been on his own for almost two years, Kiffin had become a man. Now twenty-one years old, Kiffin stood almost six-foot-two, and had grown into a strong, handsome, independent and well-rounded gentleman. But though he was finally back home, Kiffin was not done roaming. In fact, he was just beginning.

Chapter Ten

The die is cast.

After spending Christmas with Loula, Kiffin headed to Atlanta to see Paul, who had been living there for the past year or so. As a newspaper man, Paul cut a dashing figure about town, where he was known as "genial, always smiling and always dressed to the minute," with "a weather eye ever skinned for the girls...."[1]

Paul worked as a reporter for several Atlanta papers, starting with the *Atlanta Georgian*, an afternoon newspaper with a penchant for sensationalizing the news.[2] Earlier that year, Paul had covered the Leo Frank trial – if you have heard of it, you know it needed no sensationalizing.[3] By the time Kiffin showed up – on January 1, 1914 – Paul had begun working for the *Atlanta Constitution*.[4] Paul later said he would never forget that New Year's Day when Kiffin arrived in Atlanta:

I had been up late the evening before, properly ushering in the New Year, and was asleep at the Georgia Tech chapter house of our fraternity when I was awakened by the feeling that someone was watching me. I opened my eyes, and there stood Kiffin at the foot of my bed, with an amused expression on his face. I was amazed to see how tall he had grown; he was then a little over six feet two inches, having grown fully three inches since I had seen him.

We spent the day talking over anything and everything. I was full of curiosity as to his impression of the places he had seen, and Kiffin wanted to know if I really liked Atlanta well enough to make it my home. We agreed never again to part company, but to live together, and began making plans for leaving the fraternity house and finding a suitable bachelor's apartment.[5]

The brothers soon located a little apartment on West Peachtree Street, which they rented for $20 a month.[6] They also hired Jim, a "fairly efficient" young black man, as their "cook, butler, and general factotum," and Kiffin began looking for work.[7]

Kiffin's first visit was to St. Elmo Massengale, the owner and president of

Massengale Advertising Agency, to whom he carried a letter of introduction from a friend in Asheville.[8] Only thirty-eight years old, Massengale had started his ad company – the first and largest in the South – at the age of twenty, and in the ensuing years had built it up through hard work and his embrace of advertising as a means to raise the standard of living.

Believing that increased competition reduced the cost of living, Massengale was convinced that advertising particularly helped the poor. His philosophy was straightforward: "the more the wealthy spend money for automobiles, diamonds, [and to] build houses, the more employment it gives the laboring classes."[9] Massengale handled the first national advertising campaign for Coca-Cola, and also worked with other well-known brands, such as R.J. Reynolds, Red Rock Ginger Ale, Nunnally's Candies and the Cheek-Neal Coffee Company, which was becoming famous for its Maxwell House Coffee.[10]

In addition to his advertising agency and outdoor bulletin system, Massengale was the founder and president of the Atlanta Ad Men's club, the director of the Georgia State Chamber of Commerce, and a prominent member of Atlanta's social clubs. He had political connections, too. A loyal Democrat in the largely one-party South, Massengale would later serve as Secretary to the Georgia Democratic Executive Committee.[11] In his first foray into politics, later that year Massengale would take over the Fulton county operations of the gubernatorial campaign of Judge Nathaniel E. Harris, helping him successfully carry every ward in the city.[12] In short, Massengale was a good person for Kiffin to meet.

In Kiffin, Massengale saw a young man much like himself. Young, energetic and brimming with confidence, Kiffin impressed Massengale so well that he immediately offered Kiffin a job.[13] Thereafter, Kiffin "made good quickly," and, according to Massengale, "was the most successful solicitor" he ever had on outdoor advertising in Atlanta.[14] Massengale quickly came to know Kiffin as "serious and dignified, gentlemanly and modest," and considered him to be "a good business man."[15] In only a few months' time, Kiffin developed a strong relationship with Massengale, and they would keep in touch even after Kiffin left for France.[16]

Like Massengale, Kiffin saw plenty of opportunity in Atlanta. The city was the burgeoning capital of the South, and attracted many visitors for various activities and events, big and small. In February, the Atlanta Merchants and Manufacturers Association hosted "merchant's week" in Atlanta, drawing more than 1,500 business leaders from across the South. There were also events more to the liking of the area's less genteel folk. For example, in the same month the business elite turned out for merchant's week, the Old-Time Fiddlers Association held their convention, which included a contest that drew more than fifty fiddlers trying for prizes, as well as one 16-year old boy whose father swore he could play "Swanee River" on one end of the mouth organ and "Dixie" on the other – "at one and the same time."[17]

Baseball was becoming increasingly popular in the South, and the Atlanta Crackers regularly drew large crowds from all classes to their all-wood stadium. On opening day in April, the civic-minded Massengale shut down his business to try to help the Crackers win the Southern League attendance award. Unfortunately, the game against Chattanooga was rained out, so Massengale closed his business early again the next day. Given that he had the day off, presumably Kiffin was there to see the Crackers win the attendance award, as well as an exciting game, six to five.[18]

* * * * *

Kiffin quickly made connections among the Atlanta social scene, where he became known for having "a homely wit and an eye for beauty."[19] On many evenings and weekends, Kiffin and Paul played cards with their fraternity brothers at the Georgia Tech frat house; it was later said that no small number of "poker sharks" marveled at Paul's prowess at the game.[20]

Kiffin and Paul also enjoyed vaudeville performances at the Forsyth, a beautiful theatre designed by A. Ten Eyck Brown, the architect of several prominent buildings in Atlanta. The Forsyth had opened a few years earlier at the corner of Luckie and Forsyth streets, across the street from the Piedmont Hotel. It now sat next door to the new Ansley Hotel, which had been completed right around the time Paul came to the city. Paul worked a few blocks down the street, in the *Atlanta Constitution* newspaper building.

The *Constitution* ran frequent ads for the Forsyth, "Atlanta's busiest and most popular theatre," where matinee shows were twenty-five cents, while evening shows cost double or triple that amount. B.F. Keith's vaudeville outfit toured many urban centers at the time, and the 1200-seat Forsyth was its Atlanta home. One wonders what Mr. Massengale must have thought of the theatre's less-than-stellar slogan "Always a Good Show – Often a Great Show." Surely there were some great shows – many performers who later became big-time stars came through the Forsyth during Kiffin's time in Atlanta. For example, a young Mae West played the Forsyth in the late Spring.[21] A cowboy comedian named Will Rogers appeared there in July.[22]

During this time, Kiffin was finding his place among the up-and-comers in the growing city. A reporter friend of Paul's remembered Kiffin as "a droll, good-natured sort of chap, who once loafed along Whitehall street, in this shop and that, with a bill folder under his arm, soliciting advertising when he wasn't up to some other commercial scheme."[23] Of course, given his restless nature, Kiffin was always on the lookout for other "commercial schemes," so even while working for Massengale, his mind was often engaged elsewhere.

For example, he discussed with Paul the idea of starting some sort of magazine, and in early 1914, together the boys put out "a rather unsatisfactory paper" intended to boost their adopted city.[24] In May, Kiffin left Atlanta for a brief visit to W&L.[25] Upon his return, Kiffin decided that his job was no worse than any other peace-time profession, and tried to reconcile himself to being an "ad man." To boost his skills, he even enrolled in a correspondence course on modern advertising.[26]

Nevertheless, as the days ticked by, Kiffin could not shake his feelings of restlessness and unfulfillment. While he worked hard, enjoyed his job, and was good at it, Kiffin could not see himself selling advertising bulletins the rest of his life. Instead, he longed to make a difference and to accomplish something worthy of praise. Kiffin was still thinking of his future when he decided to return to Asheville to see his mother over the Fourth of July weekend.[27]

Before he left Atlanta, Kiffin probably had not seen the *Constitution's* July 3 front-page story about the recently-assassinated Archduke Ferdinand.[28] The heir to the Austrian throne and his wife had been gunned down on June 28 by a young Serbian anarchist. In its coverage of the event, the *Constitution* suggested that the tragedy would likely "embitter still further the none too friendly relations between Austria and Servia."[29] In Asheville that weekend, Kiffin was reminded of the slayings when the local papers carried stories about the funeral services for the murdered royals.[30] Still, the incident seemed not much more than a minor happening on the world stage, and Kiffin never gave it a second thought as he enjoyed his brief visit home, with Independence Day celebrations in which "fireworks were burned in large quantities."[31]

The Fourth was on a Saturday that year, so the next day Kiffin would have attended church with Loula, as well as Agnes and Paul, who were also home.[32]

One of the local Sunday papers carried an account of President Wilson's high-minded Fourth of July address on "The Meaning of Liberty," delivered at Independence Hall in Philadelphia the day before.[33] In his speech, Wilson asserted "it is patriotic sometimes to regard the honor of this country in preference to its material interest," and that "the most patriotic man" was the man "who goes in the direction that he thinks right even when he sees half the world against him, because it is the dictate of patriotism to sacrifice yourself if you think that is the path of honor and of duty."[34] Kiffin couldn't have said it better himself.

Kiffin also agreed with Wilson's statement that "America will come into the full light of day when all shall know that she puts human rights above all other rights and that her flag is the flag not only of America but of humanity." Continuing, Wilson declared his "dream" that the world would "turn to America for those moral inspirations which lie at the base of all freedom." After all, Wilson proclaimed, "To what other nation in the world can all eyes look for an instant sympathy that thrills the whole body politic when men anywhere are fighting for their rights?"[35]

The sentiments pronounced by President Wilson perfectly coincided with Kiffin's beliefs. However, the world would soon realize the president meant his words more aspirationally than literally.

* * * * *

After church, that afternoon Kiffin prepared to return to his job in Atlanta. He was beginning to feel resigned to his life as a salesman at the Massengale agency, and reluctantly began to think of settling down. While waiting on a street car to take him to the train station, Kiffin sweetly asked his mother to quit working and come to Atlanta and make a home for himself and Paul. But Loula declined, telling him she wanted her boys to get married, and to establish their own homes and families. She gave Kiffin a hug and watched as he boarded his streetcar. Loula did not know it at the time, but this was to be the last time she would ever see her son.[36]

While Kiffin returned to Atlanta, Paul remained in Asheville a few days longer.[37] The assassination of Franz Ferdinand had already dropped from American front pages – the day after Kiffin left, had Paul chanced to look in the "market news" section of the *Asheville Citizen*, he would have seen the following note in the middle of a piece on financial issues:

At Paris there is still some tension owing to an uneasy political situation, but financial affairs generally on the continent are settling down, and the calmness with which the assassination at Sarajevo was received shows that no serious complications are yet in prospect.[38]

A bit further south, Kiffin was already back at work, hustling up and down the streets of Atlanta and studying the principles of modern advertising via his correspondence course. Upon Paul's return, he and Kiffin visited the Forsyth, where they saw a dancing novelty and musical comedy performance starring Ralph Riggs and Katherine Witchie, along with Will Oakland, a tenor making his first visit to Atlanta.[39] Along with the rest of Atlanta, the boys surely enjoyed Walter S. "Rube" Dickinson, a popular character comedian of the time, who performed his show "The Ex-Justice of the Peace."[40] Later that month, the whole city was buzzing over Dickinson's impromptu marriage to Laura Grant, a girl Kiffin's age whom Dickinson met one night after his show and proposed to the next day. Grant accepted, a municipal court judge was summoned, and the pair were married next to their dinner table on the roof garden of the Atlanta club, in front of nearly a hundred surprised diners.[41] Dickinson and his new wife departed Atlanta the next day to finish his summer bookings.[42]

But soon no one would be discussing Rube Dickinson's marriage to Laura Grant.

* * * * *

As July rolled towards August, the Atlanta papers carried increasingly ominous mentions of the escalating tensions between Austria and Serbia, and the saber-rattling of the old European powers. On July 24, the *Constitution* noted that Austria claimed it "was unable longer to pursue an attitude of forbearance" with Serbia, to whom it had sent a humiliating ultimatum.[43] The very next morning, the front-page proclaimed that "Austria's Ultimatum to Servia Over Archduke's Assassination May Loosen War Dogs in Europe."[44] The accompanying article noted the "extreme gravity" of the situation, stating that unless the crisis were "handled with great delicacy it is not unlikely that others will become involved in war."[45] Just two days later, the headline banner across the front page of the evening's *Atlanta Journal* said it plainly: "Darkest War Cloud In Several Years Is Hanging Over Europe."[46]

In the midst of these issues of worldwide importance, tragedy of a personal nature struck the Rockwell boys – on July 26, 1914, their grandfather Enoch

Shaw Ayres passed away. The old soldier's last words were: "I'm in harmony with everyone and am ready to meet my God."[47] To Paul and especially Kiffin, their grandfather had been a hero and example. Kiffin was surely at a low point and felt the need to *do something*. Not long after, he would write to his mother that he had been "dissatisfied with the course my life was taking," and the death of his beloved grandfather only made worse the unshakeable feeling that he was meant for more.[48]

The day after Enoch's death, the frontpage headline of the *Atlanta Journal* blared: "All Nations of Europe Make Preparations for War."[49] Although war in Europe appeared increasingly likely, the paper also carefully noted that the United States would take a "hands off" approach in the threatened conflict – indeed, President Wilson had already emphatically affirmed the traditional policy of the United States "not to mix in European affairs."[50] However, despite Serbia's surprisingly conciliatory response to Austria's ultimatum, on July 28 the conflict sparked into war between those countries. The next morning, the *Constitution* reported: "Europe Quakes as Austro-Servian War Begins."[51] All eyes now turned to Russia, Germany, France and Britain, each of whom held alliances or had assumed obligations with Austria or Serbia, or their allies.

As a reporter, Paul was keenly following the unfolding events in Europe, and could scarcely believe what was happening.[52] Kiffin was also paying attention, and as tensions escalated and events snowballed towards war, he began formulating plans about his future – plans that did not involve correspondence courses on modern advertising. The death of his grandfather had sharpened his resolve, and Kiffin was starting to think that he might participate in the upcoming war. He had always dreamed of proving himself on the battlefield, as had both his grandfathers; and the looming conflict seemed to offer a real chance to seize the life he had always wanted – the life of a soldier.

Perhaps to take his mind off things, that night Kiffin took in another show at the Forsyth. He saw "That Funny Fellow" Jack Wilson, a comedian who, according to the review in the *Constitution*, was "doing the best set he has ever given Atlanta."[53] In addition, "Those Kidlets," a clever boy and girl dance act, presented a "treat for the ladies and children."[54] This was to be the last show Kiffin would ever see at the Forsyth.

On July 31, alarmed by the doubling of the English bank rate to 8% and news of bank runs in London and Berlin, the governors of the New York Stock Exchange hastily voted to close.[55] The exchange would not reopen until

December, still the longest stoppage in its history. It was obvious now – the great powers of Europe were preparing for hostilities, and practically no hope was held out for peace. The world anxiously awaited declarations of war.

* * * * *

Finally, inevitably, one by one the European nations were drawn into the conflict. First, Russia announced it was mobilizing to defend the Serbs. Viewing this as a threat to Austria-Hungary, to whom it (like Russia to Serbia) was bound by treaty, on August 1, Germany declared war on Russia. Of course, France was bound by treaty to aid Russia, and had to react. Sure enough, that same day, France posted on every public building and post office in Paris and the provinces an order calling for the mobilization of all French troops.

Along with the mobilization order, the Ministry of War also posted a proclamation reminding citizens that "mobilization is not war," and that the government still hoped its diplomatic efforts would succeed. But no one believed it – as one French journalist stated, if mobilization "was not war, it was certainly something terribly near to it."[56] That is, everyone knew that once started, the machinery of war would be difficult if not impossible to stop.

More convincingly, the proclamation affirmed that France counted on "the patriotism of all Frenchmen, knowing that there is not one of them who is not ready to do his duty." It ended with this call to arms:

At this hour there are no parties. There is France eternal, France peaceful and resolute. The fatherland of right and justice is entirely united in calm, vigilance and duty.[57]

Recognizing war was at hand, in Paris, the English-language *New York Herald* solemnly opined:

The die is cast. All Europe is under arms, and only a miracle can now prevent the outbreak of the tremendous conflagration which the world has so long dreaded and for which the European nations have been preparing for so many years.[58]

Back in Atlanta, Kiffin read the news that Germany and France had both mobilized.[59] On the first day of August, the *Journal* reported that French officials felt "it would now be folly to rely on any hope of a peaceful outcome," and thus "war seemed to be only a question of hours."[60]

War was overtaking Europe. As one by one the dominoes fell, darkness threatened to engulf the entire world. Kiffin's moment had arrived.

Chapter Eleven

I felt the call of opportunity.

The causes underlying the war's outbreak were numerous and complex. Suffice it to say that the war came. It was immediately called the Great War, and great it was, in the best and worst senses of the word. Over the next four years, monarchies fell, borders were erased, and the seeds of revolution were sown. The costs were incalculable – on top of the property, money, assets and cultures of the peoples of Europe, the war wiped out a considerable portion of an entire generation of young men, changing the globe forever. Countless soldiers faced the terrible horrors of mechanized war, and sacrificed all so, as many of the participants saw it, civilization itself might survive.

But in the fateful summer of 1914, most young men in America had other things on their minds. While a European war seemed a terrible affair, it was literally an ocean away, and surely the parties would come to their senses sooner or later. No one imagined the initial puffing would draw in millions of soldiers, or that it would eventually bring death and misery on a scale never before seen. To most, then, the squabbling over the death of one measly archduke did not seem worth getting too worked up about.

Things were different for the Rockwell brothers. They foresaw the potentially drastic consequences and the certain involvement of their favorite among nations, France. And because both of them, but especially Kiffin, were grateful for the noble part France had played in America's war for independence, they felt an obligation to repay that debt.[1]

As the war clouds gathered, on Sunday afternoon, August 2, Paul and Kiffin invited a few friends to their Atlanta apartment for a mid-day meal. Reflecting on their French ancestry, the Rockwells spoke of how interesting and exciting it would be to go and fight for France if that country became directly embroiled in the escalating conflict. Their lunch guests agreed that someone needed to stand up to the German onslaught, but like most Americans had other personal concerns that seemed more important.

But Kiffin had already reached his decision – he pulled Paul aside and said he had thought it over, and "his mind was fully made up to go."[2] Kiffin felt that any war would eventually involve the United States, and convinced Paul they should act now and fight for France.[3] Listening to the Rockwell brothers as they talked, one of their friends became caught up in the spirit of the thing and declared that he too would join up.[4]

The next day, realizing it could not wait for the full mobilization of the Russian forces, as this would mean fighting on two fronts, Germany declared war on France. The *Journal* announced: "Armageddon has come. The greatest war since the fall of the Roman Empire is on in Europe."[5] That was enough for the Rockwell brothers – they quickly composed a letter to the French Consul in New Orleans. It read as follows:

Dear Sir:

I desire to offer my services to the French Government in case of actual warfare between France and Germany, and wish to know whether I can report to you at New Orleans and go over with the French Reservists who have been called out, or must I go to France before enlisting?

I am twenty-five years old, of French descent, and have had military training at the Virginia Military Institute. I am very anxious to see military service and had rather fight under the French flag than any other, as I greatly admire your nation.

If my services can be used by your country, I can bring several friends who are also desirous of fighting for the French flag.

Trusting to receive a favorable reply from you soon, I beg to remain,

Yours most sincerely,

Paul A. Rockwell[6]

Clearly, the brothers meant what they had said the day before – they were going to enlist and fight for France. Indeed, on Tuesday, the *Journal* carried an article noting that Kiffin and Paul intended to "shoulder arms in defense of France."[7] When he heard of it, Massengale tried to talk Kiffin out of his plans. But Kiffin was adamant, telling his boss "he had made up his mind he must go[.]"[8]

* * * * *

However, the American government had other ideas. The same paper that announced the Rockwells' intention to fight for France also noted that

President Wilson had just issued a proclamation of American neutrality, forbidding American citizens from "enlisting or entering into the service of either of the said belligerents as a soldier" or in any other capacity.[9] Wilson later declared that the country "must be neutral in fact as well as in name during these days that try men's souls," and even that Americans "must be impartial in our thought as well as in action, must put a curb on our sentiments as well as upon every transaction that might be construed as a preference of one party to the struggle before another."[10] In short, Wilson had no intention of choosing sides, much less entering the fray.

Apparently, neither did the young man who just two days earlier had told Paul and Kiffin he would go with them.[11] When, despite Wilson's neutrality proclamation the boys moved forward with their plans, their friend began to have second thoughts. As Paul later recollected, their acquaintance "was one of the big talkers we encounter in life. He evidently thought Kiffin and I were discussing volunteering to fight for France just to be talking, and he was all for going with us. When he found out we were in earnest he dropped out of the picture."[12]

Of course, Kiffin was having no part of Wilson's "neutrality" poppycock, and you can bet he was not about to "put a curb" on his sentiments. A clash of civilizations was underway, all Europe was in arms, and Kiffin did not intend to wait on the sidelines.

Thus, even as Germany was invading neutral Belgium, Kiffin and Paul were at a travel agency on Peachtree Street inquiring as to any steamships leaving for Europe. In the few days since war had been declared, ocean liners headed across the Atlantic had suddenly become scarce. In fact, other than an American Line vessel sailing from New York in exactly two days, the boys were told that "there might be no more ships Europe-bound for some time."[13] After begging the agent to telegraph New York to determine whether any berths were still available, at 10:00 a.m. on August 5, Paul and Kiffin learned they could secure two spots in a cabin on the *St. Paul*, leaving New York in forty-eight hours.[14]

But they would have to hurry – to reach New York by the morning of August 7, the boys would have to take a 20-hour train ride from Atlanta to Washington, D.C., and another train from there to New York City. The brief stop in D.C. would also allow them to obtain their passports. If all went according to plan, the boys would arrive in New York the night of August 6. But the train to the nation's capital left that afternoon.

The next few hours were a whirlwind, as the boys hastily prepared to leave. Intent on making the afternoon train, Kiffin and Paul raced home and spent the next several hours packing their bags and ordering their affairs.[15] Many of the things they couldn't carry they left with their butler Jim who, predicting he would never see them again, broke down in tears as the boys said their farewells.[16] Paul stopped at the newspaper offices and told his colleagues: "I'll meet you boys in France."[17] Before they caught their train, Kiffin also went to say goodbye to his boss and co-workers. Massengale later said he "would never forget" the day Kiffin left:

I asked him if he realized he might be killed and he said he ... was not afraid at all – that he believed whatever happened would be for the best. That God knew when and where his time would come, whether here or there; in peace or war, and that he thought his duty was to go....[18]

"He thought his duty was to go." That simple statement perfectly explains why Kiffin decided to fight for France. Thus, the day after President Wilson forbid Americans to enlist as soldiers for any of the belligerent nations, Kiffin left Atlanta, intending to do just that. He had $12.95 in his checking account at the Fourth National Bank of Atlanta, and still owed money on his correspondence course and the typewriter that came with it.[19] Moreover, he wasn't even sure the French would accept his offer to fight on their behalf. But right now, those were secondary concerns – the world was at war. And strangely, finally ... Kiffin was at peace.

* * * * *

The boys made the afternoon train, which rolled northward from Atlanta all night long, arriving in Washington, D.C., on Thursday morning, August 6. Scrambling from the station, Paul and Kiffin roused their congressional representative, a man named William Schley Howard, out of a committee meeting and induced him to help expedite their passports.[20] On House stationary, Howard quickly scratched out a note to the Assistant Solicitor at the State Department, Richard W. Flournoy, Jr., which read:

My dear Mr. Flournoy:

This will present messieurs K.Y. & Paul A. Rockwell of Atlanta, Georgia, who are desirous of obtaining passports. Will appreciate any courtesies extended them.[21]

The boys raced to the State Department, where Mr. Flournoy questioned them as he filled out their passport applications. Paul gave his occupation as "reporter," saying he intended to return to the United States within 6 months, while Kiffin said he was in "newspaper work," and intended to return within 2 years.[22] It is unknown whether Flournoy directly asked the boys what their intentions were in traveling abroad and at the time the American passport application did not request such information, but the law deemed an American citizen to have expatriated himself "when he has taken an oath of allegiance to any foreign state."[23] In any event, both boys signed the Oath of Allegiance appearing on their passport applications, swearing to support and defend the Constitution of the United States, whereupon Flournoy endorsed as notary and issued the boys their passports.[24]

Having acquired their travel documents, Kiffin and Paul stopped by the Treasury and exchanged their paper money for gold.[25] The boys then rushed to catch the train to New York City, where they arrived later that night. Upon their arrival, the pair made their way to the Hotel Imperial, where Kiffin would spend his last night on American soil.

* * * * *

That night, Kiffin was restless and full of nervous energy. Realizing they had not even told their mother they were leaving, Kiffin stayed up late writing her a letter. He decided the blunt approach was best, and so began like this:

Well, Paul and I are sailing on the American liner St. Paul *tomorrow morning at ten o'clock. We would have gone by home and seen you and explained things if we had had the time. But we had to do some hurrying to catch this boat and it was practically our only safe chance. It is the only boat leaving here in two weeks' time flying the U.S. flag, and we didn't want to wait two weeks.*[26]

Kiffin hinted he would not have brought Paul along, except he felt it could help get him "into the line of being a good short story writer."[27] Kiffin's own reason for going was consistent with his adventurous spirit – like Lafayette, he had found a unique opportunity to distinguish himself, and could not pass it up: "You know I have always been a great dreamer and I just couldn't keep myself from going on this trip, for I felt the call of opportunity."[28]

Reminding Loula she had always claimed great faith in his future, he declared: "well, now is the time for you to prove your faith by not worrying any about me."[29] Then, softening his tone a bit, Kiffin almost apologized:

All of my actions have always appeared as if I didn't care much about you and the rest of the family, but it isn't that way. It is just that I must and will live my life as I think best even though I am often mistaken.[30]

Exhausted after the two-day journey to New York, Kiffin explained that he couldn't write a good letter just then, being "completely tired out [with] so many things to think about."[31] So he asked his mother to please not worry too much and put down his pen. Utterly drained, Kiffin closed his eyes and drifted off to sleep.

* * * * *

The boys arose early the next morning and excitedly made their way through the city to Pier 62, on the east bank of the Hudson River.[32] They must have been in awe when they first took in the huge *St. Paul*. The twin-screw, double-funnel ocean liner stood more than six stories high and was a full 535 feet long on the water line. With a crew of nearly four hundred, the ship could accommodate more than 1300 passengers, with 366 berths in first class alone. The boys had secured two first-class tickets, sharing a four-berth room with two other passengers.

Pushing through the throngs of people, the brothers boarded the massive vessel and handed off their "not wanted on voyage" baggage to the steward. Dropping their remaining bags in their stateroom (No. 124), the boys headed to the promenade deck to see the crowds gathered to witness the ship's departure.

At 10:00 a.m., the *St. Paul* pushed away from the pier and steamed south down the river. From their places along the guardrails, Paul and Kiffin waved to the crowds on shore until the ship pulled into New York Harbor, and churned past the Statue of Liberty. The boys knew the magnificent robed statue had been a gift from the people of France commemorating their nation's alliance with America during its fight for independence. Miss Liberty, as she was then called, had only recently completed her exquisite oxidization process, transforming from her original dull bronze to a smooth blend of green, and stood as a beautiful and vivid memorial to the long-standing ties between America and France.[33]

As the ship moved past the monument, the boys could make out the date July 4, 1776, inscribed in Roman numerals on the tablet she held in the crook of her left arm. The date brought to mind America's struggle for freedom, in which France and especially General Lafayette played such a glorious role, and of which the splendid statue was an unmistakable reminder. Now, almost one hundred and forty years later, France was facing her severest test, and at least two passengers on the ship, brothers from the South, remembered and felt obliged to repay their portion of America's debt. Gazing up at the monument commemorating the sacred bond between the two countries, Kiffin couldn't help wondering whether the anticipation he felt meant he had at last found his calling.

As the *St. Paul* pulled into open water, Kiffin felt the cool morning air breezing past his face. Looking up, he saw the American flag on the mast unfurl, revealing its 48 stars. As America slipped from view, Kiffin's last sight was of the torch held aloft by Miss Liberty. He smiled, and turned his eyes eastward, towards France.

End of Part One

Enoch Shaw Ayres, image courtesy of Washington and Lee University.

Loula Ayres Rockwell, courtesy of Sybil Rockwell Robb.

James Chester Rockwell, image from the State Archives of North Carolina.

(left to right) Kiffin, Agnes and Paul Rockwell, circa 1899. Image from the State Archives of North Carolina.

Kiffin at age 14 in Asheville. His mother's scrapbook notes this photo was taken "in the days we called him Senator Smoot." Image from the State Archives of North Carolina.

Kiffin (left) at age eighteen. The caption in Loula's scrapbook states: "Kiffin out West, getting out advertising editions of paper." Image from the State Archives of North Carolina.

Σ Φ E

Sigma Phi Epsilon fraternity photo from The 1910 Calyx. Kiffin is in the back row, middle, while Paul is in the front row, far left. Image courtesy of Washington and Lee University.

My favorite photo of Kiffin, this is him at age 17 during his time at W&L. Image from the State Archives of North Carolina.

Part Two – The Boys Who Remembered Lafayette

"Ladies and Gentlemen, in international conflicts it is not
the most highly evolved nation that has the choice of weapons.
And so when a nation which is still in the backward stage
of preferring violence to peace attacks a peaceful and more
advanced nation with violence, then that nation must either hit
back or go under – and we are not disposed to go under."

- Christabel Pankhurst, October 24, 1914[1]

"So ask the travelled inhabitant of any nation, In what
country on earth would you rather live? &—Certainly in my
own, where are all my friends, my relations, and the earliest
& sweetest affections and recollections of my life. Which
would be your second choice? France."

- Thomas Jefferson[2]

Chapter Twelve

The cannon must speak.[3]

Former (and future) Prime Minister Georges Clemenceau was right – the cannon would speak. In Paris, the hour was one for action, and above all else the need was for soldiers. And so, shortly after Germany invaded Belgium (and right around the time Paul and Kiffin were packing their things in Atlanta), Clemenceau issued a stirring call, a beacon signaling all Frenchmen to the defense of their country:

And now to arms, all of us! I have seen weeping among those who cannot go first. Everyone's turn will come. There will not be a child of our land who will not have a part in the enormous struggle. To die is nothing. We must win. And for that we need all men's power. The weakest will have his share of glory.[4]

While rousing rhetoric such as Clemenceau's certainly helped, the French people needed no prodding. Everywhere in France, men were enlisting, trains were rolling, machines were humming, and flags were waving. According to one observer, "there never was a thrill like the early days of August, 1914, in Paris."[5] Another noted, "Everywhere, war fever is now turning. Here and there a shop is closed and a scrap of paper on the door explains the reason – the owner is at the front."[6] And not just Frenchmen – foreigners all over France felt the call, and volunteers of many different nationalities came forward.

However, the Foreign Legion required a five-year enlistment, and many foreigners did not want to sign on for that length of time simply to fight in what many of them were sure would be a brief conflict.[7] And so, on August 3, the French minister of war proposed instead that enlistments into the Foreign Legion be for the duration of the war, rather than the standard five-year engagement. This would, he predicted, "attract to the legion a large number of foreigners desirous of giving in the great circumstances faced by the country proof of their attachment to France."[8] President Poincare quickly adopted the proposal, and it was printed in the *Journal Officiel* on August 8.[9] But to avoid overcrowding the railroads, barracks and training camps already inundated by the ongoing deployment of the French army, it was decided that no foreign recruits would be accepted until twenty days following the mobilization order.[10]

In the midst of the fervor of mobilization, a group of American students living in the Latin Quarter of Paris gathered at the *Café du Dôme* to discuss the question of volunteering.[11] The meeting was crowded; as one New York paper put it: "One would have thought that half the American art students in the quarter had turned out."[12] An American woman living in Paris must have passed by some of the students; she recorded in her diary:

Today a gay crowd of Americans, all decorated with French and American colors and flags, went by singing and clapping their hands – as they had no musical instruments – cheering for La France and for the United States. They carried an enormous canvas (contributed by the artists) with Vive la France *– Vive l'Amérique – Bless 'em!*[13]

Two days prior, an American citizen living in Paris had publicly called for volunteers. Published in the *New York Herald* on August 3, the letter read:

In the war of Despotism versus Equality, Justice, Liberty and Fraternity which noble France and her allies have undertaken to defend, I am prepared, like a true-spirited American, to offer myself as a volunteer, and abide by any orders the Ministry of War may give.

Surely there will be other Americans to share my sentiment – Americans who, apart from considering France a second Motherland, have for years enjoyed the great freedom and hospitality of this glorious Sister Republic.

Able-bodied American citizens residing in France who desire to manifest the brotherly feeling existing towards the citizens of France should not hesitate to enlist as volunteers.

Georges Casmeze[14]

Born in London to a Turkish mother and an American father, Casmeze was a "strange combination," at least according to his friend, a fast-talking motor car salesman and opportunist named Bert Hall, who just happened to be living in Paris when war broke out.[15] Apart from his exotic ancestry, Casmeze was described as "cool, modest, and sparing of words, but with a remarkable reserve of energy and the instincts of leadership."[16] An American citizen, Casmeze for two years had lived in Paris representing American manufacturers and handling American goods.[17] After writing the above letter, Casmeze offered his business office as a recruiting headquarters for what he dubbed the American

Volunteer Corps.[18]

Many American students and university men could be found in Paris, along with others vacationing or residing there for business, and some of these felt a strong desire to fight for France. In addition to Casmeze and Hall, this group included men like Kenneth Weeks, a former Harvard, M.I.T. and *Ecole des Beaux-Arts* student and the author of several volumes of short stories and plays.[19] Weeks told his mother: "Paris is wonderfully calm, as is all France. Naturally, perfect confidence exists and, God be praised, the barbarians will be crushed flat."[20]

Another was F.W. Zinn, who in June had graduated from the school of engineering at the University of Michigan.[21] Within two weeks of his commencement, Zinn left America on a long-planned trip around the world.[22] Having booked a cheap ticket to Antwerp via London, Zinn was stuck in London when the war started. He crossed to Paris where, speaking with some French students, he became thrilled by the prospect of war – enthusiastic enough to fight against Germany, the country of his ancestry.[23]

John J. Casey, a popular artist deeply sympathetic to the French cause, drew newspaper illustrations for the *New York Sun* and other papers.[24] He had exhibited his work in America and France and even displayed a canvas in the 1914 Salon earlier that year in Paris.[25] Like many of the others, Casey also lived in the Latin Quarter. So did David Wooster King, a dry wit who would later write an engaging book about his experiences. Only 19 years old, King had recently finished up his sophomore year at Harvard, where he had been a member of Cercle Francais, the French club on campus.[26] Casey and King both signed up.

Alan Seeger, another Harvard alumnus, had been a classmate of T.S. Eliot. Since graduating in 1912, he had been living in the Latin Quarter, writing poems and hobnobbing with intellectuals.[27] In fact, Seeger had just returned to Paris from London, where he had been seeking a publisher for his first manuscript. On his way back to Paris he left it with a printer in Belgium, which was now being overrun by the Germans.[28] Upon his return, when he could not find his friends at his favorite café, Seeger hastened to join them in "playing soldier."[29] Along with these men, many others among the American colony in Paris inquired about volunteering, and applications came pouring in to the recruiting office.[30] As a group, most of the men felt as did Kenneth Weeks, who told his mother that "in defending France, I hope to defend you."[31]

As Hall put it, "[e]veryone wanted to fight, but the problem was to find out how, when and where to begin fighting."[32] Wanting to enlist but unsure of the effect it might have on their American citizenship, a few volunteer-minded individuals went to visit the American Ambassador to France, Myron T. Herrick.[33] Eager to follow the French soldiers to war, they inquired whether they had a legal right to fight for France. Many years later, Herrick still remembered the emotional meeting:

I got out the law on the duties of neutrals; I read it to them and explained its passages. I really tried not to do more, but it was no use. Those young eyes were searching mine, seeking, I am sure, the encouragement they had come in the hope of getting. It was more than flesh and blood could stand, and catching fire myself from their eagerness, I brought my fist down on the table saying, "That is the law, boys; but if I was young and stood in your shoes, by God I know mighty well what I would do."[34]

That was good enough for the Americans, who began streaming in to Casmeze's office at *11 Rue de Valois*, now the recruiting headquarters for the American Volunteer Corps. Fortuitously, his office opened directly into the arcade and gardens of the *Palais Royal*, where the American volunteers quickly received permission to begin drilling each day at two o'clock.[35]

In charge was Charles Sweeny, a former underage fighter in the Spanish-American war who supposedly had the extraordinary distinction of having been kicked out of West Point – twice.[36] Nonetheless, Sweeny would prove to be a real soldier and, along with Bert Hall, Hall's friend Rene Phelizot, a well-known hunter of big game in Africa, and James Bach, a mechanical engineer who had lived for some time in Europe, took charge of the training and drilling of the American recruits.[37] But first, the excited volunteers purchased the largest and best American flag they could find in Paris – a four-foot beauty – and hung it over the door of the recruiting office.[38]

The committee also sent out several appeals for volunteers, expressly recalling the service Lafayette had rendered to America in its time of need. Published in London, where many expatriate Americans were located, one such appeal read:

Can Americans remain deaf or indifferent to the appalling drama – unprecedented in the annals of history – that is now being unfolded on the Franco-German frontier?

Should not a sentiment of gratitude vibrate within the heart of every true

American, and an eager feeling burn within our bosoms in recognition of and to reciprocate in a measure the gallant service noble France rendered when the great General Lafayette, with an able army of men, drilled and equipped, crossed the Atlantic to aid our immortal Washington?

No! If the United States as a nation must remain deaf, many of its able-bodied citizens will heed the call "Aux armes, Citoyens!" It is our brothers' call, and the call of many mothers, wives, children and sweethearts of our second motherland.

Quite a number have already enrolled. More are wanted, so as to form a league worthy of the name American. As soon as the lists are prepared the names of those enrolled and those who have promised to aid in equipping those enrolled will be duly published.

American Volunteer Corps[39]

The committee had published a similar appeal in several Paris papers the day before. Written in French, the plea emphasized "the most imperious duty of American citizens: to recruit, equip and exercise an American legion by adopting the martial costume of the bold companions in arms of General Lafayette," who when needed had traveled to the United States "to offer our immortal Washington the assistance of their sword."[40] The committee ended its request by asking members of the American colony to join their enterprise:

Citizens of the United States, we appeal to your uprightness, your love of freedom, the sacred memories of our history and its martyrs! France, our sister Republic ... is in danger. The French people, like one man, went to the frontier to defend it against invasion, and to punish a people perverted by pride and unavowable envy. This is the time when every American citizen should do his duty by uniting with us. Our confidence remains intact, and it will not be said that the generous American colony of Paris and France will have done less for its benefactor, France, than the other foreign colonies.

Long live immortal France! Long live the American colony![41]

This appeal, like the other, was signed by Casmeze, Hall, Phelizot and a gentleman named Paul Testard, an engineer from Union University in New York by way of Montreal.[42]

Enthusiastic and ambitious Americans from all over Paris and beyond responded, and the roll of volunteers rapidly grew to more than 120 names.[43] As Hall noted, "applicants came in droves," and the project "seemed to be an assured success."[44] But while mostly young and healthy, the men were hardly soldiers, and sorely needed instruction. Zinn later recalled the volunteers were made of "wonderfully good material but *so* raw...."[45] Even gung-ho Sweeny admitted "no crowd ever looked less soldierly than we did."[46]

But they were willing to learn. Many had French parentage, others had been living in Paris as students or for business reasons and volunteered out of a desire to aid France. Zinn, the recent Michigan graduate, noted that he and the others "felt toward France precisely as they would have felt toward their own country in a similar crisis."[47] In fact, as one reporter noted, many of the Americans "propose[d] in small measure to repay the service Lafayette rendered the United States."[48] Sweeny later recalled the spirit that animated the volunteers:

We meant to fight for France. We loved France. Something in each of us, voiceless and confused as we were, told us that the world would be the gainer if France won and immeasurably the lower if France were crushed. I do not know that many of us carried the argument further.[49]

Although a bit older than most of the others (he was a married father of two), Sweeny had charisma, guts and – most importantly – prior experience. He would earn the respect of all the men, and before the war was out, would become the first American volunteer to become a commissioned officer of the Foreign Legion.[50] With the help of some French drill manuals, he began to work the men into shape.[51] Although they had no uniforms, little equipment and no rifles (it was understood the French would supply those once the men were officially enlisted), soon enough the group drilled so well they were actually applauded by the Parisians who gathered in the gardens of the *Palais Royal* each day to watch.[52]

* * * * *

As the various units began to coalesce, Casmeze began receiving letters and telegrams from others eager to volunteer, even from abroad. For example, Victor Chapman, a rich young American who would later become an aviator and one of Kiffin's closest friends, cabled from London stating simply: "I am coming over. Can I bring anything with me?"[53] One James Frazer of Ohio also reached out, stating he wished "to fight or do anything for right and justice."[54] Bob Scanlon, a large Southern black man and prize fighter well known in both London and Paris, was once described by one of his peers as "a coal-black human mountain."[55] Living in Paris at the war's outbreak, Scanlon signed up because he "wanted to see a bit of fun."[56]

William Thaw, another future comrade of Kiffin's, was also in Paris. In a note to Casmeze, he explained the essential sentiments underlying his enlistment: "[m]y love for France and my hatred for Germany inspire me to volunteer."[57] Having just turned twenty-one on August 10, Thaw was a former Yale footballer and the son of a wealthy railroad executive. A budding aviator, Thaw caused quite a stir at the beginning of his sophomore year when he arrived on campus in a hydroaeroplane he had purchased with an inheritance.[58] Shortly thereafter, Thaw made news in New York when he became the first pilot to fly under the four bridges spanning the East River, and topped it off by circling both the Statue of Liberty and an inbound steamship.[59] He soon dropped out of Yale to pursue his interest in flying, and was next seen in Palm Springs, Florida, ferrying high-society folks around the beaches in his flying boat.[60]

Earlier in 1914, Thaw traveled to France with his younger brother Alexander Blair Thaw, hoping to market an aircraft stabilizer Alexander had invented.[61] The brothers planned to enter the balancing device in a safety contest sponsored by the Aero Club of France.[62] In addition, Thaw accepted the invitation of the Aero Club of America to represent the United States in the Jacques Schneider Cup, a hydroaeroplane race in Monaco.[63]

Although Thaw was not able to start the race, he did acquire his French pilot's license, and was widely covered in the French press.[64] He also probably met several French flyers, including Roland Garros.[65] Thaw and his brother spent the care-free summer of 1914 in Southern France, flying and carousing around its beautiful beaches and resorts.[66] Friends of the swashbuckling young pilot began referring to him as "The playboy of the Riviera."[67]

When war broke out, Thaw was in Paris with his mother, sister and brother. Despite his mother's misgivings, Thaw told her "this was not a time for patriotism, but for principle" and offered both his flying machine and his services to the French.[68] France accepted his plane, but at the time was not able to accept Thaw in aviation. Thus, Thaw signed up with the American Volunteer Corps, from which he would enter the French military service as a simple soldier, with the expectation that he would "be put in the Aviation Corps later."[69] Although young, Thaw was a natural leader, and was immediately viewed as such when he arrived at *11 rue de Valois*.

In addition, several steamships that left America after the outbreak of war began to arrive in Europe, bringing further recruits.[70] One of these recruits was

Dennis Dowd, a 27-year old Brooklyn lawyer.[71] When the conflict began, Dowd devoured the dreadful news out of Europe, and could not sleep for four nights. He finally told his family he "wanted to get into it for France." Thinking it was only an outburst of enthusiasm, his father advised him to "wait till your own country needs you."[72] But when Dowd saw mention of the American volunteers in a New York paper, he "decided that his place was in their ranks."[73] Having made up his mind, he approached his father during an after-dinner smoke, and calmly told him "Dad, I'm going to France to join in the fighting."[74] He told his mother he felt he was doing his duty.[75]

But to his friends Dowd said only that he had urgent legal business in Europe that could not be postponed.[76] Quickly securing a passport, he booked passage on the August 11 crossing of the *Rotterdam*, the first ship to leave Hoboken, New Jersey after the war began.[77] Dowd got a taste of the changed circumstances of the world when a riot broke out just before the ship's 1:00 a.m. departure – it seems the ship's officers had denied entry to three hundred German reservists, who "gave vent to their indignation" until the police were called to disperse the belligerent crowd.[78] When the *Rotterdam* docked in Plymouth, England on August 19, Dowd made his way to London and then Paris, arriving just before the volunteer corps was to officially enlist.[79]

Dowd immediately offered his services to the group, and on August 21 joined with the Americans as they trooped over to the *Hotel des Invalides* (the residence of invalids) to enlist. Louis XIV had built the *Invalides* in the seventeenth century as a sort of hospital and retirement home for his wounded soldiers. Encompassing a huge complex of buildings, grounds, and two beautiful chapels, since the mid-nineteenth century the *Invalides* had also housed Napoleon's tomb. In the early days of the war, the French used the complex as a medical examination center and clearinghouse for enlistees. Just after Dowd's arrival, word came down for the volunteers to present themselves at the *Invalides* for evaluation and assignment.[80]

Predictably, now that the time had come officially to commit, about half the group suddenly had other things to do. As Hall put it: "when we were sent over to the *Invalides* to take the oath of allegiance ... many of our good boys fell ill or had business engagements, or family matters or any one of a thousand other things that prevented them from taking the final step."[81]

Nonetheless, those willing to go forward fell in and marched in smart columns towards the *Invalides*, Sweeny in command. The next day, *Le Figaro* noted how the Americans "excited admiration by their superb outfit," and that a considerable crowd had followed the various groups to the *Invalides*.[82] The men surely got caught up in the moment – Paris was ablaze with war time fervor, and a spirit of invincibility prevailed. While waiting to enlist, a large volunteer seated on one of the old cannons in front of the *Invalides* shouted to an elderly French gentleman: *"On va taper sur les Boches, mon vieux!"* – we're going to hit the Boches, old man![83]

At the *Invalides*, the American recruits passed the necessary physical examinations with flying colors, at least as compared to volunteers from some of the other nations. Whereas other groups saw up to thirty percent or more of their recruits rejected, only two American volunteers were turned away.[84] One later legionnaire described the process:

After being stripped and examined as carefully as a horse, and given a certificate of "aptitude," I went to another place and was sworn in. A little old man with two medals and a glistening eye looked over my papers, and then in a strong voice asked if I was prepared to become a soldier of France, and, if asked to, lay down my life for her cause. Then I signed, and was told to report the next morning, and be prepared to start training at once.[85]

Many of the Americans had little understanding of the papers they signed, as they were written in French. Bill Thaw, whose knowledge of the language was limited at the time, later described what he comprehended of the pledge:

I met, as I understood, the requirements of the French authorities in order that a foreigner might become a French soldier. I understood this oath to be one of obedience and loyalty to the French during the war, and [that it] did not include my renunciation of allegiance to the United States, and that all my rights as a citizen of the United States [were] fully retained.[86]

Having signed the pledge, each volunteer was given their first day's pay and told to await instructions on when and where to report for training.[87] The recruits were officially admitted into the Foreign Legion on August 24 and departed for their training facility the next day.

* * * * *

As the time approached, surely the volunteers contemplated their individual reasons for the action they had taken. For many of the men, especially among the students in the Latin Quarter, signing up was the natural, easy choice – most of their classmates had already done the same. For example, Casey, the blond, athletic artist, remarked that he had a lot of "awfully nice" French friends, and just before embarking to the front gave this straightforward explanation for his decision: "They've all gone – I can't stay behind. So off I'm going!"[88]

Seeger invoked similar reasoning, albeit with prettier language, as the rationale underlying the enlistment of many of the volunteers – namely, that after "that memorable day in August," it was unthinkable for them "to go on enjoying the sweet things of life in defence of which [their friends] were perhaps even then shedding their blood...." "Face to face with a situation like that," wrote Seeger, "a man becomes reconciled, justifies easily the part he is playing, and comes to understand, in a universe where logic counts for so little and sentiment and the impulse of the heart for so much, the inevitableness and naturalness of war."[89]

Of course, Seeger took his own choice to enlist quite seriously. The contemplative and idealistic poet said he "joined up in order that France, and especially Paris which I love, should never cease to be the glory and the beauty which they are."[90] Even after more than a year of fighting in the trenches, he reminded his sister: "My being here is not an accident. It is the inevitable consequence ... of a direction deliberately chosen."[91]

At least one of the volunteers was not so reflective. After he signed up, David W. King sent a cable to his brother at Harvard. It read: "The joke is on you. I enlisted and am in the Foreign Legion."[92]

Chapter Thirteen

Let us do what Washington would have done.

As all of this was taking place in Paris, London was also experiencing a rapid transformation from peace to war. The city was packed with soldiers, and a tense anticipation reigned everywhere. A letter home from an American in London depicted the scene:

As you know by this time, there is "something doing" in England. But you are so far away that you can have but little idea of the excitement which prevails here. In less than a week the country has been plunged into a war that bids fair to be the greatest in all history. Only a few days ago, life went on as placidly as could be; and now the streets are filled with soldiers, all the trains are loaded with them, business is pretty much at a standstill, we are expecting every day to hear of a great naval battle, and are already getting accounts of the fighting in Belgium where the Germans have thus far been unsuccessful in their attacks upon Liege.[1]

Not long after, another American correspondent described his experience:

After the first few days of panic and readjustment London has settled down to a calm that is more significant than all the cheering and shouting and enthusiasm in the world would be. The English people are grimly, determinedly, methodically and intelligently going about their war. It is a job of work to be done – a bloody and a desperate job; but if it can be done they intend to do it, and they are not counting the cost in men or in money, in blood or in treasure. In the incredibly short space of a week the country has been put on a war basis and the people have taken up the task of maintaining the British flag on the sea and of holding the vast empire intact – taken up that task solemnly, patriotically and loyally.[2]

English Prime Minister H.H. Asquith showed great awareness of the stakes. In an address to the British Parliament on August 6, he expressed the grim determination of the English people:

I do not believe any nation ever entered into a great controversy – and this is one of the greatest history will ever know – with a clearer conscience and a stronger conviction that it is fighting, not for aggression, not for the maintenance even of its own selfish interest, but that it is fighting in defence of principles the maintenance of which is vital to the civilization of the world.[3]

Kiffin felt much the same – when he departed America, he left with a strong conviction that he was doing his duty, going to fight for liberty against oppression. Now, only a week later, he and Paul were skimming across the Atlantic Ocean towards England, anxious for information about the war. Although they received bits of news from passing ships through the Marconi Wireless Telegraph System on board the *St. Paul*, the boys were largely without reliable information during the week they spent crossing the ocean. On August 13, when the ship came in range of Crookhaven, Ireland the first "Marconigram" received aboard brought news sure to cheer the Rockwell brothers: "Liege forts still intact. German advance in Belgium checked."[4]

Having spent a solid week at sea, Kiffin was eager to disembark. The first three days of the voyage had been pleasant, with light breezes and smooth seas. But after an iceberg was spotted the morning of August 10, it became rather cold and overcast, with strong winds.[5] Later that day, they ran into a storm which lasted for two days and made "at least two thirds" of the passengers seasick. However, Kiffin reported that he and Paul were "good sailors," and so "did not feel the effects of it."[6]

The *St. Paul* was originally scheduled to dock on the Southern coast of England, at Southampton, but due to the closure of the English Channel the ship was forced to detour to Liverpool, on England's northwest coast. Accordingly, on August 14, Kiffin and Paul were crossing the Irish Sea, due to come ashore at six o'clock that evening. Kiffin took this opportunity to write his mother:

I have spent a week of absolute rest and quiet, thinking neither of the past or future. Paul and I both feel the best we have for years. I think I must have gained at least ten pounds.[7]

Kiffin excitedly told about the "cosmopolitan bunch" on board the *St. Paul*. In addition to "Her Grace the Duchess of Marlborough, two or three Lords, several Ladies and a few Knights," there were also "French and English reservists and adventurers of all description, and several war correspondents."[8] One of the journalists was Irvin S. Cobb, an author, humorist and former editor for the *New York World*. Cobb was rather famous and would visit France several times throughout the war as a correspondent for the *Saturday Evening*

Post.[9] As onboard entertainment one evening, Kiffin enjoyed a mock trial for which Cobb served as the presiding judge. Cobb would later write a book publicizing the exploits of several recipients of the *Croix de Guerre.* Little did he know at the time, but a future recipient of that distinguished medal (Kiffin) was watching his mock trial aboard the *St. Paul.*

While there is no record of it, on their way across the ocean Kiffin and Paul probably met two brothers, descendants of John Adams, Ellingwood Hubbard Towle and Francis Bartram Towle from New York.[10] Once in France, the Towle brothers would enlist in the Foreign Legion, and end up in the same unit with Paul and Kiffin.[11] But Ellingwood was invalided out early on, and Kiffin never really hit it off with the younger brother Bartram.

Other passengers included a supposed Brazilian count everyone had down "for being a faker," but with whom Kiffin admitted being "quite friendly."[12] There was also a Hungarian officer in the Red Cross who Kiffin suspected "might be a spy."[13]

As the ship drew near to Liverpool, from which place the boys intended to go to London for a week and then on to Paris, Kiffin finished up his letter. Once again, he sought to reassure his mother, and wrote: "This is a great trip for both of us and so far I don't regret it, if you will only realize that it is all right and not worry."[14]

* * * * *

The boys would not make it into Liverpool that night. As the *St. Paul* approached the port, instead of coming in, it dropped anchor about three miles out. The next morning, a British cruiser put aboard a few officers to inspect the passengers. It turned out that Kiffin was right about the Hungarian officer – he was arrested, along with a few Germans.[15]

The delay meant the boys did not arrive in Liverpool until noon on Saturday, the fifteenth, and by the time their baggage was inspected, it was after four o'clock. Once on land, they quickly made their way to a train and arrived in London at 10:45 that night.[16] There the boys rented a little two-bedroom apartment in Torrington Square for the low price of twenty-five shillings a week.[17]

In short order, Paul and Kiffin found their way to the French Embassy, where they learned that although France had agreed to accept foreign volunteers, this would not be effective until twenty days after mobilization. As the boys now had a little time, they left their names and addresses, and set about exploring London.[18]

Over the next week, the two brothers saw a great deal of the city, including the River Thames, Westminster, Big Ben, and the Tower Bridge. They spent a whole day at the British Museum just a short walk from their apartment; Kiffin reported it was "the most wonderful thing we have seen."[19]

The boys also spent time at the Savoy Hotel with the many stranded Americans.[20] On the whole, Kiffin found the group anxious to get away, an idea he considered foolish, since in London they could "really see a little excitement." And excitement was certainly the order of the day – as Kiffin told his mother, "everything in the city is topsy-turvy." Although it was hard to get any definite information, the general belief was that the war would last a long time, an opinion given credence by the large numbers of troops they saw "marching through the streets at all times."[21]

In all, the boys would spend ten days in London. At some point near the end of their stay, they received word from the French Embassy that they were now able to join its fighting forces. Paul later asserted that he and Kiffin could have joined the British forces earlier, but they "wished especially to fight for France."[22] As a consequence, they were forced to wait in London until the French authorities there gave them a visa to enter France.[23] Finally, on August 24, they went by the consulate and, as Kiffin put it, "had our papers fixed up."[24] The endorsement on their passports allowed them to cross the Channel into France, and the next day the brothers left for Paris.[25]

Some may wonder why the boys spent ten full days in London before going on to Paris, eager as they were to get to war. Two reasons seem primarily responsible – first, the French strictly enforced the 20-day waiting period from the date of mobilization for accepting foreign volunteers, and second, in the rush of mobilization it is perfectly understandable that it took the French authorities a week or more to process their papers, make contact with Paul and Kiffin and grant their visas.

However, at least three other possibilities for the delay exist, and they are not mutually exclusive. First, perhaps the brothers simply wanted to take what would likely be their only chance to do some sightseeing in London. After all, Kiffin and Paul had always been interested in history, and how many chances would they have to see London? When Kiffin wrote Loula shortly after they arrived there, he told her they had "decided to stay here a while before going any further," and had been "on the move, seeing all the city we can."[26]

A second possibility is that the boys were detained by the authorities. There is one source for this, a newspaper article stating that Kiffin and Paul had been "held in London for ten days because they were found in company with a German spy, but were later released."[27] While this is possible – after all, Kiffin himself noted that several Germans and the Hungarian officer had been arrested before leaving their ship – it is not likely that this accounts for their extended stay in London. To begin with, if the detention were linked to their arrested shipmates, it seems more likely the boys would have been kept in Liverpool where they came ashore, rather than allowed to leave immediately for London. Moreover, the brothers carried not only American passports, but letters of introduction to the American ambassadors to both England and Switzerland – not something many German spies would have in their possession.[28]

The third possibility is that by this time, Paul may have intended to go to the war only to observe, rather than fight, and to further his long-held goal of becoming a writer. At the very least, it is not entirely clear by the time they made it to London that Paul still planned to enlist, and in this period (if not before) it seems that Kiffin led and influenced Paul, rather than the other way around. Solid evidence supports this hypothesis.

For example, back on August 2 in their apartment in Atlanta, Kiffin had pulled Paul to the side and said he had made up his mind to fight for France. In his letter to Loula the night before they sailed from New York, while Kiffin told her that *he* "felt the call of opportunity," he also stated he "wouldn't have come with Paul if I didn't feel that it was a really great opportunity for him." Kiffin then explained to his mother his true motive for bringing Paul – he thought it would get his older brother "into the line of being a good short story writer."[29] So from the time they left New York, Kiffin intended to enlist, and may have brought Paul along only because he thought he could help him achieve his goal of becoming a writer.

In addition, near the end of August, the *Asheville Citizen* reported that in recent letters to friends there, the boys had "stated that they intended to tour Europe on a pleasure trip while Paul Rockwell planned to furnish Atlanta newspapers with stories of the conflict from time to time...."[30] Similarly, just before departing London, Paul's old employer the *Atlanta Constitution* quoted him as saying:

We came over to Europe just for a pleasure trip, but made up our minds we want to fight for the allies. Belgium won our admiration by her game fight. France is in the thick of the fight and we want to help her out as best we can. We desire to get into action right away and the French army seems to be the place for us. We realize how serious the game is, but are willing, if necessary, to offer our lives for the allies.[31]

So, perhaps the brothers (or Paul, at least) were not one hundred percent convinced they would actually fight. Maybe Paul had changed his mind, and intended only to write, rather than enlist. Maybe when they got to London, Paul learned he needed a visa to enter France and travel as an American, even if he were only going to report. And maybe when Paul saw his little brother Kiffin ready to go off and enlist, he once again felt the need to protect him, as he always had when they were little boys, playing at war back in the mountains of Tennessee.

Of course, the two earliest pieces of solid evidence – Paul's letter to the French Consul and the *Atlanta Journal* article from August 4, 1914 – show clearly that Paul always meant to fight.[32] And a fair review of the available sources leads to that same conclusion, although the truth may include elements of some or all of the possibilities. Thus, whatever their motives for pausing in London, and whether or not Paul wavered on his initial commitment to fight, by the time they left London for Paris, Paul and Kiffin were both fully dedicated to shouldering arms in defense of France, just as they had declared back in Atlanta.

Papers all over America, including their hometown papers in Asheville, picked up the story of the brothers' decision to throw in with France.[33] The *Asheville Citizen* noted the news would "come as a surprise to their friends at this city, who were not aware of their intention of taking up arms for the allies."[34] The next day, an editorial in the same paper recalled how "[e]very American youth is taught in his school that in the days when these young colonies sought to gain independence it was France who came to their aid, with men, ships and purse," and proudly conveyed its best wishes to "the young Rockwell brothers, boys from our own city of Asheville, who have joined, or will join the Foreign Legion in France."[35]

* * * * *

Kiffin and Paul traveled to Folkestone, England, and from there took a channel boat across to France. After a mild crossing, the boys landed at Boulogne-sur-Mer, a coastal city through which many of the allied armies traveled at the outset of the war. Due to ongoing fighting in the area just a few days after Kiffin and Paul entered France there, the port was first cleared, then completely shut down as the Allied forces fell back ahead of a German advance.

The boys did not linger in Boulogne, but immediately embarked on a train bound for Paris. On their trip south, the pair witnessed some early scenes of the young war. Paul described how "[a]t every station, women and children, and sometimes whole families, crowded into the compartments. For the most part the picture was of a fine farming country, with crops even now ripe for harvest, but bare of harvesters, ruining for want of men to gather them. Occasionally we would see a woman gleaning, patient, stolid, understanding nothing of war save its effect on her and hers."[36] The train wound its way by Amiens, near which heavy fighting was in progress, and finally rolled into Paris. It was August 26, 1914.

What an impressive sight Paris must have been to Paul and Kiffin. The city was virtually humming with activity, awash in recruits and soldiers of all types, and everywhere the cry was war. Recent reports had made clear that France's fate hung in the balance of the battles now raging, a fact reflected in the absence of most fighting-age French men from the city. A good number of the French troops had already moved through Paris to the front, and now the country was ready officially to admit the many foreign volunteers.

Paul and Kiffin arrived five days after the American Volunteer Corps had marched to the *Hotel des Invalides*, and just two days after the recruits had been officially accepted into the Foreign Legion after three weeks of drilling and waiting. Only the day before, on August 25, those recruits had assembled for the last time at their headquarters on the *Rue de Valois*. They planned to march to the train station, from which they would be transported to Rouen to be "weeded out according to ability" during the anticipated six to eight weeks of training.[37] But first, Georges Casmeze treated the whole corps to lunch at the *Café de la Regence*, at the foot of the *Avenue de L'Opera*.[38] No speeches were made at the luncheon, which grew quiet and serious as the men absorbed the gravity of their decision.[39]

Following the meal, the volunteers gathered outside and unfurled the French and American flags, after which they "spared a few minutes to be photographed" by the inevitable newspapermen.[40] One recruit remembered "wearing the oldest clothes we had," as they expected shortly to throw them away, to be replaced by the uniform of France.[41] As they prepared to march, elephant hunter Rene Phelizot raised the American flag (the same one that had hung over the door of the recruiting offices), the volunteers fell into marching order behind it and, accompanied by martial music, proceeded up the *Avenue de L'Opera*.[42] The gathered Parisians cheered the marchers all along the route, and many emotional young girls and women wept, some coming forward to hug the Americans.[43] One reporter described the scene that warm, sunny afternoon:

The citizens massed on the sidewalks and applauded frantically. Girls rushed forward to hand flowers to the volunteers, to pat them on the arm, to stammer the few words of English at their command: "Good luck!" "Come back safe!" "Brave Americans," etc. Women in their private carriages and in taxicabs ordered the drivers to keep pace with the marching men, while they leaned out, fluttered their handkerchiefs and threw kisses. A courtly old Frenchman ... rose from the terrace of the Café de la Paix *and raised his hat to the American flag. "Gentlemen, France thanks you!" he cried.*[44]

As the procession reached the *Gare Saint-Lazare* station, there occurred the one aspect of the occasion Paul and Kiffin were probably glad to have missed – the band struck up "Marching through Georgia" as a compliment to the Americans.[45] A reporter for the *New York Sun* saw the volunteers there, and gave this description:

The Stars and Stripes were waving beside the Gallic tricolor and the yard in front of the station was crowded with Americans who had come to bid them 'Godspeed.' Women showered them with flowers and men shook them by the hands. They were a well set-up lot of fellows and ought to be able to give a good account of themselves.[46]

As the recruits readied to board the train that would take them to the front, several American women appeared and pinned bunches of flowers to the now-drooping American and French banners. Before departing, one of the women "gently lifted the folds of the Stars and Stripes and impressed a fond kiss there."[47] The American volunteers boarded their train to Rouen, and as the train pulled out, enthusiastic women and children waved their *adieus*.[48] Along the route to Rouen, the proud Americans hung their flag out the window of the coach.[49]

* * * * *

All this – the procession up the *Avenue de L'Opera*, the flags, flowers, and fluttering handkerchiefs – occurred the day before Kiffin and Paul arrived in Paris. But they soon learned about it courtesy of the English-language *New York Herald*. The morning of their arrival in Paris, the *Herald* printed one of the pictures its photographer had taken of the volunteers marching to the station, under the headline "Parisians Accord Hearty Ovation to Departing American Volunteers."[50]

Kiffin must have thrilled at the paper's description of the "scenes of wild enthusiasm" as the volunteers departed for Rouen, as well as the accompanying report:

Paris was stirred by their fit and lighthearted appearance as they swung along, the Stars and Stripes and the Tricolor carried side by side, and all along the route from the rue de Valois, where they assembled, to the railway station they had a triumphal passage, cheered on their way by men, women and children, who appreciate their courage and sympathetic cooperation.... They are a particularly fine lot of men, recruited from high and low, all keen and determined, and a credit to France as well as to the country which gave them birth. Today's contingent is the first and it is hoped that others will follow.[51]

Kiffin and Paul intended to do just that – follow the first group of recruits to Rouen. To do so, they first had to enlist. Luckily, although Casmeze had already gone with the rest of the volunteers, he had arranged to keep open his recruiting office at the *Palais Royal*, where applications were being taken Mondays, Wednesdays and Fridays from ten to four.[52]

As they had arrived on a Wednesday, Paul and Kiffin were able to proceed immediately to the recruiting office to volunteer. They stopped off at the Hotel Beauvais, then went straight to the offices on the *rue de Valois*.[53] In taking this step, the boys paid no mind to President Wilson's proclamation of neutrality. As Paul later recalled, "Although Wilson had declared his neutrality, [and] we risked losing our citizenship.... all they could do was threaten you. That didn't do any good."[54]

Wilson's strict idea of neutrality – just the week before he had asserted that Americans "must be impartial in our thought as well as in action" – was not well taken among the expatriate Americans in Paris, either. In fact, the very day that the Rockwell brothers were applying at the recruitment office, the *New York Herald* published several letters urging Americans to remember the assistance France had rendered in America's time of need, and scoffing at the notion of neutrality being peddled by President Wilson.

One writer confidently asserted that "not one American in Europe ... remains impartial," and exhorted "real homemade Americans" to side with France.[55] Kiffin (one of those real homemade Americans) surely agreed with the writer's scornful statement: "That the United States can pretend to stand for all the principles of right and justice, and yet look calmly on and cry 'impartiality' is beyond my comprehension."[56]

Another letter writer noted "our handsome starry union would have very possibly been scattered if it had not been for our gallant French friends and allies in the time of our sore distress," before continuing:

France is fighting the fight of Liberty and bursting asunder the iron bands, badly forged and full of flaws, thank God! with which the pleased-with-themselves 'hobereaux' have been trying to girdle the world. By all means let Americans worthy of the name express themselves on the side of Right, Justice and Liberty. Vive le France et ses allies![57]

A professor from the Union Theological Seminary in New York staying temporarily in Paris wrote a letter with which the Rockwell boys surely agreed. Charles P. Fagnani's epistle deserves to be quoted in full:

Sir:

The neutrality of the American Government is one thing – that officials and representatives of the United States should be circumspect and correct in speech and conduct is of course imperative – but this does not and cannot involve that private citizens should not think and feel and speak according to their own ideas of what seems righteousness, justice and truth.

To be impartial and neutral when the cause of civilization, liberty and democracy are at stake; to be calmly judicial when domineering brutality attacks by foul means a long-suffering and patient neighbor; to be indifferent and a well-wisher of either side equally, when the one stands for freedom, fraternity, and peace, the other for despotism, militarism and the mailed fist – this is asking more than the liberty-loving spirit of the individual American can concede.

Who of us has been privileged to witness here at close range the behavior of the French has not been amazed and overwhelmed with admiration at the sight of their marvelous self-control, their poise, their grim determination, their heroic consecration.

No, we cannot, despite the official utterance of our Chief Magistrate be "impartial in thought or speech" so far as concerns our status as private individuals.

Vive la France! Vive la Liberte![58]

A final letter writer noted that his sixteen-year-old son had asked him: "if George Washington were alive, on which side do you think he would be?" Suggesting the answer in his stark description of the two sides, the author wrote:

On the side of a cruel, arrogant, military despotism, cynically trampling underfoot the sacredness of treaties, butchering innocent victims and violating the territory of a brave little country it was bound to respect, nay, laying waste its fields and cities, or on the side of a country who is defending Right, Justice, Civilization and Liberty, the land of Lafayette and Rochambeau? Let us do what Washington would have done.[59]

Sharing these same sentiments, Kiffin and Paul went ahead with their plans. However, like the other recruits, they were not examined and did not officially enlist until the next day, due to the legion's old rule "that an applicant will not be examined or accepted until the day following his application."[60] Thus, the Rockwell brothers officially enlisted in the Foreign Legion on August 27, 1914.[61]

Neither of the Rockwells left a detailed account of their enlistment process, but assuredly it was like that of the other volunteers. Paul recalled that the authorities at the *Invalides* "looked at our passport[s] and gave us a very thorough physical examination, [asking] the usual questions."[62] The brothers pledged to obey orders and maintain discipline, swearing "fidelity, unto death, if that shall be necessary, to the French flag."[63] The boys were given their first day's wages and told to report at the *Gare Saint-Lazare* early the next morning.[64]

At 8:00 a.m. on August 28, just three weeks from the day they had left New York, Kiffin and Paul were on a military train rolling out of Paris towards Rouen.

Chapter Fourteen

What a fellow can learn being thrown in with a bunch like this!

The Paris train carrying Paul and Kiffin arrived in Rouen that afternoon. Along with the other recruits who had arrived a few days earlier, the Rockwell boys were quartered in an old school building for young ladies, the *Ecole Professionnel pour Jeunes Filles*.[1] The school was built in the shape of an L, and two dilapidated one-story buildings enclosed the yard on the other two sides. One entered through large wooden swinging doors about twelve feet in height, located at the angle in between the two buildings.[2]

Kiffin and Paul were assigned to the *2nd Regiment Étranger*, grouped with about twenty other Americans and 60 to 70 soldiers of other nationalities. Billeted in a large rectangular auditorium in the school, the new soldiers were given straw, blankets and sleeping bags and told to make their beds against the walls, where each man was allowed three feet of space.[3] One recruit soon reported that although the Americans "all sleep on straw laid over the floor," they were "as fresh and fit as paint."[4]

Fit as paint, but not close to fighting condition. As Bill Thaw presciently remarked, "it will be weeks, perhaps months, before any of us even resemble soldiers." Remaining optimistic, he noted, "of course it's just a matter of working up to it, though there's plenty of hard work ahead, believe me."[5] Sweeny noted that on their arrival at Rouen "[m]ost of us slouched. We were to get rid of that fault."[6]

Drilling started immediately. The new recruits arose at five in the morning, had a little unsweetened coffee and bread, and the bugle sounded "fall in" at six.[7] After morning roll call, they marched out to a quiet section of the city to be instructed in formation, marching and turnings. According to Sweeny, "At first we stumbled out of the school. As the days went on we emerged from our straw more alertly, for our physical condition was bettering."[8]

This was likely due to the marching; in just the first few days they went on several eight and ten-kilometer hikes. Sweeny remembered "walk[ing] five to ten miles out in the country and back again each day." But now, unlike their march up the *Avenue de l'Opera*, there was no music, pretty girls, or cheering crowds – simply put, "there was no time for bands."⁹ As Edgar Bouligny, an American recruit of French descent, disappointedly said: "What a gyp for an American who had expected to drop into a mass of military color and an atmosphere of hip, hip, hooray!"¹⁰

Bartram, the younger Towle brother, who had been on the *St. Paul* with Kiffin and Paul, wrote of their time in Rouen, and the wake-up call it was for many among them:

*We marched ten miles a day, drilled, had heavy setting up exercises, [and] all did solid fatigue duty, besides other details. We slept on a brick floor in the school house. After a week of it, most of the fellows began to see the error of their ways but repenting and repining were too late to help. So we are being turned into soldiers of France.*¹¹

The men usually marched for three hours in the morning, including a one-hour stop along the way to drill. After the morning march, they generally had from nine to ten-thirty to clean up and rest, before the first meal was served at ten-thirty. Kiffin found the food "good, wholesome and well-cooked," and overall, was enjoying "living the army life," except for the fact that they had not yet received their uniforms.¹²

All told, the American recruits marched and drilled about six hours a day and had three hours free to themselves. The rest of their time was "filled up with odd chores and loafing around the barracks."¹³ These included being assigned as *hommes de soupes*, charged with getting the food for others, and *hommes de chambre*, detailed to sweep out the room.¹⁴

The rookie legionnaires soon learned the dangers of volunteering. On one of their first mornings, a French sergeant awoke the soldiers with a call for two good men. D.W. King jumped to the ready, sensing an important mission filled with glory. Instead, he and the other volunteer were led to a row of filthy latrines and given a mop and bucket. King had learned his first lesson: "when sergeants are wandering around collecting men, pick up anything in sight and look busy."¹⁵

* * * * *

Arising at five makes for a long day, so the men usually went to bed between eight and nine at night, flopping down on their army blankets on the straw-covered floor. Paul found the early hours irksome at first, but soon discovered he "could fall asleep at 8 o'clock, or, for that matter, the first minute I got the chance, as easily and unconcernedly as an animal that is fed and warm."[16]

On their fourth day in Rouen, Kiffin found a little time to write home. Paul had apparently already informed Loula about their enlistment in the Foreign Legion, so Kiffin chose not to dwell on it. He wrote:

I think Paul wrote you about our joining, and as it is very hard to get letters through and we are not allowed to write much about what we are doing, will only tell you that both of us are well and feeling fine. It is of course a little rough but it will make a man of both of us.[17]

The pair had become acquainted with the other recruits, whom Kiffin noted were "congenial and good-humored, all trying to make the company a good one."[18] As Paul observed, the volunteers were of every nationality and color, and "all trades, callings and professions were represented."[19] Kiffin excitedly told of the wide variety of Americans, which included "several fine fellows" from Yale, Harvard, Michigan, Cornell and Columbia.[20] Kiffin and Paul would get on good terms with most of the men. Once the men were divided into smaller groups, they both were assigned to the Ninth Squad, where Kiffin became close with Georges Delpeuch, Ferdinand Capdeveille, Dennis Dowd, and Bill Thaw.

At just seventeen years of age, Delpeuch was the youngest American volunteer. Although born in Paris, Delpeuch had lived most of his life in New York, where his father was the chef at the *Hotel Lorraine*.[21] Just after the war broke out, along with more than eleven hundred French reservists and two other American volunteers (Ferdinand Capdeveille and Charles Trinkard), Delpeuch boarded the SS *Sant' Anna* bound for France.[22] As the ship pulled from the pier, the sky echoed with the sound of the *Marseillaise*, being sung by the two thousand passengers as well as many more on the shore.[23]

Born in New York to French parents (his father was a fencing master), Ferdinand Capdeveille was with the Americans from the beginning, and would quickly be promoted to first-class soldier, as would Thaw.[24] Capdeveille worked with Charles Trinkard at the Compagnie Generale Transatlantique in New York, and shortly after the war began, he and Trinkard headed for France with Delpeuch.[25] Trinkard had been born in Switzerland and lived for some time in France. "Tiny Trink," as he was known – he stood just five feet, five inches – would become one of the best-liked American volunteers.[26]

Another among the shorter American volunteers was five-foot six-inch

Robert Soubiran. Soubiran was born in France but grew up in New York City and had lived for some time in South Boston. The blue-eyed, fair-faced auto mechanic and race car driver traveled to France and joined up with the legion at the outset of the war to fight for the land of his ancestors.[27] Once the French learned of his mechanical abilities, they tasked him with running a threshing machine to harvest the wheat still in the fields.[28]

Speaking of the tremendous mixture of enlistees, the former Yale man Thaw exclaimed: "talk about your college education, it isn't in it with what a fellow can learn being thrown in with a bunch of men like this!"[29]

* * * * *

With three hours on their own each night, Kiffin and Paul had time to roam the interesting and picturesque streets of Rouen. On Sunday, the soldiers were free from 11:00 a.m. until 8:00 p.m., which time the brothers spent "looking over the town." The "most interesting thing" to Kiffin was seeing the dungeon where Joan of Arc had been held prisoner prior to being burned at the stake.[30] The brothers also took in the famous cathedral *Notre-Dame de Rouen*.

Just a few days after Kiffin and Paul went by the beautiful church, the newly-arrived American Ambassador to France, who had not yet assumed his post, traveled to Rouen on one of his first visits. Long after the war, William Graves Sharp would remember that city with its narrow, crowded streets and especially its magnificent cathedral, whose "very impressiveness impelled me to enter."[31] The striking scene created by the many soldiers and townsfolk inside made a lasting impression on the new diplomat:

Some were in the uniform of commissioned officers, others dressed as simple poilus. *About them, kneeling in devotion or passing out as new ones came in to take their places, were dark-veiled women and old men bent with age – the mothers and fathers of young soldiers already at the front. He who would properly assess the heroic part played in this great war by the soldiers of France, must not ignore that element which contributed quite as much to its winning as their courage – their religious fervour, which seemed to gain strength from the very dangers before them. As our little party left the portals of that temple of worship, I carried away a lasting remembrance of the sweet music softly diffusing itself from the great organ above me. But I had witnessed also the visible evidence of that faith which did so much to sustain the spirit of France during the four awful years to follow.[32]*

It was while making their initial pilgrimage to see the cathedral that the Americans became aware of a quaint little café just off the square in front of the church. The *Café Paul* quickly became the Americans' gathering place on their nightly excursions into town, mainly because the owner agreed to provide their meals at a reduced price. During their short stay in Rouen, the American recruits took most of their evening meals there.[33]

Rouen was teeming with soldiers and stragglers, either heading to or coming from the French, British and Belgian units in duty at the front. The anxious legionnaires met numerous retreating English soldiers, many of whom were wounded, and all of whom were exhausted. Hearing the tales of these soldiers convinced Thaw he was "going to take a part, however small, in the greatest, and probably last, war in history, which has apparently developed into a fight of civilization against barbarism."[34]

Kiffin saw the conflict in those terms, as well, although he didn't want to concern Loula. He told her only not to worry about him and Paul, "as this is a great thing for both of us."[35]

* * * * *

The recruits remained at Rouen not even a full week. On Tuesday, September 1, *reveille* roused Kiffin and the other soldiers out of bed at 4:30 in the morning, whereupon they were ordered to hurry up and get ready. The men were told they were leaving Rouen, but no one knew where they were headed. As Thaw put it: "One of the most interesting things about being a soldier is never knowing what is going to happen next."[36]

Events were making it necessary to move the recruits along, despite the fact they were not yet trained soldiers. As German troops steadily advanced across northern France, it began to look as if Paris itself might fall, and the French government was compelled to flee to Bordeaux. As a precaution, it was thought best to move the training facilities out of the danger zone, as well.[37] Orders were hastily given, and the legionnaires training at Rouen moved out, as Paul put it: "France judging that we would be more useful to her after we had learned more of the science of warfare than at the present."[38]

As the men were preparing their things to leave, Phelizot brought out the American flag that had flown over the recruiting headquarters and that he had carried down the *Avenue de l'Opera*. The son of a former editor of *La Petit Journal* in Paris, Phelizot was already well-liked by the other Americans.[39] Born in France, the land of his father, Phelizot grew up on Division Street in Chicago with his mother (maiden name Noonan) a New York-born daughter of Irish immigrants. Even when young, Phelizot was an adventurous sort. At thirteen he ran away to take a position as cabin boy on a Mississippi River passenger boat, and at fifteen worked his way across the Atlantic on a freight steamer to France. One passenger list shows him as a stowaway on a boat from Liverpool to Boston just before Christmas 1900, when Phelizot was nineteen years old.[40]

At some point, Phelizot studied engineering and worked with the United States Steel Corporation. He also joined the Illinois naval reserve and spent some time as a sailor before drifting into the Congo district and becoming an ivory hunter.[41] Drawing on his past as a world traveler and big-game hunter, Phelizot had a great many stories to tell, especially of his time spent in the African jungles and deserts. Having accumulated a small fortune in the ivory trade, he always saw that the less fortunate volunteers were looked after.[42] Since their arrival in training, he had become something like the flag's guardian.

Sensing the opportunity to seize and record an important moment, Phelizot wrote in indelible ink across the flag's top white stripe: "American Volunteer Corps Rouen September 1, 1914."[43] He then had each American volunteer sign his name on the same white stripe.[44] Phelizot kept the flag and openly displayed it during their training until just before the unit headed to the front, when orders came down that "all foreign flags must be discarded in order that no international complications might ensue if any of the men were captured with the colors of their native countries on their persons."[45]

Many of the Americans who signed the flag that day would go on to fame and glory during the war. Some others would not last as long, their desire to serve proving stronger than their powers. Among the former who gained recognition and fame during the war were Sweeny, Thaw, Seeger, and Kiffin. Among the latter who either dropped or were invalided out for one reason or another were Paul, Ellingwood Towle, and Georges Casmeze, as well as two more Harvard grads: James Stewart Carstairs, an artist from New York who had been living in Paris, and Joseph W. Ganson, a one-time tutor to the children of Vincent Astor.[46]

Just six months after signing the flag, Phelizot would die an untimely and senseless death. The other signers would fight long and hard for France, and "[t]heir record as a whole is one that their country can be proud of."[47] Among others, Capdeveille, Casey, King, Scanlon, Dowd, Zinn and Herman Chatkoff of Brooklyn, who had been washing automobiles in a garage in Paris when the war started, fall into this category.[48] The signers deserve credit as the first American volunteers in the war, and even now their flag is on display in the *Invalides* museum. About the only signatures that can still be made out are those of Paul, Kiffin and Bob Scanlon.[49]

* * * * *

After signing the flag, the men gathered their belongings. Later that morning they marched through the city to the train station. One of the recruits half-jokingly noted the "striking appearance" of the marchers:

About noon we were marched to the station, and a striking appearance we displayed, marching with our blankets rolled and thrown across our shoulders, carrying our own belongings wrapped in a bundle or in a suit case and dragging with us our water canteens, dinner pails and bread. However, we were stout of heart and kept step well, notwithstanding the hot sun and our inconveniences during the half hour's walk to the station.[50]

At the station the men were packed into freight cars approximately 8 feet by 38 feet, with as many as forty men crammed into each one. They had just enough space to lie down and sleep, which one recruit noted "wasn't so bad, because they allowed us plenty of hay and straw to sleep on, and that made it nice and snug."[51] The men "felt pretty bad" when they learned they would be going in the opposite direction of the fighting, but were told "it would only be for a short time."[52]

Each soldier was issued one tin of "bully beef," containing enough meat to feed one man for four days, three kilos of bread, a can of sardines, and a canteen for water.[53] As the weather was very hot, the officers told the men to form groups of four and to open only one tin of meat each day. However, several of the Russian volunteers, apparently distrusting their comrades, each opened their own tin. By the third day on the train, many of them had developed ptomaine poisoning and several were later rumored to have died.[54]

For nearly 500 miles, the train slowly rolled south across rural France, taking more than 55 hours to cover the distance.[55] With the number of soldiers crowded into each car, the quarters were less than comfortable, and over the course of the long trip, the tight compartments began to close in. In his characteristic style, Bert Hall declared that the journey was "just the sordidest, uncomfortablest road to glory ever trodden by American adventurers."[56]

At night, a few of the men climbed on the roof of the train, seeking repose and fresh air, but according to Thaw, they "found more fresh air than repose on the roof of that car, believe me."[57] To make matters worse, the men were still not told where they were going. Not knowing their destination seemed to make the trip even longer; at times, the train chugged along so slowly it seemed almost not to be moving at all.

The trip was not all bad, however. Thaw recalled that in the daytime, he and others sat on the edge of the car and waved at the girls, who at every stop happily gave the troops red wine, fruit and smiles.[58] Another said the Americans "had a lot of fun cracking jokes with the girls along the road," who "regarded us as the saviors of France."[59] The monotony of the ride was further broken up by the appearance at intervals of soldiers returning from the front who, although they looked "much worse for the wear" were "always cheerful."[60]

Finally, the train came to a halt, and the recruits were ordered out at a station where the sign read *Toulouse*. Marching off the station platform and through the city's streets, Seeger felt the men "were sorry sights indeed. Grimy, unwashed, unshaven, we looked more like hoboes than the gallant defenders of France we were supposed to be...."[61] As they walked, the voice of a single Egyptian soldier pierced the silence, singing of *"La Civilization Nouvelle,"* the new civilization for which the men had committed to fight. Entranced, the marchers quietly listened to the soaring notes; one later described that in that moment he felt he had "touched the soul of France."[62]

With renewed vigor, the travel-weary volunteers made their way to the Perignon Barracks on the outskirts of the city where, for the first time since leaving Paris, they slept in beds.[63] Paul spoke for most of the men when he said, "we welcomed our quarters in Toulouse almost as eagerly as a devout Mohammedan might welcome Paradise."[64]

Chapter Fifteen

No address except France.

At Toulouse, the *"bleus"* (as the new recruits were called) quickly became accustomed to the routine of a soldier.[1] The Perignon Barracks accommodated around 5,000 infantry soldiers – rather small for a military base, but plenty big enough for the recent civilians to get accustomed to soldierly life. Built in a square, the barracks, canteen, shooting range, stables, storehouses and prison surrounded a tree-lined courtyard, presided over by a large clock in the center of the facing building.[2]

From their new home, the men would train within sight of the Pyrenees mountain range separating France from Spain. In a letter to his sister, Seeger described the surrounding countryside, filled with lush fields and vineyards, as "very smiling and beautiful."[3] He also wrote of the setting in his diary:

The landscape is very beautiful here, especially seen from the ridge behind the caserne. There is an open field here, the ground sloping down abruptly on three sides. We have often drilled here in the early morning, climbing up to it facing the rising sun. For a while before the haze rises one can see the Pyrenees far to the south, capped with snow. These mornings will be my fairest memory of Toulouse.[4]

As noted, the *caserne* offered a large courtyard, and as their training intensified the men drilled on it almost constantly. Chatkoff would later write, "at Toulouse, we first really became soldiers, or rather began a soldier's life."[5] As Paul put it, "now our real training began, making all our previous drill seem like a child's game, something akin to the military maneuvers at my brother's school."[6] Bartram Towle added:

Here we drilled and drilled on the slopes of the Pyrenees.... Rouen was child's play to training here. Close order, extended order, attack, and general bayonet drill, trench digging and heavy marches. For a rest we did fatigues, policed barracks and mounted guard.[7]

Kiffin and Paul slept next to each other on iron cots topped with straw mattresses. Their large room contained forty men of twenty-eight different nationalities, drawn from every class of society. According to Paul, a "more conglomerate and diverse lot of mankind was never thrown together in the same room."[8] Even more colorfully, Casey described the volunteers as "an astounding, appalling admixture . . . of all manner of breeds and men and rakehells, of professions honorable and proscribed, of virtues and fatuities."[9]

Seeger wrote home that on the straw mattress next to their corporal was the cousin of Harry Thaw, who had dominated the headlines in New York and America in 1906 when he murdered his wife's lover.[10] The person on the straw mattress, of course, was William Thaw, famous in his own right as an aviator. Seeger reported Thaw had "left his automobiles & aeroplanes and racehorses to follow a new caprice – a worthy representative of that strange family."[11]

In these close quarters, one soon developed a strong sense of private property and personal space. As Paul noted, "[e]very man was suspicious of his neighbor, and we watched each other with the covert glances that animals give each other."[12] Not that they had much – most of the men didn't even have full uniforms, as supplies had run short at Rouen. Many had only a *kepi* (cap), or nothing at all. For the majority, the only equipment worth protecting was the army-issue blankets, and the mess gear each had been provided – a *gamelle* (tin-plated pail with a cover), a *quart* (a tin cup, holding a quarter liter), a fork, and a spoon.[13]

But in the Foreign Legion, one's mates are not a matter of choice and anyway, as Fred Zinn recognized, "one cannot judge a regiment by the same standard that he would a social club."[14] And so, by and large the widely diverse lot got along well enough and, as is usually the case when men constantly together are focused on the same tasks and goals, there soon began to develop an *esprit de corps*.[15]

Within a few days the men were issued coarse fatigues, supposedly white, but in many instances quite something else, having been left filthy by prior occupants.[16] The drab blouse and trousers reminded J.W. Ganson of home, as they "resemble[d] those used by the New York street cleaners[.]"[17] The legion also provided socks, shoes, underwear and shirts, or made cash payments to the men already possessed of suitable items.[18] Later each of the men would draw from the arsenal a *capote* (great coat), a shell jacket, belts, cartridge pouch, rifle, bayonet and haversack. D.W. King recalled the variety of equipment and uniforms issued by the sous-officers, joking "we felt like Christmas trees as we staggered out."[19]

* * * * *

"Oh, the potatoes," lamented Bartram Towle, "the endless spuds that we did peel daily!"[20]

Feeding an army takes food, and lots of it. Other than black coffee served at dawn, with which most of the men finished any remaining bread from their previous days' ration, the legionnaires received two meals per day, referred to as "*soupe*." While the menu varied slightly, the primary vegetable served with both meals was potatoes. While no one liked peeling potatoes, few could escape the task, as spuds were in constant need. Accordingly, the younger Towle brother was not the only one lamenting the chore known as "*corvée de patate*."[21]

The first meal was served late in the morning, and generally consisted of soup or stew with meat, and potatoes, of course. Corporals served their own squads, ladling the food into each soldier's *gamelle*.[22] In addition, each man was granted one half loaf of good French bread per day, portioned out according to his own hunger.[23] Occasionally, the men were given a tin of sardines or the cook would make some sort of pudding.[24]

Second *soupe* was served late in the afternoon before dusk. This meal was much like the first, usually consisting of a meat goulash with potatoes, lentils, beans or rice, served with coffee. Red wine called *pinard* was regularly served with this second meal, and sometimes with the first.[25] Typically, the men received a piece of cheese, fruit or chocolate for dessert.

The soldiers were also issued emergency rations, which consisted of two blue tins of preserved meat (the men called it *singe*, or monkey meat), twenty hardtack biscuits, and a small bag of sugar and coffee. The penalty for unauthorized use of these provisions was eight days in military prison.[26]

Although they had plenty to eat, the men were allowed to go into town at night, where any with money could dine at one of Toulouse's well-known restaurants. While in the city, the men mingled with the crowds in the streets and cafes, watching for bulletins from the newspaper offices and eagerly listening to the tales of the soldiers streaming back from the front. Those who had already been in the fight "were always listened to with great interest and respect."[27] The returning soldiers' accounts caused Alan Seeger to wonder whether he "would have the courage – *cran*, the French call it – to face bullets

129

and shrapnel." He supposed he would find out in the not too distant future.[28]

In no time, the men fell in to the monotonous training and barrack routine, so different than the glorious adventure most of them had imagined. At the end of their first week, Kiffin got off a postcard telling his mother he and Paul were "fixed more comfortably than at Rouen," but were "working hard" and had "very little spare time." Kiffin was entirely in his element and loved it. He told Loula the soldier's life "agrees with Paul and I," and that they were "getting strong and a healthy look in our faces."[29]

* * * * *

While the men were still settling in at Toulouse, France was fighting for its life. The Germans' onslaught had advanced nearly to the gates of Paris, and only a furious push by the French managed to drive the enemy back. During that first week of September, French reconnaissance planes spotted something odd – rather than continuing straight on to Paris, the German right flank had veered toward the southeast, apparently pursuing the retreating French troops.

Sensing an opportunity, General Joffre formulated a counterattack and hurried more soldiers towards the River Marne and the now exposed German flank. Joffre's order of the day on September 6 grimly informed the troops under his command of the gravity of the situation:

At the moment when a battle upon which depends the salvation of the country is being engaged, it is important to recall to all that the moment has come when one must no longer look back. All efforts must be employed in attacking and throwing back the enemy. A troop which will not be able to advance further must, at whatever price, hold the ground conquered and be killed on the spot rather than draw back. In the present circumstances no faltering can be tolerated.[30]

On that day, as Winston Churchill later wrote, "all the French armies between Verdun and Paris, together with the British Army and the French forces in Paris and to the north of Paris, turned upon their pursuers and sprang at their throats. The Battle of the Marne had begun."[31] The stakes were enormous, the battle furious, and the slaughter immense, but over the course of the next few days, the desperate determination of the French successfully pushed the Germans back forty miles to the Aisne River. On September 13, an American living in Paris wrote the following in her diary:

Just a week ago we were all terrified. The enemy was so close to Paris, just outside the fortifications. It was the blackest hour ... and the worst seemed near, but now we breathe again.[32]

* * * * *

France had also recalled from North Africa the legion's Second Foreign Regiment. The unit arrived in Toulouse shortly thereafter, enthralling the Americans with their grand entrance. Five hundred strong, the group marched into the courtyard at *reveille* accompanied by a drum and bugle band, keeping perfect step to the music. With their spotlessly clean uniforms, the bearded *anciens* (veterans) "made a striking impression on the untrained, unkempt neophytes."[33] Edgar Bouligny drew the obvious comparison:

Their dark-blue greatcoats held in by broad blue sashes around their waists, their white tropical trousers, their highly-polished black shoes and black leather leggings, their rifles and side-arms gleaming like silver in the dawn, their famous banner bearing the motto 'Valor and Discipline' flying, they presented a startling contrast to our rabble.[34]

The officers distributed the veterans among the three companies of recent volunteers, and very quickly the *bleus* realized that the old-timers "were soldiers in every sense." One of the Americans later remembered: "Everything they did was marked by efficiency and precision. Even when they handled the broom policing their tents they did it with an air that showed how well they knew their business."[35] The veteran legionnaires certainly proved quite useful in the seasoning of the new recruits, although "the outlook, mentality and social backgrounds of the 'Africans' were so radically different from that of the new men that the amalgamation promised to be a stormy one."[36] The example and experience of the *anciens* helped familiarize the *bleus* with their duties, which masked for the moment the ever-present tension between the groups.[37] This would not always be the case.

Owing to the strict censorship of the camp, along with bits of real news, "rumors flew everywhere."[38] Thus, when on September 12 a call was made for volunteers with prior military experience to join with the veterans and be expedited to the front, although the men could "not tell how heavily France had lost," they imagined "the losses must have been very serious." Seeger drew the obvious conclusion: "This means that they need every man they can get, and that they must utilize every man that they have."[39] Still, while few if any of the Americans had any wartime experience, nearly all of them were eager to get

131

into the fight. Paul described their response:

We never had been under fire or in any army, but we volunteered. Every American but two lied like a gentleman and said he had seen service.[40]

As the Americans stepped forward, their "gentlemen's lies" were dutifully recorded by the French officers. One man claimed to have served with the Salvation Army, while several others, including Kiffin, Paul, Alan Seeger and Bill Thaw, professed to have served in Mexico.[41] Questioned later by their corporal as to why they drilled so poorly, the men explained the fighting in Mexico had been with the guerillas, who knew very little of military drill.[42] But, as D.W. King noted, the French were looking for anyone willing to go to the front, and "the words *ecole militaire* work wonders."[43] Bouligny, one of the few men with any real experience, later wrote: "Apparently the officers went on the theory that a man willing to lie to get to the front would be willing to fight."[44] The men were told that if anyone wanted to leave, he needed only to say so and he would be given five francs and a ticket back to his point of enlistment.[45] Some took it.[46]

* * * * *

As the ranks thinned, the training grew even more demanding. To build the men's endurance, the drills and marching became more strenuous, the loads heavier. Thaw wrote: "Every day it's get up at 4:45, work, work, eat and then some more work, and go to sleep at 9; then get up again at 4:45 and do it all over again."[47]

Around this time, the boys received a note from a friend in Paris asking whether they were "fully equipped, with rifle, uniforms, etc. The rumors say that the army is short of guns – is it so where you are?"[48]

It was not. Each legionnaire carried an 1886 Lebel, "a beautiful piece of machinery," according to Dowd.[49] The bolt-action rifle held ten rounds – eight in its forestock tubular magazine, one in the carrier, plus one more in the chamber.[50] All told, the weapon weighed over nine pounds, and with the bayonet affixed, measured six feet from butt plate to bayonet tip.[51] The return march from the arsenal had been very trying, as each soldier carried two of the heavy guns. Many of the men found it difficult to keep in step for half an hour with a heavy gun on each shoulder. While most managed to do so, "there were quite a number of sore shoulders the next day."[52]

Ammunition was given only at the rifle range, and a strict count kept – the men were required to return their empty shells as they fired.[53] At the range, the soldiers-in-training became familiar with the roar of the Lebel; once they reached the front, they were easily able to distinguish it from the crack of the German-made Mauser.[54] The Americans rapidly developed a reputation for being excellent shots; Chatkoff noted: "If shooting alone made a soldier, we would be ready for the front. But it takes much more. However, we are willing pupils, all of us."[55]

The instructors hastened the training of their willing pupils, using all available time to prepare the men for combat. In addition to target shooting, the men spent most of their time drilling, or in other tasks such as mock bayonet charges, in which they would jump into trenches and stab straw-stuffed dummies.[56] Preparing for warfare the way it had been practiced up to that point, the men were trained extensively in the use of the bayonet, once called "the last argument of the common soldier."[57] A sign on the wall of their barracks read: "A bullet is crazy; a bayonet is sane."[58] One soldier provided a full description of the thing to his father:

This is a murderous weapon, and I do not blame the Germans for being afraid of it. It is about a foot and nine inches long and comes to a needle point. It has four grooves, and each edge is a quarter inch deep and one-eighth inch wide at the hilt. It is half an inch in diameter at the hilt.[59]

The French troops nicknamed the 20½-inch bayonet "Rosalie," while the Germans dubbed it "the knitting needle."[60]

In preparation for the front, the men began regularly rising at four in the morning and working as many as 14 hours a day. Thaw noted the days were filled with "hard work but lots of fun, marching, drilling and playing war all over the country, capturing farms, target practice, etc."[61] Kiffin displayed the same positive attitude, telling his mother he and Paul "have been working very hard since being here, but it seems to agree with [us] as we are always in fine condition. My feet have bothered me a little from a forced march we took the other morning, but that is all and they are doing fine."[62]

Kiffin was not alone with his sore feet. Sweeny recalled that "[a]ching muscles and stiff joints and swollen eyes were the rule those days."[63] Blisters were another common recurrence among the men. One experienced corporal showed his men how to treat blisters by passing a greased thread through them, then cutting the ends off each side, creating a drain, and smearing the inflamed part with tallow to prevent chafing. This done, the soldier could put his boots back on – "painful, but easier than doing it next morning when feet have had a chance to swell."[64] One exception was Bob Scanlon, who sometimes amazed the others by taking off his boots during a march, carrying them in his free hand or lacing them together and letting them dangle from his neck.[65]

The *bleus* also learned how to handle the invariably bug-infested cots on which they were sleeping – by scorching the beds with improvised torches and then painting them with kerosene, burning the straw, and boiling the canvas bags used as mattress covers.[66]

Paul looked back longingly at the few days they had spent at Rouen, for "to rise at 5 o'clock was luxury now, since oftener our day's work began at 4, to continue for twelve or fourteen hours."[67] Later, quoting a French author, Paul referred to the legion as "that hospital whose sole remedy for all maladies is work."[68] Forced marches were taken every day, and it seemed the distance and load always increased. The recruits were now marching as much as twenty miles a day, carrying up to one hundred pounds of equipment.[69] Thaw summed up their existence: "march, drill, eat and sleep."[70]

Certainly, the men were being pressed harder than ever. Seeger told his mother they had been "putting in our time here at very hard drilling and are supposed to have learned in six weeks what the ordinary recruit takes all his two years at. We rise at 5 and work stops in the afternoon at 5. A twelve-hour day at one *sous* a day."[71] As their officers attempted to cram in as much training as possible before shipping the men to the front, circumstances forced the recent civilians to rapidly transform into soldiers. Thaw wrote "In the last two weeks we have done three months' work, and are beginning now to be a little like soldiers."[72] The *anciens* assisted in this process; D.W. King wrote: "Dry-nursed by the old legionnaires we began to shape up."[73]

One command seemed to elude the recruits, that of "*en tirailleurs.*" This was the order to spread out to escape the deadly fire of machine guns, which must be done quickly to be effective. Chatkoff explained:

We, however, do not seem to be able to do it even half quick enough, and it must be very discouraging, as I say, to our officers. We stop to observe whether we have run far enough, find we haven't, start again, stop again, start again, stop again and then find we are too far (which isn't possible) and return again. However, we'll learn, I hope.[74]

As Seeger noted, the pay in the legion was one *sous* – or one cent – per day. On that lowly salary, one soldier joked that he was "getting now so I know the value of money."[75] Although he hoped to earn higher wages after the war, Seeger "never expect[ed] to work harder."[76]

Kiffin was also learning the value of money – not long after, he asked Loula to send a few dollars, saying it "would come in handy," as the "French Army only pays one cent a day and we are both broke."[77] Out of the ten cents he was paid every ten days, the common soldier had three cents taken out for tobacco, whether he smoked or not.[78] In exchange for the three cents, the government issued a package of *Scaferlati des Troupes* – cut strips of tobacco which, with some effort, could be rolled into cigarettes. Hardly of exceptional quality, King described the stuff as the stalks of tobacco plants, and noted "you had to spread it on a handkerchief, pick out the longer pieces, and chop them up before you could possibly roll it into a cigarette."[79] Another American volunteer noted he "had practically stopped smoking" due to the difficulty of getting the French tobacco to burn, and its "strong, bitter taste." But after receiving some American tobacco from a relative, he mixed the two and, "with a little rum to flavor" was now "happy as a chimney."[80]

* * * * *

On September 17, the men were finally issued their full uniforms, and "began to feel that they were really soldiers."[81] Although it had only been six weeks since the first volunteers had begun drilling at the *Palais Royal*, it surely seemed much longer. Seven of the men who had been around for those heady early days on the *rue de Valois* got together in Toulouse and had their picture taken. Wearing their dark blue greatcoats with madder red trousers and *kepis*, the men not only felt like real soldiers, they now looked the part as well.[82]

They had hardened into soldiers, not only in body but in mind, and the military life had knocked the rough edges off their civilian habits. For example, the *bleus* had quickly realized that "cleanliness was as necessary for the sake of others as for oneself." Thereafter, the order and routine of the soldier's life further refined their behavior and attitude. As Herman Chatkoff put it: "Ordinary bad habits ... died a natural death during our training."[83]

In short, they had learned discipline. This was so despite the fact that the French officers treated the Americans appreciatively, recognizing that they had enlisted of their own volition. For example, most minor infractions were generally punished less severely, and there was slightly less formality in the regiment. Still, orders were enforced, and officers expected their commands to be followed. As one recruit said of Toulouse, "[h]ere, there was discipline...."[84] Another soldier stated that though an officer might address the men familiarly, "when an order is given I have not yet seen a man obey it except with all the alacrity possible."[85]

By the time they had trained with the regulars for a few weeks, the *bleus* had come to understand that soldierly discipline precedes and begets duty. Chatkoff later recalled their transformation:

When we entered the army we were thrown in among all sorts and types and thus obtained our first benefits, association with others. The second benefit was to learn what true discipline means. We learned for the first time what it is to obey, even those of us who had never been called disobedient before. From discipline we learned respect. At first we had no respect for our immediate superiors, corporals and sergeants. They were legionnaires, perhaps with histories that would not bear telling; often they were our inferiors in many ways, but not as soldiers. Then came duty. It was our duty to do this or that, and we soon learned that we must do it, even if it could be shirked without danger of discovery. It became a habit to do things without asking why and wherefore, and to do them at once and thoroughly, not merely well enough to satisfy ourselves but to satisfy others who had an interest in their being done.[86]

Zinn credited the *anciens* with their rapid progress, saying it was "due to them that we were able to train and get to the front in a third the time that it would ordinarily have taken."[87] In this short time, the individual volunteers had learned discipline and duty, and been molded into a cohesive unit in which each man knew his role and was prepared to fill it.

Kiffin and the others were now ready. They had become soldiers of France.

* * * * *

The day the *bleus* received their full uniforms, Kiffin wrote a brief postcard home. He told Loula that the unit was now "fully equipped and pretty well drilled," and that they expected to leave Toulouse soon. As always, he reassured her that "Paul and I are both feeling fine."[88] But amidst all the commotion and excitement, Kiffin failed to mention Loula's birthday – she had turned forty-six the day before. In his defense, it seems Kiffin was so caught up in his training and preparation for the front that he also forgot his own birthday just a few days later – Kiffin turned twenty-two years old on September 20. Only five years earlier, he had been languishing at Werntz Academy, contemplating resigning his appointment to the Naval Academy for fear of not seeing any action in that branch. Now, he was a full-fledged soldier of the Foreign Legion, on the cusp of being sent to the front in the biggest war mankind had ever known.

Around this time, Paul wrote a letter to a friend back in Atlanta stating that both he and Kiffin were in good health "and enjoying life immensely." He may have stretched things a bit when he boasted that there were "large numbers of black-haired lassies and huge quantities of red wine" in their territory.[89] Although true, the statement probably implied too much – with all the work he was doing, it is unlikely Paul had much time for wine or women.

On September 25, the regiment assembled in full field dress for its final grand inspection. While the men were ready to go, none of them counted on having it easy. Far from it – as Thaw indicated, they all understood that now "the real work was coming."[90] And while everyone knew they were going to be sent somewhere, no one was sure where. As Kiffin wrote his mother, "Tomorrow we leave here, after that we have no address except France."[91]

Chapter Sixteen

If anything will make a man of me, it is this.

Around the time of their final inspection, Kiffin and Paul received their first letter from Loula, which had been forwarded from their prior London address. When her sons left for the war without saying goodbye, Loula described herself as "almost frantic with grief, for I felt that I should never see them again."[1] It must have been difficult, as she had also lost her father only a week before Paul and Kiffin left for Europe without telling her. While no copy of her letter has survived, it must have laid bare the emotions of a heartsick and worried mother. The letter also caused Kiffin to further reflect on his decision to enlist, as it made clear Loula wanted her boys to come home. Kiffin let her know that was not going to happen, and why. He replied:

I realize, and did before joining, how you feel, but I don't think you should worry or feel bad because I have such a temperament that if I didn't do things that seemed funny to you, I could never be satisfied myself, or make a success of my life. You would not want my life to be a failure in my own mind, even if by doing so I lived many years and was always with you.[2]

In essence, Kiffin felt he was meant for more than what he had accomplished before he left for Europe. He explained his reasons for joining the war effort, and how it had already changed him, and again linked his decision to how Loula would feel if Kiffin were unhappy with his life:

I was dissatisfied with the course my life was taking but now this is changing it. If by chance I am killed in this war I will at least die as a man should and won't consider myself a complete failure. I know you must think me selfish and inconsiderate of your feelings, but I am not. You expect great things of me and I want to do great things, and can see a great future before me. If I am killed in the attempt to attain that future, I have at least done my best; that is all any of us can do. Since being here I have taken more interest in life than ever before. It has brought out new feelings and thoughts in me. I think if anything will make a man of me, it is this.[3]

While in Loula's mind, their enlistment seemed pointless – for what could her boys possibly mean to France? – to Kiffin the war and, more importantly, his service in it, had clarified his purpose as never before. This statement to his mother reveals the true Kiffin Rockwell: a striving idealist, wanting so much to succeed and firmly convinced of the justness of his cause, committed to do his utmost and see it through, no matter its end.

In closing, Kiffin again emphasized his commitment, and showed some tenderness for his mother's feelings: "It is going to be a life of hardships but I am willing to go through them, and actually enjoy them. [T]he only thing that bothers me is you, but I hope you will turn to feeling proud of me instead of worrying."[4]

Kiffin and his new friend Alan Seeger must have been talking, and boosting one another's confidence and spirits, for around the same time, Seeger expressed similar sentiments to his mother: "I hope you see the thing as I do and think that I have done well ... in taking upon my shoulders, too, the burden that so much of humanity is suffering under and, rather than stand ingloriously aside when the opportunity was given me, doing my share for the side that I think right."[5] Seeger's confidence was full to overflowing; he told his sister he felt "on a plane above fear these days. I am ready for anything that comes."[6]

Paul marched next to the loner poet on many of the Ninth Squad's excursions, and recalled that although Seeger rarely said anything, when he did the usual topic was "the glory of death in battle."[7] Paul later told a friend he considered Seeger to be "a genius," whose "greatest ambition was to be a good soldier."[8]

Like their friend Seeger, Paul and Kiffin were eager to do their bit. As they prepared to leave Toulouse on September 27, the men were each given three days' emergency rations, consisting of a tin of beef, a small package of soup tablets, six hard biscuits and a small bag of coffee and sugar.[9] The wagons were laden and the horses requisitioned. Everything was ready, and then, as is often the case in the military – nothing. Twice at roll-call orders to leave for the front were read out, and twice the men were disappointed. As Paul expressed two days later, now they were just "eager to be in the midst of it and have it over."[10]

* * * * *

Finally, on September 29, the order was given that they would depart for the front the next afternoon. Upon hearing this, the entire section "was lifted up on a mighty wave of enthusiasm, which thrilled us all, the oldest legionnaire as well as the youngest recruit."[11] Paul captured the excitement of the men:

Everyone was as gay and excited as if it was some long anticipated 'lark' we were starting upon, instead of the very serious business of fighting. Personally, I felt so happy at the prospect of getting away from Caserne Perignon *that after we were dismissed for the afternoon I adjourned to the washroom and shaved off a week's accumulation of beard, something I had lacked the energy to do before.*[12]

One soldier who didn't shave was Thaw, who probably provided the evidence for Paul's later statement that "the better a man's education and the gentler his breeding, the more unkempt and wild he gets to look when in a war."[13] Not long after they reached the front, a fellow soldier wrote that "Thaw's best friends wouldn't know him now; he has grown a jagged beard, and any stranger seeing him would suspect him of almost any crime which could be accomplished with a blackjack or a knife."[14] Thaw was beginning to look worthy of his boast of having been disinherited four times before reaching the age of twenty-one.[15] Former tutor Joseph W. Ganson also grew a scraggly beard; the white patches in it earned him the sobriquet "Papa Ganson."[16]

Having made it through their initial training, the soldiers – with or without beards – were now worthy of the famous name given to all common French soldiers – *poilu*. Translated literally, *poilu* means "a being covered with hair," and was shorthand for "hairy ones."[17] But the term predated the "*Grand Guerre*," and was not solely meant as a comment on the bearded status of many of the French soldiers.[18] Instead, the general connotation of the term meant "he has hair on his chest" – i.e., is tough, courageous, brave.[19]

Nevertheless, over time most of the men grew facial hair, causing one to assert that "you would have a hard time picking the Americans out from the veterans, except that we are taller than most of the others."[20] Combined with his height, Kiffin's stubble caused some of the French officers to refer to him as *la grand avec la barbe* – the tall fellow with the beard.[21]

As a general rule, the Americans were taller than their non-American counterparts, but the Rockwell brothers stood out even among the Americans. As a fellow soldier noted, Kiffin and Paul were "the tallest among us, both over six feet."[22] That means Kiffin was likely the tallest man in the company – standing between six foot one and six foot two, he was about an inch and a half taller than Paul, who was six feet even.[23] Kiffin was skinny, too; Bert Hall used to call him "the living hall tree," and joked that "if he could keep side on to a German it would be impossible to hit him."[24] Kiffin stood six inches taller than the average American soldier, with an even greater disparity between himself and the French soldiers.[25]

Many of the tallest men in Battalion C of the Second Marching Regiment, including Kiffin and Paul, were grouped together in the Ninth Squad. The other Americans among its members were Alan Seeger and Charles Sweeny (both 6 feet even), Bill Thaw and J.S. Carstairs (both 5'11"), the lawyer Dennis Dowd and the engineer Fred Zinn (both 5'10"), Ferdinand Capdeveille (probably also about 5'10"), and Harry Collins (height unknown).[26] The squad consisted of six others in addition to the ten Americans: two English, one Norwegian, one Swede, one Serbian and one French old-timer. These sixteen were all under the command of Corporal Ferdinand Weidemann, a former German national who sometimes muttered that although the Germans would win the war, "I have given my word to France, and will keep it."[27]

According to D.W. King, Weidemann was "born and bred to soldiering," and so "it was the only life he knew or cared about." Notwithstanding this, he still had "unlimited patience with stupid recruits."[28] The men all believed Weidemann had been in the legion fifteen or sixteen years, but his service card shows he enlisted in Oran, Algiers, in 1907.[29] Paul remembered Weidemann as "absolutely fearless," and although born in Saxony, he was fully devoted to France.[30] Paul said:

The old corporal, as we called Weidemann, never smiled. He had no friends among the old legionnaires and his name was never called at the daily distribution of mail. With his men he was a strict disciplinarian, but absolutely fair and impartial. When he served the 'soupe' he always gave the same portion to each of his men as to himself. He did not admire his men because, to his eyes, we were not soldiers. But let one of us get a bruise or injury and [a] woman could not have been more gentle or solicitous in bandaging the hurt.[31]

"Entirely the soldier," Wiedemann's "only hobby was collecting postage stamps, of which he had a fine assortment."[32] Zinn remembered their corporal as a "pretty rough specimen," but with one good trait that outweighed all the bad – after all his years in the legion, "he was still honest."[33]

But whatever the men thought of him, Weidemann was not well-liked by his immediate commanding officer, a sergeant "who delighted in passing on to him all the work possible."[34] This would result in many of the unpleasant chores falling upon the shoulders of the Ninth Squad, keeping Kiffin, Paul and the others quite busy.[35]

* * * * *

The soldiers were awakened at five a.m. on September 30. After coffee, they were sent to the company's storeroom to be doled out the remainder of their equipment before leaving for the front. Each soldier received 120 copper-jacketed cartridges, "one-sixth of a tent, with a two-piece tent pole and stakes, a package of bandages, and leather strap for use if wounded, and rations for the trip – a loaf of bread, tin of beef, and small bit of cheese."[36]

The troops gathered in the courtyard of the barracks and assembled into marching columns as the various battle flags were presented. Finally, at twelve noon the legionnaires marched through the streets of Toulouse behind their *clairons*.[37] Overhead flew the famous battle flag of the legion, as well as the French, Belgian, Russian, British and American flags. Once again, Rene Phelizot was proudly carrying the stars and stripes.[38] Paul later commented:

The flag had already been carried through the streets of Paris, Rouen, and Toulouse by men in civilian garb; now it floated over a band of American citizens in French uniform and fully armed, ready and eager to fight the Germans. The shades of Neutrality must have shivered.[39]

This march to the train station was much more somber than the procession down the *Avenue de l'Opera* just thirty-six days before. Although many of the townspeople of Toulouse stood and watched the troops file past, they were generally subdued. After two months of blood and carnage, these French citizens were terribly aware of the probable fate awaiting these men come to fight for France. Thus, as the legionnaires tramped along the cobble-stoned streets, the residents respectfully and sadly bid them *adieu*. Staring quietly, a few young school children sorrowfully waved as they passed. Chatkoff remembered all along the route being "hemmed in by silent crowds. Almost every woman was weeping."[40]

The troops stopped briefly at the town hall, where the mayor and town council held a short ceremony. Presenting the soldiers with a silken flag, the mayor spoke of his wish that it would soon be raised "over territories liberated from the *boches* by the bayonets of these brave and noble young men of

La Legion."[41]

As the soldiers left the town hall and headed towards the station, the gathered crowds did their best to lift the men's spirits. Some tried to cheer, and here and there a black-haired maiden with flowers would run out to the marching soldiers, keeping pace with them for a few steps to say farewell. Still, as Paul noted: "The sun was hot, and the way to the station long, and it takes more than cheers and flowers to make a soldier forget his seventy-five-pound load. By the time the station was in sight we were sufficiently fatigued to welcome any resting place, even a hard bench placed lengthwise in a freight car."[42]

The men finally reached the waiting trains and clambered on board, waving their goodbyes. Thaw wrote that after all this "regular soldier stuff," they "finally got packed away in our box cars and started north."[43] Although they were still overcrowded, unlike the train to Toulouse these cars had benches on which the men happily sat as they unburdened themselves of their heavy canvas knapsacks.

The Americans again put their flag on display during the trip. Later in the war, still waiting for their home country to awaken to its duty, Paul remembered:

For three days we swung this beautiful American flag from the French troop train, and no diplomatic episode so far has resulted. We are afraid none ever will.[44]

* * * * *

The train pulled out of Toulouse and rolled north, towards the front. At each stop, "the townspeople turned out and gave the train a great ovation, passing around all kinds of good things to eat and drink."[45] At some of the stations, Red Cross girls gave the men hot coffee, ripe peaches and postals to send home.[46] At one of these stops, someone snapped a wonderful photo of clean-shaven Paul sitting on the floor of the train car, his long legs dangling from the side of the train.[47] The serious and thoughtful look on his face matches well the description he gave of his feelings on the eve of reaching the front. He wrote:

Whether we would have chosen this profession if we had known two months ago what we know now is beside the question. So far, it has been all gain for me. The exercise and regular life has built me up physically, and the experience has enriched me mentally beyond all my hopes. [But] I do not feel any less human or have any less love for my fellow-men than I had before I enlisted[.][48]

Paul and the rest of the legion men rolled inexorably towards the front, each sitting and thinking his own thoughts. Some wrote letters home, while others slept or played low-stakes poker, although some cars were too cramped to afford this luxury.[49] Thaw spoke for most of the Americans when he wrote that at least now they were "going in the right direction and felt like regular 'sojers.'"[50]

Chapter Seventeen

We have come to the point where fighting is the only thing to do.

After a cramped, cold ride lasting two days, the train creaked to a halt on a dark, windswept plain. It was not yet dawn, but the glow in the east foretold the sun's imminent appearance. The men were told to gather their belongings, as they would soon arrive at their destination. The morning mist still hung in the air as the sleepy soldiers peered out from the rail cars at the surrounding countryside. Portions of the battle of the Marne had been fought in this area, and traces of the campaign were discernible all around – twenty yards from the tracks, the men spotted a French flag stuck in a mound of earth covered with flowers: the makeshift grave of eight dead combatants. In the distance, a small group of houses had been razed to the ground by gunfire.[1] Paul would never forget looking through the open door of the box car at "the fresh graves of soldiers, covered on one side of the track by German helmets and on the other by French *kepis*."[2]

As the men prepared to disembark, the train again lurched forward, and a short while later rolled into the railway station. The men grabbed their gear and stepped out of the cars and into the early light of dawn. Just outside the station, they were greeted by a long, recently-filled trench, in which stood a large cross made of railroad ties – another fresh grave for an unknown number of dead.[3] Everywhere was evidence of the recent battle, from the shabby crosses marking soldiers' graves, to discarded backpacks, German and French rifles, uniforms and pieces of shell.[4] Many of the station buildings and village houses bore shrapnel scars, further evidence of the furious fighting which had recently taken place. Paul noted that "if we were not actually on the firing line, we were at least near enough to smell the powder[.]"[5] And it couldn't have come soon enough – Paul had just written home that when he and Kiffin had left Atlanta "we thought we were going to see the war," but two months later, although "much wiser about war," of "what most people mean when they say war we have yet to get our first glimpse."[6]

In the distance, the men could make out a number of tents and newly-constructed concrete buildings, which comprised Camp de Mailly, their new home. It was the morning of October 2, exactly eight weeks since Paul and Kiffin had left America for Europe. The battalion had at last arrived in the warzone.[7]

* * * * *

As Seeger correctly surmised, Mailly was "about the furthest point reached by the Germans before the French success in the battle of the Marne forced them to retreat."[8] The day after their arrival, the men heard cannon for the first time, and the occasional rumble of heavy siege guns from the direction of the frontier.[9] From this point on, that sound would become so commonplace that after a while the men hardly noticed it.

On a wood-gathering expedition shortly after they arrived, Dennis Dowd, Frederick Zinn, and a few of the Englishmen captured a German soldier hiding in the scrub pines.[10] Another was lying dead among the trees. The surviving German was nearly dead from hunger and exposure, and told his captors the reason he had not surrendered was because "their officers had told them that they would be shot."[11] The legionnaires gave their new prisoner "chocolate and cheese and made him very happy."[12] He would not be the last gaunt and ragged German they would find straggling around the lines, and although they had no sympathy for the starving enemy combatants, still the legionnaires "admired their pluck."[13]

The early days at the camp were "passed in exercises and sham battles in the pine woods around the camp. The underbrush was full of relics and wreckage of real battle, cast-off French and German haversacks and other equipment, broken guns and bent bayonets, unexploded shells, and occasionally a dead body, overlooked by the burying parties. The continuous rumble of cannon in the distance added to the reality of the scene."[14]

The weather that first week in Camp de Mailly was beautiful, and the troops enjoyed the lovely autumn conditions prevailing in the French countryside. Seeger described the "frosty nights and sunny days and beautiful coloring on the sparse foliage that breaks here and there the wide rolling expanses of open country."[15]

But the men were not sent immediately to the front. Instead, they were "kept in fine trim by heavy field exercises[.]"[16] The French military authorities continued to press and push, preparing the men for the front lines. As Kiffin noted, he and the others were "still working very hard, as France anticipates a long hard war and wants her men well trained so as to stand the hardship of it."[17] Edward Mandell Stone, a Harvard alumnus born in Chicago, who would later be the first American killed in the war, wrote a similar letter home, telling his mother that the men were "working very hard going through exercises of all sorts, as I am glad to say that the French Government has no intention of sending us to the firing line without thorough preliminary training."[18] Seeger wrote his mother simply that they had been engaged "in the hardest kind of hard work."[19]

On October 10, a seven-hour march tested the company's endurance more than had yet been called for, but only one man fell out.[20] As the hike was all cross-country through heavy brush, and each man carried a fully-loaded pack, Thaw considered it "a pretty good tryout." Indeed, the former Yale left tackle noted that, "in comparison a game of football is almost a joke, for you don't get a rest every 15 minutes, and a game doesn't last seven hours."[21]

The tired soldiers marched to a high field where the officers ordered them through the entire exercise of bivouacking. After setting up camp, they unpacked and stowed everything and even lied down six to a tent. Then, just when the men figured they were spending the night, the order was given to break camp, and "in a few minutes all the orderly labor was undone." The company quickly formed up in columns and tramped their way back to camp.[22]

In addition to the constant marching, the troops fired dozens of blank cartridges at one another in splendid sham battles.[23] At the rifle range, the soldiers were each given eight real bullets to shoot at a silhouette set up in a trench two hundred and fifty yards or more distant. The target would show for ten seconds and then away for ten seconds, and no scores were allowed but bullseyes. One day, three of the American volunteers made perfect scores, further burnishing the reputation of the Americans as excellent marksmen.[24]

Mostly, the men got too little rest, did too much work, and unlike their time in Toulouse, had not enough good food to eat. As many of the railway lines had been damaged or destroyed, necessities were in short supply, and foraging parties were sent out to locate food.[25] After one morning spent tramping and scavenging, Thaw reported the company had only acquired "a few potatoes and cabbages." He wrote:

Beef has ceased to exist around here; in fact, I'm getting very fond of horse meat, of which there's plenty, as there are still lots of wounded horses in the stables that aren't dead yet, which is one way, though far from humane, of keeping the meat fresh! But this is war, and a very terrible one, and the men must have food. It's a pretty hard life and most of the men are harder.[26]

As Thaw indicated, the Germans had cleaned out everything they could find, so for several days the men were served horse stew. Paul, for one, liked it, finding the horse meat had a "good flavor," although it was "somewhat more tough than beef."[27]

* * * * *

The field exercises continued, and the men were always on the move. They marched through ruined villages, crossing over temporary structures standing in place of the many destroyed bridges. Passing by streams of wounded and returning soldiers, they could plainly see the terrible toll being taken all along the western front. Any who originally believed the war would end quickly had by now been disabused of the notion. But Kiffin was prepared to go through whatever was necessary. In fact, the closer he got to the front, the more he seemed to thrive. In a rare letter home from this period, Kiffin told his mother of the challenging work, and its effect on him:

I have been feeling better physically than ever before in my life which means a lot. I think that I will be able to stand all the hardships of the war. Of course, there is the danger of the bullets, but, as I wrote you in Toulouse, I am ready to take my chance and will go through everything willingly, always doing my best.[28]

The other men were also feeling healthier than ever. For example, Seeger told his mother that the "hard work and moments of frightful fatigue have not broken but hardened me," so she could rest assured he would "play the part well for I was never in better health nor felt my manhood more keenly."[29] Similarly, Charles Sweeny, the former West Pointer, wrote his mother that he was "very well, never been better in my life," and "doing my duty as I see it, but taking no useless chances so do not worry about me."[30] As for the other fellows, everybody was cheerful, and the spirit and morale were high. Sweeny felt "sure to win with such men."[31]

The day after Kiffin wrote home about how good he felt, it was announced that the regiment would start its march to the trenches the next day. In a letter to his mother, Seeger showed his eagerness to get into the thick of things. He wrote: "imagine how thrilling it will be tomorrow and the following days, marching toward the front with the noise of battle growing continually louder before us."[32]

As the men prepared to leave for the front orders were issued that all foreign flags must be discarded to avoid international complications if any of the soldiers were caught bearing emblems from "neutral" nations.[33] Of course, Phelizot still had the flag he had everyone sign at Rouen and was not about to discard it now that they were heading to the front. Instead, he disobeyed the order, and thereafter wore the flag around his body as a sort of sash or belt.[34]

Thus, on Sunday, October 18, the American flag accompanied the Americans as behind Phelizot they marched out of Mailly. No one knew for sure where they were headed, but the fresh troops were eager finally to be taking a real part in the war. In a letter to his sister, Alan Seeger wrote "whatever we are going to, we are going triumphantly."[35] Marching along in the bright morning sunshine, the men cheerfully shouted out the legion's famous marching songs. Kiffin called his favorite *Le baptême Français* – the French baptism. It went something like this:

Nous sommes soldats (we are soldiers)

Soldats de la Legion ètranger (soldiers of the Foreign Legion)

N'ayant pas de patrie (having no homeland)

La France est notre mère (France is our mother)

Nous avons là bas (we have over there)

Conquis dans le combat avec succès (conquered in the fight with success)[36]

* * * * *

The soldiers marched northwest for almost fourteen miles before stopping for the night in Fère-Champanoise, where they spent the night in the loft of a barn. The next day, they trudged through Marsain and Bergéres; in these shelled-out villages they saw "[n]othing but blackened walls and here and there the inhabitants standing with sullen faces in their ruined doorways."[37] In a postcard to his sister, Seeger conveyed well the feel of the cruel landscape over which the men had passed: "All our way has been one immense battle-field, little villages that are nothing but heaps of ruins, fields torn with artillery fire and heaped with the fresh graves of the soldiers, buried where they fell, a rude cross above and the *kepi rouge*."[38] Paul added that "signs of life were few everywhere,"[39] while Bert Hall described the trek in similarly bleak terms:

Along the roadside lots of trees had been smashed by shell fire, and there were hundreds of graves with rough crosses or little flags to mark them, and every now and then we passed a broken auto or a dead horse lying in the gutter.[40]

Unaccustomed to long marches weighed down with full field equipment and pack, a few of the British and American volunteers made their way to sick call when halt was called for the night, victims of blistered feet and aching backs.[41] A British legionnaire once said of his blisters: "You dare not take your boots off, for your feet would swell so you could not put them on again. It is terrible work but it is grand."[42]

Despite their aching feet, on the men marched. Not that they had much of a choice – at one point along the way, two Americans who had had enough (probably D.W. King and J.S. Carstairs) sat down beside the road to rest their feet. King remembered his shoes feeling as if they had been "filled with painful marmalade."[43] But the pair were not sitting long before a French colonel rode up on horseback and, with pistol pointed, ordered them to stand and march. They did.

One bright spot had emerged – as the soldiers passed fully into Champagne country, they "had the pleasure of picking Mumm's luscious grapes as we marched."[44] They ate their fill as they passed through Vertus, Chouilly and Epernay, "where lots of troops lined the sidewalks and watched us pass."[45] Eventually they stopped outside Hautvillers, where they built a nice bonfire in the courtyard of the *Abbaye Saint-Pierre d'Hautvillers*, a Benedictine monastery where Dom Perignon once served as cellarer. Afterward, they spent the night on the plentiful straw in the loft of a nearby barn.

The next day, the tired and frayed regiment marched another thirty kilometers across the mountainous terrain, through Louvois to Verzy. It was a hard walk, and many of the men fell out.[46] During their last halt before reaching the town, the sergeant informed the men they were not going to stay in Verzy, but would leave immediately for the trenches. Upon hearing this unexpected news, the legionnaires marched into town amid a drizzling rain which had begun to fall. The battle-line was just below Verzy, and the "smell of powder and of war was in the air."[47]

But only half the regiment was sent to the trenches that night. The other half was again quartered in houses, lofts and barns, and told to sleep in their harness – "that is, wearing the cartridge belt with sack and gun at our head."[48] The tired men objected when Zinn crawled in amongst them, as he had a terrible snoring habit.[49] After he became an officer, Edward Morlae, a former business owner and one-time soldier from Los Angeles, had Zinn arrested for falling asleep on guard duty and snoring.[50] For this and many other reasons, many of the men grew to dislike Morlae. As usual, Kiffin seemed to have Morlae's number early on, and would have his own run-in with Morlae later.

Zinn's snoring may have been a nuisance, but the men wouldn't get much sleep anyway – it was cold, and at four in the morning they were awakened for a sunrise march to Verzenay, just a few kilometers around the mountain. On the way, the numerous passing wagons and cavalry served as constant reminders of their proximity to the front. The point was forcefully driven home when the troops paused for a brief rest and noticed three fresh graves by the side of the road. A placard above read: *Espion, traitre a son pays* – Spy, traitor to his country.[51]

* * * * *

In Verzenay, the soldiers were billeted in a long shed and building at the end of the *Rue de la Veuve Pommery*.[52] The plentiful vineyards in the area began abruptly at the end of the street, directly across from their lodgings. The men stood guard duty and watched the anomalous sight of grape pickers singing in the fields as the artillery batteries boomed on the opposite slope.[53]

Their quarters provided a wonderful vantage point, giving the men a broad, uninterrupted view across the vineyard-covered valley. They could plainly see the frontline trenches, the flash of the German artillery and the puffs of smoke from the bursting shells, but as the wind was from the other direction could hear the distant booms only faintly. They also spotted big columns of dirt shooting skyward from the ground near the German lines, evidence of the French response.[54] The men gathered in the street and watched the ongoing shelling into the evening, which Paul later described:

The panorama from in front of the building occupied by the Americans was wonderful. The battlefield could be seen for miles and miles: to the left, almost to Reims, and to the right, stretching away as far as the eye could reach toward the Argonne. Flashes from rifles and machine guns twinkled up and down the valley like intermittent fireflies, while less frequently came the lights from the bellowing cannon and exploding shell. Very lights and star rockets cast an unearthly glare over the scene from time to time. Veteran officers and men ... watched the spectacle with as eager an interest as the greenest volunteer.[55]

Paul wrote "For most of us, this was the first real glimpse of war, and a very convincing glimpse it was."[56] The attacks continued the next day. The thumping of the shells ripping through the crisp autumn air made the men feel more alive, even as they had drawn closer to potential death. As Bartram Towle put it: "Now it was real war...."[57]

Having witnessed it for themselves, the men were certainly persuaded of the reality of war and understood with clarity the dangerous role they were to play. Despite this knowledge, the Americans kept up their high spirits. A comment from Seeger to his mother may not have been typical, but it displayed an attitude not uncommon among the men – he wrote that he was "feeling finely, in my element, for I have always thirsted for this kind of thing, to be present always where the pulsations are liveliest. Every minute here is worth weeks of ordinary experience."[58]

Their excitement (and fear) surely increased when their corporal told the remaining men that they would be sent forward themselves at any minute, and that of the half of the regiment previously sent to the trenches, already twelve had been killed and forty wounded.[59]

* * * * *

As usual, however, the plans were changed, and the Americans were not sent to the front lines. Instead, the legionnaires were given their first day of repose since signing up, "a relief after weeks when we have scarcely had a minute to ourselves."[60] Except for a few *corvees*, the men were free to sit around or forage through the little town where one could "buy chocolate & cheese and other little luxuries."[61] Several of the *anciens* tracked down some wine – not hard to do in Verzenay – and the night rang out with drunken merriment, squabbles, and singing. Seeger remembered the laughter and revelry, a by-product of the "girl grape pickers" who "mingle[d] freely with the soldiers."[62]

Not every repose would be so pleasant. Paul later recalled that more often than not, rather than rest, repose entailed "working harder than one works when in the trenches – digging, cleaning, grinding coffee, sawing wood, doing many things."[63] Another soldier later reported that repose generally meant joining "the pick and shovel contingent" – that is, digging trenches.[64]

Following their rest, on October 25 the company filed out to perform some maneuvers, traveling through the woods on the heights above Verzenay. From the open crests the men caught excellent views across the valley and could even clearly see Reims and its famous cathedral.[65] Germany's shelling of this cultural and artistic treasure the prior month had provoked great outrage and helped swing world opinion in favor of France. One reporter expressed the prevailing sentiment:

How any commander could have trained his guns on the Cathedral of Reims passes human understanding. If it had been in Bible times that such wanton sacrilege took place a plague would have overtaken the guilty people. The gun-pointer would have been struck blind as he took aim.... It is one of those crimes which are so great that they stand outside the human catalogue. For this scandalous sacrilege there is no atonement.[66]

German aeroplanes passing overhead put off the expected maneuvers. Instead, the men gathered wood for the kitchens, and then watched the lines from the grassy knolls.[67] They spent the next few days shooting, taking soldierly lessons and performing various tasks, a few of which seemed designed just to keep the men busy.

A typical day's schedule looked something like this: 7:00 – 7:45 a.m.: theory lessons on patrol work, 7:55 – 8:30 a.m.: theory lessons on firing and ammunition supplies, 8:40 – 9:10 a.m.: fencing and section drill, 9:20 – 9:50 a.m.: firing theory and pointing correction, 10:00 a.m. – 12:00 p.m.: free for lunch, 12:00 to 4:00 or 5:00 p.m.: 12-mile marches with full kit, shooting practice and taking cover. A few other "amusements" included "practicing putting up tents (which will never be used), practicing getting aboard trains, loading wagon and various gymnastics. Even Sunday is not a free day."[68]

On October 26, the men of the Ninth Squad were roused at sunrise. While the rest of the soldiers were placed in buses for the front, the squad was required to act as *garde de convoi*, traipsing alongside the pack train and the rolling *mitrailleuse* section.[69] After a cup of warm coffee, Kiffin, Paul and the others threw their sacks into the supply wagons, and fell in behind the procession. Although they were not carrying their equipment, "a long day's march was promised us to counteract the comfort of marching without sack."[70] In fact, by the next morning, the men would march fifty-six kilometers (almost 35 miles) on empty stomachs. In his diary, Seeger recorded it as "the hardest day we have had."[71]

The convoy trooped over a plateau, in a sort of semi-circle around Reims. From this height, the marching men had a clear view of the city and its wonderful cathedral.[72] In addition to the views of the famous church and a quaint (and somehow, intact) windmill outside Verzenay, there was plenty to interest the men as they followed the caravan. As an occasional aeroplane flew overhead, the marching legionnaires passed soldiers of all kinds, including colonial troops from Senegal and squadrons of Dragoons and Hussars, each with their brilliant uniforms. Batteries of heavy and field artillery rolled along, and encampments of Zouaves, regular infantry, and Arabs from northern Africa lined the roadsides. As Paul put it: "all the romance and color of a world war was there."[73]

The men began to grumble when, after stopping at three o'clock for lunch, they received no meal – something had gone wrong with the food supply, and the weary marchers were provided only a half tin of sardines. The few who had saved any ate the remainder of their bread from the day before.[74] Following this short break, the hungry soldiers marched on with "[n]o food except the scraps we had in our *musettes*."[75] While only a few of the men complained, their grumbling was useless, for "the corporal had his orders, which were to follow the convoy."[76]

Throughout the afternoon and into the evening, the heavy booming of the guns increased as the men drew closer to the front lines. While at Mailly the men had been conscious of the roar of the artillery, it had mostly served as mere background noise, more noticeable by its absence than its presence. Now, as they drew ever closer to the front lines, and could not only hear but *feel* the booms and whistles, it seemed that the ongoing cannonade might suck the air right out of the sky.

Late in the day, one of the mule-drivers started a rumor that the men would rest for the night at Fismes. However, by the time the convoy and guard reached that village shortly after dark, they still had not received orders. Eventually, a cyclist appeared with a dispatch ordering the men on towards the Aisne sector. Once again, the weary men arose and marched. Paul remembered:

By now the mules themselves could scarcely walk, and their drivers were swearing as vociferously as their exhausted condition would permit. The men of the Ninth Squad were so sodden in misery that they could not complain, but staggered on in a sort of daze. Every half hour, ten-minute halts were made, and the men threw themselves down and slept, on rock piles or anything else at hand to keep them out of the mud.[77]

Finally, at 10:30 that night, a true halt was called next to a waterlogged field. Having been told to spread their blankets in the field beside the road,

Thaw "lay right down in the mud by the roadside and went straight off to sleep[.]"[78] The mules and horses slept where they stood, while Kiffin, Dowd and Seeger were posted to guard the wagons, and the rest collapsed into sleep.[79] The few men remaining awake could hear the crack of the rifle, the rat-tat of the *mitrailleuse*, and the boom of the artillery, and see the magnesium lights fired above the battlefield from the trenches.[80]

After being relieved at midnight, Kiffin, Seeger and Dowd laid down on the wet ground to get what sleep they could. Three hours later, the squadron was roused and again set forth in the darkness. Taking a wrong turn at a crossroads, the marchers were heading straight for the German lines before a mounted sentry stopped them and turned them around.[81] A few hours and another ten or twelve kilometers later, the weary men stumbled into the "wretched village" of Cuiry-les-Chaudardes, just behind the lines.[82] Here the soldiers were stationed in the dirty stables, loft and outbuildings of a large abandoned farmhouse, and given a day and a night to rest before they were to go to the front lines. Anticipating this, Seeger wrote "at last we shall be under fire."[83]

* * * * *

Following their brief rest, the men made ready for their first trip to the trenches. The officers issued extra rations, and gave instructions not to smoke or talk, and to fasten down loose articles. As the legionnaires trudged their way to the front that night, even though they were probably several kilometers from the closest German, Trinkard gave Zinn a dressing down when his *gamelle* chain kept clanking.[84]

Zinn had a good excuse, for the way to the trenches was not easy. The farmers had not had the opportunity to harvest their crops, and the road cut through the fields was almost impossibly muddy and still full of sugar beets. The protruding beets probably explained Zinn's clanking *gamelle*; in a letter home, he noted they stuck up through the mud "like doorknobs set in a field of butter."[85]

The men made their way through the marshy fields to the base of a hill overlooking German-occupied Craonnelle, where "with the quiet swiftness of a pantomime," they silently crept forward to relieve the French army personnel huddled in muddy ditches and rude dugouts.[86] Suddenly, finally, the boys were in the trenches.

In his diary that night, Seeger bluntly stated "We have come to the point where fighting is the only thing to do."[87]

Chapter Eighteen

Monotony and vermin and mud and cold...

Whatever Paul had intended when he embarked for Europe with Kiffin, he was no longer a tourist. He later wrote of his first morning in the trenches:

The first night we got to the trenches, Kiffin was sent out all night on petite post, so when he came in at dawn, he had to get into a trench about 250 yards from me. Our trenches were in the edge of a wood, on the slope of a hill. I didn't know the first morning just where the 'Boche' trenches were, so I climbed out of my trench, which eight men shared with me, to hunt Kiffin. I hadn't got ten feet before a blamed sniper spotted me and 'zip' – whizzed a bullet just by my ear. My first thought was: 'what in the dickens is someone shooting at ME for?' but coupled with the thought was the impulse to drop. I ducked to the ground and snaked my way back to my hole, and I spent most of my time in said hole thereafter.[1]

A Belgian soldier named Arthur Vandevelde was not so lucky. He was killed by a shrapnel ball while standing in the door of his hut just 15 or 20 yards from Seeger.[2] Trinkard saw him go down and shouted: "*Homme blesse!*" But nothing could be done, and the 24-year old died right there.[3] A short time later, a Spaniard was shot in front of Phelizot and King as they climbed out of their dugout.[4] Overall, the company would lose two killed and nine wounded over their four days spent in the trenches.[5]

Later that first day, the men tried to count the numerous shells fired by the German artillery, estimating the thousands of dollars it must have cost to drop bombs all around them to seemingly little effect. Indeed, the only discernable result from the cannonade was a wounded cow wandering about three hundred yards from their lines. That night, Paul and the others slipped down and killed the cow; the next day the men enjoyed fresh beef.[6]

Paul was not the only one who had to get used to living in a hole. Not long after, Chatkoff described their circumstances: "we are groundhogs, venturing forth as necessity compels us and only then."[7] The big boxer Scanlon compared himself to a different animal, saying "We live in the trench, just like rabbits, with only enough water to drink."[8]

At the outset of the war, France pushed back the invading Germans the only way it could – by throwing impossible numbers of men directly into the fray. Once French blood halted the German onslaught, the republic and its allies began the terrible task of rolling back the invader and the lines began to harden into the defensive stalemate of trench warfare. Initially, the trenches were essentially holes covered with logs and earth, reinforced to protect the occupant from shells and shrapnel. One of Kiffin's comrades put it well when he said that the earthen walls of the trenches suggested "nothing more forcefully than the sides of a prodigious grave [one] has had to dig for his own body[.]"[9]

The soldiers quickly realized that this was to be a war of digging in, and rather than the Germans, they would do battle with mud, rocks, trees and earth. Accordingly, the pick, the axe and the shovel would figure far more prominently than the rifle and bayonet. Upon the legion's arrival at the front, the trenches were poorly made, still too shallow and narrow. Seeger gave a good description:

The typical trench dugout resembles catacombs more than anything else. A long gallery is cut in the ground with pick and shovel. Its dimensions are about those of the cages which Louis XI devised for those of his prisoners whom he wished especially to torture, that is, the height is not great enough to permit a man to stand up and the breadth does not allow him to stretch out. Down the length of one curving wall the soldiers sit huddled, pressed close, elbow to elbow. They are smoking, eating morsels of dry bread or staring blankly at the wall in front of them. Their legs are wrapped in blankets, their heads in mufflers.

Slung or piled about them, filling every inch of extra space, are rifles, sacks, cartridge belts and other equipment. A villainous draught sweeps by. Tobacco smoke and steaming breath show how swiftly it drives through. The floors are covered with straw, in which vermin breed. The straw is always caked with mud left by boots which come in loaded down and go out clean. To get new straw we sometimes make a patrol in the night to the outskirts of a ruined village in front of our lines and take what we need from a deserted stable. It is our most exciting diversion just now.

The roof of the dugout is built by laying long logs across the top of the excavation; felling trees for these coverings occupies a large part of our rest intervals. On the completeness with which these beams are covered with earth depends the comfort and safety of the trench. Wicker screens are often made and laid across the logs, sods are fitted over the screens so as to make a tight covering and then loose earth is thrown back on top. This is an effective protection against all but the heaviest shells. If the roof is badly made, out of branches, for instance, the rain drips through and makes life even more miserable inside.[10]

Elov Nilson, a Swede in the Ninth Squad who had claimed to be from Wisconsin in order to join up with the Americans and learn English, judged the existing trenches "worse than none at all."[11] And so the men spent their first few days perfecting the shelters, covering them with the thick trunks of trees, large branches and straw, with mounds of dirt piled on top to keep out the water.

Given all the work to be done, especially on the legion's first few trips to the front lines, it seemed their sole recreation was digging.[12] But in no time at all, these soldiers of France built, enlarged, and fortified their dugouts and carved ever longer interconnected trenches through the muddy clay. In front of these sculpted ditches, Kiffin and his colleagues placed seemingly endless amounts of barbed wire, "through which a jack rabbit could not go without getting hung up."[13] Later in the war, one legionnaire described the web of trenches that had sprung up across the front lines:

Back of the first line trench is the second, back of that a third. In some places, there are a dozen lines of trenches, different distances apart, varying with local conditions. From the rear, at right angles, interweaving like meshes of a net, are the communication and auxiliary branches through which men bring up supplies, provisions and ammunition.[14]

* * * * *

The regiment's first stint in the frontline trenches lasted four days. On November 2, they were relieved, and the soldiers again trudged back to Cuiry-les-Chaudardes, about five kilometers behind the lines. According to Paul, the place was really just a small group of farmhouses, "too small to even be called a village."[15] Still, the tiny hamlet would serve as the legion's headquarters for the next several months and, although there was not even a store, the men were happy to find that the owner of one farmhouse was selling wine, cheese, sugar, chocolate and other soldiers' luxuries.[16]

Seeger now had a little time to record his impressions of their first trip to the front lines. He noted that their initial fortification of the shelters had been time well spent, as the Germans, "informed no doubt by their aeroplanes that buzzed continually overhead," turned their guns on the trenches instead of continuing to fire at the French batteries behind. Thus, after their first day or two, the men spent most of their daylight hours hunkered down in the dugouts trying to sleep, despite the "magnificent orchestra of war."[17] And they needed the rest, because they were kept awake most of the night:

Darkness would hardly begin before a fusillade would start from the lines nearby. The cry of "aux armes, aux tranchées!" *would run from door to door and we would hasten out into the night to wait in the muddy ditches while the bullets whistled about us. But the fusillades would always die out, provoked probably only by German patrols seeking to discover our situation. After the first experience we were forced to stay up all night, but later we became used to it and were allowed to go back to our holes to sleep. In this way we would hustle out into the darkness four or five times in a single night, at first a little uneasy, but in the end only bothered. In the daytime we slept, oblivious to the shells that burst around us.*[18]

During their rest periods in Cuiry-les-Chaudardes, the men spent much of their time digging trenches, building dugouts and sawing logs. When not working on the ever-growing network of trenches, a soldier might be found cleaning his gun, greasing his boots, patching his uniform, grinding coffee, or peeling potatoes. But whatever they were doing, the men were always occupied; as D.W. King put it, "the word 'rest' was euphemistic."[19] In a letter home, Robert Soubiran emphasized that he had learned that "what one requires most of all is sleep, not food, when doing this sort of thing."[20]

Americans in the *1st Regiment Étranger* were having a similar experience. Victor Chapman, who had been assigned to the Third Company, found it "simply appalling how hard it is to have time unobstructed to oneself."[21] Not long after, Kenneth Weeks (serving in the Second Company) would write his mother: "The last two months have been hard, too hard, especially lately; no rest, not enough food, too much work and anxiety. I am exhausted."[22]

Weeks' experience was typical of most of the Americans. He told his mother he had become a "miner – a day labourer. In fact, I have learned all the labours: cook, miner, tailor, woodcutter; the soldier's life is not all uniform and glory. It is uncommonly hard, but forced labour is better than idleness here."[23] Kiffin and his fellow legionnaires were adjusting to life at the front, which meant many things, but mostly it meant continuous hard work. Their work and proximity to the Germans further hardened the men, and as their time at the front lengthened, their mood became more somber, their faces more drawn. The approach of winter promised to make their lives even harder.

But not everything at the front was worse. For now, at least, the food had gotten better, and more plentiful. The general bill of fare included cabbage soup, beef stew, bean soup, hard bread, coffee and a pint of wine a day.[24] Not that the soldiers were in any position to complain – as Paul put it, "Trench digging will make anyone like any food."[25] One correspondent wrote around this time:

The food is a revelation to one who has read of hunger among the Germans. Whoever read of soldiers getting bars of chocolates, wine, cognac and other delicacies? We do. We get sweet coffee, sometimes with milk, and at other times we get tea. We always have excellent meat, potatoes and rice. Food! Why, one cannot possibly be hungry; in fact, I have not eaten lunch today because I am not hungry, so I am writing this instead.[26]

In addition, the men received from friends and family numerous packages bearing various treats. For many commodities, the law of supply and demand took over, and an informal "exchange" developed on which items such as liquor, cigarettes, chocolate, cheese, sardines, jam and other indulgences were bartered. The day's trading session generally opened at first natural light, when coffee and the days' rations were distributed. Thaw and Casey usually tried to corner the market on rum, which Bert Hall (who never drank), King, Towle, Chatkoff and Dowd were happy to give up. Trinkard, Morlae, Soubiran and Capdeveille were always seeking cigarettes, with Seeger, Towle and Chatkoff on the selling end. Dowd typically tried to secure a stash of chocolate, and most of the men wanted jam. One participant stated that the daily "riot" usually lasted half an hour, after which everyone "settled back satisfied."[27]

* * * * *

Kiffin's company returned to the frontline trenches on November 5 for what Seeger called "five days and nights of pure misery." Due to their exposed place on the line, Seeger, Kiffin and the others were confined morning to night in "very formidable bombproofs." As they were located only a few yards from a large pit marking the spot where a few days earlier a German mortar had killed several soldiers from another battalion, the men expected heavy shelling.

However, due to nearly continuous fog throughout their five days on the line, the firing was less frequent than anticipated, although they received their share.[28]

When it began to rain, the uncomfortable trenches got even worse. According to Zinn, their dugouts "were leaky and were invaded by everything that creeps and crawls."[29] Of course, natural aggravations such as weather and bugs were not their only, or even chief, concern – they were also dealing with German-made nuisances. The Swede Nilson may have summed up the unique misery of the saturated trenches in a single sentence, written in his diary: *Det regnar, både vatten och granater* – It rains, both water and grenades.[30]

A few days after their second trip to the front line, Kiffin scratched out a short note letting Loula know he and Paul were "both well and safe." Hiding the true nature of their duties and placement, Kiffin lied that they were spending most of their time in the reserve trenches, away from danger. He admitted the hardships were severe, but reassured Loula he and Paul were "standing them well and the outlook is bright." Closing with "love to all," Kiffin again reminded his mother not to worry, "as we will come out ok."[31]

As winter approached with no action, Seeger wrote of the toll the colder weather and waiting were taking on the men:

It is a miserable life to be condemned to, shivering in these wretched holes, in the cold and the dirt and semidarkness.... The increasing cold will make this kind of existence almost insupportable, with its accompaniments of vermin and dysentery. Could we only be attacked! I would hear the order with delight. The real courage of the soldier is not in facing the balls, but the fatigue and discomfort and misery.[32]

Having envisioned bayonet charges and offensive actions, shivering in the mud like animals was not what the men had in mind. As Fred Zinn noted, contrary to their expectations at the time they enlisted, "we found ourselves simply an insignificant link in a human chain that reached from Switzerland to the Atlantic. After our happy dreams of sharp engagements and swift marches ... this was, to put it mildly, a terrible come down."[33] One soldier conveyed the general mood of the men in a letter published in the *New York Sun*: "So the days and nights pass. There is little excitement, less danger, and no adventure."[34]

The soldiers were learning that life in the trenches is a study in contrasts. While every moment was potentially one of life or death, and anything could happen, for the most part it never did. Charles Sweeny captured well their daily existence:

Monotony and vermin and mud and cold and thrills and dulling work and hunger and that gambler's happiness which only the soldier knows in its fullest perfection – all these things enter into life in the trenches.[35]

For many, boredom became a constant companion and second enemy. One Englishman put his finger on it when he stated that trench life "is as dull as the ditch-water which trickles plentifully away along the gutter at the bottom. There you fight and live and sleep and eat and smoke, and it is not long before the sleeping and eating and smoking come to seem by far more important than the fighting."[36]

Not that the men were doing any fighting. Many, including Kiffin and Paul, had not even fired their rifles. Like others, Kenneth Weeks decried this fact in a letter to his mother: "There are long days of inactivity that become monotonous to despair, and an attack, an ambuscade, a lively cannonade are really welcome."[37] Simply put, having been trained for combat, the men wanted to engage. But instead they had been placed in defensive positions and were tasked merely with holding the line. Thus, they whiled and wasted away the hours, and began to feel as if they were never going to see real combat. Still, the somber soldiers tried to stave off discouragement by telling themselves that this was "the great European war we have always heard, read and talked about, and that everything is on so gigantic a scale that we must wait before our own particular small section can accomplish anything."[38]

Staving off discouragement got harder when the food situation changed. First, the fact that Cuiry-les Chaudardes had no store and was overrun with troops made scarce the little luxuries which to that point had helped make trench life tolerable. Seeger described the conditions in a letter to his mother, written in French:

We are now in a country harassed by war. The villages in which we are billeted, if not burned and demolished, are absolutely deprived of all provisions and merchandise by the continual passage of troops. There is not even a drop of wine or a morsel of bread to buy. The poor inhabitants live for the most part on what the soldiers who are lodged with them bring them.[39]

But the "real inconvenience," according to Seeger, occurred when the regular hot meals coming from the legion's galley were disrupted. Their rolling kitchen, having been placed too close to the front, was shelled by the Germans, after which it was moved several kilometers behind the lines.[40] Thereafter, the food was cooked and brought up from the rear on an "almost impassably muddy" path, which was "ill-defined [and] hard to follow after dark, so that most of the wine & coffee would be spilled on the way."[41] The three to four kilometer distance meant the food was usually lukewarm and often cold before it reached the waiting soldiers. Hoping to eat while it was still hot, the men eagerly listened to "hear the clink of the pails returning in the dark."[42]

Many of the men were bored enough to make an exception to their general rule against volunteering and offered to make the regular walk back to the kitchen just to have something to do. Seeger wrote:

At night we can have a little more freedom. The cannonade ceases with daylight, and we prepare ourselves for the nightly fusillades that may mean an attack or simply the passing of a patrol. There is the corvee de soupe, *when we start for the kitchen two or three miles back at three o'clock in the morning and at sundown for no one can cross the open spaces with safety in daylight; the half-dozen or so men who bring back the provisions and meals for the section are willing to face the hardship of bringing a heavy load back over the dark, muddy path, just to have a little action.*[43]

The ever-cheerful big-game hunter Rene Phelizot tried to bring some levity to their circumstances. When anyone complained about the rain, the bitter cold, the mud, the lukewarm meals, the lack of fighting, the monotony, or anything else, Phelizot would invariably respond "It's the fortunes of war, my boy."[44] This catch-phrase became something of a running joke among the Americans. But soon enough, they would have even more to complain about.

* * * * *

While serving in the trenches with the *1st Regiment Étranger*, Victor Chapman wrote his mother that "the soldier at the front is about the most picturesque animal I can think of."[45] But there were many at the front lines in France in late 1914 who would have taken exception to that rosy sentiment.

To begin with, already cold and rainy, the weather turned and got even colder. On November 16, the first flurry of snow blanketed the trenches.[46] Within days, an early winter had set in, freezing the roads. Crammed into their filthy trenches, with shells falling and snipers sniping, the men were constantly cold, hungry, and tired. In a letter to his mother, Alan Seeger gave a good description of what the men were going through and of how hard things had become:

We are now in the field all the time, under the gray November skies, the fog and the rain. I write this from the trenches, where we are lodged elbow to elbow in the dark, cold bombproof. I have no inclination to describe to you at length the nature of our life under these conditions (nor is it possible to write at length) though such a description would be very novel and interesting to you. It would be simply the description of taxing human endurance to the utmost and the proof of how much sheer misery and discomfort the human organism can support. We are confined continually to the underground shelters, unable to show our heads on account of the shrapnel of which we are in continual danger and which daily takes a little toll from the imprudent.[47]

The squalid conditions made many of the men miserable. It was not just the cold weather and tough surroundings, however, but the drudgery of trench life. Seeger told his father it was distressing "being harried like this by an invisible enemy and standing up against all the dangers of battle without any of its exhilaration or enthusiasm," adding that "a bayonet charge would be desirable and the command welcome to us all."[48] In a letter to the *New York Sun*, Seeger captured well the feelings of disenchantment felt by those in the trenches:

This style of warfare is extremely modern and for the artillerymen is doubtless very interesting, but for the poor common soldier it is anything but romantic. His role is simply to dig himself a hole in the ground and to keep hidden in it as tightly as possible. Continually under the fire of the opposing batteries, he is yet never allowed to get a glimpse of the enemy. Exposed to all the dangers of war, but with none of its enthusiasms or splendid élan, he is condemned to sit like an animal in its burrow and hear the shells whistle over his head and take their little daily toll from his comrades.[49]

One member of the Ninth Squad, having had enough of life in the trenches, feigned madness in an attempt to be relieved of his duty. On a freezing night, Harry Cushing Collins stripped naked, grabbed his bayonet and swore he would kill anyone who approached him. He then picked up his clothes and ran into the woods.[50] A few days later, Zinn came across Collins in the infirmary. Calling Zinn to his bed, Collins whispered to Zinn to "[t]ell the boys I'm not crazy. I've had all I want of this show, got all the glory I'm after, and I'm going to get out."[51]

But his ruse did not work – after being placed under a doctor's observation for a few days, Collins was sent to a disciplinary battalion in Northern Africa.[52] Later in the war he wrote a long article in the *New York Herald*, claiming to have been the founder of the American Volunteer Corps. The Americans remaining in action "laughed long and loud" over this ridiculous claim.[53]

Collins was not alone in wanting out – the bitter cold caused even Paul to have second thoughts. Around this time, he wrote to a former classmate from Washington and Lee that "[i]f the men who sit by the fireside and direct the campaign desired peace as heartily as we poor devils who freeze in the trenches, the war wouldn't last long."[54] Despite the wishes of the troops, however, the war rolled on, for reasons no one could quite grasp. F.W. Zinn gave as good an explanation as any when he later said that "a nation looks on war like a man does on his religion – it seems a kind of sacrilege to apply common sense to it."[55]

Paul also wrote an article for a major London paper, his first published piece of the war. In it, he described the situation faced by the men:

The weather had turned freezing cold, the Germans had burned all the straw stacks in the vicinity, and there was little straw in our trenches, which were practically open, so the suffering was intense.... The battalion lost some killed and wounded, and still more succumbed to the cold and exposure and had to go back to the infirmary.[56]

While Kiffin's infrequent letters from this time say nothing about it, there is strong evidence that Kiffin was one of the many sent back to the infirmary, and that he even returned briefly to Paris.[57] One contemporary account notes that a sore heel of Kiffin's had blossomed into an inflamed leg and blood poisoning was feared, resulting in his being sent behind the lines for about ten days.[58] However long his absence, Kiffin returned to his unit around November 22, and assured his mother he was "getting along fine."[59]

* * * * *

Kiffin must have dreaded returning to the unclean, even unsanitary conditions prevailing in the trenches and dugouts, but there was not much that could be done. Like the other legionnaires, Kiffin understood that at the front cleanliness was not next to godliness, it was next to impossible.[60] Lice were a fact of life throughout the conflict, and conditions in the trenches proved ideal for their spread.

The little monsters collected and bred in the straw on which the soldiers slept, or in the seams of filthy clothing, thriving on the body heat and close conditions of the men who in the cold often huddled together for warmth. Seeger had been the first victim, but at one point or another all the men were plagued and scratching.[61] In an effort to avoid the creatures many of the men had their heads shaved, but quickly learned the nasty things enjoyed other parts of a soldier's body just as well. Even worse, the lice were hard to kill, and the eggs laid by the females provided ready reinforcements for those squished or burned out by the infected soldier. Paul later said his memory of the trench vermin "still makes me shudder," and that he would "rather be blown to bits by shells than suffer again the terrible torment" of the big body lice with which they were infested.[62]

Down through the century since, one name for the critters has stuck – cooties. But at the time, the Americans gave them plenty of other names. Early in the war, some men referred to the bugs as "seam squirrels," while others called them "Russian deserters."[63] Bert Hall called them "totos," or more formally, "Monsieur Toto."[64] Long after the war, Paul Rockwell termed them, simply and descriptively, "the soldier's greatest pest."[65] But a poem written by one trench veteran may have supplied the most appropriate name for the infernal beasts. Titled "The Immortals," the poem ends like this:

> I used to think the Devil hid
> In women's smiles and wine's carouse.
> I called him Satan, Balzebub.
> But now I call him, dirty louse.[66]

Lice were not the only vermin; there were rodents, too. Hall said the trench rats "nibbled on everything" and "made our nights impossible with their scurrying and squealing."[67] Russell Kelly, a former VMI cadet, enlisted in November 1914 and was assigned to the *1st Regiment Étranger*. A few months later, he found himself at Verzenay. In a letter written from the nearby trenches, Kelly remarked on the great nuisance created by the large numbers of rodents – so many that he "often wished there was a Pied Piper amongst us."[68] Instead, one sergeant had a pet ferret and a fox terrier; the ferret to drive the rats out and the fox terrier to catch them.[69] Some of the legionnaires rigged up a sign in French over their catches – it read: *Hotel du Rat Mort – prix fixe – déjeuners et diners á toute heure* – hotel of the dead rat – fixed price – lunches and dinners at any time.[70]

* * * * *

There were also a few internal troubles, and the men learned that vermin also came in human form. In the large and motley force several spies were discovered, and some, wondering why these men walking around in French uniforms were unable to speak French, even suspected the Americans. Morlae, although American himself, seemed to have it in for the poet Seeger, and accused him to the legion officers of communicating with the Germans after he wandered off on one of his solitary jaunts. Morlae had been advanced to first class soldier and then corporal, and once given a little authority delighted in lording it over the other Americans. Coming on top of his having had Zinn arrested for snoring, several of his countrymen began to develop a strong dislike for Morlae.[71]

Many of the *anciens* were also something less than upstanding moral individuals. Zinn commented that it was "not particularly pleasant to be a trench-mate with a man who escaped prison by outrunning the police, nor to take orders from a sergeant who has forgotten his real name[.]"[72] Nearly all of the regulars were rough characters and a fair percentage were nothing more than common criminals, even fugitives from justice.[73] According to Ganson, they were "men who had reasons for disappearing, in many cases."[74] Although there was no question as to their ability – all recognized the *anciens* as superior soldiers – there was a wide gap between the ideals of the American volunteers and the situational ethics of the veterans.

Among men such as this, it is not surprising that theft was an issue, both during training and at the front. Indeed, Bert Hall may not have been too far off when he said that many of the foreigners in the legion were "hard customers" who "would steal anything from a cancelled postage stamp to a modern dreadnought."[75] Most of the men remembered Conti, an Italian soldier and professional bicycle thief who Hall said "would steal a part of my equipment every other day and sometimes had the nerve to steal the same piece of equipment two or three times in succession."[76] Others were victimized, too. Not long after they reached the trenches, someone relieved Dowd of his blanket. In a letter home, the chagrined soldier wrote:

While ordinarily this is termed "stealing," in the Foreign Legion it is regarded as O.K., and euphemistically called "providing for oneself by the notorious 'System D.'"[77]

As Corporal Weidemann had explained early in the recruits' training, "System D" was shorthand for *debrouillez-vous*. Translated literally, the phrase means to cope, untangle or straighten out, but in practice it meant to be resourceful, "to shift for yourself, to take the initiative, to do your own thinking."[78] Under System D the men were forced to fend for themselves in nearly everything they did, from finding their own supplies to constructing trenches to keeping warm. In fact, as Ganson later remembered, especially during their training "the only answer we could get to any question was System D."[79] While overall, the system taught the men to think for themselves and prepared them to adapt to any situation, it was certainly subject to abuse, especially when used to justify outright theft.

For these and other reasons, when the Americans were first thrown in with the hardened *anciens* there was a bit of a culture clash, and the stark differences in the mens' social backgrounds, financial circumstances and soldierly training sometimes led to jealousy and misunderstanding. For one thing, the American volunteers were idealists fighting, as they saw it, for civilization and liberty. In sharp contrast, many of the veterans were crusty mercenaries, fighting for no better reason than it was all they knew. In addition, many of the Americans were both wealthy and college boys, whereas very few of the *anciens* were either. The mixture resulted in poor leadership, low morale, and regular friction between the volunteers and the old-school legionnaires.[80] Although many of the veterans were jealous of the newcomers and asserted that distinctions were made in their favor, according to Paul, "the old timers g[o]t all the easier jobs."[81]

Over time, cramped quarters and strenuous conditions bred disagreements, and petty quarrels were common. While physical altercations were rare, they did occur. In one rough fight, the boxer Scanlon was forced to intervene against a drunken Serbian legionnaire attempting to gouge out Seeger's eyes.[82] Fighting according to gentlemen's rules, Seeger was in danger of succumbing to the brawler's tactics. After stepping in and knocking out the Serb with a single punch, Scanlon explained to the complaining Seeger: "But he was at your eyes. Who ever heard of a blind poet?"[83]

While the Americans eventually earned begrudging respect from the regulars, and some genuine friendships were formed, the line between the two groups was never fully erased, as the Americans – particularly the flag-wearing Rene Phelizot – would discover.

But first, on November 15, the men were again reminded of their common enemy. That day, Edgar Bouligny became the first American wounded in the war when a German shell splinter smashed his leg while on outpost duty.[84]

Chapter Nineteen

C'est terrible, l'est guerre...

From the time he entered the legion, Bill Thaw had always expected to be transferred to aviation. After waiting patiently through their two months of training, Thaw's desire to serve as an aviator was rekindled when, not long after the group reached the front, he and the other men witnessed their first aerial battle above the trenches.[1] Eager to fly, he sought and was granted permission for himself, Bert Hall and Jimmie Bach to walk approximately sixteen kilometers to the nearest airfield at Merval, where *Escadrille D.6* was stationed. There, the three soldiers spoke with senior officer Lieutenant Felix Brocard and requested transfers to aviation.[2] Thaw and Brocard had crossed paths before the war, and Brocard may even have given him a chance to go up in one of the two-seater Deperdussin planes, despite the fact that Thaw's proficiency was limited to the slower-moving flying boats he had used for joyrides and sightseeing excursions before the war.[3]

Although it is very likely that only Thaw had actual flight experience, Brocard agreed to assist the trio with their efforts to transfer to aviation.[4] Upon hearing the positive news, the men excitedly returned to the trenches, expecting transfer orders and a rapid end to their anonymous trench existence.[5] But no such orders came, and every day the filthy trenches seemed more discouraging. As they continued slugging it out in the mud and cold, a few of the legionnaires began to turn their gazes upward, toward the inviting French sky.

* * * * *

Back in America, on the north shore of Boston, another red-blooded American was also looking toward the French skies. Norman Prince – "Nimmie," as many of his friends called him – had spent much of his youth and many hunting seasons at the luxurious Pau estate of his father and considered France his "second country."[6] Norman's father was Frederick Henry Prince, the investment banker, financier and industrialist. Frederick was the son of the former mayor of Boston and one of the richest men in America, having earned his vast wealth investing in the stockyards, slaughterhouses and meatpacking operations around Chicago.

Being the son of a millionaire had its advantages, especially for an adventurous boy like young Norman. In addition to private tutors, race horses and flitting between Europe and America, when he was just 15 years old Prince became the youngest automobilist in Massachusetts, "scorching along at high speed and showing considerable nerve in races," according to one Boston paper.[7]

Although not overly tall (various accounts give his height at 5'5" or 5'7½"), Prince was quite handsome, with "very strong, muscular shoulders" and "the poise of an athlete."[8] He was intelligent, too – he studied in Germany and at Oxford, graduated *cum laude* from Harvard in just three years and then earned his law degree from Harvard Law.[9] While in law school, Prince became intensely interested in flying. But as aviation was still in its infancy and popularly regarded as a mere sport, rather than a profession with any practical utility or future, Norman's business-minded father – who thought aviation would "distract his attention from the more serious concerns of life" – forbade him to waste his time with it.[10]

Despite his father's prohibition, in the winter of 1910 Prince began flying lessons under an assumed name at the Wright brothers' flying school in Augusta, Georgia. Prince accompanied family friend and expert yacht builder W. Starling Burgess there when Burgess traveled to the school to learn to fly. After becoming interested in airplanes, Burgess founded the Burgess Company & Curtis, perhaps the first licensed airplane manufacturer in the United States.

In 1911, still flying under his assumed name of George H. Mannor, Prince qualified for his flying license.[11] However, knowing it would come as a "great surprise" to Prince's friends, few of whom knew that he had been taking instructions in the art of flying, a reporter on the scene spilled his secret and announced that Prince was a "full-fledged aviator."[12] It was also a great surprise to Prince's father. Hoping to trim his son's dangerous flying proclivities, Frederick Prince sent Norman off to Chicago, where he secured a spot for Norman with the prestigious law firm of Winston, Payne, Strawn & Shaw.[13]

It is not clear how much law Norman practiced while in Chicago. However, he did continue his thrill-seeking activities and became quite popular in the aero, athletic and country clubs.[14] In 1912, hoping to help keep an international cup in America, Prince and a friend hired Burgess to build and enter a plane on America's behalf in a flight competition in Chicago, but Prince was turned down as a last-minute substitution for an antsy pilot.[15]

Prince also continued to vacation in Pau, France, and to race horses at the sporting club there where his father was master of the hounds.[16] As a pilot, racer, sportsman, polo player and lawyer, Prince was a brash, confident gent – one French publication later described him as "young, rich, and full of vigor."[17] He was remembered at Harvard as "genial, a dispenser of good cheer, [and] reticent, like most normal young Americans, as to the deeper vein of seriousness which only his friends appreciated."[18]

He was also an idealist, with a strong sense of patriotism, and of right and wrong. Shortly after the war broke out, Prince took off for Montreal where he hoped to enlist in the "Canadian flying corps" but was disappointed to learn "there was no such animal[.]"[19] He then announced he was heading for France, but his father, who had already asked Norman to wait a reasonable length of time for his mother's sake, "arranged matters so that his son would not be in possession of sufficient financial means to take care of a trip to France."[20]

Not to be deterred and hoping to further refine his aeronautical skills while he saved the money on his own, Prince enrolled in the Burgess Flying School started by his old friend Starling Burgess in Marblehead, Massachusetts. During his training, Prince asked a young stenographer employed at Burgess' airplane factory to hold little bits of money he set aside; in a short while he had accumulated almost two hundred dollars for his trip.[21]

While at the flight school, Prince also came in contact with fellow Harvard alum Frazier Curtis, whose brother was connected with Burgess' airplane manufacturing business. The 38-year old Curtis was also eager to assist the allies. In fact, he had already sailed for England and attempted to enlist in the admiralty's aviation branch. However, the director turned down his request, bluntly telling Curtis there were "no vacancies and your age precludes you entering the Air Service."[22] Disappointed but determined to keep trying, Curtis returned to America and continued flying at the Burgess flight school, where Norman Prince had recently started his own training.

While flying with Curtis in November of 1914, Prince sketched out an inchoate plan he had conceived – an aero squadron composed entirely of Americans to serve France in her hour of need.[23] While Curtis thought Prince's idea splendid, he was not very enthusiastic – unlike Prince, he did not speak

French, and he still hoped to secure a spot with the English. Having already been turned down by the Royal Naval Air Service, Curtis "realized that getting into the service was no cinch," and felt he needed to concentrate on his own flying prospects rather than attempting to organize an entire squadron in a foreign military.[24]

Nonetheless, Prince pressed ahead, motivated by his belief that Americans owed France for her help during the Revolutionary War. Telling a friend "the decent thing for us to do is to go over there and help them what little we as individuals can," against his father's wishes Prince began making travel arrangements to France.[25] He also had a sense of humor to go with his idealism – asked on his passport application to state the object of his visit abroad, Prince wrote "For my health."[26]

Prince's quip failed to convince R.W. Flournoy, the same official who had signed off on Paul and Kiffin's passports a few months earlier. Perhaps the authorities were growing leery as to the plans of adventurous young Americans but, whatever the reason, the passport application form now included a line specifically requesting the applicant's purpose for traveling. Accordingly, Flournoy requested further assurances as to Prince's reasons for going to Europe. To satisfy Flournoy, Prince supplemented his application with a sworn affidavit stating that he intended to visit relatives in France and that he might take orders for an American manufacturing concern, "if I am able to do so." Most importantly, Prince affirmatively asserted he had "no arrangement or prospect of enlisting in a foreign army," which was probably technically true at the time he swore to it.[27] But while he may not have had a definite "arrangement or prospect," Prince certainly meant to assist France in whatever way he could, and intended to seek out any opportunity to do exactly that.

Whether the young lawyer's fib constituted an act of perjury or bravery is for history to decide. However, one thing was clear – like Kiffin, Paul, and the other Americans already in France, the talented and accomplished rich kid Norman Prince was ready to take his stand. And he meant to recruit other Americans to help.

* * * * *

In Asheville, a snowstorm the week before Thanksgiving prompted Loula to write her second letter in two days to her boys. The newspapers had all been reporting the hardships faced by the soldiers in Europe, and with the falling snow, Loula could not help but think of Paul and Kiffin. In her letter, she wrote:

The papers say the soldiers in France and Belgium are covered with snow, cold to the marrow, and wet through, standing in trenches of mud to the knees and that much pneumonia prevails. It is needless to ask you to think of my mind for you know it. Yet I am trusting God not to give any of us more than we can bear.[28]

She advised Paul and Kiffin to "never lose sight of one another," and suggested that if they were caught by the enemy they should "beg to be sent home," as maybe the Germans "would let you come rather than take even prisoners' care of you." She closed "let me hear as often as you can and be sure your mother's heart is with you all the time."[29]

Thanksgiving fell on November 26 that year. On Thanksgiving morning, Mrs. Rockwell wrote another letter to her "darling boys." In it, she said that although she and Agnes expected to have "a fairly good dinner," they were sure to be "lonely and wondering what our boys are doing."[30] The day before, Loula had mailed Kiffin and Paul a box for Christmas, containing knitted socks and other useful items for them to enjoy.

The brothers could have used the socks, as the bitter cold at the front was exacerbated when two more inches of snow coated the trenches on Thanksgiving.[31] Bartram Towle later recalled the day: "We celebrated Thanksgiving under fire, in a muddy dug-out, shells bursting around us. But it was a real celebration – we got up a meal, Bill Thaw conducted a little service and read the Bible aloud, and we all sat round and sang the old home songs."[32]

Although he was not overly religious, Thaw was the natural choice to lead the short ceremony.[33] Not only had he been promoted to first class soldier a month earlier, but he carried in his pocket a prized bible given to him by his mother.[34] Obliging the boys, Thaw called everyone together and read a few passages from his bible.[35] Perhaps he read these lines from Deuteronomy:

When thou goest out to battle against thine enemies, and seest horses, and chariots, and a people more than thou, be not afraid of them: for the Lord thy God is with thee…. Let not your hearts faint, fear not, and do not tremble, neither be ye terrified because of them; For the Lord your God is he that goeth with you, to fight for you against your enemies, to save you.[36]

The Americans in the *1st Regiment Étranger* also recognized the holiday. Along with two of his countrymen, Victor Chapman rounded up several stray chickens and a goose and arranged a little feast in their hut. According to one of the Americans, the others in the squad "didn't know what Thanksgiving was, but they knew chicken when they smelled it, so we invited them all."[37]

* * * * *

Although President Wilson had appointed William G. Sharp to serve as his ambassador to France in June, Sharp's wife had been ill, and the eruption of full-scale war had prevented a normal transition. The day before Sharp finally sailed for Europe on August 26, Secretary of State William Jennings Bryan sent a telegram to Republican holdover Herrick (the same man who told the initial volunteers he knew "mighty well" what he would do) asking him to continue to stay on:

Ambassador Sharp is sailing tomorrow. The president earnestly desires that the rules of etiquette followed in ordinary time may be suspended on this occasion in view of the extraordinary conditions to be met. He desires that you shall continue to hold office of Ambassador until a time shall have been agreed upon for the transfer to Mr. Sharp.[38]

Sharp would not officially present his credentials until December 4, 1914, so Herrick remained in place until the week prior.[39] As his time as ambassador neared its end and he prepared to leave Paris, on Thanksgiving, Ambassador Herrick and his wife had a final intimate gathering with a few friends and staff in the "bare and dismantled" dining room of the embassy. The only decoration consisted of two little flags at each plate – one American, the other French.[40]

* * * * *

While the food and fellowship on Thanksgiving brought a bit of home to the trenches, it did not fill every need of the men. Around this time, one of the men wrote "it is unbelievable what prices are offered for cigarettes unavailingly. When a fellow receives some by mail he is a prince."[41] The day after Thanksgiving, the twenty-six American volunteers remaining in the regiment wrote a letter to the *New York Herald* to inform "well-meaning Americans" of their presence in the trenches and to request "cigarettes, tobacco, sweaters, woolen helmets, warm gloves, chocolate, etc."[42]

Even when the soldiers had cigarettes or tobacco, they sometimes lacked matches. Bob Scanlon noted "My pipe is my only comfort, when I get a light, but there are no matches to be had."[43] On November 28, another man wrote that matches were "scarce and candles scarcer," and there was "a great demand for tinder and cigarette lighters."[44] Often, the matches were moist and would not burn, and the officers yelled at the men if they used lighters, as the tinder acted as a flashing signal to the enemy.[45]

Chocolate never lasted long with the soldiers. While they sometimes received it as part of their rations, during long stretches in the front-line trenches chocolate became "much more valuable among us than silver."[46] Dowd explained that its increased value at the front stemmed from the fact that the men could not "venture from the trenches in the daytime to search for food."[47] Not only chocolate, but sweet things in general were in demand; everyone knew when Phelizot received a packet of Domino sugar.[48]

But the lack of chocolate was far from the most pressing problem facing the men – as winter set in, so too did colds, rheumatism, and frozen feet. Bartram Towle wrote home that "[o]utside everything is frozen, the ice is strong enough to walk on."[49] Finding the short leather leggings supplied by the French government "not much good, as the water gets in between them and the shoe," one legionnaire asked a friend to send heavy puttees as "cold feet, in their literal sense, are what we all fear."[50]

The Americans in the First Regiment had it equally as bad. Victor Chapman wrote that the legionnaires there were living "more or less like cattle" and that "[e]at, sleep, and warm wet feet is one's first preoccupation when not working with pick and carrying huge logs."[51] Kenneth Weeks wrote a succinct note in French to his mother:

Always very cold. When will this war end? All suffer. Nothing new at the moment. I embrace you.... Your son, Kenneth[52]

The physical strain, mental stress, hard work, muck, vermin, cold food and cold feet made conditions in the trenches quite intolerable. Living constantly in an atmosphere of mortal danger, the soldiers were coming to grips with the fact that men only yards away could at any moment charge forward, or they could be ordered to charge themselves. The proximity to the enemy and the open trenches meant nearly everyone had to stay on guard and awake at night, and sleep during the day. The stressful conditions pushed many of the soldiers to their limits.

Kiffin and Paul had envisioned man to man fighting and dashing to exaltation in a glorious bayonet charge, not shivering in frozen and muddy holes. But the reality of trench warfare proved quite different from their imaginings – the only enemies they had encountered so far were cold, dirt and lice.

Well, cold, dirt, lice … and cows. Having received some "sure dope" that there would be an attack one night, Morlae, Thaw, Hall, Bach, and Trinkard went out as an advance guard into an open trench one hundred meters in front of the lines where they could provide early warning of the expected German attack. Billy Thaw described what happened:

It was a peachy idea, but "les Boches" never showed up, and the "exciting experience" consisted in standing for thirteen hours in three inches of water and nearly dying of fright when a dozen cows came browsing across the meadows in perfect skirmish order.[53]

As the cows meandered towards the trenches, thinking perhaps the Germans might be using the cows and the dark as cover, Morlae crept forward to investigate. Just then, another section began firing, supposing the cows were the advancing enemy. Dodging bullets from their own men, the small squad had a "close call" making it back to their lines unhurt.[54]

Hall later joked that Morlae had been "attacked by a gentleman cow," and that "the cows were the only enemy we sighted all night."[55] On the bright side, however, Hall noted the "considerable casualties among the attacking force," and "for a week at least the American section of the Foreign Legion had an ample diet."[56] The fresh beef was quite a treat, and that area of the trenches was thenceforth dubbed *Les Tranchees des Vaches'* – the Cows' Trenches.[57] In a letter home, Thaw summed up the whole event: "'*C'est terrible, l'est guerre,'* as we Frenchmen say…"[58]

Chapter Twenty

They cannot mean much to France one way or another...

As November turned into December and the cold deepened, it became apparent that some of the men were not cut out for life at the front. Simply put, under the severe conditions they faced, many of the volunteers could not hold up. For example, J.S. Carstairs and J.W. Ganson left the front "for a rest."[1] At the same time, Achilles Olinger, a French language professor at Columbia University, transferred back to headquarters to become a field telephone operator or, as some of his fellow soldiers called it, a "hello girl."[2] Because of his mechanical ability, Robert Soubiran had also been transferred, and was running a threshing machine to harvest the wheat left in the fields.[3] Charles Beaumont had injured his heel, and was sent to the hospital around this time.[4] A few others had dropped out earlier at Toulouse, including Georges Casmeze, the founder of the volunteer corps, who took sick, and Thomas F. McAllister of Grand Rapids, who had broken his ankle in training.[5]

Bartram Towle's older brother Ellingwood experienced knee problems and had also been left behind at Toulouse.[6] Then just before Thanksgiving, the volunteers received word that Ellingwood had been declared unfit for service. Most of the Americans were relieved, "for the possibility of two brothers never returning home seemed to us too great a sacrifice."[7]

They likely felt the same sense of relief when Paul was sent to a field hospital just after Thanksgiving. On November 28, one of Paul's comrades wrote that Paul was "likely to be declared unfit for service, as his health is not standing the strain."[8] One account states that previously Paul had "dropped in his tracks" while on one of the legion's long forced marches, and had to be carried back by two comrades.[9] This led to an incident with one of the officers:

Fatigued from hard fighting and frozen from exposure, he was taunted by a corporal who had been in the army twenty-five years. "If I were no better soldier than to drop on a forced march, I'd desert," cried the corporal to Mr. Rockwell, to which the latter replied: "And if I had been in the army twenty-

five years and had attained no higher place than that of corporal I'd get in front of a bullet and stay there until it struck me."[10]

On December 1, Thaw wrote that "about a dozen men" had already been "sent back with frozen feet."[11] Paul must have been one of these, for that same day Kiffin wrote Loula the following:

Go back in the trenches tonight. We are so safely entrenched that there is practically no danger at all. Our losses have been mostly through sickness, as conditions are bad in that respect. I suppose Paul has written you that he is out of it, but there is nothing seriously wrong with him. I haven't heard from him but am hoping he was sent to Paris.[12]

* * * * *

As Kiffin indicated, by December 1, Paul was indeed "out of it." With his long history of pneumonia and weak lungs, perhaps it is surprising that Paul made it as far and as long as he did. Paul seems to fit the description of the spirit being willing, but the body being weak.[13] But the precise cause of Paul's exit from the front (and ultimately the legion) has received little scrutiny.

It is often asserted that Paul was "seriously injured at Craonnelle in December 1914 in the course of a patrol in advance of the lines," likely based on a citation Paul received with language to that effect.[14] Most authors have simply repeated this claim in one form or another.[15]

However, while he may have hurt his shoulder carrying his heavy pack or digging trenches and it appears certain he suffered from exhaustion and prolonged exposure to the harsh conditions, no evidence supports the notion that Paul was wounded in combat.[16]

To begin with, had Paul been wounded during a patrol that fell under attack that fact would have been recorded in the regimental journal. However, the journal makes no mention of Paul being wounded, although it meticulously records all casualties suffered in the regiment.[17]

Contemporaneous newspaper accounts further dispel the notion that Paul was wounded in action. For example, on December 30, 1914, the *Atlanta Constitution* – where Paul had worked less than five months before – quoted the following from a postcard written by Paul on December 7:

The cold has been terrible and we have suffered much. Just now I am in a hospital. The doctor says I will be O.K. by Christmas. Kiffin is in the trenches. He was in good spirits and health when I left.[18]

While Paul's postcard did not state whether he had been wounded, according to his former colleagues at the paper the quoted passages seemed "to indicate that he is ill from exposure to the wintry weather."[19] The same paper later confirmed that Paul's hospital stay was attributable to exposure, and reported the following:

Paul Rockwell is no longer eligible for service by reason of a dislocated shoulder and a weakened physical condition brought on by severe exposure during the campaign of last winter. In the trenches he was forced to undergo many hardships and his breakdown was complete. The heavy knapsack which he was forced to carry strapped to his left shoulder caused the dislocation, and it was soon after he entered the hospital to receive treatment for the injury that he suffered the breakdown from exposure.[20]

Further evidence regarding the nature and origin of Paul's injury comes from a chance encounter between Paul and a pair of husband and wife evangelists working with the YMCA visiting French hospitals just before Christmas.[21] By February of 1915, the evangelists (Mr. and Mrs. Ralph C. Norton) had returned to America and traveled to Atlanta where they spoke of their fortuitous meeting with Paul. While the story relayed by the Nortons cast Paul in a very favorable light, it made clear he had *not* been wounded. Rather, Paul was in the hospital because, like many others, he had succumbed to the severe conditions prevailing at the front.

The Nortons had traveled to France with another well-known evangelist, and were near Rheims distributing khaki-bound scriptures to soldiers when a nun asked if they would like to speak with some of the wounded. They assented, and the nun led the Nortons to a "cold, insanitary little convent" in Montmirail where about one hundred and fifty sick and wounded soldiers were receiving care.[22] There an English legionnaire named Hadley told them about a young American from his battalion in another part of the building.[23] The Nortons described their meeting with this "young American":

Stretched on a hard cot, with a dirty blanket thrown over him, was a gaunt weather-hardened man – he seemed 45 years old – with a full heavy black beard on his face and dressed in a torn long blue coat, and the worse-for-wear red trousers of the French infantryman. His shoes were worn and he had no socks! He had been borne there almost bodily by two stronger comrades. He said that although he had had many narrow escapes, he had not been wounded, but that the severe winter weather with inadequate clothing and the long foot-weary miles of a retreat had done for him.[24]

Hoping to make their new friend more comfortable, the Nortons suggested they could make arrangements to have him moved to the American Hospital in Paris. But Paul – for it was Paul on the cot – was intent on returning to the front, and responded:

You'll do nothing of the sort, please. I came over here of my own accord to get into this war, and I'll see it through as long as I last. In a few days I'll be all right again and I'll go back to the front with my battalion and with Kiffin.[25]

As it was just a few days until Christmas, the Nortons bought a few sweets, post cards, grapes and little items to cheer up the soldiers. When they presented a small package to Paul, he smiled and thanked them. Then, with tears in his eyes, he said: "Oh, I'll get along all right, but there's a French youngster back yonder dying. Give it to him." The Nortons took the package to the French soldier, a "pale little fellow" who could not understand but tried to thank them.[26] Although they knew Paul for only a brief time, the Nortons stated that the incident "has since seemed to us typical of Paul Rockwell."[27]

Perhaps far less typical of Paul, a few months later he apparently embellished the origin of his maladies and asserted that in fact he had been wounded on the battlefield. In May of 1915, the *Atlanta Constitution* published an April letter from Paul to an Atlanta friend in which Paul made the following claim:

I was coming in from petit post *one night across an open field. It was pitch black dark when, all at once, those fellows turned a searchlight on us and opened up with rifles. Also the shell fire began just then. We were absolutely in the open and began hot-footing it for the pines. A 'marmite' exploded near me just as I started to jump into an open communications trench. I was blown into the trench and cracked my left collar bone. I knew my shoulder was hurt, but thought it nothing serious, so I stayed in the first line until my company's six days were up. When we went to leave I found that I could not carry my sack. I also had the rheumatism and two toes were nearly frozen, so I have had a spell in the hospital.*[28]

Paul was not the first soldier to exaggerate the details of his service and perhaps he really did dive into a trench and hurt his shoulder. But the impression that has carried through the years – that his stay in the hospital and ultimate discharge from the legion was the result of being wounded in action – is not supported by the evidence.[29]

Whatever the origin of his injury, the fact that Paul and many of the others left the front is hardly surprising – the conditions were harsh and unforgiving. By mid-December, Dennis Dowd reported that eight more of the twenty-six Americans who less than a month earlier had signed the letter published in the *New York Herald* "dropped out for one reason or another, either wounded or worn out by the hardships that are the natural exigencies of a campaign such as this."[30] Around the same time Kiffin noted that the "American bunch has dwindled, only about 15 of us left. The others are either reformed or sick in hospitals or have gotten easier jobs. Only one wounded."[31]

When the unit was called to formation one morning not long before Christmas, the remaining volunteers realized how depleted they had become: "We started out a section of sixty odd, and at the review numbered only thirty-seven. This certainly opened our eyes somewhat."[32] One of the men described the scene:

We made a sorry sight, formed on a square, each squad forming a side. Everybody was muddy, for the mud cannot be got off. Buttons were missing, leggings and shoe laces gone.[33]

* * * * *

Back in Asheville, Loula was anxious for news. Every day she eagerly watched for the mail, but because it usually took about three weeks to make the voyage from France to North Carolina, as of yet she knew nothing of Paul being sent to the hospital. Moreover, the papers carried news of "bitter weather, hardships and fighting," which did not ease her mind.[34] While she wrote Paul and Kiffin that "all America sympathizes and weeps over Europe," Loula also recognized that, nearly alone among American mothers, she had a direct stake in the affair.

All in all, Loula had held up remarkably well in the months after Paul and Kiffin unexpectedly departed for Europe, even though she simply "could not see where my two boys meant anything to France, whereas they meant everything to me."[35] It helped that for the most part, her friends in Asheville felt towards the Rockwell boys the same way they felt towards the other Americans volunteering to help – proud.[36]

Still, some were critical of her boys' decision and as the news from Europe grew darker throughout the autumn and early winter, Loula's distress intensified. While she was far too strong-willed to be influenced by the few who were unsympathetic to Paul and Kiffin's decision to enlist with a foreign army, she was distraught at being suddenly – and perhaps permanently – separated from her darling boys.[37] Despite her strength, one thing is certain – especially during those first few months, Paul and Kiffin's decision took a hard toll on their mother. The tenderness of her feelings is captured in two letters she wrote to her "darling boys" in early December:

We do not like the war news we get. How I long for it to be over, how I long for my boys. Three weeks from tomorrow is Christmas, but we do not expect any pleasure this year.... How I hope you can be spared to come home well, and unscarred. God in his mercy can take care of you, my own dear ones.[38]

Loula also saw to the more mundane matters the boys had left behind. For example, she tried to recover the trunks and other belongings they had left in Atlanta and London. She also forwarded to Kiffin a letter sent by a collection agency seeking the return of his correspondence course books and typewriter. The agency asserted it would "leave no stone unturned" to secure the return of the items, but would also "be glad to cancel the account on the payment of a small fee."[39] Loula advised Kiffin to take care of the matter, telling him he could not "afford to let his honesty be questioned, or be considered slack or crooked."[40]

* * * * *

But in the cold trenches of France, Kiffin had more important things to worry about and somehow typewriters, books on modern advertising and collection agencies ranked well below German bayonets, mortar shells and trying to keep warm. Happily, Kiffin's hard work had made keeping warm a little easier. As he wrote to Loula on December 10:

I have spent 21 out of [the] last 24 days in trenches. At first suffered some from cold, but the trenches are now fixed up for winter, and we are able to have fires at night when the smoke won't show. I am in the best condition have ever been in – in a comfortable point now. This is my "Merry Xmas" and "Happy New Year" to you all.[41]

Unfortunately, on their next rotation, the troops were moved to a new spot in the woods facing Craonnelle. There, instead of snug dugouts, they were housed in carelessly made huts whose roofs "offered no protection against shrapnel or even rain." "In some respects," Seeger noted, this was "the worst situation we have occupied."[42] While the interdiction against flames had been removed, this allowance turned out to be premature when two fires got out of control.

The first happened in the dark just after they were transferred to the unfamiliar huts. Casey lit a piece of paper to see where he was, but accidentally caught the dry branches and straw overhead on fire.[43] Although it was quickly put out, Morlae accused Casey of being a German spy and of starting the fire to try to signal the enemy.[44] Like his accusations against Zinn and Seeger, this allegation was groundless, and put further distance between Morlae and many of the Americans. Many were happy when Morlae was sent off to non-commissioned officers' school.[45]

The other fire destroyed a hut quartering four of the legionnaires. The soldiers fell out and "worked like beavers" to put it out, carrying water from a nearby stream in their empty food pots, while Bill Thaw soaked his trench mate's blanket and used it to fight the flames.[46] The bright blaze soon drew the attention of the Germans, and the men had to extinguish the flames while under a different kind of fire. According to Seeger, the "hurried call to arms amid the fusillade and the crackling of the fire was not a pleasant experience."[47] Once the blaze was out, Thaw's friend could not help suggesting that Thaw "might have used his own blanket[.]"[48] Seeger guessed (correctly) that these incidents probably meant "the end of fires and a return to sleeping in the cold."[49]

* * * * *

Although Thaw still had his blanket, he was just about sick to death of trench life. Having waited almost a month to be transferred to aviation, he wrote home just after Thanksgiving: "War is wretched and quite uninteresting. Wish I were back, dodging street cars on Broadway for excitement. Am that tired of being shot at!"[50]

Two weeks later, Thaw grew even more frustrated when aviation transfer orders arrived for Jimmie Bach, but not for him. While Bach was an engineer and spoke fluent French, unlike Thaw, he had no experience as a flyer.[51] Bert Hall had not received a transfer either, but had been sent to the American Hospital in Neuilly with the mumps.[52] Trying to figure out what was going on, Thaw again trudged to Merval to meet with Lieutenant Brocard.[53]

The lieutenant informed Thaw that he and Hall had been accepted into aviation and would soon receive their transfers.[54] Sure enough, a few days later on Christmas Eve, Thaw received orders transferring him to *Escadrille D.6* where he was to serve as an observer while waiting for a spot to open up in one of the military flying schools so he could earn his military license.[55] Thaw left the legion that very day, saying "I am sorry to leave you boys, but I am glad to get back at my old job."[56] His parting words to Kiffin and Charles Trinkard were that he would do his best to get them into aviation with him.[57] Hall received his transfer on December 28, while still in the hospital with the mumps.[58]

A few days later, the *Boston Globe* noted the Americans who had made the jump to flight training, stating: "It will do this nation no harm to have a few men know by actual experience how aviation is utilized in war."[59]

* * * * *

Back home, Loula Rockwell was having fits. On December 18, she must have gasped when she read in the *Asheville Citizen* an article headlined "Asheville Soldiers Sent to Hospital." The piece noted that Kiffin had recently returned to the front after his stint in a field hospital, then stated:

Paul Rockwell is now in the hospital, it is learned, although it is not thought that he is seriously hurt. He is again able to write, and in a letter to an Asheville friend, which was received here yesterday, he stated that he hopes to be back in the trenches within the next few days.[60]

An ocean away from her darling boys, Loula felt helpless knowing they had both been sent to hospitals, and one was still there. More than ever, Loula just wanted her sons home where they belonged. Not knowing what else to do, she wrote out a plea to the newly-installed United States ambassador to France, William G. Sharp, who had only recently assumed the duties of his office.

"I come to beseech your interest in my two boys now in the French Army, to ask that you use your influence to give them an honorable discharge," Loula began. Asserting her status as a widow and a mother, she told the ambassador how after losing her husband at a young age she had by her own efforts raised and educated her three "delicate children," and explained:

The oldest boy has had three attacks of pneumonia and one hemorrhage from the lungs. The youngest has a similar tendency and I am trying to save the daughter from tuberculosis.[61]

"As soon as the war broke out," she continued, "these boys without consulting me or older, wiser friends decided to go to Europe and sailed from New York on August 7, on the American S.S. *St. Paul*." Now, having learned that "both have been in the hospital as a result of exposure," and that Paul was still there, Loula was frantic to have her boys back home. She ended with her plea for the ambassador's help, underlining the words she wished to emphasize:

Now, I do not think it possible with their constitutions for them to live through a long war even if they are not killed. Should they possibly live, it seems inevitable to me that they will come back ruined in health.

I need them, I need their support, their sister needs them. They cannot mean much to France one way or another, but they mean all to me. They should have known that, they were young and [their] judgment wrong....

They have never intimated that they would change if they could, they are too brave for that. But I believe they know their mistake, and realize that their duty is to me.

Because I am a widow, a mother, I ask that you be patient with my request that my boys be allowed to come back to me, or at least get out of the trenches. Can you, will you help me? I need the boys.[62]

This was just one letter among several Loula wrote seeking the return of her boys.[63] She must have written Kiffin as well, begging him to come home. While it is not known exactly what she said, Loula probably expressed something similar to what she had written Ambassador Sharp: that in leaving, her boys "took away from me my life, my all."[64]

Whatever she told Kiffin, it made him feel awful – on the envelope of his next letter home, Kiffin scrawled "Please don't write such pitiful letters."[65]

Chapter Twenty-one

Joyeaux Noel

At the end of the year, one of Paul's former fraternity brothers in Atlanta saw Paul's postcard published in the *Constitution*. Many others must have seen it, too, for when Lionel K. Anderson, Jr. wrote Paul, he passed along best wishes from "fifty or sixty others," telling him "You do not know how popular you really are until you become a soldier."[1] Whether due to their status as soldiers or not, the Rockwells were certainly popular in Atlanta; Lionel said he was constantly receiving inquiries about Paul and Kiffin from both girls and boys.

Lionel was Paul's fraternity brother, fellow poker player and all-around comrade-in-arms; Paul called him by his nickname, "Shine." In his letter, Shine informed Paul of all the news from Atlanta, centering mostly on his poker winnings from the old fraternity gang. Shine was also close with Kiffin, and asked Paul to tell his younger brother "not to become too much in love with soldiering that he cannot settle down to private life again."[2]

According to Shine, Paul and Kiffin were "getting plenty of free advertising here in this old town," via the recent article detailing how the YMCA evangelists had met Paul in France. He wrote:

[T]here was a good writeup about you in the Constitution *telling of their meeting with you over there in the hospital and they said some damn nice things about you: how you were over there in this hospital and so cheerful and unselfish etc. Oh, it was a peach of a writeup and one that people will always remember you by. I am going to send the clipping to your mother so that she may see just what these people think of you.*[3]

Knowing Loula was consumed with worry over her sons, in closing Shine urged Paul to "be careful and get back to this country alive and whole for your mother worries about you all the time – you see, I can tell from her letters that she thinks of nothing else so when this business is over beat it this way at once."[4]

Although Paul optimistically expected to be out of the hospital by

Christmas, as the day approached he learned he would be sent to a *chateau* for some more rest. This and the relative comfort of the little convent kept Paul from complaining as his hospital stay lengthened over Christmas.

* * * * *

On Christmas Eve, Bill Thaw arrived at the airfield in Merval, where he began his service with *Escadrille D.6*. The next Christmas would find Thaw back in America where, along with two other American aviators, he would be the toast of New York and featured on front pages across the country, but for now he was an observer only.

In his first letter after his transfer, Thaw told his friends not to worry about him, for "in this war, 'the higher, the safer,' say I."[5] But while he was definitely higher, Thaw was slightly disappointed that he was not yet a pilot.

Still, the change was much to Thaw's liking, "if only from the point of personal comfort," for now he could "at least keep clean." Moreover, the work was "considerably more interesting" and "easier than handling a pick and shovel all day, or standing four hours' sentinel duty on a cold, rainy, sleety night." Despite the hardships he had experienced, Thaw did not regret his four months in the infantry for, he said, "if I picked up some bad French, I think I got also some good training, physical and otherwise."[6]

* * * * *

While Paul was spending Christmas in the convent-turned-hospital, at the front Kiffin labored on with his comrades in the legion, where bad French and standing sentinel was the best he could hope for. Christmas morning found Kiffin feeling "pretty rotten," still nursing a lingering cold that had plagued him for the prior week, during which he and his unit had spent every day digging trenches behind the lines in Cuiry-les-Chaudardes.[7] As Kiffin told his mother, their repose in the village "was supposedly six days of rest, but each day at eleven o'clock we have gone out with our guns and picks and shovels and dug trenches until four o'clock."[8]

They were supposed to dig on Christmas as well, but instead most of the Americans "slipped off and spent the afternoon at a farmhouse, drinking coffee and rum."[9] Kiffin mentioned his truancy in his letter to Loula, but only told Paul the part about the rum.[10]

Excusing themselves from duty was a rare occurrence for Kiffin and his fellow soldiers; the officers must have exercised some leniency due to it being Christmas Day. Spending Christmas in the trenches was not what the common soldiers on either side had expected back in the early days of August, and many observers had predicted that a day of peace might materialize among the weary men on the front lines.

For example, on Christmas Eve the *New York Sun* reported that the soldiers in the trenches expected to observe the sacred day such that "habit and thoughts of home will accomplish what diplomacy and the Church failed to do – produce a brief truce."[11] The paper continued:

There is a very definite belief here that neither Germans nor Allies will on Christmas Day actively pursue their business of killing each other, and that choruses of old songs will supplant momentarily the thundering guns and popping corks the fusillades of rifle fire.[12]

Similarly, the Christmas Eve edition of the *Daily Mail* stated:

There should be some quaint scenes and sounds in the forests of the Argonne where French and German lines have been established so close to each other that the men are getting quite well acquainted. The gay soldiers of France will not forget to fête Noël with songs, and the Germans may be depended upon to reply. Whatever commands may come from headquarters, it will be odd if the eve of Christmas is not kept as an informal truce.[13]

In the First Regiment, Victor Chapman witnessed this firsthand, and wrote to his uncle of their "interesting but not too exciting" Christmas in the trenches. It began on Christmas Eve, when men in opposite trenches began calling to each other, and progressed from there:

Christmas morning a Russian up the line who spoke good German wished them the greetings of the season, to which the Boches responded that instead of nice wishes they would be very grateful to the French if the latter buried their compatriot who had lain before the trenches for the last two months. The Russian walked out to see if it were so, returned to the line, got a French officer and a truce was established. The burying funeral performed, a German Colonel distributed cigars and cigarettes and another German officer took a picture of the group.... No shooting was interchanged all day, and last night absolute stillness, though we were warned to be on alert.[14]

Citizens of all countries sought to bring Christmas cheer to the combatants and the mail systems were flooded with packages filled with warm clothing, socks, hats, boots, knitted items, such as scarves and mittens, as well as sweetmeats, wine, coffee, tobacco and most of all, candy. A poem written by a French volunteer nurse and included with a pair of knit mittens exemplifies the tender care and emotion with which many of these items were made and sent:

> Soldier, Soldier, dear Unknown,
> I wonder as I knit.
> Will you be a corporal
> Who will wear this mit?
>
> Will you be a captain?
> Tell him, Mitten, pray,
> That in your simple meshes
> I wove my heart today.
>
> Wove it warm and throbbing,
> O gallant soldier mine!
> Praying that it strengthen
> That strong right hand of thine.
>
> Strong to strike and swift to strike,
> And drive the foe away,
> Lay on, lay on, my Soldier,
> Lay on, and win the day!
>
> And if my little mitten
> Be dyed a deeper red
> Its saffron turned to crimson
> With blood in honour shed.
>
> The radiance of that scarlet,
> The glory of that stain,
> Would make my little work-bee
> Seem like a sacred fane!
>
> So here's my little mitten,
> Wool to keep you warm,
> Kisses in the meshes,
> To keep you, dear, from harm.[15]

Although the mail was congested, on Christmas Day Kiffin received a letter from Paul.[16] He also received and read an article Paul had written about the legion's training and time at the front, which appeared in the *Daily Mail*.[17]

In addition to Paul's letter, the Americans split the contents of two packages that got through to the trenches. This meant the group had new clothes and plenty to eat for Christmas, including candy, nuts, jam and cheese. An English soldier even gave Kiffin an orange, a special treat. Best of all, an American doctor serving in the legion provided the group "a good Virginia ham ... which we all enjoyed very much."[18] They also managed to rig up a Christmas tree and one of the boys played Santa Claus in a suit sent by a woman in Paris.[19] To top it off, a few soldiers found some excellent champagne in the village. Overall, the men judged the days' festivities to be "a bully time."[20]

* * * * *

In a letter to Paul the day after Christmas, Kiffin noted Thaw's departure to join the aviation corps and reluctantly stated that he was thinking of getting out of the legion as well:

The English expect to be transferred to the English Army soon. They took the names of all the English, and I gave my name.... I had rather stay with France but this is such a damn rotten outfit that I figure I had better get out if I can.[21]

But the English were not leaving any time soon, and Kiffin and his company were sent back into the trenches that night. Soon enough, the men settled back into their monotonous existence, broken only occasionally by the cry "to arms!" As Seeger put it:

So the old routine begins again – days with the whistle of shells overhead, and nights of intermittent fusillades, the only diversions being when the shells land close, or when the fusillades provoke that thrilling cry Aux armes! ... which I do not think a soldier ever grows too inured to hear without a momentary qualm, as it tumbles him from a profound slumber out into the perilous dark.[22]

Although the weather was very bad, by their third day back on the lines Kiffin and a comrade had "fixed up a dandy little trench" where they were "snug and comfortable."[23] After five mostly uneventful days, on New Year's Eve they left the trenches and tramped back to Cuiry-les-Chaudardes.

On New Year's Day, the whole section was roused before the sun came up and marched to an abandoned sugar refinery outside Maizy. The refinery was situated by a canal that ran alongside the River Aisne and had excellent bathing facilities, including hot showers. There, Kiffin rang in 1915 with his first honest to goodness bath in three months.[24] After washing up, the boys took a "pleasant diversion" to purchase hot coffee and bread from a woman selling her goods from a barge moored on the side of the canal.[25]

Back in Cuiry-les-Chaudardes that night, the men enjoyed the government's "splendid" extra dinner as well as "lots of cakes and home-cooked delicacies sent out fresh from the ovens of the American colony in Paris."[26] To celebrate the New Year, French War Minister Millerand even had champagne and fruit sent to the troops, so the day was "spent in good eating if not feasting on the French side."[27] The next day, the troops were inoculated against typhoid and Kiffin and a few of the others spent two days with sore arms and mild fevers. But the side effects came with a silver lining, at least as Kiffin saw it: "we got two days rest – the first since being in the army."[28]

* * * * *

As 1914 slipped into the past, any soldiers who had not already realized it began to comprehend that their expectations for a short conflict were mistaken – 1915 had dawned, and still the thing raged and swelled. And although they had already been through much, the participants sensed the undertaking would require more, both individually and collectively. More time, more blood, more guns, more men, more sacrifice, more sorrow, more courage, more loss.

A. Piatt Andrew, a former Assistant Secretary of the Treasury who in 1915 would head up the American Ambulance Field Service, initially volunteered to drive an ambulance and arrived in France just before the end of the year. In a letter written from Paris on New Year's Eve, he described the complete determination of the French people:

They are confident that, cost what it may cost, they are going to win. They realize that the war must last indefinitely. They know that more and more of their boys have got to die.... They know how terrible the price of victory must be, but life without it – life under German domination – would be unsupportable, and they are ready to pay the cost.[29]

Yet even while the French understood and accepted the terrible price to be paid, they and the world still held out hope that the conflict could be resolved, that the warring parties could be brought to their senses, that the slaughter could be stopped. Of this time, Winston Churchill would memorably write:

> [I]n January, 1915, the terrific affair was still not unmanageable. It could have been grasped in human hands and brought to rest in righteous and fruitful victory before the world was exhausted, before the nations were broken, before the empires were shattered to pieces, before Europe was ruined.
>
> It was not to be.[30]

Chapter Twenty-two

We have reached the point where our hardships are real and not imaginary.

During their first two months at the front, the Americans had rotated through several different locations within sight of Craonnelle, a small village from which the French had only recently pushed out the Germans. The *"boche"* had bombed their way into the village, and occupied it until the French bombed them out, so the whole place was largely in ruins. While they could not tell the full extent of the damage, from their various emplacements Kiffin and the others could make out the battered houses and shops, as well as a large burned-out *château* just outside of town.

Although the French had dislodged the Germans from Craonnelle, the retreating army had not gone far – it halted and dug in outside town along the *Chemin des Dames* (the ladies' path, named for two daughters of Louis XV who used to walk along the route). This road ran along the ridge on the edge of the plateau of Craonne, an excellent defensive position and one of strategic importance due to its elevation. Recognizing this, once the Germans took control of the plateau, it quickly became another link in their chain of increasingly hardened trenches which soon stretched across Northern France. This meant Craonnelle was now situated in the valley directly between the redrawn lines of the two armies, in a pocket cut at angles by a series of lowered crests. Because of this, according to Seeger, Craonnelle was "the most advanced [and] the most dangerous point of our sector."[1]

On January 4, Kiffin and the others were repositioned again. For the first time, they were ordered to relieve the French troops occupying and holding the village itself. Around midnight that night, the men nervously marched out of the reserve trenches, making their way in the brilliant moonlight. After a while, they turned into the woods and slogged their way through several miles of muddy trails and swamps. The route was not easy, as the entire area was wooded and hilly, and cut through by lines of abandoned trenches littered with knapsacks and equipment, another sign of the desperate fighting that had taken place. Eventually the men reached a good highway, but still had to steer clear of marmite holes, broken barricades and fallen trees. Three hours after they left the reserves, the men followed the highway into the ruined village of Craonnelle.

The rising moon provided light for the legionnaires as they made their way. According to Fred Zinn, the dead town "was a sight that one could never forget ... the moonlight and the silence and the awful devastation made a combination that was simply weird."[2] Seeger also wrote of their "stealthy, silent" entrance and first close-up view of the destruction only glimpsed from prior emplacements:

I had become familiar in our march to the front from Mailly with the tragedy of these pretty centers of peace and happiness made desolate by war. But no scene of ruin that we passed through exceeded the spectacle that met our eyes here.... [T]here was literally not a house that had not been riddled with shrapnel or disemboweled by the deadly 'marmites' that must have fallen on it in a perfect inferno of fire. Picking our way through the debris that littered the streets we filed in through that picture of desolation that makes always so striking a background for a column of infantry advancing.[3]

Kiffin described Craonnelle as "once a prosperous village but ... now just a mass of ruins."[4] Similarly, Dowd called the place a "ruined city," with not a single building at least partially destroyed, the whole town "absolutely without inhabitants, simply deserted, except for some French troops."[5] The detritus left behind by the retreating fighters made the streets nearly impassable. As they filed in, Zinn recalled "zig-zagging from one side of the street to the other to avoid the barricades and heaps of ruins."[6] Kiffin later told Paul "[t]he whole town was demolished; everywhere were barricades and dead bodies."[7] The lifeless soldiers lying amid the rubble provided graphic evidence supporting Kiffin's judgment that the advanced post was "kind of a death-trap for the troops here."[8]

* * * * *

Craonnelle was home to two bombed-out *châteaux* in which the troops were to be lodged. The first, considerably larger than the second, had been visible to the men for some time from their prior positions in the sector. It was located just outside town, so the men staying there – including Kiffin and the rest of the Ninth Squad – passed straight through the village and headed towards the large heavily-wooded estate enclosing the grand *château*.

The impressive place was known as the *Château du Blanc Sablon*. In the moonlight, the building reminded Kiffin "very much of the white house"; he guessed it had probably belonged "to some millionaire."[9] Seeger suggested it was "the pleasure retreat of some man of wealth and taste."[10] Neither knew it, but whoever the owner was, he was dead – a young French soldier occupying the home a few months earlier recorded in his diary that the master of the *château* had been shot, explaining bluntly: *"C'était un espion"* – He was a spy.[11]

Remarkably, although the *château* had been heavily bombarded and its interior completely gutted by fire, the framework and outer walls were still largely intact. In fact, in the dark and from a distance one could almost believe nothing was wrong with the place. But it was just an illusion of the moonlight. David King described what happened as they approached:

It gave us comfort and cheer to see the château lighted as we filed through the gates of the park. The glass [gateway] was intact, and so little damage seemed to have been done to the façade that it was hard to realize we were only a few hundred yards from the front line. We turned the corner, and as if by black magic the lights went out, and the place became a gutted ruin. It had only been the moon shining through empty windows.[12]

The wrecked manor sat on hundreds of acres and boasted a massive lawn sloping down to an artificial lake. Numerous paths crisscrossed the lawn and gardens, on which were interspersed ornate benches and fountains among a few summer and guest homes. A high stone wall – to his sister, Kiffin described it as "like the walls built around castles in medieval times" – surrounded the entire estate, forming a part of the French line of defense.[13] In fact, the *château* was the closest French position to the German lines for miles in either direction, and within twenty meters on the other side of its stone wall the German trenches radiated out in a semi-circle through the surrounding woods and hills.[14] The estate was near enough to the German-occupied crest that the men would soon become accustomed to the enemy patrols that came down every night to harass the legionnaires in what Seeger called "the most nerve-racking kind of warfare."[15]

The smaller *château* was located in the town itself and had suffered less from the falling shells. Only one side had been knocked in and the structure had not caught fire so, at least compared to the trenches, the *petit château* was in fine shape.[16] One of the men remarked that it was a good place for snipers.[17] The men quartered here found all manner of loot among the now-displaced family's possessions. Sheets, pillowcases, cards, furniture, photographs – everything lay scattered knee-deep throughout the residence.

The soldiers also located "the remains of a beautiful library, the last thing to be violated by the rude hands that have ransacked everything else and left not a bottle of wine in the whole town."[18] In the library Zinn found a fancy book detailing the inner workings of the court of Louis XIV while Seeger dug up some old historical and political works, including "immaculate sets" of Rousseau, Voltaire and other authors.[19] The poet could not resist taking a few volumes with him "esteeming that the pious duty of rescuing an old book doomed otherwise to certain destruction might absolve me from the gravity of the charge that such an act made me liable to."[20]

A piano in the *petit château's* upper section provided some welcome amusement for the fatigued soldiers. Once the men got going, they ended up singing songs until *soupe* time. Zinn wrote home of their songfest:

The Germans in the advanced post must surely have wondered what they were up against if they were able to hear the choice collection of hymns that were rendered. Everything from 'The Old Maid's Ball' on down to 'Tipperary,' not forgetting the 'Marseillaise' nor even 'Die Wacht am Rhein.'[21]

* * * * *

Kiffin's section was billeted in the only remaining habitable part of the larger *château* – the wine cellar. But even the cellar of a bombed-out *château* is preferable when the alternative is muddy and freezing trenches. Happily, this particular cellar turned out to be very nice – its vaulted ceilings had been relatively untouched by the shells that destroyed the upper portion of the mansion, and the furnishings were first class. Zinn described the contrast between the dirty soldiers and the luxurious surroundings:

It was surely quite a place. Some of the furniture had been moved down during the bombardment, and the rich plush chairs and inlaid tables were so at variance with the service-worn uniforms and unkempt beards of the men that it made a fellow think of his kid dreams of robber caves.[22]

Thus, even though they were directly in harm's way, Kiffin and the rest of the Ninth Squad were pleased to be stationed below the ruins of the *Blanc Sablon*. A short time later, Seeger noted the incongruity of this opulence so close to the enemy:

Here the soldiers have been able to bring straw, coal and candles, and with a good roof over their heads, safe from shells and from rain, enjoy a degree of comfort quite exceptional for a position where the crack of the German mausers as they snipe at sentinels seems at our very doors and where the mitrailleuse *upon the hillside could rake our cellar door itself were it not for the encircling groves.*[23]

Seeger especially appreciated their new quarters, writing that even if the men returned to the comforts of peace, "we will never think without fondness of the luxury it was in these days of strenuous toil and robust health to lie down after a night's watch in the straw-covered cellar bottom of our ruined *château.*"[24]

* * * * *

Due to their proximity to the German front lines, in Craonnelle the men were largely free from artillery attacks. However, skirmishes with German patrols were a constant possibility and often a reality. In addition, the men were cautioned to stay out of sight during the daytime, as the German sharpshooters held the advantage of the higher ground.

Kiffin learned this last point the hard way. Immediately after their arrival that first day, around four a.m. he and another member of his squad were placed on guard duty along the stone wall. Just before sunrise, they were instructed to return to the *château* and fetch food for the sentries. After securing the meals, Kiffin and his fellow guard started back for their posts just as the sun came up. Kiffin described what happened next:

We came out of the woods toward the wall where we saw that we were exposed to fire from three directions and that the German trenches were real near the wall. About that time the bullets began to 'whizz' and we ducked and ran to the wall and then along the edge of it about 200 yards to the petit post. *All that day we crouched in little dug-outs and cursed our officers for putting us in such a death-trap without more men and without telling us the real situation.*[25]

Thereafter, the legionnaires stayed out of sight or slept during the day, coming out only at night to stand sentry duty and man the "*petit post.*" The phrase literally means "small post," and was usually the furthest forward-stationed troops, serving as a sort of combination lookout and alarm system. Zinn described it as "what you might call a finger tip of the army pushed out into the space between the lines."[26]

Each night the officers would select several small parties of four to six men to serve guard duty along the high stone wall surrounding the large *château*, where they would take up positions on scaffolding (usually planks laid across barrels) rigged up alongside the wall to provide a view of the surrounding country and hillsides. Given their advanced position so near the enemy, guard duty ceased "to have the air of a mere formality," and the soldiers began to recognize in it "a grave danger, a terrible responsibility."[27] Dowd remembered the awful anxiety, saying that "the keeping on the *qui vive* every second, the expectancy, the tenseness of it all – is what wears on your nerves."[28]

Being so close to an enemy on the prowl could fray one's nerves. On moonless nights, the sentries would peer over the wall towards the plateau above the town, scanning the fields and conjuring up a thousand imaginary dangers:

As the night wears on the tension begins to tell. The senses of sight and hearing become subject to strange hallucinations. Surely someone is whispering out there in the darkness. Or else it is a low whistle, or such signals as pass between the members of a patrol. A black spot in the night takes shape and seems to move. A human form detaches itself from a tree trunk. As a shot rings out nearby along the wall the sentry's hand tightens on his rifle. The very suspicion of a sound, a broken twig or a trodden stone, may startle him so that he can hear his heart beat. And so, with finger on trigger and every nerve tense he waits, alarmed enough to entertain the illusion but master enough of himself not to fire till the mark is sure.[29]

Frayed nerves and overactive imaginations had been a danger even prior to the legion's installment at Craonnelle. A few days after Christmas, there was a little scuffle one night between the French *petit post* and a German patrol. All the men were called out, expecting an attack, but nothing happened. Just as the French soldiers turned to head back to the trenches, the moon came out, making the trees in the distance "look like a vast wave of men coming across the field." Kiffin told Paul what happened next:

Two or three officers yelled "aux armes!" with their voices full of terror and there was much excitement for a few minutes. We were commanded not to fire until they were close and then the mistake was discovered.[30]

Several months later, in another location close to the trenches, Harvard volunteer Henry Farnsworth wrote his family a description of what it was like to serve guard duty:

As the night grows and you stand crouching and watching for any sign of life ahead of you, the very air seems to come to life. All is still, nobody talks above a whisper, and all lights are out. From trenches, all along the maze of line, shots crack out and stray impersonal bullets whiz by on unknown errands. A huge rocket candle shoots up and hangs for a moment above the earth lighting up a section of the country; big guns boom out, and shells, like witches riding to a feast, whiz by.[31]

Other times, a soldier serving sentry duty could find consolation in "a kind of comradeship with the stars," as Seeger called it.[32] He wrote:

Then there is the nightly sentinel duty when one stands for two hours alone or with a companion in some dark corner under all kinds of weather. Sometimes on such lonesome vigils the winter clouds will roll back and the northern stars will blaze out in all their familiar beauty. On such moments, after all the dirt and fatigue and cold, I can have still emotions of real sublimity, feeling under the stars myself filling an appointed place in the universe. And so one watches while the Great Bear wheels slowly upward and every now and then the bleak hillsides will be lit up by the magnesium rockets from the German trenches, where they too are watching, fearful of an attack.[33]

But at the *Château du Blanc Sablon*, guard duty was not always sublime, and the dangers were not only in one's mind. Kiffin and the others would soon learn firsthand of the very real threats they faced so close to the front. As lawyer turned soldier Dennis Dowd put it, at Craonnelle the men had "reached the point where our hardships are real and not imaginary."[34]

Chapter Twenty-three

My fighting blood is up now.

The night following their first day at the big *château*, Kiffin was again placed on sentry duty by the stone wall. Facing another long and sleepless night and already worn out by the march to Craonnelle and guard duty the prior night, just before heading out Kiffin remarked to one of the Americans that he "wished the Dutchmen would come," or that something else would happen "to keep me awake."[1]

He would get his wish.

Under the command of Corporal Weidemann, that night Dowd, Capdeveille, Zinn, King, an Englishmen named Buchanan and Nilson the Swede were assigned *petit post* duty and stationed in the northwest corner of the estate along the stone wall. Some scaffolding had been erected there in the angle where the wall turned sharply, although even from this vantage point the men could not see immediately on the other side. They worked in rotating two-hour shifts, so a few of them manned the scaffolding while the others stayed below in dugouts, resting and awaiting their turn.

Along with Kiffin and Seeger, this handful of untested soldiers "had to watch a wall practically half mile long, right under the nose of the enemy, with hundreds of men in the rear of us subject to a surprise attack."[2] Kiffin was posted about a hundred meters down from the *petit post* at a breach point where a falling shell had blown a good-sized hole in the wall. The hole had been covered with a few boards and a large door serving as a makeshift barricade. A small gap on one side of the door allowed the sentries to peer through and look in the direction of the Germans.

Although it was a clear night and the moon was already up, like the men at the *petit post*, Kiffin could not see much on the German side of the wall. Due to the slope of the land, all that was visible through the opening on the side of the door was "a bit of the landscape beginning some hundred meters off; but of the space immediately outside, nothing at all."[3] Moreover, no scaffolding had been erected here. Instead, every few minutes Kiffin would climb a ladder propped against the barricade and scan the terrain below.[4] The raw soldiers on duty that night did not fully comprehend it, but their officers had poorly positioned the sentry posts, leaving them particularly vulnerable to ambush.[5] They would soon learn how exposed they were.

* * * * *

Seeger was the communication sentinel that night and so moved between the *petit post* and the other sentries, which consisted of Kiffin at the hole in the wall and another guard a couple hundred yards further down. For this reason, he stayed only briefly with Kiffin before heading down the path to check in with the next sentinel, leaving Kiffin as the sole soldier along that portion of the wall. The distance Seeger had to walk before reaching the next post alerted him to "how insufficiently the line was being guarded."[6] Kiffin later told Paul there were "three men watching a position where there should have been twenty."[7]

Around 10:30 p.m., Seeger returned to the hole in the wall by which Kiffin was posted. The two men had just resumed their discussion when suddenly a heavy object dropped between them, landing at their feet with a thud. The startled pair looked down and saw the device sputter out. Puzzled, Kiffin bent to look at the thing. As he picked it up, Seeger hissed "Good God! It's a hand-grenade!"[8]

Kiffin tossed it away as the pair came to the sickening realization that the Germans had slipped up on the opposite side of the wall and were only steps away, right on the other side of the makeshift barricade. Seeger figured "Our conversation, or that of the preceding sentinels, had given away our post. A bolt out of the blue could not have astonished us more."[9] Unfortunately for the two soldiers, given their poor position, they had no angle from which to see the grenade-throwers, much less return fire. Seeger explained their predicament:

What was to be done? The imbecility of such a post did not permit much. Open fire through the barricade? There was no chance of hitting your mark. Cry to arms? To what good! There was no line of fire that commanded the spot where the enemy was crouching two meters away outside the wall. He could have laughed at us & stayed where he was with impunity.[10]

In his typical understated style, Seeger later wrote "It was a moment for quick decision."[11] Hurriedly conferring, the two decided that as the *sentinelle mobile*, Seeger would run and alert the corporal while Kiffin stood his post.[12]

Kiffin watched as Seeger ran down the path and disappeared in the night. Clutching his Lebel rifle, he turned and stared hard at the barricade, a lone legionnaire straining to see, hear or even smell the enemy soldiers he knew were on the other side.[13]

* * * * *

Corporal Weidemann did not know what to think when Seeger came panting up to him, gasping in French about hand grenades and Germans. Nonetheless, he quickly buckled on his gear, took up his gun and came with Seeger back down the path. The few minutes Kiffin was alone at the barricade must have seemed like days, and he felt great relief as he heard the corporal and Seeger approaching. Unfortunately, the Germans must have heard them as well – Seeger and Weidemann were about 20 meters away when they spotted a fuse whirling through the air over the wall. "*Gardez-vous, Rockwell*," shouted the corporal. The warning had hardly escaped Weidemann's lips when "the grenade burst with a terrific report."[14] Kiffin explained what happened:

*I jumped over the ladder toward the corporal [and] as I reached his side the bomb exploded. We both hollered "*Aux armes.*" We had no more than done this when the door gave in and a rifle barrel entered the side of the opening. The corporal and I both were in an open position at their mercy, so we turned and jumped towards cover.*[15]

Seeger distinctly saw more burning fuses passing over the wall, and realized the Germans were tossing additional grenades. As the little bombs exploded on their side of the wall, he cried out to the corporal "*qu'est ce que nous devons faire?*" – what do we do?[16] But Corporal Weidemann was looking about "in a bewildered fashion," completely caught off guard and unsure of what was happening. Sadly, this was the last time Seeger would see him alive.[17]

As the German soldiers began shooting through the opening, Weidemann and Kiffin broke towards the cover of the nearby woods. Kiffin made it less than ten feet before a rifle flashed and he instinctively dropped to the ground. The corporal fell beside him but Kiffin could tell by the way he fell that he was dead. Leaving the corporal, Kiffin "crouched and ran, three bullets whizzing by me, but I made it to the woods."[18] As more Germans pushed through the barricade, Kiffin lay in the woods "not daring to move, as I would be seen."[19]

Amidst the grenades and gunshots, and fearing a general attack, like Kiffin, Seeger had but one thought: "to get away from the immediate vicinity of the wall." As they scrambled to find a defensible position, the two soldiers met up on the border of the woods. In between breaths, Kiffin fretfully whispered the awful news of their corporal's death, telling Seeger "[t]hey have done for old Weidemann."[20] They both crouched in silence as they peered in the direction of their comrades at the *petit post*.

The men there had heard the commotion and pursuant to their pre-arranged plan of defense, those not already on duty scrambled out of the dugouts. Expecting an attack from the other side of the wall, the legionnaires immediately grabbed their weapons and clambered onto the platform atop the scaffolding.

They soon regretted it, however. The moon had come out, and according to Zinn, "it was as if a big searchlight had been turned on behind, silhouetting us against the white wall."[21] Immediately, German bullets hissed by the men, ripping holes into the stone wall and causing the plaster to fly off in all directions. Some of the plaster chips from the wall temporarily blinded Dennis Dowd, and Buchanan (the Englishman) had his rifle shattered by a bullet.[22] As they had not been expecting an attack from inside the wall, the men now exposed on the scaffolding were unpleasantly surprised to learn that "instead of the expected direction," the bullets "came from the wood almost behind us."[23]

The continued crack of multiple Mausers and the bullets spattering all around the men quickly convinced them they were in the wrong spot. Attempting to dodge the bullets and flying plaster, a few of the men fell off the platform where they lay flat in the mud, afraid to fire lest they hit Kiffin and Seeger, who they knew had been posted in the direction from which the Germans were now shooting.

Those that didn't fall off the platform soon jumped. Zinn reported "we got off that scaffolding with some haste, so to speak, and down on the ground in position to stand the enemy off as long as possible."[24] Only then did he realize a bullet had nicked him between the little and ring fingers on his right hand.[25]

Although the men were back on the ground and no longer spotlighted on the scaffolding, they were still cornered against the wall. With no idea how many Germans were inside the park, they feared the worst. Dowd later quipped that during the attack he "felt very much like the man who fell from a ten-story building, and when passing the fifth floor was heard by a window washer to say: 'So far all's well.'"[26] Capdeveille, who had received a deep scratch on his scalp by his ear, formed up the men to face what they were sure must be a full brigade of bloodthirsty Germans.

Instead the attack ended as suddenly as it had begun. The firing ceased, and what must have been a small patrol of Germans slipped back through the barricade.

* * * * *

Just as the shooting stopped, a French sergeant and two other soldiers from the *château* came rushing through the woods where they ran into Kiffin and Seeger. With bayonets fixed, the little group advanced back to the post. There they saw the large door barricade had been pushed aside. Sadly, in front of the "gaping breach in the wall" they found Corporal Weidemann's bloody body "stretched ghastly in the moonlight, his head crushed in, and his *capote* torn off."[27]

Apparently, while Kiffin and Seeger were crouched in the woods and the soldiers at the *petit post* were pinned down in the mud, the Germans had dragged Weidemann's body back towards the breach and brutalized it. Kiffin disgustedly told Paul they had "knocked the top of Weidemann's head off with the butt of a rifle, took his gun, coat and equipment, and all got away."[28]

The legion reinforcements soon came up and Kiffin helped put the door back in place over the hole. All the men were either posted along the wall or sent out scouring the grounds and woods for Germans. Kiffin resumed his post with his corporal's disfigured body still lying in the moonlight. Understandably shaken by the death of his officer and the narrowness of his escape, Kiffin asked his commander to be relieved "as my nerves had gone all to pieces on me."[29] Permission was granted, and Kiffin went back to the *château* to make a report, returning to his post half an hour later. The rest of the night, all the men were keyed up and on guard, apprehending another attack.

Kiffin and the others recounted the events to one another, trying to piece together what had happened. Seeger gave credit to the German patrol, calling the episode a *"coup d'audace,"* or a "bold stroke."[30] Still, the men couldn't help feeling they had fallen short. Zinn noted they had been under fire before, "but it had never been as embarrassing as this." In a letter to a friend back home, he reported "frankly, they pulled out of it with more glory than we did."[31] Kiffin was also ashamed of their performance, particularly his own. He told Agnes:

The affair was rather a disgrace for all of us. I made mistakes in my actions due to not being well versed in all kinds of warfare. The corporal acted wrongly through ignorance and astonishment.[32]

Although no further attack would come that night, the event was already seared in Kiffin's memory. Even worse, about two hours after the incident, floating down the hillside from the trenches came "the most diabolical yell of derision I ever heard." It was Weidemann's killers, mocking his last words, his call to arms. The cry penetrated through the men, striking fear, revulsion and anger in the hearts of all who heard it. Kiffin said "it practically froze the blood to hear it."[33] Zinn likewise stated, "In all my life I never before have heard such a diabolical yell."[34]

King described it as "something new, but very old," a "long wolf-like howl, half human, half beast – derision, triumph, and revenge – straight back across the ages from ape-man and wolf-pack."[35] Seeger felt the cry was "more like an animal's than a man's, a blood-curdling yell of mockery and exultation." It chilled him to the bone:

In that cry all the evolution of centuries was levelled. I seemed to hear the yell of the warrior of the stone age over his fallen enemy. It was one of those antidotes to civilization of which this war can offer so many....[36]

With the yell, all conversation ceased, and the men helplessly listened to the terrible jubilation of their enemies. Rene Phelizot broke the stony silence that followed, saying "Well, fellows, we're in it for keeps."[37]

That was certainly true for Kiffin. The incident deeply affected him and proved to be a turning point for the young soldier. It refined his motives, strengthened his conviction, and aroused in him a righteous desire to avenge the awful death, and to see the war through right to the end. A few days later, Kiffin expressed his deepened commitment to his sister Agnes:

The whole thing impressed all of us more like a murder than warfare. The Germans had no military point to gain by doing what they did. It was done as an act of individualism with a desire to kill.... Up until that minute I had never felt a real desire to kill a German. Since then I have had nothing but murder in my heart, and now no matter what happens I am going through this war as long as I can.[38]

The incident also left Zinn with a new hatred of the other side; afterward, he wrote a friend the following note:

Previous to this affair I had held much the same feeling toward the enemy that I had toward the disappearing targets on the rifle range at Toulouse and Camp Mailly – they pop up and we shoot. But ever since I stood there by

Weidemann's body and heard the howl of triumph I have sort of felt the blood lust, the desire to go out and kill somebody, and I am sure the other fellows feel the same.[39]

* * * * *

Kiffin spent the next three days and nights on guard, as did everyone else, except those on patrol "prowling in search of Germans."[40] For nearly eighty hours, Kiffin hardly slept. The one chance he got to close his eyes was cut short when "some excitable fool hollered a false alarm" and he couldn't get back to sleep.[41] He told Paul it "was a hell of a time, and everyone's nerves were shattered...."[42]

Kiffin felt lucky to have survived the incident, and given the multiple grenades and point-blank volley, he was.[43] He summed up his feelings in a letter to his sister:

There is nothing that could be worse than those four days and nights. The uncertainty of it all—lying in the rain and mud, eternally watching and listening, knowing that everywhere men were prowling, trying to slip up on one another in the dark and kill.[44]

The confusion surrounding the embarrassing attack lingered. Not yet knowing all the details, Seeger confided in his diary that "the gravest accusations" might be made against Kiffin, and initially thought he needed to shield Kiffin from a possible inquest by keeping his silence.[45] But Seeger preferred to "make allowances for poor human nature for almost any conduct determined by so difficult a situation," and believed there was a "still graver responsibility of those who assigned the sentinels to a post where through no fault of theirs the enemy could approach to within two meters of them without their knowledge."[46]

Upon further reflection, Seeger backed further away from blaming himself or Kiffin even partially and, like the others, focused on the vulnerable situation into which their officers had placed them. Looking back on the incident a few months later, Seeger had become much less "inclined to blame my action and the more the incompetence of those who were responsible for placing this post so foolishly.... As it was, the sentinel had absolutely no chance."[47] This judgment was confirmed by Dowd, who wrote that the placement "constituted one of the worst death traps that I have seen or heard of."[48] Zinn too, said the men realized they "had been sold a pup." He explained the problem in a letter to a friend back home in Michigan:

A hundred meters farther along the wall [from Zinn's place at the petit *post] there was a gap that had been barricaded by an old door, and here we were supposed to post a couple of sentries besides keeping those on the scaffolding. But – this was the bad feature – at neither point was it possible to look over along the outside of the wall. And, worse yet, we were the only guards for a stretch of at least a quarter of a mile.*[49]

Despite their own feelings of humiliation, perhaps the soldiers were too hard on themselves – a few days after the close call, one of their section mates wrote "Rockwell and Seeger have their coolness and agility to thank for being alive today."[50]

Like Kiffin, Seeger felt fortunate to have survived that winter night at the *Château du Blanc Sablon*. In a letter to his father telling of the experience, he minced no words: "Believe me, I have had a narrow escape."[51] He would later write one of the most famous poems to emerge from World War I. It may be that his close call at Kiffin's side near the hollowed-out *château* served as inspiration for the poem, which begins: "I have a rendezvous with death, at some disputed barricade."[52]

Later in 1915, Seeger would again write of death. And once more, it is easy to imagine his feelings were influenced at least in part by his near-death incident with Kiffin:

If it must be, let it come in the heat of action. Why flinch? It is by far the noblest form in which death can come. It is in a sense almost a privilege to be allowed to meet it in this way. The cause is worth fighting for. If one goes it is in company with the elite of the world.[53]

* * * * *

The men buried Corporal Weidemann in the courtyard of the *château*.[54] The fact that it might just as easily have been Kiffin, Seeger or any of the others under the little mound and rough wooden cross made the occasion even more somber.

After they laid their corporal to rest, Kiffin and the others moved to the *petit château*, where Kiffin was again put on guard duty. Coming in from the long night, he desperately needed sleep, but a false call of *"aux armes"* prevented it. Trying to keep his mind occupied, Kiffin sat down in the blown-out window of the *château* to write Agnes a letter about the events of their first few days in

Craonnelle. However, when he got up to get more paper, German sharpshooters began potting the position, ending Kiffin's letter writing for the day.[55]

About the time the German snipers in Craonnelle were preventing Kiffin from writing home, in Asheville Loula sat down to write to her boys. She had just awakened from a dream in which they were both with her, safe and sound, and she felt the need to write.

Loula was still struggling with Paul's hospitalization and the knowledge that – by his own choice – Kiffin was thousands of miles away on the frontlines of a war more deadly than any that had preceded it. She was trying to keep her spirits up, but had not received any response to her letters to the French and American government officials, and had heard nothing from Kiffin for nearly a month. To make it worse, in recent days the Asheville papers had been reporting on the fighting taking place around Craonne.

Near her breaking point, Loula later confided that the "first awful winter of the war came near costing me my mind and my life."[56] Her dream brought some temporary peace and, hoping to calm herself further, she decided to again put pen to paper. Perhaps a mother's intuition had given her some hint of Kiffin's close call. She wrote:

I long to hear that my youngest who is in [the] trenches is o.k. as well as his brother. My brave boys!! How I pray that all may go well with you! ... I dreamed last night you were both with me. At times I feel I must go to you. Would if I were stronger.... I look at my shelves of sweets and wish they were with you or you with them.... Stand by each other my boys. Devotedly, Mamma[57]

After a few more days spent on patrols between the two *châteaux* in Craonnelle, the fatigued legionnaires were finally sent behind the lines for a few days of well-earned rest. Dowd spoke for them all when he said "[i]t was good to get back to a place ... where there were signs of life."[58]

During this short repose, Kiffin received Loula's earlier "pitiful" letter begging him to come home. However, the corporal's death and his own close call had stiffened Kiffin's resolve. He had chosen his course and was not looking back. While he was sorry she felt the way she did, Kiffin now spoke like a true Rockwell: unflinchingly, he told his mother he had "no intention of trying to get out of the war, as my fighting blood is up now."[59]

Chapter Twenty-four

It's the fortunes of war, my boy.

Kiffin and his cohorts settled into their routine – usually four to six days encamped in the wine cellars of the two *châteaux* followed by a like period behind the lines in the reserves. Before long, the route between Cuiry and Craonnelle would become so familiar to the men that Zinn would say it was like commuting from New Jersey to New York, "but once a week instead of every day."[1]

On their next trip into Craonnelle, Kiffin again spent four straight days on *petit post* in the "village death trap," during which he got a total of about five hours sleep.[2] The death of their corporal served as a teaching moment for the men, and they no longer viewed the risks associated with guard duty as theoretical.

For his part, Seeger wrote a few weeks later that his nerves were still very tense while on watch, as the danger was "very real." In fact, he confided to his diary that "the fear of another grenade has always kept me on the alert and startled me at the smallest sound and made sleep the last thing I had to fight against."[3] Kiffin too, remained alert – the *Atlanta Constitution* printed in its film section a quote attributed to him: "I see movies every night on picket duty. They are Dutch, and move about stealthily, silhouetted in the moonlight, looking for me with bullets, sometimes bombs." The paper commented: "And we complain about one-reelers!"[4]

In addition, the officers warned the men that when assigned watch they had better stay put. As Kiffin reported, "our duty is to stay there, regardless of what happens elsewhere. If we are attacked, they will send reinforcements, if possible, but whether reinforcements come or not, we stay there, dead or alive."[5] Under these orders, as part of a five-man squad Kiffin spent one night "crouched by the wall for fourteen hours in the sleet and snow, with my gun cocked and the magazine open."[6] The post was shot up fifteen minutes after Kiffin's squad was finally relieved; when he wrote Paul two days later, Kiffin was not sure how many had been killed.[7]

The once-prosperous village was still the most advanced point in the entire sector and according to Seeger, life amidst its ruins was "as tense & exciting as that in the trenches was dull & monotonous."[8] During daylight hours there was plenty of sniping and sharpshooting, and a German machine gun placed in the sloping orchard overlooking the town opened fire "whenever it [saw] a good mark."[9] Even though the men were too close under the ridge where the Germans were dug in to worry about artillery fire, every night enemy patrols came down to engage and harass the legion troops, and in such circumstances "the war of ruse, surprise and ambuscade prevails."[10]

During the night, the Germans sent patrols down from the nearby hillsides to probe the lines while the French dispatched their own patrols to protect the perimeter. According to Zinn, a "patrol" was the "general name applied to any excursion outside your own lines – it may be nothing more than a hasty scurry around the outposts, or it may be a trip right up to the enemy's lines to get a sample of his barbed wire, or it may be anything between the two extremes."[11]

Such patrols carried increased risk; to Zinn they were "a game of hide and seek where the advantage is all with the hunted and not with the hunter."[12] Another soldier wrote that on patrol "there is all the danger and excitement that you care to have. Talk about your frontiersman or sneaking Indian warfare: they are not in it with patrolling."[13] The Americans' poor showing the night of Corporal Weidemann's death confirmed the low opinion held by many of the *anciens*, who thereafter constantly reminded the volunteers they were "no good." To rebuild their reputation, the Americans were willing to take a few risks and even concocted plans to capture and bring back alive a German sentry.[14]

Instead, one of their first patrols ended uncomfortably among a trench full of German corpses. Zinn told the story:

We had just ascended the second ridge and were crossing one of the old trenches. The Germans opposite got nervous and began sending up one of their great calcium flares. These throw out an intense white light that illuminates the country for miles around. No one in the party needed to wait for orders – in five seconds every man was in the trench. At first sight it seemed that we had landed among a lot of old clothes, but very shortly we realized that the clothes were still occupied. However, there we were, and there we had to stay, whether we liked it or not. It was a half hour before things had quieted sufficiently to let us get out and go on. And you can take my word for it, that never in my life was I so glad to quit a place.[15]

Seeger felt the night patrols were one way to "pursue more primitive and more exciting methods of warfare."[16] While the firing lines were fixed, Kiffin's description of the patrols sounded more like guerilla warfare:

We send out a small bunch of men at night to prowl around the German lines, and the Germans do the same. If we meet, there is a scrap. We learn the location of one of their posts and go up to wipe it out or shoot them if possible.[17]

At daybreak, Kiffin and his mates would return to whichever *château* in which they were quartered, "gather around, have our coffee, rum, wine and bread, and tell of our night's experiences." For Kiffin, this was "the most interesting time in the life."[18]

* * * * *

When not on guard duty or night patrols, the men spent much of their time fortifying defenses, which generally included various tasks such as strengthening the barricades, laying out stakes and putting up barbed wire. If they had any spare time, some of the men liked to "pitch pennies" in the woods near the large *château*. But there was precious little spare time. Instead, their routine consisted of guard duty, patrols, work, sleep, repeat.

Although he was working harder than ever, Kiffin managed to keep his sense of humor.[19] In a letter to his old boss St. Elmo Massengale, to explain the non-stop nature of his duties Kiffin referenced a Billy Murray song popular before the war, "Nothing to do until Tomorrow." Kiffin asked Massengale if he remembered the hit, saying "well, that's the kind of job I have now. But I don't mind it."[20] The song's lyrics show how much work Kiffin was doing:

Gee but I'm a lucky man, as lucky as can be
No one in this town has got a job the same as me
All the easy jobs, you see, are hardest when compared
With the job that I secured, I'll tell you don't get scared.

I get up at four in the morning, bring in the water and the coal
Cut ten acres of hay by twelve in the day
The boss is a grand old soul, God bless him
Five minutes for dinner then it's noon time
And back to work feeling fine

Then I clean all the windows and I sweep up the floors
Polish all the handles of the big front doors
Gee but I'm a lucky guy
Nothing to do until tomorrow.

This week I have had it cinched, I hardly worked at all
Monday, Tuesday, Wednesday I just built a three-mile wall
Thursday, Friday, Saturday I'll work all night again
Which makes it easy Sunday I'll just work from twelve to ten.

I get up at four in the morning, bring in the water and the coal
Cut ten acres of hay by twelve in the day
The boss is a grand old soul, God bless him
Five minutes for dinner then it's noon time
And back to work feeling fine

Then I go to the stable and I hitch up the mule
Dress up twenty children and I drive to school
Gee but I'm a lucky guy
Nothing to do until tomorrow.[21]

* * * * *

One bright spot in Craonnelle was the abundance of food. According to Kiffin, the legion fed the men well and provided "plenty of booze."[22] In addition, the troops supplemented their rations with carrots, turnips, potatoes and other vegetables from area farms and were well supplied with tea, coffee and sugar, so there was "no letup in the dining hour." Some of the men fixed up a messroom in one of the spacious halls of the *petit château* with "real plates and dishes from the houses about town," and they even had a dinner bell.[23]

As January neared its end, indications were that soon something big would occur along the line. Kaiser Wilhelm's birthday was approaching, and the French expected the Germans to attempt to secure some kind of victory for the occasion. On January 25, Seeger reported violent cannonading and rifle fire all afternoon and evening, while the men worked feverishly stringing barbed wire and digging trenches in the park outside the larger *château*.[24] The night before the Kaiser's birthday the Germans commenced a "fairly heavy attack" to the right of the legion. Zinn wrote that the "regiment next to us was getting a pretty heavy pressure and every minute we expected to get in on that."[25] The attack ultimately receded, however, and they were not needed.

Kiffin told Paul that the "battle was raging on every side of us ... yet we didn't fire a shot." Instead, the artillery did all the damage and Kiffin and the other legionnaires sat underground "with our rifles in our hands ... ready to go out any minute and fight, but that was all."[26] Once again, the men were disappointed to miss out on the "real action," as shown in a letter written by one of the soldiers:

A fight had been raging on and off for days. The cannonading, sometimes coupled with rifle fire, was incessant for hours at a time, but we got no part of the actual fighting. A half hour walk to the right would have brought us into the thick of it, but we had to do our share by awaiting a counter attack, which was never really attempted by the infantry, although the artillery, both our own and theirs, kept up a steady roar both day and night....[27]

Exactly at midnight on January 27, the Kaiser's birthday, the French launched a series of twelve volleys from their 120mm gun to greet the occasion.[28] In a letter to the *New York Sun*, Seeger wrote "[t]he enemy did not respond. And so the long night wore away and the day came and passed without incident for us."[29] His personal diary entry gave a few more details:

Day & night of extraordinary calm. Mounted guard behind the park wall at two hour stretches all the night. Relief intervals in a wine cave in the park. Stove there & warmth & comfort. Something sinister about the profound silence punctuated by hardly a rifle shot. Bright moonlight. The enemy is probably as anxious as we are, for they kept sending up magnesium fusées all the time. This morning our four days were over but no one expected relief. On the contrary the town is full of reinforcements & we are here indefinitely.[30]

When they finally finished their extended stint, Kiffin sent a letter home that began "Suppose you are a little worried about me, owing to recent happenings, but have spent eight days in a position where we couldn't send any mail." As usual, he protected his mother from the dangers he encountered at the front, telling her only that they had given "the Germans a nice birthday present all around where I was," and that he had come "awful close" to firing his rifle. Kiffin also told Loula not to worry about his welfare, adding "the more I see the more convinced I am that I am coming through safe and whole."[31]

Kiffin wrote the above words to Loula on January 31, 1915. He had just completed his third full month at the front, and his fifth in the legion. It was very cold, and a heavy snow began falling – "not a flurry like we have had several times, but real snow, a white blanket covering the ground."[32]

* * * * *

Around this time, Edward Stone, a Chicago-born Harvard graduate in Kiffin's battalion, wrote a letter in which he complained that they had been near Craonne for some time with "very little action" and "practically no ground lost or gained." Even so, they had been "under fire more or less continually," and the constant pressure of warfare had "tired out" most of the men.[33]

Entering his sixth month in the legion, Kiffin had proven himself a capable soldier and hard worker. Still strong and healthy, he withstood the tough conditions at the front better than most. In a letter to Paul, he stated he was "stronger now than I have ever been in my life, but without one exception I am the only one."[34] But even Kiffin was susceptible to the relentless stress. Earlier, he had written Paul:

I have been well ever since you left, perfect health, have gotten strong and hardy and stood it better than anyone, but the mental and physical strain we have been under this month is breaking us all down. It has been worse than if we had been having big battles. I have experienced more and done more work and guard than anyone else in the section and it is telling on me now.[35]

Kiffin was not alone. No matter how tough, the strain and stress of war gradually took its toll on everyone. Kiffin told Paul how "all the fellows we thought strong have gone backward and have been sick a lot. Out of the 18 men of the Ninth Squad, there are only six of us in it now...."[36] Those few who endured did so through obedience and indifference, two qualities good soldiers developed in abundance. This was the case with Kiffin, who bluntly told Massengale that although he was still in "fine physical condition," he had "reached the point where I don't give a damn."[37] He also wrote his mother that "we feel more like real soldiers than ever. We no longer grumble or kick, as we have found it does no good. We do everything now with a 'I don't care' spirit, and that is one of the main qualifications of a good soldier – not to care."[38]

While he maintained discipline, Kiffin's close call at the barricade had soured him on the officers in the legion. Just two weeks after the incident, Kiffin asked Paul to see about getting him transferred to a regular French regiment, as he felt the legion was "no good; the officers are no good. It is just luck I am not dead, owing to their damned ignorance and neglect."[39] In Kiffin's view,

Corporal Weidemann's death had cost the legion a solid and well-liked officer and his replacement fell far short of that standard. He told his mother:

When we lost our old corporal we lost one of the greatest characters in the legion. We often compared him to an eagle with the squad as his young. We later got a corporal who was the exact opposite in every respect. We thought of a sparrow instead of an eagle. He was a faker, lazy, a coward and a crook. He did not last long, however, before he became 'sick' and was evacuated. They say it was the Ninth Squad that made him sick.[40]

Kiffin was not alone in his attitude. Among his fellow soldiers, he guessed there were "not five here but what would get out if they could."[41] Rumors were going around that the whole regiment was to be reorganized and that the English volunteers would be sent off to the English army. Kiffin, who spoke very little French, figured he might have a shot at a leadership role with the English, and so considered going with them.

Once the rumors were confirmed, however, rather than leave with the English volunteers, Kiffin decided he would instead "stick it out in the legion."[42] The morning of February 1, the regiment's commanding officers spoke a few words to the 150-200 departing English soldiers, "the Captain expressing his regret that the company should be broken up in this way."[43] The Major told the English troops "how pleased he was with them, what a fine lot they were, what good soldiers they had been, and what good service they had done."[44] He shook hands with each of them as they left amid the cheers of the remaining soldiers: "*Vive la France!* Hip! Hip! Hurrah! and *Vive l'Angleterre!*"[45] That day, Kiffin wrote a letter to Paul, a portion of which read:

The English left this morning. I was given the option of going or staying, and it may have been I am foolish, but I stayed. I figured that I came over to join with France and had stuck it out five months, so might as well continue.[46]

In a letter to Massengale a week later he gave a similar explanation, hinting at the good opportunity he had passed up:

I had a chance last week of being transferred to the English army. I would have had a good chance there for a command, whereas I will never get above a common soldier here, owing to a lack of knowledge of the French language, if for no other reason. Yet I didn't go. I decided that as I came over to fight for France, I would stick it out.[47]

Bartram Towle did leave with the English. Ever since he and his brother Ellingwood had enlisted, their parents had been doing everything possible to get them out. Ellingwood hurt his knee and did not make it out of Toulouse, but younger Bartram stuck around much longer. At some point after they reached the front he wrote his father, "You want me home again, but I love this life. I am learning a lot. I am happy, so you must be too. This was my choice and I still love it."[48] But by the end of January, Bartram was ready to go, writing: "The real war seems now to have shifted to the British front so with some Englishmen I applied for a transfer to the English army. Even seeing friends killed or wounded and taking chances hourly cannot repay for trench inaction month after month."[49] Once Bartram was with the English, his father finally succeeded in having him discharged and returned home.[50] Bartram seems to have been one of the few Americans with whom Kiffin did not get along; Kiffin ended his letter to Paul by saying "Young Towle left with the English, a good riddance."[51]

Kiffin's decision to decline the transfer and honor his commitment to the Foreign Legion and to France echoes the decision of his father when he was just seventeen and overwhelmed with his failing literary journal. James Chester Rockwell's words to his mother could have been written by Kiffin almost 30 years later:

I cannot bear the thought of failing, of having to give up. While I might find an easier way to support myself than this is, still I had rather toil day and night, and go through untold trouble, than to give it up and seek some easier path. I have found my sphere, and I am going to stay in it.[52]

Even in difficult circumstances and with every reason to go, Kiffin viewed leaving the French as giving up. And much like his father, Kiffin could not bear the thought of giving up. Instead, he had found his sphere, and was going to stay in it.

* * * * *

Paul, however, was a different matter, at least as far as Kiffin was concerned. Paul's letters suggested he meant to return to the front, something Kiffin opposed. Recollecting his own recent brush with the wages of war, Kiffin responded on January 21: "In regard to your coming back, I will say for the last time, don't be a fool. If you try hard enough, you won't have to." Kiffin did not mince words with his older brother:

You have not the physical or mental makeup to stand this life, something I have realized for months but didn't realize before we joined. If you come back you will be no good inside of a month and it will be harder to get evacuated the second time so you will suffer a lot and finally reach the point where they will have to send you back. I know what I am talking about. I have told Dr. V[an] V[oast] and the boys that you were trying to come back and not a one of them but has said that they thought you had more sense.[53]

Loula was also worried about Paul and begged him to make sure he told the doctors all his "past troubles" so he could receive the "most scientific treatment possible." She also warned him: "Don't try to go in ranks when not able."[54] Not long after, Kiffin reiterated to Paul "[t]he reason I keep writing you to get out is because I know that you are not able to stand it, and then there is absolutely no romance or anything to the infantry."[55]

Kiffin and Paul had signed up to fight in a different war – a nobler, cleaner war, like their grandfather had told them about, one where men fought and died like men. Instead, they got long periods of boredom punctuated by pointless skirmishes where most of the fighting was done by the artillery. Kiffin told Paul he now believed it "possible to go through the war without ever taking part in the kind of fighting we imagined we would do."[56]

While Paul did not lack fighting spirit, Kiffin knew he was not physically able to keep up with the soldier's life in a time of war. Indeed, for Kiffin, whether Paul returned to the front was "not a question of bravery," but simply "a question of being a good day laborer." Believing his brother could not meet the demands, Kiffin instead advised Paul to "get into something that requires education and not brute strength."[57]

Even before Kiffin rendered this advice, Paul had already started writing articles about his experiences, including the one Kiffin read on Christmas in the *Daily Mail*. Over time, Paul would continue writing and became a good source for information due to his many contacts in the legion. When he was officially invalided out of his unit in the first half of 1915, Paul took Kiffin's counsel and moved to the information and propaganda section of the French Army. By the fall of that year, he got into another line that did not require brute strength – he became a war correspondent in Paris with the *Chicago Daily News*, located at *10 Boulevard des Capucines* on the second floor of the northeast corner of the *Place de l'Opera*. The paper's office overlooked the *Avenue de L'Opera*, down which Rene Phelizot had carried the stars and stripes that exciting day in August 1914.

Alan Seeger, who had walked right behind Phelizot as he carried the flag, was already doing a little writing of his own for the *New York Sun*, as were

Chatkoff and some of the others. In late February, Seeger made the front page of that publication, but not for his writing ability. The headline read "Alan Seeger is Hit by German Sniper."[58] It seems that while coming in from sentinel duty on February 20, Seeger paused in a communication ditch to allow a fellow soldier to pass by – but those few brief seconds in the open were long enough for a Mauser sharpshooter to nearly take him out of the war for good. In a letter to his father, Seeger told him the German sniper

came within an ace of getting me. The ball just grazed my arm, tore the sleeve of my capote, and raised a lump on the biceps which are still sore, but the skin was not broken and the wound was not serious enough to make me leave the ranks.[59]

To convince the Red Cross medics "it was all nothing," Seeger waved his arm around, proving he could still move it. The next day, all he had to show for his brush with the bullet was a large blue-black bruise on his upper left arm.[60]

* * * * *

In early February, Kiffin's issue with the quality of the officers was exacerbated when Edward Morlae was promoted from corporal to sergeant.[61] Morlae had from the beginning played up his supposed experience as an officer in the U.S. Army and won his promotions by convincing the commander that the American volunteers wished to be led by an American.[62] But once given a little authority, Morlae "took advantage of his grade to mistreat and humiliate his countrymen in all possible ways."[63] He always seemed to be issuing orders, cursing the men or handing out prison sentences. By the time he tried to have Zinn court-martialed and shot for falling asleep on sentry duty, most of the Americans were sick to death of him.[64] Seeger, whom he had accused of being a spy, called Morlae "the very soul of vindictiveness."[65] Things eventually got so bad that Dowd later said, "the Americans considered their lives unsafe so long as they were in the same regiment with the man."[66]

In a move in keeping with the estimate of his former legion subordinates, in late 1915 while on leave, Morlae deserted the legion, fled to Spain and returned home to America where he wore the *médaille militaire* and posed as a war hero.[67] A few months later, he wrote an article for *The Atlantic Monthly* which was not well-received by his former comrades in the legion. Zinn wrote a response in *Leslie's Weekly*, declaring it "unfortunate that the man whose accounts of the legion were most widely circulated in America should be a deserter."[68]

Charles Sweeny happened to be in Washington, D.C. when Morlae's first article came out. He told Benjamin Thaw (Bill's brother) of Morlae's "untrustworthy character," and further stated that Morlae "was not wounded, has absolutely no right to wear the *médaille militaire*, and is, in fact, a deserter, having escaped to this country through Spain while on leave."[69] Later, future pilot James Norman Hall learned from the Americans in Paris that Morlae was "a deserter, never received a decoration of any kind, was never wounded and the men say that a good deal of his narrative is fiction."[70]

Paul had taken an instant dislike to Morlae from the moment they met.[71] Kiffin and Morlae never really saw eye to eye, either. They had yet another run-in shortly after Morlae was promoted to sergeant. In a letter to Paul, Kiffin recorded his feelings and uncannily predicted what eventually happened. He wrote:

The Americans here now are Cap[deveille], Zinn, Dowd, Seeger, Trinkard, King, Phelizot and Chatkoff. Morlae is also here, he just came back the first of the year after studying a few weeks in a corporal's school. He is now a sergeant in charge of this section and a bigger son of a b***h than ever. He takes every opportunity to insult the Americans in front of superior officers so as to try to curry favor with them. He and I are always at swords' point and I have told him that someday we will both be back in America. The first thing I [will] do when we are back there is to beat the sh*t out of him. None of us has any use for him. But you know how it is in the French army. A sergeant has it over a private. I have even been thinking of changing my company because I might really lose my temper some time and kill the son of a b***h, and you know what that would mean for me. I want you to keep this letter ... and if by any chance I don't get back to the states, and he tries to get a lot of cheap notoriety over there, like he is after, this is what the Americans think of him.[72]

Kiffin ended his letter by asking Paul: "Just what are the chances of another regiment; if not a regular French Regiment, the First *Étranger?*"[73] Whatever efforts Paul had been making to get him into a new unit, Kiffin's comment that he might kill Morlae caused Paul to redouble his efforts seeking a new spot for his brother.

* * * * *

Eddie Stone was wounded in action on February 15. Around five thirty that night, seven German shells fired from the crest of Craonne hit Stone's machine gun section, wounding him, another private and the corporal.[74] Carried via stretcher back to the *Blanc Sablon*, the examining doctor there found Stone "with a hole in his side made by a shrapnel ball, which had probably penetrated his left lung."[75] Stone was taken far behind the lines to a hospital in Romilly-sur-Seine, where his condition deteriorated. At dawn on the morning of February 27, Stone died from his wounds and pneumonia which had settled in both lungs.[76] He was buried in the military cemetery in Romilly, his family feeling "sure that his own wish would have been to lie in the country which he loved and served."[77]

Stone was the first American to die on behalf of France in the First World War.[78] When the sad news reached Boston, a former classmate of Stone's wrote the following to the editor of *The Harvard Crimson*:

We do much talking around the Yard about the war, taking sides (usually the same side) with earnest eloquence; but here is a fellow, happy, rich, strong, with a promising life before him, who did not hesitate to volunteer under a foreign banner and sacrifice his life for the cause he thought (and most of us think) right. Let undergraduates and professors and alumni take off their hats in reverent memory of their brother who by dying for his ideals has brought honor upon himself and upon the University he so nobly represented.[79]

In the meantime, Kiffin was still working and waiting for Paul to come through on his transfer request. However, due to Kiffin's having "got his number" on a few things, Morlae had suddenly become "exceptionally friendly" towards him.[80] As a result, Kiffin had much more latitude within the section, and suddenly he and Capdeveille were "practically running" the Ninth Squadron.[81]

Although Kiffin had forced Morlae to back down, there was still some tension in the unit. Given their vastly different backgrounds and socioeconomic status, many of the regulars still resented the Americans, believing they often received special consideration and privileges. While over time the friction between the two groups ebbed and flowed, it never completely went away.

* * * * *

The tragic death of Rene Phelizot brought the rift between the regulars and the Americans into the open. Kiffin wrote Paul that their friend died "as a result of foul play in a scrap between him and two Arabs of the [*mitrailleuse*] section, which afterwards turned into a battle royal between the two sections."[82] Paul later learned more details, which he included in one of his first stories for the *Chicago Daily News*.[83]

It happened in early March, behind the lines in Cuiry-les-Chaudardes, where the legion was preparing to return to the front. Some of the men were gathered around a coffee wagon trying to keep warm when two drunken Arab legionnaires began making disparaging remarks about the Americans, boasting that each could "single handed and in a fair fight" dispatch any seven of them.[84] Stone had served in the same machine gun section as the drunks and, perhaps still sensitive from Stone's very recent death, the normally irenic Phelizot told the Arabs he would take them both on and prove otherwise. A crowd of partisans quickly formed, cheering their side, and the two drunk regulars and Phelizot cleared some space in the courtyard. In his article, Paul described the incident this way:

The fight started well for Phelizot, who was no mean boxer. He speedily knocked down one of his adversaries and was severely punishing the other. At this moment a third legionnaire, a pal of the two Phelizot was fighting, entered the courtyard. Seeing one of his friends sprawled out on the ground and the other in a fair way to join him there, the newcomer ran up behind Phelizot and, swinging by its leather strap his two-liter metal canteen, which was filled with wine, he struck him a crashing blow on the head. Phelizot fell unconscious.[85]

The third legionnaire's unfair blow from behind the unsuspecting Phelizot caused tensions long bubbling just beneath the surface to boil over. According to King, immediately "a general riot broke loose – our section against the machine gun outfit."[86] The brawl was broken up only when officers separated both sections and placed them in isolated quarters.

Phelizot was unconscious for an hour before the men could revive him and by the next day "was almost crazed with pain."[87] He reported ill at the infirmary, but after a cursory examination the doctor said nothing was wrong and refused to excuse him from service. That night with his company Phelizot marched back to the front. When on the second day his pain got even worse, eventually a sergeant sent him back to the infirmary. Although he must have been in agony, Phelizot walked the five kilometers alone and presented himself before the same doctor. However, he was again declared fit for service and ordered back to the trenches.

Unfortunately, Phelizot never made it back. The blow from the canteen had fractured his skull and, left untreated, tetanus had set in – later that day an officer found him collapsed by the side of the road leading towards the *Château du Blanc Sablon*, already partially paralyzed. Phelizot was taken to the nearest military hospital at Fismes, but it was too late.[88] Unable to speak and drifting in and out of consciousness, he suffered for two more days before passing away on March 6. Just before he died, Phelizot "raised up out of bed, ... pulled the Amer[ican] flag from around his waist, and cried out, 'I am an American.'"[89]

The death of the patriotic and always-smiling Phelizot permanently marred relations between the American volunteers and the regulars. The following days were tense and physical violence again flared up; Kiffin reported the Americans were "practically under arrest now," prevented from mingling with the regulars in the *mitrailleuse* section "because it would mean a war."[90] The hard feelings continued, and on their first repose after Phelizot's death, Chatkoff immediately "hunted out the man who had struck the fatal blow, knocked him down and was literally walking on him when he was pulled away."[91]

Phelizot was buried in the soldiers' cemetery in Fismes, his grave marked by the flags of France and the United States. Showing how highly they thought of him, the Americans took up a collection to get a handsome tombstone to denote the grave of their friend and countryman.[92] Everyone mourned the loss of their ever-cheerful comrade; they could almost hear Phelizot's voice calling out the familiar phrase now sadly applicable to his own fate, "it's the fortunes of war, my boy."

Like the death of Weidemann, the deaths of Stone and Phelizot within a single week marked something of a turning point for the remaining Americans in the legion. Two of their countrymen now lay in the soil of France, and those who had trained and fought by their sides were no longer innocent, no longer unscathed by the hand of war. In a poem titled "My Hate," one of Phelizot's officers provided a glimpse of the loss felt by those who knew him:

Somewhere in the trenches
Along the western line of war,
A soldier brave has met his death
Beneath the cannon's roar.

A braver and a truer heart
By God was never made,
And a greater price of sacrifice
To God was never paid.

From time immortal have the bards
Portrayed the 'Hate' of war,
And sung the praise of those
Whom we should see no more.

I read, and reading pondered
'Tis a song of the departed,
Little thinking at the time
'Twas the cry of the brokenhearted.

But now I know
And understand, too late,
The fiend of war has taken my friend
And thereby sealed my Hate.[93]

Chapter Twenty-five

Alone in Paris, with all hopes of forming a squadron blown to the winds.

While Kiffin and the others were scraping by in the wine cellars near Craonnelle, William Thaw was enjoying the high life at the Hotel Ritz in Paris. Since leaving the legion just before Christmas, Thaw had been serving as an observer-gunner at Merval, waiting for his chance to take a military license and become a full-on pilot. When a slot opened up at the end of January, the French initially were inclined to send him to aviation school at Pau. But Thaw did not want to waste his time at school and so requested to be sent directly to Buc to fly Caudrons – and by convincing his superiors his full name was W. Caudron Thaw, he "finally persuaded them to give me a try."[1]

As the Buc airfield was not too far from the old city, Thaw figured he really ought to sleep in Paris. Accordingly, using his "fluent, though at times amusingly incorrect" French, Thaw talked his commandant into letting him set up at the Hotel Ritz. Thaw chalked up to good will the commandant's acquiescence, stating "anyone, especially a foreigner, who voluntarily passes ten weeks in the trenches is looked upon either as some guy or a bit nutty (I can't make out which), so here I am."[2] So Thaw spent his nights gallivanting about Paris, sleeping at the Ritz, then arising early to head out to the airfield.

At Buc, Thaw put his favorite motto (try anything once) to the test. After a ten-minute ride as an observer, he was stuck behind the controls and told to pilot the Caudron, a rather ugly, rotary-engined bomber. While this was the opportunity he sought, it was not without risk – before the war, Thaw had flown only a Curtiss hydroaeroplane, and he had no experience with this type of aircraft.

In a letter home, Thaw confessed he was "rather up against it," as he had "never flown on land, never with a rotary motor, never with the propeller in front, and never with that control...."[3] Despite his inexperience, Thaw was able to get off the ground in control of his plane and land without causing any damage. Once he had shown he could take off and land without killing himself, the rest was easy – after flying alone twice, Thaw was told he could test for his military license on the first good flying day. He happily let his family know that he hoped soon to be back at the front, "this time with a good job instead of being a ditch-digger."[4]

Thaw progressed rapidly and on March 15 received his *brevet d'aviateur militaire*, number 712, the first American to be licensed.[5] Around this time, he was transferred to Le Bourget, a commune in the northeastern suburbs of Paris. He stayed in a little place near the airfield, and occasionally took the short tram ride into Paris, where he could speak English with other Americans over dinner at *Ciro's*. By the time he left, Thaw had become a "sort of assistant instructor, teaching green *observateurs* how to observe."[6] Bill Thaw was likely the first American pilot to fly for France.[7] But he would not be the last.

* * * * *

Back in America, Norman Prince was moving forward with his idea for an all-American squadron. Having further honed his skills on the Burgess-Dunne hydroaeroplane and having squirreled away enough money to finance his trip to France, Prince traveled to New York, where on January 20, 1915, he boarded the French Line ship *Rochambeau* embarking for Havre.[8] While a few close friends in Boston whispered that Nimmie intended to join the French Aviation Corps and take part in the European war, Prince's father insisted there was "nothing unusual" in his son's trip to France, as the family had often spent the winters hunting at their large estate in Pau. But those who knew Prince best knew he was not going hunting – as the *Daily Globe* noted shortly after his departure:

One thing is certain: he is not going abroad to hunt this year, as there is no hunting at Pau. Next to the chase, war is probably the most exciting occupation he could get into.[9]

On the *Rochambeau*, the underfunded Prince traveled second class, where he would meet Edmond Genet, an idealistic American who had just turned eighteen. The young sailor was of French ancestry, a descendant of "Citizen Genet," the former French minister to the United States after the French Revolution. After completing a year in the U.S. Navy, just a few weeks earlier young Genet had abruptly decided to head for France. He recorded his thoughts in two diary entries at the end of 1914:

At one p.m. today I took the most daring and decided step of my life. I left ship with a furlough paper for ten days in my possession, with the convinced feeling that I would never return. Something bigger and sterner was calling me. It was the great world conflict raging across the Atlantic. How I was to get to it I knew not; neither did I know in what way I could help if I got there; but these seemed surmountable barriers. I would go, and somehow, someway, I would help that glorious French nation, the nation of my ancestors – of Citizen Genet – no matter what the cost to myself, what the price to be paid later for my deliberate act of desertion....

I want to do my part in that great cause of Right and Justice to the world of civilized peoples, even though my own beloved country has refused to stand up and fight with those who are striving heroically for Justice. I am an American, but I am also a civilized human being. Should my service – my very life – go to America or to Humanity, first? The answer is plain to me.[10]

Now officially a deserter from the navy, Genet got his things together, said goodbye to his friends and paid seventy dollars for a one-way ticket to France. The *Rochambeau* was supposed to sail at three in the afternoon on January 20, but it was past five o'clock before they got underway. Due to the late departure, those on board had a lovely view of Manhattan's electric-lit buildings in the early dark of the cold winter evening. As the statue of liberty appeared over the ship's starboard side, Genet stared up at her lighted torch, saluted, then went below decks.[11] The deserter was reporting for duty.

During their trip across the Atlantic, Prince shared his plans with the like-minded Genet. When the ship docked in Havre on January 29, Genet wrote in his diary that he had come ashore with "a fine young fellow by the name of Norman Prince, who comes from Massachusetts, is an aviator, and intends to join the French aviation corps for the war."[12] In a letter to his mother he described Prince as "a rich young fellow ... very quick and sensible," and predicted "He will have some exciting experiences, I feel sure."[13]

* * * * *

While Genet went to join the legion, Prince set up shop in a Paris hotel and threw himself into implementing his idea. But first, he wrote his mother that he hoped "papa has not taken too much at heart my leaving home," but that he believed he could "find a place to do some efficient and useful work for the cause to which I am so deeply devoted."[14] Prince had a lot going for him – he had spent enough time in France to speak French well and, due to his family's tremendous wealth, moved in high society on both sides of the Atlantic. In other words, he had the fluency, contacts and social standing to be taken seriously and was also a Harvard-trained lawyer when that meant something.

Figuring that organizing a squadron would be better accomplished from the inside, Prince's first task was to put in a request to join the *Service Aéronautique*. In the meantime, Frazier Curtis had gone to England to make one last attempt to join up with the British. When he was again rejected, Curtis came straight to Paris to assist Prince with his efforts to get up an American squadron among the French.

At the American embassy, secretary Robert Woods Bliss introduced Curtis to the American naval attaché, who in turn introduced him to Thaw, Bach and Hall, each of whom Curtis learned had recently transferred into the French aviation service. Thus, when Curtis met up with Prince at the Hotel D'Orsay, he excitedly told him about the three American men who had already enlisted among the French flyers. Prince was glad to learn that, counting himself and Curtis, they already had five of the six Americans they would need to form a full squad.

By this time, Prince had discussed his idea for an American squadron with brothers Jacques and Paul de Lesseps, two wealthy aviators serving in the Paris Air Guard. In mid-February, Prince and Curtis had lunch with Paul de Lesseps at *Fouquet's* and the next day dined with both brothers at Jacques' flat where they discussed the possibilities for a sixth pilot for the squadron. Eventually, they decided to ask Prince's old classmate Elliott Cowdin, a volunteer ambulance driver with the American Ambulance Corps who had graduated a year behind Prince at Harvard. Cowdin had recently returned from the Belgian front to Paris, where he was staying with Robert Chanler, the uncle of legionnaire Victor Chapman. Although Cowdin was not a pilot, neither were Hall and Bach, and the French had allowed them into aviation training. In the circumstances, Prince was looking only for promising material, and Cowdin fit the bill.[15]

The son of a wealthy businessman, Cowdin was well known among the New York society set. A handsome man with light brown hair, green eyes and an athletic build, Cowdin stood five foot ten inches, with an oval face, roman nose, and strong chin.[16] Like Prince, his pal at Harvard, Cowdin was a polo player, all around sportsman and man about town.[17] Since November, he had been attached to the 1st Division Cavalry of the Belgian Army. In a letter home, one of Cowdin's ambulance corps comrades relayed "an interesting experience" involving Cowdin and another American volunteer near Veurne, Belgium:

They wanted to have a look at the trenches and started out one morning toward the front. Before long they came to some well concealed trenches and looking in were surprised to find that no troops were there. It seems that these troops had been shelled out some time before by the Germans. After looking around for a while they concluded that there was nothing of interest to be seen and started to go back, but they had no sooner come out of the trenches when bang! a German shrapnel exploded right over them. It seems that the Germans had observed them and, thinking that the troops had gone back into the trenches, they began firing. The shells now began to come thick and fast and exploded all around them and they ran back toward the farm house as fast as their legs could carry them. When they got back they were greeted with cheers by the Belgian officers, who had seen the whole performance and thought it a great joke on the fool Americans.[18]

At a dinner party that evening, the de Lesseps brothers helped Prince and Curtis put together in French a letter to the Minister of War, Alexandre Millerand. Curtis remembered the "very noisy evening," with many toasts being made and the talk half-French and half-English. According to Curtis, the most memorable toast was one he made in jest to the "*Escadrille Escroquerie*" – the Fraud Squad.[19]

Prince did not have to wait long for a response to his request that he and the other five Americans be allowed to form their own aerial squadron. According to the definitive account:

This letter met with a very discouraging response. The Americans were told that no volunteers could be admitted to the Aviation, owing to the popularity of this branch with the French soldiers, hundreds of whom – far more than could be used – were applying for training as pilots.[20]

Although disheartened, Prince continued to press his idea with anyone who would listen, until the diplomat Bliss introduced he and Curtis to Jarousse de Sillac, at the time the Under-Secretary to the Minister of Foreign Affairs.[21] This was a fortuitous introduction – the first biographer of the squadron would later write that "it was almost entirely due to the efforts of M. de Sillac that the consent of the French government to the plan for an American squadron was gained."[22]

Fortunately, de Sillac immediately recognized the potential propaganda value in having American boys flying for France. Accordingly, on February 20, 1915, he wrote a colonel friend in the Ministry of War that the previously-rejected offer put forth by Prince and Curtis could prove very beneficial to France:

It appears to me that there might be great advantages in the creation of an American Squadron. The United States would be proud of the fact that certain of her young men, acting as did Lafayette, have come to France to fight for France and civilization. The resulting sentiment of enthusiasm could have but one effect: to turn the Americans in the direction of the Allies.[23]

Knowing that the de Lesseps and de Sillac were using their influence to press his case with the French, but anxious to get in the air as soon as he could, Prince decided to get in some flight time in England. The same day that de Sillac wrote his letter endorsing the idea of an American *escadrille*, through an old English friend from his hunting days in Pau, Prince was admitted into the Royal Flying Corps and left for England to, as he put it in a letter to his friend Starling Burgess, "look over the situation."[24]

Prince soon found himself at the Brooklands aerodrome, near Weybridge, England, with the understanding that the R.F.C. would release him if, as hoped, the French government acted favorably upon his outstanding request. As it turned out, approval came more quickly than he anticipated – Prince made only four flights in England, all on a 1913 Maurice Farman, before receiving word that the French had accepted his plan. The delighted Prince immediately handed in his resignation to the Royal Flying Corps and returned to Paris.[25] On March 4, 1915, he enlisted with the French, emphatically declaring *jusqu'au bout* – until the end – when taking the oath of allegiance.[26] Prince's plan for an American squadron was taking shape.

* * * * *

With Cowdin and Curtis, who had also enlisted, Prince immediately transferred to the *service aeronautique*, and the trio prepared to enter flight training. In addition, Prince requested the transfer of Thaw, Bach and Hall to the training facility at Pau so all six Americans could train together. Beginners Bach and Hall enthusiastically agreed, but Thaw was "very lukewarm" towards Prince's idea, as he was already flying well at Buc and on the cusp of receiving his military *brevet*.[27] So instead of joining the other Americans, Thaw made it as far as the depot at Lyon before convincing his superiors to allow him to finish his license at Buc and then transfer to the front as part of a French squadron.[28]

In Paris, the American enlistees were becoming quite fond of Robert Chanler, with whom Cowdin had been staying. Avowedly pro-French, Bob Chanler was a rich artist and socialite, and proved to be of great help to Prince in pushing the idea for an American squadron. Chanler's views were probably not far from those of his brother-in-law John Jay Chapman, the father of Victor Chapman.

John Jay Chapman was perhaps one of the most intensely principled men in history. A famous author, essayist, and social critic, Chapman was the son of a former president of the New York Stock Exchange, and the great-grandson of one of the Founding Fathers, the first Chief Justice of the United States, John Jay. While he initially talked his son Victor out of fighting with the French, at his wife's urging he relented, and Victor hurried to Paris to sign up with the Foreign Legion – it was Victor Chapman who in August 1914 telegraphed George Casmeze from London: "I am coming over. Can I bring anything with me?"

Once Victor committed, John Jay did, too. He wrote a letter to the editor of *The Times* stating that by its treatment, Germany had become "the enemy of mankind," and that "unless the neutrals join ... in putting down a nation which claims to be above law, international law will cease to exist."[29] By November, Chapman declared in the *New York Times* that if neutrality meant "national self-effacement in the presence of insult," he wished that God would "raise up some other neutral nation that will protest in a manly way against these things."[30] He continued:

If it be a breach of our own neutrality to protest against Germany's declaration that she will not be bound by treaties, then our neutrality is a suicidal thing, it consents to the death of all neutrality.... Is it not time that we all acknowledge openly what every American knows in his heart, namely, that France and England are fighting our battles? By their blood they are saving our institutions.[31]

Like his brother-in-law, Robert Chanler despised what he saw as America's weak-kneed neutrality, and so did all he could to help Prince and the others. But that may not have been his sole motivation – he also hoped to secure his nephew a spot in the *escadrille* once it came to fruition. Just after the first Americans were sent to flight school, Victor Chapman received a note from his other uncle, William Astor Chanler, suggesting that he "write to Norman Prince at Pau, where he is getting up an American aviation." Chapman did write to Prince, but told his father it would probably "be more trouble than I am worth" to get out of the legion.[32] It is pretty clear that his family wanted to get Victor out of the trenches and, if possible, into the skies – a few weeks later, Victor's younger brother wrote that he hoped his father and uncles succeeded "in either getting you a furlough to recuperate or else into the American Aviation Corps."[33]

But Bob Chanler's help was not limited to making connections for his nephew, or arranging meetings and interviews with important officials – he would also see to it that the budding pilots were well taken care of during their journey to Pau and their training; the Americans jokingly dubbed Chanler *maître de logis* (master of lodgings) and "lord high treasurer."[34] The night before they left Paris for flight training, Chanler took everyone to dinner at *Maxim's* to celebrate, where Curtis reported (complete with the quotation marks) that "a pleasant evening was had."[35]

* * * * *

The next day, the group left for Lyon, where they were to receive their official assignment. Bert Hall embarrassed the others when he showed up with a "lady friend," then brought her along for the trip. Curtis reported they were all "rather bored" with Hall's behavior, but things got even worse after they arrived at Lyon – when the Americans went to headquarters to get outfitted with their blue cloth uniforms and sign some additional paperwork, Hall cursed out the French officers for keeping the group waiting, saying he "would not be bossed by any damned frogs."[36]

From Lyon, the Americans took a long train ride to Pau, where Hall's big talk was about to catch up with him. While organizing the American Volunteer Corps back in Paris, Hall had claimed to be a pilot flying with the famous French aviator and airplane manufacturer Maurice Farman, but more likely was selling motor cars or driving a cab.[37] After he entered the legion, Hall continued to brag, telling the others that he had been a race car driver and, after "one peach of a smash-up in a famous race," had been flying for three years.[38]

Although Hall had been well-liked in the legion, even his friends took his tales with a grain of salt – D.W. King later referred to Hall as an "ex-racing driver, and God knows what besides," and in a letter home, Thaw called him "an expert crook and all around good fellow."[39] Although his solid record and fast talking eventually got him transferred to aviation with Thaw and Bach, it is probable that Hall had never actually flown an airplane.[40] Nonetheless, as he had most of his life, Hall would skate by on sheer guts. One of his former legion mates wrote of Bert's experience upon his arrival at flight school:

Bert's debut was typical. He climbed into the machine, had the controls explained to him, and started off... Full speed ahead, up, and then down with a crash. After they had extracted him from the debris, the officer in charge questioned him.

"What went wrong?"

"I don't know."

"Haven't you ever been in a plane before?"

"No."

"What in God's holy name do you mean – starting off like that?"

"Well, I thought I might be able to fly."[41]

Crawling from the wreckage, Hall "took his bawling out philosophically."[42] According to D.W. King, the French decided that the braggart "had enough nerve to be worth training."[43] Ultimately, they were right – although he and Jimmie Bach took longer than the rest, later that summer the tenacious Hall would earn his military aviator's license.

* * * * *

The Americans stayed in a hotel in Pau and either biked or bummed rides to the airfield eight miles outside of town, at least until Robert Chanler paid a visit and put them up in the fancy English Club, a handsome home near the old *château* of Henry IV.[44] Chanler also arranged a nice lunch with the mayor and the general commanding the district, an event reported in several French papers.[45] Following this lunch, Prince, Cowdin and Curtis were the first American aviators to be photographed wearing French uniforms.[46]

The French officers and men welcomed the trainees into the school, along with Andrew Ruel, an Alsatian-born Chicagoan who Prince "naturally signed up" to fill the sixth spot left open by Thaw.[47] The Pau aerodrome offered ideal flying conditions, with calm air and two large, flat fields surrounded by numerous hangars. Planes and pilots were everywhere, with sometimes as many as fifty machines in the air simultaneously.[48] The Americans were delighted with the place and, excepting Hall and Bach, all made rapid progress. A couple weeks into their stay, the *New York Sun* quoted Curtis on their treatment:

Everybody is doing the utmost possible to rush our training. There is an astonishingly large number of fliers who speak English, and they help us a great deal in an unofficial way. Besides this, everybody is most friendly and very appreciative.[49]

Four of the six men – Prince, Curtis, Cowdin and Ruel – quickly worked their way through the lower power Penguins and Bleriots to the eighty horsepower Caudron. Hall and Bach, however, were "flying only two or three times a week, making little progress," causing Curtis to remark that he "could not see that they would be of much use to us."[50] In April, the advancing aviators were sent to Camp d'Avord but, according to Cowdin, Bach and Hall were "very slow in qualifying and we were forced to leave them at Pau."[51]

Boasting a very large aerodrome surrounded by flat country, Camp d'Avord was an excellent ground for the learner pilot. Living in bungalows on the edge of the field, here the flyers would learn to handle Voisin bombers, as well as the technique of volplaning, from the French phrase *vol plane*, literally "glided flight." Although Hall and Bach were lagging behind, things were looking good for Norman Prince's plan and for the first time the New York press took notice of the ongoing efforts in France "to form a distinctively American aerial squadron."[52]

Unfortunately, their very first day at Avord, Ruel had a "terrible smash," breaking his leg in two places as well as his arm.[53] Then Hall caught up with the men at Avord, and must have continued his antics – in a postcard to his wife, Curtis wrote "Hall's adventures here interesting."[54] In addition, although Cowdin received his *brevet* on April 29 and Prince received his two days later, by his own admission, Curtis "was not having an easy time of it."[55] In fact, while testing for his military license, Curtis had two rough accidents resulting in a week-long hospital stay.[56] Following his second accident, his nerves were shot, and he was granted a 45-day sick leave.[57] Thereafter, although he would continue to assist with the organization of the squadron, Frazier Curtis would never return to active duty.[58]

With Curtis and Ruel out, and Bach and Hall still struggling, by early May, Prince's planned squadron had dwindled to two pilots. Although Thaw was already at the front, and doing well, the prospects for an American *escadrille* looked bleak. Cowdin later wrote that he and Prince "found ourselves alone in Paris, with all hopes of forming a squadron blown to the winds."[59]

Chapter Twenty-six

It is no rumor this time.

By early March, Kiffin had been in the trenches almost five months. While he had experienced much and greatly matured as a soldier, at least geographically Kiffin had not progressed much at all – as he wrote in a letter around this time, "the trench I am now in is about seven hundred meters from the first trench I was ever in."[1] Although still in fine condition, he was hoping for a change in sectors, and had requested that Paul see about arranging a transfer for him. But nothing happened, as Paul had learned that French law made it impossible to get Kiffin into a regular French unit. While disappointed, Kiffin said he "had about made up my mind to be contented with where I was."[2]

But after Rene Phelizot's death in early March, the friction in the unit grew worse than ever and Kiffin again began hoping for a change. A few days later as he came in from working on some trenches, Kiffin was pleasantly surprised to learn Paul had come through with a transfer – orders reassigning him to the First Regiment had arrived, and he was to leave in two hours. Kiffin hurriedly packed his sack (forgetting some of his unwashed clothes), said his goodbyes, then jumped in the first wagon to the rear. From there, over the next two days he took a series of automobiles and limousines to his new regiment.[3]

Kiffin's exit from the Second Regiment, while welcome, must have been somewhat bittersweet. He had spent five months at the front among these men, and their common suffering had surely created some attachment. In places with names like Verzenay, Cuiry-les-Chaudardes and Craonnelle, Kiffin and his legion cohorts had become soldiers and men. A few memorable lines from Alan Seeger's poem *The Aisne* hint at the relationships that had there been forged, and that Kiffin now left behind:

Craonne, before thy cannon-swept plateau,
Where like sere leaves lay strewn September's dead,
I found for all dear things I forfeited
A recompense I would not now forego.

For that high fellowship was ours then
With those who, championing another's good,
More than dull Peace or its poor votaries could,
Taught us the dignity of being men.[4]

* * * * *

As much as Kiffin had learned of life, strife and war in his prior unit, he found in the *1st Regiment Étranger* better discipline, officers and soldiers – "men you would have confidence in in case of action," as he put it.[5] Kiffin judged this new group to be "a better lot than the Americans in my old company."[6]

Some of Kiffin's good feelings surely stemmed from his elation at getting out of the Second Regiment, where he had suffered under the poor leadership of men like Morlae. As Kiffin told Paul, "I had little regrets leaving the outfit, although things were at the best stage for me there they had ever been in."[7]

Kiffin and his new American mates had a few things in common, too. For example, Russell Kelly attended VMI a year or two after Kiffin and was pleased to have another former "rat" in his squad. In a letter home in early April, he wrote:

We were scheduled to leave town one night for the third line of defense and had our packs made up when in came a fellow who wanted to see the Americans. He was an American from the Second Regiment Étranger, *and had been transferred at his own request, and as the authorities are following a plan of segregation by nations, he was sent to our squad. I was agreeably surprised to learn that he had been at Virginia Military Institute; he is Kiffin Y. Rockwell.*[8]

In November 1914, Kelly and his chum Lawrence Scanlan had together worked their way across the Atlantic on a cargo boat carrying six hundred and fifty horses for the use of the French army.[9] They both enlisted in the Foreign Legion just before Thanksgiving and arrived in the frontline trenches near Verzenay a week before Kiffin showed up.

In addition to Kelly and "Larney" Scanlan, there were three other Americans in Kiffin's new squad. The first, a soldier calling himself John Smith, admitted his real name in a letter opened upon his death in battle a few months later – John Earl Fike from Wooster, Ohio. He had enlisted under the name of his grandfather, Captain John Smith, who served with an Ohio regiment of volunteers during the Civil War.[10]

Like Kiffin, Kenneth Weeks of Boston had just transferred into the squad. During their time together, Kiffin and Kenneth developed a close friendship and Kiffin would later become like another son to Kenneth's mother. Weeks was the author of several books, one of which had come out just after he enlisted with the French at the beginning of the war.[11] Paul Pavelka, the other American in the squad, said Kenneth Weeks was "a nice fellow, sociable, well educated," and "believe me, through him our library is well stocked."[12]

The others all called Pavelka "Skipper," a reference to his sea-going past. In the legion, he entertained his friends with tales of his pre-war life, primarily a 159-day trip on the ship *Dirigo* from Seattle to England via Cape Horn.[13] The adventurous Pavelka was born in New York and grew up in The Bronx, where he attended the public schools. After living for some time in Madison, Connecticut, he left home as a teenager due to conflicts with his stepmother. Pavelka traveled across America, making his way west and sending picture postcards to a friend back home. On one card Pavelka had written: "I don't know where I'm going, but I'm on my way."[14]

That pretty much summed it up for Pavelka. He was always doing something new, always on the move. He held numerous jobs on his journey west, working "among the cow punchers" as a sheep-shearer and cowboy in Montana, as camp cook at a lumber camp in Washington, and even as an assistant nurse in San Francisco. He eventually worked his way down to the Panama Canal Zone, before crossing the Pacific to see Australia and Japan. Suffice it to say that on his own account Pavelka made his way around America and the world. When the war broke out in 1914, he was back in New York, staying at the Seaman's Church Institute at 25 South Street.[15] When a recruiter came by rounding up hands for a Canadian transport ship carrying horses to the British Army, Pavelka signed up and headed for England. There he was the only American to enlist with the pro-French army of the Republic of Counani, a group raised under the Belgian flag. After making his way to France, Pavelka enlisted with the Foreign Legion in November.[16] Kiffin described "Skipper Pavelka" as a "sailor and bum, [who] has never had any ambition, otherwise could probably have made a success as he has quite a lot of genius in several ways."[17]

The night Kiffin arrived, his new unit went into the trenches where it stayed for the next twenty-two days. Kiffin described these trenches as very close together in a level field and "laid out so that it is almost like an underground city." Eight feet deep and just three feet wide, the trenches wound around "in every direction so that you can walk for hours, all of them leading into the front combat trench." During their stay in the trenches "things were rather quiet," so Kiffin "had it pretty easy."[18]

In his haste leaving the Second Regiment, Kiffin had left some of his things behind and so asked Paul to send him some socks and underwear.[19] Kiffin preferred light-weight, two-piece BVD's, finding them easier to wash and "easier for catching the lice[.]"[20] While the company did not advertise its underwear as easier for catching lice, Kiffin would have been happy to know that in one ad back in America, his preferred brand was described as the "underwear of red-blooded, right-living men who find clean fun in keen sport, from tramping to camping."[21]

* * * * *

Kiffin was surely doing his share of tramping and camping, and in the process, he and the small group of Americans were becoming fast friends. A month after his arrival, Kiffin told Paul "the six of us stick together pretty close and get a little pleasure out of being together."[22] Kiffin also liked his new officers, particularly Corporal Didier, "a huge Moor, who had lived in London and New York and was very partial to the Americans."[23] In what must have been a significant contrast with the Second Regiment, Kiffin told Paul that no officer had raised his voice since he had transferred to the First Regiment, and that the corporal had even showed "a little favoritism towards me, more than to anyone else in the squad."[24] Things were going well; the sergeant even asked Kiffin if he wanted to be a candidate for corporal. But Kiffin declined, as it meant extra drilling and he was still unsure of his command of the French language. Still, he confided to Paul "if I could speak a little more French, I would make a better officer than some of them."[25]

Language-wise, Kiffin was probably on the wrong side of the war – he had taken two years of German in high school and finished near the top of his German class at VMI. A few months before, Kiffin had expressed to St. Elmo Massengale his feeling that he would "never get above a common soldier here, owing to a lack of knowledge of the French language," and subsequently asked a friend in Paris to send him a beginner's French grammar.[26] Once Kiffin began to focus on learning French, his two years of high school Latin surely helped, as not long after he reported that of the five other Americans in his new squad, four of them could not speak French as well as he could.[27] By April 17, he wrote

Paul that while at first he had been "handicapped very much by not knowing any French," now he could "speak a little and understand more."[28]

Maybe it helped that his new friend Kenneth Weeks spoke "perfect French" – the two often served guard duty together and undoubtedly their conversations helped Kiffin pick up the language.[29] One night they must have spoken of the *Rubaiyat*, as each of them requested copies, Weeks from his mother and Kiffin from Paul.[30] Weeks also had "plenty of money," and he and Kiffin shared what they had with the others, none of whom had any means.[31] In short order, the other men began to look to Kiffin and Weeks as the *de facto* leaders of the Americans.

Their first repose was spent in Verzenay, the same town where Kiffin and Paul had stopped just before their first trip to the trenches what to Kiffin must have seemed a lifetime before. There the dirty men were treated to a "great event" – a bath. One soldier held a hose with a sprinkler attachment while two others worked the pump. Kelly admitted it was "rather a crude method, but as the water is hot we are very thankful for it."[32]

* * * * *

During the early months of 1915, Paul was writing articles and sending them home for his mother and sister to try to sell. Around the turn of the year, he had been transferred from the convent at Montmirail to a sanitary hospital being set up at the *Château de Lamothe* in Villeneuve-sur-Lot in Southwestern France.[33] The *château* was owned by Georges Leygues, a prominent French cabinet minister and chief of the foreign affairs committee who would later become Prime Minister of France. Early in 1915, Leygues returned from Paris to oversee the transformation of their family home into a volunteer hospital founded by his wife Anne, assisted by their pretty daughter Mademoiselle Jeanne Leygues.[34]

Just twenty-three years old, Jeanne was a few years younger than Paul, who had turned twenty-six on February 3, 1915.[35] She was also petite and attractive, with a dark complexion, soft features, short brown hair and deep brown eyes. Serving in the hospital as a nurse volunteer, she soon became acquainted with the tall and handsome American. Paul could think of worse ways to spend his convalescence than practicing French with his winsome nurse, while to Jeanne, Paul must have seemed the bravest man in the world, come from across the ocean to rescue her homeland.[36]

Wartime romance is as old as war, and Paul and Jeanne soon realized they were in love. In fact, within a few months of their meeting the young nurse and her charge decided to marry. Her father must have approved of Paul, as it was likely through this powerful new connection that Paul was able to effectuate Kiffin's transfer, and to meet many prominent French citizens. It is also probable that his father-in-law-to-be helped secure Paul's release from the Foreign Legion and found a spot for him in the propaganda and information section of the French Army, where he could utilize his writing skills and contacts in the legion.[37]

Right around the time he got engaged, Paul developed bronchitis and spent three weeks at the American Ambulance hospital in Neuilly-sur-Seine, a western suburb of Paris.[38] The driver who transported him to Neuilly was Jim McConnell, a bagpipe-playing, fun-loving jokester from the University of Virginia, now serving as a volunteer in the American Ambulance.[39]

McConnell was born in Chicago, where his father Samuel was a Cook County judge. Samuel was the son of General John McConnell, a Union cavalry officer during the Civil War. As a successful young lawyer, Samuel had married Sarah Rogers, the daughter of Judge John G. Rogers, chief justice of the circuit court of Cook County and grand-daughter of the Chief Justice of the court of appeals of Kentucky. Samuel soon built up a successful practice; at the time it was said that "no member of the Chicago bar ... more fully command[s] the respect of his professional brethren" than Samuel P. McConnell.[40]

Young Jim grew up in Chicago until the family moved to New York City during his teen years. Later, he attended the University of Virginia, where he was well-known on campus, serving as the editor in chief of the yearbook and as King of the "Hot Foot Society," a secret society for upper classmen. He also helped found and was president of the Aero Club.

When the war began, McConnell was employed as the land and industrial agent for a railroad company in Carthage, North Carolina. A few months later he left for Europe, telling his friends: "These sand hills will be here forever, but the war won't; and so I'm going."[41]

McConnell had a brilliant mind, was an excellent writer and always fun to be around. But his quick wit and penchant for clowning around sometimes led those who did not know him well to dismiss him as not serious. But this was a mistake, for in his core, McConnell was solid as a rock, all commitment and ideals. Paul immediately recognized this, and from the beginning saw Jim more as a brother than a friend. McConnell acted on his ideals when in early February 1915 he was among a contingent of six Americans who boarded the S.S. *Chicago* and headed for France to serve as the first volunteer drivers in the newly-formed American Ambulance corps. After getting to know Paul, he wrote a chum back home:

I've made an awfully good friend of Paul Rockwell of the Foreign Legion who is at our hospital. He is simply a wonder and when he tells of his experiences, he makes one mad, you envy him so. He's only potted in the shoulder; will be made réforme *and is to marry one of the richest and most prominent girls in France.*[42]

Kiffin had also just received the surprising news of Paul's engagement; he told Paul "I could hardly believe my eyes when I read it."[43] His feelings turned from surprise to relief when he learned of Paul's impending discharge. "That is what I have been wanting to hear all along," he told Paul, "for I knew you were not physically able to come back to the trenches and stand the life." More importantly, Kiffin knew his anxious mother would be thrilled by both pieces of news, telling Paul it would be "one of the happiest moments of mamma's life when she hears."[44]

Paul must have mentioned that Kiffin could get out, too, but Kiffin wasn't going anywhere. He was committed to seeing the war through, especially since Paul was now safe and could take care of their mother, whatever happened to Kiffin. He wrote:

In regard to seeing the [doctor] and getting evacuated, I have never reported to the [doctor] once since you left. I may be a fool, but I have been conscientious about doing my best ever since I enlisted.... Being in the war is probably the only good thing that I have ever done or ever will do, so while I am in it I want to always do my best, and if I am killed in it, I will be perfectly contented to die, more so now that you are getting fixed right and will be in a position to prove to mamma that her sacrifices and work have not been wasted. Even if I come out of the war, I am afraid that will be up to you, for I have lost my ambition for what the world calls success.[45]

In other words, Kiffin was never going back to modern advertising, sales, or correspondence courses. He was playing his part, however small, in freedom's ongoing life or death struggle. And that was the only place he wanted to be.[46]

* * * * *

With spring in the air, a new infection began making the rounds in the trenches, at least among the Americans – baseball fever.[47] With nothing else to do, during one break the handy Pavelka manufactured a homemade baseball by winding worsted and thread around the "business end of a cartridge," then sewing it up with leather cut from a puttee. With the whole company watching, the men enjoyed a wonderful time until "Home-run Scanlan" drove the ball into the canal, breaking up the game.[48]

Although the weather had turned, the war stayed the same – exactly ... the ... same. The continued lack of action caused some of the men, tired of the tedium of life at the stalemated front, to look for ways to break up the monotony. As Pavelka said in a letter from this time, "most all of our boys are slowly acquiring the recklessness of true legionnaires."[49] For the most part, however, they had simply gotten bored with the daily routine, and were just seeking a little more excitement than a baseball game. The situation had been so quiet for so long that, as Weeks told his mother, "it is hard to believe that we are at war sometimes, especially these balmy days."[50] Nonetheless, he knew it was "only the ennui that is a bore, and that cannot last."[51]

Weeks was right.

In late April, the men were taken out of the trenches and told they were to be given a rest at Lyon then sent to the Dardanelles. The day before they were to be moved, many of the Italian volunteers that comprised a large portion of the company began drinking, perhaps to celebrate the rumor going around that Italy had (finally) declared war on Austria.[52] A few of the Italians started picking on a smaller and weaker soldier and, not liking the unevenness of the fight, Weeks took up for the smaller man. In the end, his efforts to keep the peace failed, and a large Italian walloped Weeks in the jaw. Showing how close the small band of Americans had become, they all immediately jumped in to defend their comrade. Russell Kelly described the melee that took place:

In a fraction of a second it was the biggest free-for-all I was ever in or hope to be in. We battled around the yard to a fare-you-well and in no time the guard was on the scene with fixed bayonets, but we still kept on.... The guards eventually separated us, but the Americans carried the day.[53]

Perhaps the soldiers simply needed to let out a little aggression, for once the fight was ended, they all "shook hands and called it square."[54]

* * * * *

The next morning the regiment was loaded on a train of box cars and informed that they were heading to Lyon for a rest. But their orders were evidently changed while en route, for after the train passed through Paris around midnight on April 26, it turned north toward the front rather than south toward Lyon. For the next few days, the men bounced between camps behind the rear of the lines, with no one knowing for sure just what was going on or where they were headed. Kiffin told a friend he was "very puzzled as to what we are up to, as we keep moving around."[55]

They eventually settled just behind the lines north of Arras, on a little spot known as Berthonval Farm, located between Mont-St.-Éloi and Neuville-St.-Vaast. The censor-conscious Weeks relayed to his mother only that they had ended up "far from where we were, and in a livelier section."[56] And a livelier section it was – the mass movement of equipment and artillery, the newly constructed evacuation hospitals and trainload after trainload of arriving French, English and Belgian troops convinced the men they would soon see real combat.

This was confirmed when the officers told the men to rest up, for they were going to participate in a great attack on the Germans. Kiffin told his mother he expected to go into "hard action at any time[.]"[57] As usual, he was more blunt with Paul. He wrote:

I hate to think of what is going to happen soon, for we are all going into hard action. A big battle is going to commence soon, and we have already received instructions as to just what our position will be in it and what we have got to do. It is no rumor this time.[58]

Chapter Twenty-seven

A nice clean bullet

In preparation for the upcoming battle, the men were given a few days to relax, which included all the wine they wanted, and even special foods and treats. With this abundance, the legionnaires spent the first four days in May "eating and drinking to a fare-you-well."[1] Kiffin used this time to cut his beard and shave for the first time since his enlistment. He told Loula that he had a "fine beard, but it made me look very old." Perhaps for the first time, his fellow soldiers realized Kiffin was their age: clean-shaven, he looked fifteen years younger.[2]

Around this time Kiffin learned from Paul that the Atlanta papers had published a few of his letters home. For example, at the end of February the *Atlanta Constitution* printed one of his letters to Massengale, and in April the *Atlanta Journal* published his letter to Agnes about the night Corporal Weidemann was killed.[3] Kiffin was not happy about this and wrote a note chastising his mother:

Paul wrote me that the Atlanta papers had been giving me quite a lot of publicity and that the Journal *had published my letter to Agnes. Others have also written me, and all of you write and act as if you all thought I came over here for notoriety and to try to be a hero. It has hurt me and made me mad also to think how few people there were that gave me credit for any strength of character. Maybe the life I have led justifies all in their opinions. However, I am sorry that such is the case and it means to me that I will never try to live in the South.*[4]

Simply put, Kiffin did not like the idea of being classed with those who (like Morlae) had come to France merely to get their name in the papers. Having acted on principle, he was disappointed to learn that some saw his decision as a stunt or lark. A few days later, he wrote a slightly less forceful rebuke to his older brother, making it clear he did not want his letters publicized this way:

I am glad to hear that you are making a success with your writing, but I don't want any publicity or fame so don't want to write for the Journal *or any paper. Was sorry to hear that my letter to Agnes had been published.*[5]

But however much he wanted to avoid publicity, Kiffin's actions would soon make the papers again.

* * * * *

The night of May 3, Kiffin and a few others were sent out to work in between the lines, tasked with putting up earthworks to serve as protection for their upcoming attack. Out in the open less than eighty yards from the German trenches, the group worked under continual fire, forced to lie on their stomachs "and throw up the dirt with one hand."[6] The danger was real; Kiffin wrote Paul that the "bullets were pretty thick" and a friend of his – one of the Italian soldiers – was killed near him.[7]

Two days later, Kiffin's squad was sent back into the trenches, again less than one hundred meters opposite the Germans. They spent their time standing guard and digging tunnels towards the German lines. But at the end of what was to have been a forty-eight-hour stint, rather than being relieved, the unit was informed that the attack would begin the next night at midnight and that their battalion was to lead the regiment into battle. Everyone scrambled to get extra cartridges and food, as well as to build up an embankment that stretched nearly all the way to the barbed wire in front of the Germans. This exposed work again drew the fire of the German marksmen – Kiffin said that he "spent three hours at it and didn't like it a bit."[8]

Once everything was ready, the men settled down to await the bombardment that was supposed to precede the attack. However, no bombing commenced and a couple hours later they were informed that the attack had been postponed. Disappointed, they spent the rest of that night on guard duty in a temporary trench before being relieved the next morning. After marching twelve kilometers to the rear, that night Kiffin laid down exhausted, hoping for a good night's sleep, as he had only five or six hours of sleep in the prior three days.[9] Of course, that did not happen.

* * * * *

At one in the morning on May 9, the sleeping soldiers were awakened and told to get their sacks ready at once. They hurriedly gathered their things and took their positions in the second-line trenches just as daylight pierced the sky.

Within minutes, the French artillery began a stupendous bombardment – to Kiffin, the barrage sounded "as if all hell had broken loose."[10] For the next several hours shells of all calibers rained down on the German earthworks and lines. Kelly said the continual rumble and vibration was "beyond description," while Kiffin remembered that along the entire German line one could see "nothing but smoke and flying debris."[11] Then, just before ten o'clock, the booming guns fell silent.

Kiffin stood in his second-line trench looking over the field. He and the others in Battalion B were slated to advance third, behind Battalions C and A. Fixing his bayonet, he watched as the men from Battalion C clambered out of the ground and charged. He later described the event to Paul:

At ten o'clock, I saw the finest sight I have ever seen. It was men from the [First Regiment] crawling out of our trenches, with their bayonets glittering against the sun, and advancing on the 'Boche.' There was not a sign of hesitation. They were falling fast, but as fast as men fell, it seemed as if new men sprang up out of the ground to take their places. One second it look[ed] as if an entire section had fallen by one sweep of a machine gun. In a few minutes, a second line of men crawled out of our trenches....[12]

By the time the men of Battalion A charged onto the field, it was clear that the French bombardment had not taken out all the German guns. While some of the attackers were able to make it through, it seemed that at least as many fell in a terrible hail of bullets.

Watching the carnage, Kiffin drew in a deep breath. He and his brethren were next. At precisely seven minutes after ten, the Captain called out "*en avant!*" (forward), and the men of Battalion B dashed down to the combat trench, "the German artillery giving us hell as we went." Just as they reached the first-line trench, a shell burst near the captain, leaving his face cut and bleeding. Wiping his hand across his face and seeing the blood, the French officer muttered something under his breath. Kiffin was close enough to hear what he said: "*cochons*" – pigs.

Raising his head, the captain looked straight into Kiffin's eyes as he ordered the men over the top.

* * * * *

With the others, Kiffin scrambled up the ladders and out of the trenches. According to Kiffin, "from then on it was nothing but a steady advance under rifle, machine gun and artillery fire. We certainly had the *Boche* on the run, but at the same time they were pouring lead at us."[13] Kelly also remembered taking heavy fire as they charged across the field, saying "I will never be able to satisfy myself how so many of us got through safely."[14]

But many did not make it through, leaving the field strewn with the dead and dying. Across this bloody terrain the soldiers advanced in fits and starts, first one section, then another. Everywhere soldiers were dropping due to the return fire of the German guns. Seeing this, the men scurried forward using their sacks as shields, hitting the dirt when the bullets got too thick. In this way, they took the field twenty-five to fifty meters at a time, like running the bases on a baseball field. As Kelly put it, "talk about Ty Cobb sliding into second base, it isn't a circumstance to the way I hit the grit."[15]

Kiffin had dreamt of this moment his whole life, so despite the noise, smoke, danger and death, he saw nothing in it but glory. He later wrote:

To think of fear or the horror of the thing was impossible. All I could think of was what a wonderful advance it was, and of how everyone was going against that stream of lead as if they loved it.[16]

The initial rapid charge of the legionnaires caused scores of casualties from friendly fire as the French guns, directed behind the lines to prevent German reinforcements from coming up, instead hit the fast-advancing legion. Despite this, the attacking line continued to press forward, and took the small hamlet of La Targette, along with one thousand German prisoners. As more legionnaires swept past, a few of the captured men called out, urging them to "push on to the Rhine and end the war."[17] By this point, the legion's numbers had dwindled considerably and most of the surviving attackers were thrown together in a mix with the remaining men from other regiments.

Five hours into the attack, Kiffin and "Skipper" Pavelka found themselves hunkered down with their sous-lieutenant on the outskirts of Neuville-Saint-Vaast, a small town situated in the foreground of the Legion's objective: Vimy Ridge, a strategic hill rising high in the distance. As the French advanced, the frontline Germans fell back to the heavily fortified village, which one officer described as "a mass of machine-guns and bomb-throwers."[18] This description was accurate, at least from Kiffin's perspective – he, Skipper and their officer were pinned down taking heavy fire from several positions in the end of Neuville still held by the Germans.

As they lay there, a messenger arrived to tell the sous-lieutenant that both the captain and lieutenant had fallen, so he was now in charge of the company. After taking a moment to process the news, the sous-lieutenant stood and ordered Kiffin and Pavelka to follow him. Steeling himself, Kiffin jumped up and turned to Pavelka. "We might as well get it over at once," he said with a wan smile. Grabbing his sack and rifle, Kiffin dashed after their officer, with Skipper right behind.[19]

* * * * *

The boys were moving fast, but not fast enough – they made it only 20 meters before a bullet caught Kiffin through the fleshy part of the thigh, causing him to topple over. Pavelka dropped next to him to help bandage the wound, but Kiffin waved him off, saying "Go on and give them hell."[20] As his friend hurried after the sous-lieutenant, Kiffin turned his head away, not wanting to see Skipper catch his own bullet.

Looking for a place to escape the terrific firing, Kiffin spotted a marmite hole and crawled into it. Momentarily safe, he examined and lightly bandaged his wound before turning his attention to another soldier laying in the pit. The man was in bad shape – he had been shot through both hips and a piece of shell had ripped through his stomach. Kiffin later wrote to Paul:

I tried to bandage him up but he was dying and I couldn't do any good. He wanted water, but I had none and couldn't get any for him. That was the cry going up everywhere – for water. I stayed there until he died.[21]

Kiffin expected to die as well, but not from his bullet wound – shells were dropping all around, and he felt certain one had his name on it. He told Paul of the experience:

While I was laying there, three shells exploded within ten meters of me, each time covering me with dirt. The last one landed within five or six meters of me. I would hear them coming and would say to myself, 'Well, it's over,' and shut my eyes. Then I would brush the dirt off and find that I was all right.[22]

After things died down a bit, Kiffin made his way out of the hole and crawled "snake fashion" towards the rear, stopping at a haystack to rest with some other wounded men.[23] While he was there, a Red Cross medic came by and told them there were so many wounded it would probably be the following day before they could be picked up and taken to the rear. On hearing this, Kiffin improvised a cane and hobbled along another kilometer or two until he came to a farm with many wounded soldiers.[24]

Kiffin spent the night at the farm, and the next morning hitched a few rides until he made it to an evacuation center near Abbeville. There he was able to quickly jot down a few lines on a post card:

Am en route to some hospital, having received a nice clean bullet through the thigh day before yesterday. We made one glorious advance, breaking the German lines, driving them out of the trenches and advancing over open country, fighting every step of the way.[25]

From Abbeville, Kiffin was put on a train, expecting to be sent to the American Ambulance hospital just outside Paris. Instead, he eventually ended up in a military hospital in Rennes, in Western France. Two days into his journey, Kiffin could barely move his leg, and by the time he finally received treatment in the hospital, it had been four days. Although the wound had festered, and the doctors initially suspected they would have to reopen and clean it, Kiffin assured Paul it was "nothing bad and I will soon be all right."[26]

Kiffin particularly welcomed one aspect of the hospital, and began his first letter from there to Paul with this sentence:

Well, I am lying between two nice, clean sheets now for the first time for nearly nine months, so I guess you know how good it must feel.[27]

So Kiffin's nice clean bullet had led to nice clean sheets. For a boy raised on gallant tales of combat, it is hard to say which of these pleased Kiffin more.

* * * * *

In the hospital, Kiffin had time to reflect on the war, write a few letters, and catch up on the news. The information he received confirmed what Kiffin had already sensed – the battle had gone well. The French troops had taken La Targette and half of Neuville-St.-Vaast, wiped out the enemy works south of the Souchez-Carency road, and pushed the Germans out of the eastern part of the village of Carency.[28] Describing the battle as a "brilliant success," the Paris papers reported the capture of a dozen cannons, sixty machine guns and as many as 3,400 German soldiers, including fifty officers and one colonel.[29] The attack on La Targette, in which Kiffin participated, was singled out for specific praise, with one report stating it had been "conducted with remarkable audacity and complete success."[30] On Kiffin's first day in the hospital, the *New York Herald* ran this description of the attack, taken from official French communiqués:

At ten o'clock, two regiments left their trenches at Berthonval. The artillery, particularly efficacious, opened up their road. The barbed-wire fences were destroyed. In a magnificent charge, the trenches, whence the Germans continued to fire, were overrun. Our men ran on past them, only stopping to surround the shelters containing whole sections of the enemy. The Germans who barred the way were struck down by bayonets and on went our men.[31]

At the time, the papers did not highlight the deep losses suffered by the French, particularly in the Legion. But Kiffin soon heard that only seven hundred of the more than four thousand legionnaires who had gone into battle came back fit for service, with more than eight hundred killed outright and about 2,500 wounded over the course of the four-day fight.[32] For its work, Kiffin's regiment was cited in Army orders:

Second Marching Regiment of the First Foreign Regiment: Ordered, May 9th, under the orders of Lieutenant-Colonel Cot, to take with the bayonet a very strongly entrenched German position, launched itself into the attack, officers leading, with a superb enthusiasm, gaining in a single bound several kilometres of terrain, in spite of an extremely strong resistance of the enemy and the violent fire of his machine guns.[33]

Of his own role in the battle, Kiffin said he had only "a little old wound" that would allow him to "take life easy" for a month or two before rejoining the fighting.[34] Several months later, he told a friend of the glorious attack: "There is nothing like it, you float across the field, you drop, you rise again. The sack, the 325 extra rounds, the gun – have no weight. And a ball in the head and it is all over – no pain."[35]

Although he had not yet learned the fate of his squad mates, Kiffin was very proud of the work of his fellow soldiers. Not long after the battle, Kiffin wrote to a friend that the men in his unit had "engaged out of love and admiration for France, and because they knew they were right. They were men who had the courage of their convictions and were willing to die, if necessary, to prove it. So the day we were called upon to attack, every man went into it willingly with the determination to do his best, and humming the *Marseillaise*."[36] He surely would have agreed with a statement made by another American volunteer, who later said "as long as you are soldiering, I think it as well to do it with people who are soldiers to the very marrow of their bones."[37]

Finally, on May 30th Kiffin received good news from one of the other Americans in his squad. Remarkably, all five had come through unscathed, which to Kiffin seemed "a kind of miracle."[38] Russell Kelly, who helped take the crest of a hill just before dusk on the first day, said he would never forget the "nightmare" scene as he looked back across the field in the fading light.[39] Weeks could not believe he had not been hit. "Not a scratch," he told his mother, adding that this "seem[ed] miraculous to me in such a hell of fire and shells."[40] Pavelka was also surprised to have made it through, telling a friend he could not account for it, "except that my day has not been intended to come quite yet."[41] Several Americans in other battalions were injured, and Kiffin's friend Zinovi Pechkoff, the son of the famous Russian Maxim Gorky, who was serving as a corporal in Battalion D, had his right arm shot away at the shoulder.[42]

At the hospital, Kiffin saw wounds even worse than Pechkoff's – crippled and disfigured soldiers, along with other "pitiful examples of the effects of the war."[43] As he contemplated their sacrifice, and the greater sacrifice of those killed in the fight, Kiffin knew that these men had accomplished something truly meaningful. Thus, the soldier who just three weeks earlier told his brother Paul he had lost his ambition for what the world called success now seized on his own definition – to Kiffin, success meant something lasting, something permanent, something done for others, rather than for oneself.

In a letter home later that year, Harry Butters, an American volunteer fighting with the British Army expressed similar feelings. He told his parents:

I think less of myself than I did, less of the heights of personal success that I aspired to climb, and more of the service that each of us must render in payment for the right to live and by virtue of which, only, can we progress. Yes, my dearest folks, we are indeed doing the world's work over here, and I am in it to the finish.[44]

Like Butters, Kiffin was not in France for himself, or for any personal gain – nor for fame, publicity or any other self-serving reason. Rather, he was there to make a stand for the benefit of generations to come. For this reason, Kiffin's natural revulsion to the massive death he had witnessed was overshadowed by his pride and admiration for those who had given their lives for something more important than themselves. As he explained to a friend:

This life does not hold such great value in my eyes as it does in some people's, and I feel that those men who died that day, died having made a success of their lives ... doing something for the world, for posterity, and that their characters are their souls which will forever live and be passed down from generation to generation. So, is not that success! And what more can a man ask for his life than success?[45]

While many who witnessed the wanton bloodshed of war became disillusioned, for Kiffin, the conflict – even the seemingly senseless killing – served to reveal a higher and greater purpose for his life. As Paul would later write, Kiffin had "a spirit which could rise high above the grim horror and miserable sordidness of war and see all the glory and wonder of it."[46] While some might view it as naïve, Kiffin felt that in fighting for France, he was in some measure refining his soul. He was doing something *right*. Something *good*. And most importantly, something that would matter long after he was gone.

* * * * *

His injury once again landed Kiffin in the Atlanta papers, one of which informed its readers that he had been wounded "in the desperate fighting around Arras."[47] Kiffin even made page two of the *New York Sun*, which reported:

Paul Rockwell, one of the Americans in the Foreign Legion, has gone to Rennes to see his brother, Kiffin, who is in the hospital there. Kiffin was with the First Regiment of the Foreign Legion, which suffered severely in the recent fighting at Arras. After five hours of hard fighting his thigh was shattered and it will be two months before he will be able to return to his regiment.[48]

Despite this report, Kiffin's thigh was not "shattered" – luckily, the German bullet had missed Kiffin's bone, although it had torn through the muscles and left a rather large exit wound on the other side. Ultimately, the doctors determined debridement was not necessary, and decided simply to allow the wound to heal on its own. Still, it took time for the muscles to mend, and it was several weeks before Kiffin could again move around on it.

Paul hurried to Rennes as soon as he received word of what had happened. With his brother to keep him company, Kiffin had a pretty good setup as he recovered – he was well looked after and had plenty to eat. In the mornings, he read the French papers and a wide variety of English magazines and books. Before the war, Military Hospital No. 101 had been a large school for boys, and Kiffin spent his afternoons with Paul and other visitors in a very pleasant garden. All in all, Kiffin was treated rather royally and felt he was in a "regular paradise."[49]

Every day from noon to five, the hospital orderlies carried Kiffin down to the garden to visit with Paul. The two brothers enjoyed their time together as they had plenty to discuss, including Paul's fiancée and upcoming marriage, their former comrades in the Second Regiment and Kiffin's war stories. Paul told Kiffin all about his new friend Jim McConnell, who had just written Paul to express his sympathy and admiration:

I don't know whether to be happy that your brother escaped being killed after such a grand and terrible fight or to be sorry that he is so wounded. God Almighty, it must have been wonderful.[50]

Paul also told Kiffin how their mother's earlier entreaties seeking their release from the legion had gained them a small measure of notoriety among the officials in Paris.[51] Kiffin sternly addressed this with Loula in his next letter home:

Paul tells me that when he arrived in Paris he found we were quite well advertised, but not to our advantage, by a number of rather wild letters you had written to everyone you could think of. If you had understood a little more about war and diplomatic affairs, you would have known that the ambassador could be of absolutely no assistance to us while we were in the army.... Now, we appreciate the fact that your efforts are out of love for us, but there are a lot of things you do not understand in regard to conditions over here and the war, and it is hard for a person to give advice on something they know nothing about.[52]

In addition to his brother, many English-speaking residents of the town regularly came to see Kiffin, offering to do whatever they could to make him comfortable.[53] Several of the nurses at the hospital spoke English, but Kiffin also had plenty of opportunities to practice his French – one pretty blonde Alsatian came to sit with him every afternoon. Her later explanation as to why she admired Kiffin so dearly was surely true for many other grateful French citizens:

I happened to meet him when he was wounded for the first time in 1915. As he felt rather lonely in the hospital, I liked to come and talk to him. I like my country very dearly and admire our brave French soldiers. Still, how much more to be admired are those who could have remained absolutely out of the war and instead, came forward for the triumph of a great ideal: freedom and civilization![54]

Chapter Twenty-eight

The cause of all humanity

On May 1, 1915, eight days before Kiffin charged into battle near La Targette, the following advertisement ran in several New York and Washington, D.C. papers:

NOTICE!

TRAVELLERS intending to embark on the Atlantic voyage are reminded that a state of war exists between Germany and her allies and Great Britain and her allies; that the zone of war includes the waters adjacent to the British Isles; that, in accordance with formal notice given by the Imperial German Government, vessels flying the flag of Great Britain, or any of her allies, are liable to destruction in those waters and that travellers sailing in the war zone on the ships of Great Britain or her allies do so at their own risk.

IMPERIAL GERMAN EMBASSY
Washington, D.C., 22 April 1915.[1]

That same day in New York City, many of those boarding the British-flagged ocean liner *Lusitania* had seen the warning. As the great ship prepared to depart for Liverpool, a number of passengers received telegrams at the pier, "advising them not to sail, as the liner was to be torpedoed by submarines."[2]

Alfred G. Vanderbilt, the heir of Cornelius Vanderbilt and one of the richest men in America received one such telegram. It read: "The *Lusitania* is doomed. Do not sail on her. Mort."[3] In French, *mort* means death. As he boarded the ship, Vanderbilt crumpled the telegram and tossed it away.[4]

Six days later, with more than nineteen hundred persons on board, the *Lusitania* sank off the coast of Ireland after being struck by a torpedo fired by a German U-boat. In Paris the next morning, the *New York Herald* ran one of the first accounts of the sinking, including an initial mistaken report that all the passengers and crew may have been saved by other boats. Still the paper declared: "the question on every tongue is, as the threat to commit this terrible crime – the murder warning – was published in the American press, what will America do?"[5]

* * * * *

By the time Kiffin was receiving his wound in battle, the world had learned that a substantial majority of the passengers on board the *Lusitania* had perished, including 128 Americans. In the face of this provocation, the *Herald*, which had always held a decidedly pro-French view, began to campaign more aggressively for America to respond.[6] On May 9, the paper quoted former president Theodore Roosevelt's characterization of the attack as "warfare against innocent men, women and children on the ocean and on our own fellow countrymen and countrywomen." The *Herald's* Paris readers assuredly agreed with the rest of Roosevelt's sentiment: "It seems inconceivable that we should refrain from taking action. We owe it to humanity and to our own national self-respect."[7]

Undoubtedly, Germany's sinking of the *Lusitania* was a direct challenge to President Wilson's declared policy of neutrality. Many assumed that Wilson would at least have to issue a very firm rebuke, or even declare war. For example, Edmond Genet wrote in his diary the day after the sinking: "What will our Government do now? Surely there will be immediate war."[8] But Wilson said nothing, even while the world condemned the deaths of almost 1,200 people.[9]

The day Kiffin arrived in Rennes, news of the glorious advance of his unit appeared on the front page of the *Herald*. Right next to it, in an article titled "Germany's Insult to America," Kiffin read this:

[T]he people of the whole civilized world … have their eyes turned on the White House, waiting for the answer to the question: 'What is President Wilson going to do about it?'[10]

Three days after the sinking, President Wilson finally broke his silence. During a speech before a group of recently naturalized citizens at Independence Hall in Philadelphia, Wilson asserted that America must be a "special example" because "peace is the healing and elevating influence of the world and strife is not." Although he did not mention the incident directly, most people took Wilson's next comments as responsive to the *Lusitania* provocation. He said:

There is such a thing as a man being too proud to fight. There is such a thing as a nation being so right that it does not need to convince others by force that it is right.[11]

254

Kiffin had been thrilled when, speaking in the same place less than a year earlier, Wilson had declared that America would "come into the full light of day when all shall know that she puts human rights above all other rights and that her flag is the flag not only of America but of humanity."[12] Now, however, she was too proud to fight.

Wilson's weak response disgusted Kiffin. In a letter to his mother, Kiffin suggested that if Italy joined the Allies, as was widely reported at the time that it might, the war would soon be over. With a touch of bitterness, he added: "If the U.S. would show a little self-respect it would end quicker."[13]

* * * * *

Colonel Roosevelt, as the press often referred to the former president, despised a government "pledged to the ignoble policy of neutrality between right and wrong," and responded fiercely to Wilson's weak comments.[14] Just two days after the event, he began selling a five-cent pamphlet titled *Murder on the High Seas*. In it, he wrote:

[W]e earn as a nation measureless scorn and contempt if we follow the lead of those who exalt peace above righteousness, if we heed the voices of those feeble folk who bleat to high heaven that there is peace when there is no peace.[15]

On Kiffin's first day in the hospital, he read in the *Herald* what Roosevelt thought of Wilson's assertion that one could be too proud to fight. Declaring that "the policy of blood and iron cannot be met efficaciously by a policy of milk and water," Roosevelt suggested that peace (so-called) could come at too high a price:

I do not believe the firm assertion of our rights means war. But we shall do well to remember there are things worse than war. Let us as a nation understand that peace is of worth only when it is the handmaiden of international righteousness and national self-respect.[16]

In the same edition, the *Herald* published a letter to the editor written by an American expressing support for Roosevelt's tough talk. A portion of it read:

It is too bad, indeed, that Roosevelt, or a man of his type, is not president. We want a man whose motto is to act, not make timid half-hearted protestations.[17]

Kiffin wanted action, too – not cowardly and shameful words. Indeed, during his time in France, Kiffin increasingly found himself at odds with his party's steadfast neutrality. Paul later wrote that after the sinking of the *Lusitania*, Kiffin felt "deeply humiliated and outraged" when Wilson refused to lead the American people into the war. He said Kiffin "was especially hurt because, being a Democrat by birth and tradition, he felt that the party had been betrayed by its leader."[18]

Now, as he lay wounded in a French hospital bed, Kiffin could not help siding with Roosevelt over Wilson. Reaching for some stationary, Kiffin composed his own letter to the *Herald*. Surely it laid out the case for America to act in the face of this insult and to aid its longtime ally. Surely it rebuked President Wilson and his "too proud to fight" nonsense. It must have been superb. Paul later said:

I have often wished I had kept a copy of a letter Kiffin wrote in May 1915 from the Rennes Hospital to the Paris edition of the New York Herald. *The* Herald *made a practice of printing letters from readers, but it never published Kiffin's, as it was too stern and too just an attack on Wilson's peace policy.*[19]

While written much later in the war, Edmond Genet's letter to a friend back home following Wilson's reelection in late 1916 probably catches some of the spirit of how Kiffin felt. Genet wrote of the "unthinking, uncaring voters," who had reelected the man, saying: "Where has all the old genuine honor and patriotism and humane feelings of our countrymen gone?"[20] He continued:

It couldn't be possible for Americans in America to feel the same bitter way as Americans over here among the very scenes of this war's horrors. It's not comprehensible over there where peace reigns supreme. Come over here and you'll be engulfed like the rest of us in the realization of the necessity of the whole civilized world arming itself against this intrusion of utter brutality and militaristic arrogance.[21]

While Kiffin was a Democrat, first and foremost he was an American, and his roots and soul were red, white and blue. While nothing could ever change that fact, in the world's fight for liberty, it was not America but France putting it on the line, so with France is where Kiffin stood. Indeed, in large part, Kiffin's identity as an American is what led him to volunteer – in his mind, signing up was the *American* thing to do, as no true liberty-loving patriot could stand aside at this critical moment in history.

America's failure to live up to its principles and aid France had been troubling enough in the first nine months of the war, but in the face of the outrageous murder of more than one hundred Americans, Kiffin simply could not comprehend President Wilson's mild response, or his fellow citizens' steadfast aloofness. Paul felt likewise. He once said that the "bitterest regret" of his life was that "so few Americans have come here to help France. When we … needed help, Lafayette and his followers were a hundred times as many...."[22]

While his faith in his party, president and country flagged, Kiffin still held out a slight hope that America would eventually awaken to its duty. On June 8, he wrote Loula:

We are all watching the U.S. now. If she wants to keep up her name as a nation and be respected by other nations, I don't see how she will keep from fighting. But I haven't much faith in her.[23]

Around this time, still under pressure, Wilson determined to send another diplomatic note, seeking assurances that Germany would henceforth safeguard American lives and American ships. Finding even this meek request too forceful, William Jennings Bryan, Wilson's Secretary of State and *de facto* leader of the "peace at any price" wing of the Democrat party, refused to sign the note, and instead resigned his portfolio. But the letter was sent anyway, signed by Robert Lansing, serving as *ad interim* Secretary.

Bryan saw the issue as one of force versus persuasion, with force representing the "old system" that he felt certain was passing into history. In a note explaining his decision to resign, Bryan described how he would have liked America to respond:

Some nation must lead the world out of the black night of war into the light of that day when swords will be beaten into plowshares. Why not make that honor ours?[24]

Reading this, Kiffin surely gagged. There was no honor in humiliation. Had Bryan suddenly appeared in front of him, Kiffin may have beat his head into a plowshare.[25]

* * * * *

His good friend Kenneth Weeks was a lot like Kiffin – he too was still hoping his country would take its place among the warring nations. In a letter to his mother dated May 14, 1915, he expressed a sentiment with which Kiffin surely agreed:

Thank you for your letter about the Lusitania. *I am doing my best to revenge that and all else. Do you not now understand me, and what I engaged for?*[26]

Then, in early June, Weeks wrote: "It looks really as if America might get mixed up in the war after all. I hope so; I want to see the whole world with us."[27] Hoping the resignation of Bryan would perhaps cause the president to take a firmer stance against Germany, Kiffin now noted that he had previously "thought Mr. Wilson a good man and maybe he still will not disappoint me."[28] Similarly, Edmond Genet wrote in his diary on June 11: "news came today that Mr. William Jennings Bryan, our choice Secretary of State, has at last resigned. We may have war with Germany yet, if Wilson makes good at last, now that he isn't influenced by peaceful Willy Bryan."[29]

One of the men in Kiffin's old unit, the Second Regiment, wrote a letter around this time which probably captured much of the thinking then current among the American volunteers. The letter said:

One of our chief matters of discussion is whether we shall leave to fight under our own flag, and since the Lusitania *sinking we have often pictured ourselves making our entry into the United States army. Of course, we do not really expect that it will happen, but as we talk and talk of the possibility of fighting under the Star-Spangled Banner, much as we love the French army, our hearts beat high.*[30]

Kiffin also still hoped to fight under the stars and stripes. He felt that if the United States declared war, it would be "easy" to get a good commission and he could provide "quite a lot of assistance when the troops arrive."[31] Although he suspected American troops would not be arriving any time soon, this did not faze Kiffin – as he explained to his mother, he was "just following out my old theory that we are a part of this whole scheme of affairs," and so "if one is going to fight, I don't see why the *country* should have as great an influence as the *principle*."[32]

Fighting for principle was probably just as well, for it seems that the outrage of the sinking was already fading a bit, at least in America. Kiffin's disappointment grew when he received a letter from an old fraternity pal back in Atlanta stating that although Germany "had incurred the displeasure of 90% of American people" when it torpedoed the *Lusitania*, the likelihood that America would sever diplomatic relations seemed "less imminent now than it was a week ago." Nevertheless, Kiffin's friend felt America would eventually have to take some action. He wrote that "it seems we will have to do something in [the] nature of establishing peace, or we will have to enter [the] war ourselves. I do not believe the U.S. can stay neutral."[33] In closing, he told Kiffin to "take a drink of French wine and think of an old friend."[34]

While Kiffin was not likely to let French wine dull his memory of the international slight, he slowly made peace with the fact that the United States was not going to step into the conflict. As time marched on, the deep disappointment he felt in his home country stood in sharp contrast to his increasing loyalty towards France. Under the circumstances, and given the sacrifice he had made, it is not surprising that Kiffin began to see in France all that he hoped for America. By the end of June, he told his mother he would "rather be fighting for France than doing anything else now," and just after Independence Day, he wrote "every day I am gladder that I came over and am fighting for France. I have grown to love the people and the country more than I ever loved America."[35]

Kiffin was by no means the only American who had soured on America's leadership. Many Americans in France began to direct their patriotism towards France, feeling that if America would not defend its allies, at least it could defend its dignity. After spending the Fourth of July in Paris, A. Piatt Andrew, by then in charge of the American Ambulance Field Service, wrote a letter worth quoting at length, as it gave voice to the frustrations of many Americans feeling the shame of their country's failure to take an active part in the war. He wrote:

Yesterday, we celebrated the "Glorious Fourth," but alas, I must admit that I felt there was but little glory for us Americans to celebrate. The United States have had a great past – they are destined, I feel confident, to have a great future – but for the present I feel only a haunting sense of humiliation and regret. The only glory about the Fourth for me is the glory of France fighting the world's battles with indomitable courage and silent determination and without a murmur of complaint, although not properly supported by any of her allies.[36]

Along with a collection of other Americans in Paris, Andrew had gone to visit the grave of Lafayette on the morning of the Fourth. He expressed the dissatisfaction they all felt at the wishy-washy words of the American ambassador, meant to mark the occasion:

With the French and American flags we marched through the cemetery to the tomb of the great Frenchman who spent so many years in the service of the United States during the grim years of our struggle for freedom. Here we were, a little group of Americans, trying in our turn to do our little for

France in her desperate effort to throw off the yoke of her aggressors. But our Ambassador was our spokesman, and he spoke without imagination, without comprehension, without sympathy. It would have been easy for any intelligent man with a heart to recall in terms of living sympathy the story of Lafayette and of the past friendship of France and the United States without in any way violating our present official neutrality. But Mr. Sharp was not the man to do so.[37]

Andrew's letter a month later sounds so much like Kiffin, it could have been written by him. On August 5, he wrote:

I love my country. I am proud of her past. I have great dreams for her future, but, somehow or other, I must confess it beyond my power to defend the policies of "our" Mr. Wilson, or the competence of men like "our" Mr. Bryan and "our" Mr. Sharp, whom he has chosen for positions of the highest responsibility. Jealous for my country and wanting always to defend her, I am unhappy, indeed, when I think of the role she has been forced into by her representatives in this the most crucial, transitional period of all the world's history.[38]

Kiffin could not have said it better himself.

* * * * *

Back at the hospital, Kiffin was healing well and finally getting around on his own. Near the end of May, he wrote a friend that he wouldn't be surprised if Paul returned to Paris, as he suspected his brother found it rather dull in Rennes. He must have been right – Paul dutifully hung around until June 5, then returned to Paris. Kiffin kept busy with his reading, visits from the nurses and townsfolk, and exchanging letters with his friends in the Legion. Two of those letters came from his friends Weeks and Pavelka, both of whom informed Kiffin that all the Italians in the unit had been liberated to go and fight with their country, which had finally officially declared war against Austria. He must also have written Russell Kelly, for on June 10, Kelly told a friend that "the ball that hit Rockwell's leg just missed the bone, so he is recovering rapidly and hopes to be back with us soon."[39] By mid-June, Kiffin was able to take walks around the hospital, and optimistically told his mother that in a week or two she would not be able to tell he had been wounded.[40]

Around this time, Kiffin received a letter Loula had written when she first learned of his wound. Kiffin could tell she had been letting her imagination run wild, and so responded gently. But having had a month to contemplate his place in both the war and the universe, Kiffin took the opportunity to explain to his mother why he was doing what he was doing, and made clear that his death in France, should that happen, would not be cause for sadness. Whatever President Wilson or his fellow Americans thought of the war, Kiffin was convinced that he was doing what he was meant to do, and if it cost him his life, he was willing to pay that price:

When you write of the chances of my being killed I can see that you have a great horror of it. I don't see anything so horrible in death. Of course, anyone with any feeling at all hates to see anyone they love or all their friends die. I didn't watch a friend of mine continue on after I was wounded because I didn't want to see him if he fell. But if he had fallen, I would have felt proud of him because he did his duty and would have died brave[ly]. So if I was killed I think that you ought to be proud in knowing that your son tried to be a man and wasn't afraid to die, and that he gave his life for a greater cause than most people do – the cause of all humanity. To me that doesn't appear a bad death at all.[41]

Kiffin's straightforward and heartfelt explanation of his motives had one immediate effect – Loula ceased her embarrassing letter-writing campaign to have her boys sent home. But more importantly, it convinced her to see past her fears and glimpse the conflict through Kiffin's eyes. She later said that after reading it, she saw, "for the first time, what impelled" her sons "to go to France, and saw it in the light that they saw it." This proved to be a pivotal moment, not only for Kiffin but for Loula. She explained:

It was this letter that brought me to myself. I realized that my sons were no longer boys to be dictated to, but men, and I felt the seriousness of their purpose. I was proud of their forefathers' fighting spirit that I saw in them, and I honored them for the vision of justice and right that they had caught.[42]

Henceforth, Loula came fully to understand the depth of Kiffin's commitment. Not only that, she also became converted to the justness of his cause, the cause of France. Or, as Kiffin now expressed it, the cause of humanity.

During the ten months her sons had been in France, Loula's osteopathic practice had been sidetracked by her worry and fear, and she eventually left her partnership with Dr. Meacham.[43] Having put her emotions in check and now seeing things as Kiffin saw them, Loula's life began to return to normalcy. She realized she could move forward comforted by the knowledge that whatever came, her sons were where they wished to be, doing what they wanted most to do.

Now working on her own, Loula again picked up the reins of her practice. That summer, she attended the North Carolina Osteopathic Society's convention in late June in Wilmington, where she presented an "exceedingly interesting" talk on "Uterine Displacements." Afterward, the *Osteopathic Physician* reported that "Dr. Rockwell has had a great deal of experience in this work and her talk alone was worth the trip to the city by the sea."[44]

Kiffin also received further support from home. One interesting note came from J.A. Susong, his banker uncle in Newport, Tennessee. Susong noted the change in Loula, saying she had "become more reconciled" to the fact that Kiffin and Paul were in France. He also had a few things of his own to say of the war:

It has given you boys an opportunity that you never would have had otherwise, and as you are now in it, make the very best you can of it, and act in a way that if you should live through the war ... you will come out with bright colors. In other words, whatever you do, do well. Be true, honorable and upright in every respect. Remember that God, who knows all things, is guiding your destiny, and will protect you against scrapnell and bullets, if it is for the best.[45]

* * * * *

In mid-June, two sous-lieutenants from Kiffin's old battalion showed up wounded at his hospital in Rennes. From them Kiffin learned the "very bad news" that his unit had engaged in another big battle a few days earlier and had been, for the most part, wiped out.[46] It seems that after the squad surged through a big hole in the German lines, they had been cut off after reinforcements failed to come up, causing very heavy losses. Based on this new information, Kiffin worriedly told Paul, "I can't see how the Americans could escape at least being wounded."[47] Concerned about the fate of his friends, Kiffin dashed off a letter to Skipper Pavelka.

But Pavelka had already written Kiffin and their letters crossed in the mail. As it turns out, Skipper had been wounded, and was himself recovering at a hospital at Nogent-le-Rotreu. Charging through heavy fire, he had reached the second line of the enemy trenches when a German soldier sprang up and stuck his bayonet through Pavelka's left leg. Skipper reacted like a soldier, and later told another friend that his assailant would never again "stick anyone else on this earth with a bayonet or anything else."[48]

Pavelka's letter also advised Kiffin that their captain had been killed and that Russell Kelly and "John Smith" (really John Earl Fike) had both been wounded. While he did not know about Kenneth Weeks, he hoped to hear good news. Skipper closed his letter:

Well Boy, keep up your courage, and get better so we can go down and pay them back in full. I will try my best not to die in the trenches.[49]

Dying in the trenches was precisely what Kiffin was afraid may have happened to his friend Kenneth Weeks. On the same day Kiffin wrote Pavelka, he also wrote Weeks, hoping to reach him "in some hospital," as Kiffin now considered that a best-case scenario.[50] He offered to send anything Weeks might need, and ended his letter:

Sincerely hoping that this will find you, if not entirely O.K., only slightly wounded,

I am, your friend,

Kiffin Rockwell[51]

Unfortunately, Kiffin's letter was returned bearing a stamp in purple ink: *Retour a l'envoyeur* – return to sender.[52] Kiffin did not yet know it, but his friend was dead. And Kenneth Weeks' passing would have a significant impact on the rest of Kiffin's life.

* * * * *

The year 1915 was half over, yet the war raged on and neither France nor Kiffin showed any signs of backing down. As he neared the end of his eleventh month in France, Kiffin had almost fully recovered from the bullet wound in his thigh. Despite the sacrifices he had made, and the friends he had lost, he did not want out. Indeed, he wanted to get back to the front, and so did his comrades like Pavelka. Although the fighting continued unabated, Kiffin was more committed than ever to France and her cause.

Written by Barrett Wendell, a poem using the year *1915* as its title wonderfully expresses the firm resolve of both Kiffin and the country he had come to love:

Though desolation stain their foiled advance,
In ashen ruins hearth-stones linger whole:
Do what they may, they cannot master France;
Do what they can, they cannot quell the soul.[53]

Chapter Twenty-nine

The time is now ripe for putting through our project.

Back in March, when Norman Prince was pushing to consolidate the Americans in a single flying school, William Thaw, eager to get to the front, had requested instead to be placed with a French *escadrille*, rather than waiting around with the neophyte Americans. Thus, the French assigned Thaw, who had just earned his military brevet, to the newly-formed *Escadrille C.42*, flying under the command of Captain Frank Delaney.[1] This unit was originally placed in Nancy, but relocated about 30 kilometers southeast in early April. Even though he was now a full-blown licensed military aviator, truth be told, Thaw was still rather raw – after he flew his Caudron plane to the new aerodrome in Luneville, he wrote home that "although I am supposed here to be a pretty good *pilote*, it was my first cross-country flight."[2] But he would soon show the French they had not misplaced their trust.

Four days after his arrival, Thaw made his first flight behind the German lines, flying reconnaissance. Although he and his observer were "fired on considerably," they were able to bring back some pretty valuable information. That night, Thaw happily wrote a letter to his folks, telling them, "well, at last I've flown over the Germans, and, believe me, after eight long months of work and waiting, it certainly seems good to feel you're really doing something."[3]

On April 15, Thaw reported he had encountered his first flying Dutchman. He wrote:

Met my first and only "Taube" last Thursday morning and, believe me, I was scared. But so was he, and he beat it straight down, much to my relief, as we were 40 kilometres from our lines.[4]

Escadrille C.42 was used primarily for *reglage* – directing artillery fire. In this task, Thaw and his observer, Lieutenant Andre Felix, rapidly built a record of success. Within two months, Thaw was promoted from private to corporal and from corporal to sergeant. He and Felix performed some brilliant work over the German lines regulating the French artillery fire and were twice mentioned in the orders of the day. According to the citation they received on May 9, the pair flew for more than half an hour "in the midst of explosions," always returning to their point of observation, showing "a tenacity without fear, worthy of praise."[5]

Thaw was rewarded with the *Croix de Guerre,* for which he received all kinds of positive press back in America. The Associated Press picked up the account, and numerous papers ran with the story, all lauding his skill and daring.[6] Two weeks later, a reporter from the *Chicago Daily News* tracked down "the only American aviator actually at the front" with the French. Thaw showed him a square six-inch patch on the lower wing by the fuselage, explaining it was "where a bit of a shrapnel shell came through."[7]

When the reporter pointed out that it must be disconcerting to have shells bursting around one like that, Thaw modestly gave Lieutenant Felix most of the credit:

At first I imagined I was several kinds of hero, but we soon get accustomed to it. The main thing is to have an observer who doesn't lose his nerve. You see, it is harder on him than it is on the pilot.... The observer, not the pilot, is the man who usually signals to return to camp when the shrapnel gets disagreeably close. But the observer I have now absolutely does not seem to have the slightest feeling about it at all. Nothing would cause him to wish to turn back.... Once when shrapnel was bursting within fifty or seventy-five feet of us, four shells at a time, I touched him on the shoulder and inquired by signs if he wished to go back. He merely smiled, shrugged his shoulders and went on with his work. That sort of thing gives a pilot a lot of confidence. So, you see, much depends upon the observer.[8]

Thaw also got along well with the other pilots in the squadron, including Georges Thénault, a French pilot promoted from lieutenant to captain around the same time Thaw was made sergeant.[9] Later that summer Thénault would be given command of *Escadrille C.42,* and over time he and Thaw would form a strong friendship. Like everyone else, Thénault surely appreciated his American friend's sense of humor – with the other pilots at a feast celebrating his promotion, the ever-witty Thaw observed the fancy spread and quipped, "It is hard, the life of the aviator at the front."[10]

* * * * *

Although the reporter from the *Chicago Daily News* did not know it, Thaw was not the only American aviator at the front. After they received their military licenses, Norman Prince and Elliott Cowdin had both been sent to the depot at Le Bourget to await assignment. A week and a half later, they were ordered to fly two planes to Bruay-en-Artois, a district northwest of Arras, where they were to join *Escadrille V.B.108*, a Voisin bomber squadron flying missions over German lines. Thus, by the end of May there were actually three American pilots at the front – Thaw, Prince and Cowdin.[11]

By June, Thaw was contemplating transferring to Italy or the Dardanelles to fly hydroaeroplanes, as he had before the war,[12] but Prince and Cowdin were still hoping to form an all-American squadron. Cowdin said he and Prince had been "promised that as soon as the other American pilots were ready we would be recalled to Bourget that we all might start aviation work as an American unit."[13] However, it was not clear when that would be – Bach and Hall were still struggling through flight school, while Ruel was recovering from his broken leg and Curtis was in a military hospital, too nervous to fly after his smash-ups.

While waiting for the lagging aviators, Cowdin and Prince settled in at Bruay-en-Artois with *Escadrille V.B.108*. A month and a half after their arrival, Cowdin wrote that he and Prince had been "sitting tight, doing our work and waiting for an opportunity to present itself whereby we may either form the *American Escadrille* or better ourselves."[14]

For those first six weeks, there was more of an opportunity for the latter than the former. The two Americans were kept quite busy flying bombing missions over the German lines in Voisins, a lumbering, French-made bomber. Prince wrote one of his cousins in Boston that flying the Voisin was "just like flying in a locomotive," as it gave one "a feeling of unlimited power."[15] But Cowdin did not care for the Voisin at all, saying it was "a great heavy slow machine which makes but 80 kilometres an hour," and was "very difficult [and] tremendously fatiguing to pilot."[16]

Nonetheless, located about ten miles from the German border, the men were "in the thick of the fighting" which, Cowdin said, "keeps us busy and on the jump."[17] The day they arrived was the first time Prince had seen the front and the first time he heard "the never-ending boom of guns." "This is war in dead earnest and right at hand," he relayed to a family member. Within a week, he told his brother Freddy he had "become quite accustomed to being shot at."[18]

From the beginning, Prince and Cowdin went on bombing runs at least once a day, sometimes twice, striking ammunition depots, railroad tracks, trains and *"Boche"* headquarters, when they could find out where they were located. Sometime after their arrival, Prince wrote that he and Cowdin had "done eight bombardments in seven days and are 'in right' here."[19] On these missions, they took plenty of shells from enemy "verticals," the numerous anti-aircraft gunners. Prince found it "very curious" how the shells could "explode near us and not cripple the machine enough to cause it to come down in German lines."[20]

He later referred to his first flight over the lines as his "baptism of fire," admitting that though he felt "confident and unafraid, my legs began to tremble." In fact, Prince's legs were at first "so wobbly from nervous excitement" that he tried to hide them from his observer. Still, he kept straight on course, saying "I would not have changed it for the world."[21] After just a month at the front, Prince became a bit more accustomed to the shells, and felt it would take a "very lucky punch" to bring him down. "Nowadays," he said nonchalantly, "I smoke my pipe quietly, and if a shell bursts too close I change my direction."[22] Around this same time, he wrote:

Every other time out, just about, we get shrapnel holes somewhere in our machines, but so far have had the good fortune not to be brought down. Since our arrival our captain and two of the under officers of our escadrille have been brought down, but only one had to land in Bocherie – as we call the other side of the German lines.... We think nothing here of breaking machines or gripping motors: it is part of the game. You can't cook an omelette without breaking eggs.[23]

Early on, according to Cowdin, the German aeroplanes would "turn tail and descend as soon as a French machine appears."[24] That was just as well, given the slowness of the Voisin. But when the Germans began to attack from the air as well, things could get rather dicey. Cowdin wrote that he had several "narrow escapes due entirely to lack of speed."[25] According to Cowdin, his most "interesting & formidable experience" came on June 26 when he was attacked by a pair of two-gun Aviatiks twenty kilometers behind enemy lines. He described it this way:

[Aviatiks] are very fast machines so naturally we are at a tremendous disadvantage & the only chance we have is to face them. So after facing the one nearest me on my left, we all started blazing away & fortunately my passenger was a good shot [and] brought him down. [The Aviatik] turned over & with his motor all ablaze plunged down 2600 metres to the earth

below us, a wonderful sight. But this did not happen until they had filled us full of lead. My radiator, engine & left aileron were smashed to pieces, to say nothing of bullet holes in our wings, four in the casque of my passenger & one in mine. Of course, I had to return by volplane, always under a heavy shell fire & when I crossed the German lines at 1200 metres the mitrailleuses in the trenches all showed me [their] best intentions. I don't know to this day how we ever managed to land safely just back of our lines. For this little experience [and] my other raids, I may add that I have been proposed for sergeant and given a citation a l'ordre des Armees with the right to wear the Croix de Guerre with a palm.[26]

The feat landed Cowdin on the front page of the *New York Tribune*, although it failed to mention his observer – in the paper's telling, Cowdin had supposedly brought down the German while operating his plane with one hand and a machine gun with the other.[27] Regardless, he was maturing into a fine pilot; his friend Prince noted that Cowdin was "flying very steadily," and had taken well to "getting saluted" while flying over the enemy's lines.[28]

Prince was closing in on his own citation, and in June participated in more bombings than any pilot in the entire *Third Group de Bombardement*. On July 2, the *escadrille* took part in a bombing raid of a German aviation field, about which he reported "we raised hell with it, two hangars burning while I was there."[29]

Prince had also been promoted (to corporal), and overall, he and Cowdin were making a name for themselves, both in France and back home. Still in full pursuit of his goal of forming an American squadron, on July 8, Prince wrote a letter to a friend summarizing where things stood:

Our plans – and we have been assured lately they would be carried out – are to form an Escadrille Américaine *as soon as all eight Americans are ready. Six of them already have their 'brevet militaires' and four of them are at the front. Two of them (Cowdin and Thaw) have been decorated. Not so bad, is it?*[30]

Just two days earlier, Cowdin had written John Jay Chapman, providing details as to the "present standing and whereabouts" of each of the American pilots. He wrote:

Thaw [has] been on the front for some time in the south of France flying Caudrons. Bach and Hall have both passed their brevet militaires and are at Le Bourget waiting for orders and flying Caudrons. Curtis is in Paris, finishing his last days of a forty-five days convalescence and will return to Avord to rejoin Ruel, who has now recovered from the effects of his broken leg, in trying to pass their brevets militaires again on [the] Voisin.[31]

Asserting that Curtis and Ruel had "failed utterly and miserably in their first attempt," Cowdin did not have much faith that those two men would succeed upon their return to Avord. He suspected (correctly as it turned out), that they had lost all confidence in mastering the Voisin, and so imagined there would be "a repetition of their last disgraceful and unfortunate performances." He charitably noted, however, that at Pau the two pilots had passed their *brevet militaires* on the Caudron.[32]

Accordingly, Cowdin felt that if all the men were put on Caudrons, he and Prince could quickly get their squadron formed, for even Curtis and Ruel had achieved their licenses on those machines. Speaking bluntly, he told Chapman: "Prince & myself are both young & naturally ambitious & we want to do something worthwhile. Now that the opportunity has arrived we want to form the American *Escadrille*..." Stating that he could take Chapman's son Victor as his observer, Cowdin suggested that all the American pilots could do likewise – that is, adopt an American observer. Then, once they reached the front, they could teach those observers to fly and double the *escadrille* in no time. "The first thing you know," said Cowdin, "we will have a large American Flying Squadron. Why not?"[33]

With things progressing nicely (at least for he and Prince), Cowdin confidently told Chapman, "the time is now ripe for putting through our project."[34]

* * * * *

As his own and Ruel's injuries caused Frazier Curtis to worry about the future of the *escadrille*, he had begun pushing Prince to enlarge the squadron to account for attrition among the volunteers. But according to Curtis, Prince "was opposed to this increase, which caused considerable coldness" between he and Curtis, as well as Cowdin, who sided with Prince.[35] Despite this opposition, while in Paris at the beginning of his 45-day medical leave, Curtis spoke with de Sillac about enlarging the planned American *escadrille* to a full corps.[36]

Having from the beginning sensed the potential impact of an American unit, de Sillac liked the idea of a bigger group staffed and paid for by Americans. He suggested to Curtis that they prepare a pamphlet to send to the best university men in America, recruiting them to come and fly for France.[37] Still on convalescence and not flying, Curtis assured de Sillac he would work on it. He also spent some time in Neuilly, a suburb of Paris, canvassing for possible aviators among the university men who had signed up with the American Ambulance.

While spreading the word among the volunteer drivers, Curtis heard about Dr. Edmund Gros, an official of the American Hospital, founded in 1908 for expatriate Americans in Paris. Many of Doctor Gros' patients were drawn from the wealthy elite of America, and he was well-connected in both American and French society. When the war broke out, Gros and a group of wealthy Americans immediately proposed to equip and maintain at their own expense a hospital for French soldiers, if the French government would provide a building suitable for that purpose.[38]

The French readily accepted the offer, and so turned over the nearly complete campus meant for the *Lycee Pasteur*, a secondary school not far from the hospital in Neuilly. The Americans quickly transformed the buildings into "a vast hospital, with every improvement then known to the world."[39] It was known as the American Ambulance.[40]

Gros was pro-French and pro-American. Following the sinking of the *Lusitania*, along with one hundred other Americans in Paris, he signed a cablegram stating, in part, "in order to preserve our self-respect we must voice an energetic and indignant protest against the sinking of the *Lusitania*, an act pre-eminent in its savagery, and which places the responsible Government outside civilized humanity."[41] In early and mid-1915, as he witnessed the stream of splendid young men like Jim McConnell coming from America to volunteer as ambulance drivers, Doctor Gros began to think of them in other capacities, including as aviators. He later explained that he was "dreaming of a *squadrilla* of American volunteers who would express their sympathy for France in a material form."[42]

Having already met with de Sillac to convince him of the benefits of enlarging the planned squadron, when Curtis learned Gros had similar ideas, he wrote him at once:

Dear Dr. Gros:

I went to the Ambulance today to see if I could find any drivers who wanted to join the French Aviation Service. The government is willing to train 100 American flyers and to keep them together in one Corps. Men of flying experience would be preferred, but those of apparent aptitude (knowledge of French, gas engines, etc.) will be acceptable. [I am told] you are keen on getting up a big Corps, so we ought to be able to work together. I would like to introduce you to one of my friends who is pretty much running this enlarged Corps. I am here on sick leave, three accidents having left me pretty well jarred up. I expect to go to the seaside for a good rest in a day or two, but am very anxious to see you first.

Sincerely yours,

Frazier Curtis[43]

In a meeting which would prove pivotal to the future of Prince's planned squadron, Curtis met with Gros and introduced him to de Sillac. As the first biographer of the unit put it, "Upon meeting M. de Sillac, and a little later, Norman Prince, Dr. Gros joined forces with them, and from that time on took an increasingly active and important part in the organization and development of what was to become the Lafayette Flying Corps."[44]

* * * * *

Soon enough, Gros and de Sillac had, along with American lawyer Frederick Allen, formed the so-called Franco-American Committee to oversee the establishment of a group of American pilots. The Committee soon involved Robert Bacon in their efforts. A former State Department official under Theodore Roosevelt and ambassador to France under President Taft, Bacon met with Curtis and "agreed to do what he could" – *if* a meeting could be arranged with General Auguste Hirschauer, the director of French Military Aeronautics.[45]

However, for some reason or other (likely because he was busy fighting a war) Hirschauer was in no hurry to sit down with the former ambassador, and by the time Curtis returned from the seashore near the end of his 45-day leave, Bacon still had not met with the general. On July 6, Curtis saw Bacon at the Ambulance and learned he was returning to the states in a few days. Knowing they could not afford to lose this opportunity, Curtis returned to his hotel and wrote a letter to de Sillac "playing Bacon's friendship with [Theodore] Roosevelt as my trump card."[46] Curtis later shared what he had written in this letter:

I said that Bacon was a close personal & political friend of Roosevelt. That if Bacon could see Hirschauer [and] present a definite scheme, he could undoubtedly get Roosevelt's support. That such support meant at least 1,000 suitable volunteers [and] money enough to train them. That Bacon was a very busy man who had to leave in three days for the U.S., & finally that if France wanted to have 1,000 American pilots with all the political prestige attached, Hirschauer would have to see Bacon in three days or lose the opportunity forever.[47]

The note worked – the next day de Sillac phoned Curtis to tell him a lunch had been arranged. It would take place the following day, July 8, 1915, at the Paris home of Senator Gaston Menier. Bacon, Gros, and de Sillac were each invited, as well as General Hirschauer and various French senators and deputies. While the precise details of the meeting are unknown, Gros later wrote that Bacon and Hirschauer discussed the matter of American neutrality as it concerned the proposed flying unit and concluded "there existed no international law which forbade Americans from enlisting individually in a foreign army – as long as the recruiting was not carried out in America."[48]

Whatever else was discussed at this luncheon, those pushing the concept finally achieved some concrete results – General Hirschauer was "persuaded of the feasibility and benefits" of an American squadron and agreed to issue an order for the formation of a unit to be called the *Escadrille Américaine*.[49] From this point forward, Prince's idea was no longer a question of *if*, but *when*. Curtis, who returned to America a month later, stated: "My work in France was done. After that lunch, all hell could not stop the corps."[50]

* * * * *

As Gros quickly realized, now that they had succeeded in getting permission to form a separate American squadron, it was necessary to obtain funds "for monthly allowances, uniforms, distribution of prizes, printing of pamphlets, etc."[51] Thus, before he returned to the United States, Bacon accompanied Gros to visit William K. Vanderbilt. Bacon had promised General Hirschauer he would get "men & money," and Vanderbilt had the latter covered.[52]

Like other members of that family, William K. Vanderbilt was a very wealthy man. Having inherited a vast fortune from his father (the eldest son of Commodore Cornelius Vanderbilt), William spent much of his time building magnificent houses and engaging in thoroughbred horse racing in France, where his horses won a number of important races.[53] He was also very charitable and provided generous support for the American Ambulance when that group was organized shortly after the war broke out. Like many other

Americans abroad, Vanderbilt "was strongly opposed to the neutrality of the United States," a position which must have hardened following the death of his nephew Alfred G. Vanderbilt, who had been warned not to book passage on the *Lusitania*.[54] A warm admirer of the American volunteers in the Foreign Legion, Vanderbilt often wished there was something tangible he could do to express his support.

In short, Gros and Bacon had come to the right man. Or woman, rather – Gros recalled that the squadron's "financial question was quickly solved." He explained:

I called with Robert Bacon on Mr. and Mrs. W.K. Vanderbilt. We spoke with warmth of our plans. Our enthusiasm must have been contagious for when I appealed for funds, Mrs. Vanderbilt walked to her desk and wrote out a check for five thousand dollars – and turning to her husband said: "Now, K., what will you do?" His check read fifteen thousand dollars. With this sum in hand, it looked as though our dream was really coming true![55]

Gros later said that "from the first" Vanderbilt had "grasped the importance of the movement and had a vision of what it would mean for America in the future, because none of us ever doubted that our country would finally take her place."[56] Indeed, these initial donations were just the start of a steady stream of funds that would supply the squadron with everything it needed over the course of the war. Several months after America finally entered the war in 1917, Gros stated that the "financial side" of the *escadrille* had been "supported almost entirely by one man" – W.K. Vanderbilt.[57]

That took care of the money, now they needed the men. As a result, despite Bacon and Hirschauer's apparent understanding to avoid recruiting in America, the brief account prepared by Curtis soon became the nucleus of a recruiting pamphlet, to be sent to recent graduates of many elite American universities.[58] Indeed, someone (probably Curtis) was speaking to the press, for the week following the meeting with Hirschauer, several articles appeared in American papers mentioning the squadron, taking care to emphasize the angle most likely to skirt the messy issue of neutrality – that volunteering would assist America with its own preparedness.

For example, on July 15, 1915, the *Chicago Tribune* ran a detailed article stating that one thousand American airplanes, flown by American volunteers, were to be tendered to France, allowing American aviators to train "in the practical, perilous school that the war affords."[59] The paper assured its readers that this would benefit America, because once the pilots were properly trained, their military experience would "qualify them to become reserve aviators in the United States." Staying with this theme, the article noted that "10,000 circulars are to be issued to the graduates of Yale, Harvard and Princeton, inviting them on patriotic grounds to aid in strengthening the defenses of their country."[60]

Although the referenced pamphlet would not be issued for a few more months, it made the case that this undertaking was of great importance to America, emphasizing that "whether the United States should be drawn into the present struggle or not, they will need military aviators, and above all, they will need competent instructors in war aviation." It further asserted that "German hegemony in Europe would be a permanent menace to the liberty of the world, as well as to the security of the United States," and ended the discussion with this prescient comment:

We believe that the Franco-American Flying Corps will show the world what America could do if provoked and forced into war.[61]

Chapter Thirty

We are all changed.

By the middle of June, Kiffin's wound was almost fully healed and he was growing restless. Stiff muscles were the only lingering effect of the bullet, and Kiffin told Paul he was "tired of the hospital and either want to be where I can do as I please or back at the front line."[1] Due to some administrative rules, Kiffin first had to be transferred to a convalescent hospital before he could be discharged to take any recuperative leave. On June 24, Kiffin was finally moved, then a few days later told he had been granted a full month's permission in Paris. He eagerly awaited his papers and excitedly planned his trip.

Once the paperwork arrived, Kiffin made his way to Paris, arriving right at the beginning of July. Kiffin was delighted to have a full month off with his brother and excited to visit Paris again, as this was to be his first extended time there since boarding that troop train to Rouen a little more than ten months earlier. Somehow, he felt much older than he had during those first frenzied weeks of mobilization and war.

What a time to visit Paris – a city at once modern and ancient, sparkling and filthy, fleeting and eternal. Apropos of the American volunteers, someone once called Paris "that jewel of civilization, where each of us offers and acquires what is best in us."[2] René Besnard, who would later replace General Hirschauer as director of aviation, once said "Paris belongs to the common inheritance of mankind..."[3]

Surely many of the Americans felt that way – in a sense, Paris was the living embodiment of all they were fighting for, and when there, they must have felt a special pride and a connection to the city, to one another, and to the cause for which they were fighting. In fact, earlier that year, the poet Seeger had named loyalty to the city as the reason underlying his own enlistment and that of his former Latin Quarter friends:

Paris – mystic, maternal, personified, to whom they owed the happiest moments of their lives – Paris was in peril. Were they not under a moral obligation, no less binding than their comrades were bound legally, to put their breasts between her and destruction? Without renouncing their nationality, they had yet chosen to make their homes here beyond any other city in the world. Did not the benefits and blessings they had received point them a duty that heart and conscience could not deny?[4]

But even before he arrived at the *Hotel Beauvau*, where he was to spend the month with Paul, Kiffin could sense a different mood.[5] Signs posted on the trains and on placards all around Paris reminded travelers: "*Taisez-vous! Mefiez-vous! Des oreilles ennemies vous écoutent!*" – Shut up! Beware! Enemy ears are listening to you! And while one could still find spectators and crowds on the boulevards and at the sidewalk cafés, instead of the fresh young soldiers of August 1914, brimming with confidence and ready to hit the *boche*, now many of the few men found in Paris were either weary *permissionaires* (men on furlough) or crippled *mutilés* (men who had lost a limb). In the year since the war began, the city had grown accustomed to men in uniform – and to women in mourning. After spending a week there, Kiffin wrote the following in a letter to his mother:

Paris is very sad now and we all wish the war could end, but I have very little hope of that being any time soon because the only peace that would be any good is a peace of complete victory, which will take time, for the Germans are still strong.[6]

While Kiffin was not familiar enough with the city to realize it fully, the war had changed Paris. One volunteer soldier described the subtle transformation that had taken place:

Since the outbreak of the war, the sham Paris that was "Gay Paree" had disappeared, and the real Paris, the Paris of tragic memories and great men, had taken its place. An old Parisian explained the change to me in saying, "Paris has become more French." Deprived of the foreigner, the city adapted itself to a taste more Gallic; faced with the realities of war, it exchanged its artificiality for that sober reasonableness which is the normal attitude of the nation.[7]

"Paris is calmly waiting," the soldier concluded – "waiting for the end of the war, for victory, for the return of her children."[8]

* * * * *

Their hotel was not far from the *Champs Elysses* and the *Place de la*

Concorde, and Kiffin was thrilled to explore the city and spend time with his brother. This was the first time he had all to himself in a year, and he wanted to enjoy it. Within the first week, he met Paul's fiancée and her mother; he reported to Loula that they were "awful nice people and very influential in France."[9] Kiffin also met a husband and wife with whom he had corresponded, the Vicomte and Vicomtesse du Peloux. Loula had connected with them through a friend in Asheville, and the couple had taken an interest in her boys, sending little things to Kiffin in the trenches and handling his and Paul's affairs in Paris. Kiffin felt they were "two of the finest people I ever knew," and they treated he and Paul "as if we were their own children."[10]

While much about Paris was different, much remained the same. The theatres and shops were open and there were plenty of activities with which a *permissionaire* could fill his time. A week into his stay, Kiffin told his mother he was "always on the go," and had "hardly had a minute to myself since I arrived here."[11] Kiffin loved the city, and everyone he met treated him well. His French uniform certainly helped – as one American pilot later put it, "[a]lthough it is not as gay as in peace times, yet Paris still loves a soldier."[12]

Likewise, the soldiers still loved Paris. One of these was young Edmond Genet, who was in the city just after the Fourth of July. In his diary, he recorded one of the reasons a soldier might prefer Paris to the trenches: "The people here – particularly the ladies – are mighty nice and agreeable. They can't quite conceive of an American being in the service of the French. It strikes me as very funny of them to think that. Why shouldn't we?"[13]

Another American in the service of the French, Paul Pavelka, received seven days' leave following his bayonet injury and joined the Rockwell boys in Paris on July 14. They spent the next week together strengthening their friendship, and the little group of Americans received numerous invitations to dine. On July 18, along with Zinovi Pechkoff (another soldier from Kiffin's regiment), the three of them had lunch with Alice Weeks, the mother of their missing friend and fellow legionnaire Kenneth Weeks. Of these four soldiers, Mrs. Weeks wrote:

They are such fine fellows with the true spirit of fighting for civilization and freedom. As they say, a man can do no more, and they consider they have had a successful life even if they are killed.[14]

Following the Foreign Legion's battle north of Arras in May, Kenneth Weeks had written his mother, who evidently had been misinformed that he had been wounded in the taking of the German trenches. "No," he told her, "I have not been wounded. A chap named Rockwell was shot in the knee and [the source] mixed him up with me. If you see him (Rockwell), by the way, be kind to him."[15]

Respecting her son's request, Kenneth's mother *was* kind to Kiffin, and to Paul. On July 20, Kiffin wrote Loula that he and Paul had been spending "much time with Mrs. Weeks ... the mother of one of the Americans who was with me."[16]

Alice Weeks had traveled extensively in Europe and had access to influential Parisians. A wealthy woman from Boston, she was unafraid of speaking her mind and standing up for what she thought was right, a trait her son Kenneth obviously inherited from her. Something of her manner and feelings can be gleaned from her encounter with the American ambassador in late May, which she described in a note to her brother:

I had a talk with our ambassador the other day, and he did not seem to understand what prompted the American boys to join the Foreign Legion. He said very emphatically, 'You know our President has asked the people to be neutral.' This started me on a long harangue about our love of freedom and also our connection with France through Lafayette. I also added that those who had lived [in] and loved France before the war should be willing to fight for her and I felt proud that our boys had the courage to do what they considered was right, which after all is what our country must depend on in time of trouble. I was warm and I must say he was very patient and said, 'You know, I believe you have more power than I have over here.' I said, 'Of course, because I am a woman.' Perhaps this was poor taste on my part, but I must fight for the boys who have so often been classed as adventurers and soldiers of fortune.[17]

And Mrs. Weeks certainly did "fight for the boys." Indeed, she later became a sort of surrogate mother for many of the Americans and even some of the French, who would come to know her as *Maman Legionnaire* – the Mother of the Legion.[18] Beginning in July 1915 with Kiffin and Paul, over time her Paris home became a sort of unofficial headquarters and information exchange for legion soldiers and pilots. It was later written:

The opening of a home in Paris for the men who were associated with her son was an idea which came to Mrs. Weeks gradually but naturally. Soldiers came; they came again, bringing others.[19]

Once America entered the war, her idea eventually morphed into the Home Service for American Soldiers Abroad.[20] While Mrs. Weeks cared for all the boys, from the beginning she loved Kiffin especially, and did all she could to make him comfortable and happy. Loula later wrote to him that her "greatest earthly comfort" was that Mrs. Weeks "will do for you as if you were her own."[21] In a scrapbook she kept, under a picture of Mrs. Weeks, Loula wrote: "she made a home for Kiffin and loved him as her own son."[22]

The bond between Kiffin and Mrs. Weeks was immediate; the first letter Kiffin sent after leaving Paris he addressed to "My Dear Second Mother."[23] In Alice Weeks, Kiffin had found an advocate and ally. And she had the connections to make a difference.

* * * * *

For some time, Mrs. Weeks had been urging her son Kenneth to pursue an opportunity she had lined up for him – in aviation. In fact, less than two weeks before Kiffin came to Paris, Mrs. Weeks had written the following to her other son in America:

I have been keeping at [Kenneth] for two weeks to make out a demand for the aeroplane service. For some reason he has not sent it and says now that he will after this time at the front. I have a wonderful chance for him and heard directly from the Minister of War this morning, saying if Kenneth would send the demand, it would be all right.[24]

Unfortunately, although Mrs. Weeks did not know it at the time, two days before she wrote the above letter, her son Kenneth had been killed in battle. He had volunteered to be his squad's bomb thrower, and was last seen "running towards the third line of the German trenches, his right arm extended, and facing the enemy."[25] Just before that battle, Kenneth had written his mother that the regiment was readying for another advance and stated, "In view of this attack, I think I may as well wait until afterwards about my demand for the aviation."[26]

When Kiffin arrived in Paris just two weeks later, Mrs. Weeks had heard nothing further from Kenneth. As it turned out, that was the last letter she would ever receive from her son.

* * * * *

Passing by a Paris café one day in late July, Kiffin and Paul were pleased to see their old trench mate Bill Thaw having a glass of beer. They sat down with him and during the course of their conversation, Kiffin "complained that he wasn't able to walk very well." Thaw, who was on leave from his post at the front with *Escadrille C.42*, replied, "Well, you ought to transfer to aviation."[27]

Paul later stated that this happenstance meeting was the impetus for Kiffin leaving the Foreign Legion and seeking a transfer into aviation, and there is ample evidence for this conclusion. For one thing, Kiffin's and Thaw's time in Paris overlapped for one week, as Thaw's leave began on July 24, and Kiffin did not depart Paris until July 31, so it is a safe bet that they saw one another.[28] Moreover, as General Hirschauer had indicated just two weeks earlier that he would group the Americans together, Thaw would have learned that the squadron was at last becoming a reality and fully aligned himself with Prince and Cowdin's developing plan for an American Escadrille.

Indeed, just six weeks later Thaw was openly recruiting for the squadron. On September 8, he wrote a letter to the editor of the *New York Herald* positing the following question: how could Americans "prepare themselves to be of service to their country" in the event the United States eventually entered the war.

In answer, Thaw suggested that enterprising and patriotic American men should do as he had done – enlist with the French aviation for the duration of the war and "learn to fly in France[.]" In this way, they could "become thoroughly trained pilots" and "get some very practical experience in wartime aviation," which, Thaw said, would "be invaluable to our country in case of war."[29]

Thaw further noted that he was one of nine American aviators now serving France, with eleven more in training, each of whom had "enlisted separately at various times since the beginning of hostilities with exactly the above purpose in view." Now, he and the others were "endeavoring to get together in an American *Escadrille* to be later on enlarged by just such enthusiastic and patriotic men" – that is, those who came from America to help out.[30]

Given these facts, it is very likely that while both were in Paris at the end of July, Thaw and Kiffin discussed the possibility of Kiffin transferring to aviation and getting grouped with the American pilots.[31] But that does not tell the whole story of Kiffin's switch, for it leaves out the large role played by Mrs. Weeks.

On July 24, still not knowing of her son's death (although she learned that morning that Kenneth was officially posted as missing), Mrs. Weeks wrote that she had "become very fond of Kiffin and Paul Rockwell ... and it is going to be hard to let them go back. I am going to try to get Kiffin Rockwell into the aeroplane service."[32] That week, probably at the instigation of Mrs. Weeks, Kiffin had "a long talk" with Ambassador Sharp. Kiffin wrote his mother what had happened:

He told me that owing to the letter he received from you he went to the War Department and tried to get Paul and me released. I was awfully sorry to hear that he had done that; but he offered to do anything possible for me. So I asked him to go back to those people and explain things to them, and tell them I regret that the request had been made, very much. I hope to get a few favors from the War Department now, so want to fix things with them.[33]

Kiffin must have met with the ambassador to see about being switched to aviation, for when he left Paris, he hoped and expected to be transferred without delay. The first day after he left, he wrote to Mrs. Weeks that he figured he would "soon be changed, or returned to the front."[34] That same day, Mrs. Weeks wrote her other son, telling him: "I hope before long we will be able to get [Kiffin] into the aviation."[35] And just a few days later, Kiffin wrote Paul that "If by any chance I am not transferred to the aviation, they ought to at least put me in a French regiment."[36]

Thus, while Thaw surely had something to do with it as well, the evidence shows that Kiffin filled the aviation slot Mrs. Weeks had secured for Kenneth. Direct confirmation of this was contained in a letter Loula received a couple weeks later. While we do not have the letter itself, the next day the local paper printed the details, confirming that Kiffin took Kenneth's place. On August 17, 1915, under the title "Kiffin Rockwell to Join Air Fighters," the *Asheville Citizen* reported that Kiffin would join the French aviation service. The article contained this paragraph, obviously from information supplied by Loula, who had just received the letter from France:

The Asheville young man received this commission by reason of the activities in his behalf by Mrs. Alice Weeks ... whose son had been given a place as a member of the aeroplane fighting force. Mr. Weeks enlisted in the foreign legion at the same time that Mr. Rockwell joined it and his mother had completed arrangements for the enrollment of her son on the list of air fighters when a message from the front was to the effect that he was among the missing. It is not known whether he was killed or taken as a prisoner by the Germans. Mrs. Weeks ... sent for [Kiffin] and advised him of her desire to have him take the place of her son. He consented to do so, believing that the aeroplane service offers a great field for service. Arrangements were completed immediately for his transfer.[37]

Not only was the idea of an American flying unit taking shape, but events had transpired to make Kiffin a part of it. Kiffin's destiny was coming into sight.

* * * * *

Kiffin's last night in Paris was July 31. He and Paul, along with Pechkoff (who had lost his right arm in the same battle in which Kiffin was shot through the thigh) had dinner with Mrs. Weeks. After dinner, Mrs. Weeks and Paul accompanied Kiffin to his train. Mrs. Weeks wrote of the scene:

The station was full of women seeing their men off and the soldiers were holding their babies in their arms. A strange contrast. I was surprised to see everything so quiet. Not a sob anywhere as in the beginning. We are all changed.[38]

We are all changed.

That statement was certainly true for Kiffin Rockwell, soldier of France. The war towards which he had so innocently rushed nearly twelve months before had changed Kiffin in ways he could not possibly have imagined when he boarded the *St. Paul* in New York City. It had changed his feelings towards life and living, death and dying, and the purpose he was meant to serve on this earth. He knew what war was now, and with full knowledge of the consequences and eyes wide open, he was going back. Raw courage, curiosity and a sense of responsibility had been replaced by principle, mature reflection and his own deliberate, voluntary choice. Kiffin had finally found his place, but now knew what that might ultimately mean.

As the train began to move and he waved good-bye to his brother and "second mother" on the platform, Kiffin must have felt a swirl of emotions. Although he was excited about the prospect of transferring to aviation, the fact that his good friend Kenneth was confirmed missing and likely dead surely tempered his anticipation. On the other hand, it also increased Kiffin's desire to do the best he could, as he would be serving as Kenneth's proxy.

Once the train was underway, Kiffin opened the letter Mrs. Weeks had pressed into his hands at the station. As he read, Kiffin reflected on how the war had changed him, and everything else. Maybe he thought of those who had died, or were missing, men like Corporal Weidemann, Rene Phelizot and Kenneth Weeks. Mrs. Weeks' words struck a deep chord and, although Kiffin was never one to become emotional, he cried.

The next day, Kiffin wrote Mrs. Weeks that his train ride back to the front was "the saddest night in my life." Through the instrument of war, Kiffin had stepped into a world larger than himself and his own needs and wants. Still filled with the desire to do what he could to see that right prevailed, he again resolved to stand fast by his commitment, whatever sacrifice that involved.

Now primed for immortality, Kiffin explained to Mrs. Weeks his thoughts and feelings:

I was not sad because I was going back to the war but ... from thinking of the ones who stay behind. I was in a second-class coach and very comfortable, but I couldn't sleep. I just thought and thought all night long and couldn't keep the tears out of my eyes. I want to live now more than I ever did in my life but not from the selfish standpoint. This war has taught me many things and now I want to live to do whatever good is possible. But if I am killed anytime in the war I will not be afraid to die, and you may know that I will die like a man should, feeling that it is the greatest death that a man can die.[39]

End of Part Two

This photograph was taken near the Cáfe de La Paix on August 25, 1914, as the American Volunteer Corps crossed the Place de L'Opéra. It ran in the August 26, 1914 edition of the New York Herald in Paris, over the caption "The Departure of American Volunteers." Image courtesy of Washington and Lee University.

The caption in Loula's scrapbook states "En route to front, Oct. 1, 1914, Paul sitting."
Image from the State Archives of North Carolina.

Kiffin (left) and Paul (right) must have just received their equipment and new uniforms when this photograph was taken at the Perignon Barracks in Toulouse on September 14, 1914. Image courtesy of Washington and Lee University.

Back row, left to right: Georges Casmeze, Charles Sweeny, John Casey, Bert Hall.
Front row, left to right: J.S. Carstairs, William Thaw, J.J. Bach.

This photograph was take in Toulouse on September 17, 1914, and ran in the December 4, 1914 edition of the New York Herald in Paris, over the caption "American Volunteers in French Army."

Kiffin in the foreground, with Dennis Dowd standing to his right and Charles Trinkard visible behind. Image courtesy of Washington and Lee University.

(left to right) Dennis Dowd, Kiffin, Fred Capdeveille, Charles Trinkard and Edward Morlae, Cuiry-les-Chaudardes, winter 1914-1915. Image from the State Archives of North Carolina.

Chateau du Blanc Sablon in Craonnelle. Image taken from a postcard in the public domain.

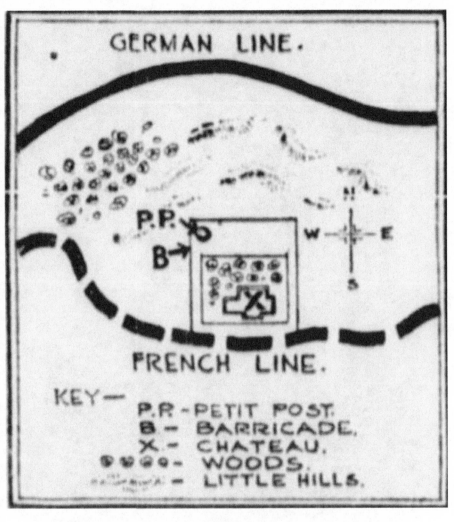

This hand-drawn map accompanied "Coolness of Americans Saves Outpost in France," an account published in the New York Sun on February 2, 1915, a little more than three weeks after the attack at the Chateau du Blanc Sablon.

Kenneth Weeks, Kiffin's friend in the Foreign Legion. Image from the State Archives of North Carolina.

Alan Seeger served in the Ninth Squadron with Kiffin and Paul. Image courtesy of the Newberry Library, from the Paul Scott Mowrer collection, box 12.

Alice Weeks, Kiffin's "second mother." Image from the State Archives of North Carolina.

Kiffin (far right), probably during his convalescence at Military Hospital No. 101 in Rennes. Image from the State Archives of North Carolina.

Kiffin and Paul in Paris, July 1915. Image courtesy of Washington and Lee University.

Part Three - Destiny

"If this war is the greatest that history has recorded, it is not because people are striking at one another for the conquest of territories, openings, the aggrandizement of material comforts, political and economic advantages; it is because they are striking at one another to settle the fate of the world. Nothing greater has ever appeared to the sight of man..."

- M. Renè Viviani, Speech in Parliament on December 22, 1914[1]

The stars are like a myriad eyes
My inmost soul to scan,
And every star a challenge cries:
"Who rides God's highway in the skies
To wage the war of man?"

- Extract from "The Airman's Creed," by Owen Oliver[2]

Chapter Thirty-one

The most interesting thing I have ever done...

Kiffin was not the only soldier looking toward the skies. In a war fought to stalemate in the trenches, aerial warfare created a new class of combatants and provided an opportunity for individual recognition entirely absent on the ground. Edmond Genet surely understated the matter when on August 11, 1915, he wrote in his diary that transferring from the trenches to aviation "would mean heaps more individuality for me over here in the service."[3] In a letter to a friend, another pilot emphatically stated, "Beyond a doubt this is the most fascinating game on the face of the earth."[4]

While aviation was even more dangerous than the trenches, many soldiers preferred the sky. One of those soldiers was Genet, who felt aviation was what one could call "the real thing."[5] While he acknowledged that flying was "the most dangerous branch of the service," Genet felt the glory "well worth the loss."[6] He surely spoke for others when he told his family: "I'd far rather die as an aviator over the enemy's lines than find a nameless, shallow grave in the infantry, and I'm certain you'd all feel better satisfied, too."[7]

Bert Hall felt likewise, and cracked, "if the Germans do wing us, it's a decent, quick finish, and I for one prefer it to slow starvation, or being frozen stiff in a stinking, muddy trench."[8] For these and other reasons, many adventure-seeking young men hoped to make the jump from the trenches to the clouds. As one pilot would later put it, "[a]t twenty, one's dream of war is either of glorious living or more glorious dying[.]"[9]

Others were motivated by a similar desire to test themselves. Asked by a friend why he was in the war, James Norman Hall responded:

Right down in the bottom of my heart, I know it was that old tremendous longing for new experience, real, vital experience that compels growth, and makes or breaks character whether one will or no.... What sort of a creature could he be who should live in daily personal contact with Death and not be steadied, sobered, purified by it![10]

Although Harry Butters volunteered with the English, his reasons for doing so echoed those of the Americans who enlisted for France. Simply put, Germany's unprecedented attack on liberty presented a unique opportunity he could not pass up. As he explained to his family:

It may seem to you that for me this is all quite uncalled for, that it can only mean either the supreme sacrifice for nothing, or some of the best years of my life wasted, but ... I firmly believe ... that never will I have an opportunity to gain so much honorable advancement for my own soul or to do so much for the cause of the world's progress, as I have here daily, defending the liberty that mankind has so far gained against the attack of an enemy who would deprive us of it and set the world back some centuries if he could have his way.[11]

Like Kiffin, many of the young men that volunteered for France did so at least partially out of a sense of obligation. They were idealists, they felt a debt was owed, and so hurried to the side of France as her sons had once come to the aid of the United States. The recruiting pamphlet that eventually grew out of the initial short draft written by Frazier Curtis posed the question: "What was the spirit that actuated these young American citizens to cross the ocean and volunteer as French aviators?" In answer, it included this quote, which must have come from Prince:

We wished to return the compliment which Lafayette and Rochambeau paid to us; we wanted to belong to that fine and sportsmanlike institution, the French Aviation Corps, and we felt that Americans ought to help a republic that was in a conflict where the liberty of all nations was at stake.[12]

While Kiffin's service was primarily motivated by his desire to repay the obligation he felt was owed to France, it surely didn't hurt that his contributions would be much more visible in aviation than they had been in the trenches. Moving from the dirt to the skies meant moving from the lowest to the highest branch of the service, and not just physically. Thaw and Hall had already made the switch, and their experience – and the esteem in which they were held, even by other soldiers – convinced Kiffin that aviation was the place he wanted to be.

Two additional reasons were more personal. First, although it had healed, Kiffin's leg still gave him a little trouble, and avoiding the long marches and constant work associated with infantry service held some appeal. Second, he felt a particular responsibility to his friend Kenneth Weeks, whose slot in aviation he hoped to fill. For all these reasons, he could hardly wait to receive his transfer orders. For the time being, however, Kiffin was still a soldier in the Foreign Legion.

* * * * *

Kiffin's train arrived in the Lyon depot at 8:00 am on Sunday August 1, 1915. Eager to move on, Kiffin hoped to minimize his remaining service with the legion. That first day, he wrote Mrs. Weeks that things at Lyon did not look good, and he "wouldn't want to stay here very long." During the almost three months Kiffin had been apart from his unit, many of his former comrades in both regiments had fallen, forcing the legion to combine its decimated ranks into a single regiment. Despite his former and current units being thrown together, Kiffin found only one man in Lyon that he knew and could not track down a few others he expected to see there. Somewhat lonely, at the end of his first day he wrote Mrs. Weeks, "I am all alone, sitting in a café writing to you[.]"[13]

Although Kiffin was still committed to the cause, deprived of all the good soldiers he had known his squad no longer seemed the same, and he soon soured on those who remained. Just a few days after he arrived, he told Pechkoff that Lyon had "absolutely the poorest collection of men … I have ever seen. And the sous officers are the worst type, continually yelling.... All of the good men seem to be gone." While Kiffin decided he would stay in hopes of receiving his transfer to aviation, if that did not happen in a week he meant to ask to return to the front.[14]

After waiting for his orders for several days without result, Kiffin wrote Paul that he was "thoroughly demoralized as far as this outfit goes."[15] Although he had spent a few evenings with Trinkard, his old trench mate from the Second Regiment, Kiffin wanted either to be switched to aviation or sent back to the front.

Thirty kilometers away in La Valbonne, Pavelka was also back amongst the legionnaires. In a letter to Paul, he confirmed Kiffin's low estimate of Lyon, and spelled out the similar reasons he disliked his current location:

Lyon is a bad hole, and this camp ranks second with it, every day we have our exercises and plenty of other work along with. Somehow, they do not take into consideration that we are old-timers, and it makes me so disgusted to have to drill with all the rookies, and take commands from men who ha[ve] never been under fire. What's more, many of these non-coms will never see the front.[16]

On August 8, hoping to improve their surroundings, Kiffin and Trinkard joined a detachment leaving Lyon for La Valbonne. After the short trip west, Kiffin was pleased to be in a new location, as the small town had plenty of cafés where one could buy almost anything. The military camp on the edge of town had its own canteen and Kiffin loved the feel of the place, which must have reminded him of Tennessee and North Carolina – he told Mrs. Weeks there were "plenty of trees and grass and you can see the Alps in the distance."[17] Once he located Pavelka and went for a drink, Kiffin told Paul he was "feeling better all around except I am still hoping the transfer will come through this week."[18]

Pavelka introduced Kiffin to "another Yankee" who had turned up, D.W. "Bill" Thorin from South Dakota. According to Pavelka, Thorin was "quite a good comrade, always jolly and never down-hearted."[19] Although he found him "a little rough," Kiffin also enjoyed Thorin's company and felt he was "a fine boy." At first his fellow legionnaires doubted Thorin's many colorful stories, but over time their skepticism faded as the details were confirmed by others and "Billy Nuts," as some of the boys called him, proved his worth.[20] Kiffin later told Paul that Thorin had "a good heart and one could not find a better comrade in a fight."[21]

Kiffin told Mrs. Weeks that he and Pavelka were "treated pretty good," as the officers regarded him well and recognized Pavelka as the best soldier in his company. When one morning a new corporal barked at Kiffin during drill, "the adjutant spoke up and said that that would do, and that he only wished he had a few more men like me in the company."[22] This episode prompted Kiffin to write:

I have learned how to handle most of the men in the legion. It is only the surroundings that bother me. I have a strong constitution and for that reason physical hardships do not bother me, whereas mental ones do very much.[23]

Up to this time, Kiffin had heard nothing about his transfer, and began to get discouraged. By August 11, he was starting to think the request would not come through. But that afternoon, an officer told Kiffin to report to the bureau, where he found an order initiating the transfer process for he and Pavelka to the aviation corps. The next day, Kiffin wrote Mrs. Weeks a thank you note:

We were so happy last night we got several of the boys together and had a regular celebration. This morning, Pavelka and I were busy signing papers at the bureau and passing the medical visit to see if we were all right. Now we are just waiting for the order to move. You can't imagine how I thank you for all you have done, for I certainly wanted to get out of this place. Yet I don't want you to think I am selfish and only thinking of myself. I have been thinking of you and of Kenneth all the time, and only wish there were something I could do for you.[24]

Kiffin eagerly awaited his final transfer order. But if there is one thing every soldier learns, it is that orders come when they come, and not before.

* * * * *

So Kiffin settled into the routine of camp, each day hoping his order would arrive. He wrote Paul of the poor general atmosphere on August 15:

There is really not much hard work to do here, and plenty of cafés right in the camp, but it seems to be in the air for everyone to be completely demoralized and it is nothing but grumbling and yelling from morning to night. Prison sentences are handed out freely on the slightest pretext.[25]

That same day, Pavelka told Mrs. Weeks that Kiffin was "very angry at the stupidity of these fellows here in the bureau."[26] A week later and still waiting, one can hear Kiffin's frustration in the words he wrote to his mother:

The life [in La Valbonne] is about the same as the life I spent at Camp Mailly last October and I don't like it a bit. The only reason I am still here is because I have been hoping that I would not return to the front in the legion. I never have liked but one part of the legion, but the men of that part are mostly killed or disappeared, so I dread the idea of staying any longer in it. However, if some kind of change doesn't come soon, I may return to the front.[27]

On top of the poor atmosphere, several specific events left Kiffin feeling rather despondent. On August 22, he read in the papers that three days earlier Germany had sunk the British White Star liner *Arabic*, killing two Americans and thirty-odd others. This surely rekindled Kiffin's anger at President Wilson; he sardonically wrote to Loula: "I am wondering today what the U.S. is going to do about this latest slap in the face Germany has given them by sinking the *Arabic*."[28]

The answer was not much. Despite the fact that Wilson had warned Germany he would hold it strictly accountable for the lives of American citizens, "nothing of a positive character was done by the United States." Instead, "[n]egotiations dragged out to a wearisome length and the submarines continued to take their almost daily toll from neutrals and belligerents alike."[29]

A few other incidents reminded Kiffin of all he hated about military life. On August 24, he witnessed a commandant berate a group of volunteer soldiers, all of whom had passed the winter in the trenches and many of whom had been wounded for France. They were receiving medical discharges, a fact which made the commandant "sore as hell." Knowing something of their sacrifice, Kiffin was disgusted to witness the scene, about which he wrote Paul:

He lined them up, some of them could hardly walk, and cursed them out. He told them they were not worth a damn, that they disgraced the legion, and that they only came here for the gamelle *– now, we have heard that from sergeants and such all the time. But for a Commandant to tell men who have ruined themselves for life out of love of France and the principles she is fighting for, I think it is going a little too far.[30]*

In another incident, Kiffin's corporal, a twenty-one-year-old Greek, was given an eight-day prison sentence for failing to report to morning exercise. As the corporal's cot was next to his, Kiffin knew the man had not slept a wink the night before owing to a toothache. The corporal, who had never served so much as a half hour's prison sentence, took his punishment badly – Kiffin held his coat as he cut off his corporal's stripes, which he threw on the floor of the bureau on the way to prison.[31] About these events, Kiffin told Paul:

Now, since I have been here, there has been no one that has said a word out of the way to me. Yet I see these things every day and never know when my turn will come. And it is such a disgrace to France for such things to happen that I wish something could be done to stop it. My idea is that the legion should be broken up, and any man that France is unwilling to accept in a regular corps be given their freedom. I can't help but believe that if enough of these facts get to the War Dep[artment], that this will happen.[32]

Kiffin had reached the limit of his patience and wanted out of La Valbonne and out of the legion. However, it had been more than two weeks since he had been told he would be transferred, and still no order had arrived. As the days turned into weeks, Kiffin felt increasing frustration and resignation, but there wasn't much he could do but work, wait and hope his transfer would finally show up. In a letter to Loula on August 29, he summed up the state of affairs:

Well I am still here at La Valbonne, doing little of nothing but drill which gets very monotonous after the length of time I spent at the front. It has been very hot all this month and I have had little energy. I thought that I was going to be changed to the Aviation Corps this last week but the transfer didn't come through. There is still hope that I will be transferred in the next week or so, if not, I will return to the front.[33]

As their time in camp lengthened, the workload increased. Night exercises, twenty-four-hour marches and trench digging reminded Kiffin of his early days in the legion. As Pavelka put it on September 1, "everything here is as usual, work and drill and plenty of it."[34] Neither Pavelka nor Kiffin had heard a word about their transfer, and because both were now booked to go back to the front with the legion on the fifteenth, it began to look as if Kiffin was not going to be transferred into aviation after all.

Having reconciled himself to whatever was to come, Kiffin wrote Paul, "I have reached my old point of indifference now, and it doesn't make much difference to me where I go or what I do. I will get along all right wherever they put me."[35]

* * * * *

Another American had a little more luck ... or pull. In early August, Elliott Cowdin succeeded in getting Victor Chapman transferred from the legion to *Escadrille V.B.108*, which a few weeks earlier had been relocated from Bruay-en-Artois to an airfield just outside Nancy. Cowdin had promised John Jay Chapman that he would make Victor his observer, but by the time Victor arrived, Cowdin had left for Paris to pick up another machine. An eager Victor wrote his stepmother from Plateau de Malzéville on August 9, "I am affected here as *mitrailleur*, and wait Cowdin's return."[36] However, once in Paris, Cowdin was ordered to train on a Nieuport, while Norman Prince "was sent North on a cannon Voisin." According to Cowdin, he and Prince "parted for the first time," and did not see one another again "until we came home on an eight-days' leave for Christmas."[37]

As Cowdin had been officially transferred, Victor was instead assigned to a young Lieutenant with whom he immediately began making trial flights as an observer and bomb-dropper. On August 24, Victor participated in his first successful raid into Germany. After scoring a direct hit on some railroad tracks, Victor settled back into the collapsible seat on their Voisin and he and his pilot celebrated with some chocolates. As the victorious pair flew back to France, Victor must have felt like a king. He wrote his little brother of the scenery, telling him "[f]rom a good altitude the country looks like nothing so much as a rich old Persian carpet."[38]

Although Victor Chapman hoped to train as a pilot as soon as possible, for now he was happy to have made the jump from common soldier to bombardier. And he was yet another American coalescing in the French aviation service.

* * * * *

While headed to his new assignment, Cowdin stopped in Paris, where he ran into Hall and Bach, both of whom had finally "passed their tests at Pau and were awaiting orders to leave for the front."[39] Realizing they at last had enough pilots to form a squadron, Cowdin arranged to see Commander Joseph-Édouard Barès, the Director of Aviation at the *GQG – Grand Quartier Général* (General Headquarters), to alert him to that fact. After making the 40-kilometre trip from Paris to Chantilly, Cowdin reported to Barès that the number of American pilots was sufficient to staff a squadron. In response, Barès explained that the aviators were currently needed at the front as individuals, but assured Cowdin that the Americans would soon be grouped together. Upon hearing this good news, Cowdin dashed off a letter to Prince, who "immediately regained his former enthusiasm for carrying the original plan into execution."[40]

It seemed that things were finally coming together for Prince. Earlier that summer he had been promoted to sergeant and on August 15 was awarded a well-earned citation for his work with *Escadrille V.B.108*.[41] Elliott's welcome news that Hall and Bach were now licensed military aviators, combined with the fact that the first three Americans at the front – Thaw, Prince and Cowdin – had all won citations surely did not hurt the prospects for an American squadron.

In fact, Prince's idea was slowly but surely progressing through the bureaucratic channels of the French government. On August 21, General Hirschauer sent a letter to the Minister of Foreign Affairs stating that his attention had on several occasions been called to the idea that France might use the assistance of citizens of the United States for the benefit of military aviation, a "process which would not fail to provoke and support the sympathies of the American public with regard to our country."[42] To that end, Hirschauer wrote, he had decided to group the American airmen currently serving France into a single squadron and to "welcome and examine" proposals made by private American citizens for "the organization of some sort of American aviation group."[43]

Prince's idea now had the money, the men and the backing of the French. In early September, he summed up their progress in a letter to his grandmother:

I am happy and in the best of health. I sleep under canvas on a stretcher bed and eat in the shed of an old farm house nearby. I have nothing to complain of. I like it. There are ten American pilots with us in the French service and twelve others in training with their number consistently increasing. Someday soon we will all be united in one escadrille – an Escadrille Américaine – that is my fondest ambition. I am devoting all my spare energies to organizing it and all the American pilots here are giving me every encouragement and assistance in the work of preliminary organization. As I have had so much to do in originating and pushing the plan along, perhaps I shall be second in command.[44]

* * * * *

In the meantime, Mrs. Weeks had again spoken to the American ambassador. While her visit likely had nothing to do with the timing, on Saturday morning the fourth of September the bureau at La Valbonne finally received a telegram authorizing Kiffin's transfer to the aviation corps. He was just about to go on guard when a staff officer "came running down to tell me to get a move on," and within an hour he was headed back to Lyon, from which place he would take a train to the aviation camp at Avord.[45] Kiffin barely had enough time to say good-bye to Pavelka.[46]

Speaking of Pavelka, poor Skipper's hoped-for transfer order had not come in, so he was left behind with the regiment at La Valbonne, knowing that if his order did not arrive by the fifteenth he was slated to head back to the front with the legion. He explained to Mrs. Weeks that while of course he would go, he wouldn't necessarily be happy about it:

I shall surely be lonesome with none of the boys around to chat with [but] shall make the best of it for as the old soldiers say, "Grumble you may, but go you must," and it is true.[47]

But for Kiffin, there was no more grumbling. In fact, that night in Lyon, Kiffin was feeling so good he decided to celebrate, and so missed his evening train. Instead, he left at five a.m. on Sunday, September 5, and arrived at Avord that night. Neither of the small hotels there had a room, so Kiffin walked the two kilometers out to the camp and spent the night at the *Poste de Police*.[48] He wrote Paul it was "such a relief to be out of that damn legion that I can hardly believe it. I think that if I had to stay in La Valbonne for a month or so longer I would have gone completely nutty."[49]

Kiffin was thrilled to have been selected for pilot training. Shortly after his arrival, he wrote Loula, telling her "I have at last gotten what I have been trying to get for the last two months. I am transferred to aviation as a student-pilot.... It is the most interesting thing I have ever done, and is the life of a gentleman, and I am surrounded by gentlemen."[50]

Chapter Thirty-two

Like a duck to water.

In 1915, French aviation training was still in its infancy. But if aviation training was an infant, aerial combat was a newborn. At the outset of the war just a year before, airplanes were viewed primarily as reconnaissance tools, useful for observation only, and aerial combat was unknown. One author said it was "a legend of the service, which ought to be true even if it is not, that at the first meeting over the fighting lines of two French and German airships, the pilots greeted each other pleasantly."[1] Of course, things escalated quickly and opposing pilots and their observers who initially waved at one another soon began to take up a variety of arms to attack the other if encountered.

The observers typically fired out of the back or side of the plane, due to the danger of hitting one's own propellers. But Frenchman Raymond Saulnier soon came up with a practical synchronization gear that allowed the pilot to shoot through the arc of the propeller, which he fitted with steel deflectors to deflect the occasional cartridge not perfectly timed to make it between the spinning blades.[2] The result was essentially a flying gun, which a pilot aimed by pointing the airplane itself.

In April 1915, former test pilot Roland Garros brought down five German planes in less than three weeks using a plane outfitted with Saulnier's synchronization system.[3] Both sides joined in the arms race when Garros' plane was brought down behind German lines by anti-aircraft fire and his secret fell into the hands of Anthony Fokker, a Dutch engineer who soon supplied the Germans with a machine gun synchronized to fire through the propeller blades. During the summer, a young German pilot named Oswald Boelcke began flying over the front in a Fokker E1 Eindecker equipped with this technology.[4]

Still, throughout much of 1915, pursuit type planes were viewed mainly as escorts for bombers, rather than as stand-alone fighters. This also was rapidly changing. In July, future French ace Georges Guynemer won his first victory, and by the fall of that year the warring nations were beginning to comprehend the strategic importance of aerial combat. As both sides built faster and better armed planes, once infrequent dogfights were becoming commonplace. It was at this moment that Kiffin entered the French aviation service.

* * * * *

But Kiffin was not the only American hoping to become a pilot. As the plans for Prince's squadron slowly moved forward, more of his countrymen began entering aviation. For example, after serving more than a month as an observer with *Escadrille V.B.108*, on September 20, Victor Chapman took "French leave," and spent the day at a nearby camp with Prince. While there, Chapman learned that Prince had secured permission for an unlimited number of Americans to train at the French flight schools and was "very anxious to get as many as possible."[5] In fact, Prince helped hustle through Chapman's own request to train as a pilot, and less than a week later Chapman would join Kiffin at Camp Avord.

In addition, Edmund Gros was also spreading the good word at the American Ambulance and assisted several drivers in switching to aviation. Among those who elected to leave the Ambulance to join the aviation corps was Horace Clyde Balsley, a graduate of the West Texas Military Academy and former student at the University of Texas. Like Kiffin, Balsley was the son of a reverend, and had volunteered out of a desire "to see the war, to see it well." That fall, he wrote home of his chance to transfer out of the ambulance service, telling his mother that he could "learn aviation, the newest game in the world," and finally "take a man's part in this war for humanity."[6]

Several other ambulance drivers also switched to aviation around this time. One was Laurence Rumsey, a hard-charging professional polo player and Harvard graduate from Buffalo, New York. Charles Chouteau Johnson, a St. Louis native, University of Virginia alum and friend of Jim McConnell's was another.[7] Only five-foot seven, Johnson had grey eyes and a mole on his right temple. Most of the men knew him as "Chute," except for McConnell who usually called him "Kid." Speaking of McConnell, he was doing well in the Ambulance. In fact, in October he would be awarded the *Croix de Guerre* for "courage and fearlessness worthy of the highest praise."[8]

McConnell was also using his writing skills and in its September 15, 1915 edition, *The Outlook*, a popular weekly magazine of the time, published an article McConnell had written about his service.[9] In a nice introduction to the piece, former president Theodore Roosevelt wrote of the "ignoble part" played by the United States in the thirteen months since the war had begun, while lauding McConnell and several other college men who had stepped forward to assist France. He encouraged others to do the same, or at least to be prepared to defend their own country:

Every young man just leaving college – from Harvard, from Yale, from Princeton, from Michigan, Wisconsin, or California, from Virginia or Sewanee, in short, from every college in the country – ought to feel it incumbent on him at this time either to try to render some assistance to those who are battling for the right on behalf of Belgium, or else to try to fit himself to help his own country if in the future she is attacked as wantonly as Belgium has been attacked.[10]

However, Roosevelt did not view a college education as a guarantee of manliness or right-thinking in every instance: less than three weeks before, he had denounced "the professional pacifists and the poltroons and college sissies who organize peace-at-any-price societies," declaring that "no man is fit to be free unless he is not merely willing but eager to fit himself to fight for his freedom."[11]

Along these same lines, in his introduction to McConnell's article Roosevelt accused the American government, still in full-on neutrality mode, of treating "empty rhetoric and adroit phrase-making as a substitute for deeds." In contrast, he praised those "few individuals" who had "to a limited extent by their private efforts made partially good our Governmental shortcomings."[12] McConnell sent a copy of his article to Paul Rockwell, telling him "you'll agree with Teddy."[13] It's a safe bet Kiffin did, too.

Others were also beginning to agree with Teddy, including clergymen back home. "Put me down on the side of Colonel Roosevelt," said Bishop Thomas F. Gailor after one Sunday service in New York. "His sentiments concerning the European war are my sentiments. I go quite as far as he does.... Our whole attitude as a nation, ever since Europe began to fight, has been altogether too negative." While Bishop Gailor understood that President Wilson hoped to be re-elected, he felt it incumbent on America to act, saying "there is a duty to civilization to perform, and it must be performed now."[14]

Another pastor was even more blunt. The Reverend Dr. S. D. McConnell (no known relation to Jim), the former rector of Holy Trinity Church in Brooklyn, stated he "was never less proud than now of being an American. Our national administration seems not to have felt for a single moment during the last year that it was sure of the difference between right and wrong. The time for talk has ceased. The time for action has arrived."[15]

* * * * *

For the most part, French aviation training was based on a simple concept – pilots would learn aviation from the ground up, as it were. One author said the French school was "like learning to swim, starting at the shallow end."[16] The students would be taught what to do to begin flying, and more importantly, what not to do.

Most pilots began their training by rolling along the ground in a so-called "penguin" – an underpowered Bleriot monoplane with clipped wings, designed not to leave the ground.[17] Even though it did not fly, handling a penguin was not as simple as it sounded. Laurence Rumsey noted that "the idea is to go fast and keep in a straight line. It looks easy but is not, as the least shift of the wings will spin it around or turn it over."[18] Clyde Balsley, the former ambulance driver, also found the penguin a difficult bird to control:

It is very hard at the beginning to keep the plane straight ahead. The tendency is to make circles called 'chevaux de bois' (wooden horse) meaning 'merry go round.' When a man makes a 'chevaux,' which he is certain to do on his first trip, he is fined a small amount in accordance with his rank, a soldier two cents, a lieutenant ten cents, etc. The money is used to buy sandwiches and wine for the class.[19]

Chapman later said he had never "heard of a man who did not, on his first start, make half-a-dozen *chevaux de bois*, like a kitten chasing its tail."[20] Balsley did a great deal worse than he expected on his first trip, making 14 *chevaux*. "However," he noted, "that doesn't break the record by a great deal."[21]

Eventually, the *élève pilote* (as an aviation student was called) learned to maneuver the penguin in a straight line across the field and back to the hangar, whereupon he graduated to a higher horsepower Bleriot *roleur*, a plane that would leave the ground, but not by much. This plane had bigger wings, and as it repeatedly left the earth and came back down, a student learned the most important skill – how to land. A reporter who witnessed many of these trips wrote that the beginner seated in one of these machines "goes buzzing about the field for all the world like a primordial grasshopper."[22]

From there, the student pilot progressed through increasingly powerful

311

aircraft which allowed for sustained flight and mastery of the plane's controls and instruments. Over time, the heights gradually got higher and the distances greater, until after sufficient experience the aviator was allowed to try for his military *brevet*.[23]

This was how things were generally done, but Kiffin was destined for the air. On the morning of September 6, as he exited the police station where he had spent his first night at the camp, Kiffin met Commandant Henry Sussigny. As the men shook hands, Sussigny asked Kiffin which plane he wanted to fly. Kiffin replied he "didn't know much difference," and so agreed with the Commandant's suggestion to learn on a real plane – a double command Maurice Farman model 1913.[24] A big biplane with dual controls and an instructor seated behind, the Maurice Farman had the reputation of being the easiest and safest to learn for a beginner.

Thus, Kiffin did not begin by driving in circles on the ground but was instead thrown immediately into the sky. It must have been daunting – Kiffin had never before been in an airplane, and knew "absolutely nothing" about motors, yet here he was on his first official day at Avord, going up as a passenger to get a feel for the machine.[25] Having handled it well, by the next morning he flew for ten minutes, getting as high as 100 meters, with an instructor directing his movements from behind.

The day after that he began twice-daily flights, going up once in the morning and again in the afternoon. Bill Thaw's former mechanic Henri Massot was Kiffin's bunkmate and his instructor was a one-time chum of Casey, another old friend of Kiffin's from the legion. Under their tutelage, Kiffin found flying to be "very easy and most interesting," and declared himself "perfectly contented."[26] He wrote Paul a short note describing the hard work of the student aviators:

We all go out on the field at four-forty in the morning and assist in moving the machines out of the hangars. Then we see that the motors, etc., are in good condition. Then we go out on the field and take turns flying with the instructors. At seven o'clock we come in for a little breakfast. At eight, we have a lecture on flying, then go out and put the machines back in the hangars. We are free until nine-thirty. At eleven, we have dejeuner. Then we usually sleep until three-thirty, when we go back on the field. We are out there then until after dark. Don't have dinner until eight or after. That is the day's routine. They are all a quiet bunch, little foolishness going on, and all intent on learning to fly as quickly as possible.[27]

* * * * *

Most of the other student pilots were officers, which got Kiffin thinking about purchasing a new uniform. The only problem was that unlike many of the Americans in aviation at the time, he did not have a lot of money. While Kiffin could never claim poverty, there is little doubt that he was in an entirely different category from guys like former Yale student Thaw – whose father was a noted Pittsburgh financier and mother a wealthy heiress.

Similarly, many of the other Americans enlisting in the French aviation service came from monied and elite backgrounds. For example, Cowdin, Chapman and Rumsey all came from very wealthy families – Cowdin and Rumsey both played professional polo – and graduated from Harvard.[28]

But Prince – another Harvard man, and polo player, may have exceeded them all. At the time, the Prince family was one of the wealthiest in America: his father was the senior member of the well-known investment firm F.H. Prince & Company, chairman of the Union Stockyards and Transit Company, and held seats on both the Boston and New York stock exchanges. One guest at the Prince mansion joked that Mr. Prince served "champagne at luncheon, tea and dinner. It is hard to say why he discriminates against breakfast."[29] Compared to wealth on this scale, Kiffin (who had not yet met these men) appeared downright destitute.

Still, Kiffin always had sufficient for his needs, and with some money received from Paul was able to order a sharp black custom-made uniform – one designated for use by a French engineering unit.[30] Although he wanted to fit in with the well-dressed officers, Kiffin told Paul there were "a lot of things I would like to have that I don't even think of getting," and assured him he was "not living a riotous life here." However, Kiffin did note that he expected "to reap the good times after once being at the front."[31]

While Kiffin was not rich, he did not envy the wealth of others and wanted only to be comfortable. Around the time he started aviation training, Loula apparently suggested she might sell some property and come to France. While Kiffin dearly hoped to see her and Agnes, his response sheds a little light on the financial status of the family as well as his view of money:

I wouldn't advise you to sell any property if you can help it, for after the war there will be little money and land is the only thing I am sure will be worth anything. I would be glad to see you stop work and am sure that we would never have to go to the poorhouse if you did. After the war I never expect to try to get rich but am sure one can always live well.... [A]t present, I am having to spend a little money on clothes and am not being paid much but as soon as I become a full-fledged pilot, I will be paid pretty well.[32]

In the meantime, Kiffin was rapidly advancing in his aeronautical training. After just a week on the double command, Kiffin's flight log recorded he had been *lâche seul sur 1913* – that is, "loose alone" on the 1913 model Maurice Farman. Clearly, the boy had the makings of an aviator. In a letter to Paul, he claimed that the first stage of flight school was "very easy and I take to it just like a duck to water."[33]

Chapter Thirty-three

Confidence is the greatest asset in this game.

Kiffin turned twenty-three years old on September 20, 1915. That same day, he made his first trip in a double command 1914 model Maurice Farman. He must have done well: after three short flights, his instructor told Kiffin he was "very good," so there was no need of his continuing under the double command.[1]

His rapid progress made Kiffin even more eager to fly. The next day when he couldn't find another airplane he decided to try a machine on which several mechanics had been working all day. Although they weren't sure it was ready, they let Kiffin take it out, warning him to be careful due to the plane's poor wheels and motor. Unfortunately, as soon as he began to taxi, the machine became hard to control and began to turn on its own. Realizing it would break if he didn't do something, Kiffin tried to get off the ground, but this only threw the plane completely around, causing him to smash it up pretty badly. He was not happy and told Mrs. Weeks:

It made me awfully mad. Although it was not my fault it does not help my record and also delays me for several days, as I must now wait for another machine. But it will all come out eventually. I am all right when up in the air, but as our machines are old and not very good, they are hard to manage on the ground.[2]

Kiffin's accident was just one of nine wrecks at the school that day. The resulting shortage of machines over the next week led to several entries in Kiffin's flight log reading *"pas vol, pas d'appareil"* – no flight, no aircraft.[3] He did manage to take his first solo flight on the Maurice Farman 1914 model on September 23, but this was followed by five straight *pas vol* days due either to no machines or poor weather.

The same day that Kiffin was making his first solo on the 1914 Maurice Farman, Jimmie Bach became the first American taken prisoner in the war. In late August, Bach had finally been sent to the front as part of *Escadrille MS.38,* flying a Morane-Saulnier monoplane. On September 23, Bach volunteered for a special mission – he and another pilot were to drop two French soldiers behind German lines to destroy a section of railway.

Bach and French Sergeant Georges Mangeot both landed without incident and dropped off their soldiers and explosives. Unfortunately, in attempting to take off, Mangeot turned over his plane, so Bach swung back around again to pick up his fellow pilot. He again landed and was able to get his French friend, but with the extra weight on takeoff, Bach clipped a tree with the wing of his Morane, bringing them both down behind enemy lines. Caught, the pair of aviators were twice court-martialed, although "owing largely to the able defense of a German lawyer, they were found not guilty."[4] Bach would spend the remainder of the hostilities as a prisoner of war in Germany.

Although Kiffin did not immediately hear of Bach's incident, at Camp Avord he nonetheless learned that in aviation the risks were real. On September 24, he witnessed two "very horrible" deaths at the base. A Morane instructor and a mechanic were heading to an accident at the end of the field when a puff of wind caught their plane, sending it straight up in the air. It then fell back to earth, trapping the pilot and mechanic in the wreckage before the whole thing burst into flames. According to Kiffin's account, the two unfortunates "were burned alive with all the men watching but unable to do a thing."[5]

* * * * *

Having secured a letter of recommendation from Prince, Victor Chapman had no difficulty being accepted for pilot training at Avord, where he arrived on September 27. Chapman soon found the only other American at the school, whom he described in a letter home as "a compatriot I am proud to own.... A tall, lanky Kentuckian, called Rockwell."[6] He advised his uncle he had met "a very decent Kentuckian, who served in the legion and was wounded at Neuville St. Vaast on May 9 when the regiment was covered with glory but very nearly annihilated."[7] Chapman bunked near Kiffin in the dormitory in which the élève pilotes were quartered and, although he incorrectly thought his new friend was from Kentucky, was quite impressed with his tales of the battle north of Arras.

Kiffin also made note of Chapman's arrival, telling Paul that an "American named Chapman ... arrived here this morning and doesn't seem to be a bad fellow."[8] Almost immediately Chapman's infectious laughter and easy-going manner endeared him to Kiffin. As time passed, Kiffin would grow to greatly admire Chapman's character and ideals, and Victor would become one of his few close friends.

Like Kiffin, upon his arrival at flight school Victor Chapman felt he was where he was meant to be. But this was not the only similarity between the two friends. For example, like Kiffin, Victor had lost a parent while young – his mother died suddenly in childbirth when he was just six. Also like Kiffin, Victor had a religious upbringing – to the end of his life he made the sign of the cross when reciting the prayers his mother had taught him in his youth, always ending with the phrase "and make me a big soldier of Jesus Christ who is the Lord and Light of the world."[9] Even in the trenches of France, Chapman kept his bible at hand, in which he pressed flowers and photos of friends.

In addition, both Kiffin and Victor were tall and strong, fond of nature and the outdoors, and unafraid to stand up for what they believed. While both boys were well-liked (with Chapman perhaps more "popular"), each had a predisposition to hold himself apart from others, and to stand on principle. A friend later remembered Chapman as having "noble and chivalrous instincts in such overwhelming proportions that it was literally impossible for him to act like the average person."[10]

Finally, both Kiffin and Victor seemed to have found their true calling in the war. In words that sound as if they could have been written by Kiffin, one month after starting flight school Victor told his father:

This is the first thing I have ever done that has been worthwhile, or may ever do, and you might just as well get the benefit of it without the heart-wringing worry.... If ever anything does happen to me, you would rather it happened than that I had never joined at all, and simply gone on living a listless, aimless existence.[11]

* * * * *

After Victor graduated from Harvard in 1913, he traveled to Paris where he "entered an atelier for preliminary studies in architecture which he was to pursue at the Beaux-Arts."[12] As the war clouds gathered in late July of 1914, he happened to be traveling with his stepmother and father in Germany. Upon mobilization, the family hastened to London and checked into the Artillery Mansions Hotel, just a half mile down the street from the Palace of Westminster. Safely in London, Victor's father John Jay Chapman indignantly wrote of Germany's rough handling of the fleeing Americans, declaring, "This is modern Germany. The armed nation has dropped the mask at last."[13]

At this early date, John Jay understood that America's history and policy forced his nation to "stand outside the conflict," despite his own conviction that "every American who understands the conditions will feel the appeal so strongly as to make him almost desire to enlist under the British Flag."[14] Accordingly, rather than joining up, John Jay felt it incumbent on Americans abroad "to explain this war to Americans at home, to the millions of our fellow citizens far away, who may think that this is an ordinary European war with which we have little to do – a European diplomatic imbroglio which will settle itself."[15]

But his son wanted to do more than *explain* the war – at 24 years old, Victor felt called to take an active part. Just days after they arrived in London, Victor read in *The Times* the appeal published by the American Volunteer Corps in Paris, urging Americans to reciprocate the "gallant service" rendered by Lafayette.[16] Then one evening Victor heard floating through the night air voices singing the Marseillaise outside parliament. The anthem's stirring chorus echoed the message set forth in the appeal made by the American Volunteer Corps: *Aux armes, Citoyens*!

His martial spirit stimulated, Victor determined to join up with the Americans in Paris before his sober-minded father talked him out of it, suggesting "it was merely a random desire to see life and get rid of his serious duties that led him to the idea of enlistment." Victor obediently muttered "no doubt this must be it," and shuffled out. But as soon as the disappointed Victor left the room, his stepmother scolded John Jay, telling him that Victor had only "submitted through his humility and through his reverence for you. But I had rather see him lying on the battlefield than see that look on his face."[17] Not long after, Victor telegrammed the American Volunteer Corps that he was coming, and by the end of the month, he was in France.

This action was not surprising, as from his youth, Chapman had a penchant for placing himself in peril. His father said that Victor "never really felt that he was alive except when he was in danger," and Victor did seem to seek out risks. Early in his time in the legion, he transferred to the *mitrailleuse* section, explaining to his Captain that it was "more dangerous."[18] One of his squad mates wrote that Chapman:

was something of a philosopher, and he used to say, 'The danger of being shot is very small, the trail of a bullet is very small, the space around you, as compared with the trail of a bullet, is as a million to one; so the chances of being hit are in that same proportion.' But it didn't work out with Chapman at all. He was hit the very first day in the arm.[19]

After catching that stray bullet in the bicep, Chapman shrugged away the surgeon's suggestion of evacuation, saying "Let me be, the boys will renew my dressings. I don't want to *embusqué* myself!"[20]

Although Chapman was extremely wealthy, he did not flaunt it, and wished nothing more than to be treated like everyone else. At the front, this desire was accommodated, and along with the other soldiers, Chapman spent a good deal of his time excavating trenches. When an inspecting officer noticed Chapman digging with such ardor, he inquired, "Say you, you must have been a navvy." To which a French comrade replied: "My captain, you're mistaken. He's a millionaire!"[21] But there were times when Chapman's money came in handy. For instance, once when a fellow machine gun operator mentioned that he had been told by the doctor that he needed milk for his stomach problems, Chapman left for a few hours before reappearing, leading a cow by a rope. "I bought her so that you could get your milk," he explained to the grateful soldier.[22]

* * * * *

At the time, Victor and Kiffin were the only two Americans going through flight school at Avord and both stayed in the dormitories with the other pilots. But unlike Kiffin, Chapman began his training on the "penguin," and found rolling along the ground as difficult everyone else. Less than a week into it, he wrote that he had "taken eight spins of ten minutes each so far and still turn more often than I go straight."[23]

Whether in the air or on the ground, at Avord there were too many pupils and too few machines, so training progressed slowly. In addition, the weather was less than cooperative, making time in a good machine even more scarce. A few of the French pilots seemed not to mind this state of affairs and advised the impatient Chapman not to worry – as the war would likely last two more years, he might just as well spend the winter there as anywhere else.[24] But Chapman held the same attitude as Kiffin towards the war, and aviation – he wanted action. Although he acknowledged that it was "better to go slow than be killed," Chapman still wished he could somehow speed up his training.[25]

In contrast, Victor's stepmother did not mind her son spending his time in flight school, as compared to being at the front. About a month after his arrival, Victor began a letter to her:

Well, it seems that our interests and happiness are dependent o[n] diametrically opposed conditions. I am only happy when I am at the front with the opportunity of sailing over the lines and you can only sleep well at night if I am chafing and idling away my time at this nest of embusques at Avord.[26]

Victor asked her not to worry about him and insisted he really was quite safe – the accidents about which she was so worried were not likely to happen to him:

This élève pilote *is a little risky if you will, but the accidents that happen come from carelessness or from the fact that the fellow was unfit ever to be a pilot, i.e., lost his head, did the wrong thing and again the wrong thing. I don't intend to be in either class.*[27]

It would not have pleased Chapman's stepmother to hear it, but on October 6 another would-be pilot went down. The unlucky flyer was a friend of Kiffin's, and the first man he knew at Camp d'Avord. He had been in a rush to finish his last test for the *brevet militaire*, and they found his body with the plane's wreckage about twenty kilometers from Chartres. Following this, Kiffin decided he would "go a little slower," as he did not want to die an inglorious death. As he explained in a letter a few days later: "At the front one thinks little of death because there is always more or less glory in it, and we feel that it is necessary there. Here, there is no glory in it, and it seems so unnecessary."[28]

Not that Kiffin had many opportunities to fly – his flight log from early October shows that about half of the time he was prevented from flying due either to lack of a machine or the poor weather. He told Paul he was "doing little or nothing here now," and highlighted the problem of broken machines – in his Maurice Farman section, the number of flight-worthy aircraft had dropped from forty-four to sixteen.[29] Still, he was making great strides for such little time in the air:

Out of the last three weeks I have fourteen days that I haven't been in an appareil *and most of the other seven days was only in odd minutes. Altogether, I have between twelve and fourteen hours (not sure exactly) of actual work in the five weeks I have been here. Yet when I do go up I shoot right up into the air anywhere from 1,000 to 2,000 meters high and I make fancy descents, showing perfect control of my* appareil. *Sat[urday] morning, the last time I have flown, I was up to 2,000 meters and came down in what is known as the "spiral," or regular corkscrew descent, round and round. I was deaf for an hour afterwards, as it is hard on the ear drums.*[30]

Despite his lack of consistent flight time, Kiffin made solid progress and was soon told by his instructor that he could test for his military license. He wrote Mrs. Weeks that from now on, any flying would be "part of the *epreuve* for the *brevet militaire*. In other words, I am a regular aviator now."[31]

* * * * *

There were generally four separate qualifications to receive a military flying license. A would-be pilot had to (1) fly above 2,000 meters for at least one hour, (2) complete a cross-country triangular flight, with landings at two different points, (3) take a direct flight to a distant point, and return, and (4) volplane down to earth from a height of at least 500 meters. Kiffin accomplished the first requirement, the "altitude" test, on October 14. The next day, he began the "triangle" test, for which he was supposed to fly from Avord to Châteauroux, Châteauroux to Romorantin, and Romorantin back to Avord.

But that's not what happened. Instead, anxious to finish his "*essai de triangle*" as quickly as possible, Kiffin took a few foolhardy risks, putting himself and his plane in danger, and ended up having to retake his test. But fate has a funny way of working things out, and the trip ended up being a great boost to Kiffin's confidence. As he told Paul, he "acted a fool" but "had more or less luck."[32]

The afternoon of Friday, October 15, was overcast and foggy at Camp d'Avord, and hardly an ideal day to fly. But Kiffin figured the clouds were high enough that he could stay below them and complete his trip. However, not long after he took off towards Châteauroux, Kiffin found himself flying through clouds much lower than when he left. Forced to rise above the cloud cover, Kiffin was no longer able to see the ground, and had to use his compass and watch to make his way. Once he reckoned he was near Châteauroux, Kiffin "shot down through the clouds, and sure enough, I was there."[33] A fellow pilot who had just broken his machine while landing urged Kiffin to remain at Châteauroux, judging it too foggy to continue. But Kiffin figured if he had found Châteauroux he could find Romorantin even easier, and so got his papers signed and took to the air again.

Unfortunately, Kiffin immediately ran into heavy fog and wind and became "completely lost." For two hours he searched for Romorantin, but could hardly see anything, and finally came down near a village he spotted. Finding he was within fifteen kilometers of Romorantin and figuring he could make it there in ten minutes, although it was now nearly dark, Kiffin again took flight.

However, night fell quickly and Kiffin "couldn't see a thing" in the dark and fog, and so flew right by Romorantin. Finally, after flying for half an hour, and realizing he was nearly out of oil and essence, he spotted the lights of a town and headed for it. Unable to see to land, Kiffin circled above the town three times, hoping someone would put out a light. But no one did, so finally he "trusted to luck and shot down."[34] He told his mother he "felt my way down, as you might say – until my instinct told me I was nearly down. Then I let my machine lose its speed and settled nicely on the ground without breaking a thing."[35] Kiffin was pleased with his "perfect landing," something he told Paul "wouldn't happen one time out of a hundred under similar conditions."[36]

He had come down just outside of Vierzon, a medium-sized town a little more than thirty kilometers past Romorantin. Many residents had heard the plane's descent and landing, and turned out to see what was going on. Kiffin got the *bureau de police* to place a guard at his plane, then spent the night in town, where he was treated like a king, and where – due to the fog – he stayed another two nights.

Well, maybe it wasn't solely the fog – the next day, Kiffin wrote Paul from the *Café du Commerce*, where he was dining with a guest. He told Paul he was "having the greatest time of my life," and described his situation:

I have the pick of the town for anything I want, girls included. I am followed by two or [three hundred] people everywhere I go. My appareil *is covered with flowers, also names of girls. People meet me in the streets with bouquets, and in all I am* bien content. *I haven't gotten drunk yet but it isn't the fault of the inhabitants.*[37]

Alongside the girls' names, the townsfolk wrote messages on his plane like "*Vive l'Aviateur Americain Engage Volontaire pour la France,*" and "*J'Adore l'Aviateur.*"[38] Kiffin was not allowed to pay for anything and the crowds that followed him everywhere made it almost impossible even to walk through the streets. He ended up staying three nights in the village, and on Sunday afternoon put on an aerial exhibition for almost a thousand residents. With the weather still too bad to leave, he repeated the performance on Monday. While in the air that morning, Kiffin decided to head back to camp and so pointed his machine toward Avord, leaving many wide-eyed Vierzon residents waving goodbye from the ground.

One of those waving inhabitants was a young French maiden. Apparently, Kiffin spent some time with the *mademoiselle* and her mother while in Vierzon; perhaps she was the resident who accompanied Kiffin to the *Café du Commerce*. While that is unknown, a few weeks later the smitten girl wrote Kiffin asking what had become of him. Near the end of her letter, she said:

My mother and I have fond memories of you and would be happy to hear from you. Be kind enough to remember us well, just as we will remember you eternally.[39]

The three days of adulation served as a much-needed shot in the arm for Kiffin. With the spate of accidents, deaths of fellow pilots, and lack of flight time due to faulty machines, Kiffin had begun to lose focus at Avord. Just before his trip, he had written Mrs. Weeks that he was doing little of interest there, stating "at times it grows very monotonous and gets on my nerves."[40]

However, after his fortuitous stay in Vierzon, Kiffin was enjoying aviation more than ever and now felt that in a plane he could do "most anything" he wished.[41] Upon his return to camp, Kiffin shared his experience with the chief pilot, who "laughed and said it was good training for me before going to the front, but that I was an old fool and lucky not to have broken my neck." But while he acknowledged his risk-taking had been "very foolish," Kiffin astutely realized that "at the same time it has given me much confidence, and confidence is the greatest asset in this game."[42]

* * * * *

Kiffin was a little sorry he had left Vierzon, as the fog and clouds prevented him from re-attempting his triangle test for a few days. He told Mrs. Weeks he could "almost forget what the sun looks like had I not once or twice been up high enough to get a peep at it."[43] Still, his new-found confidence allowed him to sail right through the assessment when he was once again able to take flight on October 20. He must have gazed down with fondness as he passed over Vierzon on the last leg of his journey.

The following day, Kiffin successfully completed the next portion of his test – flying in a direct line to Chartres, about 200 kilometers to the northwest. He spent the night in the city, and must have visited the beautiful cathedral, as he sent his sister Agnes a photo postcard of it with a brief note, proudly declaring "I am no longer a student pilot, but a full-fledged aviator."[44]

And the next day he was. In the morning, Kiffin made the return flight to Avord, then immediately took his fourth and final test, volplaning to the ground from five hundred meters. Commandant Sussigny signed off on his flight log, and on October 22, 1915, Kiffin was awarded his *brevet de pilote*, number 1827.[45]

Now an officially-licensed pilot, Kiffin was granted and immediately took an 8-day leave in Paris, where he stayed with Paul, who had recently moved into the home of Mrs. Weeks. Paul was very busy with his work for the French information section and with his writing, and around this time some of his first bylined pieces began to appear in *The Chicago Daily News*.[46] A picture of Kiffin aiming his rifle in the trenches with his old friends Dennis Dowd and Charles Trinkard accompanied one of these articles.[47] While on leave, Kiffin spent as much time as he could with Paul, but given the latter's busy schedule, Kiffin spent even more time with Mrs. Weeks.

Sadly, she had not received any further word about her son Kenneth, who was still officially listed as missing. Kiffin came at an opportune time, for it had been more than four months since Mrs. Weeks had heard from her son, and she had about given up hope that he was alive. Of course, Kiffin's arrival in Paris brightened her mood considerably – Mrs. Weeks gushed over how handsome he looked in his new uniform and helped tailor it to fit him perfectly.[48] She loved to listen to Kiffin's descriptions of flying and told her brother "when I think he has only been doing it for five weeks, I admire his courage."[49]

The boys also spent time with Bill Thorin, who had finagled a short leave and was also in Paris. Thorin was a hard charger, and quite the character. Mrs. Weeks was quite amused one morning when she came out to find Thorin sitting on the couch in her studio and her maid trying to coax him to drink some black coffee. While having their own coffee, Kiffin and Paul looked on with interest as Thorin glanced up and said, "Well, Mother Weeks, I didn't think you would get up so early, so here I am as drunk as a lord."[50]

Kiffin also met Helen Gwynne, an American woman living just outside Paris who was Billy Thorin's *marraine*, or godmother. Designed to boost morale, particularly for soldiers without any family to write them, a godmother was a sort of female pen pal for men at the front. Put in touch via newspapers and magazines, many women "adopted" soldiers to whom they would write encouraging letters or send small parcels. Helen had adopted Thorin, and through him met Kiffin.

Helen must have taken a liking to the confident pilot, for after Kiffin left

Paris, she asked Thorin for Kiffin's address. Thorin informed Kiffin he did not mind if Helen wrote him, saying "damn if I know [what] she can see in a long hayrick like you. Never mind kid, if you make me your best man it is all right, if not, the devil shall take you when I get ahold of you."[51]

During his leave in Paris, Kiffin decided to learn another machine at Avord and get some more training before heading to the front. Despite his busy brother's hectic schedule, Kiffin had a great time and his eight days passed quickly. Paul must have been hard at it, indeed, for he missed seeing Kiffin off on October 31. Of course, Mrs. Weeks accompanied Kiffin to the station.

Not long after his leave with Paul, Kiffin's aerial exploits soon found their way home. On November 8, the *Atlanta Constitution* reported that Kiffin was making two flights a day and had been advised that he might soon "enter active service to become a target for German marksmen."[52] His friends were not surprised to read that Kiffin was "delighted with the work, and expects to enjoy the hazardous duties he will perform as an aviator."[53] In a letter he had just written Loula, Kiffin expressed his own feelings about the work he was doing:

Some day the war will end with us victorious and then you will be glad of what we have done. If we should not be victorious there would be no interest left in anything to me. So I want to stake all on it.[54]

Chapter Thirty-four

Upon his return to Camp d'Avord, Kiffin found a new captain in command. Named Boucher, the commandant was very strict and represented quite a change at the school. Kiffin noted that Captain Boucher was "completely changing everything and it will be some time before things run smoothly."[1] Intent on instilling military rules and discipline, Boucher had reinstituted morning roll call and drills, and there was even talk of regulation haircuts and of changing the flight monitors. Naturally, the men did not like it. Chapman saw no use for any of Boucher's nonsense and commented to his father, "So foolish, for it is not going to make people fly quicker or prevent the simpletons from breaking their heads."[2]

Already a licensed aviator, Kiffin figured he might just as well leave for the front rather than continue to hang around Avord. Having heard that pilots on the Serbian front could earn as much as six hundred francs per month, Kiffin went to see Boucher. But the captain was unexpectedly nice to Kiffin, whose offer to go to Serbia on a Maurice-Farman took Boucher "right off his feet." He gave Kiffin "one compliment after another," telling him how proud it made him to see an American volunteer for France. The captain further informed Kiffin that if he absolutely wished to go to the front, he would send him, but if instead Kiffin stayed, the captain would let him train on any machine he wanted. So Kiffin asked to be put in the Nieuport, France's fastest pursuit plane. The captain agreed, causing Kiffin to brag to Mrs. Weeks, "How is that for diplomacy?"[3]

The recently-licensed pilot couldn't wait to get in his new plane – as Kiffin told his mother, the Nieuport "ranks as the best machine for war that the Allies have" and learning it would place him among the best pilots in France.[4] But in preparation to fly the Nieuport, Kiffin first had to enter the Morane school and pass through a few other machines. So rather than soaring higher and flying farther in the sky, he found himself back on the ground – going in circles with the penguins. And even that was hampered by the poor weather. Anxious to get going, but still optimistic, a few days later Kiffin summed up his circumstances to Paul:

I am getting back into doing nothing here. I have spent exactly ten minutes in a machine since being back. The trouble has been rain and heavy wind. If it keeps up this way I will regret that I didn't go to the front on the Maurice Farman. But when I do finish here I will be on the best fighting machine that France has and will be able to fly any machine made, so it is worth staying for.[5]

In the meantime, Captain Boucher was still rubbing everyone the wrong way. His discipline and reform measures, Chapman wrote, were "boring everybody here enormously." As a result of pushback at one of his roll calls, the captain restricted the men from leaving camp. One day, the *gendarme* tried to make the mechanics perform rifle drill during their lunch. "Of course," Chapman told his father, "pandemonium was let loose, for a 'mecano' is not that kind of animal and must be treated with reserve or they won't work."[6] But as one might have expected, Kiffin did not mind the strict policies. Speaking of the new captain, Kiffin told a friend that "most of the men have been a little dissatisfied, but he is very nice to me and I don't mind a little system to the school."[7]

* * * * *

But the two Americans had other reasons for being frustrated, and much of the month of November would pass quite drearily at Camp d'Avord. To begin with, at the end of October, the day that Chapman was to begin soloing, the machine he had been using was destroyed when two pilots ran into each other. This was on top of a slew of other crashes. In a letter to his father, a rather unsympathetic Chapman explained what he believed to be a contributing cause to the string of smashups – inaptitude:

[T]he Government needs pilots so badly now that they are taking people that are unfit, i.e., lack obvious common sense. There was an accident of that kind recently – a clear day, two fellows did not look where they were going and rammed each other over the field. Stupid, for if either had looked round he could have ducked under the other at the very last moment. Well, we had a little service – long and incoherent. But it's the kind of thing that's bound to happen now and again because they are not all intelligent[.][8]

The accidents continued, and flight time got even harder to come by when the weather turned for the worse. In a letter to his stepmother, Chapman explained his "unprecedented stroke of hard luck":

[First,] a fellow came down vertically and smashed the appareil *I was on into match-wood. Then a big storm kept us indoors two days, and finally one night off its moorings flew the big hangar in which was the double command '14 on which I had been shifted, and two of our best 'brevet appareil.' Now the weather has been bad for two days – fog and drizzle – and today the [double command] '14 which we were to borrow is not in commission.*[9]

The *tempête pluie* (rain storm) described by Chapman must have been pretty strong; Kiffin's flight log confirmed that it forced a stop to all training the weekend of November 12-14.[10] In a letter written that Sunday, Kiffin described its consequences to Loula:

We have been having a storm of wind and rain the last few days that has knocked the school out quite a lot. Friday night, about one o'clock, everyone was roused up to go out and try to keep the whole camp from being destroyed. The wind was blowing down the hangars, and aeroplanes were flying around all over the camp. We had about fifteen machines completely destroyed and I understand Chartres had twenty, so it has been rather expensive for the government.[11]

The bad weather, loss of machines and consequent lack of flying opportunities turned the time into something of a grind. Chapman found life at Avord "steeped in the most profound inertia."[12] Around this time, he wrote:

It is very slow here for there are too many pupils and not enough machines, besides the average man here takes this place as a kind of eternal rest cure. They are all contented to sit on the grass all morning and afternoon and exchange words or take recreation in horseplay.[13]

But while many of their French colleagues were content to pass their time doing as little as possible, Kiffin and Chapman were both intent on finishing their training. Chapman did not get the hang of things quite as fast as Kiffin had, so, finding the Morane school too challenging, he switched to the Maurice Farmans on which Kiffin had originally trained, telling his Uncle Willie:

I changed from the Morane division last week (it is a cranky little monoplane) to the M.F., a very amenable biplane, because the first was too hard a machine to learn without a little experience, so I shall come back to it after I get my brevet.[14]

Now on the verge of soloing and frustrated by the circumstances preventing his advancement, Chapman admitted he was "becoming a real *'gueulard'* now that I have a certain vulgar command of the French language."[15] *Gueulard* means bigmouth or loudmouth, a self-description perhaps fitting at this time – as Chapman admitted to his uncle:

I have been haranguing and almost calling every man in sight a vile embusque, but I think it has done some good. All that is left is to bugger the 'carnet de vol' so it shows I have 15 hours and a [payoff] to the other fellows to let me fly more than my turn.[16]

To escape the new commandant's military discipline, without permission Chapman had taken a room in a tiny village near the field. Kiffin – who had already received approval to sleep out – had his own room nearby and took meals with Victor and his roommate, a French marine named St. Maurice. Chapman reported they were becoming quite expert at housekeeping and told his stepmother that in the bad weather they had been "cooking three meals a day," and had "moved up from fried chops to roast beef and roast chickens."[17]

* * * * *

Kiffin just wanted to get off the ground and back into the sky. Telling Paul he was "awful bored here, and ... sick and tired of the rear," Kiffin lamented, "If we can only have a little good weather, I won't waste much time here, as I intend to go just as fast as I can...."[18] The morning of the fifteenth, Kiffin passed his *lignes droits* (straight lines) on the penguin, and that evening was finally back in the air, making three brief flights to 50 meters on a Bleriot.

The week before Thanksgiving the weather finally cleared enough to get in some regular flight time. Kiffin seized this opportunity to quickly move up to the Morane Parasol. After two days of intense fog lifted, he got in a flight the afternoon of the seventeenth. Thereafter, Kiffin's flight log records four separate flights on November 18th, four more on the 19th, nine on the 20th, and five on the 21st.[19] He told Mrs. Weeks that with five days of fairly good weather he had "gone like a house on fire," and he had, totaling twenty-three separate flights in that time.[20] Just a few days later, the chief pilot told Kiffin that as soon as the General Reserve asked for a flyer, he would send Kiffin, but in the meantime to stay and get some more practice.[21]

Along with French pilot Pierre Navarre – twin brother of the well-known war fighter Jean Navarre – Kiffin was now recognized as one of the best pilots at the school, having sailed through the bulk of his training in just three weeks. One gets a sense of Kiffin's supreme confidence in portions of three separate letters he wrote the morning of November 22. He wrote the first to his friend the Vicomte du Peloux:

I expect to go to Le Bourget most any time now. The only drawback is that they say I have learned too fast and have not enough hours of flight. The Morane is supposed to be the hardest machine to learn to pilot, and after learning it one is supposed to be able to learn to pilot any of them. Yet, so far, I have found it the easiest thing I have ever done. I do anything I want to on it in a practically perfect manner. If I do happen to break a machine now they can't say that it is because I do not know how to manage it. I suppose I am a little conceited, but everyone here regards me as un as, and I am satisfied, as I like to succeed at whatever I undertake. But of course, the way to prove it will be when I am at the front, which I await with impatience.[22]

In his second letter, Kiffin proudly told Paul that most men took "from six weeks to three months to do what I have done since being back here," and explained:

I don't know, but it just seemed to come naturally to me and I have always had absolute confidence and so have been able to do anything I wanted to.[23]

Likely thinking of his friend Kenneth Weeks, whose place in aviation training he had filled, in his third letter Kiffin told Mrs. Weeks:

Believe me, dear, I feel that I have many scores to settle, and there is going to be more than one 'boche' aviator to settle them, or I will not live to tell the tale. As the French say, I am vraiment un as *when in the air, and I am going to take advantage of it.*[24]

Kiffin even flew on Thanksgiving, taking two flights in the morning and one in the afternoon. The next day he sent Loula a brief note to let her know how well he was doing. He wrote:

I now rank as one of the best pilots and am considered as capable of flying any aeroplane. I also do whatever I want to with my machine in [the] air. I think nothing of doing things that men were paid thousands of dollars to do before the war.[25]

Although he was very close to finishing training on the Maurice Farman and qualifying for his *brevet militaire*, things had not gone as well or as quickly for Chapman. Unlike Kiffin, who as one of the best pilots could take out any machine he wanted, Chapman was "up against a solid wall of inertia, indifference and prejudice." That is, as he explained to his stepmother, there were too many men "pleased to remain back here," but too prideful to let others pass them by. Hence, he was stuck behind a glut of students waiting for flight time.[26]

In fact, the last day of November marked Chapman's first flight in a week. In contrast, although Kiffin was no longer pressing to fly – he had just written Mrs. Weeks "I stay out in the field all day and watch the others, but do little myself" – he had gone up twelve more times during the same period.[27] Kiffin was ready.

And so, on November 30, 1915, Captain Boucher signed off on Kiffin's flight log. Just above his signature, he wrote the phrase *perfectionnement terminé* – development completed.[28]

Chapter Thirty-five

The great days through which we are passing

Although Kiffin had mastered all the machines at Avord and was ready to learn the Nieuport, he preferred to wait until he got to Le Bourget where, he told Paul, "they know something about it."[1] But the General Reserve (*Réserve Générale de l'Aviation*, sometimes abbreviated RGA) at Le Bourget still had not requested any pilots, so Kiffin remained at Avord through the first week of December.

While there, Kiffin got in a couple more hours of flight time and was promoted to corporal. Now viewed as one of the top pilots, he had his own machine and all the liberty he wanted. But while he could come and go and fly as he pleased, what Kiffin really wanted was to get to Le Bourget. Frustrated with waiting, on December 6 he showed up unannounced at Mrs. Weeks' home "with a fit of the blues."[2] Kiffin's second mother grabbed her hat and she and Kiffin went to three theatres and a café before picking up Paul and having dinner at *Prunier*, even then a restaurant famous for its oysters.[3] This quick visit to Paris must have brightened Kiffin's spirits, because when Mrs. Weeks awoke the next morning, she found he had already gone back to Avord.

Upon his return to camp, Kiffin learned that the RGA had finally requested additional pilots. On December 9, he was officially transferred to Le Bourget, the depot just outside of Paris which took in licensed aviators from the flight schools at Avord and Pau and supplied the front with pilots and planes.

The airfield at Le Bourget was just four kilometers northeast of Paris, and easily reachable by tramway. Quickly built after the war began, it sat on a large site containing staff barracks, administration buildings and row after row of Bessoneau-type hangars housing Farmans, Caudrons, Breguets and, of course, Nieuports. From this location, numerous planes flew over Paris both day and night.

The day before Kiffin took his first flight at Le Bourget, he and Jim McConnell had tea with Mrs. Weeks and some of her friends who wished to see the boys.[4] McConnell was in Paris, having resigned from the ambulance service at the end of November. As "Mac" told a friend a few weeks later, "You see I thought it all out and figured that the decent thing for me to do was to fight...."[5] In a letter to A. Piatt Andrew, he gave a fuller explanation of his decision to leave the American Ambulance:

I have decided to go into the French Army. I shall be in the aviation corps and, if successful, will become a pilot. I've been thinking the matter over for a long time. I feel as strongly about the war as the French themselves. I believe it to be a war of freedom and civilization against despotic dictation and hideous ideals, and having this attitude I want to give up my capacity as a neutral – as a member of the Red Cross – and go into the fighting end.[6]

Mac was not the only ambulance driver migrating into the "fighting end." Many Americans who had initially volunteered with the ambulance service gradually came to see France's cause as their own and began to sour on their role as noncombatants. Clyde Balsley spoke for many of the drivers when he explained his feelings: "All France was aflame. She was a nation of superheroes. To us, our work appeared insignificant and unworthy, compared with all that her sons were doing."[7] In a letter to his mother, Balsley wrote of America: "If she doesn't take part in this great fight for humanity, I will be a man without a country."[8]

Like McConnell, Balsley also acted on his conviction, and left the ambulance service to become a pilot. The Christmas Eve edition of the *New York Times* reported that these two volunteers had joined what it called the "Franco-American Aviation Corps."[9]

* * * * *

At Le Bourget Field, Kiffin was gaining experience on the Nieuport biplane while waiting to be assigned to an *escadrille* at the front. Poor weather initially limited his time in the air, but by the end of December, he had put in thirteen flights on the Nieuport. For the next few months, he would serve as part of the Paris Air Guard, flying patrols around the city.[10]

Even better for Kiffin, the proximity of Le Bourget to Paris meant that he could fly during the day and in the evening head in to the city to see Mrs. Weeks. Her apartment was quickly becoming the social hub and information clearinghouse for American soldiers on leave in Paris, and Kiffin enjoyed spending time there with Paul and the variety of legionnaires, pilots and ambulance drivers who stopped by.

The opposite trip was just as easy, so Mrs. Weeks regularly came to visit Kiffin. She told her son that "every few days I go to camp in a taxi and bring Kiffin and any other aviators back home who are able to get off. Sometimes the taxi is so full I wonder it does not break down."[11] On one of these trips, someone took a picture of Kiffin and Mrs. Weeks, with Kiffin wearing a fur coat she probably got for him.[12] At the altitudes at which Kiffin was now flying, fur coats were an essential part of a flyer's gear.

Kiffin surely put the warm garment to good use, for his flight log shows he was honing his skills and flying nearly every day. At Le Bourget, Kiffin took easily to the Nieuport pursuit plane and continued his rapid development as a pilot. Back home, the *Atlanta Constitution* reported that a letter from a friend of Kiffin's had arrived in Atlanta, stating that he was "now breveted to fly any aeroplane France has," and "most anxious to get back into the line."

The letter also stated that Kiffin was making good in his new place, "winning much praise from his superiors, and the grade of corporal, with promise to be made sergeant as soon as he goes to the front."[13] In Paris, the popular American aviator was a sought-after dinner guest, and spent one evening with the du Peloux family, who lived very near the *Arc de Triomphe*. However, Kiffin declined most invitations, telling his mother that he, Paul, and Mrs. Weeks "stay very quietly at home and I usually go off to bed as soon as we have finished dinner."[14]

The week before Christmas, Victor Chapman told his mother he was going to Paris, seeking a bit of "city life and civilization." He found it at the Hotel Crillon, just off the *Champs-Elysses* at the *Place de la Concorde*. On Sunday, December 19, Victor borrowed an auto from a friend in Paris and motored out to Le Bourget to pick up Kiffin.

There Chapman learned that Kiffin had a close call on a trip that morning when his engine stopped mid-flight. As he struggled to maintain control, Kiffin had barely cleared a house before hitting a pole and breaking one of the wings of his plane. He came down on a fence, destroying it and his machine, and was very lucky to have escaped without injury. When he and Victor arrived at Mrs. Weeks' home in Paris, Kiffin announced that he had "nearly killed himself this morning[.]"[15]

Even though Victor and Kiffin were friends, there was surely some pride of competition and maybe a little rivalry between the two aviators. It is reasonable to believe that Kiffin's meteoric rise through the pilot ranks may have inflated his ego somewhat, and that Victor's slightly slower pace may have left him feeling a little envious of Kiffin's success. In a note to his stepmother, Victor confirmed that both things were likely true – somewhat unkindly, he wrote that he was "thankful to see Rockwell has had a bit of a setback. He left Avord thinking he was all hell."[16]

Mrs. Weeks enjoyed meeting Victor and added him to her growing list of "sons." She now had so many soldiers coming and going through her home that she could hardly keep up with all of them. Even so, she made sure she sent each of her boys at the front some groceries and little gifts for Christmas and kept busy planning a large Christmas dinner at her home.

One person not coming for Christmas was Billy Thorin, who was spending twenty days in jail for busting up a café in La Valbonne. In a letter to Mrs. Weeks, he explained what happened: "Some guys called us Americans a lot of fools and we smashed them up and then a gendarme on top of them. So what I heard from others they have changed their opinion about us here in La Valbonne anyway. It was a good go."[17] In what would become a regular occurrence, Mrs. Weeks, Paul and Kiffin each sent Thorin money to pay for the damage.[18]

Paul later told of another time when he gave Thorin ten francs with which to bribe his corporal to avoid an eight-day sentence for overstaying his leave. Upon learning that his friend went to jail anyway, Paul asked Thorin what happened, and why he had been unable to "fix" the corporal. Billy candidly explained, "Well, I got to thinking it over and decided I'd rather do the eight days and keep the ten francs for myself."[19]

* * * * *

Around Christmas, Kiffin received a printed Christmas card from Marion Fiedler, a girl back home. Titled "My Christmas Wish for You," the card contained the following poem:

When a body likes a body,
Just like I like you,
Then a body has a body
To send good wishes to.[20]

The card also contained a handwritten personal note:

May you have the happiest Christmas and the luckiest New Year possible. I say lucky, because every day is so full of danger, and I hope you and Paul will come through all o.k.[21]

While it is unknown how close they were, it is clear that Kiffin and Ms. Fiedler had been on friendly terms back in Atlanta. Now Kiffin was quickly gaining his share of female admirers in Paris, so it is a safe bet that warm feelings for Kiffin were not exclusive to Marion Fiedler.

For one, Helen Gwynne, an American woman living outside Paris, seems to have developed some feelings for the dashing pilot. After getting his address from D.W. Thorin, Helen wrote Kiffin that Thorin had said that "if he did give me your address, he certainly expected a bit of the wedding cake. Don't you love it?" She also reported that Thorin "didn't see what I could possibly find in you, except that your uniform was better & cleaner than his, otherwise that you were no better looking than himself!!!"[22]

In a photograph taken around this time, one can see what must have impressed Helen about Kiffin. Wearing his new uniform, standing ramrod straight, shoulders back and feet firmly planted, Kiffin's steady gaze and cool semi-smile exude confidence. Although their color cannot be made out in the black and white photo, Kiffin was quite proud of his aviator's wings, two little insignia with red and gold threads Mrs. Weeks had sewn on the collar of his uniform.[23]

The wings on his collar were a big difference between Kiffin and Billy Thorin, but probably not the sole attribute Helen found attractive about Kiffin. Whatever it was Helen saw in Kiffin, by Christmas Eve, Thorin wrote to tell him, "When you get a chance, take a run out to ... see Helen or I guess I will never get no *paix*. She is asking me about you in every letter."[24] At some point Kiffin apparently did visit Helen and may even have reciprocated some of her feelings. A little while later, Thorin asked him:

Are you in love, or what is the matter? I know I am always hot on the trail of a skirt when I am in Paris, but you didn't seem to catch up somehow. Have you got ahold of something special? ... I seen you have been out and seen Helen, she is quite stuck on your old dial.[25]

Thorin's Christmas wishes for Kiffin were somewhat different than Marion Fiedler's. He told Kiffin "to give the *Boche* hell" when sent to the front and closed his letter with this sage advice: "Don't let them drop you before you get one of them to keep you company."[26]

What a somber yet hopeful scene Paris must have presented on Christmas Eve, 1915. In England, the cry was "carry on," and that spirit also animated the feelings of the French. While surely less gay than in former times, Paris restaurants and cafés were crowded with families and friends gathering together, and all the principal churches drew large congregations for midnight mass.

On Christmas Day, Mrs. Weeks put on a splendid dinner for Kiffin, Paul, Jim McConnell and several of her prominent friends. An article in the *New York Herald* headlined "Paris, In Quiet Hope, Passes Second Christmas Eve of War," perfectly sums up the feelings that prevailed in the old city:

Though the shadow of the great war lies athwart suffering Europe and though in France there be countless homes that are mourning lost ones, yet something of the spirit of Christmas has survived the tragedy of circumstances. In Paris particularly, where weather conditions on Christmas Eve were deplorable, the unbiased observer must have been impressed by the people's fine courage and the optimism that seventeen months of warfare have not dimmed.

All day yesterday the main boulevards of the city were very crowded, and, despite the occasional rain, the booths did good business, especially among the procrastinating majority who had forgotten to buy small presents for their own or other peoples' children. There was also an eleventh-hour rush at the big stores, which, apart from the fact that the preponderance of women was even greater than usual, seemed to be as busy as in the piping times of peace. Many of the shoppers were buying gifts for the men in the trenches, and the military post yesterday and all through the past week must have dealt with a record number of parcels.[27]

As noted, the soldiers were not forgotten during the Christmas season. Parliament had passed a bill allowing parcels of up to two pounds to be sent to the front postage-free, so rather than shells and hand grenades, the troops were bombarded with two-pound packages containing cold chickens, meat pies, hams, cakes, sweetmeats and every imaginable item of apparel.

At McConnell's old stomping grounds in Neuilly, Santa Claus surprised the wounded troops at the American Ambulance with presents for all. Volunteers served a bounteous Christmas dinner consisting of turkey, cranberry sauce and the usual trimmings, as well as plum pudding and Christmas cakes. At the *Hopital de la Pitie*, a room decorated with flowers and an amusing scenic background had been converted into a concert hall where volunteer Parisian artists put on a show "enthusiastically applauded by the many wounded soldiers who filled the theatre," followed by a Christmas tree and "splendid" Christmas dinner. In other hospitals and in the trenches, the men were provided food, gifts, entertainment and other forms of Christmas cheer.[28]

*　*　*　*　*

As the calendar rolled over to 1916, the French looked ahead with increasing determination and confidence. By this time, Kiffin realized his destiny was in the sky and confidently applied himself to mastering the *chasse* plane. More than ever, he and Paul felt at home among the French people and soldiers, and even more committed to defeating Germany. As increasing numbers of Americans learned of the sacrifice being made by the French, they began to sense what those American sons there already understood – that their duty lie in France.

On New Year's Day, 1916, A. Piatt Andrew sent to some French friends a box containing a violin he had purchased in Alsace. In a letter accompanying the gift, Andrew wrote that the violin, made in the trenches by a French soldier of the 66th Division, had doubtless been played at the front and so had heard the roar of the *soixante quinze*, and of how the soldier who had fashioned it "may be among those who have already given their lives for their country in Alsace."

The conclusion of Andrew's letter epitomizes the actions of Kiffin and the other American volunteers, and seems a fitting end to 1915:

I like to think that when the war has become only a memory, this little box from Alsace may still sing to you ... of the great days through which we are passing, and that it will help sometimes in recalling one who will then be on the other side of the ocean, who shared in some degree the joys and sorrows of those days and who will always feel as tenderly toward your dear country as toward his own.[29]

Chapter Thirty-six

My! they will be feted!

While Kiffin was working his way through aviation school at Avord, the Franco-American Flying Corps was taking tangible form. In the fall of 1915, the organization opened a recruiting office and reading room on the *Avenue des Champs-Élysées* in Paris, and put out a pamphlet directed to American club and university men, highlighting the citations won by Thaw, Cowdin and Prince.[1] The circular noted that although previously many volunteers had been turned down, arrangements had now been made "to give a favorable reception to those having serious moral and physical guarantees."[2]

Indeed, witnessing the positive press reaction to its initial crop of American pilots, the French began to realize the full scope of the potential benefits in Prince's idea.[3] Hoping for even more American volunteers, in early December an order was posted at the headquarters of the Foreign Legion in Lyon informing commanding officers that "all Americans in any branch of the service may on their own request be transferred to the aviation branch without delay."[4]

In addition, seeking to generate further enthusiasm and positive press, the French hit on another idea – to send the most well-known and decorated American aviators back home to the states for a brief visit. Thus, it came about in early December that Prince, Thaw and Cowdin were granted eight-days of leave to be spent in New York. "Needless to say," Cowdin later wrote, "we were elated."[5]

Accordingly, while Kiffin was stationed at Le Bourget, flying with the air guard protecting Paris, Thaw, Cowdin and Prince left for Falmouth, England, where on December 15 they boarded the Dutch ocean liner S.S. *Rotterdam*, bound for America.[6] Before they could sail, however, an issue arose as to their status – their native country refused to issue passports for its citizens in the service of belligerent armies. To resolve the matter, France provided the trio with passports describing them as French subjects.[7]

In a letter to his stepmother on December 19, Victor Chapman mentioned his friends' trip home:

I suppose you know that Prince, Cowdin and Thaw got a week's "permission" in the U.S., voyage not included. Good for them! The only thing I fear is that some pro-German movement will have them interned. I suggest they sail by way of Canada and give out false reports as to the length of time they are staying, and the N.Y. boat they return on. However, I take it they will have sense enough for all that, and really, America is too strong pro-Ally to lift the arm of the law. My! they will be feted![8]

* * * * *

The *Rotterdam* took eight days to cross the Atlantic. According to Elliott Cowdin, although he and Prince had not known Thaw very well previously, during their trip back to America they spent much time in his company, "became great friends, and convinced him of the desirability of forming an American Squadron."[9] Thereafter, Thaw was united with Prince and Cowdin in bringing about their plans.

The ship docked in the Port of New York two days before Christmas, and even before disembarking the three men found themselves at the center of a ring of reporters and press photographers. Over the next few days, a picture of the three pilots on the deck of the *Rotterdam* appeared in newspapers all around the country, under headlines such as: "American Aviators Back from Western Front," "American War Aviators Decorated by France," and best of all, "American War Eagles Flying for France."[10]

At various points in their service with the French, each of the men had been reported as missing or killed. But, as the *Chicago Tribune* put it, "they were very much alive when interviewed and photographed on the deck of the steamship *Rotterdam*."[11] Alive, yes, but talkative? – no. The three airmen took turns deflecting questions as to the specifics of the planes they were flying, where they were based, and the service in which they were engaged, saying that "military regulations as well as modesty forbade giving out details of their military exploits."[12]

Asked about the actions for which they had each been awarded war medals, Prince again deferred, saying the answer would necessitate the telling of military secrets. Pressed further, he would say only that their medals had been "awarded in the regular course of duty."[13] The next day, one New York paper reported:

It was almost impossible for reporters to get a word from any one of the trio when they were first approached, but finally they appointed Mr. Prince spokesman. After numerous questions, the majority of which Mr. Prince said he could not answer, he was asked to tell his story his own way.

"There isn't much to say," he said. "Mr. Thaw has been with the French army since the beginning of the war, first having served in the Foreign Legion as a private. He took up aviation last March, and is now a lieutenant. Mr. Cowdin and myself have been aviators since last May. Just where we have been stationed is a secret, as is the name of the machines that we are flying. Suffice it to say that we have been actively engaged all the time and with good results.[14]

After some further persuasion, the three pilots loosened up a bit, and agreed "to give a composite interview of a general character."[15] The men answered a few questions about the various types of aviation work, the range of anti-aircraft guns, and the casualty rates for aviators, but didn't disclose much else. Although he declined to reveal much of what he saw or did, Prince did note with a smile that he and his two friends "had every reason to believe that in the end France would win."[16]

The reporters also questioned the men about the erroneous reports of their capture or death. An article in the *New York World* titled "Three Oft-Killed American Flyers Home from France for Christmas" contained the most humorous account:

These three birdmen ... who have each won the Croix de Guerre, were the center of interest on the big Dutch liner when she docked in Hoboken. All three had been reported dead on more than one occasion. They emphatically denied the rumors. Prince was the most often killed of the three. He explained that the false reports were due to the fact that [Jimmie Bach], another American flyer, fell behind the German lines and was mistaken for him.[17]

* * * * *

As they had come home to spend the holidays with their families, the men soon went their separate ways. While Cowdin remained in New York with his family, Prince (whose brother and parents had met the ship at the pier) returned to Boston for Christmas. Thaw's family had also come to pick him up and, after spending Christmas in New York City, he returned with them to Pittsburgh for a brief visit home.

The day before Christmas, a reporter caught Cowdin as he jumped into a limousine with some friends, and asked him whether a week of New York social life such as his pals had planned for him might be "just as dangerous to health as a week of aviating?" "Dangerous?" replied Cowdin. "Well, yes, I guess it is. But nothing so exciting as returning to New York has happened to me in a long time."[18] The press felt likewise, and so, wherever the men went, it seemed a reporter or two trailed along. This was understandable – in a nation thirsting for news from the war, the young pilots were demi-gods, and "from the moment of their arrival they were lionized and kept constantly in the public eye."[19]

That doesn't mean the men divulged much of significance. Asked by one of his hometown papers in Pittsburgh about the conditions in Europe, Thaw firmly but politely replied, "I am in a neutral country and I must positively decline to talk about the war. All that I have seen and heard abroad I must regard as confidential, and I can say nothing about it."[20]

Such tightlipped responses only drew more press coverage, even as the friends went their separate ways. Compelled to focus on minutiae, news hounds reported on every detail they could learn about the men, from their whereabouts and doings, to their "Joffre blue" uniforms. One account breathlessly described the small silver nameplate Thaw, Cowdin and Prince each wore on a bracelet on his right wrist "as a mark of identification in the event of death."[21]

Thaw and Prince even helped push along a burgeoning interest in wrist watches when both were seen wearing them while on leave, prompting the *Washington Post* a few months later to declare that "the wrist watch is no longer a sign of effeminacy when worn by men."[22] To the contrary, according to the *Post*, the two young aviators had during their Christmas leave vividly illustrated the manliness of such a thing:

Nobody who saw them or had heard of their record while flying for France could accuse them of effeminacy. Thaw is a young giant, and Prince has a reputation of being able to lick his weight in wildcats.[23]

If the coolest of the cool, the gods of the sky, were wearing wrist watches, then by golly, wrist watches were manly.

* * * * *

But the publicity had negative effects, as well. For one, Chapman's suspicion proved correct – German sympathizers and others who wished America strictly to maintain her neutrality saw the visit and positive press accounts as an affront to that pledge.

It probably didn't help that the boys became a bit more vocal, especially about the need for preparedness in America, and in public comments emphasized the importance of the Allied cause. One Pittsburgh paper quoted Thaw as saying that France felt "that we really ought not be so strictly neutral. Their battles are ours, they hold, and their cause ours; and we ought to come out openly and help the allies win."[24] Along the same lines, Prince told a Boston reporter that his experience in France had taught him that it was "criminal for the United States not to prepare for war."[25]

Prince even took a few (metaphorical) shots at the German forces. For example, he let slip that the American aviators had "no respect for the German airmen" who, he said, "seem to be forbidden to cross the lines alone." He paused before adding with a sly smile, "they also seem to have orders not to fight."[26] In contrast to the cowardly Germans, Prince emphatically declared that "the French fight with splendid spirit and you can quote me as saying we will win.[27] Although he was at pains to insist he was not fighting Germany or Germans, but rather "German militarism," this was not a big distinction to the pro-German sympathizers.

Sure enough, just as Victor Chapman had feared, a clamor was raised to hold the men as belligerents. The day after their arrival, George S. Viereck, editor of *The Fatherland* (a pro-German magazine established in New York City in August 1914 to promote American "neutrality"), sent a telegram to Secretary of State Robert Lansing seeking the immediate arrest and internment of the three pilots. It read:

Sir:

I respectfully call your attention to the fact that Second Lieutenant William Thaw, Sergeant Elliott Cowdin and Sergeant Norman Prince, of the French Army Flying Corps, arrived in New York yesterday on the Holland-American liner Rotterdam.

In accordance with the universally accepted canons of international law governing neutrality, I herewith request that you issue an order for their immediate internment.

These men, though of American birth, are officers in active service in the French army, and it would be a gross violation of American neutrality if they were not at once detained so as to prevent their return to the front.

Permit me to call your attention to the Convention respecting the rights and duties of neutral powers and persons in case of war on land adopted by the Peace Convention at The Hague in 1907, and ratified by the United States.

Article 11 of this Convention reads:

"A neutral power which receives on its territory troops belonging to the belligerent armies, shall intern them, as far as possible, at a distance from the theatre of war.

"It may keep them in camps and even confine them in fortresses or in places set apart for this purpose.

"It shall decide whether officers can be left at liberty on giving their parole not to leave the neutral territory without permission."

In view of the fact that the neutrality of the Administration has been seriously questioned both here and abroad, I trust that you will take immediate action in the case and that you will hold these three officers in confinement, unless they give their parole not to leave American territory without your permission.

Inasmuch as you have so ardently championed the rights of neutrals as against the Central Powers, I feel sure that you will avail yourself of the opportunity to demonstrate to the World that the United States Government is also alive to its neutral duties. In fact, I am advised that we have no choice in the matter unless we regard international conventions as "scraps of paper."

I am, sir,

Respectfully yours,

George Sylvester Viereck[28]

Viereck urged his readers to contact their representative or senator if Secretary of State Robert Lansing refused "to act in accordance with the law, or if he attempts to evade the issue by legal quibbling."[29]

* * * * *

Surely Lansing would have liked nothing better than to evade Vierick's complaint, with or without legal quibbling. He certainly did not want to intern these American heroes, and doing so surely would have created a huge outcry. Lucky for him, Viereck's telegram was not received by the State Department until 7:00 p.m. on Christmas Eve and, owing to the fact that it was a Friday, Lansing had until at least Monday, December 27 before he reasonably could be expected to consider the matter.[30]

Lansing's initial reaction was to inform Viereck that the question of internment of the three aviators "has been given careful consideration and it is the opinion of the Department that such persons are not subject to internment if they enter the country in the ordinary course of travel as individuals and not as an organized military body & if their conduct does not infringe the proprieties of international or municipal law."[31] However, by the time his letter was finalized and sent – not until Tuesday, December 28 – Lansing had settled upon a more measured approach which, coincidentally, would take a bit longer to sort out:

The Department received after office hours on December 24th your letter and telegram of that date, relating to the arrival in New York of three officers of the French Flying Corps. In reply I have to advise you that the possible violation of the neutrality of the United States by the presence of these men in the country is receiving the earnest attention of the Government.[32]

At the same time, Lansing also sent a letter to the French Ambassador, Jean Jules Jusserand. Referring to the accounts Jusserand had "no doubt, seen in the press," Lansing asked a little favor of him:

As it appears that these gentlemen are in the active service of the armed forces of your Government, I would be pleased if you could find it possible to inform me as to whether this is true and as to their purpose in visiting this country. I am desirous of having this information in the interest of protecting the neutrality of the United States.[33]

In the interim, the press had found a few lawyers inclined to engage in what Viereck would have called "legal quibbling." For example, the day after Christmas, the *New York Sun* asserted that lawyers specializing in international law "do not take seriously" the suggestion that the treaty entered into at The Hague a few years earlier required the United States to intern the pilots. The *Sun* quoted one attorney's opinion:

The duty of neutral nations is to disarm and intern belligerent forces who enter neutral territory. The three men mentioned have come here unarmed – without uniforms – not having been forced by the exigencies of war or on a military expedition, in the capacity of civilian Americans to spend Christmas with their families. If they are subject to internment so also should be the 350,000 German reservists here, not to mention German officers who are not here to spend Christmas with their families. These aviators are not troops in any sense of the word.[34]

Other papers also pooh-poohed the notion of internment, asserting that the three pilots had merely come home for the Christmas holiday and intended to return to France soon, anyway.[35] In the *Pittsburgh Gazette Times*, another attorney derided as "fantastic" the notion of applying the internment provision "to two or three of our nationals who peaceably return to this country for Christmas."[36]

But would it really have been so fantastic? Thaw, Prince and Cowdin could easily have been seen as coming within the provisions cited by Viereck. In part, Article 11 provided: "A neutral power which receives on its territory troops belonging to the belligerent armies, shall intern them...." The United States was plainly a "neutral power," and it had "received on its territory" the three aviators. The only arguable question was whether the three Americans were "troops belonging to belligerent armies."

For his part, Vierick set forth his belief that they were:

These men are troops of a belligerent nation, just as the scattered members of a defeated army are troops. If German aviators should descend for mere pleasure in Holland, they would be interned and rightly so.[37]

He further allowed that if there were any German officers in America, they should be held until the war ended, and suggested that if Lansing refused to arrest and hold the three pilots, "it proves that in his mind we are now at war with Germany."[38]

* * * * *

But in Pittsburgh, Thaw, for one, did not seem concerned. Asked his thoughts on the internment rumors, he brushed aside the possibility as "too ridiculous to be worth thinking about," and further responded that "the German newspaper that started the story may get some free advertising out of it, but that is all."[39] Reiterating the point to another reporter, Thaw stated:

All I know about any internment is what I read in the newspapers this morning. I have heard nothing about it officially or unofficially from any other source. Many friends have asked me about it, but my only answer is that I know nothing whatever about it. Mr. Vierick apparently is seeking advertising or publicity for himself or his periodical. I came over here as a civilian. I am unarmed and my mission is one of simply passing the holidays with my family.[40]

In Boston, a few remarks from Norman Prince and his father stirred the pot further, and surely made the American officials even more uneasy. For starters,

Norman stated unequivocally that after his visit home he was going back to Europe to fight for France.[41] At the same time, his father publicly wondered "Why should Germany demand that my boy and the other American aviators be interned here when there are many officers of the French army here against whom such action has not been sought?"[42]

In a speech just after Christmas, Norman strongly advocated American preparation for war, stating that "one day of warfare would be more expensive to a country than one year of preparedness."[43] When asked the attitude of France towards America, Prince replied that the French officers were friendly to the American airmen, but did not like the attitude of the American Government, and that "they would much prefer to see Roosevelt in the White House than Wilson."[44] As one paper reported, at another dinner given in his honor, Prince even suggested that grateful Americans such as himself could choose but one side in the ongoing war:

"I entered the French army because I had lived a great deal in Paris, because I was interested in aviation, and because," the gentleman grew grave and most serious, "because – there was need – for all Americans who loved France – who felt gratitude to France for certain generous chapters out of history – to do – in this deadly struggle – all that they could to help. Indeed, to one who feels as I feel, there seemed to be nothing else a man could do."[45]

This sort of talk further inflamed the pro-German forces, and a few more sympathizers lodged complaints with the State Department, or with their representatives in Congress. In addition, Viereck sent Lansing another telegram, insisting on the "necessity of urgent action" before the aviators returned to France. Viereck wrote, in part:

All three men have stated in newspaper interviews that it is their intention to return to the battlefront after a furlough of eight days. If immediate action is not taken it will be impossible to intern them. Their escape under the circumstances to which I have called your attention would constitute a grave international scandal.... [T]he United States cannot without violating both the spirit and the letter of neutrality permit these young men to rejoin the enemies of a country with which we are at peace.[46]

To this point, the State Department surely preferred simply to run out the clock and let the issue fade with the departure of the men. Indeed, a few articles had already appeared in the New York and Washington press, suggesting that Lansing would "probably reply unfavorably" to Viereck's demand, and asserting that "those returning to this country are subject to internment only if they return as members of an armed expedition."[47] In addition, it was insinuated that the State Department would "not take official cognizance of the case of the three American aviators unless demand for their internment is made by diplomatic representatives of Germany or her allies."[48]

But in the face of Viereck's renewed request and the additional demands, it became increasingly apparent that the issue was not going to be dropped. Thus, on December 29, Lansing had a note sent to the Attorney General, asking that he have the Justice Department interview the three men "for the purpose of ascertaining their connection with the armed services of France and their purpose in visiting this country."[49] The letter added that it was "especially desired that it be ascertained" whether the trio of officers had taken "any oath of allegiance to the French Government."[50]

Lansing also prepared a separate letter to the Joint State and Navy Neutrality Board, a committee constituted at the beginning of the war to render advice as to questions arising regarding the neutrality of the United States.[51] Lansing asked for a "preliminary opinion" on the issue "in order that the Department's attitude may be properly guided."[52]

Working quickly, the Board rendered its advisory opinion the next day, December 30. The three-man committee determined that "the United States has no duty of neutrality to arrest and intern the three members of the French Flying Corps referred to." While it agreed that "a German submarine meeting the three French officers in question would be entitled to capture them," it did not follow, said the Board, that the United States had a duty to intern the men. Instead, the three men were free to "remain in United States jurisdiction and depart at pleasure, provided they depart as individuals and not as an organized body belonging to a belligerent force; and provided further, that while in this country they do nothing to compromise the neutrality of the United States."[53]

This opinion quickly found its way into the press, which cited State Department officials as taking the position that since the pilots were not in America as part of an armed expedition, there was no more reason for their internment than for the other British, German, French and Russian officers temporarily residing in America.[54] In any event, said the State Department, since the men had relinquished their American citizenship upon enlistment with France, the United States did not intend to hold them.[55]

But even this was not clear – when a reporter asked about his American

348

citizenship, Prince denied forfeiting it:

I'm going to hold on to that. When I joined the aviation corps I had to hold up my hand and swear that I would be loyal to the French cause during the war. But I understand that this doesn't invalidate me as an American citizen.[56]

Thaw was also questioned as to his citizenship status. Earlier that year, the *New York American* published a story claiming that Thaw's supposed marriage had saved him from being a drunken scapegrace and turned him "from a waster into a useful citizen and war hero."[57] Thaw sued for libel, claiming the paper had mixed him up with his infamous relative Harry K. Thaw, as he had never been a drunk or a waster – in fact, he had never even been married![58]

Because he brought his lawsuit as a citizen of the United States, upon Thaw's return to the country, the opposing attorney saw his chance and put Thaw under oath, apparently seeking to lay the groundwork to argue that he had lost his citizenship by reason of his service with the French in the war. In his deposition, taken while home on leave, Thaw testified that indeed he had "signed a paper promising obedience and allegiance to the French government – but that was to have effect only during the war."[59] Asked why he joined the French army, Thaw replied: "my enlistment may be ascribed to three motives. My love of France, my dislike for Germany, and my fondness for aviation."[60]

He didn't want to create a diplomatic incident, but he was under oath, after all.

* * * * *

That was not the only time Thaw would be under oath during his leave. On January 3, 1916, the day before he and the others were to sail for France, Thaw gave his sworn affidavit to agents from the Department of Justice. Interestingly, Thaw attested that he had brought from France both his uniform and a weapon – "a small 25 mm automatic pistol" – which he had worn while traveling through England, but "upon boarding the steamer for this country, I went to my room and put on civilian clothing."[61]

As for the oath he had taken upon enlisting with the Foreign Legion, Thaw stated it "did not include my renunciation of allegiance to the United States," and so "all my rights as a citizen of the United States are fully retained." Thaw also explained his reasons for returning to America:

I came to this country to spend the holiday season with my family and came here entirely at my own expense; also in connection with some important personal litigation which demanded my attention. I am not here in the performance of any mission for the military authorities of France, nor have I any intention of rendering any such service.[62]

That same day, Lansing received the reply of French Ambassador Jusserand to his letter asking the purpose of the three aviators' visit. Jusserand's note echoed Thaw's affidavit:

From what I hear, and this I have from quite trustworthy authority, the motive of their coming, for the briefest stay in the United States, was a desire to see their relatives in this season, and they had no other.[63]

Combined with the earlier opinion of the neutrality board, these diplomatic assurances from the French government provided further cover for Lansing's inaction. As far as the State Department was concerned, the aviators' visit was merely a Christmas trip with familial motives, and that was that.

* * * * *

Not that it mattered much – by the time the State Department received Thaw's affidavit, the aviators were on their way back to France. The American pilots had reunited for New Year's Eve in New York City, where they spent the night as the guests of honor at the Yale Club.[64] Much of the city was still buzzing over a decidedly pro-French editorial printed in the *New York Tribune* a few days earlier. Among other things, the piece noted that from the "beginning of our national life, we have owed France a debt of affection and of honor," and that for many thousands of Americans, there could be "no more sincere or moving words for the New Year than those – '*Vive la France!*'"[65] Undoubtedly, this phrase must have been among the toasts offered at the Yale Club that New Year's Eve.

As Norman Prince prepared to leave, it occurred to his mother and father, staying with him at the Vanderbilt Hotel, that this could be the last time they ever saw their son. On impulse, his mother determined to have Norman's portrait painted, and at seven o'clock on Sunday night, January 2, a call was made to noted artist Frank Weston Benson to ascertain his willingness to come to New York and paint the portrait in a single day.[66] No doubt influenced by the promised $10,000.00 fee, Benson caught the midnight train from Boston and spent the whole of the next day painting Norman in his uniform.[67]

The day after that, along with his older brother Freddy – whom he had convinced to accompany him back to France to become the family's second aviator – Prince, Cowdin and Thaw boarded the *Rochambeau* bound for Le Havre. John Jay Chapman, who was at his New York home, went down to the pier to see the aviators off and to give Cowdin a pair of binoculars to take to Victor. In a letter to his son, John Jay wrote of his fears for the returning men:

I hope they won't be torpedoed. Someone says the passengers of the Rochambeau *have been warned. But we all know the Germans will sink anything they can anyway.*

Chapman was becoming increasingly disgusted with President Wilson, of whom he wrote:

It is peace-at-any-price, literally. No policy, no defence of idea, no sense of honor, no common sense. The only hope is that the experiences may be sinking into the average American [and] making him long for Roosevelt.[68]

Although the country as a whole still did not favor war, the reality of it was "sinking into the average American," as Chapman put it. Prince had changed quite a bit, too – now a war hero, he left on this voyage with the full support of his father and family and, increasingly, the people of his country. Based on the ongoing submarine warfare conducted by the Germans in the year Prince had been away, at least in the Eastern states, public opinion had swung from lukewarm neutral to decidedly pro-Allies. From the deck of the *Rochambeau*, he wrote a quick note to his "dear Mamma":

Just a line before the pilot leaves us to tell you that Freddy and I appreciate your sorrow in having your two boys go to the war. However, the greater the sorrow, the greater the joy will be when they return![69]

The *Rochambeau* had barely pulled away from America's shores when Prince was asked directly about his motives for joining up with France. Now in international waters and once again free to speak his mind, Prince replied:

I enlisted because we in America owe such a debt to France as can never be paid. My country may have forgotten what Lafayette and Rochambeau and all the rest did for us when we were in dire need – but some of us have not forgotten.[70]

Chapter Thirty-seven

All those who were indifferent are now more sympathetic.

In retrospect, the whole "Christmas leave" business appears to have been what it likely was – an attempt by the Franco-American Corps, if not the French government, to generate positive press surrounding American involvement in the war on France's behalf. If so, it worked like a charm. As one authoritative source noted, "[w]hether intentional or not, the visit to the United States was an excellent piece of diplomacy."[1]

The French authorities must have been monitoring the hugely positive press the trio of aviators garnered in the states, for upon their return to France in early 1916, the Americans would find they were now pushing at an open door. Thus, while the returning pilots had displayed their skill on the battlefront, it was their skill on the front pages that ultimately "convinced the authorities in Paris that a squadron of American volunteers would have an important influence on opinion in the United States."[2] On their way back, Thaw, Prince and Cowdin determined to combine their efforts to induce the French government to proceed with the long-promised – but just as long-delayed – formation of the American *escadrille.*

Their endeavors began even before they docked. While crossing the Atlantic aboard the *Rochambeau,* the now united aviators met fellow passenger Eugene Boggiano, an Italian reporter for *Le Petit Journal* in Paris who had traveled to America as a special correspondent for that paper.[3] The managing director of the *Petit Journal* was a former Minister of Foreign Affairs, and through him Boggiano had plenty of connections in the upper echelons of the French military. Upon their return to Paris, Boggiano arranged several introductions for his new pilot friends, among them René Besnard, who had replaced General Hirschauer as the Minister of Aviation in the Fall of 1915.

Georges Thénault, Thaw's commander with *Escadrille C.42,* also happened to be in Paris, and met with the group in the *Rue Royale,* just off the *Place de la Concorde* and steps from the Hotel Crillon, where Victor Chapman was again staying while on permission after finishing his brevet at Avord.[4] Clyde Balsley had also just received his flying license, and together with Kiffin, who came in from Le Bourget, on Sunday, January 16, 1916, the six American pilots and Thénault met with Besnard over lunch and discussed at considerable length how to go about forming their own distinctive flying unit.[5]

Although Minister Besnard had perhaps seen the photo of Prince, Thaw and Cowdin in the Paris edition of the *New York Herald* a few days before, the American pilots surely impressed him even more in person.[6] By the end of lunch, Besnard informed the group that immediate action would be taken to enroll all the American aviators into a single squadron.[7]

The boys left the meeting in high spirits: Balsley wrote in his diary that he believed they were "going to be able to arrange it so that we Americans will all be together flying the same apparatuses," while Chapman told his stepmother that he had lunched "with some big guns in French and American aviation."[8] According to Chapman there was a noticeable change in the attitude of the French officials: "All those who were indifferent are now more sympathetic."[9]

* * * * *

Of course, despite Besnard's assurances, the squadron was not immediately formed. A few days after the meeting, Chapman reported that although they had "understood the American *Escadrille* was formed and we were to be united," the commanding officer at Le Bourget "knew nothing of it and sent us off to our respective groups – Thaw to Caudron, Cowdin to Nieuport, Prince to Voisin and myself to Maurice."[10] Chapman disappointedly told his stepmother:

That means Prince and I have to go to some God-forsaken village ... and wait till the order comes through – if it does – and the ministry does not fail as it did last autumn when all had been arranged.[11]

Two days later he wrote to his father, "I cannot quite make out whether this American business is going through at once. They (Prince, Cowdin, etc.) certainly have a hand on the higher up ropes of this machine; but even then it seems to take weeks to pass an order down."[12]

Chapman's reference to the failure of the ministry was an allusion to the prior fall when Besnard replaced General Hirschauer as the Minister of Aviation, which had hindered the formation of the squadron. Chapman feared it might happen again, as Besnard had earned himself a few enemies through his push for various reforms and by January 1916, the knives were out.[13] But while the Paris press had been criticizing Besnard's aviation department for three straight weeks, Chapman cautioned his father that things were "not as bad as the French papers say." Instead, during his time in Paris, Chapman had observed that the "higher professional men" knew and did their jobs well, but over them were "bureaucrats who only put sticks in the administration wheels for their own interest[.]"[14]

Anxious to get some confirmation and movement, on January 24, 1916 the Committee followed up in writing with Minister Besnard:

The members of the Franco-American Committee wish to express to you their sincere thanks for the approval which you have given to their plan, which gives them encouragement to continue their efforts.... [We] would be grateful if you could obtain through General Headquarters the grouping of American pilots in the same squadron. This has often been promised us, and it is of the greatest importance that such a squadron be constituted.[15]

Besnard fully intended to stand behind his promise to establish the squadron, and even appointed a lieutenant to look out for the American interests. Unfortunately, before he could respond to the Committee's letter or take any additional concrete steps towards forming the *escadrille*, on the night of January 29 a German zeppelin navigated over Paris and let fall eleven bombs, killing at least seven persons and wounding many more.[16]

The next night, another zeppelin crept through the heavy fog and dropped a few bombs on the airfield at *Le Bourget*, leaving two massive craters.[17] Kiffin may have witnessed this attack up close, and probably was among those who took to the skies to chase the airship away from Paris, but due to the fog there was not much that could be done.[18] One of the pilots told of the night's events:

When the alarm was given us at ten minutes past nine, thirty aviators immediately took flight. Already comrades were patrolling above, as is the case every evening. I perceived that we were going to be handicapped by the mist, which was very thick. In fact, at a height of 500 metres I could not distinguish the searchlights, which failed to pierce the fog, and even with my light, I could not see more than about eight metres below me.[19]

In the aftermath of the bombing raids, Besnard's precarious political position worsened. One popular Paris daily editorialized:

It is not sufficient to be indignant against such tactics, which dishonor war itself. Public sentiment expects something else. It wants reprisals, immediate and redoubtable reprisals.[20]

Others also complained, and the outcry finally caught up to Besnard – on February 8, he was forced to resign from office.[21] To those with an interest, it must have seemed that the American squadron was never going to be formed.

*　*　*　*　*

Back in America, Kiffin's family was catching up on the news from France. Near the middle of January, his aunt in Tennessee wrote that Kiffin's old friends there were "glad to hear of his promotion" to aviator but did not "envy him his job" – one voiced his fear that Kiffin was "fixing to be an angel."[22] In early February, Loula must have thought the same thing when she read of the zeppelin raids. Anxious for news of her son, who she knew was stationed right outside Paris, she wrote Paul that the "papers tell of a raid on Paris the 30th and 31st that called out all the aeroplanes. We are wondering if Kiffin was in service, or if he was with you at Mrs. Weeks' or if he is at the front. It takes so long to hear that we never feel we know."[23]

Although it had not yet made it home, Kiffin had written a letter to Loula two weeks earlier telling her he was ok, and that he had started flying a new Nieuport plane. He also wrote of his respect for the French people:

Everyone seems in a pretty good frame of mind. They are all resigned to whatever is to come and confident of the ultimate victory and willing to continue just until then. The more they go through, the stronger and more determined they become.[24]

He saw this same quality in Mrs. Weeks, who had just received official confirmation of the death seven months before of her beloved Kenneth. In addition, Kiffin learned that his friends Russell Kelly and John Earl Fike had also died in the summer attack.[25] He told Loula of Mrs. Weeks' admirable response to the terrible news:

We just got news that Kenneth Weeks and the other boys reported missing were killed on June 17th. Mrs. Weeks had really had stronger hopes than any of us regarding them, and it has been very sad for all of us. However, she is an awful brave, fine woman, and her interest now is in doing all she can for the ones of us who are left.[26]

On February 4, Kiffin, Paul, Chapman, Pavelka and the others all gathered in Paris for Kenneth Weeks' memorial service at St. George's Church near the *Arc de Triomphe*. The event was noted in the Paris papers and, even though the service occurred during a big snowstorm, the church was full. Mrs.

Weeks selected for the service a portion of the apostle Paul's first epistle to the Corinthians. While typically read at weddings, that scripture well reflected the sacrifices of Kenneth (who gave his life) and Mrs. Weeks (who gave her son) for France, as they both exemplified a charity that "suffereth long," and "beareth all things, believeth all things, hopeth all things, endureth all things." In addition, Kenneth had surely "put away childish things" and become a man, as had Kiffin and the other American volunteers.[27]

The choir sang "I will lift up mine eyes unto the hills," from Psalm 121, and ended the service with the triumphant "Hallelujah Chorus" by Handel.[28] *Le Figaro* reported that it was "a very touching ceremony," and stated, "To those young men who so nobly fell, the sympathy of all the mothers of France will be given."[29]

* * * * *

Following the Friday service, Kiffin stayed the weekend with Mrs. Weeks. On Sunday he was transferred from Le Bourget to the *Groupement des divisions d'entrainement* (G.D.E.) at Plessis-Belleville, about an hour and a half from Paris – far enough that he would no longer be able to come in and stay at Mrs. Weeks' home most every night. With sadness, she saw Kiffin off then wrote her brother, "I suppose I should be thankful I have had him home two months, but he is very dear to me and it is hard to be brave all the time, is it not."[30]

At Plessis-Belleville, Kiffin would continue training on the Nieuport, as that entire division had also been transferred from Le Bourget to the *G.D.E.* And now, despite the earlier separate orders, Chapman, Thaw, and Prince were also directed to the depot at Plessis-Belleville. It seems that although Besnard had resigned, the Americans were still in good favor, and for the first time four of them were grouped together in the same squadron.

Of course, Kiffin had been flying the Nieuport – a *chasse* (pursuit) plane – for some time, but it was quite new for the other three Americans. But Thaw, Chapman and Prince would all need to learn it now, for that was the machine they would take to the front. As Chapman noted, "it has already been decided that we shall have the Baby Nieuport and be given a delightful French Captain and a good post at Belfort."[31] The day after their arrival, Kiffin wrote Mrs. Weeks to tell her of their new surroundings:

We are all settled here. Thaw, Chapman, and I climbed into the "1st class wagon" yesterday morning and had a nice trip up, taking about an hour.

When we arrived we were the first off the train and hurried over to the only hotel here, which is about two hundred yards from the Division. We found four rooms and took them all, as Prince was to come this morning. We also made an arrangement for our meals here, and it is not so very expensive, considering everything. It is a rather God-forsaken country, but could be worse. I was rather lonesome last night. We had a fire in one of the rooms and sat around and read until ten o'clock. This morning at seven, Thaw's orderly came around and woke us all, brought up the coffee and then brushed our clothes. I call that living in pretty good style; don't you?[32]

* * * * *

Back in Paris, Paul was coming into his own. His contacts among the soldiers passing through Mrs. Weeks' place in Paris proved a plentiful source for stories, and he had parlayed this into a more prominent role with the *Chicago Daily News*. He described his improved circumstances in a letter to Kiffin two months later:

I try to turn out a little work daily and always place what I write without any trouble. My finances are now much better, and if you need some money for anything all you have to do is tell me. One week I made over 750 francs, and I intend to knock out at least 200 per week right along. If a series I have submitted to the McClure Newspaper Syndicate goes well, I will be on easy street. The American public likes to read about the legion, and as I have gathered up a lot of facts and fiction on that subject I can supply them.[33]

Almost eighteen months after his arrival in France the one-time aspiring diplomat spoke the language very well, was engaged to a very prominent French girl, and was getting comfortable with the idea of staying in his new country permanently.[34] In a letter to a friend in Atlanta, Paul wrote:

I am finding life very well worthwhile over here, and I expect to make France my home most of my remaining years. I have had some very pleasant and valuable experiences; many glad days and many sad ones, all in all the kind that make life life.[35]

As usual, Paul could not help but brag on Kiffin. He informed their former friends in Atlanta that Kiffin was "doing good work in the aviation service" and had been put on the Nieuport, "the fastest ... machine in France." "Victory will surely be ours, but when is hard to say," Paul wrote.[36]

Around this time, Paul received a letter from Loula, stating "we all watch the papers and wonder each day if Kiffin is flying and, praying for his safety, we keep encouraged that you both will return when France is victorious. Surely the Allies must win, but oh, how long it all seems."[37]

Unfortunately, due to the winter conditions, none of the men were doing much flying. Kiffin told his mother that he was "feeling fairly well, but impatient at the inaction."[38] Chapman was with him, and noted that the weather was "one round of rain and wind," and with the occasional snow, the muddy airfield was often so cold that to keep warm the little dogs watching the pilots would hold off the ground first one paw, then the other. Although there was little going on in the way of flights, Chapman still felt the time was worthwhile for, as he wrote his stepmother, "I talk and think flying so much with Norman Prince that I feel I am learning just the same."[39]

Of course, Prince was still "busy pushing matters in regard to the formation of the *Escadrille Américaine*," as he stated in a letter to his father.[40] Now that they had a sufficient number of American aviators to staff a full squadron, they lacked only a French commander, and Thaw was trying to arrange things so that his former captain Georges Thénault might lead the new *escadrille*, "if it's physically possible."[41] In the meantime, the men waited for word from the French government, worried that if Thénault was not selected quickly they would instead end up with some other "service" officer who could make life unpleasant.

But for the moment, Thénault was unavailable – Thaw's old squadron, *Escadrille C.42* had been summoned to defend the fortress of Verdun, attacked by the Germans on February 21, 1916. During the numerous dogfights above the battlefield that first day, Captain Thénault was in the thick of the fighting and brought down his first German plane, an Albatros C.[42] Below the plane-filled skies, thousands of men were slugging it out in a bloody battle for the very life of France. While Verdun is sometimes crudely referred to as a meatgrinder or slaughterhouse, one ambulance driver there at the time aptly described it as "a hell of mud, blood, flames and noise."[43]

The losses on both sides were immense, and fully justify all that has been written about that campaign. The men heard the stories of the intense combat, too. In a letter to Loula one week after the battle started, Kiffin stated his belief that Germany was "just wearing herself out," and averred that even if Germany managed to take Verdun, "it won't discourage me any for I realize that it will cost her so much that we will really be the winner."[44] Even with the war raging, the only thing discouraging Kiffin was the fact that he was stuck at Plessis-Belleville, waiting for assignment.

* * * * *

The other Americans had been sent for training at Pau, and early in 1916, one by one these men received their military brevets – Chouteau Johnson and H. Clyde Balsley on January 2, Laurence Rumsey on February 2, Jim McConnell on February 6, and Paul Pavelka on February 23.[45] But while Pau may have been great for flying, it was lousy for Americans trying to pick up the French language – as they were all grouped together, McConnell complained that the aviation school was "about as good a place to learn French as a jail in Ohio. Everyone speaks English."[46]

McConnell had other problems, too. Apparently, while on leave in Paris after earning his brevet, he attended a gathering at the home of Lawrence and Henrietta Slade, Bill Thaw's sister and brother-in-law. While there, McConnell had a little too much to drink and embarrassed Marcelle Guerin, a female friend he was pursuing. In an apologetic note to Paul, McConnell allowed how it "sure was the limit my blowing around there soused," and lamented, "I should have died when I was a little baby." He even mentioned fixing up "some sort of a pledge that will result in my being sober when I go to see her."[47] While she would ultimately forgive McConnell, Marcelle initially told Paul that Jim had no excuse, as there were thirty-four other guests and he was the "only one who distinguished himself."[48] Perhaps this incident was the origin of Bert Hall's nickname for McConnell – McScandal.[49]

Speaking of Hall, he had his own share of scandal wafting around him. Having already qualified on the Nieuport, on January 1, 1916, he had been sent to work as an instructor at Avord, where Victor Chapman was one of his pupils.[50] At the time, Chapman described Hall as "a thin-faced, keen-looking fellow," and noted he was "too sharp according to rumor." The gossip going around the school was that Hall had "passed off a bogus cheque on Prince to the tune of 3 or 4 hundred francs." But the affable Chapman kept an open mind, noting that "Prince often exaggerates."[51]

Hall was still serving as an instructor at Avord in late February while Chapman waited with the others at Plessis-Belleville for official word on the American squadron. Around this time, Balsley and Johnson were transferred from Pau to Le Bourget to assist in the aerial defense of Paris. While there, they learned that the *Escadrille Américaine* was nearly formed and so quickly put in their applications to train on the Nieuport so they could go to the front as part of that squadron.[52]

As the reports of fighting at Verdun reached the aviator pool at Plessis-Belleville, the Americans grew even more impatient to get to the front. Everyone was anxious for the squadron to be formed, and they all wanted to get into the ongoing fighting. Elliott Cowdin was particularly keen to get going, and apparently passed along to the American press one of the many French promises made to the impatient pilots. Soon, the word back home was to the effect that the long-anticipated squadron had at last come into being. In late February, Chapman explained the true situation to his stepmother:

As usual, Cowdin was a little beforehand with his cable to America; the Escadrille *is not formed but only promised. We sit around in the forlorn vacant plain out here or wander back to Paris when the weather looks too uncompromising, and as today when there is snow on the ground. Cowdin himself arranged to be sent off to the East instead of waiting about here.*[53]

As Chapman indicated, Cowdin had grown tired of waiting, and on an excursion into Paris with Thaw, he telephoned Thénault hoping to get in on some of the fighting taking place around Verdun. While Thénault was unable to get Cowdin transferred to his own unit, he did manage to get him attached to a neighboring squadron at the front – on February 29, 1916, Cowdin left to join *Escadrille N.65* near Bar-le-Duc.

Cowdin's jubilant words on being transferred echoed the sentiments of Kiffin and the other Americans, who simply wanted to fight: "Thank heaven! I am going where there's something doing. What's the use of being a French army aviator if you can't be in the biggest scrap the war has produced?"[54]

Likewise, at Pau, talk of the soon-to-be-formed American *escadrille* was rife. McConnell wrote that "[e]very day somebody 'had it absolutely straight' that we were to become a unit at the front, and every other day the report turned out to be untrue."[55] All the men were sick of waiting, and with Thaw and Cowdin splitting off to go to the front as part of a French unit, the Franco-American Committee again felt compelled to remind the French authorities of their promises of an American squadron.

Accordingly, on March 3 the Committee penned a letter to the newly-appointed Director of Aeronautics, Colonel Henri-Jacques Régnier. It stated:

Following our letter of January 24, addressed to M. René Besnard, and of which a copy is attached, allow us respectfully to call your attention to the situation of the Americans enlisted in the French Army. M. Millerand, General Hirschauer, and M. Besnard, after careful study of the question, decided that the American pilots should be united in one squadron. General Headquarters also took this view, and it was furthermore decided that Americans should fly the Nieuport fighting planes. Notwithstanding this ... only four have been grouped at Plessis-Belleville. The others are scattered, and most of them have not been assigned to Nieuports.... The Franco-American Committee, which has taken upon itself the task of selecting volunteers from the United States ... would be very grateful if you could find it possible to carry out the decisions taken after careful reflection by your predecessors.[56]

As it turned out, the gears had been slowly turning behind the scenes. Colonel Régnier responded to the Committee with the good news on March 14, 1916:

Replying to your letter of March 3, 1916, I have the honor to communicate to you the following information. I had already considered the question of an American squadron, and as early as February 20, 1916, I asked the Commander-in-Chief to advise me of his intentions in this matter. General Headquarters has just replied, informing me that an American squadron will be organized, with the pilots whose names follow: William Thaw, Elliott Cowdin, Kiffin Rockwell, Norman Prince, Charles C. Johnson, Clyde Balsley, Victor Chapman, Lawrence Rumsey and James R. McConnell.... I have every reason to believe that the ... squadron will be constituted rapidly ... and I will keep you posted as to what is done in this matter.[57]

Chapter Thirty-eight

Off for the races.

By the time the Committee received Colonel Régnier's response to its letter, Elliott Cowdin was making a name for himself at the front. Piloting a Nieuport as part of *Escadrille N.65*, throughout March he participated in numerous attacks, and on April 4 while flying north of Douaumont, he attacked and brought down an L.V.G. (so called due to its German manufacturer, *Luft-Verkehrs Gesellschaft*).[1]

Following his victory – the first by an American pilot[2] – Cowdin explained the huge change that had taken place in aerial combat and the advantage of flying the latest French pursuit plane:

There was a time when the aviator on a chasing aeroplane was required to hunt the enemy's aeroplanes. Now they are as thick as bees from dawn until sunset and it is merely a question of which one to tackle and of getting him before he gets you. The majority of German aeroplanes one meets when flying in a swift Nieuport monoplane run when attacked because the Germans have nothing to equal this machine.[3]

Thaw had also been attached to *Escadrille N.65* a week earlier, and with Cowdin and their French squad mates (including Charles Nungesser, who rejoined the squadron two days after Thaw), was soon spending many hours patrolling the skies over Verdun.[4] Among his numerous fights, Thaw attacked an Aviatik which Paul reported in the *Chicago Daily News* as having dropped behind German lines.[5] However, Thaw denied bringing it down:

Despite reports to the contrary, I have not "officially" brought down an aeroplane this year, although recently I passed six hours a day in the air. Elliott Cowdin brought down his second machine the other day and I hope soon to do the same.[6]

While he could not confirm a victory, Thaw did corroborate the superiority of the new French pursuit plane – after several weeks of very heavy flight hours, he noted that the German machines were "naturally slower than the little Nieuports we have, which travel – well, quite fast enough – and, what is also very important, very slowly when that is required."[7]

The Nieuport was the newest and classiest machine France had yet launched into the skies, and its speed and maneuverability were part of a series of rapid advances in aviation brought on by the press of war. Throughout World War I, a new machine could barely assert supremacy before an even better machine took its place. As one military observer wrote in 1916, "the development of ... aeroplanes is proceeding so rapidly that it is difficult to say today what they will be capable of doing tomorrow."[8]

Nicknamed the *bébé* (baby), due to its small size, the Nieuport 11 was emblematic of this rapid development. The Nieuport was France's only pursuit plane, a *chasse*, launched into service over Verdun to combat the "Fokker scourge." Although it was quickly succeeded by the improved Nieuport 16 and later, the Nieuport 17, the *bébé* helped turn the tide in the skies and in the spring of 1916 was much sought after by French and American pilots alike. Powered by an 80- or 110-horsepower Gnome rotary engine, the agile little craft could take off in as few as one hundred feet, with an excellent climb rate and a top speed of 100 miles per hour. Chapman told his father the *bébé* was "a most delightful machine and responds so quickly and precisely. Can you figure moving at will in three dimensions?"[9] "Heaven only knows how fast it goes," said Laurence Rumsey, who further declared the machine "so small, light and fast that you have only to move your feet a hair's breadth to maneuver."[10] Another American pilot called the plane a "little hunting apparatus, the fastest war machine in the world."[11]

The *bébé* was a sesquiplane (literally, one and a half wings), but its narrow lower wing couldn't be built rigid enough to withstand too much torsion. Unfortunately, this meant "the twisting forces sometimes caused the wing to fail, which usually led to the break-up in mid-air of the entire machine."[12] Thus, while the machine was beautifully balanced, maneuverable and responsive, its lower wing had a tendency to collapse during prolonged high-speed dives or inordinately violent maneuvers.[13]

The Americans training on the Nieuport advanced to the *bébé* as machines became available, but the latter were hard to come by. Rumsey had been flying the Voisin, and on February 20 wrote that he had "asked for a Nieuport, which is the best and fastest, but everybody is doing the same, so doubt if I get one."[14] Kiffin had been on Nieuports since late November, but first flew a *bébé* on

March 1. Due to poor weather and lack of machines, he got in only 115 minutes of flight time over the next month and a half.[15]

* * * * *

Without much flying taking place, Kiffin longed for the front. He wrote Loula on March 11 that "the fighting has kept going as heavy as ever at Verdun, but we seem to be holding now. I have been kind of expecting and wanting to go down there, but so far, nothing doing."[16] Just a few days later, Billy Thorin wrote Mrs. Weeks:

Well, tomorrow is St. Patrick's Day. I only wish he had banished the Germans out of France instead of snakes out of Ireland. I would sooner see the snakes here and the Germans in Ireland, because I don't think they would stay as long over there as they have over here. I hear that they have not sent Kiffin to the front yet. I guess he will go there soon enough. Think it is going to be pretty lively on all sides soon.[17]

Over the next few weeks, Kiffin and Chapman journeyed into Paris every so often, always hoping that upon their return, they would find transfer orders. During one trip to see Mrs. Weeks near the end of March, Kiffin learned that the Germans had torpedoed an unarmed French boat in the English Channel.[18] The *Sussex* was a ferry boat, much like the one (perhaps even the very same one) that Kiffin and Paul had taken across the channel from Folkestone to Boulogne back in August 1914.

The attack killed at least fifty people and wounded two American citizens, one of whom was Betty Baldwin, a friend of Jim McConnell and some of the other Americans. McConnell was outraged – in a letter to a friend back home, he angrily wrote that he was "ashamed of my American birth and seriously contemplate becoming a Frenchman and remaining here after the war is over[.]"[19] Betty Baldwin's father, Professor James Mark Baldwin, a philosopher and member of the Academy of France, was also angry. He sent off a cable to President Wilson, which promptly appeared on the front page of the *New York Times*. It read:

A woman traveling where her right was, carrying an American passport, stricken on the Sussex, *hovering between life and death, demands that reparation for assault on American life and liberty be exacted.*

Mark Baldwin[20]

The *Sussex* incident revealed an ongoing shift in American public opinion towards more forceful measures to protect its interests and citizens. Indeed, President Wilson eventually took what to Kiffin, McConnell and the others must have seemed a surprisingly firm stance. In an address to a joint session of Congress on April 19, Wilson issued an ultimatum: Germany must cease its policy of unrestricted submarine warfare, or America would sever all diplomatic relations. Wilson declared:

[T]he Government of the United States is at last forced to the conclusion that there is but one course it can pursue; and that unless the Imperial German Government should now immediately declare and effect an abandonment of its present methods of warfare against passenger and freight carrying vessels, this Government can have no choice but to sever diplomatic relations with the Government of the German Empire altogether. This decision I have arrived at with the keenest regret; the possibility of the action contemplated I am sure all thoughtful Americans will look forward to with unaffected reluctance. But we cannot forget that we are in some sort and by the force of circumstances the responsible spokesmen of the rights of humanity, and that we cannot remain silent while those rights seem in process of being swept utterly away in the maelstrom of this terrible war.[21]

Professor Baldwin was pleased with Wilson's strong response, and with the slowly coalescing opinion of his home country. In a piece in the Paris edition of the *New York Herald*, he wrote:

There are many who have maintained – myself among them – that the people of the United States would follow the President with enthusiasm in whatever active measures he might find it right to take. The Americans have been ready for great resolves – ready for months past to follow up their sympathy for the cause of the Allies and their resentment against German intrigue and barbarity, with active and efficient effort whenever they found themselves properly led from Washington. We now see that the country is sound.

[M]oreover, what I personally know of the President leads me to believe that his determination is now based upon an unalterable conviction of duty. One may believe that this determination should have been taken long ago – when the Lusitania was torpedoed, in my opinion – and that the apparent supineness of the Administration has done incalculable injury to the country and to its good name; but if that apparent supineness turns out really to have been the moderation of fairness and of the will to act only when sure of the

will of the country, then all good Americans can rejoice both that demands of fairness have now been exercised and that the accumulating voices of protest have been heard.[22]

In short order, in response to Wilson's ultimatum the German government adopted the so-called "Sussex pledge," under which it agreed to refrain from sinking merchant and passenger ships without giving adequate warning to all passengers and crew and providing for their safety.[23] Germany's revocation of this pledge and the resumption of unrestricted submarine warfare was a primary factor in America's entry into the war nearly a year later.

While Kiffin may not have been as pleased with Wilson's response as Professor Baldwin, he was surely happy to see America finally displaying a more forceful posture towards Germany.

* * * * *

The weeks following Colonel Régnier's notification to the Franco-American Committee of his approval of the squadron passed slowly and uneventfully, with the men scattered and waiting for the *escadrille's* official formation.

In early April, Kiffin spent a few days in Paris with Mrs. Weeks. On April 2, a Sunday afternoon, she and Kiffin took a leisurely boat ride down *La Seine* towards the Île St. Louis. As they sailed down the river, taking in the beautiful blooming cherry trees and the cloudless and sunny sky, the old city must have seemed a sundrenched jewel. As shown in a letter she wrote that evening, Mrs. Weeks had an exquisite day:

Spring is in the air. Windows are open and people hanging over their balconies. Someone is playing the piano very well, and life smiles for the moment. Happy the person who makes the most of such conditions and does not wait for happiness, which never comes if sought. I find myself at times very happy, coming home in the river steamer with the sun setting behind the Tour Eiffel and the bridges arching across the gold of the sunset.[24]

I like to think that Kiffin also recognized the beauty of that day, that he soaked in its sights, sounds, smells, sunshine and spirit, and that it strengthened and sustained him. The sunset behind the Eiffel Tower must have been splendid. Perhaps Kiffin was even able briefly to forget the war and simply be happy. Life smiles for the moment, indeed.

* * * * *

Following his interlude on the *River Seine*, Kiffin returned to the patience-testing inaction of Plessis-Belleville. From there, he wrote on April 6 that he was "more or less demoralized by never doing anything and waiting each day to go to the front." There was still no word on the American squadron, nor had Kiffin received any response to several requests he had made to be attached to a regular French *escadrille*. As he told a friend, "they continue to keep us all back, waiting until the *Escadrille Américaine* is formed." He went on:

Why they don't form it, I don't know. We have enough men ready, the material ready, know who will be the captain, that we are to go to Belfort, and that our number is 'N.124.' Yet we are not sent out. In the meantime, I fly a little and spend much time in Paris. I have now written a captain at Verdun to please ask for me to be attached to his escadrille *if he has a vacancy.*[25]

The next morning, Kiffin heard that Captain Thénault (who had been given command of the American squadron) had gone to the depot at Lyon to requisition the tractors, trucks, automobiles, personnel and equipment necessary to outfit the *escadrille*. Now knowing he could be called to the front any day, Kiffin dashed off a quick note to his mother, telling her "I think everything is going through alright at last."[26]

That afternoon, Kiffin went up twice in his assigned *bébé*, carefully marking each flight in his *Carnet d'emploi du temps*. Those trips would be the last entries in his flight log. Afterward, he grabbed Chapman and the two pilots caught the train to Paris, where that evening they dined alone with Mrs. Weeks. After spending the night, they took the 6:00 a.m. train back to camp. In a letter to her son, Mrs. Weeks noted that the boys were "very happy to hear that they are to be sent to the front any day now."[27]

At Plessis-Belleville, Kiffin, Prince and Chapman were pleased to be joined by Jim McConnell, who had been transferred up from Pau.[28] In a letter dated April 10, McConnell wrote that "The American *Escadrille* thinks it will leave for the front this week and Kiffin says I can get off with them. I hope so anyway. Otherwise I may have a long wait."[29] The expectant pilots made their final preparations for the front.

But not all the Americans were as focused. Johnson and Rumsey "sneaked into Paris" without permission; causing McConnell to confide to a friend, "[t]hey are not very serious."[30] This was at least the second time Rumsey had disappeared, and may have been the reason he and Johnson were dropped from Colonel Régnier's original list of the pilots to be included in the squadron.[31] Of course, he had also wrecked two machines while testing for his brevet.[32]

Whatever the reason, when orders forming the *escadrille* finally arrived, Johnson and Rumsey were out, and Bert Hall was in. Hall had good intangibles and was included for his experience and solid skills as a pilot, despite a few dents in his reputation stemming from a wide variety of women, poker wins (and losses), and rumors about bounced checks.[33] Although some might have debated whether he was the proper choice, Hall surely had a knack for being in the right place at the right time.

Thus, on April 16, 1916, seven American pilots – Kiffin, Chapman, McConnell and Prince at Plessis-Belleville, Cowdin and Thaw at the front with *Escadrille N.65*, and Bert Hall at Avord – received official orders transferring them to the *Escadrille Américaine*.[34] The unit's official designation was N.124 – the N signifying the squadron would fly Nieuports. By coincidence, 124 was the same number as Kiffin and Paul's stateroom on the S.S. *St. Paul* on their way to France.

The pilots were to report on April 18. Back home, the *New York World* informed its readers that "[t]he All-American flying squadron is at last an accomplished fact." [35]

* * * * *

To celebrate, the next night Prince treated the others to a "hilarious dinner" at *Ciro's*, located in the ground floor of the *Hotel Danou*.[36] The fashionable restaurant – a favorite hangout of Americans in Paris – was just across the street from *Harry's* bar and not far from Paul's offices at the *Chicago Daily News*.[37] Those lucky enough to be there that evening – Kiffin, Chapman, McConnell, Balsley, Johnson, Rumsey and Michel Plaa-Porte, Prince's mechanic – wore their aviation uniforms and had a great time. The fact that it was also Chapman's 26th birthday increased the festive nature of the celebration.[38] Many toasts were offered, and the official roster of the *escadrille* was read.[39] Unfortunately, Thaw and Cowdin were on their way back to Paris and missed the shindig, as did Bert Hall, who was at Avord.[40] Thus, only four of the men present were official members of the squadron – Kiffin, McConnell, Prince and Chapman.

"[F]ull of enthusiasm, joy and eagerness to get at the foe," those four left the dinner before 9:00 o'clock and took a taxi-cab to the *Gare de l'Est* to catch their train to the front.[41] The only "sad and depressed member of the party" was Paul Rockwell, who had accompanied the aviators to dinner and to the station.[42] On the platform, the men said their goodbyes to Paul, then boarded the night train out of Paris.[43]

At last, the *Escadrille Américaine* was headed to the front. As the engine pulled out of the station, Kiffin looked around at the others and said, "Well, we're off for the races."[44]

Chapter Thirty-nine

The transport train rolled east for most of the night, arriving just before morning in Rosnay, a little hillside village only fifteen kilometers from Reims.[1] The sleepy men grabbed their things and reported to the airfield only to find they had been given incorrect orders. "[A]fter a great deal of telephoning by the Commandant," it was determined the pilots were supposed to have been sent to Luxeuil-les-Bains, well over three hundred kilometers away.[2] Chapman explained to his uncle what had happened: "With that renowned imbecility so common among bureaucrats," the aviation department had misdirected the group to the location of N.24 instead of 124.[3]

The men piled into a borrowed motor car and drove off toward Reims. Although cloth screens (to prevent the Germans from seeing the traffic) now covered the north side of all the roads leading to the town, the men got a nice view of the famous cathedral as they passed by.[4] When they drove by a detachment of the Foreign Legion on its way to dig trenches, Kiffin couldn't help but think of his early days in France, and entertained the others by telling them about his and Paul's 56-kilometre hike over the same ground in October of 1914.

From Reims the men turned south toward Epernay, passing by Hautvillers, where Kiffin and Paul had spent one night near the abbey of Dom Perignon while both were still in the legion. The four pilots stopped in Epernay for the night and boarded another train at five o'clock the next morning. Though they changed trains two more times, throughout the day their route followed the River Marne. Finally, at three in the afternoon, the men arrived in Lure, still twenty kilometers from Luxeuil. The next train was not for another three hours, so the four Americans decided to get something to eat.[5]

As they were leaving the café, the group was met by Captain Thénault, who had driven over to gather his new charges and bring them back to the airfield. He cheerfully greeted the men, telling them "Sixty-two pilots were killed last month."[6]

Shaking hands with their new commanding officer, the four Americans slipped into the soft leather cushions of the luxurious staff car he had brought from Luxeuil. As they started towards their destination, the group quickly forgot the two days they had lost and began to feel out Captain Thénault. Although they had met briefly in Paris in January, Kiffin did not know Thénault well. But he took to him right away, telling his mother his commanding officer "is a young fellow and one of us."[7] To Mrs. Weeks, he wrote that Thénault was "certainly a pearl of a fellow."[8] Kiffin would not always think so highly of the young captain.

The aerodrome at Luxeuil, where Thénault brought the men, was one of the biggest and most beautiful in all of France. The village was in a relatively quiet sector, nestled in the vestiges of the Vosges mountains, some thirty-five miles from the Swiss border. Its airfield was a choice landing spot, over two miles long and entirely flat. In the weeks and months before the formation of the *escadrille*, the men had anticipated being sent to Belfort, right on the front; now Chapman was a little disappointed to find they were slightly further back. He wrote his uncle: "Pretty little town this Luxeuil-les-Bains but *fifty-six kilometres* from the lines!"[9]

As Thénault drove the group to the aviation field, he acquainted the men with their assigned duties: the new unit was slated to fly protection for *Groupe de Bombardement 4*, a bombing squadron under the command of Captain Maurice Happe who, according to Kiffin, was "the most famous man" in French aviation.[10] Bombing squadron *GB.4* was well-known for the heavy losses it had suffered performing its dangerous work. Kiffin and the others had been ordered to Luxeuil to protect Happe's trips over the German lines.

* * * * *

Captain Happe was a legend among flyers, famous for his recklessness, luck, and – mostly – his success.[11] One soldier referred to the captain as "the most terrible adversary that ever French aviation had employed," a fair point given Happe's expressed attitude toward the Germans: "It is war," he said, and so "we must keep on continually killing the *boches*, for the dead are the ones who never return to fight again."[12]

Every aviator in France had heard of Happe's daring feats: how he had flown over the upper *Danube* and shot up German trains and factories; how he braved German bullets from the air and ground, dropping bombs from his slow-flying Maurice Farman and Breguet bombers; how he had each of his planes painted with the *Croix de Guerre avec palme*; and how he was said to have lost more pilots than any two captains in the French army.

The fact that Happe himself remained unscathed despite the heavy losses all around him only added to his aura of invincibility. The man – who "never hesitated to question his superiors" – once proposed to fly over the German lines, land at a rail center, capture the station master and fly back across the lines to wring information out of him.[13] The French authorities vetoed Happe's plan but, recognizing his courage, instead placed him in command of a bombing squadron.[14]

Due to the audacious bomber's numerous successful raids, the Germans had put a price of 25,000 marks on his head. Happe responded by painting the wheels and part of the wings of his aircraft bright red, then dropping a weighted message over a German airfield asking his opponents to spare his companions, and instead attack his own now easy-to-distinguish plane. Happe's well-known exploits and his red aircraft soon earned him sobriquets on both sides of the trenches – the French called him "*le Corsaire Rouge*" (the Red Pirate), while the Germans dubbed him "*die Roter Teufel*" – the Red Devil.[15]

Suffice it to say, Captain Happe's reputation preceded him. Now, immediately upon their arrival at the aerodrome, Thénault took his four new pilots to introduce them to the Red Pirate himself. While Kiffin and the others were certainly familiar with Happe's name, none of them had met the man, so no one knew quite what to expect. Thénault led the excited men past huge hangars and cabins still being constructed to Happe's office, located in a simple wooden shack on the airfield. As the pilots gathered behind Thénault, a man who to Kiffin "looked like an under-secretary, without any *galons* to show his grade and none of the decorations" stood to greet them.[16] This was Captain Maurice Happe.

A tall, thin man with a fierce pointed beard, Happe made an immediate and lasting impression on all the pilots, especially Kiffin, who professed: "I will never forget my first view of him and wouldn't have missed it for anything."[17]

Thénault introduced each of the pilots, and the men shook hands all around. Following the brief introductions, Happe launched into a little "impromptu lecture on the advantages of accompanying bombardment machines."[18] He told the men he knew *escadrilles de chasse* disliked such assignments, but wondered why, as he "considered that they had a better chance to get the Germans, who would be attracted by the slow [bombing] machines."[19] "Now if you had been here last time, I should not have this unpleasant task," said Happe "and you would have knocked down some *boches*."[20]

Happe waved his hand towards a table "where lay a batch of yellow envelopes and packages looking in size and shape like boxes of wedding cake."[21] Rubbing his hands together and smiling, Happe explained the boxes contained "*Croix de guerre* and letters to the relatives of the eight fellows killed" on his last raid.[22] Chapman thought Happe's "eye glittered" as he related this morbid tale; he told his uncle, "I don't know if it was the way he said it or what, but we all felt he was like a Cyclops gloating over his last victims."[23] Continuing to smile, Happe told them to "hurry up and get ready as quick as you can so that we can work together."[24]

Surely this introduction to the grim realities of aerial combat had an impact on the newly-arrived pilots. Kiffin found the conversation with Happe "interesting, and enough to drive fear in the hearts of some men."[25] McConnell relayed to a friend that he was "looking forward to my first bombardment with the same feeling that a man must have who counts the days before he sits in the electric chair."[26]

In his understated fashion, Captain Thénault later noted that "as an introductory remark," Happe's speech "wasn't very encouraging."[27] Still, Thénault took note that after Happe's comments, the four Americans "stood impassive." Sensing their courage, in that moment Thénault perceived he could trust the fledgling aviators.[28]

* * * * *

Unfortunately, the enthusiastic pilots had everything they needed but planes. As Chapman said, "The captain is here, the *personelle non navigant* (ground personnel), the spare parts and a vast formidable array of motor lorries, motor trucks, *voitures légères* (light cars) – 20 in all, but no *appareils*."[29] The fresh-from-the-factory *bébés* were being trucked in from Paris and would not arrive for two weeks. In the meantime, the boys could only sit and wait.

At least they knew the planes would be worth it – the American squadron was to be the first *escadrille* to fly Nieuports exclusively. Thénault described the awe in which a pilot lucky enough to fly one was held:

You were no longer a taxi-chauffeur, whose part is to take out an observer who does all the really useful work, but the honoured driver of the fastest racing machine whose record-breaking speed and daring turns the press celebrated.[30]

While usually the first one to chafe at waiting, according to a postcard McConnell sent to Paul two days after their arrival in Luxeuil, Kiffin was "very happy."[31] This was likely because in Luxeuil there was plenty to be happy about.

Luxeuil was built on the vestiges of the camps of Roman soldiers, who centuries before had discovered its warm-water springs bubbling to the surface. In peacetime, the thriving village served as a resort destination, and even during the war drew many wishing to partake of the community's thermal table and dietary waters to treat their rheumatism or arthritis, or just to relax. The little town was still famous for its natural thermal baths – indeed, the "*les Bains*" in Luxeuil-les-Bains means "the baths."

Kiffin, Chapman and McConnell shared rooms comprising the whole floor of a villa near the thermal baths, while the three officers installed themselves just up the hill at the *Hotel Lion Vert*.[32] In a letter to his uncle, Chapman noted that the men ate all their meals together at the *Lion Vert*, "and most excellent meals they are."[33] Given their differing nationalities, the meals were governed by an informal code under which English was spoken at noon, and French in the evening. Any infraction resulted in a two-cent fine against the offending pilot, placed into the pool to pay for their meals.[34] Thénault later wrote:

The result was that some hard-headed citizens endeavored to maintain unbroken silence but they couldn't stand the kidding of their friends which would go on until they simply had to answer; then they'd burst out into a weird Franco-American jargon that would have made the fortune of a clown in the circus.[35]

Thénault took it upon himself to calculate the meal expenses for the pilots under his command, and set up a loose system whereby each would chip in, but according to Kiffin, "the officers pay more than we do so as to make it easier for us."[36] For now, Prince was the only American officer, as Thaw and Cowdin had not yet arrived. Another French officer, Lieutenant Alfred de Laage de Meux, arrived via train on April 20.[37]

De Laage's appearance in Luxeuil was something of a surprise to the Americans, as all along they had assumed that Thaw would be second in command.[38] Instead, Thénault had secured the appointment of his "faithful friend" de Laage, whose merits he had learned to appreciate while the Frenchmen were fighting together over Verdun.[39] After de Laage was introduced as the number two, Chapman wrote that Thénault "seems to have put one over on us and hauled in a Lieutenant friend of his." Chapman anticipated this fact would be "rather hard on Thaw," who apparently assumed he would fill that slot.[40]

Soon, however, the men would come to deeply admire de Laage. The lieutenant was easy to like and spoke English well, which helped him get along with all the men. A natural leader, de Laage was just twenty-three years old. That was the same age as Kiffin, who told Mrs. Weeks that his new superior officer was "as fine a fellow as one could want to know."[41] And whatever Thaw expected, he held no grudge; he later said de Laage was "the finest chap, French or American, that I ever knew."[42]

* * * * *

With nothing else to do, the men settled in to enjoy Luxeuil. The day after their arrival, Kiffin wrote his mother that "so far, it is like being on a pleasure trip to a resort." He continued:

We all eat together at a hotel where they serve wonderfully good meals. We have a villa that has been requisitioned for us, with orderlies to clean up the rooms, our clothes, and anything else we want them to do. We go down each day about one hundred yards from here to bathe in a bath-house that is over two hundred years old. It is wonderful scenery all around here and we ride over the surrounding country with our captain and are planning to do a little fishing and hunting. So you can see that it is not much like being at war.[43]

In fact, said Kiffin, were it not for "looking in the glass and seeing myself in uniform I wouldn't be able to believe that I was at war, or that there was such a thing."[44]

McConnell was also enjoying himself. With an orderly to shine his shoes and leggings, take care of his room, run errands, and arrange for baths in the famous hot springs next door, Mac could hardly believe his good luck.[45] Always a jokester, he closed a letter to a buddy back home, "I must go out now and take a plunge in the famous baths of Luxeuil where the Romans were wont to frolic. 'War is hell!'"[46]

In addition to the orderly, the pilots were each assigned two mechanics to take care of their planes, which had still not arrived. The whole setup, said McConnell, "makes one feel quite classy."[47] He explained his great change of fortune in a letter to a friend:

In the Ambulance, I was a driver and ran around on orders. Here we have the driver come for us, an adjutant sees that our orderly does what we want and for the first few days it's hard to get used to, especially after being a 2nd class soldier at Pau. The whole thing reminds me somewhat of the custom in ancient days of treating a man like a king before the sacrifice of his blood to the Gods. But I don't care what the motive is so long as the treatment lasts.[48]

Summing up their current existence, McConnell wrote: *"C'est dure cette sale guerre!"* – it's hard, this dirty war![49]

Chapter Forty

More of a social than military outfit.

The second day after their arrival was Good Friday and April 23 was Easter Sunday. Given that France was (and still is) overwhelmingly Catholic, it is likely that the Americans attended mass with their French officers and the numerous personnel now stationed at the airfield. Saint-Pierre, the wonderful and beautiful *basilique* in town, has been in Luxeuil for centuries; its bells ringing out that Easter morning must have been something.

In addition to more than seventy mechanics, drivers, and other staff, the airfield housed everything needed to support an aerial squadron – all the brand-new tractors, cars, equipment, tools, etc. In a letter to a friend, McConnell bragged about their gear: "Our fifteen trucks are new Fiats, our hangars the latest, our staff cars are just out of the factory, and the personnel, such as mechanics, drivers, hangar-men, bureau-men, etc. is picked."[1] All in all, McConnell felt the pilots were "very well fixed" at Luxeuil, "the only drawback being we have no machines."[2]

With no planes to fly, soon enough Kiffin told Paul in a postcard it "seems to be awful slow."[3] To Mrs. Weeks he said they "couldn't be better fixed and if we can get some good work here, it will be making the war a picnic[.]"[4] With nothing else going on, Kiffin suggested that Paul and Mrs. Weeks come to Luxeuil for a visit.

But Paul was too busy with his writing, and Mrs. Weeks – who would have loved to go to Luxeuil – was not feeling well. Having grown accustomed to seeing Kiffin regularly, she wrote him a short note saying, "I hope that you are missing me and that your head needs rubbing," and cautioned him: "don't let that orderly do it will you, or anyone else."[5] In a letter he received around the same time, Loula told Kiffin what a comfort it was to know that Mrs. Weeks was "mothering my boys," and reminded him that as long as he lived he should "try to fill in her life the place left vacant by her own son's death."[6]

* * * * *

Without planes, but anxious to take to the skies, there was nothing the men could do but hurry up and wait. Not long after their arrival, Chapman heard they were "getting a couple of tired babies to play with until our good ones come," as a nearby squadron had promised Thénault a few planes on which to practice.[7] The day after Easter, *Escadrille N. 49* stationed nearby at Fontaine, sent over an old unarmed Nieuport 10. Each of the eager pilots had a turn with it, but the next day it was "on the bum."[8]

Of course, the mechanics got the machine running again, but that did not last. While complaining to a friend about their lack of planes, McConnell explained what had happened:

We had an old 18-meter Nieuport – unarmed – we had been flying, but this morning our boy Norman Prince ran into the hangars with it and smashed her to bits. He's gone to Paris on noon train. If these old pilots are no better than he is, we're going to have a rotten outfit.[9]

In a letter to his uncle in Paris a few days later, Chapman jokingly asked whether that "reprobate renegade Prince" had called on him and, if so, whether he bothered to mention he had "smash[ed] to bits the only machine we all had before leaving for Paris."[10]

Thus, a week into their stay, McConnell remarked the men were "still loafing, taking the baths and eating like summer resorters."[11] To this point, he was less than impressed by the squadron, an opinion he shared with a friend back home: "Of course the American *Escadrille* may work out all right, and I hope so, but I have my doubts. If we can enjoy the treatment and comfort and at the same time kick across with the work, *tant mieux*, but we will see what we will see."[12]

* * * * *

Without planes, there just wasn't much going on. A week into their stay, the captain and several of the boys went trout fishing, while Kiffin stayed at the villa and wrote his mother that "the last week has passed very quietly for me. We are still waiting for our machines and getting organized."[13] One gets a sense of the relaxed atmosphere from the first lines of a Victor Chapman letter to his younger brother: "Ha! A snooze and a warm bath at the cure house!"[14]

Victor and Kiffin even rigged up a target in the woods where they did "quite a bit of shooting."[15] Another kind of shooting also occupied a bit of their time –

378

Kiffin, Chapman and McConnell frequented the *Hotel Pomme d'Or*, where they shot pool and got to know the local girls.[16]

Thénault remembered the *Pomme d'Or* as "a really good old French Inn."[17] The awning stretched across the front of the café advertised beers from Le Val d'Ajol, a commune not far from Luxeuil. That little village was just one of the many beautiful spots the planeless pilots saw during various excursions through the Vosges mountains with Captain Thénault, who took the men around to point out possible places to land in case of accident. As one author described it, "from an automobile the scenery was glorious, Le Val d'Ajol unbelievable."[18]

On a few of these outings, the boys visited nearby *escadrilles* in Belfort, Fontaine-les-Bains or Romagny. Passing through Belfort, they "nearly had a calamity" when Thénault's playful wolf dog chewed up the official red paper pass that allowed the men to circulate near the front. To salvage it, they patched it together and pasted it on some celluloid, allowing them to continue their journey.[19]

Another time, they traveled to the frontier village of Rechesy, near the Swiss border. After passing the time with the officer of the guard, they stuffed the staff car full of cigars – "whose flavour was doubly good because they were contraband."[20] Thénault later fondly recalled these day trips:

The roads over which we passed were fringed with cherry trees in blossom and a hearty lunch in some Alsatian inn at Dannemarie or elsewhere would break our journey. The greeting of mine host was as welcome as his good cheer, washed down with Alsace's wine and a drop of its famous Kirsch at the end. We used to come back by the Valley of Thann or by Belfort, Giromagny and the Ballon d'Alsace. My pilots were amazed by the beauty of the country, with its torrents roaring in waterfalls over the cliffs on the steep pineclad slopes of the mountains.... In voyages like these our American comrades learned to understand some of the love that we Frenchmen bear our country.[21]

This was true of Kiffin who, after a couple of these trips, wrote Loula that the sympathy of the people of Luxeuil and the beauty of that section of the country "has made me love France more than ever."[22] Likewise, McConnell's obvious affection for his adopted country comes through in a letter he wrote at the time:

I've never had a more wonderful tour than I did through the Vosges. The myriads of little glittering cascades that tumble down avenues of green from snowcapped peaks constitute a ravishing sight.[23]

Chapman's account of one of these trips is worth quoting at length:

Yesterday we went to attend the funeral of a pilote. We went to Gerardmer and thence on to lunch with an escadrille in a nearby town. It was an even more delightful trip, principally perhaps because it was a very fine day and we had no top on the motor to spoil the view. First the low lands and foothills, with the white fruit trees and buttercups everywhere; then the narrow valleys with little streams, gray trees budding on new leaves, and finally Gerardmer Lake with fir covered hills coming down to the water's edge. Lots of swagger aviation officers with glittering decorations, and a fiery young Alpine Lieutenant who marshalled his demi-section of sallow youths about the bier. It was a short, impressive ceremony in the little grave-yard on a side hill, and once over, we continued to the nearby flying corps. We lunched – messed, I suppose I should say – with the officers there, and scrumptious food we had, the proprietor of one of the best-known restaurants at Geneva being the cook, we were told. Cigarettes, liqueurs, a view of the champs – very small – and the latest model Farman, which had fresh bullet holes from the morning's encounter. And we returned. We took another route, leading through the Val-d'Ajol, very noted, I believe, for its gorge-like sides. Little yellow jonquils and some blue flowers covering every grassy slope.[24]

* * * * *

The funeral mentioned by Chapman was not the only one the men attended – on April 28, the squadron gathered in Luxeuil to bury one of its tractor drivers, a victim of bombs dropped by the dirty *boche*. The French applied this derogatory slang to all German soldiers – shortly after arriving in France more than a year prior, McConnell had written home that the "Germans are universally known as *'boches'* here. I hadn't heard the term before I arrived."[25] The word's origin seems to be a French alteration of *alboche* – a combination of *al* for *Allemand* (German), and *boche*, short for *caboche* (cabbage or blockhead).[26]

Two mornings before, a German plane had buzzed their aerodrome, welcoming the American pilots by dropping three bombs. Six personnel coming out of a shack by the airfield were hit by shrapnel; the tractor driver – a soldier by the name of Pierre Joseph Gaston Masse – was critically wounded and later died.[27] A second bomb hit a hangar, doing no damage, while a third struck near the rail line.[28] With no machines of their own, the helpless pilots were forced to watch the bombing from their villa three kilometers away.[29]

The rude bombing and subsequent funeral made the men feel more acutely their lack of battle-ready machines. Chapman told his uncle the German bomb-dropper "would not have had the ghost of a chance of returning home if we could have given him chase."[30] Then on the day of the funeral three more boche planes – "great big slow things" – attacked, causing a frustrated Kiffin to tell Paul that "one good man with a *bébé* could have gotten all three of them before they could have gotten back to their lines."[31] Happily, the squadron received a telegram that same afternoon informing them that four Nieuport single-seaters had left for Luxeuil and four more would depart the next day.[32]

Then just after 4:00 a.m. on April 30, with the new planes still en route, the Germans again raided the town, dropping bombs near the hospital, church and seminary.[33] While no one was killed or injured, McConnell had just about had enough – he wrote Paul:

The boches come over nearly every morning and wake us up at an ungodly hour. That will stop damn soon tho[ugh] you can bet when we have our planes.[34]

Making things worse, the guys heard of several victories by the daring French aces Jean Navarre and Charles Nungesser, the latter of whom Thaw and Cowdin had flown with during their time in *Escadrille N.65*. On April 24, Navarre brought down his ninth German plane, while Nungesser brought down a *boche* flyer each of the next two days, marking his sixth and seventh official victories.[35] The Paris press loudly praised these brand-new national heroes, making the planeless pilots of Luxeuil feel very earthbound indeed.[36]

Speaking of Cowdin and Thaw, along with Bert Hall they finally arrived in Luxeuil on April 28. Cowdin had just received word that he would be awarded the prestigious *médaille militaire* and was already wearing the ribbon.[37] Still the *escadrille* was not complete, as Prince was three days late on the 24-hour permission Thénault had given him after he wrecked the loaner Nieuport. Commenting on this fact, McConnell told Paul that to date, the unit seemed "more of a social than military outfit."[38]

* * * * *

But Mac could just as easily have made the comment about himself – in a letter to his mother in early May, he described the squadron's easy existence:

I have told you, have I not, how well we live here and of the generous treatment we receive? From Pau to here was like a change from jail to a palace. Our meals at the best hotel in town are really too good, for I am eating more than I should. We are at perfect liberty and, due to the fact that we are still awaiting our machines, my life so far has been the lazy existence of a summer resorter. I get up at 8:30, my orderly orders my bath, and I go to the thermal for a dip in the warm waters that since the Romans' time have benefited the pilgrims to Luxeuil. Then I motor down to the aviation field to see what news there is of my new aeroplane and to get the mail. Then back to our villa where I write until 12. Then I walk over to the hotel, passing the thermal en route where I drink some of the water. In the afternoon I walk or practice shooting with revolver and mitrailleuse. After supper we take our coffee and liquors in a café where the seven of us Americans gather. Of course, this lazy life will end as soon as the machines arrive and then too we may move from here, but until then I am enjoying the vacation about as much as anything in my life.[39]

In addition, with no planes to fly, the boys were spending more time chasing girls than soldiering. Prince apparently had a girl in Paris, and when he again returned there, Chapman wrote his uncle that although Prince had promised to visit, he doubted it would happen.[40]

Although the town was never very large – in 1916, it had less than three thousand inhabitants – there were plenty of girls in Luxeuil, too. Due to the ongoing war, most of the remaining residents were women, so – on the ground at least (which is where they were spending all their time, for now) – the odds favored the pilots. Thus, for those so inclined, their new home "was a happy hunting ground for the lady-killers."[41]

One author described well the scene: "Physically untouched by the war, far removed from the anger of the guns, Luxeuil was safe, unspoiled and – in the eyes of the arriving Americans – a soldier's paradise."[42] The townsfolk were thrilled to have aviators in their midst, and when they learned the newly arrived pilots were American, their initial curiosity turned to something like gratitude mixed with awe. Within just a few days of the pilots' arrival, "it was noticed that some of the village belles were wearing little silk American flags as pocket handkerchiefs."[43] A week later, McConnell told a friend back home that "Luxeuil had never seen any aviators and so things are flowing our way."[44]

To another friend, McConnell confided that there were "lots of *poules* in this town."[45] *Poule* means "floozy," and Mac admitted to Paul that although he had "obliged a couple," he had his eye on a pretty Italian girl named Rosa who worked in the café where he and the boys played pool.[46] "Rosa serves beer in a home-like café on the hill, and unless they make her stop I'm going to become a beer drinker," he wrote. According to McConnell, "it mellow[ed] the beer to watch her walk toward one with it."[47]

Kiffin also met a girl in Luxeuil, probably at Madame Vosges' billiard parlor. Her name was Titine, a diminutive of Christine. Kiffin must have had feelings for the *mademoiselle*, for he wrote her at least once after the squadron left Luxeuil. Titine responded that even though they had received no further visits from "*ces cochons de boches*" (those *boche* pigs) since the Americans left town, the empty cafés made her sad. Addressed to her "dearest friend," a portion of Titine's letter read:

Mrs. Vosges told me about your card, she was very pleased by it. We speak very often of you. As you can see, we have not forgotten you and I would be very excited if I get to see you again. Despite the fact that you are at the front, I hope that luck will be on your side until the end of the war, as it has been until now.[48]

She signed a second letter "your friend Titine, who is thinking of you."[49]

Chapter Forty-one

I think that I am all ready now.

May 5 was a big day at the Luxeuil airfield. Early in the day, a *"prise d'armes"* ceremony was held at the aviation field to award Cowdin the *médaille militaire* for his victory a month prior. All three *escadrilles* stationed in Luxeuil attended.[1] Chapman gave a brief description to his stepmother:

We had all the mecanos and drivers lined up with old-fashioned guns out on the field this morning; and without very much ado Capitaine Happe read the citation and hooked on the yellow badge.[2]

That night, some of the mechanics got in trouble when they were caught out after hours with Cowdin toasting his medal – each of the French soldiers was given a four-day prison sentence.[3] In contrast, Cowdin – who had only been in Luxeuil for eight days – was granted an eight-day permission. McConnell did not have much use for Cowdin and drily noted Elliott had "beat it back to Paris before the lustre of his *Médaille* is dimmed."[4]

The same morning of the *prise d'armes*, the first batch of the squadron's new *bébés* arrived along with all the mechanics' tools, and plenty of spare parts – unfortunately, the parts were all for the older model Nieuport 10. While they had been told to expect only four planes, five showed up. Thénault assigned these machines to himself, de Laage, Thaw, Hall and Kiffin. Cowdin, Chapman, McConnell and Prince were left without, but knew another batch was coming right behind.

Along with a civilian sent from the Nieuport factory to direct their construction, the mechanics immediately set about assembling the first five machines. Kiffin could barely wait until his plane was bolted together to test it out – the moment it was ready, without waiting even for the *mitrailleuse* to be installed on the upper wing, he took to the sky.

It was a fine afternoon, and when Kiffin left the ground there was "not a breath of wind."[5] He flew around Luxeuil for a while, getting above 2,000 meters. Satisfied with his machine, Kiffin soon turned back toward the airfield.

However, just as he began his descent, the sun abruptly vanished, and a sudden and furious wind came out of nowhere. Thénault later said the "terrible storm" that occurred that day would "never be forgotten by those who experienced it."[6] On the ground, a few of the canvas hangars were ripped from their moorings, and one of the Maurice Farman planes was blown away and completely broken.[7]

Watching from the ground, the squadron saw Kiffin trying to land his machine, which was being "thrown up and down like a dead leaf" in the gale.[8] Although Kiffin worried his new plane might be "going to pieces," he kept his motor going, "turned face in the wind and just kind of dropped down to the ground."[9] Thénault described the feat this way:

The force of the wind was so great that he didn't go forward at all, but came down gradually. Our mechanics gauged the spot where this new-fangled helicopter was going to land. They ran to meet it. Rockwell landed right in their midst and immediately a score of vigorous hands gripped his fragile machine by the wheels, the wings, the supports or the fuselage – anywhere, so as to prevent it being whirled away. Rockwell got out safe and sound and his machine was uninjured. It was a splendid piece of work.[10]

All the pilots congratulated Kiffin, who told Paul he "landed without breaking a thing," and "didn't regret the event, as it gives me a good start."[11] A Maurice Farman pilot from *Escadrille MF.29* was not so lucky – caught up in the same storm and forced abruptly to land in Belfort, he broke his landing gear and three ribs.[12]

The unexpected tempest truly was quick-forming and violent. In fact, the storm came on so suddenly, many French balloonists and observers were killed, injured, or taken prisoner after their balloons broke loose and drifted towards the German lines.[13] One later source described it this way:

On May 5, 1916, 24 balloons surprised by a storm were torn from their winches, and 18 observers jumped by parachute; of these, 11 landed in French-held territory, 2 among the enemy, 2 were seriously wounded, 2 were killed by being dragged along the ground, and the last landed in free fall.[14]

Kiffin was just glad not to have wrecked his plane, as he would have had to wait a good while for another new one. The *Washington Post* reported that Kiffin had been "up in the hurricane that carried away twenty French captive balloons, and with a machine that is cranky enough in quiet weather. One gust turned him completely around."[15]

But as usual, Kiffin was not seeking publicity and told Paul he really would rather not get a lot of attention. He also responded to Paul's earlier request asking him to send pictures to sell to the newspapers back home:

In regard to photographs, every single fellow seems to be trying to beat the others in sending news to the newspapers, so there is going to be a damn sight too much publicity as it is, and every time the least thing happens, four or five will be sending telegrams to the papers. So I had rather not bother with any of it. I will be able to scrape along alright and all this junk they pull off makes me sick.[16]

A few days later, he wrote:

I will take your pictures the first good day that I am not too busy, but would really prefer that you lay off the stuff about us. Any time that one of the escadrille brings down a boche I will write you about it, but outside of that I hate to see anything at all come out about us.[17]

At least one good photo had already been taken, and on May 6, Victor Chapman sent a copy of it to his stepmother. It showed the first four American pilots at Luxeuil (Chapman, Prince, Kiffin and McConnell), along with Thénault, standing in front of a worn Nieuport 23-meter. Chapman apologized for wearing an old uniform in the picture but told his mother not to worry as there would be plenty of opportunity for additional photos.[18]

* * * * *

Two days after Kiffin's wind-blown adventure, three more *bébés* arrived. "Amazing little things," Chapman told his stepmother, so "neat and clean-limbed, the eight of them do not half fill up one shed."[19] He dubbed his plane "*l'alouette*" – the lark, as it reminded him of the numerous skylarks rising in the air around the field.[20] Prince, the only pilot left without his own machine, asked permission (which Thénault granted) to again return to Paris so he could fly one out from Le Bourget.[21]

It took the men and mechanics several days to mount, outfit, arm, adjust, and regulate the new planes, but by May 9, McConnell wrote Paul that "all of our machines are here now and work is well under way."[22] Most of the planes were colored to match the landscape, with mottled brown and green splotches – "war paint," Chapman called it, "rather handsome, savage without being garish." His was a nice solid cream color, something new the French were trying out.[23]

Every American but Chapman also chose to personalize his machine, most by having the initial of his last name painted on each side of the fuselage. For example, Cowdin had a "C," Prince a "P," Thaw a "T," Hall an "H," and Kiffin a capital "R."[24] Initially, McConnell chose his nickname "MAC," but later that summer switched to a white footprint, representing his time as king of the "Hot Foot Society" at the University of Virginia.[25]

Around this time, Kiffin wrote Loula that he was "at last ready to get down to real work, and would have made my first trip over the lines this morning if the weather had not turned out bad."[26] Two days later, he wrote Mrs. Weeks something similar, and stated that he "would like for them to signal a German so I could go up and have a try at him."[27] But although Kiffin was looking, no enemy planes could be found – as Chapman noted:

Of course, since our machines have come, nary a boche. Occasionally, one is signallé, but not located. This evening one was seen over Lure. They even blew the pompier horns here. It turned out to be only Kiffin Rockwell at a higher altitude than usual.[28]

* * * * *

Kiffin was in high spirits when the others finally got their planes ready, and early on the morning of May 12, he woke Chapman to go up with him. In a letter to his brother, Victor described their early start:

Rockwell called me up at three, "fine day, get up!" It was very clear and we hung around at Billy's, and took chocolate made by his ordonnance. Hall and the Lieutenant were guards on the field; but Thaw, Rockwell, and I thought we would take a "tour chez les Boches." Being the first time, the mechanaux were not there, and the machine gun rolls not ready. However, it looked misty in the Vosges, so we were not hurried. "Rendezvous over the field at a thousand metres," shouted Kiffin. I nodded, for the motor was turning; and we sped over the field and up.[29]

The trio soared high above the field. Chapman vividly described how things looked as they climbed through the sky and headed east toward Belfort:

The earth seemed hidden under a fine web such as the Lady of Shallot wove; soft purple in the west changing to shimmering white in the east. Under me on the left, the Vosges, like rounded sand dunes cushioned up with velvety light and dark mosses (really forests). But to the south, standing firmly above the purple cloth like icebergs shone the Alps. My! they looked steep and jagged.... Right beside the capote of my engine, shining through the white silk cloth, a silver snake: the Rhine![30]

As they turned to the north, German anti-aircraft batteries began shooting at them and nearly got Chapman's range with their first shot. Hearing a funny boom, he saw a black puff of smoke behind his tail, and "had the impression of having a piece of iron hiss by." After diving steeply, Chapman straightened out and saw "bunches of exploding shells" up over his right shoulder, near where Kiffin and Thaw were, hundreds of meters above him.[31]

Having dropped lower to dodge the shells, Chapman found it difficult to climb as high as his two friends, and eventually lost sight of them. After making his own little tour of the area, Chapman returned to the field, where he was handed a printed slip showing a telephone message from a neighboring *escadrille.* It turned out that Thaw and Kiffin had come down there, Thaw's plane having caught three pieces of shrapnel in the shelling.[32]

In fact, Thaw's propeller had been nicked and "the landing bumper on his tail shot away."[33] Ever ready with a witty remark, the *New York American* quoted Thaw as saying, "It was a good fling, but the morning was spoiled because the other fellow wouldn't come out and fight."[34]

By the time this account filtered back to America, Chapman's mother read on the front page of the *New York World* that her son's machine had also been "hit by a shell and driven out of its course, returning to its base so late as to cause anxiety for Chapman's fate."[35] A few weeks later, Chapman received a worried letter from his mother, stating "it shows us you have the upper hand of your machine if you can come safely home under such difficulties."[36] Victor wrote back:

From now on you must not believe too much of what the papers say.... The reporters in town see their chance for news; and they will soon have us bringing down a German a day a piece, and dying gloriously weekly. I am reported killed twice already, and more than one of us is severely wounded several times.[37]

* * * * *

Thénault later wrote that at the time the squadron received its planes, "few of us had ever flown a Nieuport...."[38] Perhaps this helps explain why he and the other officers (de Laage and Thaw) had, "when closeted with Happe, said we would rather not cross the Rhein or take extensive voyages behind the lines," a fact Chapman somewhat shamefacedly reported to his stepmother.[39]

But Thénault's comment about the squadron's lack of experience with the Nieuport was true only for himself and Lieutenant de Laage, who were Caudron pilots.[40] While a couple of the Americans had limited experience flying *bébés*, all of them had at least some proficiency with earlier-generation Nieuports.

For example, while Thaw and Prince were undoubtedly the most experienced aviators in the bunch, they had been flying the Nieuport only since the end of January, upon their return from Christmas leave in America. But Cowdin had already qualified on that machine, so when Prince and Thaw were ordered to Le Bourget, he requested to go back into combat.[41]

Some might be surprised to discover that (at its inception, anyway) Cowdin had the most Nieuport experience in the squadron, but it is most likely the case. After flying a Voisin over the lines the summer of 1915, he flew with *escadrilles* N.38 and N.49 in the fall of that year, and then spent seven weeks back at the front with *Escadrille N.65* before joining the Americans at Luxeuil. Around this time, Cowdin claimed to have put in more than 100 hours in the air over Verdun, a number that was probably not exaggerated.[42]

Another unlikely pilot – Bert Hall – may have ranked close to Cowdin in Nieuport flight time. Hall had trained on the Nieuport at Le Bourget in the summer of 1915 before going to the front with *Escadrille N.38* in the fall, then served as an instructor at Avord from early 1916.[43] Kiffin also had solid experience, as he had been flying the Nieuport 10 since late November and the *bébé* for more than a month before coming to Luxeuil.

On the other end of the spectrum were Chapman and McConnell. Although both had some experience on Nieuports, neither had flown at the front, and the first time McConnell went up in his new machine he told Paul, "I was worried for I'd never flown a baby, but got away with it all right."[44]

If you can, imagine being sent to the front in the greatest war the world has ever known, then thrown into aerial combat in a machine you have never flown before. That's what happened to Jim McConnell, who not long before being ordered to Luxeuil had confided to a friend in Paris that he knew he was "not good enough as yet to work over the lines."[45] Heck, less than two months before that he had not even earned his military brevet, and had written:

What I'm trying to figure out is how anyone shoots out of an aero. To run it is hard enough. Heavens, if I try to move a hand to pull down my casque *or something, the blooming thing begins to flop and dip and heave and run away.*[46]

But while he may have been a bit less experienced, McConnell's situation was not so different from the others. It is useful to remember, as Thénault emphasized, that "[a]t the beginning of the war, fighting aviation didn't exist" – that is, it was "a new science, a development of the war, and there was not a class of experienced men from which to draw."[47] Another comment by McConnell helps explain why he didn't feel too out of place:

There seems to be a fascination with aviation, particularly when it is coupled with fighting. Perhaps it's because the game is new, but more probably because as a rule nobody knows anything about it.[48]

* * * * *

After an early breakfast on the morning of May 13, Thénault ordered the squadron's first official sortie over the lines.[49] Thaw's plane was still being repaired from the shelling it sustained the day before, so he must have flown Cowdin's machine, as Cowdin was finishing his eight-day permission in Paris. According to Chapman, "We lined up, tried our motors, and left at 6:45. A circle over the town, and off we go!"[50] McConnell stated that "few of us knew anything about what should be done ... but there we were – just as if we knew something about it."[51]

Thénault selected Kiffin to head up the formation, flying in a wild-duck wedge.[52] As the pilots cleared the clouds the rookie McConnell lost track of the others.[53] By the time he finally located the group, they were crossing the lines, where a series of white puffs appeared all around the planes. The pilots realized they were being fired upon, something McConnell felt "was more amusing than alarming for they were not coming close." Recalling Thaw's shelling, he noted, "yesterday they shot better."[54] Chapman, who had been targeted in both incidents, concurred, telling his brother the bombardment "was very feeble as compared to yesterday."[55]

After clearing the anti-aircraft shells, the squadron tooled around the skies over Mulhouse, where a disappointed McConnell reported they "couldn't find a single *boche* plane."[56] Kiffin was hoping for some action, too, and "dived right down over the Habsheim aerodrome and there performed an aerial fandango to bring the *boches* out."[57] None took the bait, however, and eventually the Americans returned to Luxeuil, where Thénault declared the sortie "a promising first expedition."[58]

With the machines squared away and their first patrol under their belt, the men recognized that their days of hot baths and shooting pool were coming to an end. In a letter to a friend, McConnell lamented, "Well, the easy life is over now and we're off for the work ahead. It's up at 3 a.m. and to bed after dinner."[59] But Kiffin didn't mind – he was done preparing and wanted to fly. A few days earlier he had written Paul, "I think that I am all ready now."[60]

* * * * *

The afternoon following the *escadrille's* first sortie, Cowdin and Prince returned from Paris. With them was Jarousse de Sillac, who had been so instrumental in pushing the idea of an *Escadrille Américaine* when Prince first proposed it. Now serving as president of the Franco-American Committee, de Sillac had an "unwavering belief that ultimately the United States would be fighting side by side with Frenchmen in the great struggle for Right."[61]

Having always appreciated the propaganda value in such high-profile American involvement in the war, now that the squadron was officially formed and equipped, de Sillac meant to make the most of the opportunity. He arrived with a captain and several photography and cinema men from army headquarters, as well as an associated press reporter. McConnell noted:

Tomorrow the army moving picture outfit is to take us for the French propaganda in America. We've staged a big show in connection with the bombardment machines here. It will be very funny to go thru with it.[62]

But even before de Sillac showed up with his French government film crew, the men were receiving plenty of publicity in America. Not long after the formation of the squadron, Conrad Chapman informed his older brother of the increasing press coverage, which stood in sharp contrast with Victor's days in the Foreign Legion:

Your present position of international repute is great comfort and reassurance to all of us. As public interest centers on aeroplaning anyway (especially the American Escadrille*), it's very pleasant to feel that we shall learn, thanks to the papers, whatever you do within a day of the event. How different from the uncertain day-to-day knowledge of the trench dwellers!*[63]

The morning after de Sillac's arrival, despite some rain and low clouds, the pilots located at the airfield pulled off the simulated bombing. First, the Maurice Farmans took off over the camera crew, then the Americans in their *bébés* – Chapman told his family they would probably see it all soon, as he understood that the footage was to be given to an American cinema company.

According to Chapman, this fact got Kiffin's goat:

Kiffin and Berty Hall were much peeved to think that some [darn] person was going to make heaps of money out of us, and we'd risked our necks for nothing. (None of us liked to maneuver so close together with the plafond at 300 metres.) "Think of the honor," said I. "Oh no, give me the cash and keep it," said Bert.[64]

Later, the men heard a rumor that the pilots were supposed to get twenty percent of the moving picture returns, "but I'll bet we never see it in a million years," predicted McConnell.[65]

The footage taken that day also included many shots of the men on the ground – singly, in groups, lined up on the field, discussing their supposed raid, rolling out the planes, and always smoking. Chapman told his family he "never was so be-photo'd or ever hope to be again."[66] This was one of the few times the entire *escadrille* was together, and the crew made sure to film each of the Americans posing in front of what was probably Chapman's *bébé*.

The still-existing film belies the *New York Times'* assessment that each of the American aviators looked "more uncomfortable under the aim of the camera than he probably ever felt under the aim of a Fokker's rapid firer."[67] It is clear that the men were ribbing one another as each took his turn in front of the camera, but the film captures something more of each man's personality and character – Thaw: unassuming, but serious and exuding authority; Cowdin: smiling, proud of the medals on his chest; Prince: good looking, confident, and dignified; McConnell: goofing, laughing, and easy to like; Hall: lean, lank, and nonchalant, master of the "devil may care" attitude; and Chapman: joshing, boyish, and handsome, flashing his infectious smile.

One source noted that "clean-cut, handsome" Kiffin looked "fussed to death" when facing the camera, but to me the smiling pilot appears self-assured, smooth and strong.[68] At any rate, soon Kiffin and the other Americans would no longer be pretend airmen, staging mock bombardments and mugging for the cameras, but real fighter pilots, at war in the skies above France.

Chapter Forty-two

America is not at war with Germany, but Americans and Germans are fighting most spectacularly.

The bad weather that had threatened the propaganda filming on May 14 lingered, so for the next couple of days no flying took place. When conditions cleared early on the morning of May 17, Kiffin and Chapman took off "on a wandering route of adventure to try if perchance we could not match our skill against some doughty *boche*," as Chapman later wrote.[1]

They climbed east towards Belfort then circled together over Altkirch before turning north. As the pair neared German-occupied Mulhouse, a watchful enemy battery tucked into a nearby forest welcomed them "with salutes and bouquets of smoke." However, according to Chapman, its shots were "so far off one scarcely noticed, except by looking back, [where] a line of puffs marked roughly our path."[2] The aviators zig-zagged north, seeking an opponent. Chapman later recalled their flight: "Now Kiffin was to the right of me, now underneath, now above to the left, and so close I could see his goggles. It was hard to realize we were speeding forward at 160 kilometres an hour."[3]

The men got as far north as Saint-Dié before turning back in disappointment, having not spotted a single enemy plane. Pausing briefly at the aviation field near Altkirch, they refilled their oil and fuel, and ate breakfast and chatted with the French flyers there until eight o'clock, when three German planes were signaled. Kiffin and Victor rushed to their machines, hoping to catch one on their side of the lines. But it was not to be, and eventually the frustrated pilots made their way back to Luxeuil.[4]

Later that afternoon, Thaw had the squadron's first run-in with a German. Chapman spoke to him just after it happened, and recorded the event in a letter to his brother:

I just saw Thaw who had a good set-to with an Aviatik. He was so close he saw the passenger pointing a machine gun at him the size of a stove pipe. The latter must have emptied his roll of 500 cartridges, for Billy says he began firing at 900 metres, but when close up was silent. The pilote *ducked down and dived over the German lines. A little better marksmanship and Billy had him.*[5]

Chapman told de Sillac that Thaw had "played a *boche* in the most approved style.... Dodging to the right, then to the left, he ended under the enemy's tail, where he emptied his machine gun."[6] According to the first reports, the pilot dove toward the ground, apparently seriously hit, but able to regain the German lines.[7] Later an artillery observer phoned in that he had seen the plane going down.[8] However, the victory was never officially confirmed, and Thaw himself was unsure of the outcome. He said of the fight:

They are hard to get. I gave three of them a score or two shots each, but only one seemed to be badly hit. As he was over his own territory I cannot be sure whether he landed safely, but something hit him; that is sure from the way he dived.[9]

As Thaw's fight was not official, the *Escadrille Américaine* was still seeking its first victory. Kiffin would soon provide it.

* * * * *

Kiffin arose at daybreak on May 18, still eager to find a German and intent on heading out over the lines "to make a little tour."[10] Kiffin was the only pilot to leave the airfield that morning, and after taking flight he flew south and east towards Belfort, beyond which was the frontline. Continuing his climb, he reached 14,000 feet before turning north to make his way along the lines. On the ground, Kiffin could easily make out Mulhouse, divided by a canal running right through the town, but in the skies, nothing. After flying a little further to the north, he cursed his luck when his motor began to miss just as he crossed the frontlines. But as he banked his *bébé* to turn back, just inside the French lines near Hartmannswillerkopf – a peak in the Vosges mountains – Kiffin spotted a two-seater L.V.G. about 2,000 feet below him.

With a rush of excitement, Kiffin immediately reduced his motor and dove for the *boche* plane. At the same moment, the German pilot caught sight of Kiffin and hightailed it for his own side of the lines. However, at that altitude the L.V.G. maxed out around 84 miles per hour, so in his fleet *bébé* Kiffin was able to close the distance quickly. But the German craft still held the advantage in armament – two machine guns, one firing through the propeller, the other mounted on a rotary turret in the rear cockpit. In short order, Kiffin came under fire as the rear gunner fired over the tail of the German craft, "swinging his machine gun from side to side" in his frantic efforts to track the nimble Nieuport's movements.[11] Firing indiscriminately, the shooter probably got off two or three hundred rounds as Kiffin rapidly closed on the German plane. Kiffin described it all in a letter to Paul:

The gunner immediately opened fire on me and my machine was hit, but I didn't pay any attention to that and kept going straight for him, until I got to within twenty-five or thirty meters of his machine. Then, just as I was afraid of running into him, I fired four or five shots, and swerved my machine to the right to keep from having a collision. As I did that, I saw the gunner fall back dead on the pilot, his machine gun fall from its position and point straight up in the air, and the pilot fall to one side of the machine as if he too were done for. The machine itself first fell to one side, then dived vertically towards the ground with a lot of smoke coming out of the rear. I circled around, and three or four minutes later saw smoke coming up from the ground just beyond the German trenches.[12]

Kiffin must have been elated as he watched his foe go down in flames. By the time he got back to camp, artillery observers had already phoned in his victory.[13] The other pilots met him at the field and carried him from his plane on their shoulders. According to Bert Hall, "the girls gave him bunches of flowers and the hotel-keepers sent him bottles of champagne."[14]

Unlike Thaw's fight the day before, Kiffin's victory was officially confirmed – Chapman appended a postscript to a letter he had finished but not yet sent to his little brother, telling him: "Rockwell just came in; got an L.V.G. No doubt about it: artillery report him. He fell between the trenches. We're going to see this afternoon."[15]

McConnell immediately got off a telegram to Paul, telling him Kiffin "*a descendu un* boche. *Il a tiré a trente mètres, tué mitrailleur et pilote tombé en flammes sur les tranchées boches. Médaille Militaire propose*" – Kiffin has brought down a *boche*. He fired at thirty meters, killed the gunner and the pilot, who fell with the machine in flames into the German trenches. Has been proposed for the military medal.[16]

* * * * *

In Paris, Paul was preparing for a bath when Jim's telegram arrived. Uncontrollably happy over his little brother's victory, Paul "did a sort of barefoot war dance about the room." To Kiffin, he wrote, "I knew you would lay the *boches* low when you came in contact with one, and I am proud of you and of your feat."[17]

One of Paul's colleagues at the *Chicago Daily News* happened to be in Luxeuil at the time and immediately began pumping Kiffin for the details. Realizing there was no way he could avoid publicity this time, the normally reticent Kiffin told Paul, "Percy Noel is down here and so is going to write the story of my fight. Can't be helped."[18]

In his article cabled back to America, Noel got the facts right, emphasizing one important aspect of the duel: "Not less remarkable than the fearlessness of the method of attack was the fact that it was the first time this aviator had ever encountered the enemy in the air."[19] The story also made the *New York Times*, which reported that Kiffin had been proposed for promotion to the rank of sergeant and would be decorated with the military medal. That paper also accurately described his fight:

Corporal Rockwell engaged his opponents at close quarters. He swooped down upon the German aeroplane, facing machine gun fire as he approached. He waited until he was within thirty yards of the German machine and then opened fire. At the fifth shot the gunner of the German machine threw up his hand and fell over on the pilot, who also crumpled up as the machine began to plunge downward, in flames, to the German trenches near Uffholz.... Corporal Rockwell was compelled to turn at a sharp incline to avoid a collision with the German aeroplane.[20]

The day after his victory, a still euphoric Kiffin wrote Mrs. Weeks:

Paul has told you by now, I suppose, of my having brought down the German machine yesterday. I am very happy and think that I am the first pilot that has ever brought down one in as quick a time. It was my fourth trip over the lines and the first German machine I ever shot at and I only fired four or five shots while he fired over 200 at me. The captain sent me today two [citations] for me, one for the médaille militaire, *the other for sergeant. Even if they don't give me the medal, I get the* Croix de Guerre *with palm and my galons. I hope to get the medal also.*[21]

* * * * *

As word got out, papers on both sides of the Atlantic celebrated Kiffin's feat. In Paris, *Le Rappel*, *Le Figaro*, *La Lanterne* and *Le Matin* all ran stories, the last-named noting that Kiffin came from a family of soldiers and had been proposed for both the *médaille militaire* and the *croix de guerre.*[22] *Le Temps* published two articles about Kiffin.[23]

On May 20, the English-language *New York Herald* reported on its front page that one "James" Rockwell had brought down a German fighter plane after an exciting aerial battle.[24] Fuming at the paper's mistake, Mrs. Weeks immediately dashed off a letter, which read, in part:

There is no James Rockwell in the French aviation service. The American aviator who Thursday forced down a Hun aeroplane ... was Kiffin Rockwell of Atlanta, Ga., who offered his services to the French Republic the day war broke out with Germany.

Mrs. Weeks provided the details of Kiffin's background and family, noted he was an "intimate friend" of her son Kenneth, and asked:

Will you kindly correct your news item, as Mr. Rockwell has many friends in France and Paris who will be interested to know that he has already brought down a German aeroplane.[25]

The next day, the *Herald* ran another front-page article under the headline "American Downs First Aeroplane He Encounters." It began:

Corporal Kiffin Rockwell – not James Rockwell, as was erroneously reported in the Herald *of yesterday – who has just shot down a German aeroplane, has only been actively engaged in the aviation corps of the French army for a few days, and the machine he destroyed was the first one he encountered in combat.*[26]

While Kiffin expected to be appropriately recognized for his achievement, he wanted only what he felt he had earned – the military medal and the war cross. Privately, he told Bert Hall "that he was mighty glad to have a victory, but he hated all the ballyhooing and the publicity he was getting over it, when other men at the front were shooting down Germans every day and hardly being noticed in the orders of the day."[27] One source quoted Kiffin as asking, "Why write about us when we are doing only what our French comrades are doing every day as well as we are."[28]

* * * * *

Unlike Kiffin, his friends and comrades were thrilled with his favorable publicity. His old trench mate Herman Chatkoff wrote, "Dear Rock: My heartiest congratulations to you! Oh, old top, how happy I am!"[29] Another penned, "I was very pleased indeed to read the flattering [account] of your fight with the German plane. You're losing no time in making a name for yourself. Congratulations! May you soon have as long a list of scalps to your name as Navarre and Guynemer."[30] A French pilot friend of Kiffin's sent along a congratulatory note ending with "Hip, Hip, Hurrah! for U.S.A."[31]

Prince was still in Le Bourget retrieving a machine and sent a telegram to Luxeuil that read: *"Mille felicitations pour ton boche* – a thousand congratulations for your *boche."*[32] Kiffin's old friend Skipper Pavelka, with whom he had charged out of the trenches north of Arras just over one year prior, wrote Paul that Kiffin's victory was "about the best piece of news I have read since the beginning of the war."[33] Still going through his own aviation training, Pavelka worried that "by the time I get down there, there will not be any *boches* left."[34]

News was traveling fast in America as well – as an old fraternity brother of Kiffin's put it in a letter to him: "I see by the papers that you are pulling off some raw stunts over there. Go to it, but don't have any Germans get you."[35] On May 23, Kiffin's old boss Massengale congratulated Kiffin for his "splendid work" and sent along newspaper clippings from two Atlanta papers, both proudly proclaiming his victory.[36]

That same day in Winston-Salem, North Carolina, a reporter notified Loula that a dispatch had come over the press wire stating that Kiffin had participated in an attack on a German aircraft. As he read the account to her, the reporter noticed "an expression of great joy in her face." His article described Loula's reaction to her son's accomplishment:

"Of course, I am proud of my boy," declared Mrs. Rockwell, "but I would rather have him with me here." Continuing, she quoted from a letter in which [Kiffin] expressed his love of the work and confidence in the cause, declaring further that his faith in the whole situation is so great that he feels the assurance that God will protect him. "That is some consolation to me," said Mrs. Rockwell, "but I cannot help feeling uneasy."[37]

Not long after, Loula wrote a letter to her "darling boys," telling them:

All our folks, Grandma and all, are very proud, and it is needless to say I'm puffed up about you both.... Everybody says, "Aren't you proud of your boys?" Mrs. Ennes of Asheville is here now for me to treat her. The first thing she said is how proud all Asheville is of you. Now, aren't you glad you are avenging yourselves of the criticism heaped upon you for going?[38]

* * * * *

Usually at this point, even the best histories of the *escadrille* repeat a legend about the so-called "bottle of death," a bottle of bourbon Paul supposedly sent or gave to Kiffin to commemorate his first victory.[39] Unfortunately, while grounded in fact, the story is based on third-hand accounts and has come untethered from the actual event. Oh, there was a bottle of bourbon, and it was intimately linked to Kiffin Rockwell, but it was not tied to his first victory. Instead, it was given after his death, and was intended as a remembrance of Kiffin himself.

The basic version of the oft-repeated account goes like this:

Kiffin's brother, Paul, was working in Paris at the time of the announcement. He rushed to Luxeuil to congratulate his brother and presented him with a bottle of vintage bourbon. Kiffin poured himself a shot then handed the bottle to Victor Chapman. Chapman declined and instead suggested that the bourbon be saved "for rare occasions." He went on to explain that each pilot who shot down a German plane would be "entitled to one slug." Thus, a ceremony was instituted which saw a number of pilots drink from what was later called the "Bottle of Death" until the bourbon was finally consumed.[40]

Now, it may be that some drinking of bourbon followed Kiffin's victory, but whatever was drunk (if anything) was not presented by Paul to congratulate his brother. In the first place, Paul did not "rush to Luxeuil" to congratulate Kiffin and it seems highly unlikely that Paul could have gotten a bottle all the way to Luxeuil in such a short time, even had he tried to do so. In fact, McConnell wrote a letter on May 20 – two days *after* Kiffin's victory – asking Paul whether he had "received my wire re[garding] Kiffin's *boche*?"[41]

Obviously, if Paul had learned of Kiffin's victory and personally appeared in Luxeuil to present a congratulatory bottle of eighty-year-old bourbon, McConnell would not have asked this question two days later.[42] A letter Paul wrote to Kiffin that same day confirms that Paul was not in Luxeuil at the time and says nothing about any bottle of whiskey.[43]

In his letter, Paul told Kiffin that although he hoped that Jim and Victor would both distinguish themselves, he was "indeed proud that you are the first one since the *escadrille* was formed to down a Hun." He also noted how happy Kiffin's victory had made Mrs. Weeks and related her attempt to correct the mistake made by the *Herald*:

399

Mrs. Weeks looks about the most pleased person I ever saw, it has done her a world of good. She gave the Herald *a little interview about you, which I suppose will come out tomorrow, tho if that asinine sheet gets anything straight I will be surprised. I hope to God you get the* Médaille Militaire, *you should have gotten it long ago for your work in the legion.*[44]

As noted above, the true origin of the so-called "bottle of death" was Kiffin's own death and will be discussed later. For now, suffice it to say that Paul did not send a bottle of bourbon to Kiffin at Luxeuil as congratulations for downing his first German.

That said, had Kiffin wanted an expensive bottle of whiskey, he suddenly could have afforded one. Around this time, the Franco-American Committee decided that in addition to the one hundred francs per month it had begun providing each member of the *escadrille*, any American pilot awarded the *médaille militaire* would receive one thousand francs, with five hundred for the *croix de guerre*, and two hundred for each citation.[45] McConnell noted this decision in his letter to Paul:

Kiffin may get a thousand frcs. from the committee for reward with médaille. *Won't he be some swank tho with medals all over him! He could have had anything in this town.*[46]

More important to Kiffin than money, however, was the fact that he had avenged Kenneth Weeks and put the American squadron on the map. And now the whole world was watching.

* * * * *

Before sunrise the morning after Kiffin's triumph, seeking revenge for their downed pilots, several German planes crossed the lines, targeting the Luxeuil aerodrome. The Maurice Farmans were on guard duty that night, so the American pilots were sleeping two miles away when the Germans were signalled. Percy Noel, who was still with the men in Luxeuil, witnessed the whole scene and wrote about it in another article for the *Chicago Daily News*:

When the first bomb explosion made me leap from bed and run outside, I had a blurred vision of Lieut. Thaw pulling on his clothes, but when I turned around a moment later and spoke to him he had disappeared. "Gone to the hangars," explained Sergt. Bert Hall.[47]

Chapman also took off for the airfield, and later that day wrote a good account of his and Thaw's chase of the bombers:

I was first on the field when one bomb fell a dozen yards from me. But damn if I didn't lose sight of him when I got into the air. At 3:10, I left the ground. It was not day yet and misty. I paraded over the lines and all over the place, from St. Die across Mulhouse almost to Bâle. It was so hazy the German cannon did not even shoot at me. All I saw was a glimpse of a wing low in the Rhine valley. Meanwhile, Billy ran afoul of a second boche *and chased it all the way to the lines, the latter throwing hand grenades at him and clipping away with the* mitrailleuse. *Bill got in half a dozen shots from close range, then his gun jammed. Damned hard luck.*[48]

For their efforts, Thénault proposed another citation for Thaw and put Chapman up for promotion to the rank of sergeant.[49] The captain had also taken wing in pursuit, but "lost sight of the German in the semidarkness and returned to the aerodrome within an hour."[50] McConnell brushed off the event, telling a friend that "The *Boches* got peeved and so came over this morning and dropped bombs on us which did no damage."[51] But while it was true that the bombs had done no damage, one had landed just ten meters from the machines on the ground.[52] After watching the whole thing unfold, Noel concluded, "America is not at war with Germany, but Americans and Germans are fighting most spectacularly."[53]

* * * * *

Later that day, Thénault received orders transferring the squadron to Bar-le-duc, just behind the raging frontlines at Verdun, where the French were now three months into their valiant stand. According to Thénault, that battlefield's "already magic name made our hearts beat stronger," as Verdun was "where men seemed to die with less regret than anywhere else."[54]

All that afternoon and into the evening, in preparation for the *escadrille's* planned embarkment the next day, the soldiers packed up and loaded the squadron's tools and supplies into the tractors. That night they left the loaded vehicles lined along the edge of the airfield, where they would be ready to go first thing in the morning.

Unfortunately, the Germans came back overnight, and this time their aim was a little better. According to McConnell, the enemy planes "came in the dark and we couldn't do anything about it."[55] One explosive charge landed right among the lined-up vehicles, destroying six tractors and three trailers. As the full gasoline tanks caught fire, some devoted mechanics saved the remaining trucks by starting them up and driving them off. But the attack left five airfield personnel wounded, and another five dead.[56]

The quintet of deceased soldiers represents but a tiny portion of the gaping hole the horrible war ripped into an entire generation of the young men of France. Georges Bouteiller, a second-class soldier, was killed just two days before his twentieth birthday. Henri Emile Bohin had just turned twenty on April 14, Gaston Laine turned twenty on April 12, and Gaston Jean Nie would have turned twenty on the fourth of July. The oldest of the five was Ernest Joseph Guillang, who had enlisted from nearby Belfort. He was three weeks shy of his twenty-second birthday.[57]

All five *soldats* were posthumously awarded the *croix de guerre avec étoile de bronze* – the war cross with bronze star.

Chapter Forty-three

The greatest thing in the history of the world.

Luckily, the squadron's planes had all escaped damage in the airfield bombing, so later that morning, Thénault, de Laage and four of the five Americans flew off to Bar-le-Duc, behind the frontlines of Verdun. McConnell – who had busted two longerons on his *bébé* a few days earlier – stayed behind to wait for a replacement tailpiece to arrive.[1] As usual, Cowdin was still in Paris, and so was Prince, the latter having collided with yet another hangar while setting out from Le Bourget in his new machine. This marked the fourth Nieuport plane Prince had wrecked, including one incident where he smashed two simultaneously by landing one on top of another. Once again, however, he "did not receive a scratch," so, as Percy Noel reported, his "fellow pilots now worry less about the danger to the aviator than to the machine."[2]

While they had engaged in a few battles before leaving Luxeuil, Verdun would introduce the American pilots to "the real business of war."[3] Without a doubt, it was where the furnace of war burned hottest and, according to Thénault, in that clash not being killed "was the most one could hope for."[4] One author later declared Verdun "France's supreme sacrifice and her supreme triumph," and stated that "no battle of the whole war was more heroic or more dramatic in its course, or made so vivid an appeal to the sympathies of the watching nations."[5]

Although at the war's outset aviation was considered more sport than a true military discipline, it quickly became apparent that the old notion of a land war conducted by infantry, cavalry and artillery, was due for an update. As the conflict took shape, the engaged nations soon realized that airplanes could effectively be utilized not only for reconnaissance, but gun-sighting and bomb-dropping. Before long, aerial combat was added to the requisites of war and – mostly out of desperate necessity – airpower came of age at Verdun.[6]

Indeed, Verdun would teach the full value of airplanes as machines of war. Shortly after their massive offensive at Verdun in February 1916, the Germans had been able to gain local air superiority for the first time in the war. They did so through a combination of tactics designed mainly "to blind the French artillery by depriving it of its balloons and army corps airplanes."[7] Using heavy guns firing in pairs, the first firing a time-fused shell at a balloon already aloft and the second shooting percussion shells at the winch on the ground, the Germans were able to prevent the French balloons from maneuvering to avoid their shots. These tactics proved quite effective and rendered ineffectual the aerial views of the front on which the French depended.

In addition, the Germans concentrated their fighters to constantly occupy the sky such that French pilots found it difficult even to take flight. With neither balloons nor planes, the French army was essentially blinded – it was at Verdun that French General Philippe Pétain famously pleaded with Major Charles Tricornot de Rose: *"De Rose, je suis aveugle! Balayez-moi le ciel!"* – Rose, I am blind! Sweep the skies![8]

Major de Rose responded by gathering at Verdun all available Moranes and Nieuport XI's, with the objective of "sweeping the sky" to drive the Germans out of it.[9] Quickly assembling the best pilots of the *Aéronautique militaire*, de Rose organized them into *escadrilles de chasse*, or pursuit squadrons – the first true fighter squadrons in aviation history. The sole mission of these elite squadrons was to systematically patrol the skies, finding, engaging and shooting down the enemy. Pétain stated clearly the stakes for France: "If we're chased from the skies, then it's simple, Verdun is lost."[10]

As the French shifted their thinking, they also shifted their tactics. Soon the skies over Verdun were flooded with French aeroplanes, piloted by Frenchmen whose names would become synonymous with aerial warfare. Names like Georges Guynemer, Charles Nungesser and Jean Navarre, "the Sentinel of Verdun." Pierre Navarre, the twin brother of Jean and a friend of Kiffin's in flight school at Avord, reported in March that the fighting over that battlefield was "practically continuous," with the French aviators "flying from dawn until dark." He bluntly summed up the French mindset, telling Paul Rockwell: "The *boches* will never take Verdun."[11] Eventually, through sheer numbers and the tremendous efforts of its aviators, the French were able to roll back Germany's air superiority and regain the upper hand at Verdun.

It was as part of this ongoing effort to sweep the skies that the Americans had been summoned.[12] Verdun, and the French army's stand there, deeply impacted Kiffin. In a letter to his mother just after his arrival, he wrote: "words are impossible to express one's impressions here as this is the greatest thing in the history of the world."[13]

* * * * *

Along with their two French officers, Kiffin, Chapman, Thaw and Hall were the first to arrive at Bar-le-Duc. The city was in constant motion – troops and *permissionaires* bustling through every street, sentries posted on every corner, and everywhere signs reading *"Cave Voûtée."*[14] These placards indicated the building contained vaulted cellars, protected by sand bags, and listed the number of persons who could take shelter there should German raiding planes make a sudden appearance.

The squadron's new aerodrome was located northeast of Bar-le-Duc, at Behonne. Their hangars were within easy distance of three neighboring pursuit units, so the Americans now found themselves among some of the best fighter pilots in the war. *Escadrille N.65*, Thaw and Cowdin's former squadron, was located north of Behonne in Lemmes and commanded by Capitaine Philippe Féquant.[15] That group boasted the colorful and well-known Charles Nungesser, who had brought down his eighth German plane the day before the Americans' arrival.[16]

Escadrille N.69, another pursuit squadron, was located on the same field as *N.65*. Kiffin's friend Pierre Navarre flew with *N.69* until he was seriously wounded in March. Pierre's famous twin brother Jean was with *Escadrille N.67*, stationed nearby in Froidos, just behind the lines in the Verdun sector. Jean Navarre and Nungesser were still one-upping each other, and on May 19 – the same day Nungesser got his eighth enemy plane – Navarre brought down his tenth, the first French pilot to reach this score. Two days later, Navarre got his eleventh victory, a two-seater over Avocourt, while Nungesser bagged a German balloon marking his ninth kill.[17]

Despite this fast company, the airfield at Behonne was rather less than what the squadron had become accustomed to at Luxeuil. Instead of two miles of flat earth, well-suited for taking off and landing, the strip consisted of very rough ground which one pilot described as "badly situated on a plateau with a slice deep on each side."[18]

On the other hand, their quarters were every bit as nice as those in Luxeuil, as they were billeted in a magnificent villa overlooking the Meuse Valley. Before the war, the place had been the home of a great French engineer and was so commodious each pilot had his own room. Surrounded by scenic gardens, the villa had a studio with skylight, hot and cold running water, and a real bathtub – supposedly the only one within twenty miles.[19] Jim McConnell wrote his mother of the beautiful gardens, hot water, and electric lights, and of how their housekeeper each night left roses or baskets of cherries in their rooms – "Sherman was all wrong as far as I am concerned," said McConnell.[20] Not long after their arrival, the *Boston Globe* reported the American pilots were "installed in a villa, sleeping in real beds, shaving with hot water and eating excellent food. Gen[eral] Pétain doesn't have any of these luxuries."[21]

The excellent food surely included confiture – a jelly preparation of whole seeded currants for which Bar-le-Duc was famous. Kiffin reported that they even had their own cook, and military orderlies to serve their meals and wait on them.[22] All the men – officers included – ate together, their table and cellar abundantly supplied by generous gifts from W.K. Vanderbilt and by a common fund into which each pilot contributed a fixed percentage of his pay.[23] In short, as at Luxeuil, the Americans were surrounded with comforts, "not to be scorned even by those among them who are the sons of millionaires," as one reporter put it.[24]

The villa soon became the rendezvous point for all French pilots passing through Bar-le-Duc.[25] Soon nearly every meal saw two or three French officers dining with the men, which made it easy to keep up with news from the other *escadrilles*. One visitor admitted to being "a bit envious" when he compared the little tent and canvas-covered cot he had been assigned at his own post to the feather beds, baths and other amenities available at the pilots' villa.[26]

Kiffin described the "incongruous life" he was living in a lengthy, excited sentence:

We live like princes when we are not working, then an auto comes for us, we go up to the field, climb in our machines which the mechaniciens have taken care of, they fasten us in and fix us up snug, put the motor en route, and away we go for two or three hours, to prowl through the air, looking for an enemy machine to dive on and have it out with.[27]

* * * * *

Despite their comfortable quarters, the men would quickly become familiar with big black rats. But the villa was not infested with rodents – "black rats" was pilot slang for the large exploding shells the German anti-aircraft batteries fired at the French planes as they patrolled above the frontlines.[28]

In constant danger on their assigned daily patrols, at Bar-le-Duc the Americans "began to get a real taste of war in the air."[29] On the morning of May 22, tasked with protecting an observation machine in support of the French counterattack begun that day, Kiffin and Chapman flew low over Fort Douaumont and witnessed much of the terrible fighting taking place beneath them. Kiffin later told Paul:

This is a regular hell around here in the way of excitement and the world going crazy. Impossible to express with words one's impressions. I am badly played out for lack of sleep.[30]

At the same time Kiffin and Victor were at lower altitude protecting the *réglage* machine, Bert Hall was at fifteen thousand feet above Malancourt, fighting for his life against a German fighter. He eventually succeeded in bringing down his opponent, a two-passenger Aviatik, and later described the encounter in a single sentence: "I killed the *Boche* pilot and the whole outfit fell; nothing was left of machine or men."[31] Although his aircraft had also been hit, Hall made it back to Behonne without difficulty, where he was pleased to hear that the observation post had witnessed the skirmish – his victory was official, the squadron's second.[32]

Claimed victories were not always witnessed, and the mere fact that a plane was "driven down" did not necessarily equate to its being destroyed. Indeed, according to one contemporaneous account, "To tabulate or chronicle accurately the losses and casualties suffered by the various armies in their aerial warfare is absolutely impossible."[33] For this reason, the French required a second source, usually a ground or balloon observer, to confirm a pilot's assertion to have downed an enemy plane.[34]

The rigid standard and difficulty in verification meant that in many instances, confirmation was less than assured. As Thaw once remarked: "To drive the enemy down is comparatively simple, as usually it is only necessary to disable the machine in some part, but, really and truly, to bring down an enemy aeroplane in the way that is called 'official,' because it is duly recognized by the staff, is quite another matter."[35]

* * * * *

At the time of their arrival in the Verdun sector, Chapman was still seeking his first victory, official or otherwise. Not even three months earlier, he had flown a Nieuport less than a dozen times.[36] And although he made remarkable progress after his machine finally arrived in Luxeuil – he got in a squadron-leading 27 hours of flight time and declared he had "learned more about flying in the last five days than in the preceding five months" – Chapman recognized he was "far from being a *pilote* yet."[37] Yet here he was, thrust into the thick of things at Verdun, flying patrols between Côte 304, *Mort Homme* and Fort Douaumont. Just three days after arriving at their new airfield, Chapman told his cousin that he and the others were "really settling down to work," and he was now "actively saving France and no longer toying with her expensive utensils."[38]

The entire squadron was going through a similar transformation. Prince and Cowdin rejoined the group at Behonne on May 23 and were immediately put to work with everyone else. By the end of the month, together the squadron had logged more than 170 flight hours, a sizable chunk of which was flown over what Chapman described as the "smouldering inferno" that was Verdun – a "wasted surface of brown powdered earth, where hills, valleys, forest and village all merged in phantoms ... boiling with puffs of dark smoke."[39]

Sharing duties with the other *escadrilles* in the area, the squadron flew on a rotating schedule, staggered to keep an active patrol over the lines at all times. Pilots were generally required to cover two patrols a day and allowed to volunteer on their own in between. Kiffin and Chapman went up as much as they could those first few days, flying protection over the scarred battlefield as the French Fifth Division briefly retook Fort Douaumont before again being forced back by the enemy.

The men soon came to understand that, at Verdun, the skies were no less dangerous than the ground – as Hall put it, "every trip meant a fight, and a good stiff one."[40] Just four days after its arrival, the squadron would engage in its sharpest aerial battle yet.

* * * * *

As usual, Kiffin started the day early on May 24. He and Billy Thaw took off together at 5:00 a.m., just as the sun was coming up. Climbing over the battlefield, the pair soon spotted two German planes – a Fokker and an Aviatik. Thaw dove to attack the Fokker, while Kiffin kept the Aviatik at bay. In full-on pursuit, Thaw tracked the unaware Fokker, getting as close as fifteen yards before dispatching it at almost the first shot.[41] Thaw later recounted that he "was able to get so close to the enemy that I felt like calling to him to get out of the way before I pulled the trigger..."[42] After he and Kiffin returned to the airfield, Thaw told Thénault he was due no credit for the kill, saying "I just murdered him. He never saw me."[43]

Once Thaw and Kiffin had refilled their tanks, Thénault gave orders for the others to get ready, and at 8:30 a.m. the entire squadron took to the skies.[44] Because he was present on this occasion, Cowdin declared this flight "really the first sortie of the *American Escadrille* ensemble."[45]

As they ascended over the Verdun sector and turned towards Saint Mihiel, the patrol soon came upon a cluster of *Boche* two-seaters, flying "so low that they seemed like sheep grazing on the green meadows[.]"[46] Captain Thénault had no intention of going after the enemy, feeling the targets were "too low, too numerous, and too far behind their own lines."[47] But despite his strict orders not to attack unless he gave the signal – see-sawing his wings – Thénault's pilots proved utterly disobedient: Chapman broke ranks and took off after the low-flying Germans, and the others followed after him.[48]

Cowdin blamed Thénault's chosen formation, in which "the green young pilots, ... all keener than mustard, foolishly led the way."[49] Although he would later confront Chapman for impetuously crossing the lines, Cowdin told his father only that they "ran into a whole flock of German machines, and the fun commenced."[50]

The squadron soon found itself amongst a swarm of German fighter-planes and a general battle followed. At times four or five enemy machines attacked a single American pilot – Kiffin alone would engage in eight separate fights – and the squadron fought numerous distinct duels during the encounter. As noted by one paper, the aerial scuffle "was remarkable in that it happened for the most part at no great height – between 1,000 and 2,000 meters."[51] Thénault reported it as a "fine tussle, just over the roofs of the houses, with soldiers shooting at us with their rifles."[52]

Frederick Hobbs Allen, a retired American lawyer on the Franco-American Committee, chanced to be on the ground near Verdun that day. The "tac-tac-tac of machine guns in the air" drew his attention skyward, where he could easily make out five or six French planes engaged with a dozen or more German machines. Spellbound, and with an excellent view of the low-altitude fight, he later described the fast-flying aircraft as "dodging in and out among one another like so many swallows."[53] Cowdin also likened the aerial battle to birds, telling his father it reminded him of "the way the kingfishers used to swoop at the old Wave Crest Pond" near their home back in New York.[54]

Although their tactical approach was not as expert as it would later become, the outnumbered and fairly raw American pilots managed to make a good showing for themselves, and withdrew only after forcing down a couple more German machines.[55] Although it is hard to say for sure who got who in the intense fighting, it is likely that Cowdin and Kiffin each brought down a plane, although one source suggests the victorious pilots were Kiffin and Chapman.[56] On the heels of Thaw's kill that morning and Hall's two days before, Cowdin asserted that these victories "immediately established a great reputation" for the fledgling squadron – the French soon took to referring to the men as "the wild Americans."[57] The moniker was well earned.

* * * * *

Chapman engaged in his two maiden encounters during the mêlée, and quickly learned that the Germans were "wary beggars and damned good shots." Unfortunately, his own machine gun jammed in both attacks and his second opponent, a German L.V.G., "just pumped lead at me."[58] As Chapman scurried back towards the French lines, the *Boche* machine gave chase, firing the entire time. Even after Chapman outdistanced his foe, a German battery continued shelling him, and he had a bit of a close call. Cowdin told his father that Chapman "got his machine all shot full of holes, and he had one bullet go through his sleeve, just missing his arm. God only knows how he got home."[59]

Although Chapman would continue to place himself in the hot center of the squadron's dogfights, after this initial clash, even he recognized the need to exercise more care, and told his Uncle Willie: "We really must get less reckless or there will be serious losses soon. We have no right to attack the boches '*chez eux*' at the low altitudes we did, for the least *panne* and we remain there."[60]

Chapman credited Kiffin with excellent work in the scrap, noting he "chased off eight *boches* but had a explosive shell burst in the *capot* and cut his face up."[61] Speaking of this fight, Kiffin told his mother that while attacking a German "all of a sudden I had machines all around me shooting away and I thought for a minute or two that I was going to stay in Germany. Especially when an explosive bullet came through my windshield and exploded in my face."[62] Fragments of the bullet lodged around Kiffin's nose and mouth, leaving him momentarily stunned. However, he quickly recovered and flew back across the lines where he landed at a field ambulance station.

Although his face was quite bloodied, a Red Cross physician determined Kiffin had only superficial wounds at the base of his nose and around his lips.[63] Less than a week later, Kiffin told Loula they had removed "four or five little pieces around my mouth, which don't amount to a thing and am practically well now. But when they hit me, what with the blood and the shock, I didn't know much of what was happening."[64]

When Kiffin made it back to the airfield, he and the rest of the crew ate lunch and worried about Thaw, who had not yet returned. As it turned out, he had also been wounded, and nearly brought down – up against another Fokker monoplane and two other machines, Thaw's left arm suddenly became helpless, his elbow pierced by a German bullet.[65] Still under fire, Thaw continued to guide his machine with his good hand:

With my right arm I steered for our lines, for I saw my only chance to escape was retreat. I made what speed I could, but engine trouble developed and I had to volplane. I thought the end had come. I was faint with loss of blood and nearly lost consciousness. Finally, I landed and it was in the right place – 800 yards behind the first line trenches of the French infantry.[66]

Thaw's gas tank had also been struck, and his fuel flooded out. Although his plane escaped further damage, Thaw's rather rough landing demolished a small wireless apparatus at a station near the third-line trenches.[67] When he finally came to a stop, the woozy Thaw initially thought he had fallen in enemy territory and only "the welcome sight of two *poilus* in a nearby trench reassured him."[68]

The French soldiers transported Thaw to a field dressing station, from which he was sent to Paris for further treatment. He arrived the afternoon of Friday, May 26, and immediately went to the American Ambulance to have x-rays taken of his arm. Having confirmed the wound was not so serious as to prevent his return to the front, Thaw went to his sister's home near Mrs. Weeks to recover, telling a reporter that he "expect[ed] to be chasing Germans again within thirty days."[69] A few days later, still stuck in Luxeuil and envious of Thaw's feat of bringing down a Fokker, McConnell wrote Paul: "By George, it's some class to do that and then get a nice wound to go to Paris with."[70]

As for Kiffin, Thénault urged him to take 15 days' leave to tend to his wound and take a break from the stress of the front. Of course, Kiffin was reluctant, and only relented when Thénault ordered him to Paris, supposedly to inspect the Nieuport factory.[71] Mrs. Weeks described his arrival at her home:

About eleven o'clock we heard a noise in the hall, and in walked Kiffin. It was a great shock for he had been shot in the face.... He looks terribly with those dreadful eyes men always have after going through heavy firing. I cannot describe them. They are sunken and yet have a sharp look.[72]

Mrs. Weeks spent the next several days dressing Kiffin's wounds, during which she and Kiffin also had tea with Bill Thaw in his sister's garden. Thaw jokingly asked Mrs. Weeks if she were willing to serve as the squadron's *mitrailleuse*, or machine gunner. She laughed it off, but later wrote her son "How I wish I could accept it."[73] During their gathering, Thaw's sister, Henrietta Slade, laughingly took note of the rising public profile of her brother and Kiffin, telling Mrs. Weeks, "Think of it, we are having tea with two celebrated aviators, both wounded."[74]

And celebrated they were – over the next few days, the Paris papers were filled with stories about the squadron. On May 28, *Le Matin* ran an article headlined "*Les exploits de l'escadrille américaine d'aviation*" – the exploits of the American aviation squadron.[75] *Le Gaulois*, Paris' largest morning paper, ran stories on both the 28th and 29th, the latter titled "the American airmen worked wonders on our front."[76] But the French press had nothing on their American counterparts – on May 27 alone, Kiffin and Thaw appeared on the front pages of papers in numerous major cities across America, including New York, Baltimore, Pittsburgh, Indianapolis, Chicago and San Francisco.[77]

* * * * *

In Luxeuil, McConnell informed Titine of Kiffin's "glorious" injury. She quickly wrote a few lines to Kiffin, which she gave to Mac to deliver to Kiffin when he rejoined his squadron. A portion of Titine's letter shows the depth of her feelings for the dashing American pilot:

I congratulate you for your valiance because you really deserve it. Do not be offended by this little compliment, I know your bravery. My dear friend, I hope that your injuries are not very serious because it is difficult for me to know that you are not well. Send me a letter to reassure me about your condition.

I love you and do not forget you. Do the same and send me a letter from time to time. It will always be welcome.... I leave you kissing you very strongly.

Titine[78]

* * * * *

A few days after Kiffin's fight, his mother went to dinner at a hotel, where she found in her box a copy of the *New York Tribune* of May 27. Like many other American papers that day, on its front page was a headline praising the pilots in France – it read: "American Airmen Rout Fokkers in 8-Hour Fight." But it was the sub-headline below that caught her eye: "Single Planes Battled Five of Foe – Thaw and Rockwell Wounded."[79]

Loula's heart must have skipped a beat when she read those last two words – *Rockwell wounded*. The details of the story made her feel a bit better, but even they were alarming – a bullet had hit Kiffin's windshield and exploded, its "pieces wounding him a little in the mouth and nose."[80] She wrote her sons that "the fact that I've not heard direct makes me take courage that the wound is slight. I know every possible thing will be done for my boy and I'll try not to worry until I hear from you all about it."[81]

Loula was not the only American mother with reason to worry – Billy Thaw's mother had just received a cable from Paris, where her son was again located. It read: "Promoted first lieutenant May 23. Brought down two and was slightly wounded May 24. Left elbow fractured by bullet. No danger. Proposed for Legion of Honor. Here about six weeks. Everything fine. Love."[82]

As it turned out, Kiffin did not write his mother until May 30, by which time he had reported back to the front. He began his letter: "I suppose that the papers have given you more information than I can write, but anyway, last week was rather exciting." After providing a few details on his combat and wound, Kiffin wrote that he had gone to Paris for "a couple of days," but was "now back on the job, getting a new machine fixed up, and hope to get to work after tomorrow."[83]

By cutting short his leave and going back to the front, Kiffin deliberately chose to miss out on a wonderful ceremony in Paris, and one at which he surely would have been lauded.

Chapter Forty-four

Glory to Eternal France and to those who are dead for her.

May 30, 1916 was an important date in Franco-American relations. That day, ceremonies in Paris honored the eleven Americans who had died for France to that point during the ongoing war. Organized by A. Piatt Andrew, Charles Prince (a long-time Paris resident and the uncle of Norman Prince) and Paul Rockwell, the day was full of symbols and speeches, prayers and poems, all paying tribute to the lasting friendship between the United States and France.

"Decoration Day," as May 30 was then known, had been widely celebrated in America since the Civil War, particularly in the South. General Order No. 11, issued on May 5, 1868 by John A. Logan, commander in chief of the Grand Army of the Republic, a fraternal organization of Union veterans, designated May 30 "for the purpose of strewing with flowers or otherwise decorating the graves of comrades who died in defense of their country during the late rebellion, and whose bodies now lie in almost every city, village, and hamlet churchyard in the land."[1]

Consistent with this tradition and funded by patriotic Americans in France, the Paris Memorial Day Committee had arranged for the placement of flags and flowers on the graves of fallen American soldiers in St. Germain, Asnières-sur-Seine, Versailles, Cherbourg and Villefranche. With no such graves to decorate in Paris, a thousand or more Parisians, French dignitaries, and members of the American colony gathered at two-thirty that afternoon in the *Place des États-Unis.*[2]

A wonderful statue at the east end of that park depicts Lafayette and Washington shaking hands, symbolizing the friendship between their two republics. A fitting place for an event held, as *Le Figaro* observed, to pay tribute to "the heroes of the past and those of today; the French who fought for American independence and the Americans who enlisted under our flag."[3] By the end of the ceremonies, the monument – sculpted by Frédéric Bartholdi, the creator of the Statue of Liberty – was literally covered in enormous wreaths, floral emblems and bouquets.

Although the crowd was chiefly composed of Americans, the flowers came principally from French givers, including a superb wreath sent by President Poincare. Many members of the Senate and the Chamber of Deputies also sent floral arrangements, and Professor J. Mark Baldwin, whose daughter Betty had been aboard the torpedoed *Sussex*, sent the committee a telegram asking them to deposit a wreath "In memory of the brave Americans who have died for France, believing that this war concerns us in very fact."[4] An enormous wreath presented by the American Ambulance may have summed up best the sentiment of the gathered Americans – its banner read: "Glory to Eternal France and to those who are dead for her."[5]

* * * * *

Many of the celebrants crowded into the park that day came directly from a brief service held less than half a mile away on the *Avenue d'Alma* at the American Episcopal Church of the Holy Trinity, where Reverend Dr. Samuel N. Watson and a full choir in cassock "carried out a special service appropriate to the occasion."[6] At the subsequent event, this choir joined with one from the Chapel of the American Ambulance to sing "The Battle Hymn of the Republic," and a choir of French schoolboys followed with a hymn/poem by Victor Hugo, *À ceux qui sont morts pour la Patrie.*

The primary purpose of the ceremony at the *Place des États-Unis* was to commemorate the memory of the eleven Americans who had enlisted as soldiers of France and died on its behalf. Kiffin counted a good number of those valiant volunteers among his friends, including Kenneth Weeks, Rene Phelizot, Russell Kelly, John Earl Fike, and Edward Mandell Stone. Bill Thaw, still in Paris with his left arm in a sling, attended the ceremony and laid a wreath with another of Kiffin's former comrades, Charles Sweeny. Thaw even said a few words on behalf of the American aviators; the paper said his appearance "excited great interest among the spectators on account of his great prowess as an aeronaut and on account of his being wounded."[7]

Father Félix Klein, the chaplain from the American Ambulance, delivered a short speech in which he declared that the Americans – "the real ones, those who are Americans and nothing else" – could not forget the origin of their independence, with its "glorious bloodlines written in French blood."[8] Following a brief address given by A. Piatt Andrew, Georges Leygues of the Chamber of

Deputies (and the father of Paul's fiancée, Jeanne) rose and responded:

In the name of the French Parliament, I greet, with deep emotion, the memory of those heroes who, breaking the bonds of the dearest affections, abandoning the peace and sweetness of their homes, have crossed the seas, to bring the help of their arms to the great cause supported by the Allies and have come to fight, and die for France.

Their ashes rest in our land; they will be well guarded. Their graves are like altars raised to Franco-American friendship. Thus, through time and space, the glorious traditions created by Rochambeau, Lafayette, and Washington are being renewed for the defense of liberty and law.

[T]hese flowers will wither, the inscriptions engraved on this marble will fade, but the memory of American valor and goodness will never perish, because it will live in this thing that is immortal: the French conscience![9]

Paul's colleague Percy Noel reported that Leygues' remarks brought both tears and cheers from the assembly as he "expressed in eloquent terms the warm gratitude which France feels for the Americans who have died for her..."[10] *Le Figaro* declared that his words "went straight to the hearts of those present who, in spite of the somewhat religious character of the ceremony, could not resist the temptation to applaud them by shouting, *'Vive l'Amérique! Vive la France!'*"[11] The event proved to be a boost to the morale of the expatriate Americans who, it was noted, "left with their heads in the air, prouder of their country than at any other time since the war began."[12]

* * * * *

Only a few members of the committee realized it, but there was one portion of the festivities that did not take place as planned that day. At Paul's suggestion, the committee had asked his old trench mate Alan Seeger to write a poem for the occasion, promising him 48 hours permission to come to Paris and deliver his piece at the ceremony. Busy digging trenches and with just two days to prepare, Seeger threw himself into the project and somehow managed to compose the poem in time.

But the expected permission never arrived, and a deeply disappointed Seeger spent Decoration Day in the trenches. One account says a clerical error resulted in his permission being requested for June 30 instead of May 30, while Paul later wrote that "a careless functionary" at the French Ministry of Foreign Affairs had "confused Memorial Day with America's national holiday and had asked that the poet be given a permission on July 4."[13] Seeger expressed his sorrow in a letter to Mrs. Weeks:

What a bitter disappointment! After having worked feverishly on my poem and finished it, in spite of work and other duty, in the space of two days, behold the 29th comes and the 30th, and no permission arrives. It would have been such an honor and pleasure to have read my verses there in Paris.... They may be able to publish it in the New York Herald, *but not having graced the occasion for which it was written it is as good as still-born and shorn of all effect.*[14]

But Seeger's work was not wasted; his words were not "shorn of all effect." Titled "Ode in Memory of the American Volunteers Fallen for France," Seeger's poem is a masterpiece, and still moves a century later.

In the piece, Seeger praised France for supplying the occasion of dying in service to a higher cause and exalted those volunteers who had given "a few brave drops" and died for that fair country. And to those who wondered of indifferent America "if her manhood be decreased," Seeger answered to remember the small number of her citizens, like himself, who had not forgotten their country's "antique debt" owed to France:

Be proud of these, have joy in this at least,
And cry: "Now heaven be praised
That in that hour that most imperilled her,
Menaced her liberty who foremost raised
Europe's bright flag of freedom, some there were
Who, not unmindful of the antique debt,
Came back the generous path of Lafayette....

* * * * *

Although he was not able to recite it there himself, Seeger's poem has been read out in the *Place des États-Unis* many times since. A few years after the war, a grateful French nation erected at the end of the park opposite the statue of Washington and Lafayette a stone monument to the American volunteers fallen for France. The bronze statue atop the monument was cast in Seeger's likeness and the last lines of his ode are etched on one side of the plinth. They read:

Hail, brothers, and farewell; you are twice blest, brave hearts.
Double your glory is who perished thus,

For you have died for France and vindicated us.

Seeger's likeness stands atop the monument because just five weeks after the ceremony at the *Place des États-Unis*, this idealistic soldier was killed in combat. Fittingly, his death occurred on July 4, 1916. Like he always knew he would, Alan Seeger had kept his rendezvous.

Chapter Forty-five

The rotten day we had June 1st.

Even though Paul probably begged him to stay, by the time the Memorial Day ceremony took place in the *Place des États-Unis*, Kiffin had already rejoined his comrades at Bar-le-Duc. Upon his return, Kiffin learned three new pilots had joined the squadron.

Raoul Lufbery had arrived first, on May 24, but during the frantic events of that day, little attention was paid to the future ace. Stocky, rugged, muscular and square-framed, at thirty-one years old, Lufbery was at the time the oldest pilot in the *escadrille*.[1] He largely kept to himself, but over time would come to be respected by all the men. One Frenchman described him as "lively and energetic; but his nose, slightly flattened on his face, suggested a thoroughbred courier of the air, and his jaw great material force under the control of an indomitable will."[2]

His full name was Gervais Raoul Victor Lufbery, but he disliked Gervais and hated Victor, so Raoul it was.[3] Most of his friends called him "Luf," which one French source mistook as "*l'œuf*," which means "the egg."[4] But if Lufbery was an egg, he was hard-boiled.

Although he was born and spent the great majority of his life in France, Lufbery had been everywhere and done everything, sort of the Rene Phelizot of the aviation corps. As a youth, he helped his father through rough financial circumstances by working in several French factories making chocolates, macaroni and then shoes. After coming to Connecticut in his early twenties, he worked for a silversmith company, and in New Orleans and San Francisco as a baker and a waiter before joining the United States Army. As a soldier, Lufbery was stationed for a few years in the Philippines. Following his discharge, among other jobs he worked as a nurse in Cairo, a longshoreman in Calcutta, a railroad stationmaster in India, a mechanic and finally a pilot in World War 1. One commentator later called Lufbery "an extraordinary being who seemed to have escaped from a novel."[5]

Certainly he was something of an enigma – his own father said Raoul "was a strange boy," and "no one knew him ever," while his brother said that he "liked to be alone, and sometimes he would sit looking and say nothing."[6] His fellow pilots quickly learned that Lufbery tended personally to the upkeep of his machine, even to the point of selecting and inspecting every bullet loaded into the ammunition belts for his machine gun.[7] Other than flying, his only real activity was mushroom hunting, during which he would say nothing. As Paul would later remark, Lufbery "was a solitary soul."[8]

In short, Lufbery was different from the other American pilots, including his country of origin. Born in France, Lufbery did not set foot in America until the age of 22.[9] He spent two years with his brother in Wallingford, Connecticut, where he worked with the silversmiths Simpson, Hall, Miller & Co. making casket handles. He was known as an excellent wrestler, and spent his spare time working out, lifting homemade dumbbells made of large cobblestones and broomsticks.[10] After leaving Connecticut, he traveled to Cuba and New Orleans before ending up in San Francisco.[11] He became a naturalized American citizen by enlisting in the U.S. Army and serving a few years in the Philippines, where he was known as the best marksman in his unit.

Upon his discharge, Lufbery bounced around Japan, China and India until around 1912, when he met a French exhibition pilot in Saigon by the name of Marc Pourpe. Enthralled by the thought of flight, Lufbery volunteered to serve as the flyer's mechanic. From that time forward, he traveled with Pourpe, learning all he could of aviation mechanics.[12]

In the summer of 1914, the two men returned to France so Pourpe could acquire a new aeroplane. When the war broke out, Pourpe enlisted in the French aviation service, while Lufbery signed on with the Foreign Legion, from which he was immediately transferred to serve as Pourpe's mechanic. When Pourpe died in an accident in December 1914, Lufbery sought to become a pilot himself to avenge his good friend's death, which he blamed on the Germans.[13] One later colleague said he knew only one thing about Lufbery: that he "flew, fought and died for revenge."[14]

But at least initially, Lufbery did not prove much of a *chasse* pilot, and at one point his superiors recommended he be returned to the bombardment group. However, he stuck with it and eventually qualified as a fighter pilot. When he joined the outfit at Bar-le-Duc, however, Lufbery still had much to learn – less than two weeks before his transfer, he had wrecked an 18-meter

Nieuport at Plessis-Belleville.[15] Thénault recalled his arrival:

On the 24th of May there came to the escadrille *a pilot whom I was too busy to take much notice of the first day but who rapidly attracted everyone's attention. Simple, modest, silent and hard-working, always getting his plane ready himself – it was Lufbery.*[16]

* * * * *

The other new arrivals were Clyde Balsley and Chute Johnson. On May 25 at Le Bourget, their lieutenant told the men they would be leaving for the American squadron the next morning. As Balsley had never flown the *bébé*, the lieutenant told him to "get on and make a couple of trips," which he did. The two pilots spent the next night in Paris and arrived in Bar-le-Duc on May 27.[17]

Even with three new arrivals, the *escadrille* was only at even strength until Kiffin's return, for Thaw was in Paris on convalescence and McConnell was still stuck in Luxeuil waiting on the necessary part for his machine. Mac was even more eager to rejoin the squadron, as Lieutenant de Laage had flown back to Luxeuil and told him all about Kiffin's and Thaw's exploits at Verdun.

Unfortunately, when the component finally showed up on the 28th it was for an 18-meter machine, causing a frustrated McConnell to drive to Belfort and have a makeshift piece made. As he told Paul, "I'm damned if I'm going to wait any longer."[18] Still, as determined as he was to get to Bar-le-Duc, McConnell knew he lacked experience:

I am looking forward to Verdun with great hopes, but as I haven't yet had any practice you may see me coming in on a brancard *one of these fine days.*[19]

Although his prediction would not come true, McConnell's skills – and those of the other Americans – would be tested from the moment he caught up to the group at Verdun.

* * * * *

McConnell finally joined the rest of the squadron in the Verdun sector on the morning of June 1. He left Luxeuil the prior afternoon but had to fly low because of the cloud cover and ended up landing and spending the night in Toul. The next morning, delayed a bit by lingering mists, Mac got off around 8:30 and landed at the Behonne airfield at ten o'clock. Captain Thénault was waiting on the field as Mac touched down and immediately asked if he would be ready to go out on patrol with the squadron at 12:30 p.m.[20]

A few of the pilots had already gone up that morning, including Kiffin. While Kiffin was in Paris, the captain had given his machine to Prince who (of course) had smashed his own. Because he had returned to the front not to sit and wait but to fly and fight, as time dragged on with no replacement, Kiffin's lack of a machine would become something of a sore spot. But that morning he took Hall's *bébé*, and with Chapman and Prince went out over the lines.

Kiffin was aloft for two hours and saw a few enemy planes, but told Mrs. Weeks that "nothing came of it, except that I had to run for the first time." Separated from the others and up against three machines, Kiffin "decided the best thing I could do was to beat it."[21] Chapman was also on his own when he spotted "another fat *Boche*." As he approached under and next to his prey – like "a dory alongside a schooner," as Chapman put it – he pulled up the nose of his Nieuport "to let him have it." Unfortunately, "Crr – Crr—Crr—a cartridge jammed in the barrel." The German "jumped like a frog and fled down to his grounds."[22]

Upon arriving back at the airfield Kiffin was glad to see McConnell had turned up, but his happiness turned to disappointment when Hall indicated he would be taking his own plane on the 12:30 sortie. That again left Kiffin without a machine, so as the squadron lined up to take to the skies, he stayed behind with the two newbies, Johnson and Balsley. Although they felt bad watching as Lufbery took off, followed by McConnell and Chapman, the planeless trio would soon feel even worse.

As Hall prepared to start out, he looked up and saw a whole flock of *Boche* planes overhead. Just as he was alerting the others, German bombs began dropping on the airfield. Realizing Lufbery, McConnell and Chapman must have passed unaware directly beneath the attacking planes, Thénault, Prince, and Cowdin frantically raced to get off the ground. Thénault later recalled:

It's a most unpleasant position to be sitting out in the middle of an aerodrome in a machine whose motor is slow in starting while bombs are falling all around you. The mechanic twists away at the propeller in vain and when at last the motor does decide to fire it's a tremendous relief, for you know that at last you will be able to meet the enemy on fair terms. Until you start you keep thinking that each bomb, whose ominous whistle you hear, is coming for you and you are only reassured when once the explosion has passed. That is real torture, for our 110 H.P. machines were not very easy to start.[23]

But it was even worse for those without machines, including Kiffin. As the German bombers flew overhead, and the remaining pilots rushed to start their engines, Kiffin, Balsley and Johnson scrambled for cover. Kiffin later told Paul he thought he was "going to be killed by the bombs ... a very disgusting feeling."[24] Balsley recorded similar feelings in his diary:

Well, I have now received my baptism of fire. In all I counted ten German machines coming over the field. It was terribly mean to have to stay on the ground and see those machines all ready to bomb you. And then to see them over you knowing that the aviation field is their target and you are there. You certainly feel helpless.... Finally, four machines came right over the field. I laid down in a little ditch on my back looking up at the machines. I heard a bomb come whistling down. It seemed as though it was going to fall right on me. It hit a hangar about ten meters away.[25]

A few days later, the *New York Tribune* quoted Kiffin as saying "I thought sure I'd be killed on the ground and felt pretty sick – as when I get mine I want to be in the air."[26] But more than that, Kiffin wanted to fight – he told Paul to "tell Thaw I would have given anything if he had been here and both of us with machines," as "we would certainly have had the chance to bring down some Germans in our lines."[27]

* * * * *

According to Kiffin's account, those Americans who made it into the air experienced "a series of hard luck."[28] To begin with, having left just prior to the raid, McConnell and Lufbery were not even aware the airfield was under attack and continued on over the lines. Chapman was also unaware of the enemy raid but saw some blue puffs in the sky as he ascended, "such as one sees when the artillery has been shooting at aeroplanes."[29] Looking around, he spotted a *boche* machine above and immediately gave chase. Eventually Chapman lost his adversary over the frontlines and returned to the airfield, where he learned of the attack he had missed.

Hall understood what was happening but could not do much – not only were the Americans taken by surprise and outnumbered at least two to one, they were at a tremendous strategic disadvantage due to the fact that the Germans were already as high as several thousand meters when Hall and the rest of the squadron took flight.[30] Despite lacking altitude, as he rose Hall picked out a target but "had to sit tight" while his opponent "peppered me with a machine gun." Unfortunately, as Hall drew level with his opponent and prepared to fire, the German pilot "swung off into a cloud bank and I didn't see anything more of him until I spotted him winging back over the trench line."[31]

The rest of the squadron did not exactly cover themselves with glory, either. Captain Thénault had his gasoline reservoir punctured by a ball, causing him to descend, and Cowdin came down after his machine gun jammed.[32] The only member of the squadron to achieve any measure of success was possibly Prince, who believed he had killed an observer in one of the machines and forced another to land, but there was no official confirmation of these claims.[33] In any event, Prince was also put out of commission when his ammunition box was blown off by an explosive bullet.[34]

As for McConnell, he got lost, just as he had on his first flight at Luxeuil. One can hardly blame him, though – he wrote Paul that he didn't know the country at all, and the first time he saw the Verdun sector map was when he climbed into his machine before takeoff.[35] Already in the air and not knowing of the ongoing attack at the airfield, McConnell wandered in the general direction of the lines and eventually came across a plane he at first assumed was one of his comrades. However, upon closer inspection he saw the telltale crosses on each wing.

Sucking in his breath, McConnell cut his power and dove towards the German machine. Of the attack, his first, McConnell wrote Paul:

I hadn't the remotest idea about how to go about it. It was the first time I'd shot my mitrailleuse, first Boche *I'd ever seen. I swooped down on him and saw he carried two guns. The fellow in back opened up fire. I took a bead at 50 meters and let go a round. Then my speed carried me off.*[36]

Having shot past the plane, McConnell turned back, but immediately realized that "must have been a punk move" for he found himself directly in the sights of his opponent's machine gun, "the flames of which I could easily see."[37] The German gunner now had a "dead bead" on him, and McConnell heard bullets ripping into his machine. Firing back, he veered away, trying to escape. Creating a little space, he attempted to fire from the other side, but his machine gun failed to shoot.

As he broke away, McConnell twice tried to swap out his ammunition, but the gun still wouldn't work. Suddenly he heard a familiar "tut-tut-tut" and again "saw the German heading for me shooting." Fighting for his life, Mac disengaged and entered a steep dive at full speed – luckily, the desperate maneuver worked, and he lost the *boche* flyer, who perhaps thought the American was going down.[38] After levelling off, a rattled McConnell found a moment to check his gun. Only then did he realize that his reserve drum of ammunition had dropped overboard, and that the radiator was loose, having been struck by a bullet.[39]

Without a working gun or ammunition, Mac figured it was time to get back to the aerodrome. The only problem was he had no idea where it was, or even which side of the lines he was on. "In case of doubt, go south-west," he thought, and headed that direction. But after two hours following canals and railroads, he was still not certain whether he was in France or Germany.

Now nearly out of gas, McConnell realized he had to land. Picking out a nice long field that looked as if it was made for aviation, Mac was skimming the ground when he hit an unseen bump – the Nieuport shot up into the air, turned nose down into the ground and tipped on its back, smashed to bits. McConnell had crashed on the strip at Saint-Dizier where, as he explained to Paul, "the only way to land is from the direction I didn't take."[40] Although he was unhurt, he soon learned his machine was not. Indeed, he had been lucky even to make it to the ground, much less survive the smash-up. He told Paul:

Looked the old bus over and found nine bullet holes in upper and lower wings not a foot from each side of me. He got me well on each side, but fortunately didn't hit between.[41]

Some of the personnel at Saint-Dizier motored Mac back to the airfield at Behonne, more than twenty-five kilometers to the north. Once there, he learned that due to the length of his absence he had already been "reported missing and believed dead."[42]

Of course, McConnell took a philosophical approach to the whole thing. He told his mother he had "learned a little about fighting," and vowed "next time I won't let a German get such a steady bead on me. What a shame to have missed him – and right in our lines, too."[43] In his letter to Paul he added, "I could have bawled."[44]

* * * * *

At the aerodrome, Mac learned even worse news of what he referred to as "the rotten day we had June 1st."[45] The *boche* planes had bombed not only the airfield, but the nearby city of Bar-le-Duc. Under the headline "German Aviators Murder Innocents at Bar-le-Duc," the front page of the next day's

New York Herald stated:

The very iteration of Germany's offences against international law is apt to dwarf the importance of each new crime, but the bombardment of the open town of Bar-le-Duc, which is announced in a special aviation communique issued in Paris yesterday, must rank as one of the most wanton atrocities in the Empire's black list. For no military purpose whatever, a group of German aeroplanes attacked this undefended little town yesterday. Many bombs were dropped, and eighteen civilians, including two women and four children, were killed. Six women and eleven children were wounded by the sky-murderers.[46]

A few of the American pilots saw the attack as "an attempt to wipe out the American *escadrille.*"[47] Although he was not present when the aerodrome had been attacked in Luxeuil-les-Bains, one paper quoted Lufbery as saying "They tried to get us when we were in the Belfort sector and now they're on our trail again."[48]

Even worse, however, was the feeling that the bombing of Bar-le-Duc was perhaps due to all the publicity surrounding their squadron.[49] In a letter to his father, Chapman referenced the incident, then wrote:

Yes, this is what comes of getting notoriety. There were disgusting notices about us in the papers two days ago, even yesterday. I am ashamed to be seen in town today if our presence here has again caused death and destruction to innocent people.[50]

As evidenced by the fact that he came back from Paris rather than staying for the Memorial Day event, Kiffin didn't care much for all the hype anyway, and he certainly did not want it to affect others. In a postscript to a letter he wrote Paul the following day, he pleaded: "For Christ sakes, let's try and shut down on the publicity about the *Escadrille.*"[51]

However, it is not likely the German attack at Bar-le-Duc was due solely to the squadron's presence. As Chapman noted the next day, it was probably "a bit of self importance" to believe the bombings were their fault, as General Pétain had just moved into the area and several other cities had also been bombarded.[52]

* * * * *

While several of the men lamented missing the opportunity to fight the enemy, for the most part they now realized they still had much to learn. Betraying his neophyte status, two weeks later McConnell wrote that the only way he would be "clever enough to get a *Boche*" would be to catch him sleeping."[53]

Mac's letters to Paul prompted the latter to confide to Kiffin that McConnell seemed "to realize that he went to the front without sufficient training."[54]

But whether experienced or not, the American pilots were at a decided disadvantage in armament compared to their German counterparts.[55] In particular, while the *bébé* was by all accounts a wonderful machine, it lacked a forward-facing machine gun synchronized to fire through the arc of the propeller, such as the one created by the staff of Dutch engineer Anthony Fokker.[56] Already in use for more than a year on the Fokker E1 Eindecker, the "interrupter gear" had revolutionized aerial combat and helped bring on the so-called "Fokker scourge."

In contrast, the *bébé* was outfitted with a .303 caliber Lewis machine gun on the upper wing, fixed so as to fire over the arc of the propeller. While this avoided the problem of firing through the propeller, the drum-fed Lewis had a capacity of only forty-seven rounds, which a pilot could empty in less than five seconds of continuous firing. This constituted a strategic disadvantage, as it meant the aviator had to change out the drum in mid-flight, exposing himself to additional risk. William Thaw once remarked on the limited capacity of the "quickfirers":

It is disappointing, though, to find how quickly one loading of the machine gun is gone. It is impossible to watch for the enemy in every direction at the same time, and I never know while reloading whether the enemy is preparing to draw a bead on me. Consequently, it is safer to return to a point some miles behind the lines before undertaking to reload.[57]

As the men quickly learned, however, at Verdun one had no time to retreat behind the lines to change drums, but instead was often compelled to do so right in the middle of combat. One author described the tricky proposition:

Changing drums in the air was a feat for a contortionist. The pilot first pulled the gun down on its pivot so that the barrel was pointing straight up. Then he half stood in the cockpit and strained forward in the vicious blast of the prop wash to grasp the empty drum and replace it with a fresh one. Since a loaded drum weighed nearly five pounds and presented a flat surface to the wind, it required both strength and finesse to get the drum seated squarely on the spindle on the first attempt. More often than not, the pilot was forced to relinquish his grip on the control column with his left hand and – grasping the stick between his knees – use both heavily gloved hands to get the drum firmly seated. In the middle of combat, with a German firing on one's tail, this cumbersome procedure was a frantic business.[58]

In addition to the limited capacity of the machine guns, it seemed the ammunition was always sticking at inopportune moments. Of course, for a pilot in aerial combat, there is really no such thing as an opportune moment for a jammed gun. After one such situation, in frustration McConnell swore he had been so close to a German "that if I had had a brick I could have killed him."[59]

At the altitudes at which they were flying, there were also other issues to deal with. For instance, the cockpits were severely cold – "as cold as the North Pole," said Hall – so the pilots had "to wear all the clothes that were ever invented[.]"[60] Fur coats were standard flying gear, as were scarves, which served both to keep the wearer warm and as protection from the blowback from the castor oil used as a lubricant in the *bébé's* rotary engines.

Moreover, as most planes lacked oxygen systems until late in the war, at higher altitudes it was not unusual for a pilot to experience difficulty with his alertness and ability to function. Throughout the war, "[r]eports of strange symptoms and seriously debilitating conditions (typical of hypoxia and including cyanosis, headache, weakened muscular tone, earache, vertigo, extreme lassitude) reached medical personnel in operational areas."[61]

Over time, combined with the stress of aerial combat, the constant and drastic changes in air pressure began to take a toll on the pilots' bodies. In photographs taken during the last few months of his life, Kiffin appeared to have aged considerably, which is hardly surprising given his description of a typical day at Verdun:

Have been out four different times today, and all the while going up and down. One time I dropped straight down from 4,050 meters to 1,800 meters on top of a Boche, *but he got away. It tires you out a lot, the change in heights and maneuvering.*[62]

* * * * *

The strain of life at the front also led to tension in the ranks. Unsurprisingly, in the life and death environment of skyfighting, one man's bold maneuver was another's unnecessary risk. For example, while all the men liked and admired Chapman, after a few close encounters with the *Boche* flyers, they recognized that his fearless nature and reckless attacks put them in harm's way.

Veteran flyer Cowdin was the most agitated about it, and one afternoon not long after he joined the others at Bar-le-Duc he confronted Chapman about his tendency to rush into the fray. A reporter visiting the airfield recounted the "spirited argument" between the two pilots:

"I was just looking them over from a safe distance when I saw you volplaning down on them," Cowdin observed. "You're always trying to start something."

"Nothing like it at all," Chapman retorted, with a grin. "You had your machine gun in full swing before I was anywhere near them."

"Victor, if I took the chances you do I'd get measured for a coffin right away," was Cowdin's come-back. "Every time I try to take things easy I find you getting the Escadrille *into trouble with a whole flock of Germans."*

"Say, fellows," Rockwell's Southern drawl cut in, "don't you reckon if we hadn't started first the Germans would have finished first?"[63]

According to the reporter, Kiffin's "wise words" terminated the argument because Rockwell "generally gets listened to."[64]

Elliott was a hothead, but his remark about Chapman getting measured for a coffin would come back to haunt him soon enough.

Chapter Forty-six

There was never an American Escadrille in Germany.

Life in a *chasse* squadron was unpredictable, but this much was certain – flying above Verdun was far different than the fighting on the ground which, according to new squadron member Balsley, looked from the sky "like a broad strip of brown," with "no roads, no trees, no fields, no grass, just brown shell holes, a veritable crater."[1] In his diary, Balsley described one of his first trips over Verdun:

A bad bombardment was going on west of Verdun at Hill 304 or Mort Homme (Dead Man). All one could see under one was smoke. And now and then a flash as though the striking of a match down on the ground and I knew I had seen the 75's answering. The air over the battlefields seemed to be all nervous and troubly. I was blown around way up there like a leaf. What must it be below?[2]

Although they faced their own unique dangers, the pilots were glad not to be among the numberless, faceless soldiers taking part in the intense fighting below. Kiffin and Hall, who had been in similar circumstances, did not envy the men trudging through ruined villages, sleeping in filthy trenches or slogging it out in pock-marked battlefields.

As a pursuit squadron, the American aviators were tasked with chasing away the Germans from the lines, attacking whenever they had the chance. Bill Thaw described their work like this: "Word is flashed from the front that a German machine is rising. It may be an observer, a bomb thrower or a challenger for us. One of our machines must ascend and force him back to earth."[3] Balsley succinctly explained what he understood of his role at the front: "We were pursuit pilots. Our duty was to scout very high over the battle front, encounter enemy machines, drive them back into their own territory and destroy them if possible."[4]

While a few of the others complained of the monotony of their elevated role, Chapman – who also had served in the trenches and well understood the difference – told his father that flying was "much too romantic to be real modern war with all its horrors."[5]

* * * * *

When they were not in the air, the men wrote letters, read magazines and newspapers, smoked tobacco, and occasionally visited Bar-le-Duc's many cafés and bars. Most of the men drank, some to excess, which was just fine with Harvard grad and former professional polo player Laurence Rumsey, who joined the squadron on June 4. Standing five-foot-eight, with red hair and blue eyes, "Rummy," as his friends called him, immediately had his mechanics paint "RUM" on the side of his plane.[6]

"Rum" was a fitting handle – Rumsey was particularly close with Chute Johnson and, as Balsley noted, Johnson and Rumsey were "two men who like their liquor."[7] Along with some of the more recent aviation volunteers, these two had apparently done a little too much drinking and carousing in Paris, tarnishing the reputation of the Americans.[8]

Like Kiffin, McConnell was serious about fighting for France, and didn't see much use for additional American pilots unless they were committed to the same degree. Although his remark was directed more towards the American volunteers still in the flight schools, McConnell wrote Paul that these "see-the-war boys" would "hurt us like hell by coming in," as they would take the place of "a good Frenchman" and ultimately hurt the cause.[9] Mac wasn't known for turning down a drink, so any issue he had with the new recruits was based more on sentiment than drinking habits.

At least one of the aviators never drank liquor – Bert Hall.[10] Back in Luxeuil, Cowdin declared that "the reason Hall never gets drunk is because he is afraid of telling his right name." Hall had other rumors swirling around him as well – in addition to bouncing a large check to Prince, Chapman acknowledged that Bert had "such a weakness for lucre that he sometimes cheats delightfully at cards...."[11] According to Hall, Kiffin was a good poker player, "a game at which we spent many pleasant evenings."[12]

Chapman described one lazy day in which he sat in an upper window while "the other 'heroes' play poker, and the Captain practices scales on the piano."[13] The men gave varying estimates of Thénault's piano playing ability – Balsley described his music as "exquisite," while Hall later wrote that although Thénault wasn't much of a musician, "he was the C.O. and we had to put up

431

with it."[14] It seemed to help when there was more of an audience; Thénault fondly remembered some of the late nights the *escadrille* spent with pilots and soldiers visiting from other units:

> *Our French comrades, on their way to or back from the front, liked to stop with us for a time. We sang to the piano late into the night, so late sometimes, that the pilots who were on duty early on the next day often went to sleep in their battle-dress under the wings of their airplanes.*[15]

The squadron's musical choices expanded when Norman Prince's uncle showed up on June 5. Charles Prince, who most of the men called "Uncle Charlie," came from Paris to see his nephew and brought along a phonograph and a few records which he left behind for their enjoyment.[16] As noted by Chapman, from then on Captain Thénault's mess hall piano playing had competition. The American aviators' tastes ran to the ragtime music popular at the time, as Jim McConnell relayed in the *New York Sun*:

> *It is a queer sight in the evening to see a group of men in French aviation uniform singing "When that midnight choo-choo leaves for Alabama," or that ancient song query as to who paid the rent for Mrs. Rip Van Winkle.*[17]

* * * * *

The men might have been glad to know that a song titled "Wake up, America!" was becoming popular back home. Billing itself as "the song that inspired all America," through a series of questions the song urged Americans to remember their history and to prepare for war:

> *Have we forgotten, America,*
> *The battles our fathers fought?*
> *Are we ashamed of our history?*
> *In the peace that fighting brought?*
>
> *Must we be laughed at America?*
> *While our swords turn weak with rust?*
> *Is the blood of our fathers wasted?*
> *And how have we treated their trust?*
>
> *Is Columbia the gem of the ocean?*
> *Is Old Glory the pride of the Free?*
> *Let's forget every selfish emotion,*
> *United forever let's be!*

Wake up, America, if we are called to war,
Are we prepared to give our lives
for our sweethearts and our wives?
Are our mothers and our homes worth fighting for?

Let us pray, God, for peace, but peace with honor,
But let's get ready to answer duty's call,
So when Old Glory stands unfurled,
Let it mean to all the world,
America is ready, that's all![18]

The song reflected the growing acceptance of the gospel of preparedness, which Teddy Roosevelt had been preaching since not long after the start of the war. Having split the Republican party four years earlier in a failed attempt to win back the presidency, by 1916 Roosevelt was focused on finding a candidate to defeat President Wilson, whom he saw as insufficiently interested in standing up for American rights and preparing the country for war.

Thus, while Kiffin and the boys were listening to Charles Prince's phonograph at the airfield in Behonne, both the Republican party and Roosevelt's own Progressive "Bull Moose" party were meeting in separate conventions just one mile apart in Chicago.[19] The Progressives clearly wanted Roosevelt himself to take on Wilson, but for the Republicans – still smarting from his betrayal four years earlier – their former president was a nonstarter.

Attempting to bring both conventions together around an acceptable choice, Roosevelt recommended Senator Henry Cabot Lodge as a unity candidate. The Progressives were having none of it, however, and so within two minutes of one another on June 10, the parties selected different standard-bearers – Roosevelt for the Progressives, and (on the third ballot) associate supreme court justice Charles Evan Hughes for the Republicans.

Knowing that his candidacy would again split the electorate and re-elect Wilson, Roosevelt determined to unite the parties around the Republican-backed Hughes, provided he was solid on the two issues most important to Roosevelt – so-called "Americanism" and preparedness. In Rooseveltian language, the *New York Times* reported how the former president attempted to ensure this result:

Colonel Roosevelt sent a tentative declination of the [Progressive]
nomination, with the understanding that it was to stand if Hughes turned
out to be sound on the issues of Americanism and preparedness, and that if
Hughes turned out to be pacifistic, pussy-footed, or pro-German he would
accept and make the race as the Progressive candidate.[20]

Of course, Hughes immediately sent a telegram to the Republican
convention accepting the nomination and emphasizing a few points likely
calculated to satisfy Roosevelt:

I stand for the firm and unflinching maintenance of all the rights of
American citizens on land and sea.... I stand for an Americanism that knows
no ulterior purpose; for a patriotism that is single and complete.... I believe in
making prompt provision to assure absolutely our national security. I believe
in preparedness.... [W]e demand adequate provision for national defense,
and we condemn the inexcusable neglect that has been shown in this matter
of first national importance. We must have the strength which self-respect
demands, the strength of an efficient nation ready for every emergency.[21]

Hughes' rhetoric apparently assured Roosevelt he was not pacifistic, pussy-
footed or pro-German. But when the Democrats met the next week in St. Louis,
Roosevelt surely would have accused them of being all three.

For one thing, the single mention of the *Lusitania* by any Democrat during
their three-day convention came when Kentucky Senator Ollie James said the
following to great applause during his floor speech:

When the Lusitania *was sunk the militant voice of Theodore Roosevelt*
cried out for war, and if he had been President of the United States at that
time, today 500,000 brave American sons would be contending around the
forts of Verdun in this mighty maelstrom of blood – thousands would have
been buried in the ditches. Our President, patient, patriotic, far-sighted, the
real statesman, handled this question with the greatest ability, and won for
America its greatest diplomatic victory.[22]

But to that handful of American boys – like Kiffin and the others – fighting
at Verdun at that very moment, the humiliating episode did not look anything
like a great "diplomatic victory." It looked like cowardice. It must have appeared
that way to Roosevelt, too, for he called out the Democrats' silence as to the
victims of the *Lusitania*, and condemned the convention's applause of Wilson's
so-called victory:

The crowd roared in delighted sympathy with the men who had not dared to fight; but they uttered not a word even of regret for the women and children who had been killed because able and brutal foreigners were convinced, and as the sequel shows rightfully convinced, that the American nation could not or would not protect the lives of American citizens, and demanded of the American Government only adroit elocution, as a substitute for straightforward and efficient action. Shame is ours as a people that feelings as base as these should obtain among any of our people.[23]

In a letter written to the Progressive National Committee on June 22, Roosevelt gave his full endorsement to Hughes, and urged the party to unite behind his candidacy for president. Criticizing the Wilson administration's "timid and vacillating course," Roosevelt said the president had "lamentably failed to safeguard the interest and honor of the United States," and instead had taught that "the peace of cowardice and dishonor" was to be put above "the stern and unflinching performance of duty[.]"[24] In America, the political battle was joined.

* * * * *

While the political conventions were taking place back in the United States, two more pilots arrived at Verdun – Dudley Hill joined the *escadrille* on June 9, and Didier Masson followed ten days later. Strong and rather tall, Hill was blind in his left eye owing to an ice hockey accident in his teen years near his home in Peekskill, New York. Not long after that incident, he burst an eardrum while diving off the family yacht at Long Island.[25] Hill attended Cornell University and briefly transferred to New York University, but left in the spring of 1915 to volunteer with the American Ambulance Service. He was 21 years old.

In France, Hill performed well with the ambulance corps for several months, but in August 1915, he decided to forego his "neutral" status and enlist in the French aviation service. Despite his diminished eyesight and hearing, Hill proved a capable pilot and, after passing through flight school at Pau, he was eventually summoned to Verdun with the other Americans. Although quiet and reserved, "Dud," as the boys came to know him, was well-liked within the squadron. After America finally entered the war in 1917, General John J. Pershing would personally sign a waiver allowing Hill to serve as captain in the Signal Corps of the U.S. Air Service despite his defective eyesight.[26]

Like Lufbery, Masson was born and raised in France, and much more a Frenchman than an American. McConnell had Masson down as an "[i]nteresting, serious chap," and he was.[27] Before the war, Masson had been an exhibition flyer in America, and ended up as a mercenary pilot in the Mexican Revolution, dropping bombs from his biplane. But when he failed to receive his pay and was ordered to start bombing cities, Masson quit and shortly after the great war began he returned to fight for his native France. After earning his *brevet militaire* on May 10, 1915, Masson served in both Caudron and Nieuport squadrons before joining the *Escadrille Américaine* on June 19.[28] Over the next several months, Hill and Masson both proved to be skillful and sturdy pilots, putting in almost 78 and 69 flight hours over Verdun, respectively.[29]

However, around the time Hill first arrived, no one was doing much flying, as bad weather and intermittent rainstorms forced the idling of planes on both sides. On June 5, Paul wrote Kiffin from Paris where the weather was "vile, more like February than June."[30] Paul imagined that the poor conditions "rather gum[med] up" the squadron's flying, and he was right – a week later, McConnell told a friend that it seemed "years since we've done anything, the weather has been so bad."[31]

Even when a pilot was able to get in a flight, the results were not good. On one trip, Prince lost his way and upon being forced to land smashed his fifth Nieuport – which was really Kiffin's. On another, Bert Hall was up facing a German when his gasoline gave out. Forced to glide to the nearest landing place, Hall chuckled afterward: "that *boche* probably thought he brought me down."[32] Then, when Kiffin finally received his new machine, he got up over the lines one afternoon and saw a few Germans, but "it was too cloudy to do any good."[33]

And so, for a solid week, there was "nothing doing" at Bar-le-Duc. Instead of flying, the men relaxed in their villa, wrote letters, and taught Captain Thénault's dog, Fram, new tricks. Fram served as a sort of unofficial mascot for the *escadrille* but was not the only animal at the airfield. Thaw and Cowdin had Belgian police dogs named Pete Black and Iris, respectively, while Lieutenant De Laage owned a fox terrier named Miss Tiny. Thaw also kept a little pet fox until it was shot by a soldier while playing in a field.[34]

It was a common practice at the time for aviators to adopt pets as the mascots of their various squadrons. As noted by Bert Hall, "You'll never find a bunch of decent men anywhere, in that kind of life, that won't have annexed something that goes on four legs."[35] Indeed, Hall acquired his own unusual companion from a Senegalese regiment stationed nearby – a genet, a type of small African spotted cat, which Paul described as "resembl[ing] a skunk" but without its "disagreeable qualities."[36]

Earlier, while serving with *Escadrille N.38* in the fall of 1915, Hall apparently had a goat named Mimi.[37] He even took it up in his plane once:

I had a goat for my particular pet and, just like all the other fellows, I was crazy to take him up in the air with me. I did it once when I wasn't going too high, but when I landed he acted as if he were drunk—reeled around as if he'd been on a regular bat.[38]

* * * * *

From the squadron's inception, an easy camaraderie existed among the original seven members. Kiffin got along rather well with all the Americans but was particularly close with Bill Thaw and Jim McConnell. Perhaps his best friend at the front, however, was Victor Chapman. Kiffin and Victor roomed together at Luxeuil and again at Verdun, where Victor's bed was right beside Kiffin's.[39]

Chapman and Kiffin literally saw eye to eye on things – the olive-skinned Chapman stood almost six-foot one, just an inch shorter than Kiffin, the tallest pilot in the squadron. But Kiffin cared more for Chapman's heart than his height, and deeply admired Victor's character and ideals. In his principled friend Kiffin saw a great ally, a man unafraid and equally committed to the cause of France. The two often flew together, and in their first two months in the squadron, Chapman and Rockwell ranked first and second in both the number of flights and total flight hours.[40]

While the charismatic Thaw was probably viewed as the unofficial American leader of the unit, Kiffin was well-liked and respected by all the members of the squadron, a view bolstered by his early victory at Luxeuil. But once the *escadrille* transferred to Verdun, the strain of daily combat and the influx of six new pilots between May 24 and June 19 altered the dynamics of the unit. When, not long after their arrival at Verdun, Thaw's wounds sent him back to Paris, some personal rivalries and petty jealousies among the men manifested in disputes as to tactics or arguments about commitment.[41]

It is worth emphasizing the similar backgrounds of the eleven proper "Americans" (that is, those who were born and grew up in America) among the early members of the *escadrille*.[42] Except for Kiffin, McConnell and Balsley (who were upper middle class but could not accurately be described as wealthy), the men came from well-known or monied families and circulated easily among the upper crust, with its connections and privilege. A good portion, including Thaw, Prince, Chapman, Cowdin, and Rumsey were scions of some of the richest families in America.

Moreover, all but one of the eleven aviators were "college men" – four had graduated from Harvard and two from Virginia, while the remaining four attended Yale, W&L, Texas, and Cornell, respectively. With his hard-scrabble Missouri upbringing, Hall alone among the men neither attended college nor came from a prosperous pedigree.

Hall also wasn't helped by his well-earned reputation as a scoundrel and loudmouth, or the fact that a few of the men had their own personal reasons to disapprove of him. But Kiffin and Thaw – both of whom had served with Hall in the legion – always liked him, and Hall later wrote that he and Kiffin "were most awfully good friends."[43] Hall even indicated that by this time he and Kiffin "had been in the squadron long enough to figure out we didn't like all the members."[44]

Of course, it had been much easier to get along at Luxeuil – for much of its time there, N.124 did not even have machines; rather than being shot at, in those early days a pilot's biggest dilemma was whether to take a thermal bath before or after his late breakfast. But at Verdun, the danger was real, and the stakes were high. While men like Kiffin and Chapman were eager to fight and demonstrated their commitment to France by putting in more flight hours, a few of the others seemed more interested in basking in the favorable publicity generated by the unit than in actual combat.

Increasingly, Cowdin fit this description. Near the end of May, McConnell wrote that, "thirsty for printers' ink," Cowdin did not want anyone else as mouth piece, but wanted "to ring all the gongs himself at once."[45] A week later, in response to Kiffin's query as to where all the publicity was coming from, Paul said he had "an idea that Cowdin is press-agenting himself right along."[46]

At the same time, Cowdin regularly made excuses to avoid duty or consistently developed "engine trouble" once aloft. Faced with the awful reality of Verdun, Cowdin, who had bravely served at the front for much of the past year, suddenly took a very dim view of risk-taking, which led to his direct confrontation with the impetuous Chapman. As noted earlier, Kiffin's comment had ended the argument, but there is little doubt that the war was wearing down Elliott Cowdin. In a letter home around this time, Cowdin confided to his father that he was "just about fagged out." A portion of the letter further admitted:

I really have not been well this past month. My heart has been giving me a lot of trouble, due to the high altitude at which we are forced to fly, and my nerves – well, a June bride has nothing on me.[47]

Not long after, Paul passed along that Charles Prince had told him "that Cowdin imparted to him that he was very nervous, could not sleep, and had absolute need of rest!!!!" Rather uncharitably, he added, "Seems that worthy is always resting."[48]

While Kiffin had no problem with his nerves, a few festering issues with Captain Thénault had blossomed into an increasingly open dispute. In a letter to Paul on June 5, Kiffin wrote:

My citation hasn't yet gone through, so can't send you a copy yet. Don't think there is any doubt of the Médaille, but don't expect two citations. There is no reason why I shouldn't have them, except that we are very unlucky in having a captain who is a nice fellow and brave, but doesn't know how to look after his men, and doesn't try to. I have been fighting with him ever since being back, mainly about the fact that I have no machine, he having given my old one to Prince and not managing right to get me a new one. He acts, when I get after him about it, as if he was doing me a favor to get me one. I think that in a few weeks I will be pretty sick with the outfit. I am going to try my darndest to get another machine well down in the French lines, then I think things will change a little.[49]

Of course, Kiffin had already brought down two Germans, the only pilot in the squadron since its organization to do so. Given the way citations were given to others at the time, Kiffin surely had a legitimate complaint about not receiving two – he earned and was promised a citation for his (and the squadron's) first victory in Luxeuil on May 18, and clearly merited a second when on May 24 he brought down another plane and was wounded himself.[50] But Kiffin's initial reaction in the face of this slight was to work even harder.

The attitude on display in Kiffin's letter amply supports what a later pilot of N.124 would write of him:

In discussing men, the French used a phrase describing admirably a keen and bitter fighter – Il en veut, il fait la guerre. Rockwell had come to France to fight; not to loaf, 'swing the lead,' or pose as a hero – and when he went over the lines it was la guerre a l'outrance.[51]

The two French phrases translate roughly to this:

He wants it, he makes war.

War to the extreme.

* * * * *

By June 8, McConnell told Paul that there "seems to be a split up in this outfit," and identified two primary cliques in the *escadrille*: "Thaw & Co. v. Cowdin, Prince, et al."[52] For his part, Mac insisted he wouldn't "join either club." But in his next letter, Mac laid out how he had sized up the other pilots and made it clear which group he favored – the one most committed to fighting for France:

Kiffin, Bill [Thaw], Chapman, etc. are the most serious, Lufbery included. They are all one could ask for. Prince and Cowdin are in it for the sport, especially the latter and while they do their work, will never ring any gongs. Hall is minus a few cogs but runs along in the average. Johnson & Rumsey frankly dislike the game and I believe Balsley needs a new pair of drawers whenever he goes out. Hill is a nice sort and I believe will try hard. The only ones with the really right feeling are the first named.[53]

McConnell's summary finds support in the June flight logs of the squadron, which show that even though he was without a machine for much of the early part of the month, Kiffin, along with Lufbery and Chapman, accounted for more than a third of the squadron's 301 total hours for the month.[54] At the other end of the spectrum, Johnson and Rumsey totaled only 13 flights and 20 flight hours between them.[55]

A confidential report from an American military observer provides further corroboration of McConnell's comments. Prior to America's entry into World War I, the United States Army stationed observers in France and one of these men made a few visits to the *Escadrille Américaine*.[56] In the first of his reports to the War Department, dated June 30, 1916, Major James A. Logan of the United States Army intelligence division relayed information confidentially passed along to him by the Franco-American Committee in Paris.

Apparently, at least in the opinion of the Committee, Kiffin, Thaw, Hall, McConnell, Lufbery and Hill were "the best of the lot" among the American pilots. Johnson and Rumsey came in for criticism, as did Cowdin who, despite his "excellent record," was "supposed to be in a bad physical condition and has heart trouble." The Committee said Prince was "pretty wild," and his work, "while sometimes excellent, is a little erratic."[57]

As to this last point, it is worth noting that Prince led the squadron in both flights and hours in June. Not only that, while Kiffin had the most total hours from May to September, during the months of June, July and August, Prince logged a squadron-leading 153.9 hours, twelve more than Kiffin, who was second.[58] In fact, by the end of June, McConnell had somewhat softened his view of Prince, and wrote Paul that: "Old Norman Prince is not a bad sort at all. He's serious and works hard and tho crazy as a loon means well all the time."[59]

Over the years, a few historians have attempted to play up a supposed rivalry between Kiffin and Norman Prince.[60] However, the assertion is likely overblown – yes, Prince got Kiffin's machine while he was in Paris and turned the "R" on the side into a "P", and yes, he subsequently smashed it up, but there is no evidence that Kiffin held Prince responsible for his lack of a machine. While there may have been some friction between the two pilots at various points that summer, Kiffin well understood his true enemy was Germany, not Norman Prince.

This was true of the squadron as a whole, for at the end of the day, whatever differences existed among the elite young men in N.124, they had all been attracted to the same side in the conflict – the side of France. Thénault appreciated this fact, and drily noted, "There was never an American *Escadrille* in Germany."[61]

Chapter Forty-seven

The devil is loose on the front.

In New York, Victor Chapman's family was missing their son and brother. In a letter dated June 8, his stepmother Alce wrote:

I so often wish for you at some sunset hour, or when things look their best. I often wander into your room, too. Chanler sleeps there when he is at home. Your things are untouched on the bureau & tables, [and] I think he likes to mount guard over them & so feel nearer to you.[1]

She also mentioned the political conventions taking place in Chicago, meeting to nominate a president who Alce believed would either hinder or help the Allies' cause. Of course, Victor's father John Jay Chapman preferred Roosevelt to Hughes, viewing the latter as "a second Wilson, without Wilson's experience." In John Jay's view, Hughes' only redeeming quality was that he would have "a strong cabinet to steer him straight in international matters, which Wilson will never have."[2]

John Jay also missed his son, but enjoyed being asked about him and was proud to see him featured in the newspapers – he told Victor, "Your doings [and] the Am[erican] Aviation are on everybody's lips..."[3] Alce echoed this point, writing that "the papers give us news of you every few days & we praise God that the *Escadrille* has done such good work, & are alive & well, so far."[4]

But there's a lot of sorrow in a war, and bullets don't care about love, or the feelings of worried parents. The squadron would soon learn this lesson firsthand.

* * * * *

On June 11, Kiffin witnessed a horrible accident at the airfield involving two men from *Escadrille MF.44*. He wrote to Paul immediately after:

Just saw a pilote on a Maurice Farman do a damn stupid thing about twenty minutes ago. They have just carried the pilote and mechanician off to the hospital, and they will be lucky to live. I feel sorry for the poor mechanician, but not for the pilote, *as there is little excuse for him. He left the ground too close to the hangar, and ran full on into an iron wind indicator, then went head-on into a wall.*[5]

The pilot did in fact die, as Balsley recorded in his diary:

A pilot in an F.40 hit the weather gauge on top of a hangar on leaving the ground and his machine ran into a house. He and the passenger were terribly wounded and I heard this evening that the pilot had died.[6]

The accident was not the only thing dampening the men's spirits, for the continuous bad weather kept the squadron and neighboring squadrons grounded, for the most part. One measure of the poor flying conditions is that during the ten days from June 5 to June 14, only three claims were made throughout the entire French air service.[7] On the last day of that period, Kiffin wrote Loula that the past two weeks had been "cold and rainy all the time and I haven't felt warm once since it began."[8]

During this period, the men spent their time listening to the phonograph or hanging around the airfield playing cards. Given their fancy villa and fine dining, the American volunteers often entertained pilots and personnel visiting from neighboring *escadrilles*, with whom they discussed the latest news of the war and the gossip from the front.[9]

One common topic among the men was the prowess of their French and German counterparts. Jean Navarre notched his 12th victory and was wounded on June 17, one day before German ace Max Immelmann was brought down by two British pilots.[10] By this time, Oswald Boelcke, another famous German aviator, had racked up eighteen kills, and his black plane was well known in the Verdun sector. He would eventually shoot down forty allied aeroplanes before dying in an accident in October 1916.

Boelcke was a great airfighter, perhaps the best of his time. Even Manfred von Richthofen, The Red Baron, once said Boelcke "was the one and only."[11] During a dinnertime discussion a few weeks earlier, Cowdin had opined that although Boelcke was "the only real star the Germans have at Verdun," he was still "no better than lots of aviators on our side."[12] The Americans were about to find out how good he was.

* * * * *

Mid-month the long stretch of bad weather finally broke and Kiffin and the others were once again able to take to the skies. June 16-17 marked the one-year anniversary of the battle in which Kenneth Weeks, John Earl Fike and Russell Kelly had died, and Kiffin intended to avenge his friends' deaths – as he put it to Paul, he "would try my damndest to kill one or two Germans for the boys who got it this time last year[.]" And so, on June 16, Kiffin set out with Chapman, looking for a fight. The Germans were out in force as well, and the two aviators fought numerous duels, but without any success. In fact, Kiffin was twice caught off guard, and told Paul the "only reason that I didn't get brought down was that the *Boche* shot poorly." He explained what had happened:

Chapman has been a little too courageous and got me into one of the mess-ups because I couldn't stand back and see him get it alone. He was attacking all the time, without paying much attention.[13]

The *New York Times* reported that Chapman had been in a "perilous position" during a fight, surrounded by enemy planes, "but Rockwell came to his rescue and the two eluded the Germans without injury."[14]

Undaunted, Chapman was right back at it the next day, when he attacked and "seriously crippled" an enemy aircraft over Béthincourt, which was able to regain its lines.[15] Later, on a patrol over the right bank of the Meuse, he again broke ranks and "like a tiger" dove for a group of German machines. With Balsley, de Laage and Thénault, Kiffin followed, and his attack helped free Chapman yet again, this time from a fight with a heavily-armed, camouflaged three-seater. But instead of coming home with the others, Chapman landed at Vadelaincourt and after refueling went back over the lines alone.[16] Kiffin described what happened:

The result was that he attacked one German, when a Fokker which we think was Boelcke (the papers say he is killed, but we don't believe it) got full on Chapman's back, shot his machine to pieces and wounded Chapman in the head. It is just a scratch, but a miracle that he wasn't killed. Part of the commands on Chapman's machine were broken, but Chapman landed by holding them together with his hand.[17]

* * * * *

Kiffin was correct in surmising that Captain Boelcke had shot up Chapman's *bébé.*[18] Boelcke himself recorded that he had already been up twice that morning and was "loafing around" on the German airfield near Sivry-sur-Meuse when suddenly he heard machine gun fire and saw a Nieuport attacking one of his fellow pilots. That Nieuport was likely being flown by Kiffin.[19] Shortly thereafter, Kiffin's near-victim landed at Sivry and, "all out of breath" gasped to Boelcke: "The devil is loose on the front."[20]

The panicked German pilot informed Boelcke that six American planes were up, insisting he had even seen the American flag on their fuselages.[21] Unimpressed, Boelcke "didn't imagine things were quite so bad, and decided to go up and give the Americans a welcome." According to the brash Boelcke, "[t]hey were probably expecting it; politeness demanded it."[22]

Boelcke's version of the encounter is preserved in a letter he wrote a few weeks later; it shows how close he came to finishing Chapman:

... I met the fellows when they were still over the Meuse bend. They were flying up and down pretty impudently in close formation. I flew up to them and saluted the first one with my machine-gun. He appeared to be a fairly raw beginner; in any case I got to close range of him without any difficulty – about one hundred metres – sat on his neck and started work on him. As he was pretty helpless and flew nearly straight, I had good hopes of settling him. But Fate was unkind to me. I was using my machine for the first time after it had come back from the factory and got jams after twenty shots with the left gun and fifty with the right one.[23]

As Chapman did all he could to shake him, Boelcke struggled to clear the jams from his guns, but was unable to do so. Eventually, Chapman broke away, and Boelcke soon found "the whole swarm were after me." Still unable to fire, the German pilot tried to retreat, sideslipping down over his left wing, dropping a few hundred meters. When the planes (which were likely French pilots from a nearby *escadrille*) continued after him, Boelcke performed the maneuver again. The second time allowed him to shake off his pursuers so, catching his machine again at about eight hundred meters, Boelcke flew – "not very pleased, but at least untouched – homeward."[24]

* * * * *

In a neat quirk of fate, history preserved both combatants' accounts of the Chapman-Boelcke battle. In a letter to a friend in Paris, Chapman confirmed that his assailant was piloting an all-black machine and, given his tactics, he believed it was Boelcke on his tail.[25] He also described the dogfight and confirmed how fortunate he was to survive it:

Last Saturday, I had the narrowest escape to date. Coming home late from a reconnaissance alone, I was attacked from behind by a Fokker swooping from a great height. This, I think was Boelcke, as that is his invariable method of attack. A regular hail of bullets all around my machine riddled it. The controls were so damaged that only by holding them with the hand was I able to make a landing. I was lucky to get off with a light scalp wound, insufficient to cause me to leave the front.[26]

Chapman was indeed lucky – one of Boelcke's seventy bullets had left a two-centimeter laceration on his left parietal lobe, and he came back to Bar-le-Duc with his head wrapped in a leather and cloth bandage circling over his skull and under his lower jaw.[27] Several photos exist showing Chapman wearing his head bandages.[28]

In addition to the bullet grazing his head, Chapman's stability levers had been shot away, and the plane's wings, windshield and gun supports were all damaged. But Chapman managed to hold the controls together until he landed at a nearby *escadrille* in Froidos. When the airfield personnel saw the extensive damage done to his *bébé*, they gave Chapman a great ovation.[29]

People were applauding back home in New York, too. The *New York Sun* reported that Chapman "had to manipulate one of his ailerons with his left hand and keep control of the plane with his right," while the *New York World* stated that although the control apparatus of his plane had been shot away, "badly wounded as he was," Chapman "kept the machine's steering gear together until he descended within the French lines."[30]

The accounts brought some comfort and joy to Victor's stepmother. On June 22, she wrote him a letter from China Pond in Carmel, New York, where she was vacationing with Victor's younger brothers, Conrad and Chanler:

Well, my precious lamb, our hearts are beating high again with pride in you & thanks to God. That achievement of holding the steering gear in place with your hand after the machinery was blown away, is so typical of you as to be almost no news at all.... [Conrad and Chanler] are both in the best of spirits, so happy to be together again that it is a joy just to listen to their cooing, burbling voices as they talk & laugh & think aloud. Of course, your shadow is always at their side, [and] every hour of reunion is only a faint forecast of the day when we have you at home again.[31]

While also very proud, John Jay fully recognized the danger his son was in, and confided to a reporter: "If Victor is killed in battle I am resigned. I am proud that he joined the French army."[32]

The overriding goal of all the aviators was to bring down a *boche* and, outwardly at least, the men maintained a healthy dose of swagger and bravado. One reporter visiting the squadron around this time recounted that "the Americans were just a bunch of daredevils, ready for a fight or a frolic, preferably the former."[33] This description surely applied to Chapman, who despite his earlier promise to be less reckless, was still flying with abandon. As Kiffin noted, Victor "would attack the Germans always, no matter what the conditions or what the odds."[34]

Chapman's boldness (some might say overconfidence) was on full display following his dogfight with Boelcke. After finally arriving back at the Behonne airfield at 3:30 in a patched-up machine and with his head freshly bandaged, Victor "immediately wanted to continue his work as if nothing had happened."[35] Thénault and the others tried to convince Chapman to go to the hospital, or at least take a short rest in Paris, but he refused, and instead begged to join the next sortie touching off at 4 o'clock. His mechanic, Louis Bley, recorded that "Captain Thénault forbid this; and for his courage promised him a machine of 110 horsepower. Chapman was very happy."[36]

Their friend's lucky escape reinforced something that the men were coming fully to understand – at Verdun, they were playing for keeps. Experience is the best teacher, and Chapman's close call intensified his fellow pilots' concerns that his brashness would eventually catch up with him. As McConnell told a friend the day after Victor's encounter with Boelcke: "That fellow Chapman is a wonder. He's so brave he's unique – Kiffin says he's too courageous and will suffer for it."[37]

While Victor waited on the new machine Thénault had promised, his uncle William Astor Chanler (all the boys called him Uncle Willie) came to visit and, for a brief moment, Victor finally unwound.[38] According to Kiffin, "[t]hose first days Victor slept late, a privilege he had not taken … since being in the *escadrille*, always having got up at daylight."[39] Although Victor downplayed his wound, he knew the stakes for which he was playing, and during his Uncle Willie's visit stated in an offhand way, "Of course I shall never come out of this alive."[40]

The squadron also spent this time debunking the rumor that Boelcke had been shot down.[41] While that initial report wasn't true, the German ace's prowess and the real and imagined battles between he and the American aviators soon made Boelcke – and Max Immelmann, who actually was shot down the day after Chapman's wound – notorious back in the states.[42] A few weeks later, it was erroneously reported that Lufbery had exchanged eleven volleys with the infamous pilot's recognizable plane.[43] Understandably, Captain Boelcke was on Loula's mind, too – after a friend sent her a clipping from an Asheville paper claiming that Kiffin had saved Chapman by chasing off the famous German, Loula wrote, "I hope Kiffin can get the Captain, but I guess I ought to be happy if the Captain fails to get Kiffin.[44]

* * * * *

The day after Chapman narrowly dodged Boelcke's bullets, McConnell was at the airfield writing a letter to a friend. After describing Chapman's close call, McConnell wrote of a tough battle that morning from which Prince, Cowdin and Balsley had not immediately returned:

We are anxious about Balsley at the moment. There was a big fight and boches *were in superior numbers. Rockwell reported seeing Prince fall but Prince came in a few minutes ago. Balsley is over half an hour late. He was a little behind the others and may have fallen in with all the* boches. *Cowdin too is missing but they didn't see him in [the] fight.*[45]

Prince was all right, although he had a close call, and realized upon landing that a bullet had cut through his leather pilot's helmet.[46] By the time he closed his letter, McConnell had learned additional information about the other two missing pilots:

Cowdin showed up at a field nearby with engine trouble or something. Balsley came down back of the lines (chez nous) *wounded in the thigh. I feel relieved for I was afraid he was dead. Here comes Cowdin now – I'll see what news he has. – Nothing. He had engine trouble.*[47]

It turned out that Clyde Balsley was in worse shape than McConnell knew. He had been shot down after being ambushed by as many as forty German aeroplanes. In a letter dated June 19, Kiffin told Paul the details:

Well, yesterday, we all left for an offensive barrage over the lines. We were all supposed to follow the Captain, but only Prince, Balsley and myself did so. We four were over the lines, when we ran across about forty Boches in one little sector, flying at different heights.[48]

Balsley later recalled they were directly over Dead Man's Hill when "the clouds nearby suddenly opened, and the air was filled with German airplanes."[49]

Things must have been pretty bad; in short order, Kiffin saw one of their comrades – he didn't know whether it was Prince or Balsley – "go over in a regular death drop and thought to myself that he was killed."[50] He then lost sight of the other one, leaving just himself and Captain Thénault, who signaled from his plane: *"sauve qui peut"* – every man for himself.[51] It took all Kiffin's skill to get out of the scrape, but eventually he disengaged and with Thénault raced home, "thinking the other two were killed."[52]

But Balsley was not dead, although he was in a very uncomfortable position. Trying to fight his way free of the Aviatiks and Fokkers, his gun jammed, and he found himself "surrounded by a cordon of enemy planes" that was "impossible to penetrate."[53] He later gave this account:

I began to loop; I swung in every direction; I went into a cloud. Bullets followed. One scratched my machine, and I slipped away from the man who fired it and threw the belly of my plane upward.... It was while I was standing completely on my head, the belly of my machine skyward, that something struck me.[54]

Feeling the sensation of losing a leg, Balsley fell into a spinning nose-dive. He later told Paul: "I felt as though I had been kicked in the side by a mule. My only regret was that I was unable to get the German. As I fell I kept telling myself, 'Keep a cool head.'"[55]

Although he fell over twelve thousand feet, fortunately Balsley's feet were strapped to the controls, so he was able to work his unusable right leg with his hands. In this manner, he was eventually able to regain control of his machine and crash land in a shell pit just behind the French reserve trenches. Shortly thereafter a German battery began shelling the spot and Balsley, unable to stand or walk, crawled away from his smashed plane. He did not get very far before fainting and toppling into a small ditch.[56]

Four French *poilus* hustled Balsley to an evacuation hospital at Vadelaincourt, where a surgeon found that he had been struck by an explosive bullet and "the greater portion of one hip had been shot away."[57] Balsley did not know it yet, but his fighting days were over. A few days later, his mother received a cable from Bill Thaw, who had returned to Paris after a brief visit with the squadron. It read:

Clyde's right hip fractured by bullet. Doing well but complications possible. Receiving every care. Awarded military medal and war cross. His letters follow. Will cable developments.[58]

At one in the morning on June 30, a messenger knocked on the door of the Balsley residence at 416 Carson Street in San Antonio, Texas, and delivered a second cablegram from France, sent by the Franco-American Flying Corps Committee. Clyde's frightened mother felt certain it was a death notice and woke Rollin, her younger son. When they finally worked up the courage to open it, Clyde's mother and brother were relieved to read:

Please accept our congratulations upon the honors conferred your gallant son by the French Government also upon the rapid improvement of his wounds.[59]

* * * * *

Although they had not cared much for him at first, during his three weeks at Bar-le-Duc, Balsley earned the respect and appreciation of Kiffin and his cohorts.[60] Following his unfortunate injury, Kiffin told Paul how much he had grown to like the young Texan:

Well, yesterday was a rather bad day for us. You know we didn't think much of Balsley. It was because he is young and inexperienced, but when he got here to the Escadrille *I began to like him fairly well and better every day, as I saw he had plenty of good will to work and was not afraid.*[61]

The others had also taken a liking to Balsley, and over the next several days, a few visited him in the field hospital at Vadelaincourt. In a letter to Paul, McConnell took back "everything I said about the poor boy," and praised Balsley for being "very brave and decent during his suffering."[62] In addition, Chute Johnson and Dudley Hill dropped off some magazines before heading to Paris on leave, where they told Mrs. Weeks they had seen Balsey, who was "suffering greatly."[63]

One cause of Balsley's suffering was that, due to the nature of his wounds, he was not allowed a lot of water following his operations. Victor Chapman learned of Balsley's incessant thirst when he flew over from Bar-le-Duc to bring Balsley his toothbrush and asked if Balsley could have some oranges. When the doctor approved, Chapman told Clyde, "I'll get you those oranges if I have to fly to Paris."[64]

On June 23, intending to tour the front and then fly to Vadelaincourt to see his suffering friend, Chapman asked his mechanic to secure a bundle of newspapers, a sack of oranges and some chocolate. While the mechanic prepared his new higher-powered *bébé*, Victor discussed the wind with

McConnell, trying to figure the best direction to land at the field hospital.[65] When everything was ready, he shook hands with his mechanic, telling him "*Au revoir*, I shall not be long."[66] Then Victor Chapman climbed into his machine and, smiling, took to the French skies for the last time.

Chapter Forty-eight

These are sad days.

Captain Thénault, Prince and Lufbery had already left on a patrol over the front a few minutes before Victor took off. As the trio made their way over the lines, they spotted two German machines in the distance and dove to attack. However, once engaged, they realized at least three other enemy planes were joining the fray and, outnumbered, turned back toward the French lines. Upon landing at the airfield, the returning pilots learned that Victor had not yet made it back. But no one thought too much about it, as they figured he was still visiting Balsley at the hospital.

Indeed, Chapman was usually the last pilot to return from patrol, often coming in "with his machine all shot to hell – struts and wires and braces cut off," as Bert Hall put it.[1] But as the afternoon lengthened towards evening and Victor still had not come back, the men began to feel uneasy. Then a Maurice Farman pilot from a neighboring *escadrille* telephoned in that he had seen a Nieuport fall.

Not long after that, another call from an observer on a reconnaissance plane confirmed their worst fears.[2] From his higher altitude, the observer had seen the earlier fight involving Thénault, Prince and Lufbery; he had also seen the group attack what they assumed was two, but in fact was five German machines. As the trio of *bébés* disengaged, the observer spotted a fourth Nieuport arriving with all speed – this must have been Chapman, rushing to assist his squad mates. Thus, unbeknownst to the other three aviators, just as they pulled out and turned toward their own lines, Chapman dove into the midst of the waiting Germans.

Although Chapman fought furiously against superior numbers, the enemy were too many – the observer reported seeing Chapman's plane nosedive and go into a corkscrew, riddled with bullets. As his shot-up machine hurtled at full speed toward the earth, its wings folded up and broke apart, then the fuselage "dropped like a stone into the German lines."[3]

Victor Chapman was dead.[4]

That night, Kiffin lay in the room he had, until that day, shared with Victor. Unable to sleep, he was still awake when a terrible storm blew in around 11:00 o'clock. For half an hour, Kiffin lay listening to the thunder and rain until he heard a knock at his door. It was McConnell – a call had come in from the hospital at Vadelaincourt, and now Balsley was dying. The two friends woke Thénault, and the three men headed off in the staff car. Due to a blowout and poor driving conditions in the storm, it was 3:00 a.m. when they finally made it to Vadelaincourt where, according to Kiffin, they found Balsley "perfectly conscious to outward appearance and talking rationally and surprised to see us at that hour."[5] Not having the heart to disclose the day's tragedy, the men told Clyde to get some rest and headed back to Behonne. The worn-out group didn't make it back to the airfield until 5:00 a.m.[6]

Later that afternoon, Elliott Cowdin appeared at Balsley's bedside in Vadelaincourt. Stammering that Chapman "couldn't come today; machine's busted," he handed Balsley a small bag of oranges and abruptly left.[7] It wasn't until the following day that Balsley learned from a young French officer reading a Paris paper that Victor – "the aviator whom everyone in our squadron loved deeply" – had fallen.[8]

* * * * *

Victor's death affected the entire *escadrille*. As McConnell wrote Paul:

Somehow I can't realize he's gone, and when I think of it, I feel so badly. You know he had oranges in his machine to take to Balsley after the sortie. It was like him. We were all very fond of him. Everyone.[9]

In a letter to Victor's father, even Captain Thénault voiced his grief, saying he had "lost not only a pilot, but a comrade and friend." He also expressed his admiration for Victor:

He fell for his noble ideal, for justice and the right. When so many do not, this is enough to distinguish a man. God called him home, he could not have chosen a purer heart.[10]

Thénault telephoned Thaw, who was still convalescing in Paris.[11] The sad news came as a great shock to Thaw, who said of Victor: "He was the most fearless flyer I ever saw, and also the most conscientious. When leave was offered him to come down here for the Decoration Day ceremonies he declined, simply remarking that he thought he could be of more use at the front than

453

in Paris."[12]

All the pilots felt Chapman was special, and the whole squadron felt his loss. Bert Hall remembered Victor as "[n]ot like most of the boys, he was very settled in his habits, was never excited or mad, and I am confident he never knew what fear meant."[13] Nimmie Prince echoed Hall, telling his family that Chapman "was as brave as a lion," and had been "of tremendous assistance to Elliott and me in getting together the *escadrille*."[14] But no one in the squadron was closer to Victor than Kiffin.[15] One can get a good sense of his relationship with Victor from some lines he wrote Paul:

I would like to see every paper in the world pay a tribute to Victor. There is no question but that he had more nerve than all the rest of us put together. We were all afraid that he would be killed and I rooming with him have begged him every night to be more prudent. He would fight every boche *he saw, no matter where or what odds, and I am sure that he had wounded and killed several of them. I have seen him two times right on top of a German, shooting hell out of him, but it was always in their lines and there being so much fighting here it is impossible to tell always when you bring a machine down.... [A]s I say, he and I had roomed together and flown very much together, so I rather feel it, as I had grown to like him very much. I am afraid it is going to rain tomorrow, but if not, Prince and I are going to fly about ten hours, and will do our best to kill one or two Germans for Victor.*[16]

In a letter to Victor's stepmother, Kiffin summed up her son's impact on the squadron: he wrote that all the boys had felt Victor's influence, "and seeing in him a man made us feel a little more like trying to be men ourselves."[17] A letter he wrote to Alice Weeks the day after Victor's death gives some sense of how highly Kiffin thought of him:

Victor had about the strongest character of any boy I have ever known. He was very frank, honest and never had let anything kill his ideals and had always lived a very clean life, never doing any harm, or believing wrong of anyone and giving out a lot of good to the people around him. We used to kid him a lot and tell him that a lot of his ideals were very foolish and all, yet it didn't affect him, and he still believed these old ideals and died a glorious death.[18]

When Mrs. Weeks learned of the tragedy, she was heartbroken. She ended a letter to her son with the simple statement: "These are sad days."[19]

* * * * *

Chapman was the first American aviator to die for France, and his death was major news.[20] One tribute penned by a Parisian journalist showed the esteem in which the American volunteers were held; it ended with this sentiment: "*le roi de l'air est mort royalement*" – the king of the air died royally.[21] Stories of Chapman's death also flooded American papers. The day after his final flight, the *New York Evening World* carried Victor's photo on its front page, declaring he had saved the lives of Thénault, Prince and Lufbery before falling.[22] The same paper would later report that Chapman died while on an "errand of mercy," delivering oranges to his wounded comrade Balsley:

Sergeant Clyde Balsley, of San Antonio, Texas, wounded in a fight near Verdun, and probably crippled for life, is in a hospital a few miles from the aviation camp to which Corporal Chapman was attached. The sergeant asked for an orange, but there was none to be had at the hospital. Corporal Chapman heard of the incident and decided to gratify the desire of his comrade. He obtained a small basket of oranges and set forth in his aeroplane for the hospital.[23]

As one might expect, John Jay Chapman reacted stoically when informed of Victor's death. "Good," he said. "My son's life was given to a good cause."[24] In a letter dated June 27, 1916, John Jay wrote to the French Ambassador, Jean Jules Jusserand, "It is all as it should be and we are happy."[25] To another friend he wrote that the death of his son "was such as to leave us proud & happy – no single element that can take the sting out of death seems to have been lacking in it."[26]

Kiffin wrote Victor's stepmother, expressing his deep respect for and pride in Victor. Mrs. Chapman read Kiffin's letter aloud to Victor's two younger brothers and her husband, John Jay Chapman. In it, Kiffin wrote that his deceased friend "was one of the very few who had the strongest of ideals, and then had the character to withstand anything that tried to come into his life and kill them."[27] After telling of some of Victor's battles, he went on:

He died the most glorious death, and at the most glorious time of life to die, especially for him with his ideals. I have never once regretted it for him, as I know he was willing and satisfied to give his life that way if it was necessary, and that he had no fear of death, and there is nothing to fear in death. It is for you, his father, relatives, myself, and for all who have known him, and all who would have known him, and for the world as a whole to

455

regret his loss. Yet he is not dead; he lives forever in every place he has been, and in everyone who knew him.... He is alive every day in this Escadrille *and has a tremendous influence on all our actions. Even the* mecaniciens *do their work better and more conscientiously.... You must not feel sorry, but must feel proud and happy.*[28]

Mrs. Chapman thanked Kiffin for his words of appreciation for Victor's character and replied that if these qualities were to continue in the lives of those who knew her son, "the light has not gone quite out, but will shine still." She told Kiffin she hoped one day to meet him and all the members of the *escadrille,* for "Victor's happiest days were spent among you."[29]

* * * * *

The shooting down of two of its pilots – one seriously injured, the other dead – sobered the squadron's mood. Thénault summed up the changed outlook: "At Verdun, it was true battle indeed: in the sky, a numerous and mettlesome enemy; on the ground, an unceasing cannonade, mercilessly pounding at the soil wildly ripped open. Sacrifice had begun: to conquer or to die, such was every day's law."[30]

The loss of Chapman caused at least one member of the squadron to question his place at the front and accelerated the ongoing deterioration of the relationship between some of the men and Elliott Cowdin. "Why did I not fall instead of him?" Jim McConnell asked Captain Thénault the day after Chapman's death. "The *Escadrille* would have suffered less, for he was a better pilot than I am."[31] Just twenty-four hours later, however, McConnell's thoughts were much less noble – contradicting his normal affable nature, Mac wrote Paul:

Sometimes I keep looking over towards the lines hoping to see him [Chapman] coming. If it only could have been someone else. Cowdin, for instance, or any like him.[32]

Poor Cowdin – done in by a combination of heart trouble, ulcers, and unraveling nerves, he was truly struggling, and had begun looking for a way out. Following Balsley's horrible injury, Elliott asked for a month's leave – "Strain too great for his delicate nerves," snarked McConnell – but Thénault denied his request.[33] Once Chapman was killed, Cowdin seems to have lost his nerve altogether and, while not entirely clear, it appears that he took an unauthorized leave.

By this time, as illustrated by McConnell's shocking statement, at least some of the men in the squadron were fed up with Cowdin and his antics. During the *escadrille's* two months at the front in Luxeuil and Behonne, he had made just seventeen flights totaling 23.3 hours, and always seemed to have "engine trouble" or a jammed machine gun.[34] It didn't help that by the end of the week, Paul saw Cowdin in Paris playing tennis and frequenting the cafés – he told Kiffin "everyone is disgusted with him and he seems to be in ill favor everywhere."[35] Conscious of the public interest in the squadron, rather than have Cowdin arrested and charged with desertion, Thénault forced him out of the *escadrille* altogether, listing the official cause as "ill health."[36]

The day after Cowdin left, the squadron held another *prise d'armes*. Thaw returned for the ceremony, and with his arm still in a sling was awarded the Legion of Honor for his victory a month before.[37] Afterward, Thaw wanted to stay with the squad, but Thénault sent him back to Paris so he could fully heal.[38] Kiffin and Bert Hall were given the *médaille militaire* and the *croix de guerre*, and Kiffin, McConnell, Johnson and Balsley all passed sergeant. "Poor, old Victor" had also made sergeant, but, as Mac lamented "it doesn't help him any now."[39]

Kiffin spent that afternoon packing up Victor's things to be sent to Paris. In what was surely a tremendous understatement, he told Mrs. Weeks the task was "[n]ot a pleasant job."[40]

* * * * *

While Cowdin seems to have suffered a loss of nerve, he was not the only squadron member having second thoughts. Credible reports suggest that behind the scenes, several of the American pilots may have been angling for a way out. Indeed, Dr. Gros visited the squadron at Bar-le-Duc the day that Cowdin left, and just four days later "quite confidentially" told American military observer Major James A. Logan that "a number of these young Americans in the *Escadrille* had approached him with a view to getting released from the French service in the event of our becoming engaged in a Mexican war so that they could join our army."[41]

Similarly, the American military attaché in Paris reported that several of the Americans in aviation and other branches of the French army had "expressed their desire to join our own Army in case the United States went to war," and that "one of the aviators consulted me on this subject recently[.]" The attaché told this aviator (most likely Cowdin) to submit an application and he would see what could be done.[42]

Tensions with Mexico had been brewing since late 1915 when President Wilson officially recognized Venustiano Carranza, a rival of Pancho Villa, as head of the Mexican government. The betrayed Villa began attacking U.S. nationals and their property throughout northern Mexico, and in March of 1916, he killed eighteen people at a U.S. Army post in the town of Columbus, New Mexico. In response, Wilson authorized an expedition led by General John J. Pershing to capture Villa. By late June things had reached a boiling point in the American press, as Pershing chased Villa across northern Mexico without success.

The escalating conflict along America's southern border – in particular, Villa's ability to elude the regular troops – brought into sharp focus the country's near-complete lack of an aviation program. Right on cue, reports began appearing in major American newspapers bemoaning the sad fact and suggesting the American aviators in France owed it to their country to come home and help out. Among the clippings the pilots received from the states, one editorial in the *Chicago Tribune* caught their attention:

If active operations are to follow in Mexico, the deficiency of our army in experienced airmen will be felt.

In France, Flanders and perhaps also with the central powers, there are American aviators. They ought to return for service under their own flag as soon as possible. If they are not moved to do so in such an emergency, they do not deserve American citizenship.

The war department should get in touch with these men promptly and facilitate their release from foreign service. They are greatly needed at home.[43]

For a war-weary aviator, a potential skirmish with Mexico offered a ready-made (and face-saving) ticket out of harm's way. Around this time, McConnell wrote Paul:

What with Thaw and Balsley and Chapman I'll make a guess that some of the parade loving chaps in the A[merican] A[mbulance] that were thinking of joining the aviation are figuring that it will sound swell to say their country calls them and hie back to the land that likes only picnic wars.[44]

Needless to say, Kiffin was not among those looking for a "picnic war" – he was not interested in fighting Mexico or going home for any reason. Indeed, Kiffin and McConnell did not take kindly to the suggestion that there might be

Americans flying for Germany and felt insulted by the *Tribune's* implication that *they* were somehow shirking their duty to America, when in their view America was shirking *its* responsibility to the world. With the war waiting on America, the boys were not amused.[45]

The resentment continued to build when William Thaw received a cable in Paris from the Aero Club of America offering to pay the men's expenses to return home. It read:

Mexican trouble finds United States army with only 15 aviators. Please advise whether members of Franco-American corps can come to serve in Mexican campaign, if needed. Aero Club of America will pay transportation of six aviators.[46]

Although the cable was widely reported, the men elected not to respond publicly.[47] But at least two of the American volunteers were apparently considering using the situation with Mexico and the request of the Aero Club as an excuse to bow out gracefully. As McConnell disgustedly told a friend in early July, "two fellows are pulling the patriotic sob stuff and want to get home and fight the air above Mexico. No one to shoot at them there with machine guns mounted on swift planes."[48]

It's hard to say for certain, but it seems most likely that the two men to whom McConnell referred were Cowdin and Hall. As noted earlier, Cowdin actually left the squadron, and eventually headed back to America. As for Hall, there is some evidence that he intended to leave – for example, one American paper had just published a story detailing Hall's plan to return home and participate in a transcontinental aero race, flying a Nieuport he expected the French to loan to him.[49]

But Hall did not leave. He stuck around and for the most part continued to perform well, although his flights and hours in July were the lowest among the squadron's eleven remaining pilots.[50] The idea that Hall wanted out may have sprung from a rumor passed along to McConnell by Paul. But even Mac seemed skeptical about the idea and suspected the quitter might have been another American pilot named Carroll Dana Winslow.[51] He wrote the following to Paul on July 1:

I was greatly surprised at the developments re our boy Hall. That lemon Winslow has been pulling the same sort of line ... [a]re you sure it's not Winslow? He's gone back to Paris and is beefing about being called back for the mobilization. Norman predicted that Hall would follow in the footsteps of Cowdin and take the "cure" but it's hard to say. As we all know, he's an awful liar and hot air artist, and every time he sees a fire on the ground he comes rushing back and reports bringing down a Boche *but I believe he has the wherewithal in a pinch.*[52]

Whoever the second wavering pilot might have been, no one else left the squadron at this time.[53] In any event, in notes from his press files during the war, Paul wrote that Cowdin was "[t]he only member of the American Escadrille who has so far shown the white feather. After less than thirty hours of flying with the *escadrille*, he succeeded in getting sent to the rear; has recently been discharged from the army and has returned to America."[54]

* * * * *

Still the stories calling on the aviators to return continued. In early July, the *Tribune* ran a full-page photo spread of Kiffin, Prince, Hall and Thaw under the headline: "Their Country Needs Them." The all-bold caption under the pictures read: "THEY HAVE DONE GOOD WORK FOR FRANCE; THEY SHOULD NOW RETURN TO THEIR OWN COUNTRY."[55] The next week, the paper ran another editorial, complaining that the lack of aeroplanes and qualified aviators was "costing the American troops in Mexico very dearly."[56]

But once Cowdin was gone, the commitment to France by those who stayed outweighed any thoughts they may have had of leaving, whether to fight Mexico or avoid danger altogether. As Paul noted, the remaining pilots sincerely felt that "in fighting for the allies they are also fighting for the future safety of the United States," and that their services in France were "of much greater value to civilization and America than would be fighting against semi-barbarous Mexico."[57] While none of them intended to leave, the persistent articles finally aroused the volunteers to respond.

Serving as a conduit for the squadron via his perch at the *Chicago Daily News*, Paul relayed back to the states the great resentment the men felt towards the "bring back our aviators" talk, reporting that "virtually every man among them is anxious to serve France against the Germans until the central empires are crushed."[58] While the pilots would do what they could in case of "real need" for their services, Paul said most "would flatly refuse to leave France to fight against Mexico."[59] Paul quoted Frederick Zinn, he and Kiffin's old friend from the Ninth Squad, now in aviation training:

The people in America writing these 'our aviators' articles do not seem to *realize that the French government has spent more than $5,000 in training each of her American volunteers.... America has not spent a cent on any of them.... And to try to take them now, just when they are beginning to do things to reward France for her generous reception, would be a rotten deal. There is no danger of anything like that happening, however. America has been forgetting too many things of late years that may return to her mind.*[60]

Like Kiffin, the men felt that in fighting for France they were fighting for America. At least they were doing their part "toward re-establishing American prestige abroad," which had been "sadly lowered by the attitude of the United States government throughout the war."[61] McConnell expressed his displeasure most strongly. To a friend he bitterly wrote that America "comically puts herself up as the defender of human rights and liberties," but "sits dumbly by" while other engaged nations made all the sacrifices. With sadness, he noted that he was "getting ashamed to own up to my nationality. The good old land seems lost forever."[62]

* * * * *

Still, Chapman's death drove home an unmistakable message – this was no game. Afterward, rather than "flitting all over the heavens," Rumsey reported the men were "very careful now about staying together, as the two men we have lost got separated from the bunch and had no show."[63] Perhaps humility was the best thing they could learn – just after Chapman's death, an unnamed officer (likely Thénault, or perhaps Thaw) remarked to a newspaper correspondent that "when our boys quit taking on five *Boches* at a time they will be of more lasting use to the French army."[64]

Without a doubt the men were taking a more measured approach to their adventures. Mac noted they had absorbed a lot of hard lessons at the front, and were no longer taking unnecessary risks:

The outfit seems to have tamed down ... having learnt that there are certain precautions to follow. When we first got here no one knew anything about this aerial warfare as conducted at present and it took some while to learn.[65]

The squadron's change in attitude became apparent at the beginning of July, when Captain Thénault went on permission, leaving Lieutenant de Laage to run the unit. McConnell wrote Paul:

He's a wild one and needs a few bullets near him to tame him down. This morning he led us 20 kilometers inside the lines and we kept diving on Boches there that were in far greater numbers. [There were] three new Aviatiks that went so fast we looked as if tied, [as well as a] [c]ouple of Fokkers in the mix-up, but there was no battle. The Lieut. got into a vrille *and spun down from 3,000 meters to 500 feet. We thought it was all off. He'll keep this 'Nach Berlin' stuff up once too many times and about a half of us will stay over there. It's fool work and does no good. Kiffin's sore on him for being so wild.*[66]

* * * * *

Back in North Carolina, Loula was at dinner with a few friends when she learned of Chapman's death. Handed an afternoon newspaper, she nearly fainted when her eyes fell on the headline "American aviator killed." While relieved to find it was not her son, Loula grieved for Victor's mother, and could not help thinking of the risks being run by Kiffin. She wrote her darling boys:

Poor Chapman! It was beautiful for him to go for the oranges, but so sad for him to go down. Please let me know, if you can, if he has a mother in New York, and get me her name and address. It came so close to home to me. I sympathize with his loved ones. I notice, too, that Bach is in prison, Balsley wounded and lamed for life, and Thaw wounded – I thank the Lord every day my boy is spared. You have done so much already Kiffin, I do wish you could have less dangerous work now.[67]

But in Bar-le-Duc, Kiffin didn't feel in any danger at all – the sun was shining, and he and McConnell were resting in a tent on the edge of the airfield, waiting for their next trip over the lines. As McConnell caught up on his letter writing, Kiffin sat outside, relaxing in the warmth of the beautiful afternoon. Writing to Mrs. Weeks, Mac described how in his camp chair Kiffin looked "like a general waiting for reports."[68]

Beginning another letter, Mac expressed how lucky he was to be with the fine and brave men in his unit. At that moment, someone came in and announced that a French *pilote* of a nearby *escadrille* had collided with a Fokker, killing both combatants.[69] Turning reflective, Mac mused: "Funny life, this, you sit around comfortably and wait for your flights and you don't know whether you will come back or not."[70]

Chapter Forty-nine

If we can't have our boys here in the flesh, we will have the next best thing – see them as movie heroes.

Cowdin did make one more appearance with the *escadrille* – the morning of July 4, he attended a memorial service in Paris for Victor Chapman.[1] Thénault, Thaw, and Prince also attended the ceremony, held at the American Episcopal Church of the Holy Trinity.[2] In addition to these former comrades, the church was filled with members of the American colony, the ambassador, other embassy and consulate officials, and two French generals.[3]

John Jay Chapman later wrote that the church "became, as it were, the shrine of both nations at Victor's funeral on July 4th."[4] The chancel was decorated with French and American flags, as was the altar on which the Franco-American Committee had placed a wreath in honor of those injured and killed for France.[5] Reverend Ashman's brief eulogy noted how Victor – "unassuming, unostentatious, quietly & genuinely religious, as far removed as possible from the spirit of military braggadocio" – had served France "*sans peur et sans reproche*" (without fear and without reproach). He continued:

Truly he who loses his life shall find it. We do not know what was in store for him had he been destined to follow his art, but now, certainly, his name is among the immortals.... As for his family, they say plainly they have no regrets; on the contrary, they are proud and grateful that France has permitted them to mingle their blood with that of the French in this great cause.[6]

* * * * *

Following the short service, many of the guests, including Thénault and the American pilots, traveled a few miles to Picpus cemetery.[7] There, at 11:00 a.m. sharp, the large crowd watched as several American and French dignitaries solemnly marched to Lafayette's tomb before draping over it an American flag and placing a great wreath of roses and orchids at the base. After a brief but profound silence, H. Cleveland Coxe, the former deputy consul-general in Paris, read a cabled message from John Jay Chapman that ended "Today, France is fighting for the soul of the world and all who die in her cause are blest."[8]

Coxe then read a speech prepared by Dr. Herbert Adams Gibbons, explicitly associating the American volunteers with the illustrious Frenchman buried in the cemetery in which they were gathered:

As Lafayette and his friends went to America to fight for us, young men from America – of the same class and the same temperament – have come to fight for France.... We are glad of the opportunity to say to our brothers in France that we are proud of the blood in our veins and that we cherish our birthright. We believe that France is fighting the world-old battle for human liberty. We are with you heart and soul in the struggle.... The spirit of Lafayette is still abroad in America, stronger and more compelling than at any time in our history.[9]

The crowd then listened as Charles Prince gave a short speech.[10] Grieved by the death of Victor Chapman, with great emotion "Uncle Charlie" also connected the actions of the American volunteers with the actions of Lafayette one hundred and forty years before:

Where stand we in this Armageddon? Did Lafayette fight with us for naught? Has his chivalry, his courage, his example, his sacrifice for us been in vain? Is he but a mystic figure of the past? [J]udge us, oh France, by our hearts! The people are with you. They have proved it to you by deeds, not words.... Our sons are fighting side by side with yours in the trenches, drawn hither by the same spirit that brought Lafayette to us. Their blood has dyed the plains of Champagne and the shattered slopes of Verdun. Our ambulances are at the very front, amid the shells and carnage, saving where they can. Our eaglets – you see some of them here – are aloft with yours for the mastery of the skies. Who has not heard of Victor Chapman? That is our case, oh sister Republic! Judge it![11]

That same evening, the American Chamber of Commerce hosted the third event of the day celebrating Franco-American relations, a banquet at the *Hotel Palais D'Orsay*. At that dinner, Prime Minister Aristide Briand's toast praising the American volunteers included the following lines:

[W]e can never forget that your volunteers have fought side by side with the soldiers of our own nation in arms – and that your gallant aviators – such as the heroic Sergeant Chapman, living symbol of American idealism – have proved that their love for our cause is faithful until death.[12]

When Briand spoke of the American aviators and Victor Chapman, the assembly rose in loud cheers. "France," said Briand, "will never forget this new comradeship, this evidence of a devotion to a common ideal."[13]

* * * * *

As shown by the three public events held in Paris that day, the Fourth of July provided the perfect opportunity to sanctify an American sacrifice – the death of Victor Chapman, by laying it on a French altar – Lafayette's tomb. Through his selfless actions, as had Lafayette more than a century earlier, the young American pilot became a symbol, reminding his native country of its debt to France and simultaneously strengthening the bonds between the two countries.

Victor's death had a substantial effect on public opinion, in both France and America. After attending the ceremony in Paris honoring his son, a French woman wrote the following note to John Jay Chapman in New York:

I have just left the Church in the Avenue d'Alma, after attending the service in honor of your son. The ceremony was very touching in its simplicity.... It was a sad celebration of your Independence Day, and brought home to me the beauty of heroic death and the meaning of life.

Everyone is talking of this disinterested devotion – much greater even than that of our own men, who are fighting for their own country.... On all sides people speak with admiration and gratitude of the details, tragic and touching as they are, of his trip to his friend, of the little basket of oranges, of his headlong plunge to save his comrades.... Wherever I go I am asked about him. Never since the outbreak of the war has public sentiment been more deeply aroused.[14]

The story of Victor's death was also galvanizing pro-France opinion in America. While spending Independence Day at his Sagamore Hill home on the north shore of Long Island, Theodore Roosevelt felt prompted to write an article he titled "Lafayettes of the Air," which spoke to the feelings of an increasing number of Americans:

The American nation has had scant cause for pride during the past two years, and much cause for bitter shame and humiliation. We are therefore all of us indebted to these young men of generous soul, who showed not only that they were not 'too proud to fight,' but that they were proudly willing to die for their convictions.... [T]o the extent of their power, they have freed us from the reproach of being a feeble, greedy, and timid people: the reproach which we as a nation have earned by what we have permitted our chosen representatives to do in our name during the last two years.[15]

While perhaps not the first, the former president's piece was the most visible connection yet made in America between Lafayette and the American aviators. Roosevelt concluded with this statement:

High honor is due to the men like Victor Chapman who have shown that courage and idealism are not dead among us.

Perhaps for the first time since the furor had subsided over the sinking of the *Lusitania*, there was in America a growing sense that the country needed to act. To many, the policy of neutrality was beginning to look too much like cowardice. The spirit of Lafayette was stirring.

* * * * *

As early as May 26, John Jay Chapman had informed Victor that "all the papers are full of the American Flyers," and already the American squadron was "becoming a pet of the public." This greatly pleased Mr. Chapman, who felt the aviators were doing "more to save the shame of America" than anyone else.[16] Upon receiving his father's letter, Victor had responded, "It's too bad I'm not going into politics after the war so that I could make use of all this free advertising. I might almost run for the Assembly so as not to lose such a golden opportunity!"[17]

His death the following week added to the already widespread publicity surrounding the American squadron. Something about aviators captured the imagination, and as dangerous as aerial combat was, their choice seemed far more rational than the senseless slaughter of the trenches.[18] One major-city daily referred to the "gallant flock of airmen in France" as "the one element in this terrible war to contribute poetry and romance to the whole ghastly business," noting that in air-fighting, "something of the glamor of individual combat remains to remind one of the days of chivalry when knights engaged each other in single combat while waiting armies watched the outcome."[19] Another American reporter echoed this point, noting that the "romance of war" was "in the keeping of the aviators."[20]

With the press guiding this narrative, the idea of fighter pilots as "knights of the air" began to take root in the public conscience. And whether fascinated with war, aviation or both, the more the American public heard of its boys fighting in France, the more it wanted to hear. As noted by one scholar, the

Escadrille Américaine "caused quite a stir in the States, (not least because it caused controversy over U.S. neutrality) and raised interest in aerial combat and the war in Europe."[21]

Paul Rockwell was learning this firsthand – American newspapers were paying top dollar for news about the volunteers in France, with aviation "dope" being especially lucrative. As the war reports from Paris filtered back to the states, it became increasingly clear that the popular heroes of the conflict were young men in their twenties, wearing the insignia of wings.

* * * * *

The squadron received even more notice once the propaganda footage filmed by the French government made its way to Paris. The full movie came out to four reels, lasting about an hour, and makes for quite interesting viewing, even today. While the first three reels mostly focus on the American Ambulance volunteers and French soldiers, the last reel shows the footage of the American aviators.

It begins with Norman Prince and Elliott Cowdin at the squadron's headquarters on the *Champs-Elysées* in Paris; the remaining scenes feature the material filmed at the airfield in Luxeuil. It includes good quality shots of the "pioneers of the squadron" (Thaw, Prince and Cowdin), followed by individual photos of each of the men in front of a brand new *bébé*. Another scene shows the entire group huddled around Thénault receiving "instructions from the Captain," after which the men separate to make ready for a pretend "mission" on which they are to protect the Maurice Farman bombers. With its capital "R" painted on the side, Kiffin's machine is in full view being wheeled out of the hangar and lined up next to McConnell's.[22]

Mac would have been glad to know that his plane was also visible in the shot – when a friend in Paris wrote that she had seen the movie, he responded that she would have to tell him all about it, and asked, "Could you pick out my machine? 'MAC' was painted on the side."[23]

While it is unclear if it was shown elsewhere, the movie seems to have been exhibited at the American Ambulance hospital on June 9.[24] Bound with the tri-color, souvenir programs were imprinted with the following quote over the signature General Joffre: "The United States of America have not forgotten that the first page of the history of their independence was written with a little of the blood of France."[25]

Paul must have attended this showing, for he wrote Kiffin a few days later that the moving pictures "were very good, and yours was not bad. Your picture got much more applause than anyone else's, to my joy."[26] But that may have been due to the fact that Mrs. Weeks, Kiffin's biggest fan, was also in attendance. She urged her son in Boston to watch for the film in America, and told him that "in the aviation pictures, the tall one is Kiffin, and you will see Chapman, Thaw, Jim and Prince."[27]

* * * * *

As Mrs. Weeks suggested, soon many Americans would also see the dashing American pilots at work. The president of the American Ambulance Hospital was Robert Bacon, the former ambassador who had played a key role in the pivotal meeting at Senator Menier's home the previous July. Having seen the film, he recognized it as a means of generating both financial and moral support for the American efforts in France. Thus, not long after it was shown in Paris, through Bacon's efforts the Triangle Film Corporation secured the rights to release the movie in America.[28]

"Moving pictures" were still something of a novelty, so "real" images of the war promised to be especially enticing to American audiences – Triangle immediately began promoting the film to exhibitors as "official pictures of the actual conditions and ... work that is being performed by the American boys at the front."[29] In addition, Bacon and other like-minded individuals formulated plans to increase attendance by organizing local committees of influential men and women "to stimulate interest in the pictures and the patronage of the theatres where these may be shown."[30]

One of those influential women was Anne Vanderbilt, who served on the Board of Governors of the American Hospital and, with her husband William K. Vanderbilt, was already doing so much to finance the American Ambulance and the *Escadrille Américaine*. Asked about the Americans serving in France, she replied that it was unfortunate that those young men "had to go to another country to learn the meaning of the word patriotism," but was glad they were "showing the world what stuff Americans are made of[.]" Mrs. Vanderbilt added that she was hoping all "good Americans" would see the film.[31] The death of Chapman further increased the already significant press coverage of the *escadrille*, so the film seemed certain to find a large audience.

On July 5, 1916, the movie – now bearing the title *Our American Boys in the European War* – opened in America, premiering in New York before a large and enthusiastic crowd of two hundred and fifty invited guests in the ballroom of the old *Hotel Majestic*.[32] In a short introductory address, former ambassador Bacon paid tribute to Victor Chapman and praised "the fitness of these young Americans giving their services to France, the bulwark of our common ideals."[33]

Hungry to see the war "in action," particularly the young American flyers, the crowd at the *Hotel Majestic* was thrilled to see the supposed live-from-the-front footage.[34] The next day's *New York Times* commended the "views of the Franco-American Flying Corps, with individual pictures of some of the most famous aviators from these shores," and noted that the crowd broke into "prolonged applause" when Victor Chapman was shown on the screen.[35] Coming on the heels of that young New Yorker's death, the movie was an immediate hit.[36]

It also proved to be a catalyst for further preparedness efforts; one industry magazine declared the film "just the thing to arouse interest," while another pronounced the pictures of the aviators and their machines "a wholesome lesson in preparedness."[37] The next week, the *New York Times* encouraged "[e]veryone in the city – literally everyone" to go see *America Preparing*, a movie with a similar message being shown at the Lyric Theatre."[38] According to one film scholar, these two movies "plotted an emotional path away from detachment and toward involvement." That is, they helped soften the American attitude against joining the war effort:

Their overriding themes included a strong, historically conscious patriotism which emphasized military deeds and might; [and] a firm appeal to democratic spirit, in that the films sought to make every citizen conscious of the looming crisis and of his responsibility to meet that crisis[.][39]

* * * * *

As its proponents hoped, many members of leading Eastern society clamored to sponsor exhibitions of *Our American Boys in the European War*. A large contingent of the monied elite had sons, friends or relatives among the volunteers, prompting one society matron to say, "If we can't have our boys here in the flesh, we will have the next best thing – see them as movie heroes."[40]

The first sponsored showing of the movie – held at Newport, Rhode Island in the magnificent ballroom of Beechwood, the summer home of Vincent and

Helen Astor – proved to be the biggest event of the social calendar. It also doubled as a fundraiser for the American Ambulance volunteers in France – the sale of tickets at $2 a piece brought in more than one thousand dollars.[41] Bound by a laurel wreath, the French and American flags adorned the cover of the ornate, eight-page program printed on gray-blue vellum, which listed inside a complete roster of the Americans serving in France.[42]

The event was held on Saturday, August 19 and, according to *Moving Picture World*, it seemed "as though all the notables in the blue book of society were present."[43] It really must have been quite an affair; another publication reported that "over six hundred devotees of society forsook the polo (for the Newport Cup), the tennis finals and other events of importance" to see the film. An alumnus of the American Ambulance provided some introductory remarks for the audience, which included many friends and relatives of the volunteers.[44] The showing was a smash success, and by the end of the month other elite members of high society were similarly sponsoring the film in fashionable seaside resorts up and down the coast.[45]

In early September at the summer colony in Bar Harbor, Maine, the movie proved so popular that a second screening was quickly arranged. One patroness reported that when Victor Chapman appeared on the screen, "the entire house rose to its feet and tendered a very wonderful and reverent ovation to this splendid young hero," adding that "[e]very boy there wanted to be off for France, or do something for his own country."[46]

The favorable publicity resulting from the movie not only helped raise funds for the Ambulance volunteers, it also began a process of converting the innate sympathies of the American people towards the Allies into concrete action. The newly-opened *Rialto* theatre on Broadway in New York City announced plans to feature the film, and another private showing among prominent members of the New York Stock Exchange raised thirty thousand dollars for the American Ambulance Field Service.[47]

After attending a special screening at the Triangle company's offices in New York, Theodore Roosevelt rendered this opinion: "There isn't an American worth calling such who isn't under a heavy debt of obligation to these boys for what they have done.... No nation is worth preserving if its young men have not in them the spirit that these young men, whose deeds we have seen on the screen, have shown...."[48]

Chapter Fifty

The war has grown to be kind of a habit, and I don't suppose we would know what else to do.

Given the sacrifice made by so many of its young men, judged by Roosevelt's standard the nation of France *was* worth preserving. Paul Rockwell certainly felt so – as he would later write, "the war continues no matter who dies."[1] That is not to say death did not sting – after attending the memorial service at the American Church in Paris on July 4, Paul expressed to a friend the "great loss" Victor's passing was to himself and Kiffin.[2]

He must have been thinking of Victor's untimely end when, in the same letter, Paul noted how his little brother was now an officer, eligible to win the Legion of Honor, and "in the stride that will win it, *if he lives.*" He also spoke of how being away from Kiffin was more difficult than when they had been together in the fighting: "It is a very dangerous game, and I live under quite a suspense. If I were all the time out with him sharing every danger, it would not be hard, but back here – well, I have to take what fate has handed me and do the best I can."[3]

But on the fourth of July, Paul had every reason to be happy, for the next morning he was headed back to the front – not to fight, but for a brief visit with Kiffin. By promising not to write of what he would see, Paul had somehow secured special permission from the Minister of Foreign Affairs to visit N.124 at the front.[4]

He took the morning train from Paris and arrived in Bar-le-Duc on Wednesday, July 5. For the next five nights, Paul would sleep in Kiffin's room on the little iron bed previously used by Victor Chapman.[5] Fascinated with the daily life of the air fighters and the inner workings of the aviation camp, Paul hung around the aerodrome, with its distinct smell of gasoline and burnt castor oil, watching the men and planes come and go, taking pictures of everything.

Sadly, the weather was rather poor for several days of Paul's visit, limiting the squadron's activity over the lines. For this reason, one of Paul's pictures showed Kiffin, Chute Johnson, and Bert Hall at the hangar engaged in another popular pastime – playing poker on the lower wing of an idle aeroplane.

One day the clouds cleared, allowing Kiffin to go aloft. Paul was waiting at the airfield when Kiffin came back down and snapped a few photographs of his "bad landing" – somehow, Kiffin ran into and damaged one of the bombers taxiing down the strip.[6] Although his own *bébé* was unhurt, the accident exacerbated a growing rift between Kiffin and Captain Thénault, who had just returned from Paris.

Not long after, Kiffin and Thénault had what Kiffin called "a hell of a scrap" about the *popote*, or the squadron's mess fund. Just before his nephew's death, William Chanler had promised Victor one thousand francs toward the account. After Victor died "Uncle Willie" instead sent the money to Kiffin as "Chef de la *popote*," telling him to "make the boys' life there a little more comfortable."[7] While it is unclear exactly what happened with Thénault, after the fight Kiffin "refused to have anything more to do with it."[8]

* * * * *

Paul enjoyed seeing Kiffin again, and their time together buoyed one another's spirits. On July 9, Kiffin wrote Loula that Paul was with him, and that "everything is going along alright with me and the war seems to be going entirely in our favor at present so naturally everyone is hopeful."[9] Later that afternoon, however, Kiffin was able to make another sortie, and had quite a close scrape with several enemy fighters.

As Kiffin and Dudley Hill attacked an observation machine they had spotted behind German lines, two Aviatiks came to aid their comrade, and Norman Prince arrived to support Kiffin and Hill. In the skirmish that followed, Kiffin and Hill chased off one of the Aviatiks, while the other quit the fight. The trio of Americans then turned their guns on the observation machine, and eventually forced it to descend in its own lines.[10] Back at the airfield, Paul was both proud and nervous when he saw the evidence of his brother's fierce contest – Kiffin's machine was punctured with several bulletholes, one of which may have taken a piece out of his coat.[11]

Although he really wanted to stick around for an impending award ceremony at the airfield – for which William Thaw had again come back from Paris, briefly returning the squadron to full strength – Paul's safe conduct pass expired on July 10 and he left Bar-le-Duc that evening.[12] Two days later, Kiffin, Hall and Thaw were further decorated in an "informal affair" that McConnell described as "better than having a lot of swank."[13]

What swank there was at the *prise d'armes* was likely supplied by the flamboyant French ace Charles Nungesser.[14] In the course of bringing down two Aviatiks on June 22, Nungesser – who now had eleven kills to his credit, second most in the entire French air service – had once again been injured.[15] Although he was supposed to be on convalescent leave, on July 12, the blond-haired pilot instead attached himself to the American squadron.[16] With his elegant black uniform and ability to tear a deck of cards in half with his bare hands, Nungesser exuded coolness.[17] The Americans were also impressed by his numerous victories and multiple combat wounds – one author described him as "displaying a noticeable limp, scarred face, and a gleaming row of gold teeth to match the row of medals on his chest."[18]

Not long after the medal ceremony, Thaw again returned to Paris and the remaining American pilots returned to work – or, as Rumsey described it, "flitting up and down and trying to entice a non-suspecting German near enough to our lines so that we can go after him." But even with Nungesser at their side, the men did not find much success – as Rumsey noted, the Germans "very seldom come across, except in swarms, and then they beat it back quick before we are up...."[19] Not that Rumsey was up all that often – among the squadron's pilots in the month of July, he tallied the third lowest hours and flights, topping only Chute Johnson and Bert Hall.[20]

For at least a couple of their flightless days, Rumsey and Johnson had an excuse, albeit a poor one – they were too hung over. Nungesser was known to enjoy his libations as much as some of the party-minded Americans, and two days after his arrival the squadron's Bastille Day celebration apparently got a little out of hand. As McConnell put it, "We had a big time on the 14th in honour of France. With the result that Rumsey and Johnson couldn't fly for a while."[21]

* * * * *

At the other end of the spectrum, Kiffin was more focused than ever, and flying with an additional purpose – to avenge Victor's death. Accordingly, once the bad weather subsided, Kiffin was alert to every opportunity to go aloft. In fact, by the end of the month, he had put in more flight hours than any pilot in the entire French air service. On the strength of Kiffin's numbers, and those of stalwarts like Lieutenant de Laage and Norman Prince, the squadron as a whole flew more hours in July than any other unit at the front – even without counting Nungesser's contribution.[22] The *Escadrille Américaine* was hitting its stride, and Kiffin was leading the way.

On July 21, Nungesser finally ended the squadron's dry spell, bringing down a German two-seater while on patrol.[23] That same day, as Nungesser notched his twelfth victory, Kiffin nearly got his third. In the morning, after getting within close range of a German machine, he pumped it with more than forty bullets before veering off. According to Kiffin, the pilot "certainly had a lot of luck," for even after Lieutenant de Laage followed with another eighty shots and Bert Hall twenty more, "the damn *boche* went on as if nothing had happened."[24]

Around mid-day, Kiffin and Hall went out again. Kiffin explained to Paul what happened after they crossed over the lines:

I found an Aviatik and dived on him. Two Fokkers dived on me; Bert dived on the two Fokkers, and two more Fokkers went on him. In that line of battle we went down through the air about 2,000 meters.[25]

Kiffin closed on the Aviatik and got within ten meters, shooting his entire belt into the plane, after which it "wavered, tilted up and then headed down as if its pilot had lost control."[26] While watching the plane go down, the Fokkers on Kiffin's tail began firing, forcing him to seek refuge in a nearby cloud. Hall tried to help out but had to dive into the clouds himself to avoid two more Fokkers right on his back.[27]

The *New York Sun* reported that the German machines came so close to Hall, "it is a miracle he was not killed or wounded."[28] Kiffin echoed this point to Paul, telling him that the Germans "came damn close" to getting Hall, and "plugged a lot of bullets around him in the machine, but he wasn't touched."[29] McConnell summed up the encounter in a letter to Mrs. Weeks:

Kiffin has as usual been doing fine work. Yesterday he and Hall were together when he dove on a boche. *Kiffin didn't see the Germans higher up. Down he came, a* boche *followed, Hall dove on the* boche *and two more dove on Hall. It was a parade downward, everyone shooting at once. Hall got ten holes in his plane and Kiffin and he got away by hiding in the clouds.*[30]

The worst part was that although Kiffin felt certain he had brought down the Aviatik, an observation post later said that the pilot had readdressed before hitting the ground, denying Kiffin an official victory.[31] But Kiffin kept working, and the next day put in an astonishing eight hours in the air. In one of several fights that day, along with Lieutenant de Laage and Dudley Hill, Kiffin attacked and helped force down a German machine. Hill was closest to the enemy fighter during the attack, and Kiffin and the Lieutenant decided to give him the credit, hoping to help him earn a citation.[32]

The citation was well-deserved – having spent a month and a half with the *escadrille*, Hill was earning a solid reputation as a hard-nosed fighter. Around this time, McConnell wrote that Hill was "good, and a nervy pilot. I hope he smears several *boches* – but God in Boston, it's a hard job."[33]

As McConnell indicated, bringing down a German machine took a tremendous amount of skill. Occasionally, however, the feat involved a surprising degree of luck. Bert Hall, who spent his whole life repeatedly proving the importance of luck, did it again on July 23, when he shot down a Fokker in a morning patrol above Fort de Vaux.[34] Unseen by three enemy planes due to cloud cover, Hall dove on one he later described as being "decorated up like a new saloon."[35]

Hall opened fire at forty yards, and at almost the first shot the nose of the German machine turned upward, exposing its white belly before it slipped back and fell, spinning downward. The plane slammed into the ground on a scarred band of earth where recent fighting had taken place.[36] Later, Hall admitted to McConnell that he "was just shooting to bother the German when a lucky ball hit him."[37]

Still seething from an incident with Hall a few days earlier, Thénault attempted to deny Hall formal credit for his second victory. It seems that after overstaying his permission, Hall had come back spinning a "yarn about chasing a spy for four days," as McConnell put it.[38] Before Prince stepped in and "saved his hide for him," Thénault had been ready to charge Hall as a deserter.[39] Eventually the angry captain relented, so despite flying the least among its pilots for the month, lucky Bert Hall – still in the right place at the right time – recorded one of the squadron's few official victories in July.

* * * * *

For the rest of the *escadrille*, there was a lot of hard work, but not a lot of concrete results. The aviators had settled into a daily routine, which went something like this: arise before daylight, down a few swallows of coffee, motor to the field, don one's flight gear, consisting of fur-lined combinations, fur shoes, leather hoods and gloves, test fire the machine guns, start the engines, get aloft and climb steadily towards the front, then rove about, crossing and re-crossing the lines, seeking enemy machines. After two hours of flight, the pilots would return to the aerodrome, remove their flying clothes and rest up in their field tents to prepare for the afternoon sortie, usually undertaken after a break for lunch back at the villa. In between patrols, those not sleeping would write letters, play poker or chess, regulate their machine guns or compare notes from the morning's flight.[40]

An American military observer wrote the following about the daily patrols, which involved both a French squadron near Triancourt-en-Argonne and the Americans from Bar-le-Duc:

Each of these squadrons maintained a patrol practically constantly during the hours of daylight along the French front from St. Mihiel to the Argonne. Every two hours and a half during the daylight, three baby Nieuports would leave each of these aerodromes in a group and would mount to a height of between 3000 and 4000 meters, and make the round trip from one end of the French front and back again to the aerodrome. Their orders were to attack any German aeroplanes seen, and from time to time they would receive particular instructions to protect other French aeroplanes at certain sectors which were engaged in regulating artillery fire. The tactics used were those of the hawk. The three machines in each group would fly at different altitudes at intervals of about 200 meters on the perpendicular. If a German machine were seen below, the lower machine would dive for him, followed by the one next above; the remaining machine would remain above so that, in the event of a German chasse machine coming on the tail of the two attacking machines, it could follow the German machine. Wherever possible, advantage was taken of clouds to conceal the position of the chasse group. We spent a number of hours at the aerodrome at Bar-le-Duc, and, during this period, saw a number of groups of three aeroplanes leave the aerodrome on this patrol work.[41]

Of course, aerial combat was still in its earliest stages and constantly evolving, both in fighting methods and tactics. Although the pilots tended not to speak much of death, their entire existence revolved around the knowledge that every trip might be their last. As one correspondent put it, "In an air duel the prize is life, the penalty death. The Darwinian dictum, the fittest shall survive, finds no more conclusive illustration than the air battle."[42]

* * * * *

As for tactics, Kiffin followed one simple policy – attack.[43] Bert Hall also favored the rapid, decisive attack, or what he dubbed "the quick dive, fire and pull-away method."[44] Because aerial combat was "a thing of seconds," Hall preferred not to wait for his enemy to strike, but instead to "go after him just as hot as I could."[45] This approach – for it can hardly be called a tactic – was widely shared among the earliest fighter pilots. One later remarked, "I just play the game the same as the rest of the *escadrille*. Our motto is 'get the other fellow before he gets you.'"[46] "Usually," said Hall, "it's all over in twenty seconds – either it's a victory or you go down afire."[47]

Given this reality, it is easy to see why so many aerial bouts seemed more a test of reflexes than anything else. McConnell described a typical encounter this way:

The majority of attacks are made from above, machines swooping down like plummets on the enemy planes. For a few fleeting instants there is the hammering "tut-tut-tut" of the machine guns of both sides, and then positions being lost the combat is over.[48]

One experienced French captain who chalked up twenty victories said it was impossible to overemphasize one principle – "attack ahead while looking to the rear."[49] During his time with the *escadrille*, Cowdin agreed with this approach, advising other pilots to "Keep your eyes fastened to the back of your head."[50] This was good advice – unlike the German pilots, who often flew in two-seaters, accompanied by machine gunners, the Allied *chasse* airmen flew alone. Kiffin always felt that despite this disadvantage, their skill and initiative made it an even match.[51]

Thaw also stressed the individual nature of aerial combat, saying: "Our machines are the swiftest and lightest in the service. We are alone in them. The left hand manipulates the motor and the right the machine gun. We go out to individual combat, meet a foe similarly equipped ... and it is up to us to send them back."[52]

For Thaw, once an enemy plane was sighted "the fun begins," and would conclude only "when one or the other gives up the chase or descends because of exhausted gas or mechanical trouble."[53] Although it was deadly serious stuff, Thaw likened it to an athletic contest, and once said:

If it were not war – and, really, it is like a game sometimes – I might say that chasing enemy aeroplanes is great sport. It is much more interesting than duck or other bird shooting. I am sure that I am not blood-thirsty or brutal, but I like it even when swinging the aeroplane around so as to get between the sights that part of the enemy's fuselage where the pilot and observer sit. I do not have the slightest compunction, when I think I have the range, in pushing a little lever like a bicycle brake, which, by a wire connection, sets the quick-firer rattling.[54]

Although his words sound rather cold-blooded, Thaw had merely acclimated to the single, pitiless rule governing aerial combat – *kill or be killed.* For this reason, he bluntly acknowledged his objective in any fight was to "kill the pilot." His reasoning was simple: "Shooting into the wings or mechanism of a machine means nothing. The most vulnerable thing in a flyer is the man who directs it, and it is to him that our attention and machine guns are directed."[55]

* * * * *

Of course, the Germans were governed by the same rule and, if only by virtue of the amount of time he spent in the air, Kiffin was perhaps the most vulnerable pilot on the Western Front. Not only that, other than its speed, the *bébé*, being primarily constructed of steel tubes, wooden frame, aluminum cowling, fabric and plywood, did not offer much protection. About the only part of the machine that could stop a bullet was the rotary engine, and too many such stops could put one right out of commission.

But vulnerability was something to dwell on in between fights, if at all – as Edmond Genet noted, in the moment, there was simply no time: "Aerial combats certainly are exciting, and soon over. They try one's nerves to the limit, but there is very little, if any, time to think of danger to one's self."[56]

While not reckless in combat, Kiffin was not known for his cautiousness. His favorite tactic was something like a controlled headlong plunge; if possible, he would close to within ten meters of his foe before firing. This method caused Jim McConnell to remark that Kiffin "shoves his machine gun fairly in the faces of the Germans."[57] Despite this predilection, Bert Hall praised Kiffin's marksmanship and "cool steady control of his plane."[58]

Without a doubt, Kiffin favored a bold fighting style and immediately pressed every advantage, which sometimes led him to leap before he looked. He told of one such occasion in a letter to Paul:

Very early one morning, Lieutenant de Laage and I went on patrol together. Over Etain, I saw a Boche *underneath me. I immediately dove on him, and when I was just about ready to open fire, two other Germans, who I* had not seen, attacked me, filling my machine full of holes. I thought that my last hour had surely come. Lieutenant de Laage had already had a combat and his machine gun was jammed. But although it was impossible for him to fire even one shot, he dove on the two Boches who were trying to bring me down and drove them off. I am certain that at that moment he saved my life as he has done many times before.*[59]

Still Kiffin did not slow down, and his fighting skills were on full display throughout the latter half of July, 1916. He spent hour after hour chasing and attacking Germans from one end of the Verdun front to the other, prompting McConnell to tell his mother, "Kiffin Rockwell is a wonder at this game and it is only hard luck that has kept him from bringing down four or five *boches*.... He's in the air all the time."[60]

During this period, Kiffin was the busiest pilot on the Western Front. Paul remained anxious for inside "dope" about the squadron, but a half-annoyed Kiffin curtly brushed aside his requests, telling him:

In regard to the news from this escadrille *and all, I think you had better fix up an arrangement with Jim or someone to keep you posted, or quit trying to handle it. When I have a machine that flies alright, I fly two or three times more than most of them do, and for that reason don't have time to write letters or think much about it, and I don't go to Bar-le-Duc once a week whenever I am flying, where[as] the others do.*[61]

In a letter to Loula in early August, he briefly summarized the tremendous amount of work he had put in:

Last month, in spite of a lot of bad weather, I flew 81 hours over the lines and had between thirty and forty fights with German machines, an official report being made on twenty-one of them. Practically all, however, were in the German lines, so it is impossible to know the real results...[62]

Even after he wore out his machine and had to wait for a new one, Kiffin remained focused on his part in the seemingly endless conflict. He closed his letter home by writing:

All the news is very good from all the fronts, but still no one has any idea as to when the war will end.... It has grown to be kind of a habit, and I don't suppose we would know what else to do.[63]

Chapter Fifty-one

If such a fate awaits us who are yet alive and serving France, should not we be contented?

Balsley's wounds and Chapman's death were not the only reminders the men had of their own mortality. At the front, there was always a fatality, injury, mishap or accident to focus the pilots on the fact that one mistake could cost them dearly. On July 24, the men learned that a favorite sous-lieutenant, Jean Chaput, from neighboring *escadrille* N.57, despite being terribly wounded in combat, had somehow managed to make it back to the aerodrome near Lemmes.[1] On July 28, most of the squadron motored over to Souilly to see one of the new German Albatross planes which two French aviators had forced down intact; the German pilot was wounded, but the observer was uninjured.[2] A few days later, the *escadrille* heard about a French pilot who intentionally collided with a German machine over Minaucourt, killing two German airmen.[3]

Two near-misses on their own airfield reminded the men of the need to always pay attention. While landing one afternoon, Prince "damn near ran into" McConnell – although he managed to swerve and avoid the collision, Prince tipped over his *bébé*. Luckily, neither party was hurt.[4]

The same day Raoul Lufbery miraculously "survived an accident such as is seldom experienced without resulting in death or severe injury," as the *New York Sun* put it.[5] Apparently, he was just taking off when a Farman landing from the wrong direction forced him to attempt a quick, climbing turn to avoid a collision. Unfortunately, he was still too low – his wing hit the ground, spinning the aeroplane around and smashing it "into bits of wood, iron and cloth," as Lufbery put it. He told a friend he "wasn't scratched, but it was a miracle since I was traveling at 160 kilometres an hour."[6] The *Sun* explained what had happened:

Lufbery was racing across the field to start for the lines and had just attained top speed – well over one hundred miles an hour – when he saw a large biplane directly fronting his, coming to land. It was too low to pass under and too close to go over. Lufbery, fearing a collision would result in both machines being set afire, tried a sharp turn. During this act, the wing of his machine touched the ground. The machine made two complete circles, turning on its back and plunging its nose into the ground, then turned over again. The motor was wrenched from the machine, the wings were shattered and the aircraft's body was crushed. Men rushed to the spot and raised the wreckage. They found Lufbery pinned under the steel struts, to whose strength he owes his life. Gasoline was pouring over his face. He was extricated and was not even bruised.[7]

The destroyed aeroplane must have looked awful; Mac told Paul they all thought Lufbery was "dead, but he hadn't a scratch." However, for several days afterward, the lucky pilot was sick from the gasoline he swallowed.[8] Thereafter, he returned to the skies over Verdun, much to the immediate regret of four German pilots.

* * * * *

Meanwhile, Kiffin continued his torrid pace, regularly participating in three or even four patrols a day. On July 25, one patrol which began as a mission to protect Prince while he attacked a German observation "sausage" ended as a "thrilling battle in the air" behind German lines.[9] As the *New York Sun* reported a few days later:

While Prince and De Laage fought two of the Germans, Rockwell dived under the third machine and attempted to cut off its tail. The fire from his mitrailleuse raked the German machine from tail to motor. Rockwell, however, had two scares, one when he missed by inches striking the German with his propeller and the second when, in the course of the maneuvering, he found himself facing the enemy's mitrailleuse. It was an uncomfortable second, he relates, until he discovered the operator was sitting dead at his post.[10]

In a letter to his brother, one can almost hear Kiffin's soft Southern drawl, telling Paul that he "liked to have run into" the German plane.[11] It's a good thing he was able to avoid it, as Kiffin's plane was one of only four operable planes in the squadron, the other seven all being out of commission for one reason or another.[12] But Kiffin's near-constant flights necessitated repairs to his machine a few days later. In the meantime, however, he kept flying. In a July 26 letter to Loula, Kiffin sounded overworked, and frustrated with the lack of concrete results:

Have been so busy for the last week that haven't kept up with anything going on around me. The weather has been fine, and I have flown between 40 and 50 hours over the lines, and have attacked over twenty German machines, shooting a lot of them up very badly but never having the luck for one of them to fall over the trenches.[13]

Kiffin expressed his frustration a little more openly to Paul, and it seems that Captain Thénault's refusal to recognize his hard work was getting under Kiffin's skin. He told Paul that although he had "about twenty fights lately," he had not "had the luck to have one of them smash to pieces in our trenches, so as far as thanks go could not have done anything."[14]

The very next day, however, Kiffin had some real success, helping to bring down two German machines. The first was a joint effort, Kiffin combining with Lieutenant de Laage to shoot down an Aviatik over Ornes-Bezonvaux, just the other side of Fort Douaumont.[15] Immediately after that fight, Kiffin forced down another German machine behind the lines.[16] However, Thénault apparently denied Kiffin any recognition and refused to give him official credit for either feat.[17] In a letter to Paul, Kiffin's frustration finally boiled over:

Am pretty disgusted; have been working my fool head off lately, and don't even get 'thank you' for it. I may ask any day to change escadrilles. This outfit is on the bum, everyone scrapping and discontented and me about the worst of any. This damn Captain does everything in the world to try to discourage us from trying to do anything. It is hard to understand him except that he is a selfish, stupid fool....

This morning Lieutenant de Laage and I brought one down in their lines. I attacked him first and he went over on his nose. As he came up, the Lieutenant opened up on him and he fell. The Lieutenant deserves all the credit one gives him, but I certainly ran the most risk this morning, and if I didn't hit him myself, which I may have, I made it possible for the Lieutenant to hit him. Yet do you think I get any credit for it? Not at all!

Fifteen minutes later I made another German land just in his lines, having attacked two, and was seen by Prince, but nothing is said about it. The trouble is that I fight all the time with the Captain, instead of taking him down to a whorehouse and buying him a drink....

I think the best thing I can do is go to another escadrille, but I hate to lose what work I have done here, and tell you the truth, I want the Legion d'Honneur and a sous-Lieutenant's grade. I don't give a damn how conceited it may appear, but I think I have well earned the two.[18]

Upon reading Kiffin's letter, Paul was livid. He suggested that Kiffin take leave and come to Paris, where they could approach cabinet minister Georges Leygues, the father of Paul's fiancée, about getting Captain Thénault removed. Paul angrily told his brother that he "might work out there forever, but with an ass in charge it'd be no use." Kiffin could come with him to the country, said Paul, and "by the time you get back the boys will get credit for their work."[19] Kiffin responded that he did not want to leave just then, and fleshed out the background of the problem he and several others in the squadron had with their commanding officer:

Right now, I don't care to take a permission, *as I want to keep up with everything that goes on around here. You can just tell M. Leygues that I want to be changed to a French* escadrille *unless the Captain is changed and that several others will follow my example... [T]here is not a man here who likes the Captain. Then Colonel Barès did not want to give him to us at first, but only did it because Thaw asked it.*

I think that I have the most hours and the most fights for the month of July on the Verdun front of any Nieuport pilote, *but am not sure. I don't think, however, that a full report of my work has gone out of this office, and a number of times my report on a fight has been changed. The machine that Hall brought down the Captain did his damndest to prove that it wasn't brought down, and so far hasn't proposed Bert for even a citation.*

But this morning he showed a change. Lufbery is a quiet boy who does good work and when he says he has done something we all believe him. He doesn't like Thénault but doesn't show it so openly as some of us, so Thénault kisses his ass. This morning Lufbery brought down a German machine ten kilometres in the German lines. We all know he did because he wouldn't lie about it, yet not a soul saw it. If any of the rest of us had done it and even if it was seen by a second one of us, Thénault would only sneer about it, yet he immediately went in an automobile to the commandant of this Armee *and proposed Lufbery for the* Médaille. *All of us will be damn glad to see him get it as he deserves it, yet the principle is all wrong.*[20]

The tension between Kiffin and Thénault seems to have been building for some time, but it was not until he witnessed firsthand Thénault's unfair treatment in the handling of claims that Kiffin openly groused about his leadership. Bert Hall, whose recent victory the Captain had apparently tried to disprove, was a good friend of Kiffin's, and clearly on his side in the dispute. He later said that he and Kiffin "were not very popular with our captain, as we told him and everyone else what we thought."[21]

Prince was apparently on Kiffin's side, as well. Indeed, Paul even suggested that Prince might want a friend of his from *Escadrille N.69* to take over leadership of the American unit.[22] Despite this evidence, over the years, many have supposed that the discord in the unit at this time was between Kiffin and Norman Prince. This is probably true on some level, but it seems clear that the primary conflict at this time was instead between Kiffin and Captain Thénault, with most, if not all of the squadron – including Prince – siding with Kiffin.

It should be conceded that Thénault was in a difficult position – having been instructed not to be too strict on the foreign volunteers, he surely had his hands full with the brash, confident Americans.[23] Surely anyone in his situation – commanding a group of men just a few years younger than himself, primarily speaking another language, while flying the newest and fastest flying machines above the most violent battlefield in the biggest and worst war in the history of the world – would have faced some degree of internal conflict. Indeed, it would be surprising to find the absence of conflict under such demanding circumstances. Thus, the quarrels and disagreements that existed merely confirm the expected state of affairs and bring to mind a phrase Victor Chapman penned to his father a few months earlier: "All war is a tumbling down of the established order."[24]

* * * * *

So Captain Thénault should not be judged too harshly. This is especially true since some of the dissension in the unit, or at least the conflict between Kiffin and the captain, stemmed from the competition for recognition under the elastic standards employed by the French aviation service in determining official victories. From the flyers' point of view, the standards had two primary defects – namely, they were less than generous but susceptible to easy manipulation. Thus, whether or not a victory counted as official oftentimes depended more on luck or good graces than on one's skill, or the "facts in the air."

For example, in early August, Kiffin told Paul "you never know when a machine brought down is official or not." "Sometimes," Kiffin said, "they report a machine brought down without anyone seeing it, and then again they don't."[25] Kiffin went on to describe how a couple of "well known French pilots" had recently claimed and been given credit for a phantom "victory" he knew beyond doubt was not legitimate. He then laid out both the uncertain nature of the standard, and his related determination to take a well-earned break:

So all in all, you can't tell much about what is going on in the aviation. Sometimes a man will work his head off and get no credit or recompense, and then later, when he least expects it, he will get everything. I worked damn hard last month and got absolutely nothing in the way of credit for it. Well, now I am going to take it easier this month and I bet I gain more by it. I stayed in bed this morning until ten-thirty, and am taking life easy at present until they give me a new machine.[26]

While Kiffin was relaxing and waiting for a new machine, Chapman's replacement showed up – Paul Pavelka, fresh from the *G.D.E.*[27] Thénault assigned Hall's old machine and Victor's mechanic to Kiffin's former legion mate.[28] Kiffin was glad to have another friend at the front, and Pavelka was pleased to have an experienced pilot to show him the ropes. William Thaw would also soon return to active duty with the squadron and was immediately placed into the regular patrol rotation alongside Kiffin.

In the meantime, Kiffin was able to catch up on some correspondence.[29] He wrote his mother that he had been "taking things very quietly lately," and would probably go to Paris on permission soon.[30] Paul forwarded a few letters from Loula; in one, she mentioned an old friend of Paul and Kiffin who had informed her that "all Atlanta is praising you boys and claim you."[31] A letter Kiffin received from his former boss in Atlanta, St. Elmo Massengale, confirmed this; Massengale wrote that "all of your friends here are very proud of your achievements."[32]

Noting all the press coverage Kiffin was receiving back home and how the whole country was proud of him, Loula observed, "Our N.C. people do not like it when Kiffin is commented on as from Atlanta – Asheville wants that honor...."[33] But even though she preferred North Carolina, Loula now offered to go to Atlanta with Kiffin after the war, if that was what he wanted:

Kiffin, you mentioned a letter from Massengale. I imagine his business has increased wonderfully – I hear so. The past year has been one of unprecedented prosperity in this country. If you could have kept on with him, you would have gotten rich. But I guess you are doing the work intended for you. If after the war you want to go to Atlanta, I'll go with you if you wish it. We will see what comes and what seems best if the struggle ever ends.[34]

Loula's willingness to move to Atlanta represented a significant change in attitude and showed how much she missed her youngest son. Recall that the very last time she had seen Kiffin was while waiting on a streetcar in Asheville, when he had asked her to come live in Atlanta with him and Paul. She had turned him down then, saying she wished for he and Paul to marry and establish their own families.[35] But after more than two years without her "darling boys," all Loula really wanted was to be with them again, wherever and whenever that was. She closed her letter with these lines:

Paul, send this on to Kiffin and both of you write and tell me everything about yourselves. I love you both and rather live in a hut with you than a palace without you. If it were [mine] to do over, never would I be without you as I was in your childhood.[36]

* * * * *

Around this time, Paul could not resist bragging to a friend back home that Kiffin had "brought down three Hun machines and shot the gunners out of several others," and "been honored with two war medals." Based on the recent time he had spent with Kiffin at the front, Paul reported that "Aviation is a most dangerous and nerve-wrecking game, but the pilots are well-quartered and excellently fed. They all enjoy the life and are very much in earnest."[37]

Kiffin's resolution to take it easy while waiting on a new machine was probably not a bad idea. Paul was right – aviation, particularly in wartime, truly was a nerve-wrecking game, and it is likely Kiffin needed the rest. World War I aviators faced an incredible amount of combat stress, and many experienced hypoxia, exhaustion, and fatigue. The enormous mental and physical strain affected every pilot to one degree or another.[38] Aerial combat had a significant and usually deleterious effect on airmen and their outlook, as illustrated by the following quote from one later American flyboy: "I have never been serious about anything in my life, and now I know that I'll never be otherwise again. Here I am, twenty-four years old. I look forty and feel ninety. I've lost all interest in life beyond the next patrol."[39]

Kiffin had his own reasons to feel a bit melancholy. In early August, he received a letter from Mrs. Chapman, reminding him of Victor, "the best friend I ever had," as Kiffin put it.[40] He had also heard of Alan Seeger's death, and then on August 11, Dennis Dowd died in an aviation accident.[41]

Dowd and Kiffin had become good friends during their service with the

486

legion in the early days of the war.[42] Dowd had been among the first American volunteers, marching down the boulevards of Paris waving the American flag with Seeger almost two years before, and his loss was another blow to Kiffin. Like many others, Dowd eventually transferred to aviation, and at the time of his death was seen as one of the most promising pilots in the flight school at Buc, near Paris.[43]

Coming on the heels of the deaths of Chapman and Seeger, Dowd's death caused Pavelka and Kiffin to ponder their own fates. On August 18, Pavelka confided to Paul a reflective moment he and Kiffin shared:

It is sad about poor Dowd.... Kiffin and I were talking about him last night. It is hard on both of us to see all of our old comrades going. Yesterday I received news of three more legionnaires being killed. Kiffin knew them, they are Lindal, Jorgensen, and poor Larsen, who had his jaw shot away last June. They were all killed in the Somme.[44]

Once again, a funeral was held at the American church and, once again, the Americans in Paris gathered to honor one of their own, dead for France.[45] Dowd's fellow pilot-trainee Edmond Genet felt the need to do something more and wrote a moving tribute to his dead friend. While it is unknown whether Kiffin ever read or heard Genet's words, he surely would have agreed with them. The tribute's conclusion served as both a nice eulogy for Dowd and a stirring call for the rededication of those volunteers who remained behind, fighting for France:

'Greater love hath no man than this, that a man lay down his life for his friends.' Such is one of the great declarations of Jesus Christ. Surely there is no greater sacrifice which a young man can make, and yet did not Dowd do even more than that when he gave his life for strangers in a foreign land? Surely his reward must be great in the life beyond. If such a fate awaits us who are yet alive and serving France, should not we be contented? If we can serve France and the Allies as well as has Dennis Dowd, then we shall do well our small parts in this great strife. The spirit of Lafayette still lives – a thousand-fold increased. May it bind forever the two sister republics in love and fraternity.[46]

Chapter Fifty-two

The news is very very good for us now and everyone is happy.

It was just as well that Kiffin took things a bit easier in August. Not only was he without a machine but, as one American military observer noted, "since the end of July, the Germans had displayed very little aerial activity" in the Verdun sector, where dogfights had become "very infrequent as the Germans had been declining combat."[1] As Pavelka told Paul in mid-August, the "*boche* seem to stay at home since I have come into the *escadrille*."[2]

Of course, their opponents suddenly had another very good reason to stay home – immediately upon recovery from his airfield accident, Raoul Lufbery began shooting down every German he encountered, a string of victories that saw him rack up four kills in less than ten days. The former maker of handles for caskets was now driving up demand for both.

During his first two months in the squadron, Lufbery had established a reputation as a workmanlike pilot, maintaining his own machine with precision and handling the high altitude better than most. But although he had a taste for combat, he had not as yet brought down a German. Perhaps the gasoline he swallowed revved him up, for suddenly Lufbery became a force of nature in the skies – "a living example of audacity," as he was once called.[3]

His first victory came on the last day of July, while patrolling alone near Etain.[4] A few days later, the *New York Times* reported what it described as the downing of Lufbery's "first German flier":

He dived immediately behind the hostile machine, opening fire as he passed close to its tail. So swift was the dive that the American was able to fire only seven shots from his mitrailleuse, *but his aim was good. The pilot fell forward over the controls, and the plane dropped headlong, bursting into flames as it struck the ground.*[5]

Later in Paris, Lufbery was asked by a reporter about his "sensations" during this, his first successful aerial combat. His answer was reminiscent of the dogfight – brief, blunt, and entirely lacking in emotion:

Didn't have time for sensations. I began firing at him. Then we both circled, firing all the time. Suddenly, his machine seemed to turn all white. He was upside down. Then he caught fire. He fell, reminding me of a smoking cigarette butt dropping through the air. Then I came home.[6]

From that moment forward, Lufbery preferred fighting to all else. Thereafter, he stalked the skies over France, relentless, remorseless and unstoppable. One author, in a book for young people, perhaps captured the legend best when he wrote that Lufbery flew "as if he wanted to destroy Germany all by himself."[7] In one of his last letters, Lufbery explained to his sister-in-law why he would not be returning to Connecticut any time soon:

I could wish to see Wallingford again. But it is not for me now. I like the game here, thank you – I prefer to perch among my clouds and shoot at Boches even to passing a pleasant hour with you all. I cannot come now. After the war we shall see – but I shall not, I think, live so long.[8]

* * * * *

On August 4, Lufbery scored the squadron's first "double," bringing down two enemy planes on the same day. In the morning, while on patrol with McConnell, Luf performed his "favorite manoeuvre" to attack a German from below and behind while Mac attacked from above. The damaged plane slipped into a corkscrew dive, falling over 4,000 feet before dropping from sight.[9] Just an hour later, Lufbery teamed up with Adjutant Victor Sayaret of neighboring *Escadrille N.57* to bring down another *boche* machine over Avocourt.[10] This second battle was confirmed by a French observation balloon.[11]

While one authority suggests that Lufbery's initial four victories occurred on separate dates, a letter Kiffin sent to Mrs. Weeks corroborates the "double" on August 4. That day, Kiffin wrote:

This morning, the boys had several flights. Mac and Lufbery attacked one German that they think fell. Then Lufbery with some pilot from another escadrille attacked another one that they think dropped. Nothing official yet.[12]

Another reliable source also confirms two victories for Lufbery on August 4.[13] However, there is some dispute about this, and it may be the case that Lufbery was only later credited with the unofficial victory in which McConnell assisted.[14] Whatever the precise dates, Lufbery had already gained three kills by August 8, when Kiffin wrote Paul to tell of Lufbery's fourth:

Lufbery brought down a machine this morning that burned up over the trenches. Lufbery is a very good man and we all like to see him get credit. He has been very lucky, however, in them giving him credit for all his work and they count this as his fourth Boche.[15]

If you hear a touch of jealousy in Kiffin's words, it is probably due to Kiffin's perception that Thénault treated Lufbery's claims more deferentially than he did those of others in the squadron, including his and Bert Hall's. Judged by the same standard, Kiffin likely could have laid claim to five, six, or maybe even seven victories. Even so, Kiffin did not begrudge Lufbery the recognition, he just wanted to be treated fairly.

In any event, McConnell witnessed the August 8 fight, having left on a sortie with Lufbery just before noon. But after crossing the lines, the two airmen lost sight of one another. With no Germans in view, Mac spent his time hovering near the French observation machines. Then, as he turned back southward toward the French lines, Mac spotted a plane falling through the sky, its white belly flashing as it twisted and fell.[16] According to McConnell, the machine "did not drop whirling as is usually the case, but in long glides and curves," indicating that the "aviator must have gripped the controls in death." Following it down, he saw the damaged plane smash into the ground, "bursting into a great sheet of flame and smoke."[17]

Later, Lufbery gave his own account of the event. After becoming separated from Mac, he came upon three enemy planes, one somewhat detached from the others. His chosen target must have been piloted by a novice, for Lufbery was able to place himself about thirty yards behind and slightly above it without any notice being taken of his approach.[18] With his typical bluntness, Lufbery described what happened next:

Finally, my adversary saw me, but it was then too late. Vainly the pilot sought to turn his machine in order to enable his gunner to fire. It was no use. Their lack of vigilance was to cost them their lives.[19]

He pressed the trigger, following the machine as it plunged downward. Mac also watched the doomed plane "outlined against the shell-racked earth like a tiny insect, until just northwest of Fort Douaumont it crashed down upon the battlefield."[20] Lufbery's streak vaulted him into a lead he would never relinquish – he now had four victories to Kiffin's three. Five victories made one an "ace," and McConnell noted that when Lufbery "bagged" one more, he would be "mentioned by name in the *communiqué* and take his place as a new star in the galaxy of French aviators."[21]

While Luf was delighted with yet another *boche* machine to his credit, at the airfield during lunch Mac heard him murmur half to himself, "Those poor fellows!"[22]

* * * * *

Although he had put in the second-most hours through the squadron's first three months at the front (Kiffin was first), as July rolled into August, Norman Prince was still in search of his first combat victory. As the *boche* pilots were venturing over the lines less and less, Prince instead set his sights on a so-called "sausage" – the German *Drachen* kite-balloons which hovered high above the German lines conducting aerial observation. Used for artillery spotting and ranging, observation balloons were ubiquitous along the front. Because of their strategic importance, these balloons were heavily defended by ground-based anti-aircraft guns as well as patrolling airplanes, which meant that attacking them could be quite dangerous.

Nonetheless, Prince had his Nieuport armed with *Le Prieur* "sky rockets," and in late July began his quest to bring down one of the "aerial frankfurters," as McConnell called the balloons. Intended to ignite the hydrogen gas which kept the balloons aloft, the sky rockets looked like oversized firecrackers – with the devices protruding from each wing of his *bébé*, Mac said that Prince "resembled an advance agent for Payne's fireworks more than an *aviateur de chasse.*"[23]

The squadron's other top flyers, Kiffin and Lieutenant de Laage de Meux, often accompanied Prince on his runs, providing guard service while he sought his elusive observation sausage.[24] But the balloons were much harder to get than one would think – according to one scholar, although they "made a spectacular show," the rockets "were wildly inaccurate and seldom effective even at close range."[25] In addition, at the first sign of French planes the German ground crews used power winches to rapidly return the balloons to earth.[26] Nonetheless, Prince stuck with it, and after several failed attempts finally satisfied his appetite for sausage – as McConnell wrote:

He found one just where it ought to be, swooped down upon it, and let off his fireworks with all the gusto of an American boy on the Fourth of July. When he looked again, the balloon had vanished.[27]

The next thing to vanish was Prince, who a few days later was reported missing after a fight over the German lines.[28] Apparently, his motor had stopped, forcing him to volplane over "no man's land," landing in a shell-pitted field half a mile behind the trenches. He lunched with the officers of a French battery and was able to reach the squadron by telephone to report that he was alive and well.[29]

* * * * *

While Mac is probably due some credit for helping Lufbery with the first of his victories on August 4, he seemed more adept at wrecking his own machines.[30] In late July or early August, while landing in the early evening at another field, McConnell misjudged the distance and had what he called "another beautiful smashup."[31] He described what happened in a letter to a friend:

I saw soldiers running to be in at [the] finish and I thought [to] myself that James's hash was cooked, but I went between trees and ended up head-on on the opposite bank of road. My motor took the shock and my belt held me. As my tail went up it was cut in two by some very low phone wires. I wasn't bruised even. Took dinner with the officers there, who gave me a car to go home in afterwards.[32]

Although McConnell did not realize it at first, he had sprained his back. He was lucky it was not worse – according to Hall, the mechanics could not repair Mac's badly busted up machine, and only kept it around "in case they need[ed] any of the uncracked parts."[33] Mac continued to fly in borrowed machines, but his wrenched back grew more painful day by day.[34] Finally, hoping some rest would allow it to heal, in mid-August, McConnell took a week's permission in Paris.[35]

In the meantime, Kiffin's new machine had arrived, and he took Pavelka up to show him around on his first flight over Verdun.[36] For the next couple days, they had to hold off flying due to rain, but Kiffin didn't mind, as a long dry spell had made the ground very hard for landings.[37] Around this time, Kiffin received a letter from Mrs. Weeks – yet another friend of her son Kenneth had been killed and, feeling blue, she asked Kiffin to come visit.[38] She was also contemplating a trip back to America and wanted to see Kiffin before she left – she told him she "would not ask it if I thought you could not come."[39]

Of course, Kiffin could not say no to Mrs. Weeks, and so not long after Mac left, he began his own eight-day leave in Paris. He had not been back to the city since being wounded in May and was glad to have a real break. Even better, he found Paul well and everyone in an "optimistic mood." A few days into his leave, Kiffin told his mother that he "was very busy having a good time and not worrying about work."[40] He also wrote a short letter back to Massengale in which he modestly attributed his tremendous success to luck:

I have worked very hard in the aviation corps this summer and have had a great number of air fights in which I have, so far, been very lucky. I am spending this week in Paris on permission, and am enjoying it very much, as Paris is the liveliest now since the beginning of the war.[41]

The first portion of Kiffin's stay at Mrs. Weeks overlapped with the end of Jim McConnell's leave. Unfortunately, Mac's strained back was still declining, rather than improving – sometimes he would sit up all night in pain, and in the morning Kiffin and Paul would have to help him dress. Things deteriorated to the point that at times Mac could walk only with the support of a cane.[42]

Accordingly, Mac spent much of his time writing, and had an interesting article published in the *Chicago Daily News* detailing the daily routine of an airman at the front, under a nice picture Paul had taken of the entire *escadrille*.[43] He also wrote a lengthy feature for a popular American magazine; the article came out in the November edition of *The World's Work* and eventually led to a full-length book.[44] Still, bad back and all, Mac must have found some time for socializing – he told a friend back home that he had met "a young Russian lady in Paris who is quite interesting but with too many brains for war time."[45]

In between assisting Mac, keeping his numerous lunch and dinner appointments, and catching up with Mrs. Weeks, Kiffin spent as much time as he could with Paul, who by now felt very much at home in Paris and greatly enjoyed showing Kiffin around. Not long before, Paul had written that the morale of the soldiers was high, and that the French people had settled down patiently to wait for victory, without complaint. "Paris," he said, "does not look like there is a war on just a handful of miles away."[46]

The same could not be said of Kiffin.

A few days into his leave, Paul snapped a photograph of his brother while on one of their jaunts around Paris. Although he was wearing a new uniform, one cannot help but notice how much Kiffin had aged since first going to the front more than four months earlier – most people probably would have guessed that Kiffin was Paul's older brother, rather than the other way around.[47] Although he had grown a mustache, it does not obscure the slightly drawn and careworn look in his face. Overall, one senses tension – Kiffin's eyes stare straight ahead, his mouth refuses to smile and his fist looks to be involuntarily clenched. No, for as much as he enjoyed his brief respite in Paris, Kiffin looked *exactly* like there was a war on just a handful of miles away – it was *his* war, and he knew now he was never leaving it.

* * * * *

Mac returned to the squadron on August 24 and immediately got into an argument with Norman Prince. Apparently, there was some bad blood brewing between Prince and the Rockwell brothers, and word had drifted back to Paris. The roots of the conflict went back to Elliott Cowdin's dismissal from the squadron and Paul's desire to print the true facts about what had happened.

The exact details of that dismissal have always been quite murky. So murky, in fact, that it may even be the case that Cowdin was temporarily placed in jail – when on Paul's behalf McConnell confronted Prince at dinner the night of his return, Prince told him that all he had against Paul was that he "wanted to send a cable about Cowdin being in jail." One can hardly blame Prince for being defensive, however, as he was surely correct in his belief that such adverse publicity would hurt the *escadrille*.[48]

After dinner, Mac had another disagreement, this one with Thénault. Seeing McConnell wincing as he walked, Thénault questioned his fitness for flight. Mac claimed that "not being able to walk does not prevent my flying," to which his understanding captain softly replied, "Jimmy, go to bed."[49]

The next day, Thénault sent McConnell to the hospital at Bar-le-Duc from which place he was sent to the *Depot d'éclopés* (the depot of cripples) at Vitry-le-François. Before he left, Mac wrote a letter to Paul, telling him about his confrontation with Prince the night before. He also announced that Prince was claiming to have finally scored his first victory:

[Prince] was out [this] morning and claims to have brought down a Boche. *He acted like a wild man on landing, turned summersault and yelled.* Boche *was so far in [the] lines no one saw him. Don't know if it will be official or not, but anyway Norman beat it immediately on permission.... [He] will probably look you up to apologize.*[50]

Several solid histories of the squadron assert that around August 23 (two days earlier), Prince had forced down an Aviatik in a meadow outside Verdun.[51] This seems unlikely, however, for when Prince wrote his mother on September 2, telling her that he had been "fortunate enough to run across a German the other day who didn't see me approaching," he indicated his victim fell in a forest well behind the German side of the line.[52] Thus, if Prince did get a *Boche* the morning of August 25 (and I believe that he did), it was his first, and McConnell's letter confirms that it was unwitnessed.[53] Mac's report is reinforced by an account in the *New York Sun*, which reported that "the machine fell so far behind the German lines that no French observation officer could see it clearly and it could not be recorded officially."[54]

Kiffin returned to the squadron a day or two later, and soon wrote Paul that "no one thinks Prince got a German, in fact, everyone is sure he didn't." Nonetheless, and despite there not being a single witness to his claimed victory, Thénault proposed Prince for a citation and was going to propose him for the *médaille militaire* until the rest of the squadron warned that if he did, "they would quit."[55]

As seen in Kiffin's letter, the acrimony in the unit was growing and beginning to center on Prince. Not only did the other American pilots not trust Prince's claim of bringing down a German, they did not like his cozy relationship with Thénault. Cowdin's earlier crack-up seems to have undermined Prince's position in the squadron and left him without a strong friend or ally among the men. Moreover, with Thaw out for much of the summer and an entire new group of pilots coming in, it seems plausible that Kiffin and Prince had gradually become rivals, each vying to be recognized as the squadron's unofficial leader.

Astonishingly, Prince's standing had deteriorated to the point that Kiffin and the others even discussed running him out of the *escadrille*, and Kiffin told Paul he was "going to have to murder" Prince when he returned from his leave for talking "awful big" behind Kiffin's back while he was away.[56] Thus, whether it was simply a personality conflict magnified by the pressures of the war or something deeper, things seemed to be coming to a head between the two headstrong flyers.

One sign of the ongoing rancor is that rather than going to Paris to apologize to Paul (as Mac had assumed), Prince instead took his leave in the upscale seaside resort of Deauville. In a letter written to his mother while on the French coast, one can detect Prince's desire to escape the hard feelings and pressures of the *escadrille*:

One soon gets enough of Paris in summer and in wartime. Here no one pays the slightest attention to the war. There are few militaires – mostly civiles from Paris and their amies. Good bathing, – golf in the afternoon – many good-lookers, making the plage rather good fun.[57]

Still, whatever their differences, there was no daylight between Kiffin's and Norman's respective views toward France, or their own part in the war. And even if Prince sometimes came off as wild, at other times brooding, he was a solid pilot and his intentions were always honorable. An anecdote related by Paul from his visit with the *escadrille* earlier that summer demonstrates this beyond doubt:

When I visited the American squadron at Bar-le-Duc last July, Prince told me that he did not expect to live to see the end of the war, but he was happy to think that his death would come while he was aiding the French troops toward a victorious triumphal parade along the Champs Elysees *after the signing of peace.*[58]

* * * * *

Back in America, the campaign for president was heating up. Justice Hughes formally accepted the Republican nomination at Carnegie Hall at the end of July. In his acceptance speech, Hughes garnered the most prolonged applause of the evening when he condemned President Wilson for his alleged diplomatic weakness, declaring:

Had this government ... left no doubt that when we said 'strict accountability' we meant precisely what we said, and that we should unhesitatingly vindicate that position, I am confident that there would have been no destruction of American lives by the sinking of the Lusitania.[59]

At the end of August, Teddy Roosevelt gave his first campaign speech on behalf of Hughes. As expected, he blasted Wilson even harder than had Hughes. Speaking before a raucous crowd in Lewiston, Maine, Roosevelt continued hammering the theme of American preparedness:

Thanks to the fact that President Wilson has sometimes led us wrong, and sometimes not led us at all, and that at the best he has merely followed afar off when convinced that it was politically safe to do so, we are at this moment no more prepared to defend ourselves than we were two years ago when the world war broke out.

Roosevelt then went after Wilson's supposed lack of leadership, directly attacking the incumbent president's popular campaign slogan:

At this moment Mr. Wilson, and Mr. Wilson's fuglemen, advance as his greatest claim that 'he has kept us out of war.' This claim can be seriously made only by individuals who indorse President Wilson's belief that deeds are nothing, and words everything.[60]

Around the same time, Victor Chapman's father, who certainly appreciated the power of deeds and words, was pushing for direct American involvement, suggesting it was the only way to save America's soul. Responding to a letter of sympathy from a French society, he wrote:

That our country should have a share in the grief of this war is the only way in which it can partake of the blessings that lie concealed behind the tragedy. It is a kind of world sacrament.... My son, who hated newspaper talk, as apparently all true soldiers do, used to write savage letters complaining that the American aviators were given far more credit than they deserved, surrounded as they were by Frenchmen, their equals and superiors, whose doings excited little attention, but passed in the day's work. I could not grieve over his complaints, however, because I was aflame for America to take some part in the great struggle between light and darkness for her own soul's sake. Here was an influence which the intrigues of politicians could not benumb, nor the dead hand of consolidated interests neutralize. The elemental fire was in it.[61]

* * * * *

Although poor weather limited the squadron's flight time for a few days, upon his return from Paris, Kiffin immediately returned to form. On one of his first trips over the lines, he chased three enemy aeroplanes out of the sky around Samogneux.[62] He remarked to Paul only that he "found a number of Germans and fought with them for a long time, but couldn't do much as I was all alone."[63]

Around this time, the unit received notice that it was being transferred to another sector, to be replaced at Behonne by *Escadrille N.12*. Notably, they were to leave their Nieuports behind, and each pilot would be allowed to pick out a brand-new machine at Le Bourget. Best of all, this meant the entire squadron would be in Paris together for a few days.

Hoping to squeeze in some more work during the *escadrille's* few remaining days at Verdun, even though it was very foggy, Kiffin, Thaw and Johnson went on patrol the morning of September 2. However, the sky proved to be too hazy, and the group stayed up only 25 minutes before returning to base. The trip went into the logbook as *R.A.S.*, short for *rien à signaler* – nothing to report. Kiffin and Thaw went back up that afternoon, but once again, the patrol was uneventful – *R.A.S.*[64]

There was, however, one thing worth reporting from that day – Kiffin learned that Thénault had proposed him for another citation in the Order of the Army. Perhaps seeking to bury the hatchet, or perhaps finally realizing Kiffin's importance within the *escadrille*, Thénault extolled him as a "pilot of the very first order," and praised his "unsparing efforts" that summer in the skies over Verdun.[65] Whichever sentiment motivated Thénault's belated action, the positive news largely repaired the rift between the two and once again put Kiffin in high spirits – he told his mother:

Before leaving here they are proposing me for another citation in the order of the army, which pleases me, as it means another palm on my Croix de Guerre *and shows appreciation of the work I have done here. The news is very very good for us now and everyone is happy.*[66]

In the same cheerful vein, Kiffin wrote a friend in Atlanta, telling him the tide of war had turned against Germany. In closing, Kiffin said he would soon write again, "unless the Germans get me."[67]

Chapter Fifty-three

One cannot doubt that the spirit of Lafayette is among our youth.

In the meantime, Hall had brought down his third *Boche* machine, tying him with Kiffin for second place in the squadron.[1] Hall's kill marked the squadron's fifteenth victory, broken down like this:

Lufbery – 4

Rockwell – 3

Hall – 3

Thaw – 1

Prince – 1

Cowdin or Chapman – 1

de Laage de Meux – 1

Nungesser – 1[2]

Believing it was their last day at Verdun, on September 3, Kiffin could not be kept from the sky. Since Thaw's return to the unit, he and Kiffin had resumed their status as regular patrol-mates and the two friends went out together again on the first tour that morning. But after an hour and a half in the air, there was nothing doing – another *R.A.S.*

Both pilots stayed on the ground just over an hour before going back up, this time joined by Pavelka. On this sortie, both Kiffin and Thaw attacked enemy machines, with Thaw forcing his opponent to dive toward the lines. Coming down at two o'clock, Kiffin quickly refueled and was back in the air alone by two-thirty. He found and attacked another *Boche* plane but had to pull off after his machine gun jammed. After landing, Kiffin went up with Thaw one more time, but both men experienced engine trouble and had to come back. All told, Kiffin participated in four separate patrols that day, spending a total of six and a half hours in the air.[3]

The morning of September 4 dawned under a sullen rain that would linger for the next two days. When the squadron received the order to clear out of

Bar-le-Duc a few days before, Thénault had immediately telephoned each of the men then on leave – de Laage de Meux, Prince and Lufbery – to notify them of the coming change in sectors and order them to return.[4] Despite this, by September 4, out of his three *permissionaires*, only Lieutenant de Laage de Meux had made it back.

Prince was still in Deauville, and Thénault had received an interesting message from Lufbery the day before. Written in French, the telegram read: "*Suis retenu dans un local disciplinaire place de Chartres, Eure-et-Loir* – I am detained in a local disciplinary place, Chartres, Eure-et-Loir."[5] It seems that Lufbery – "a pretty sudden proposition when he was roused," according to Thénault – had gotten himself arrested after knocking out a few of the teeth of a railway employee who put his hands on the newly-decorated aviator in the course of demanding his papers.[6]

Well, calls were made, strings were pulled and soon it was decided that it would not do to have one of France's leading flyers locked up. Although it took a little convincing, eventually the local *gendarme* agreed to release the pugilistic pilot. By the time Lufbery rejoined the squadron, Thénault had received word to stay in Bar-le-Duc to await new orders, and Lufbery had been given a new nickname – "jailbird."[7]

* * * * *

Kiffin took full advantage of the extra time in the Verdun sector, taking to the air as soon as the rainy weather allowed. On his first sortie, Kiffin immediately got excellent position behind a German *avion*, but his machine gun jammed with the first bullet and several times thereafter, forcing Kiffin repeatedly to clear it before resuming his attack. Three times he got position and fired, but each time his *mitrailleuse* failed. Frustrated and fuming, Kiffin returned to the aerodrome.[8]

While alone on the day's first patrol the morning of September 9, Prince shot down a Fokker for his second victory.[9] Not to be outdone, Kiffin went up with Thaw and Lufbery on the second patrol. West of Verdun near Vauquois, at about three thousand meters, Kiffin dove on a German two-seater he spotted flying just beneath him. He killed the gunner with his first volley, and must have wounded the pilot, too, as the plane began to descend in a circular spiral. Plunging in pursuit, Kiffin caught up with the falling machine and finished it off around 1,800 meters.[10]

Kiffin was nearly finished off himself when two Fokkers surprised him as he watched his victim drop near the first-line trenches. Caught off guard and attacked at close range, Kiffin was forced to disengage when he ran out of ammunition and had to bank his *bébé* almost vertical to escape. Following this narrow scrape, back at the airfield Kiffin learned he still had one bullet in his machine – put there by one of the Fokkers. Happily, he also learned that the French 71st Infantry Division had witnessed his victory, which meant official confirmation.[11]

Kiffin's fourth victory not only tied him for the lead in the *escadrille*, it solidified his status back home as one of America's preeminent war heroes. For example, the *St. Louis Post-Dispatch* ran a large front-page photo of Kiffin over its article headlined, "Rockwell Drops His Fourth Enemy Flyer."[12] On the same day, Kiffin appeared on the front pages of the *New York Sun*, the *New York Tribune*, and the *Washington Post*, and his achievement was prominently covered in the *New York World*, the *New York Times*, and the *Chicago Daily News*.[13]

Kiffin was officially a celebrity fighter pilot – the *Chicago Tribune* noted that with this fourth win, he now held "the championship among his compatriots."[14] Of course, this was not wholly accurate, as Lufbery also had four victories. However, Kiffin's total was all the more impressive when one considers that he had first flown in an aeroplane just one year and three days before. By way of contrast, Hall (who had three victories) had been training or flying as an aviator since at least early 1915 (and supposedly much earlier), as had Lufbery, and Prince and Thaw were licensed aviators well before the war. Despite their headstart, Kiffin led them all.

The squadron was also showing well and had become widely respected among the French officers and pilots even prior to its pair of victories on September 9. And for good reason – during its tenure at Verdun, the *Escadrille Américaine* ranked fourth in total victories among the twenty-three *chasse* units with at least one victory.[15] Thénault referred to the squadron's time at Verdun as "its glorious prime," and it was.[16]

The strength of the squadron's reputation in those early months is best illustrated by an anecdote involving Jean Navarre, one of France's best-known aces. Late one night near the end of August, Navarre entered Gerny's restaurant and bar in the *Rue de Port-Mahon* in Paris and, after a glass of vermouth and handshakes all around, proclaimed his admiration for the work being done by the American unit:

The Americans are certainly wonderful flyers. Some of them have bagged three Fokkers already, and they have not been fighting in the air for a year. All the French pilots with a string of boches to their credit have been in the game two years since the beginning of the war. For the first year none of us scarcely did anything. It was only after a year and a half of experience that we began to get going good. It was back in February last that the first Frenchman was officially mentioned in the communiqué. That was when Guynemer shot down his fifth. Now there are a score of French pilots who have five boches to their credit, but after a much longer preparation than the Americans, who have three. I should not be surprised to see Americans with records of a score or more by next summer.[17]

At the time Navarre spoke, Kiffin was one of just three pilots in the squadron with at least three victories to his credit. Given that the other two pilots were Lufbery (who had four, but was likely not seen as an "American" by Navarre) and Hall, it is not a stretch to believe that Navarre, who knew Kiffin well, had him in mind when he responded to an American reporter asking whether he or Guynemer would have the most victories at war's end:

I think it will neither be Guynemer nor myself who will hold the record for boche machines when the war is over: I think it will be one of your countrymen – one of the men in the American escadrille.[18]

* * * * *

In September 1914, Kiffin had been an unknown common *soldat* in the Foreign Legion. Now, just two years later, he was a world-famous aviator, seen by many as the face of America in the war. But Kiffin's motivation for going to war had been clear from the beginning – as he stated in Atlanta two days before leaving for Europe, he was determined to fight to show his "gratitude to France for the noble part she played in the winning of American Independence..."[19] Throughout his enlistment, whenever the topic came up Kiffin repeatedly said he was paying his part of the debt Americans owed Lafayette.[20]

Of course, Paul was already proud of Kiffin, but wanted everyone to know the contribution being made by his little brother and the other Americans. He wrote a friend back in Atlanta that there was "a fine bunch of young American boys over here fighting for France, and the entire United Sates should be proud of them."[21]

Paul and his journalist comrades were doing what they could and, helped by the favorable publicity they generated on behalf of the squadron (and the movie now making a splash with the upper crust of high society), convinced many in the United States to see the war, and American involvement, the way Kiffin saw it – that is, as a debt owed to France, invoked through the symbol of Lafayette.

One example of the change in public opinion occurred a few days before Kiffin's fourth victory. On September 6, 1916, many high-profile citizens gathered in New York and other American cities to celebrate the 159th anniversary of the birth of Lafayette. In New York, the Lafayette Day Citizens' Committee put on a ceremony that afternoon, and the France-America Society sponsored an elaborate dinner that evening. The guest of honor at both events was the French Ambassador to the United States, Jean Jules Jusserand, for whom the day was "a continuous ovation," as the *New York Sun* put it.[22]

The afternoon event took place in the aldermanic chamber at city hall, decorated with the tri-color and the Stars and Stripes. The first speaker, former Ambassador to France Robert Bacon, referred to the relations between America and France as a "perpetual alliance of two peoples evidenced ... by no scrap of paper, but inscribed in the hearts of every American."[23]

Dr. John Huston Finley, the New York Commissioner of Education also spoke. Pointing to the example of the volunteers in France, Finley asserted that "one cannot doubt that the spirit of Lafayette is among our youth." He then declared:

But our supreme task is to make that spirit universal, as it is in France today, to stir our youth to see that here we have the glorious thing for which Lafayette offered and risked his all, and to make every youth ready and willing to give his all for 'this glorious thing.'[24]

More than eight hundred prominent guests attended the dinner held that night at the Waldorf-Astoria. Throughout the evening, the fates of France and America were implicitly linked, not least by the imagery of the French and American flags which hung side by side on the speakers' platform and around the great room. A great wave of applause several minutes long greeted Ambassador Jusserand as he took the stage. Here is a part of what he said:

If there is among the virtues of the American people one which cannot be contested, it is her gratitude, the pleasure she takes in being grateful.... No tokens of friendship, of sympathy, of good will, have touched France more deeply than those coming from this Republic, which persists in remembering Lafayette and his companions. Under very many forms American citizens have shown what they feel for the old ally. Their approval, eloquently worded, has been for us a comfort! Americans understand that what is at stake is that same question of independence for a nation, of freedom for citizens, for which our common ancestors had fought in the same fight. They took pride in seeing that to make a good stand, to arrest the invader, to act unanimously with a single purpose, men needed no autocratic organizations holding them together. The love of country, the attachment to sound principles, is between them the strongest of ties.

Referencing those serving in the ambulances, battlefields and trenches, and of course "the plucky aviators," Jusserand then expressed the gratitude of his own country for the actions of the American boys fighting in her behalf:

Never in my country will the American volunteers of the great war be forgotten.... Serving in the ambulances, serving in the Legion, serving in the air, serving liberty, obeying the same impulses as those which brought Lafayette to these shores, many young Americans, leaving family and home, have offered to France their lives. Those lives many have lost, and never was there shown such abnegation and generosity, such firmness of character as that of men like Victor Chapman who died to rescue his American and French co-aviators.... America has shown tonight that she does not forget; France will show she remembers.[25]

Many Americans in Paris also celebrated Lafayette's birthday. Professor Mark Baldwin spoke on behalf of the American colony before a gathering of many prominent French and American citizens at the *Maison de Balzac*. To great applause, Professor Baldwin spoke of the many young American volunteers fighting in the ranks of the French army, expressing "the hope that out of their number would emerge a hero whose prowess would repay the debt which America owes to France for the deeds performed by her glorious son Lafayette."[26]

That hope was about to be fulfilled.

Chapter Fifty-four

The blow has fallen again and Kiffin has gone.

The American Squadron arrived together in Paris on September 11. Rather unsentimentally, Hall said, "We packed our stuff in a motor truck, gathered up 'Fram' – Captain Thénault's police-dog – and that was the end of our stay at Bar-le-Duc."[1] Freed from the pressures of the front, all the boys were relaxed and joking on the train ride, and by the time they arrived in Paris, the entire corps was ready for a good time. Jim McConnell was still in the hospital at Vitry-le-François, but the rest of the squadron was turned loose in Paris.

According to Thénault, the men viewed the trip as a "great favour" and everyone thought it "a piece of wonderful luck" to be together in the city they loved.[2] As he explained it:

Think how different was Paris from the spectacle we were accustomed to see. No more butchery, no horrors, but among the yellowing chestnut trees of the Tuileries, *the Autumn sun gilding the marbles, while in the Avenue spanned by the* Arc-de-Triomphe, *carriage after carriage sped swiftly by.*[3]

Kiffin was in high spirits. To a friend in Atlanta, he declared that "the war is running along well for us," and that "every day the allies are growing stronger, every day the *boches* are weaker."[4] Kiffin had several personal reasons to be positive – not only had he brought down another German flyer, but Thénault had proposed him for second lieutenant for his work.[5] Kiffin told his mother the good news a few days after they arrived:

Well, I am in Paris again. We stayed at Bar-le-Duc a week longer than we expected but I didn't mind it, as last Saturday morning I brought down a German machine in their first line of trenches. I have been proposed for sous-lieutenant for having done it and am well pleased.[6]

While all the men had visited Paris individually or in small groups, this was the first time the entire *escadrille* had been there all at once. The simultaneous leave was welcomed by all and went some distance toward shoring up the diminished morale of the unit. Given the favorable notice taken of them everywhere they went, the American aviators must have felt like gods as they strolled the boulevards and visited the cafés and theatres.

The purchase of a fierce new mascot further strengthened the *esprit de corps* among the men. The day after their arrival in Paris, one of the boys saw an ad in the *New York Herald* for a four-month old lion cub and had the brilliant idea to get it to take the place of Thaw's police dog, which had recently died of pneumonia.[7] Thaw, Hall, Hill, Johnson and Kiffin all chipped in to buy the animal, which they named "Whiskey."[8]

The cub was supposedly born in the port of Marseilles, its mother belonging to a lion tamer on his way to America. Its direct provenance, however, was from a Brazilian dentist, who sold it because its cries disturbed his clients. They also disturbed Mrs. Weeks' cook, who was nearly frightened to death by its roar when the boys brought the lion back to the apartment.[9] However, Whiskey proved to be quite tame and drank milk from a bottle – eight quarts daily.[10] As one might guess given the name they chose for it, the lion cub was not the only one drinking from a bottle – the boys were regulars in the Hotel Chatham and the New York Bar, and brought Whiskey along on their excursions.[11]

The little beast proved very popular and, according to Paul, "got pretty well acquainted with the city" during the squadron's time in Paris.[12] Even before the week was out, the press took note of the Americans' new pet:

The cub has been bought by the American Aviation Squadrilla as a mascot and has been equipped with a gorgeous suit of dog harness. It is a jolly little cuss, playful as a kitten, and romps about with a couple of dogs, which have already become its inseparable companions. It is the intention of its owners to take the cub out to the front, where it will certainly run the risk of being killed with kindness – to say nothing of the shells. In the meantime, it is being introduced to Paris, and already knows the Bois de Boulogne *and not a few bars – not cage bars, but those where tea and other drugs are dispensed.*[13]

Speaking of the press, one day near the end of their visit Kiffin had lunch with Paul Scott Mowrer, a reporter and friend of Paul's at the *Chicago Daily News*. Kiffin said little until the conversation turned to air fighting. As Mowrer later related:

Finally, we spoke of death, and I remarked: 'The man who enters this war should consider himself dead from that moment. Every day thereafter that he lives should be accounted as so much good luck – as so much to be grateful for.'

Rockwell made no answer but looked me straight in the eyes with his mysterious smile. This man did not fear death, for he had faced it too often. He was brave among the brave and besides he loved the cause – the cause of France, which for him was the cause of all mankind.[14]

* * * * *

Rumor had it that the squadron would be sent back to Luxeuil but, expecting little activity there, Kiffin instead hoped for the Somme, where a major battle was still raging.[15] The rest of the squadron felt the same, and all the men were slightly let down a few days into their leave when the rumor was confirmed – Luxeuil it was.[16]

Mrs. Weeks had been away, traveling in London, and upon her return was pleased to find Kiffin and Skipper Pavelka staying at her home with Paul. In a letter to her brother, one can hear her delight at seeing her favorite pilot:

I am home again and so happy to be. I found Kiffin and Pavelka both here on their way to Luxeuil.... Kiffin has brought down another German machine, and has another palm, and has been made Sous-Lieutenant, and now I have to be very polite to him.[17]

The day before they left, Bill Thaw came by to take the group on a tour of the Nieuport factory and testing grounds at Issy-les-Moulineaux. The boys were quite impressed with the Nieuport 17s, which were rapidly replacing the *bébé* as the machine of choice for *chasse* pilots at the front. Kiffin could hardly wait to try out his own new model – in addition to the standard Lewis gun mounted on the top wing, it carried a Vickers machine gun synchronized to fire through the propeller.[18] With firepower like that (Kiffin must have thought), he would get his fifth victory and become an "ace" in no time.

Knowing they were leaving early to make the train the next morning, that night Mrs. Weeks set an alarm for six o'clock. But instead of sleeping, she worried all night that Kiffin was again headed for the front. Finally, unable to sleep, at four o'clock she got up and made breakfast for the boys. Afterward, she gave Kiffin a kiss and watched as he and Skipper drove off in a taxi with Paul, who accompanied the group to the train station. Exhausted but happy, Mrs. Weeks "went to bed and had a good sleep."[19]

On Sunday morning, September 17, a little party gathered on the platform at the *Gare de L'Est*, waiting for the train to Luxeuil. In addition to the "newsman" Paul, the group included the following aviators: Kiffin, Paul Pavelka,

Didier Masson, Raoul Lufbery, and one brand new pilot – Robert Rockwell, who had just been assigned to the squadron.[20] Rockwell was from Cincinnati and had recently completed his flight training at Pau. A distant cousin of Paul and Kiffin, Rockwell soon picked up the nickname "Doc," as he had attended medical school at New York University prior to coming to France.[21]

As the men boarded the train, Paul's face must have shown his disappointment at again being separated, for Kiffin felt the need to lighten his spirits. "Cheer up," he said as he shook Paul's hand and bid him farewell. "I'll be back again soon on permission."[22]

It was the last time Paul would see his little brother alive.

* * * * *

Although they would have preferred to go to the Somme, the other squadron members also began making their way to Luxeuil. Well, all except Thaw, who had been thrown off his train while trying to pass off Whiskey as an "African dog." Betrayed by the little lion's roars, Thaw failed to convince the stationmaster to allow Whiskey to remain in the coach and had to wait in Paris while a strong cage was made.[23]

Their new planes had not yet come in, so the arriving pilots spent the next day or two speculating about the rumored "great mission" for which Captain Happe had again summoned the Americans to Luxeuil.[24] In addition, the men got to know the bomber pilots from the British Royal Naval Air Service now sharing the airfield – mostly Canadians and, according to Pavelka, "just like Americans."[25]

This being their second time in Luxeuil, Kiffin, Prince, and Hall showed the rest of the squadron around the lovely resort town. One of the newcomers wrote that they were "all in one hotel and everything is fine as to grub, service, loafing, etc."[26] Rather than the villas at the baths, Kiffin and the others were staying at the *Hotel Pomme d'Or* where, as he told Jim McConnell, the food was even "better and cheaper than at the *Lion Vert*."[27]

On September 19, a convoy of cars sent from the *RGA* rolled into Luxeuil, bringing six 110-horsepower Nieuport 17s.[28] The new single-seat planes could rise to seven thousand feet in just six minutes. As there were not enough to go around, Thénault parceled them out by rank and seniority; Kiffin was assigned machine number 1811.[29] The next day, Kiffin's twenty-fourth birthday, he wrote Paul:

I have gotten my machine, which is the best they have, and have it fixed
up with two machine guns. But I don't expect much work here, as I fear the
weather is going to be bad most of the time. I found a number of people glad
to see me back, and think that I can get along all right if we are forced to stay
here for the winter.[30]

As the mechanics unpacked and assembled the planes over the next two
days, they realized they had received only two cartridge belts for the Vickers
machine guns. As Kiffin and Lufbery were the leading pilots, they exercised
first claim on the ammunition and immediately wanted to take to the air to try
out their new synchronized weapons. As Thénault noted, "think of restraining
fanatics like Lufbery or Rockwell when they had at their disposal superb new
machines, fitted with the latest devices."[31] The two friends went on patrol
together on both the morning and afternoon of September 22, each time
drawing heavy anti-aircraft fire over Mulhouse.[32]

That night, some of the pilots got together for dinner. When, somehow or
another, the discussion came around to death, Kiffin stated that "should he be
killed and have the good fortune to fall within our lines, he wanted to be buried
where he fell."[33] In such a case, he said, the others should use any money found
on him "to drink to the destruction of the Germans."[34]

* * * * *

Perhaps affected by Kiffin's comments the night before, the next morning
one of the men – probably Kiffin's mechanic, Michel – begged Kiffin so sincerely
not to go up that he nearly convinced him to stay on the ground. But after
hesitating a little, Kiffin decided he was going. With a strange little smile on his
face, he turned and walked to his plane.[35]

Once again, Kiffin and Lufbery were the only two pilots taking to the air.
Together they climbed through the eastern sky towards Hartmannswillerkopf,
where Kiffin had earned his first victory four months earlier. Both pilots were
surely thrilled when they spotted a patrol of three Fokkers coming up to meet
them. Signaling one another, Kiffin and "Luf" each picked out an adversary and
swooped towards it. Unfortunately, during the attack Lufbery's new machine
gun immediately jammed, and he took three bullets in his cowling before
disengaging. Forced to beat a hasty retreat, Lufbery swung around towards
Belfort before descending at Fontaine where *Escadrille N.49* was stationed.[36]

After following Lufbery to Fontaine, Kiffin turned back toward the lines alone. As he again approached "Old Armand," as the *poilus* called Hartmannswillerkopf, he came upon a single Aviatik two-seater, flying just below him at about three thousand meters on the French side of the lines. Without hesitation, Kiffin dove straight at the German plane.

As Kiffin rapidly closed the distance between himself and the enemy machine, the German tailgunner began hammering away with his machine gun. Paying no heed to the bullets, Kiffin headed directly for his opponent, firing only as it appeared the two planes would collide. Pavelka later told McConnell that Kiffin came so close to the German it "was a case of one or the other," and a French captain who watched the fight through his field glasses said that Kiffin "flew so close to the Hun machine" he feared a collision.[37]

The planes exchanged several volleys, and for a moment the field officer thought the German had been hit. But then the French machine tilted and plunged towards the earth. The watching officer later told Paul:

One wing was torn off in the speed of the descent and drifted sideways ... on the breeze, while the aeroplane itself ... dropped like a stone and struck near a little wood just behind the lines.[38]

It turned out that Kiffin had been hit in the right breast by an explosive bullet, leaving a hole about the size of the bottom of a large glass.[39] His machine fell on its nose and dropped through the sky. Kiffin was dead long before it slammed to earth in a crocus-covered meadow just outside Roderen.

Several French infantry soldiers who had witnessed the battle recovered Kiffin's body, which they would return to Luxeuil later that evening, draped in the French flag.[40] In the meantime, they phoned in a report of Kiffin's death to the aerodrome. Upon receiving the call, their shaken captain gathered the pilots together to tell them the awful news. Bert Hall later gave this account of Thénault's words to the assembled men:

'Mes enfants, *boys – gentlemen – boys – it's Kiffin. Kiffin. He's dead –* hors de combat.' *And, by God, he had tears in his voice.*[41]

* * * * *

Thénault also passed along the tragic report to Thaw, who was still in Paris and immediately went to break the sad news to Mrs. Weeks. Of course, she was devastated. She wrote her brother:

The blow has fallen again and Kiffin has gone. Lieutenant Thaw came for me. We had to find Paul to tell him, and, well what can I say.[42]

Although Mrs. Weeks left it unstated, the news of Kiffin's death also hit Paul very hard. He confided to a friend, "I could not have had a harder blow than losing Kiffin...."[43] In letters he wrote not long after, one can hear both the awful grief and the great pride Paul felt:

No one ever had a dearer brother and truer friend than I had, and when Kiffin fell, something went out of my life that can never return in this world. But Kiffin went so bravely and so willingly for what he knew to be right, that I can only attempt to bear his loss with a courage worthy of him. His life was full of fine deeds, if not of long years, and since Fate willed that he die young, I am glad that it was fighting for France and humanity that he met his death.[44]

He loved life and had more to live for than anyone I knew. Yet he was an idealist and willing to die for what he knew was just. I miss him greatly, but I am proud of his life and proud of his death. A braver, more unselfish and more self-sacrificing man than Kiffin never lived.... He is gone from me, but I hope to live the battle of life well enough to merit, at the end, the paradise reserved for such as Kiffin. He was so brave and fine that perhaps some of his heroism will help me.[45]

The news also distressed others close to Kiffin. Pavelka wrote a pal back home of the death of "one of my best friends, Kiffin Y. Rockwell." He continued:

He was one of the noblest and most courageous men I have met in my life. I learned to admire and love him from the time we first met each other in the Légion Étrangére. He did a great many things for me, especially while I was lying wounded in the hospital at Nogent-le-Rotreu. His kindness, as well as that of his brother, I shall never forget, and his name and memory will always be honored by me, as well as by other American volunteers who are fighting in France. Of course, we get so that we expect tragedies – that is War. Nonetheless, it does not make them any easier to bear, and when it is a fellow like Kiffin, it hits us hard. To me he is a great loss, and I am sure he is also a great loss to the escadrille and the cause.[46]

Even Billy Thorin, the rough-hewn soldier from South Dakota was affected. He told Mrs. Weeks he couldn't help feeling sorry, "because it ain't every day you meet fellows like Kiffin." Still, he was proud that "like a man" his fallen friend had "done his duty."[47] The anguished Thorin surely spoke for many when he wrote: "Kiffin was a good boy, one of the best."[48]

Chapter Fifty-five

We all loved him and admired him.

Kiffin's death greatly affected his comrades in N.124, as shown by the letters they wrote after learning the news. One pilot (probably Chouteau Johnson or Dudley Hill), wrote a friend that Kiffin "was a man in every sense of the word," and declared that "If France were made up of Rockwells this war would have been over the day it started."[1] Skipper Pavelka told Mrs. Weeks his "heart [was] breaking," and wrote McConnell, "God almighty! Jim, I feel terribly broken up about Kiffin's death."[2] McConnell himself later wrote, "No greater blow could have befallen the *escadrille*. Kiffin was its soul."[3]

All the men wanted to even the score, but half the squadron still lacked machines and no one besides Lufbery even had bullets! A frustrated Pavelka wondered, "How in hell can we avenge Kiffin under such circumstances? Five machines for twelve pilots, and only a few cartridges."[4]

Seeking revenge with the squadron's last 100 rounds of ammunition, Lufbery took to the skies alone on September 24. Once again, he drew anti-aircraft fire over Mulhouse, but failed to find any German machines. Along with Prince, Lieutenant de Laage, and Thaw (who had accompanied Paul back to Luxeuil), Lufbery went up again the next morning.[5] But none of the men spotted any Germans before they had to return to earth to finish preparations for Kiffin's funeral, which was set to take place at 10:00 a.m.[6]

The funeral was a grand thing, worthy of a general. Along with an honor guard provided by a regiment of territorials and a battalion of *Chasseurs Alpins*, France's elite mountain corps, the procession turned out much of the civilian and military population of Luxeuil.[7] Many of the townsfolk donated flowers to decorate Kiffin's bier, and dozens of French and British soldiers and pilots marched with his American comrades behind the horse-drawn caisson that bore Kiffin to the cemetery directly up the hill behind the *Lion Vert*.

Upon reaching the place, the mourners gathered round the freshly-dug grave, decked with flowers and wreaths. There, the silent crowd stood with bowed heads before Kiffin's coffin, draped with a large French flag on which were pinned his military medals. It fell to Captain Thénault to deliver a tribute. Among his words were these:

Here, by this tomb so soon to be closed, we meet today to pay our final respects to our comrade.... [Kiffin] was a great soldier with a high sense of duty. This he accomplished simply and valiantly, without boasting and without ambition. 'I am paying my part of our debt to Lafayette and Rochambeau,' he would say. He gave himself to France, and for France he sacrificed himself. ... Glory be to him who fell nobly in the pursuit of his dream of love and justice. He met the death he so desired.[8]

Thénault concluded his eulogy with this sentiment:

And to thee, our best friend, in the name of France I bid thee a last farewell. In the name of thy comrades, who have so often proved that they know how to keep their promise, I salute thee reverentially. And with the memory of those who have fallen, and whom we here invoke, we swear faithfully to guard thy memory and to avenge it.[9]

Reflecting on his speech, the captain said he "could give no higher praise than to tell simply what [Kiffin] had done."[10] Just after the funeral, Thénault told a French reporter he had "never known a better pilot, a braver soldier, or a more generous and frank nature." Lieutenant de Laage also praised his fallen American friend, stating that "Kiffin did not know the meaning of danger and fear.... We all loved him and admired him."[11]

* * * * *

Poor Jim McConnell was still laid up in Vitry-le-François and did not learn of Kiffin's death until he read about it in the paper the morning of the funeral.[12] Immediately he wrote Mrs. Weeks, telling her that "[w]ith Kenneth, Victor and Kiffin gone, I feel ashamed of myself for living."[13] After begging for and receiving a convalescent leave, a few days after the funeral Mac came to Paris to stay with Paul and Mrs. Weeks, to whom he confided, "[t]his new sorrow makes it hard for me to be alone."[14] Paul later wrote that he, Jim and Kiffin "had been just like three brothers over here, and I think Jim grieved over Kiffin's death as deeply as I."[15]

In Luxeuil, Norman Prince reconciled with the lone remaining Rockwell brother. Pavelka told McConnell that Prince had apologized to Paul, whose "kind heart forgave him for all the injustice that he had done."[16] On behalf of the entire squadron, after the funeral Prince wrote Mrs. Weeks a note telling her that Kiffin "was buried today in the way he had wished to be.... He died like a hero and was given the burial of a French hero."[17]

Then, remembering Kiffin's desire that they use his money to drink to the destruction of the Germans, his fellow flyers solemnly did so while swearing an oath of vengeance. In fact, the boys went a step further, and resolved to commemorate Kiffin on an ongoing basis. A reporter at the *Chicago Daily News*, who must have learned of it directly from Paul, described the *escadrille's* decision like this:

A bottle of old bourbon whiskey, which had been given Rockwell by an American in Paris, will be opened hereafter when members of the squadron bring down Germans. On these occasions a few drops will be poured out for the victor in honor of Rockwell's memory and then the bottle will be resealed.[18]

The day after the funeral, Thénault drove Paul and a few of the others out to see where Kiffin fell. The crew of the .75 battery that had recovered his body had already placed a wooden cross on the spot, giving physical form to the wartime idiom that a dead man had "gotten the wooden cross." Kiffin's machine had already been taken away, but they found bits of the propeller strewn about, and the deep hole where the plane's motor had embedded itself. There were also pieces of the canvas canopy, most of which, according to Pavelka, were covered by Kiffin's blood.[19]

Kiffin had fallen in a little meadow of a beautiful valley, overlaid with blooming purple crocuses.[20] Upon seeing the scene, Paul was quite overcome – to remember the place, he pressed a few of the flowers between the pages of a book. He later told a friend there was "no lovelier spot in the world."[21]

Hoping to lighten the mood on the way back to Luxeuil, Thénault decided to take the scenic route through the mountains. Around noon he stopped at the crest of the *Ballon d'Alsace*, where the men ate their lunch at the foot of the beautiful monument to Joan of Arc. Recalling this day, Thénault later wrote:

Our hearts were very heavy, but nature all around us was full of life and sunshine and during so pitiless a war one had to force one's self to give way to sorrow.[22]

* * * * *

When Paul returned to Paris a few days later, he found many notes of sympathy and condolence waiting for him. He and Kiffin's old legion comrades Jack Casey, Charles Trinkard and Edgar Bouligny signed one that said, "we are using this note to carry our expressions of grief and heartfelt sorrow to you and your family, for a fine brave boy, lost to us forever."[23] Trinkard also wrote a separate letter, saying "I know the sad news about Kiffin. I hope you'll bear it bravely. Kiffin died heroically, I only wish my finish'll be the same." He closed with words to which so many had been forced to cling during the two long years of war: "Courage and Hope."[24]

Laurence Scanlan, Kiffin's friend from the *1st Regiment Étranger*, wrote Paul from his hospital bed that Kiffin had met "a fine death, a death we would all be proud to meet in a cause that is dear to us all."[25] An American aviator still in flight training asked: "Could one who has shown all of us what it is to live like a man and a gentleman, die in a more noble or glorious way?"[26]

There was also a letter from Edmond Genet, the young sailor who had deserted the United States Navy to come fight for France. "Try to brighten up, dear Paul. Your brother has found a glorious end – a soldier's death," he wrote.[27] When Genet himself died the next year, Paul's words to Genet's mother doubtless reflected his thoughts following the death of Kiffin. He wrote:

I think that one enters eternity with the same force and strength that one quits this world with, and that one falling in battle in the full bloom of youth and energy has a better place in the next world than those who linger here and die of illness or age. Anyhow, I would change places with any one of the boys who have died so gallantly.[28]

Judging by that last line, Paul must have felt a touch of guilt knowing he lived while his little brother died. Not long after Kiffin's death, he had written to a friend in Atlanta:

Kiffin's death has hit me hard, yet I know that he fell as he wished, facing the enemy of civilization. Kiffin was an idealist and he was ready and willing to die for the cause he knew to be just. For me, I find it harder to live than it would be to die, now that he has gone and I cannot take up arms again. Yet we must all face life the best we can, no matter how hard fate is. I have much to console me in the knowledge that Kiffin did not fail his fellowman in the greatest crisis the world has ever known.[29]

On October 5, Paul received another expression of sympathy, cabled from the United States by John Jay Chapman. The telegram read: "Victor's soul is but a little way above [Kiffin's] head and stays for his to keep him company."[30]

In response, Paul told Mr. Chapman that he took comfort in his conviction that Kiffin and Victor were "together where the good soldiers of this life go."[31]

End of Part Three

Kiffin in December 1915, as a member of the air guard of Paris. Image from the State Archives of North Carolina.

Alice Weeks and Kiffin, probably at Le Bourget Field around December 1915. Image courtesy of Washington and Lee University.

(left to right) Norman Prince, Elliott Cowdin and William Thaw on the deck of the Rotterdam, December 23, 1915. Image from the George Grantham Bain Collection in the Library of Congress.

The original members of the Escadrille Américaine: left to right, Victor Chapman, Elliott Cowdin, Bert Hall, William Thaw, Georges Thénault, Alfred de Laage de Meux, Norman Prince, Kiffin Rockwell and James McConnell, in Luxeuil, May 1916. Image courtesy of Washington and Lee University.

(left to right) James McConnell, Victor Chapman, Madame Vosges and Kiffin Rockwell, Luxeuil, April or May 1916. Image courtesy of Washington and Lee University.

The so-called "tragic" photo, as all four Americans in it died in France. Left to right, James McConnell, Kiffin Rockwell, Georges Thénault, Norman Prince and Victor Chapman. Victor apologized to his mother for wearing an old uniform. Image courtesy of Washington and Lee University.

(left to right) H. Clyde Balsley, Raoul Lufbery, James McConnell and Norman Prince.
Taken in Bar-le-Duc, June 1916. Image courtesy of Washington and Lee University.

James McConnell, approximately June 1916. Image from the State Archives of North Carolina.

Victor Chapman, approximately June 1916. Image part of Bob Ford personal collection

Norman Prince, around the time he qualified for his original aero license in August 1911. Photo illustruation by Eleni Trapp from a photograph printed on the front page of The Boston Daily Globe, August 29, 1911.

Paul Pavelka, circa August 1916. Image from the State Archives of North Carolina.

Norman Prince is on the far left of this photograph, while Didier Masson is on the far right. The guy in the middle with all the medals is Charles Nungesser. This picture was likely taken in Bar-le-Duc in July 1916. Image courtesy of Washington and Lee University.

Raoul Lufbery. Unfortunately, I cannot pinpoint the provenance of this photograph.

Kiffin was wearing this uniform when he was shot down and was buried in it. This photograph was taken on August 28, 1916, while Kiffin was on leave in Paris. Image courtesy of Washington and Lee University.

Part Four – Lafayette, we are here!

"But you, young men, whose country was not threatened, whose lines were cast in peaceful labour, what brought you to the fields of battle? The voice of your dead makes reply: for reasons of sentiment, of honor, for the holiness of the cause."

- M. René Besnard, speech delivered at the Comedie Francaise, January 21, 1917.[1]

"Lafayette, we are here!"

- Colonel Charles E. Stanton, Picpus Cemetery, July 4, 1917.[2]

Chapter Fifty-six

I wish I had a dozen more Kiffins to give to my country and the cause of liberty!

In early September in North Carolina, all seemed to be going well for Loula Rockwell. Now spending most of her time in Winston-Salem, Loula had established a small practice and was preparing to speak at the upcoming state osteopathy conference. On September 14, the local paper ran an account of Kiffin's fourth victory, making sure to mention that he was Loula's son.[3] Then, the day before her famous son's twenty-fourth birthday, the same paper ran another article discussing the accolades and awards Kiffin was winning in France.[4]

The morning of September 23, Loula was delighted to receive a letter Kiffin had written three weeks earlier.[5] She smiled upon reading how her youngest had spent his eight-day leave in August with Paul and shared Kiffin's joy that Thénault had proposed him for another medal.[6] Just a few hours later, however, her life was changed forever by a telegram from Paris, sent by William Thaw. Its single sentence surely shattered Loula's heart:

Kiffin killed this morning aerial battle in Alsace.[7]

Overcome with grief, Loula hoped against hope that it was somehow a mistake. But the next day another cablegram from Paris arrived – this one was from Mrs. Weeks, who confirmed the terrible verdict in two words: "Great sympathy."[8]

* * * * *

Letters of condolence poured in from everywhere, both from those who knew Kiffin or Loula, and from a few who did not. Demonstrating how renowned Kiffin had become, one letter addressed only to "Mrs. Rockwell, The Aviator's Mother," made its way to Loula all the way from France. It was sent by a "very young French nurse," who had gotten to know Kiffin while he was recovering in the hospital at Rennes. She told Loula: "Perhaps it will help you to know that we French sympathise and do value to its fullest extent the noble sacrifice they make, those who give their life on our side, for the freedom of the world."[9]

Loula also received many sympathetic notes from Kiffin's associates and fraternity brothers, as well as from her own friends and relatives. One wrote "what a wonderful thing it must be to be the mother of a man of such courage. Even though this cup of bitterness is the price."[10] Another reminded her to "be most thankful that you believe in a future life where, in a short time ... we shall be reunited with those who have preceded us."[11]

Undoubtedly, Loula knew that she would see her youngest son again. Her preacher husband had once sermonized that although all would surely die, just as surely "the slumber of death will not last forever" – rather, resurrection morning would dawn at last, and "like Lazarus, we too must arise at the voice of the Lord...."[12]

Perhaps Loula took further comfort in a poem James had written before they were married. Called *Shall We Meet Again*, it surely brought her a measure of peace:

Must the parting last forever?
Shall we never meet again?
When we pass beyond the river,
Will our longings prove in vain?

Sweet the answer floateth downward,
From the distant pearly gate,
"Doubting heart press ever onward,
For your coming I await."

Ask no more, O heart that bleedeth,
Weep no more, O blinded eyes.
Answer comes to those that pleadeth,
"Ye shall meet beyond the skies."

O my heart, be still and listen,
Angels whisper through the air,
"Ye shall meet again in Heaven,
And shall live forever there."[13]

* * * * *

Having given his life for their cause, the French people honored Kiffin's sacrifice. Not long after an Atlanta businessman-turned-ambulance-driver returning from France noted that Kiffin "was a great hero" there, "and justly so. He is known throughout the nation."[14] Many important persons took note of his death. The French Ministry of Foreign Affairs cabled American Ambassador Sharp, regretting to inform him of the decease of Sergeant Rockwell who had "died for France."[15]

Ambassador Jusserand sent a telegram directly to Loula stating, "All France mourns with you. Your son will live forever in the hearts of the French people."[16] Loula also received a note from the Marchioness of Anglesey, Marjorie Paget, written from Paris: "Will you allow an unknown compatriot to offer her deepest sympathy for the loss of your splendid son. It must be some consolation to a mother to feel that her sorrow is shared by a grateful nation – and that she gave to the world for a glorious cause, a son whose name will live in history among those heroes who have died that France might live."[17]

On October 11, yet another memorial service was held in Paris, this time for Kiffin. It was a big deal, and the Minister of War was officially represented.[18] Although devastated, Mrs. Weeks put on a brave face and greeted Kiffin's fellow aviators who came to honor him.[19] Shortly after the ceremony, she confided she had "been through so much I feel numb."[20] As for Paul, he was pleased that Kiffin would "not soon be forgotten here in this land where brave men are honored and appreciated."[21]

* * * * *

Most of the letters Loula received recited words of encouragement, and many noted how Kiffin's noble sacrifice established a standard the rest of the nation would do well to follow. On a larger level, Kiffin's death further galvanized public opinion on the side of France and stirred many Americans to reflection on the role of their own country. Sympathetic words written by one of Loula's friends hint at the slow but certain ripening of American sentiment: "As this terrible struggle goes on, I feel more and more that deep, vital principles are involved which do not appear on the surface, and it is wonderful to know that here and there one of our own men has thrown himself in on the right side."[22]

John Jay Chapman had long advocated for further American involvement. Immediately after Kiffin's death, he sent Loula a telegram advising her to "take heart," as her dead son and the other American volunteers were "not only saving France they [were] saving the soul of this country."[23] According to

Chapman, these boys were "the spark that shows America is alive" and those "giving their lives in awakening their countrymen to the great truth couldn't be better employed." As a result of the very public sacrifices of his son Victor and Kiffin, Chapman hoped that more Americans would be willing "to take up the work."[24]

As Mr. Chapman hoped, beginning with the death of his son Victor and accelerating with the death of Kiffin, more American citizens sensed that the entry of the United States into the war was not a question of if, but when. And with this realization, people began to associate explicitly the sacrifice being made in the battlefields of France by American boys such as Kiffin with the invaluable assistance Lafayette had rendered their own nation generations earlier.

One of the earliest and best examples of this is "For Lafayette," an editorial written at the death of Kiffin, probably by W.A. Hildebrand, the editor of the *Greensboro News*. Hildebrand had at one time published the *Asheville Register*, and surely knew folks in Kiffin's adopted hometown. Published just two days after Kiffin's death, Hildebrand's piece glorifies the sacrifice made by Victor and Kiffin and is worth quoting at length:

Yesterday, only ordinary American boys, with little to distinguish them from the mass of their fellows; today they are legendary heroes of two nations. One stride through the opal gates has carried Rockwell into the company of ... Lafayette. He is a man transfigured from an ordinary North Carolina boy into a martyr of liberty in the eyes of the French, and into the coin in which we have paid for Lafayette in the eyes of his own countrymen.

There will be those who will assert that after all he was merely an adventurous youngster, whom love of excitement carried into the war. That is as it may be, but it is well to remember that so late as 140 years ago that was the spirit that was expected of every well-born youth; and their own countr[y] regarded the Frenchman ... whose memor[y] America honors as actuated by much the same motives. The fact remains that when he decided to fight it was France that Rockwell chose to fight for: and France cannot forget.

In years to come when old men who fought in the war of 1916 grope back in their memories for the outstanding incidents of the collision to which Verdun has given its name, they may forget how many thousands of guns were employed, they may forget the fury of the assaults, they may forget how many of their own countrymen lie buried on the field, but they will remember that among the dead were two young foreigners, come of their own free will out of democratic America to fight for democratic France. Living, Rockwell and Chapman were only two adventurous youths; dead, they are links that bind more closely the two greatest republics of the world. Living, they accomplished only microscopic things in the elemental struggle about them; dead, they have accomplished what all the kaiser's men and all the kaiser's guns in 25 months have not been able to do – they have made France bow her head.

Ah, well, they are gone – dead, and yet not mourned, indeed, not missed. For in their going they have left a thing infinitely greater than themselves – a tradition of heroic proportions that shall only increase as the years go by.[25]

* * * * *

By the time Hildebrand's editorial was reprinted in a local Asheville paper three days later, Loula was responding to another letter, its strangely slanted print its own poignant reminder of sacrifice. Zinovi Pechkoff, who had served with Kiffin's company in the Foreign Legion, had to write his condolences with his left hand, his right arm having been amputated at the shoulder following a wound received at Arras the same day Kiffin was shot through the thigh.

In his peculiar scrawl, Pechkoff told Loula that he had always seen Kiffin "at the height of the task and duty that he voluntarily put on himself," and assured her that every soldier would envy Kiffin's end – "a happy, heroic death while fighting with the awful foe." He closed his letter with this declaration:

The name of Kiffin Rockwell and of all the heroic and noble American volunteers will go far in history and proud may be every family who can say: my son fought for justice and civilization.[26]

Like many Americans, Loula's view of the war had changed in the two years it had persisted. In response to Pechkoff's letter, she referred to the cause for which her son had fought and died, the same cause to which she now dedicated herself:

Ah, yes, my great loss is all the greater because Kiffin was just the boy he was, but I am not rebellious. Just before going to the front last May with the American escadrille he wrote me these words – his last that referred to death – "If I die I want you to know that I have died as every man ought to die – fighting for what is right. I do not feel that I am fighting for France alone, but for the cause of all humanity – the greatest of all causes."

So my brave boy is gone, but he leaves a beautiful memory.[27]

Loula had long since embraced the righteous purpose underlying Kiffin's military service, and his death only solidified her own commitment to the cause of France – within a year, she would proudly declare: "I wish I had a dozen more Kiffins to give to my country and the cause of liberty!"[28]

Chapter Fifty-seven

The business of neutrality is over.

The 1916 presidential campaign proved to be a tight race, and as it entered the home stretch some observers believed that Justice Hughes might have gained the upper hand. The close contest provided good cover when President Wilson called his ambassador James W. Gerard back from Germany in late September. The story was that Gerard was to be of service in the remainder of the campaign, but in truth he carried an overture of peace from the German government.[1] Gerard's absence left his aide Joseph Clark Grew as the *Chargé d'Affaires*, in command of the embassy in Berlin.

Little did Grew know that the death of an American aviator in France was about to bring Germany to the brink of war against the United States. As Grew stated in a cable to Secretary of State Lansing:

The submarine question had appeared to be in abeyance and matters between the United States and Germany on a temporarily quiet footing when, on September 29th, came the unexpected anti-American outburst in the press, based on the report of the death of the American aviator Rockwell in the service of France.[2]

The "submarine question," as Grew called it, was shorthand for whether German submarines would ruthlessly attack and sink all ships supplying England, including even merchant ships or, in accordance with the *Sussex* pledge made to President Wilson less than five months earlier, provide sufficient warning and protection to passengers and crew of such vessels prior to sinking them.

For some time, much of the press in Germany had been pushing for a resumption of indiscriminate submarine warfare, including against commercial vessels, as the only sure means of bringing down England and defeating France. However, although a majority of the German public favored the effective reversal of the *Sussex* pledge, most realized the inherent danger in sinking neutral ships, and everyone was wary of drawing the United States into the ongoing conflict. But supporters of unrestricted submarine warfare among the German navy and admiralty staff were becoming increasingly vocal, calculating that any American mobilization would be too late to stop their expected quick victory on the Western Front.

Those advocating for the abandonment of the *Sussex* pledge saw in Kiffin's death an opportunity to further inflame German public opinion against America. Hoping to weaken the chancellor at an upcoming meeting of the Reichstag during which the "submarine question" was to be debated, at a daily press conference in late September a pro-reversal military representative forced the news of Kiffin's death past the German Foreign Office censors.

Thus, on the first day of the ambassador's absence from Berlin, Grew received a call from a frantic Associated Press correspondent, who told him: "You have a pretty scandal on your hands already."[3] The correspondent informed Grew that the German press, normally prevented by the powerful Foreign Office from printing anything which might tend to stir up public sentiment against the neutral United States, was intent on publicizing Kiffin's death as a way to highlight and condemn the participation of American aviators on the side of the French. Indeed, many German papers were about to use the information as the basis "for a virulent attack on the neutrality of the United States."[4]

* * * * *

Sure enough, "[p]ractically every newspaper in Germany came out with hostile editorials."[5] As reported by the *Chicago Tribune* a day later, with one voice the Berlin papers declared that "moderation in the use of Germany's undersea weapons merely serves to further American assistance to the entente allies in men and munitions."[6] As just one example, the *Lokal Anzeiger* had written:

With a naivete, which must appear astonishing even in a war which overturns ordinary conceptions of international law and neutrality, the Paris Matin announces that Aviator Rockwell, one of the best known of the American airmen, has fallen in an air battle. The Matin does not attempt to dispute the fact, long known to us, that at Verdun an aero troop under the name of American Aviation Squadron participates in the fighting....[7]

Not surprisingly, the American-manned squadron proved to be the primary focus of the Germans' ire. The military critic at one German daily denounced "the appearance of American aviators in the ranks of our enemies," while another paper declared that "the presence of Rockwell and others in camps of the enemy cannot be regarded as the acts of individuals," but was instead proof "that America sends its own citizens to European theaters of war to fight Germany."[8] Finally, in an article on Kiffin's death, the influential *Tageszeitung* proclaimed:

It is self-evident that this unneutral favor and support of our enemies cannot be permanently permitted by Germany. America itself cannot doubt that its conduct arouses universal indignation in Germany. We are convinced that the whole German nation is united in believing that just as the American deliveries of munitions laugh to scorn American assurances of humanity and love of peace, so this support of our enemies by American aviators constitutes an insult to neutrality.[9]

Sentiment in Berlin was certainly running high, and following this firestorm in the German press well informed persons in Germany "were of the opinion that a grave political crisis was impending."[10] Correctly surmising the political motive underlying the uproar over Kiffin's death, Grew "went immediately to the Foreign Office and told them that these attacks on the United States must cease[.]"[11] The chancellor and Foreign Office were themselves greatly perturbed "and took immediate steps to suppress all further comment in the press." The Chancellor even referred the matter to Kaiser Wilhelm himself.[12]

Notwithstanding these actions, at the beginning of October, the outlook was serious, and Grew fully expected the German navy to resume its prior policy of *rücksichtslos* (ruthless) submarine warfare, even against neutral commercial ships. He wrote Secretary of State Lansing on October 1:

The general attitude of the press together with confidential information received leads me to believe that an early resumption of indiscriminate submarine warfare is not unlikely. It is doubtful whether the Chancellor can continue to withstand the steadily increasing public sentiment in favor of such a step, in view of his increased weakness in the Reichstag.[13]

However, the government's muzzling of the press as well as some skillful political maneuvering by the Chancellor, caused the crisis to subside at least temporarily. The fragile nature of the German position maintaining the *Sussex* pledge was correctly described in a prescient cable Grew sent to Secretary of State Robert Lansing on October 16:

Whether the issue has been laid in abeyance indefinitely or whether it has been postponed merely for a certain period, say until after the Presidential elections in the United States, or longer, it is as yet impossible to ascertain.... I wish, however, to repeat what I have endeavored to indicate in my various confidential telegrams to the Department, that while the political outlook is for the present moment reassuring, there is no permanent security to be looked for in the situation [and] our government should therefore be fully prepared for an eventual resumption of the indiscriminate submarine warfare against commerce in violation of the rights of neutrals on the high-seas.[14]

* * * * *

Meanwhile in Luxeuil, Pavelka and Lufbery were surprised when they showed up at Kiffin's grave, intent on fixing it up, but found that "someone had beaten us to it." The boys asked the local florist, who told them of a mysterious woman, "a lady, who had come from Paris the day after the funeral, [and] left orders for him to take care of the grave, and to place cut flowers on it every week." He refused to tell them who she was, divulging only that "she was a cousin of Kiffin."[15]

Having received ammunition and a few more machines, the squadron had finally gotten to work. By the first week of October, de Laage, Lufbery, Prince, Masson and Thaw all had their own planes, and Bert Hall and Pavelka were taking turns on Thénault's machine while he was on leave in Biarritz. With Thénault on permission, Lieutenant de Laage was in charge and refused to let any of the men go out alone, as the sector had suddenly become much livelier.

On the morning of October 6, a *boche* plane was signaled and Pavelka and Thaw "went out to meet the scoundrel." Although the German pilot never came within range, finally getting off the ground helped Pavelka begin to "get back to myself again."[16] Prince went out later that day and was nearly shot down, "returning in a most miraculous manner," his lower right wing shot to pieces and one of the steel cabin supports cut in two.[17] Perhaps realizing how close he had come to joining Kiffin, Prince was uncharacteristically shaken up and stuttered as he explained that as he attacked one German plane another had fallen on him from behind.[18] It was a narrow scrape, to be sure.

A few days later, those still without their own machines went to Bar-le-Duc to pick up their Nieuports. Hall snagged a nice new one, but the others – Pavelka, Chute Johnson and Dudley Hill – ended up with the old 80-horsepower models.[19] Poor weather prevented their immediate return, so the four pilots were not in Luxeuil when the rest of the men finally learned the dangerous reason Captain Happe had summoned them to the Vosges sector – to fly protection for a huge bombing raid on the Mauser arms factory behind the lines in Oberndorf, Germany.

The N.124 pilots still in Luxeuil – Lieutenant de Laage, Didier Masson, Raoul Lufbery and Norman Prince – all took part in Happe's October 12 mission.[20] Unfortunately, the factory was more than 100 miles from Luxeuil, and the complicated operation did not go as smoothly as hoped. Although some of the bombers found their targets, the French side lost fifteen aircraft and twenty-one airmen that day.[21]

Prince, Masson and Lufbery fought valiantly, and each brought down a German foe during the lengthy sortie. However, by the time they returned to their forward station it was early evening and oil fires had to be lit on the airfield to help guide them down. Sadly, in the dim light Prince's landing gear caught on a utility cable, flipping him out of the cockpit and breaking both his legs.[22] Somehow a blood clot formed on his brain, and on October 15, with his brother Freddie and uncle Morton both by his bedside, Norman Prince, the founder and originator of the *escadrille*, passed.[23] Like Kiffin three weeks before, he had fallen one victory short of becoming an official "ace."

A few weeks later there was scarcely an American in Paris not present at Prince's memorial service, where it was reported that "the quantities of floral offerings, entwined with the Tri-color and Old Glory, were magnificent."[24] His devastated but proud father later wrote a friend that his son Norman had "fulfilled his task and duty by giving his life to the cause he loved."[25]

* * * * *

Despite the diplomatic assurances given to Grew by Berlin, it was becoming obvious to nearly everyone, including President Wilson, that sooner or later Germany meant to resume its policy of unrestricted submarine warfare.[26] Sensing that "he kept us out of war" might ultimately prove untrue, Wilson must have felt the need to tack away from his primary campaign slogan, which to many of his detractors sounded increasingly like moral cowardice or outright pacifism, rather than principled statesmanship.[27]

Less than two weeks after the death of Norman Prince, Wilson had his chance. In an address to the Women's City Club in Cincinnati, one of the strongest German communities in the country, the president startled the audience by declaring "this is the last war of the kind or of any kind that involves the world that the United States can keep out of." He continued:

I say that because I believe that the business of neutrality is over; not because I want it to be over, but I mean this, that war now has such a scale that the position of neutrals sooner or later becomes intolerable....[28]

While continuing to cling to the idealistic notion that he could bring the warring parties together before America was ever forced to choose a side, Wilson asserted that "the world's peace ought to be disturbed if the fundamental rights of humanity are invaded," and further that "America must hereafter be ready, as a member of the family of nations, to exert her whole force, moral and physical, to the assertion of those rights throughout the round globe."[29]

As his campaign neared the finish line, Wilson's statement that America's position as a neutral would, sooner or later, become intolerable was something of an admission against interest, likely made only because he suspected events inevitably would bear out that assertion. In any event, when President Wilson spoke the words "the business of neutrality is over," somewhere Kiffin heard them and smiled.[30]

Chapter Fifty-eight

There is no question about going to war. We are at war now.

Although due to the crackdown of the German government the furor in the Berlin press had abated, widespread sympathetic accounts elsewhere of the deaths of Kiffin Rockwell and Norman Prince led German diplomats to protest officially against the so-called American squadron, particularly its pilots' country of origin – the allegedly neutral United States.

Just before the election, the German complaints bore fruit. On November 2, the Associated Press reported from Washington:

The famous American aviation corps of the French army probably soon will lose its distinctive title as a result of protests to the State Department that use of the name is not compatible with American neutrality. There will be no formal exchanges on the subject, but the State Department will suggest informally to the French foreign office that mention of the 'American' corps in official communiques places this country in an embarrassing position. There is no doubt here that this point of view will be appreciated in Paris.[1]

One disgusted citizen who read the report in the *Tribune* was moved to write a letter to the editor. It read in part:

Till today I thought it impossible that as an American I could feel deeper humiliation than I did already. I was wrong.

On the front page of this morning's Tribune *I read that "the famous American Aviation Corps of the French army probably soon will lose its distinctive title as a result of protests to the State Department that the use of the name is not compatible with American neutrality."*

There is no doubt that Gallic esprit will appreciate this delicacy to the full. It will be appreciated here also. It will be appreciated by the parents of Victor Chapman and Kiffin Rockwell. It will be appreciated by Americans who have hitherto felt that on the battlefields of France something of the ignominy of the American name was being redeemed.

Sometimes a single incident, like a rocket, lights up a whole situation.[2]

Norman Prince's uncle Dr. Morton Prince had just returned to Boston when he got wind of what he viewed as the craven action of his government. In response, just three days before the election a still grieving and now angry Dr. Prince threw back at President Wilson his weak "too proud to fight" phrase and railed against so-called "hyphenated Americans":

Our Administration may be 'too proud to fight' for the honor of America and the rights of humanity, but those young men who have formed the 'American Aviation Corps' and those who have joined the British and French regiments in the trenches have shown that the American spirit still lives and that Americans as individuals are not 'too proud to fight' for democracy and the cause of mankind.

The name of 'American Aviation Corps' was granted by the French government at the request of the aviators themselves, who were inspired by the old American spirit. If in response to hyphenated Americans this name is now protested by our government, that failed to rise to the opportunity and prevent the violation of Belgium and throw its moral support against the advance of the Hun, it will make a most painful impression upon the friends of the United States in Europe.[3]

Despite this controversy, consistent with the request of the American diplomats, Thénault would soon receive orders changing the squadron's name to *Escadrille des Volontaires*.[4] But William Thaw, who had again returned to the states for another visit, denied the prior name was ever used at the front:

Americans with the French flying corps are called members of the American squadron in this country only, and consequently there was no need for the recent request by Washington that they be officially designated by another title. In France, this squadron is known as Escadrille N.124.[5]

It made little difference – according to McConnell, the new name "never had a chance to take."[6] Within a few weeks it was changed again, this time to something more appropriate – *L'Escadrille Lafayette.*[7]

* * * * *

The presidential election was held on November 7, 1916. Early reports gave the victory to Hughes, only to be followed by those confirming Wilson's narrow win. In fact, the outcome was not clear until two days after the election, when the results from California came in. Wilson defeated Hughes by less than four thousand votes in that state, and this made the difference – had California gone to Hughes, he would have pulled out a narrow victory in the electoral college. Once the results became clear, Loula wrote John Jay Chapman, telling him that although it had greatly upset her, she felt about the election as she did the war: "God is in the Heavens, and all is well."[8]

Not long after, the *New York Times* published a letter to the editor from a Connecticut reader. The letter writer referenced Kiffin's death and that of Harry Butters, an American killed while fighting with the British, before bitterly noting: "'He saved us from war' was not a satisfactory slogan for these noble young Americans."[9]

Assured of a second term, Wilson continued to hope for a negotiated end to the war. But while the American president nursed his dreams of mediating peace, the German shipyards were arming for war, building submarines at a clip of two per week. Unfortunately, the United States remained as unprepared as ever. On December 14, one of Wilson's closest advisors confided to his diary the following unflattering assessment:

He has had nearly three years in which to get the United States into a reasonable state of preparedness and we have done nothing. Neither the Army nor the Navy are in condition to meet an enemy of the class of Roumania, or Bulgaria provided they could reach us.... We have no air service, nor men to exploit it, and so it is down the list.[10]

A few days later, hoping to jumpstart some form of peace talks, Wilson sent a note to the warring nations asking that they state their terms for peace. But by the end of 1916, according to one scholar, the results of the president's peace diplomacy "appeared ... to be nil," and even he "could sense that his time was running out[.]"[11]

Indeed, on January 9, 1917, Wilson's time did run out. That day the German government decided to reinstitute its policy of unrestricted submarine warfare, although it did not inform Wilson for three more weeks. The next day, January 10, through the French the Allies rebuffed Wilson's December offer to state peace terms, instead asserting they were "determined, individually and collectively, to act with all their power and to consent to all sacrifices to bring to a victorious close a conflict upon which they are convinced not only their own safety and prosperity depend but also the future of civilization itself."[12]

The famous "Zimmermann telegram" was sent (and intercepted by the British) a short while later. While the British were trying to figure out what to do with the explosive note – in which Germany urged Mexico to make war on the United States and dangled Texas, New Mexico and Arizona in return – the German ambassador on January 31, 1917, bluntly informed the United States that beginning the next day, "[a]ll ships met within" the warzone, including neutrals going to and from England and France, "will be sunk."[13]

* * * * *

With the *Sussex* pledge in tatters, war with Germany was plainly visible on the horizon. Still Wilson stubbornly refused to accept that Germany meant what it said, and in a speech to Congress on February 3, he declared that "only overt acts on their part can make me believe it even now."[14] Thereafter, according to one prominent Wilson scholar, he "maneuvered in every way possible to stave off war."[15]

Another historian summarized what he called the "pathetic" quality of Wilson's "last stand against America's involvement in World War I":

While refusing to acknowledge to others, and probably to himself as well, that the end had come, he provided little reason for others to believe that America's intervention in the war might still somehow be avoided. Although the desultory diplomatic efforts of February were barren of results, Wilson clung desperately to convictions that the course of the war had suddenly and rudely shaken. Unwilling to abandon the views and the hopes of earlier months, he remained for a time unwilling to accept the measures a new reality demanded. It was a position that could not be sustained. "He does not mean to go to war," Henry Cabot Lodge wrote at the time to his friend Theodore Roosevelt, "but I think he is in the grip of events."[16]

A staff member of the British embassy in Washington put it even more bluntly, telling the permanent undersecretary at the British Foreign Office that Wilson was "the most agile pussy-footer ever made, and when any serious decision is taken, always tries to unload the responsibility on to someone else, and has been doing so this time again."[17]

But Germany's "overt acts" were piling up.[18] In February, German U-boats sank the Cunard-line *Laconia*, on which two American citizens died, as well as two American merchant ships. Then in mid-March, its submarines aroused tremendous anger when on three consecutive days they sank three more American ships – the steamer *Vigilancia*, the passenger ship *City of Memphis*, and the tanker *Illinois*.[19] Fifteen crew members on the *Vigilancia* drowned, including six Americans.[20]

The American press was apoplectic and wondered how much longer President Wilson could avert his eyes. "Is President Wilson still doubtful of Germany's sincerity in its submarine war against the United States?" asked the *New York Sun*. Like most Americans, the paper saw "the incidents of the last six weeks" as Germany's clear answer to what it called Wilson's "generous incredulity."[21]

An editorial in the *New York World* on March 19 spoke for many: "The facts must be accepted as they are," it solemnly asserted. "Without a declaration of war, Germany is making war on the United States."[22] That same morning the *Brooklyn Daily Eagle* intoned, "It is war pure and simple, war levied without a declaration, but none the less war directed coolly and deliberately against the people and Government of the United States."[23]

In a private conversation that afternoon, President Wilson lamented that he had "considered every loophole of escape and as fast as they were discovered Germany deliberately blocked them with some new outrage."[24] But a tipping point had been reached and even President Wilson could no longer avoid the truth – like it or not, America was at war.[25] Reluctantly, he advanced from April 16 to April 2 a special session of Congress to address that body "on grave questions of national policy."[26]

At a rally held in Madison Square Garden the night of March 22, Philadelphia lawyer George Wharton Pepper read a letter from Colonel Roosevelt labeling the actions of the Germans "overt acts of war, just as much as the fight at Lexington or the bombardment of Sumter." Roosevelt continued:

The nation which tamely submits to such conduct forfeits what should be its most precious possession, its own self-respect.... There is no question about 'going to war.' We are at war now. The only question is whether we shall make war valiantly or make war feebly.... Germany has made and is making war upon us. Let us face this as an accomplished fact, and ... teach those who assail us that they do so at their peril.[27]

* * * * *

Convinced that war was imminent, and trying to scare up an aviation corps, the United States War Department seized on an idea that would have made Frazier Curtis smile – they hoped to have certain of the American pilots then training in France or flying with the *Lafayette Escadrille* relieved of service there to accept commissions with the Aviation Section, Signal Officers Reserve

Corps. Upon their return to the United States, the aviators would serve as flight instructors for the neophyte American forces.

In internal discussions with the Adjutant General, H.P. McCain, Chief Signal Officer George O. Squier specifically inquired about thirteen American pilots – among them, Thaw, Lufbery, McConnell and Kiffin. He wrote:

The following Americans are now serving in France in the French Army aviation service. These men are highly trained aviators who have had a wonderful experience in flying under all conditions of war with the French Army. The experience that they have acquired would be of invaluable assistance to the Aviation Section of the Signal Corps in the development and training of military fliers for the United States Army[.][28]

McCain's response is interesting, as it shows that it was still an open question whether the men had lost their American citizenship as a result of their service to France:

The individuals in question may not desire to withdraw from their present activities and obligations for the purpose of becoming members of the Officers' Reserve Corps.

It has been held by the Judge Advocate General, under date of August 7, 1916, that to become eligible for appointment in the Officers' Reserve Corps, an applicant must become a citizen of the United States – which opinion would materially affect the men covered in the letter ... in case it is determined that due to swearing allegiance to a foreign power, they have forfeited their United States citizenship.

It is not believed desirable to attempt to ascertain the attitude of the French Government, as requested by the Chief Signal Officer, until the answer to the foregoing question regarding the men themselves is obtained.[29]

The fact that Kiffin was on the list of requested pilots shows that, unlike his countrymen, his government was not yet aware that Kiffin had died. But it didn't matter – he wouldn't have come home.

Chapter Fifty-nine

How impossible it is to put an end to a really fine life...

Not long after Prince's death, the *escadrille* was relocated to the Somme where, on November 11, Jim McConnell finally rejoined his comrades.[1] The squadron had undergone a marked change, what with Chapman, Kiffin and Prince all gone. Kiffin's death had left an especially large hole and McConnell immediately noticed the difference. In a letter to Mrs. Weeks, Mac confided that he was "quite lonely," and that it no longer seemed "like the *escadrille* now that Kiffin has gone. It has a very different atmosphere, if I can use the word."[2]

A reporter who had spent much time with the squadron also noticed the "great change" that had come over the group. In a November 12 article, he wrote: "The loss of Chapman and Rockwell and Prince has set its stamp on even the youngest and least experienced of them, and the frolicsome spirit has gone for good. They are all doing their duty doggedly, but it isn't fun any longer."[3]

Perhaps Paul was looking for a change, too, for he and his long-term fiancée Jeanne Leygues decided to marry. The civil ceremony took place on December 2 in the office of the mayor of the seventh district of Paris, and the religious ceremony followed on December 4 in the *Sainte-Clotilde* Basilica.[4] As they were still in mourning, other than the bride's family, just a few guests attended, including Mrs. Weeks, along with Herman Chatkoff and Fred Zinn, Paul's old friends from the legion.[5]

Jim McConnell made it back from the front and served as Paul's witness.[6] In a letter two weeks later, Mac thanked Paul for the gold cigarette case Paul had sent as a keepsake from the wedding, telling him he would "treasure it all my life and think of you, my best friend, whenever I use it."[7]

While Paul and his new wife honeymooned in the south of France at her family's estate, McConnell finished up *Flying for France*, a book about his experiences with the *escadrille*.[8] Although he and the others flew as much as the weather allowed, they fought the bitter cold more than the Germans. But even with limited flight time, Lufbery brought down his sixth official German on December 27, and had several other unofficial kills, while Pavelka also scored a probable victory.[9]

At their *dîner de Noël* on Christmas Day, McConnell noticed there were thirteen pilots seated around the table and commented to Lieutenant de Laage that, according to superstition, this unlucky number meant one of them would die within the year. "Well," replied the lieutenant, "it will hold good with this crowd, but, unfortunately, there will probably be more than one."[10]

* * * * *

On January 21, 1917, the *Comédie Française* paid tribute to the memory of the American volunteers who had died for France. The main speech was rendered by René Besnard, surrounded on stage by American volunteers seated around him in an arc. Among the aviators there were Thaw, McConnell, Lufbery and Chute Johnson, as well their former comrade H. Clyde Balsley, who received a big ovation from the crowd when, on crutches and wearing his aviation uniform with the *croix de guerre*, he hobbled to his place on the stage.[11]

Several former legionnaires were also seated behind Besnard, including Paul Rockwell, Charles Sweeny, George Casmeze and Herman Lincoln Chatkoff, the last of whom pronounced Besnard's speech "a dandy."[12] Besnard rendered high praise to those fallen Americans, declaring that "[t]heir undying heroism has united forever in a common grief all that is noblest and best in our two countries."[13] Following Besnard's oration, Eugène Silvain, dean of the *Comédie Française*, read in French Alan Seeger's poem "Champagne, 1914-15."[14]

The poem is wonderful. It ends with the dead poet's instructions to those seeking to honor the fallen soldiers, suggesting they do so "not so much with tears and flowers," but:

Rather when music on bright gatherings lays
Its tender spell, and joy is uppermost,
Be mindful of the men they were, and raise
Your glasses to them in one silent toast.

Drink to them – amorous of dear Earth as well,
They asked no tribute lovelier than this –
And in the wine that ripened where they fell,
Oh, frame your lips as though it were a kiss.[15]

When Paul learned of Germany's decision to resume unrestricted submarine warfare, he hoped the United States would at last take "stern action[.]"[16] McConnell happened to be on permission in Paris on February 3, living it up on the first royalty check for his book, when President Wilson broke off diplomatic relations with Germany.[17] Of course, he and Paul talked much about their desires to see their own country finally enter the war. Mac's views were no surprise – he wrote a friend in America that he could not "reconcile a break in diplomatic relations with a pacific attitude. Logically, war should follow. If a state has reason enough for a break it has cause enough for war."[18]

On the last night of his Paris leave, McConnell and Paul went to the home of a good friend. While waiting on coffee in the living room, the discussion turned to the deaths of Kiffin and Victor Chapman. The talk put McConnell in a reflective mood, and as he stood with his back to the fireplace, he said in a quiet voice: "Well, I suppose I'm the next one to go."[19]

Unfortunately, McConnell's prediction would come true. On March 19, while on a sortie over Ham he was hit and fell behind the German lines. Three days later, after the Germans had retreated, a French cavalry patrol found Mac's body lying beside the wreckage of his machine on the outskirts of Petit Detroit. The men made a rude coffin from the doors of a ruined dwelling and buried Mac off the side of the road.[20] After decorating the spot with French and American flags, as well as flowers, at the foot of his makeshift grave they placed Mac's mangled machine gun.[21]

According to Paul, the telegram announcing Jim's death "turn[ed] a knife in the cruel wound caused by the death of my own brother, Kiffin, which had not healed and never can heal." Still, he took some comfort knowing that his friend had died content, as he knew Mac's "love for France was stronger than his love for life...."[22] Paul had good reason to believe this – as he explained:

I looked through the diary that Jim had scrupulously written up every day since coming to France. He was thirty years old on March 14. The last sentence he wrote in the diary of his twenty-ninth year is: "This war may kill me but I have to thank it for much."[23]

* * * * *

Witty to the end, McConnell left a note to be read in the event of his death. "I have no religion and do not care for any service," he told his friends, but "[i]f the omission would embarrass you, I presume I could stand the performance."[24] Of course, his fellow pilots wanted to honor his memory, and so on the morning of April 2, Paris was again the scene of a memorial for a fallen American. Like the others before him, McConnell's service was held at the American Church on the *Avenue d'Alma.*

Everyone from Ambassador Sharp to French dignitaries and officials such as Jean Jules Jusserand was there, as well as nearly all the American aviators and ambulance men.[25] The American and French flags stood on opposite sides of the chancel, while lilacs, lilies and other flowers banked the steps and rails, stretching all the way into the aisles. According to one attendee, the bishop "delivered a magnificent speech."[26] Another said the bishop had thrilled the assembled congregation with the splendor of McConnell's sacrifice, and reminded them "how impossible it is to put an end to a really fine life...."[27]

After the service, a newly heartbroken Paul wrote to Mrs. Weeks, who was back in America raising money to assist her efforts in France. Lamenting that he "never had a better friend except Kiffin," Paul told Mrs. Weeks "I am glad you were not here when [Jim] was killed."[28] In America, Mrs. Weeks wrote a letter to the editor of the *Asheville Citizen,* which ended with these words about her favorite boys:

These men have done all they could for France, but they have done a greater thing for their own country in keeping the bonds between the two countries strong, and in not forgetting the debt we owed to France, without whose aid we might never have been. They are the proof, too, that our wings of idealism are not lost but clipped and their lives and glorious deaths are an example for us to follow.[29]

* * * * *

Within hours of McConnell's memorial service in Paris, night was falling in Washington, D.C. as President Wilson addressed a joint session of Congress. He informed the assembled legislators that the American people could no longer "suffer the most sacred rights of our nation and our people to be ignored or violated." He then set forth the purpose of his speech – to ask Congress to declare war:

With a profound sense of the solemn and even tragical character of the step I am taking and of the grave responsibilities which it involves, but in unhesitating obedience to what I deem my constitutional duty, I advise that the Congress declare the recent course of the Imperial German Government to be in fact, nothing less than war against the Government and people of the United States; that it formally accept the status of belligerency which has been thus thrust upon it, and that it take immediate steps, not only to put the country in a more thorough state of defense, but also to exert all its powers and employ all its resources to bring the Government of the German Empire to terms and end the war.

Two days later, the Senate voted overwhelmingly to declare war on Germany. Two days after that, on April 6, 1917, the House did likewise. America had officially entered the war.

On April 15, Edmond Genet, who had been on patrol with McConnell when he fell, wrote a letter to his mother, telling her that the American decision for war was "the crowning assurance for all of a sure and complete victory." He also described the tremendous change the declaration had brought about:

I got to Paris just a few days after war was declared, and what a change I found there! American flags were flying everywhere among those of the Allies, and everybody was feeling far brighter and more cheerful than I have ever seen them before. It was fine to see Old Glory waving everywhere, Mother. We've waited so long for it to fly over here and all Americans have had to be restrained before. Now it's entirely changed and all are happy and contented and hopeful. One can see that it has made a big moral impression on the French soldiers.[30]

Genet's plane went down the next day, making him the first American to die following the United States' declaration of war.[31]

Chapter Sixty

Vive l'Amerique!

Led by General John "Blackjack" Pershing, American troops began arriving in France in numbers in June of 1917, and on July 4 in Paris, the grateful nation extended its official welcome.

Anticipating the days' events, just after dawn large crowds began gathering on the streets of Paris and outside General Pershing's hotel at *73 Rue de Varenne*. Street hawkers were already doing a brisk business in tiny United States flags designed to be worn in buttonholes, and larger versions hung from nearly every window and building.[1] At precisely 8:30 a.m., a French military band in the hotel's courtyard played a fanfare that brought General Pershing out on his balcony to acknowledge the crowd. The band struck up *The Star-Spangled Banner*, at which the crowd all took off their hats and bowed their heads, while the military men present stood at attention and saluted.[2]

Soon a car arrived to take General Pershing the short distance to the *Hôtel des Invalides* where an impressive ceremony would take place. A large contingent of American soldiers was already assembled in the court of honor, having arrived in twenty motor trucks from the Latour-Mauborg barracks, where they had spent the previous night. French troops from the 237th division were also on hand, and the esplanade in front of the *Invalides* had been overrun with citizens and spectators.

A great cheer went up when President Poincare entered the courtyard, followed successively by Ambassador Sharp, Marshal Joseph Joffre, and other civil and military officials. But the greatest applause was reserved for General Pershing, as he walked to his place with General Augustin Dubail, the military governor of Paris. Once the officials were seated, the French military band again played *The Star-Spangled Banner*.[3]

After a review of the troops drawn up in square columns, representatives of the Society of the Cincinnati presented General Pershing two guidons of command, which had been embroidered by French and American women.

General Pershing was visibly moved by the tokens, and expressed thanks to the group, comprised of descendants of French officers who had fought for American independence under General Washington.[4]

At that point, the Reverend Samuel N. Watson of the American Church in Paris stepped forward to present to General Gustave Léon Niox, the director of the *Musée de l'Armée* at the *Invalides*, the banner carried by the first American volunteers in the Foreign Legion.

This was the same flag that had hung over the offices of the "American Volunteer Corps," that Alan Seeger and Rene Phelizot had carried down the *Avenue de l'Opera*, that had traveled with the men to Rouen, Toulouse and Craonnelle, and that Phelizot had raised up just before he died, proclaiming: "I am an American."

The flag had accompanied the Americans into the battle of Champagne in September 1915 and following America's declaration of war, had recently been brought to Paris and given to Reverend Watson with the hope that it might be given a place in the French military museum. It had last been in the *Invalides* on August 21, 1914, when the first little band of American volunteers had carried it there on the day of their enlistment. Now, nearly three years later, the flag was back in the court of honor.

All the American volunteers had been given 48-hours leave for the occasion, and most were on hand for the ceremony at the *Invalides*. In fact, further heightening the emotion of the affair, several men whose signatures appeared on the flag – including William Thaw, Frederick Zinn, Jack Casey, and Ferdinand Capdeveille – stood near Watson as he presented it to the French general.[5] Paul was there, too, and surely had tears in his eyes as he thought back to the day he and Kiffin had affixed their own signatures to the emblem. Then, they had been new recruits, preparing to leave Rouen for Toulouse. Now, Kiffin was dead, resting under the flags of both nations, as were several of their friends who had also signed that day – Alan Seeger, Dennis Dowd, and Rene Phelizot among them.

The crowd fell silent as Reverend Watson stepped forward. Being careful not to slight the newly-arrived American leader, he spoke first to General Pershing:

It is my privilege, General, as representing our American Legionnaires, those Americans who for the love of France and of Liberty entered the French Army in 1914, to present to France this flag, their flag and our flag. They were the pioneers of that great American Army which is coming following your lead as their General. And now they, the Advance Guard, are leaving to you and to your troops the task which they began so bravely; now your new Standard will replace their bullet-pierced flag; whilst theirs is confided to France whom they loved with deathless eagerness, and it will be guarded forever in that Shrine of the Nation, the Musée des Invalides.[6]

Then, turning to General Niox, Reverend Watson said:

Mon Général, it is my duty as well as an honour which I appreciate most deeply to bring you today, on behalf of a little group of my countrymen, this flag which they loved. They wrote their names on its bars of white, and they signed it with their blood. It was not their privilege to carry it with them as a battle flag [but] more than one of them was wounded, more than one of them was killed with this flag wrapped about his body. It was thus that our Stars and Stripes received their Baptism of Blood in this struggle for Right against Might. I beg that you will accept it in the name of France, and I ask that it may be placed where it will be a perpetual inspiration to those who follow on to be worthy of those who have gone before them to pay the eternal price of the Liberty of Nations.[7]

General Niox gratefully accepted the flag, and for a second or two there was an almost sacred stillness that washed over the crowd. Then the stirring chords of the *Marseillaise*, the only sound that could properly break such a silence, called the ceremony to a close.[8] As the columns of French and American troops, unified in solemn purpose, began their exit, that anthem surely sounded more beautiful, more righteous than it ever had before.

It must have been quite a moment. Shaking hands with General Pershing, a deeply affected Marshal Joffre repeated several times two words: "Beautiful ... unforgettable."[9] General Pershing was also impressed; he later recalled that no other occasion "was more significant or more clearly indicated that depth of French sentiment and affection for their old ally."[10]

* * * * *

One more visit was necessary to complete the occasion – the tomb of Lafayette at Picpus cemetery. And so, following behind their French hosts, the beaming khaki-clad soldiers proudly strode across the esplanade and the beautiful *Pont Alexandre III* to the *Place de la Concorde* before turning right on the *Rue de Rivoli*.[11]

Hundreds of thousands of cheering Parisians filled the sidewalks along the approximately eight-kilometer route. The Tuileries Gardens and other vantage points were all densely packed with men, women and children, while many more watched from windows, balconies and rooftops as the columns of marching Americans made their way through the city.[12] Along the way, not a few grateful citizens rushed forward to shake hands, toss flowers or march with the troops.[13] One Paris daily described the massive crowd, which was nearly mad with excitement:

With all their strength they shout their joy, their exultation, their intoxication! Never has the sky of Paris shuddered under such tremendous clamor! The air vibrates endlessly with a fantastic thunder of human voices, all of which utter the same cry: "Vive l'Amerique!"[14]

For many among the huge throng, the sight of the "Teddies," as they called the newly-arrived Americans, meant nothing less than a rebirth of hope.[15] In his memoirs, General Pershing fondly remembered the scene. He wrote:

The humbler folk of Paris seemed to look upon these few hundred of our stalwart fighting men as their real deliverance. Many children dropped on their knees in reverence as the flag with the stars and stripes went by. These stirring scenes conveyed vividly the emotions of a people to whom the outcome of the war had seemed all but hopeless.[16]

One American who had recently arrived in Paris en route to his aviation training walked alongside the soldiers from the *Place de la Concorde* to the *Hotel de Ville*. In a letter home, he told his family of the pandemonium surrounding the procession as it streamed through Paris:

I never saw such a demonstration. Everywhere were American flags. Everybody was yelling, jumping, and shouting all through the three hours' parade. French poilus *burst into the lines and took our boys by the arms, marching and singing with them. Women did the same, and all the women were weeping. Then they came to the* Hotel de Ville *and the "Star-Spangled Banner" was played. Every Frenchman, Englishman, Belgian, and American bared his head and silently stood at attention. The music stopped and for a few moments there was silence; then the crowds burst again into a tremendous cheer, and the parade went on to the tomb of Lafayette. Paris was wild, frantic. I never saw anything like it. They are crazy over the Americans. 'Vive l'Amerique!' seems to be still buzzing in my ears. I can't begin to describe the wonderful effect our declaration of war has had on the French. It has given them new courage. We came in at the psychological moment. France weeps for happiness; cheers for joy; rekindles her spirit and cries "Vive l'Amerique!"*[17]

* * * * *

Eventually General Pershing and the other dignitaries arrived at the high-walled cemetery, which was surrounded by and filled with several hundred American and French citizens. Adorned with the French and American flags, a small raised platform had been erected in front of Lafayette's grave, on which General Pershing and his staff officers gathered with "Papa" Joffre and other French officials.

After a few brief remarks, the time was turned over to the Americans. General Pershing had delegated the task of speaking to his aide, Colonel Charles E. Stanton, who stepped before the crowd. Although he spoke in English, judging by their wild cheers, the French immediately understood the now-famous line with which the colonel ended his speech:

America has joined forces with the Allied Powers, and what we have of blood and treasure are yours. Therefore, it is with loving pride we drape the colors in tribute of respect to this citizen of your great Republic, and here and now, in the shadow of the illustrious dead, we pledge our heart and our honor in carrying this war to successful issue. Lafayette, we are here![18]

Seeing the crowd's reaction and overcome with emotion from the day's events, Pershing – who had not intended to speak – took the stage and expressed gratitude for the reception Paris had given he and his men.[19] The general said:

I did not intend to speak today, but the occasion is rather overwhelming. No one could have attended the ceremony at the Invalides this morning and witnessed the touching scenes that occurred there, no one could have followed the procession from there to this cemetery and witnessed the enthusiasm with which our own troops were greeted without having a swelling of the heart, without having a feeling of pride to which he could not adequately give expression, in the fact that we have joined hands and arms side by side with France in the great struggle for liberty. It seems fitting that the entrance of our troops into this war should be made an occasion to celebrate or to commemorate the memory of the great patriot who set out from France to obtain our liberty. Today really marks the entrance of the United States into this war.[20]

By May of 1918, more than one million American troops were stationed in France; a good portion would take part in the Allied victories at Cantigny and Belleau Wood. That fall, led by General Pershing, hundreds of thousands of the American "doughboys" played a decisive role in the Battle of Saint-Mihiel and in the Meuse-Argonne offensive. On November 11, 1918, at the eleventh hour of the eleventh day of the eleventh month, the guns of war finally fell silent.

In America a few months after the end of the war, a new song was released that quickly grew in popularity. Titled "Lafayette We Are Here," its chorus went like this:

Lafayette, Lafayette, we've paid the debt we owed,
That we never could forget.
Our honor we upheld and we're now on the road,
So goodbye to your France, Lafayette.[21]

The End

This photograph shows Kiffin Rockwell's funeral procession entering the cemetery in Luxeuil, September 25, 1916. While not certain, the first line of men entering the cemetery appear to be Captain Thénault, Lieutenant de Laage de Meux, Paul Rockwell, Raoul Lufbery, William Thaw and Paul Pavelka. Image courtesy of Washington and Lee University.

Kiffin Rockwell's funeral procession passing through Luxeuil, September 25, 1916. I thank Beverly Leroy from iCare for permission to reprint the photograph.

Captain Thénault (right, back to camera) delivering his eulogy for Kiffin in the Luxeuil cemetery, September 25, 1916. Paul Rockwell is to Thénault's right, and William Thaw is on Paul's left. Image courtesy of Washington and Lee University.

Paul at Kiffin's crash site, September 26, 1916. I believe Chouteau Johnson is to the left and perhaps William Thaw to the right, but it is hard to say with certainty. Image courtesy of Washington and Lee University.

James McConnell and Paul Rockwell at Paul's wedding, December 1916. Image courtesy of Washington and Lee University.

General John J. Pershing, middle, in the Invalides on 4 July 1917. Photograph originally appeared in L'Illustration, 7 Juillet 1917.

American troops entering the Invalides on 4 July 1917. Photograph originally appeared in L'Illustration, 7 Juillet 1917.

General John J. Pershing, middle, in the Invalides on 4 July 1917. Photograph originally appeared in L'Illustration, 7 Juillet 1917.

American troops marching down the rue de Rivoli on 4 July 1917. Photograph originally appeared in L'Illustration, 7 Juillet 1917.

General John J. Pershing, middle, speaking at Picpus Cemetery on 4 July 1917. Image from the George Grantham Bain Collection in the Library of Congress.

Afterword

My wife and I visited Luxeuil in May of 2017. I still remember following *Rue Sainte-Anne* up the hill behind the *Hotel le Lion Vert*, where we had spent the previous night. At the crest of the hill we turned right and walked along the cemetery's stone wall. We stopped about halfway down where, above the wall's coping, I spotted an American flag, gently flapping in the light breeze. "There he is," I thought. I felt like I had found a little piece of myself.

Of course, France rightfully claims him, too, and so the French flag also flies above Kiffin's grave, side by side with the Stars and Stripes. Both are appropriate, and together form a fitting monument for one of the best young men of his generation. Kiffin gave his life for France, and his death should ever be a reminder of the principles for which his own republic's flag stands – liberty and justice for all. I agree with Theodore Roosevelt, who at Kiffin's death said he had been "true to American ideals" and that "every American owes him a debt, because by his example he has helped this nation to save its own soul."[1]

With those of other American volunteers, Kiffin's name is also etched in a stone monument placed opposite the statue of Washington and Lafayette in the little park in the *Place des États-Unis* in Paris. A bronze statue in the likeness of Alan Seeger, Kiffin's guardmate that long-ago night in the ruined village of Craonnelle, stands atop the stone.

A third symbol can be seen at the *Invalides*. Following the beautiful ceremony there on July 4, 1917, the flag carried by the original American volunteers was hung in the hall of honor. Sometime after the war, it was placed in the museum itself, where it is still on display among the tokens from the war which will forever define France.

I felt a rush of emotions when I stood in front of that splendid symbol of the "boys who remembered Lafayette." About the only signatures still visible today are those of Kiffin and Paul, who both signed the flag on September 1, 1914 – when they, like the war, were young. Frederick Zinn, another signer, surely got it right when, many years after the war, he wistfully recalled, "what a bunch of really innocent children we were...."[2]

* * * * *

In early 1920, Loula finally visited France for the first time. She stayed with Paul and Jeanne, and her new grandbaby, a little girl her parents had named Françoise Jeanne Anne Loula Rockwell. Naturally, Paul and his mother visited Kiffin's grave and reflected on what might have been. But perhaps more importantly, as I have tried to do in this book, they reflected on what *had* been.

Standing proudly by Kiffin's graveside, Paul noted how his little brother had "fought with an ideal and a vision such as few others were capable of."[3] For her part, I suspect Loula recalled Kiffin's words to her while lying wounded in a French hospital, responding to her worries that he might be killed in the war:

[I]f I should be killed I think that you ought to be proud in knowing that your son tried to be a man and wasn't afraid to die, and that he gave his life for a greater cause than most people do – the cause of all humanity. To me that doesn't appear a bad death at all.[4]

Her travels in France lent Loula a perspective that helped her better appreciate the sacrifice her son had made; she later wrote that, having seen where Kiffin "fought, fell and lies," she thought she could "understand why the cause of liberty was so sacred and dear to him."[5] Loula always hoped others would "see in my boy something far beyond a spirit of mere adventure, as so many were prone at first to see."[6] I hope this book helps accomplish this.

* * * * *

There is little doubt that, as Paul later asserted, the sacrifice and service of Kiffin and the other American volunteers had a great moral effect in the United States. Paul firmly believed that the deaths of Victor Chapman, Kiffin Rockwell, Norman Prince and James McConnell "did more than anything else" to induce the people of the United States "to side with France and her allies, in force as well as in sympathy."[7] Captain Thénault agreed, and stated that the deaths of those four men had "aroused their compatriots from the doubt of neutrality to a comprehension of the vital issues at stake.... The sacrifice of their young lives stirred their countrymen beyond all argument of words – theirs was the propaganda by deeds, and they won out."[8]

While the United States probably would have gone to war in any event, the example set by Kiffin and the other brave volunteers surely played a role. Their actions during the first two and a half years of the war helped crystallize American public opinion in favor of the Allies and prepared many citizens for their country's eventual decision to take an active part in the conflict.

One can debate Kiffin's precise impact on the war, but judged by his own terms, Kiffin led a successful life. Speaking of those who had died "doing something for the world, for posterity," he asked, "is not that success! And what more can a man ask for his life than success?"[9]

Kiffin and the other boys – "Who, not unmindful of the antique debt, came back the generous path of Lafayette," – unfailingly gave thanks for the opportunity they had been given to sacrifice themselves for an ideal. Kiffin's friend Alan Seeger captured this gratitude, probably the volunteers' most remarkable attribute, in two lines of his splendid *Ode in Memory of the American Volunteers Fallen for France*, written for the Paris memorial service for which he could not get leave:

Now heaven be thanked, we gave a few brave drops;
Now heaven be thanked, a few brave drops were ours.

* * * * *

Six decades after his service in World War I, Paul Rockwell was asked why he and Kiffin had enlisted with France. He answered "Well, because we were brought up differently from most people today."[10]

That was true in 1976 and is even more true today. But while Kiffin and Paul were surely raised differently than most, they were not the only volunteers. One hundred years ago, many American sons – a good number from some of the wealthiest and most privileged families of the time – felt it their duty to repay a debt incurred nearly 140 years prior when Lafayette came from France to assist America in her war for independence. And so, they traveled to France to fight and, in many cases, die for the liberty of that land.

What has happened to our nation in the past one hundred years? Today, many American youths would not even fight for their own country, much less another – although perhaps they could be roused to post a hashtag. Masculinity is now scorned as "toxic" and, especially among the so-called "elite" – the college-educated, the wealthy and politically connected – the concept of repaying a debt to those who made their own nation and freedom possible is unthinkable. Little wonder, for among much of this crowd, the thought of

American exceptionalism is anathema, and words like duty, honor and sacrifice merely outdated concepts in unread history books. I suspect Wilson's "too proud to fight" would suit many of today's self-obsessed Americans just fine – they would rather, in the words of one well-worded article, "ignore stupendous facts in [their] myopic quest for tiny excuses."[11]

But not Kiffin, or the other American volunteers. Faced with the monumental struggle between right and wrong, these boys took a stand on the side of liberty and right, their enlistment "a revolt against their homeland's apathy to an armed threat ... aimed at the heart of mankind."[12] Through their actions and sacrifice they became men, real men, men worthy of admiration and emulation. Many years after the war, Captain Thénault inscribed one copy of his book "in memory of some Americans who could not stand to be neutral."[13] In the end, that may be the most fitting description of the boys who remembered Lafayette.

I believe, as did one who knew many of them well, that these boys "are not dead, their spirits still live, inviting us to higher ideals, nobler aspirations, and unwavering patriotism."[14] I only hope I have told their story in a manner worthy of it.

The Boys Who Remembered Lafayette

This book is a tribute to those Americans who volunteered to defend France in her darkest hour, a reminder that *non exercitus neque thesauri praesidia regni sunt verum amici* – neither armies nor treasure protect a country, but its true friends.[1]

I agree with Edmund Gros, who less than a year after the war ended wrote the following to John Jay Chapman: "The splendid heroism and sacrifice of these young men who came as volunteers, when nothing forced them to enter the strife, should never be forgotten, and, in my opinion, it is our duty ... to do all that will fix their names on the tablets of time."[2]

And so, here they are – the workmen of the first hour. The boys who led the way. The boys who remembered Lafayette.

Jules James Bach*	H. Clyde Balsley
Charles Beaumont*	Edgar Bouligny*
Ferdinand Capdeveille*†	J.S. Carstairs*
John J. Casey*	Georges Casmeze*
Victor Chapman†	Herman Lincoln Chatkoff*
Elliott Cowdin	Frazier Curtis
Georges Delpeuch*	Dennis Dowd*†
Henry W. Farnsworth†	John Earl Fike†
Joseph Ganson*	Edmond Genet†
Bert Hall*	Dudley Hill
Chouteau Johnson	Russell Kelly†
David W. King*	Fred Landreaux*
Raoul Lufbery†	Didier Masson
James McConnell†	Achilles Olinger*
Paul Pavelka†	Rene Phelizot*†
Frederick Prince	Norman Prince†

Kiffin Rockwell*†

Paul Rockwell*

Robert Rockwell

Andrew Ruel

Lawrence Rumsey

Lawrence Scanlan

Bob Scanlon*

Alan Seeger*†

Robert Soubiran*

Edward M. Stone†

Charles Sweeny*

William Thaw*

D.W. Thorin

Bartram Towle*

Ellingwood Towle*

Charles Trinkard*†

Kenneth Weeks†

Frederick W. Zinn*

* *signed the flag of the American Volunteer Corps*
† *died for France*

Deeds never die.

– James Chester Rockwell[3]

Heroes

I SEE them hasting toward the light
Where war's dim watchfires glow;
The stars that burn in Europe's night
Conduct them to the foe.
As when a flower feels the sun
And opens to the sky,
Knowing their dream has just begun
They hasten forth to die.

     * * *

Like meteors on a midnight sky
They break—so clear, so brief—
Their glory lingers on the eye
And leaves no room for grief.
And when to joy old sorrows turn,
To spring war's winter long,
Their blood in every heart will burn,
Their life in every song.

    - John Jay Chapman

Author's note

In writing this book, I made a conscious decision to let the boys tell their own story to the greatest extent possible. This meant the use of lots of quotes. I relied on primary sources wherever I could, including many of the letters the men wrote during their service. In seeming vindication of these decisions, during my research I stumbled across this neat passage about letters written home during the war:

In nothing else does the soul of this world war speak so frankly as in the field post letters sent by officers and men to their dear ones at home. It is in them that you find the naked thought. It is from them that the future historian, if he takes his task seriously, will have to glean the facts, rather than from the official reports, army orders and proclamations solely, for those are dressed for the occasion.[4]

Being a lawyer by trade, of course I tried to cite a source for every statement. I hope the reader finds it helpful and not distracting. Finally, although he denied doing so, Paul edited Kiffin's letters prior to publication. Where there are differences between the published version and the actual letter, I have included the actual text.

Acknowledgements

Although I am sure to leave someone out, the following people have contributed to this work in ways large and small, for which they have earned my thanks and gratitude.

To begin with, the staff at the Special Collections and Archives at Washington and Lee University have been so wonderful throughout the lengthy process. Lisa McCown, Byron Faidley, and Seth McCormick-Goodhart were always responsive to my many requests and more than willing to promptly provide research materials. Tom Camden was especially encouraging of my efforts and always willing to speak with me about Kiffin and the boys. The Rockwell papers at W&L are an invaluable resource, and the staff proved equally indispensable.

I also benefited greatly from the Alan Seeger diary and papers and the John Jay Chapman collections at Houghton Library at Harvard University, where the staff was entirely first class. The same was true of the staff at the University of Virginia. The Newberry Library in Chicago houses microfilm copies of the *Chicago Daily News* and proved to be a wonderful resource.

I visited or contacted many other archives and had uniformly positive interactions with each one. I especially thank Mary Laura Kludy at VMI; Linda Gass at Carson-Newman University; Rebecca Petersen May at the Z. Smith Reynolds Library at Wake Forest University; Elyse Rives at the Southern Baptist Historical Library and Archives; Anna Mullen Villareal and Debra Loguda-Summers at the Museum of Osteopathic Medicine in Kirksville, Missouri; Nicole Milano at the Archives of the American Field Service; Debbie Seracini at the San Diego Air and Space Museum; Jelena Fay-Lukic at the National Air and Space Museum; Katie Jean Davey at the Minnesota Historical Society; Anne Causey at the Albert and Shirley Small Special Collections Library at the University of Virginia; Brendan Kieran at the Massachusetts Historical Society; Helen Matthews at the Atlanta History Center; Rachael Zipperer at the Georgia Historical Society; Colin Reeve at the Ramsey Library, University of North Carolina – Asheville; Mary Jones at the Senator John Heinz History Center; and the staff at the United States Naval Academy library in Annapolis.

The National Archives is another wonderful resource, and I had great interactions with several individuals there. John P. Deeben and Robert Thompson both went above and beyond, and Rebecca J. Crawford located Loula's letter to the French ambassador – what a delight it was to receive that!

Another memorable day occurred when I received a response to my numerous inquiries with the French diplomatic authorities, asking about the letter Paul and Kiffin had sent to the French Consulate in New Orleans in August 1914. Imagine my joy when Delphine Fourrez of the Centre des Archives diplomatiques de Nantes sent me a copy of Paul's actual letter!

Vann Evans was particularly helpful in securing resources from the State Archives of North Carolina, and Allison Haack provided many of the letters from the James Norman Hall archives at Grinnell College. I express my gratitude and thanks to Cindy Rutgers, Hall's grand-daughter, for permission to quote from several of those letters. Ronald Poteat graciously provided several letters of Jim McConnell from his private collection.

Paul Grasmehr and Lindsey Sturch at the Pritzker Military Library were always helpful, and without fail the entire staff at the Glenview Public Library located and acquired the many items I requested.

Many local historians and societies provided useful information or records, including Betty Lou Barclay, Dillon County Historical Society; Helen Moody and Jo Church Dickerson, Pee Dee Genealogical Society; Meghan Jordan and Ann M. Broadbent, Old Buncombe County Genealogical Society; Duay O'Neill, Newport, TN; Mark Laughlin, Kirksville, MO; Stephanie Henry, East Tennessee Historical Society; Clay Krummel, First Baptist Church in Morristown, TN; Robert Prince, First Baptist Church in Waynesville, NC; Wren Williamson, Bear Swamp Baptist Church, SC; Cindy Lane, Hamblen County Archives; Mary Dixie Dysart, Air Force Historical Research Agency, Maxwell Air Force Base; and Helena Hayes, Galesburg-Charleston Memorial Library.

Several individuals provided translation assistance to the project, including Jenny Fichmann (who also proved a terrific researcher), Fanny Gaston and Kayla Gabbay. I thank them for their insights.

I benefited greatly from conversations and exchanges with the following scholars, each of whom was happy to share his time and knowledge: Steve Suddaby, Marc McClure, Chuck Hess, Steve Tom, Bill Jackson, and Raoul

Lufbery, III. Mr. Lufbery also sent some additional resources, as well as a wonderful photo of his aviator ancestor and namesake. In addition, Alan Toelle and Dennis Gordon each responded to email inquiries, and Mr. Toelle provided a neat photo of Victor Chapman from the Bob Ford personal collection.

My wife and I met Jeannine Pairron and her husband Guy in Luxeuil, and again when they visited Chicago, bringing many useful materials for my research and even gifts for my family. We were able to share Independence Day with this wonderful couple, a memory I will always treasure.

Sybil Rockwell Robb was a wonderful resource and sounding board throughout this process and, along with her husband and daughter, even entertained my wife and I in her family home. I thank her for blessing my use of the Rockwell materials and trusting me to tell her family's story.

I also wish to thank my friend Earl Ternieden, who read a good chunk of an early draft manuscript. His words of encouragement meant a lot to me and helped me to continue writing. My mother also read an early draft and cheered me on as I approached the finish line. Dawn McCauley lent her Microsoft Word expertise to the project. From a few conversations, photos and letters my daughter Eleni created the perfect cover for the book. She also typeset and formatted the entire text and photos; her talent never ceases to amaze me.

Finally, as in everything else, my wife and children have been a tremendous support to me in this project. Karina has believed in me from the beginning, and never once complained when I spent so many nights and weekends with Kiffin and the boys. Likewise, the rest of my family has never grumbled about the time I spent talking their ears off or typing away. Always willing to overlook my shortcomings, they have provided encouragement and inspiration every step of the way. Their love and support mean more to me than I can express.

Mark Trapp
July 4, 2019

Works cited

Rockwell Papers, WLU

Paul Ayres Rockwell Papers, WLU Coll. 0301, Special Collections and Archives, James G. Leyburn Library, Washington and Lee University, Lexington, VA.

KYR Papers, NCDNCR

Military Collection WWI, Private Collections, Kiffin Y. Rockwell Papers, Box 32, State Archives of North Carolina, North Carolina Department of Natural and Cultural Resources.

James Chester Rockwell Papers, WFU

MS78, James Chester Rockwell Papers, 1886-1890, Z. Smith Reynolds Library Special Collections and Archives, Wake Forest University, Winston-Salem, North Carolina, USA.

McConnell Collection, UVA

James Rogers McConnell Papers, 1915-1917, Accession #2104, etc., in the James Rogers McConnell Memorial Collections, Albert and Shirley Small Special Collections Library, University of Virginia Library, Charlottesville, Va.

Rockwell Files, VMI

Records, papers and photographs of and relating to Kiffin Rockwell, Preston Library, Virginia Military Institute, Lexington, Virginia.

JNH Papers, Grinnell

James Norman Hall Papers, 1906-1954, Collection MS 01.01, Burling Library Archives, Grinnell College, Grinnell, Iowa.

Alan Seeger Papers, Harvard

Alan Seeger Papers, 1907-1937, MS Am 1578.2, Houghton Library, Harvard University, Cambridge, Mass.

Alan Seeger Diary, Harvard

Seeger, A. (1914). Diaries: Manuscript, 1914-1915, MS Am. 255.2, Houghton Library, Harvard University, Cambridge, Mass.

Lafayette Escadrille Scrapbook, MHS

Frazier Curtis, *Lafayette Escadrille Scrapbook, 1914-1917*, Massachusetts Historical Society, Boston, MA.

William Thaw Scrapbooks, HSWP

Papers of the Thaw Family, 1792-1981, MSS# 29, Historical Society of Western Pennsylvania, Senator John Heinz Pittsburgh Regional History Center, Pittsburgh, Pennsylvania.

John Jay Chapman Papers, Harvard

John Jay Chapman Papers, 1841-1940 (MS Am 1854). Houghton Library, Harvard University.

John Jay Chapman Additional Papers, Harvard

John Jay Chapman Additional Papers, 1841-1940 (MS Am 1854.1). Houghton Library, Harvard University.

William Roscoe Thayer Papers

William Roscoe Thayer Papers, (MS Am 1081). Houghton Library, Harvard University.

Relevé des vols effectués pendant le mois de mai – aout 1916, records of the 2nd Armée.

Relevé des vols effectués pendant mois de mai – aout 1916; le chef d'escadron commandant l'aeonautique de la II armee; Hoover Institute at Stanford University, Microfilm collection 91053, Box 4, 19N 491. Ordres d'operations de l'aeronautique, execution des missions, reconnaissances aeriennes, avionsd'artilleries, releves des vols executes 1914 September – 1918 October.

Papers of Edwin A. Alderman

Papers of Edwin A. Alderman, Accession #1001, Special Collections, University of Virginia Library, Charlottesville, Va.

Albert Hatton Gilmer Collection

Albert Hatton Gilmer Collection, MS 062, Skillman Library, Lafayette College.

The Triangle, Triangle Film Corporation

P-L TRI.01, Margaret Herrick Library, Academy of Motion Picture Arts and Sciences, Beverly Hills, California.

Horace Clyde Balsley Personal Papers

Horace Clyde Balsley Personal Papers, SC.10013, San Diego Air & Space Museum Archives.

James Rogers McConnell Collection

James Rogers McConnell Collection [Truitt], NASM.XXXX.0232, National Air and Space Museum Archives.

Endnotes

1 The actual telegram is preserved in the Paul Ayres Rockwell Papers, WLU Coll. 0301, Special Collections and Archives, James G. Leyburn Library, Washington and Lee University, Lexington, VA (hereafter Rockwell Papers, WLU). *See also* "Kiffin Rockwell, Famous Atlanta Flyer, Is Killed," *The Atlanta Constitution*, September 24, 1916, p. 1.

2 James Chester Rockwell, "After the Wreck," *The State Chronicle*, November 9, 1888, p. 4. I have quoted only a portion of the poem.

3 "True Nobility," *The Belles Lettres*, August 15, 1885, p. 6.

Introduction

4 James Norman Hall & Charles Bernhard Nordhoff, *The Lafayette Flying Corps.*, Vol. 1, p. 407 (1920).

5 Arch C. Whitehouse, *Legion of the Lafayette*, p. 118 (1962). The fellow pilot was Chouteau Johnson.

6 "Paul Pavelka, A Soldier of Fortune," *The New York Sun*, December 30, 1917, Sec. 5, p. 4.

7 Bill Thorin to Alice Weeks, September 27, 1916, Alice S. Weeks, *Greater Love Hath No Man*, p. 171 (1939) (hereafter "*Greater Love*").

8 *See e.g.*, "My Most Thrilling Sky Fight," *Sky Fighters*, p. 85 (August 1936).

9 This story appeared in the popular comic-strip "Strange as it Seems." The cartoon showed a fistfight in a German plane, and the accompanying text read: "Turnabout capture! While being flown to German HQ by the enemy pilot who took him prisoner, flier Kiffin Rockwell knocked out his captor and flew pilot, ship and all back to his home airdrome!" "Strange as it Seems," *The Roanoke Times*, March 1, 1948. This cartoon seems to have had its origin in an article printed during the war three decades earlier. *See* Edward Lyell Fox, "U.S. Leads in Air-War," *Illustrated World*, p. 667, 672 (July 1917).

10 Carl B. Ogilvie, "Kiffen Rockwell," *Aces*, p. 37, 40 (January 1931).

11 Just a few months after his death, a magazine that billed itself as "the companion for all the family" paid homage to Kiffin and two other pilots of the *escadrille*. *See* "Three Heroes," *The Youth's Companion*, Vol. 90, No. 46, November 16, 1916, p. 666. By 1918, George Sully & Company, a New York based publisher, began putting out a series of "books for boys," based on aviation during the war. Published under the pseudonym Charles Amory Beach, the first book of the series was titled *Air Service Boys Flying for France, or The Young Heroes of the Lafayette Escadrille*.

12 Thomas E. Smith, Jr., "Remarks upon the dedication of the Kiffin Yates Rockwell Memorial Exhibit, Florence Air and Missile Museum, April 25, 1977," in Rockwell Papers, WLU. At the time, Smith was a South Carolina state senator.

13 *War Letters of Kiffin Yates Rockwell*, p. 2 (Country Life Press, 1925) (hereafter "*War Letters*").

14 *War Letters*, p. xv.

15 Georges Thénault, *The Story of the Lafayette Escadrille*, p. 78 (The Battery Press, reprint 1990).

16 Chouteau Johnson, quoted in Whitehouse, *Legion of the Lafayette*, p. 118; and Hall & Nordhoff, *The Lafayette Flying Corps.*, Vol. 1, p. 407.

17   Jane Dixon, "Death For One, A Bride for the Other," *The Atlanta Journal*, December 3, 1916, in Rockwell Papers, WLU. *See also* "Kiffin Yates Rockwell," *The Sigma Phi Epsilon Journal*, p. 194, 207 (December 1916).

18   John Jay Chapman, Prefatory Note, in *War Letters of Edmond Genet*, p. ix (Grace Ellery Channing, ed.)(Charles Scribner's Sons, 1918).

19   Harvard was once such a place that in the course of honoring several of Kiffin's companions, it could print the following sentiment in the pages of its *Graduate's Magazine*: "But the vital human being can never be neutral, and if his vitality be at so low an ebb that he takes no side, is inspired by no vision, seeks no great truth, then he, and only he, will be lonesome and neglected when the crisis is passed. True sons of Harvard, therefore, can no more be neutral today than they were [in the Civil War]. They look upon a world at war and they must, perforce, take sides, for no true-hearted man can wash his hands, like Pilate, and disclaim responsibility in the struggle between right and wrong...." "From A Graduate's Window," *The Harvard Graduate's Magazine*, Vol. XXV, 1916-1917, p. 184 (Dec. 1916).

20   Paul Ayres Rockwell, "Our Pioneers in the Air," *The Franco-American Weekly*, March 2, 1918, p. 3.

21   John Bowe, *Soldiers of the Legion*, p. 72 (Peterson Linotyping Co., Chicago, 1918).

22   I've borrowed this profound thought from Robert C. Brooks. Shortly before America entered into World War II, he wrote: "If democracy fighting for its life proves to be spineless and cowardly, why should any future generation wish to revive it? On the other hand, if it goes down fighting gloriously to the last ditch, it will not lose the power to fire the hearts of some future generation." Robert C. Brooks, "Reflections on the 'World Revolution,'" *The American Political Science Review*, Vol. 35, No. 1, p. 16 (Feb. 1941).

23   David McCullough once said that one of the most important things in understanding the people of the past is to remember "that they had no more idea of how things were going to turn out than we do. They had no way of foreseeing what was over the horizon, any more than we do." David McCullough, speech given on April 29, 2010 to the National Genealogical Society, available on the DVD, *A Celebration of Family History* (Family Search International).

24   One source suggests that about one thousand Americans volunteered for France before their own country entered the war, but admits this number is "difficult if not impossible to certify today[.]" Axel Jansen, "Heroes or Citizens? The 1916 Debate on Harvard Volunteers in the 'European War,'" chapter 9 in *War Volunteering in Modern Times* (Krüger & Levsen, ed. 2011), p. 150.

25   http://encyclopedia.1914-1918-online.net/article/war_losses_france

Prelude ~ War

1   S.L.A. Marshall, *World War I*, p. 7.

2   "Thrilling Scenes Caused in Europe by Appeal to Arms," *The Atlanta Constitution*, August 2, 1914, p. 1; "'On to Berlin!' Thousands Shout in Streets of Paris," *The Atlanta Journal*, August 2, 1914, p. 5.

3   *War Letters*, p. xvii.

4   *The Atlanta Journal*, August 2, 1914, p. 1.

5   "Russia, France and Servia Will Battle Germany and Austria," *The Atlanta Journal*, August 2, 1914, p. 1.

6   *The Atlanta Constitution*, August 2, 1914, p. 1.

7   *War Letters*, p. xvii.

8   *War Letters*, p. xviii.

9   One of their lunch guests was a reporter who participated in the conversation that Sunday afternoon. *See* Paul Rockwell to Dr. James Patton, April 27, 1959, in Loula Ayres Rockwell Recollections, #3119-z, Southern Historical Collection, The Wilson Library, University of

North Carolina at Chapel Hill. He wrote that the boys had determined to fight for France "as evidence of their gratitude to France for the noble part she played in the winning of American Independence..." "Three Young Atlantians Would Shoulder Arms in Defense of France," *The Atlanta Journal*, August 4, 1914, p. 5.

10   *War Letters*, p. xvii-xviii.

11   "Germany Declares War; First Skirmish Fought," *The Atlanta Journal*, August 2, 1914, p. 5.

12   *War Letters*, p. xviii.

13   "War Bulletins," *The Atlanta Constitution*, August 3, 1914, p. 2.

14   "Three Young Atlantians Would Shoulder Arms in Defense of France," *The Atlanta Journal*, August 4, 1914, p. 5.

15   *Id.*

16   "Wilson Proclaims Neutrality of U.S. During Great War," *The Atlanta Journal*, August 4, 1914, p. 1.

17   The names of Kiffin and Paul appear on a supplemental passenger list, showing they were added just prior to passage. American Line list of passengers for S.S. *St. Paul*, August 7, 1914, in Rockwell Papers, WLU.

Part One

1   David A. Clary, *Adopted Son: Washington, Lafayette, and the Friendship That Saved the Revolution*, p. 13 (2007)

2   Paul Rockwell to John Jay Chapman, October 5, 1916, in John Jay Chapman additional papers, 1841-1940. MS Am 1854.1 (660), Houghton Library, Harvard University, Cambridge, Mass. (hereafter "John Jay Chapman Additional Papers").

Chapter One

3   Henri de Bornier, *La Fille de Roland: drame en quatre actes en vers*, p. 63 (New York: Jenkins, 1886). An account of an Englishman who joined the French Foreign Legion contains a close variant of this phrase: "To those of us wanderers who love France the idea of invading Germans within her frontiers is intolerable. It is as if some large and brutal individual had deliberately slapped some charming woman friend. To England one rallies as one would to some strong and manly friend beset by numbers, but to France one brings a chivalrous affection which justifies the epigram: 'All well-bred men have two Motherlands, their own and France.'" "Mixed Company: Some of my Friends in the Foreign Legion," *The Daily Mail*, January 14, 1915, p. 4. When Minister to France, James Monroe expressed a similar sentiment: "Republics should stand shoulder to shoulder; this maxim applies specially to the American and French Republics; their governments are of a very similar nature; they are both built upon the same foundations: the equal and inalienable rights of man." As quoted in M. René Besnard, *Speeches Delivered*, p. 14-15 (Paris, 1917).

4   *Honorable Daniel Webster, at the celebration of the New England Society at Washington, on the 22nd of December, 1845.*

5   Paul Rockwell to Robert House, September 29, 1920, in Military Collection WWI, Private Collections, Kiffin Y. Rockwell Papers, Box 32, Correspondence with Fred Olds & Robert House, State Archives of North Carolina, North Carolina Department of Natural and Cultural Resources (hereafter "KYR Papers, NCDNCR"). The Rockwells were well aware of their family history. In a letter to her brother Chester Rockwell during the Civil War, Sarah Rockwell wrote that she would send to him "a genealogical history of the Rockwells from their first landing in this country to the present time[.]" Sarah Rockwell to Chester Rockwell, letter misdated October 15, 1865, should probably be 1863, in Rockwell Papers, WLU.

6   Donald Shumway Rockwell, *Eleven Centuries of the Remote Ancestry of the Rockwell Family*, p. 6 (The Gillick Publishing Co., Berkeley, California, 1914).

7   Rockwell, *Eleven Centuries of the Remote Ancestry of the Rockwell Family*, p. 8. Kiffin was aware of the family's Norman origins; he had once told Robert Rockwell, a fellow pilot who joined the squadron shortly before Kiffin's death, that "he was sure they were from [the] same ancestry – Normandy France was the home of their ancestors." Mary F. Rockwell to Loula Rockwell, September 24, 1916, in KYR Papers, NCDNCR. Paul was familiar with his family's "ancient motto," and said a few short years after Kiffin's death "I think that Kiffin lived up to it perfectly; although not having a king, Kiffin substituted for the 'Roi' his ideal of civilization." Paul Rockwell to Robert House, September 29, 1920 in KYR Papers, NCDNCR.

8   Apparently three "knight's fees" of land "is as much as three yokes of oxen can plow in one season." "History of the Rockwell Family" by Eleanor Lexington, in KYR Papers, NCDNCR.

9   Paul Ayres Rockwell, *Three Centuries of the Rockwell Family in America, 1630-1930*, p. 9 (privately printed, Paris, 1930) (hereafter "*Three Centuries*").

10   In some accounts, Rockwell's wife is listed as Susanna Capen.

11   Discourse of Reverend Thaddeus Mason Harris, delivered July 4, 1830, *Memorials of the First Church in Dorchester from Its Settlement in New England to the End of the Second Century*, p. 7 (Boston, 1830).

12   *Id.*

13   Psalm 90:16-17, King James Version.

14   *Three Centuries*, p. 25.

15   *Three Centuries*, p. 24.

16   "One Line of Rockwells in America," undated sketch by Paul Rockwell, in family records, courtesy of Sybil Rockwell Robb.

17   *Three Centuries*, p. 32, 34.

18   *Three Centuries*, p. 34.

19   *Three Centuries*, p. 37.

20   "Notes – Kiffin Yates Rockwell," p. 3, typewritten notes in biographical files, KYR Papers, NCDNCR.

21   *Three Centuries*, p. 37.

22   Gladwin Hill, "Avocation is Soldiering," *The Charleston Evening Post*, December 20, 1940, p. 4C.

23   William Ray, "Wake Forester," *The Wake Forest Magazine*, p. 1 (Summer 1976).

24   *Three Centuries*, p. 37.

25   Whitehouse, *Legion of the Lafayette*, p. xiv.

26   "Notes – Kiffin Yates Rockwell," p. 3, typewritten notes in biographical files, KYR Papers, NCDNCR. *See also* Johnston, Henry P., ed.. *The Record of Connecticut Men in the Military and Naval Service During the War of the Revolution 1775-1783. Vol. I-III.* Hartford, CT, USA: 1889, p. 654.

27   Sarah Rockwell to Chester Rockwell, letter misdated October 15, 1865, should probably be 1863, in Rockwell Papers, WLU.

28   Hannah Rockwell to Chester Rockwell, December 17, 1839, in Rockwell Papers, WLU.

29   *Three Centuries*, p. 41.

30   Edward A. Oldham, "North Carolina Poets, Past and Present," *The North Carolina Poetry Review*, p. 67 (Jan-Feb 1936).

31   Paul Rockwell to Robert House, September 29, 1920, KYR Papers, NCDNCR.

32   *Three Centuries*, p. 41.

33   Undated sketch Rockwell Papers, WLU.

34   *Three Centuries*, p. 42.

35   Oldham, *North Carolina Poets, Past and Present*, p. 68. *See also Three Centuries*, p. 43, 75.

36   *Three Centuries*, p. 76.

37   *Id.*

38   William Kenneth Boyd, *North Carolina on the Eve of Secession*, p. 177, reprinted from the Annual Report of the American Historical Association for 1910, pages 165-177 (1912)

(available at http://docsouth.unc.edu/nc/boydw/boydw.html#p177).

39 *Three Centuries*, p. 44.

40 Henry Clay Rockwell to Chester Rockwell, September 6, 1863, Rockwell Papers, WLU.

41 Grant, Ulysses S., *Personal Memoirs*. New York: C.L. Webster, 1885–86; available at www.bartleby.com/1011/55.html (visited July 8, 2017).

42 Henry Clay Rockwell to his sister Mary, August 9, 1864, Rockwell Papers, WLU.

43 *Id.*

44 *Id.*

45 *Id.*

46 *Three Centuries*, p. 56.

47 "Columbus County and the Lower Cape Fear," *The Wilmington Journal*, October 3, 1873, p. 2. Thomas Ritchie – or Old Father Ritchie, as he became known – was the Democratic editor of the *Richmond Enquirer* from 1804 to 1845. Through his editorials, Ritchie exerted great influence over the Democratic party, and his opinion was respected and repeated throughout the South.

48 Paul Rockwell to Robert House, September 29, 1920, KYR Papers, NCDNCR.

49 *Three Centuries*, p. 56.

50 "Premium List: Fourth Annual Fair Cape Fear Agricultural Association," *The Weekly Star* (Wilmington), November 29, 1872, p. 4.

51 "Columbus County Letter," *The Observer* (Raleigh), September 29, 1878, p. 2.

52 "Further Notice," *The Wilmington Journal*, March 20, 1874, p. 3.

53 "Correction," *The Eagle* (Fayetteville, NC), October 9, 1873, p. 3.

54 "Columbus County and the Lower Cape Fear," *The Wilmington Journal*, October 3, 1873, p. 2.

55 "Columbus County Letter," *The Observer* (Raleigh), September 29, 1878, p. 2.

56 "Charleston, S.C., Oct. 10," *The Eagle* (Fayetteville), October 16, 1873, p. 2; "Distiller's Convention," *The Daily Journal* (Wilmington), October 11, 1873, p. 1.

Chapter Two

1 "Thursday – Night Session," *The Baptist and Reflector*, October 20, 1892, p. 4.

2 Ben W. Hooper, as quoted in Paul Ayres Rockwell, "James Chester Rockwell: A Memoir," p. 8, MS78, James Chester Rockwell Papers, 1886-1890, Z. Smith Reynolds Library Special Collections and Archives, Wake Forest University, Winston-Salem, North Carolina, USA (hereafter "James Chester Rockwell Papers, WFU").

3 Handwritten history, in James Chester Rockwell Papers, WFU.

4 "Death of Captain H.C. Rockwell," *The Daily Journal* (Wilmington), March 5, 1874, p. 3.

5 "Material Available for a Sketch of the Life of James Chester Rockwell," in family records, courtesy of Sybil Rockwell Robb.

6 *Id.*

7 Henry and Sallie J. Rockwell had six children together, so apparently one predeceased Henry.

8 "Material Available for a Sketch of the Life of James Chester Rockwell," in family records, courtesy of Sybil Rockwell Robb. Paul said Council "was what is known as a 'poor manager.'" "James Chester Rockwell: A Memoir," p. 1, James Chester Rockwell Papers, WFU.

9 Census records from 1880 show Sarah Jane Council – along with 12-year old J.C., his younger brother Robert, and his two half-siblings, all listed as living with their grandfather in Whiteville, North Carolina. *See* Census records available on Ancestry.com, *1880, Whiteville, Columbus, North Carolina*; Roll: *959*; Page: *105C*; Enumeration District: *053*.

10 *Three Centuries*, p. 76.

11 "Columbus County Letter," *The Observer* (Raleigh), September 29, 1878, p. 2.

12 *See* T.B. Murphy, *Kiffin Rockwell, The Lafayette Escadrille and the Birth of the United*

        States Air Force, p. 10 (McFarland & Co., 2016).

13   *Three Centuries*, p. 58.

14   E.C. Brooks, *North Carolina Poems*, p. 108 (Raleigh, N.C. 1912).

15   Handwritten history, James Chester Rockwell Papers, WFU.

16   "Commissioner's Sale," *The Wilmington Morning Star*, July 8, 1884, p. 4.

17   "Weeds" by James Chester Rockwell, "An Idle Afternoon," KYR Papers, NCDNCR.

18   "Death of Rev. J.C. Rockwell," *The Biblical Recorder*, September 27, 1893, p. 3.

19   Handwritten history, James Chester Rockwell Papers, WFU.

20   "James Chester Rockwell: A Memoir," p. 1, James Chester Rockwell Papers, WFU.

21   "Editorial Correspondence," *The Reidsville Review*, October 13, 1893, p. 1.

22   "Spirits Turpentine," *The Wilmington Morning Star*, July 9, 1885, p. 1.

23   "False Destiny," *The Belles Lettres*, August 1, 1885, p. 7. He also quoted a snippet of *Lucile*, an awesome poem by Owen Meredith. A portion of the poem goes like this:
        How blessed should we be, have I often conceived,
        Had we really achieved what we nearly achieved!
        We but catch at the skirts of the thing we would be,
        And fall back on the lap of a false destiny.
        So it will be, so has been, since this world began!
        And the happiest, noblest and best part of man
        Is the part which he never hath fully played out,
        For the first and last word in life's volume is – Doubt.

24   "False Destiny," *The Belles Lettres*, August 1, 1885, p. 7.

25   As quoted in "James Chester Rockwell: A Memoir," pp. 2-3, James Chester Rockwell Papers, WFU.

26   "James Chester Rockwell: A Memoir," p. 3, James Chester Rockwell Papers, WFU.

27   Handwritten history, James Chester Rockwell Papers, WFU.

28   "Dead!" *The Belles Lettres*, August 15, 1885, p. 4. In another section of the same paper, Rockwell displayed his still intact sense of humor, writing: "Some people seem to think that their 'best wishes' are sufficient to support a paper, whether they subscribe and pay for it or not. If you will give them a free copy they are lavish with their praises. They think that an editor can get along all right without any pocket-change, if he is only kept supplied with praise. But it is not so. If you really want to make an editor feel happy, just mingle a little cash with your compliments." *Id*. at p. 6.

29   Handwritten history, James Chester Rockwell Papers, WFU.

30   *Id*.

31   *Id*.

32   Glenn Tucker, "James Chester Rockwell," NCPedia, available at https://www.ncpedia.org/biography/rockwell-james-chester (visited April 18, 2019).

33   James Chester Rockwell, "Hearts and Faces," *The State Chronicle*, April 22, 1886, p. 1.

34   Oldham, *North Carolina Poets, Past and Present*, p. 68.

35   *Three Centuries*, p. 58. Rockwell himself said he had spent the season in "the mountains of Western North Carolina whither I had gone to search for health." Handwritten history, in James Chester Rockwell Papers, WFU.

36   Untitled, *The Davie Times* (Mocksville, NC), August 20, 1886, p. 4.

37   For example, J.C. wrote a tender poem following William's death:
        Nay, question not, God knoweth best,
        We should not murmur when we weep:
        His feet were weary, let him rest,
        "God giveth his beloved sleep."
        Aye, it is hard, but God is just,
        And well we know his ways are wise;
        And someday from the dreamless dust,

Our fondest hopes again will rise.
We can but trust, and trusting wait,
And waiting will not be in vain,
Some day we'll read the book of fate,
And God will make his purpose plain.
"Death of Rev. J.C. Rockwell," *The Biblical Recorder*, September 27, 1893, p. 3.

38 "James Chester Rockwell," *The Biblical Recorder*, March 17, 1915, p. 5. Much later in his life, Paul wrote that his father "was brought up in the Presbyterian Church, [and] became a Baptist in 1886." Paul Rockwell to Eleanor Susong, March 30, 1966, copy in special collections at Carson-Newman University.

39 Handwritten history, James Chester Rockwell Papers, WFU.

40 "James Chester Rockwell," *The Biblical Recorder*, March 17, 1915, p. 5.

41 Handwritten history, James Chester Rockwell Papers, WFU.

42 Handwritten notes, James Chester Rockwell Papers, WFU.

43 *Id.*

44 Untitled, *The Western Sentinel*, December 16, 1886, p. 4.

45 "Personal," *News and Observer* (Raleigh), December 14, 1886.

46 "State Items," *The Weekly Sentinel* (Winston, N.C.), March 3, 1887, p. 4. *See also* "Personal & Other Items," *The Biblical Recorder*, February 23, 1887, p. 2; and "Personal & Other Items," *The Biblical Recorder*, February 16, 1887, p. 2. One record states that J.C. preached in Bogue Chapel, Porter Swamp and Griffin's Cross Roads in Columbus County. *See* John R. Sampey, *Southern Baptist Theological Seminary: The First Thirty Years, 1859-89*, p. 173 (1890).

47 "Mother" by James Chester Rockwell, "An Idle Afternoon," KYR Papers, NCDNCR.

48 "Material Available for a Sketch of the Life of James Chester Rockwell," family records, courtesy of Sybil Rockwell Robb.

49 Oldham, *North Carolina Poets, Past and Present*, p. 67.

50 "Chrystella: The Echo of a Dream," by James Chester Rockwell (Rockwell, Taylor & Company, 1887).

Chapter Three

1 Proverbs 31:29, King James Version.

2 W. W. Sellers, *A History of Marion County*, p. 166 (1902).

3 Freeman Irby Stephens, M.D., *The History of Medicine in Asheville*, p. 399 (2013). *See also* "Dr. Loula Rockwell to be Buried Today," *The Kingsport Times*, July 30, 1959, p. 12.

4 Duay O'Neill, "Newport's Kiffin Rockwell Carried on Family's Military Traditions," *The Newport Plain Talk*, January 28, 2010, p. 2.

5 One local account states that Loula was known as "Granny Rockwell" in her later years, and that she "had a large following" for more than four decades. *See* Stephens, *The History of Medicine in Asheville*, p. 398.

6 *Three Centuries*, p. 72.

7 F.A. Thompson, "Color Goes to State Senate With Harry Kemper Cooke," *The Charleston News and Courier*, September 26, 1932, p. 7.

8 Loula Ayres Rockwell, "The Election of General Wade Hampton," p. 1, Loula Ayres Rockwell Recollections, #3119-z, Southern Historical Collection, The Wilson Library, University of North Carolina at Chapel Hill.

9 Edward Stanley Barnhill, *The Beatys of Kingston*, p. 118. *See also* Kate Lilly Blue, "Lincoln Opposed by 3 Generations," *The Charleston News and Courier*, December 3, 1933, p. 3B.

10 *North Carolina Baptist Almanac for 1882*, p. 34.

11 Barnhill, *The Beatys of Kingston*, p. 118.

12 Paul Ayres Rockwell, "The Reverend William Ayres," p. 2, manuscript on file with the Dillon

County Historical Society, special thanks to Betty Lou Barclay.

13   N.S. Watson, "A History of Bear Swamp Baptist Church," *The Robesonian* (Lumberton, NC), March 19, 1931, p. 7.

14   *North Carolina Baptist Almanac for 1882*, p. 34.

15   Sellers, *A History of Marion County*, p. 166.

16   "Personal & Other Items," *The Biblical Recorder*, October 25, 1882, p. 2.

17   Haynes Lennon, "For the Recorder," *The Biblical Recorder*, September 23, 1863, p. 2. Reverend Ayres is buried in the Bear Swamp cemetery; engraved on his gravestone are these lines: Although he sleeps, his memory doth live, and cheering comforts to his mourners doth give: he followed virtue as his truest guide, lived as a Christian – as a Christian died.

18   Paul Ayres Rockwell, "The Reverend William Ayres," p. 2.

19   D. Augustus Dickert, *History of Kershaw's Brigade*, p. 567 (1899).

20   *Id.* (listing Ayres, D.D. as private in Company L of 8th Regiment). *See also* Kate Lilly Blue, "Lincoln Opposed by 3 Generations," *The Charleston News and Courier*, December 3, 1933, p. 3B.

21   Paul Ayres Rockwell, "The Reverend William Ayres," p. 3.

22   Kate Lilly Blue, "Lincoln Opposed by 3 Generations," *The Charleston News and Courier*, December 3, 1933, p. 3B.

23   Paul Ayres Rockwell, "The Reverend William Ayres," p. 3.

24   *Id.*

25   Kate Lilly Blue, "Lincoln Opposed by 3 Generations," *The Charleston News and Courier*, December 3, 1933, p. 3B.

26   *Three Centuries*, p. 83.

27   Loula Ayres Rockwell, "The Election of General Wade Hampton," p. 1.

28   Sellers, *A History of Marion County*, p. 17-18.

29   *Three Centuries*, p. 82.

30   Loula Ayres Rockwell, "The Election of General Wade Hampton," p. 1-2.

31   *Three Centuries*, p. 83.

32   "The Rockwell Brothers," *The Charleston News and Courier*, January 26, 1917, p. 6.

33   Loula Ayres Rockwell, "The Election of General Wade Hampton," p. 2, 5.

34   *Three Centuries*, p. 83.

35   Betty Bryant Overturf, *The History of Bear Swamp Baptist Church*, p. 190 (1985). The record shows a visit to Bear Swamp from Pastor Ivey in December 1878, when Loula would have been 12. *Id.*, p. 38.

36   Notably, the church had long accepted blacks into full membership even before the Civil War freed the slaves. N.S. Watson, "A History of Bear Swamp Baptist Church," *The Robesonian* (Lumberton, NC), March 19, 1931, p. 7.

37   Overturf, *The History of Bear Swamp Baptist Church*, p. 33, 43.

38   Loula Ayres Rockwell, "The Election of General Wade Hampton," p. 2.

39   "Mrs. Mantha Ayres," *The Charleston News and Courier*, August 8, 1931, p. 3.

40   "Commencement at Murfreesboro, June 23 and 24, 1884," *The Biblical Recorder*, July 1, 1885, p. 2.

41   "Chowan Baptist Female Institute," *The Biblical Recorder*, July 3, 1886, p. 2.

42   The article suggests that Henry Clay Rockwell met Enoch Shaw Ayres when the former was called to defend Charleston in 1863 as part of the 51st North Carolina. Kate Lilly Blue, "Lincoln Opposed by 3 Generations of Marion Family," *The Charleston News and Courier*, December 3, 1933, p. 11B. This could very well be true, but the account loses credibility by stating that after the Civil War, the men were guests in one another's homes and swapped stories about their service while their grandsons Paul and Kiffin listened. *Id.* While the former assertion could be true, the latter cannot – H.C. Rockwell died in 1874, and Paul and Kiffin were not born until 1889 and 1892, respectively.

43   "Personal & Other Items," *The Biblical Recorder*, January 26, 1887, p. 2.

44 "Personal & Other Items," *The Biblical Recorder*, February 23, 1887, p. 2; "State Items," *The Weekly Sentinel* (Winston, NC), March 3, 1887, p. 4.

45 One record from the Southern Baptist Theological Seminary states that J.C. preached in Antioch Baptist Church in Marion County during 1887 and 1888. *See* Sampey, *Southern Baptist Theological Seminary*, p. 173.

46 Bear Swamp is only half a mile from the North Carolina border, and drew many of its congregants from that state. In fact, from early in its history, the church was affiliated with North Carolina Baptist bodies. N.S. Watson, "A History of Bear Swamp Baptist Church," *The Robesonian* (Lumberton, NC), March 19, 1931, p. 7. Thus, it makes sense that J.C. would have come into contact with the Ayres at this time.

47 James Chester Rockwell, "King and Queen," *The Wilmington Morning Star*, May 25, 1887, p. 3.

48 "Whiteville – Fair Bluff – Spring Branch," *The Biblical Recorder*, September 14, 1887, p. 2. The pastor who spoke this praise (A. W. Price) had baptized James in October of 1886, and would ordain him to the ministry in September of 1887. "Ordination to the Ministry," *The Biblical Recorder*, October 19, 1887, p. 3.

49 "Sunday School Institute," *The Biblical Recorder*, May 11, 1887, p. 3. The Reverend James A. Smith, who would later officiate at Loula and J.C.'s wedding at the Ayres' plantation, was also an instructor at this meeting. *Id.*

50 "Outlines," *The Wilmington Morning Star*, June 2, 1887, p. 1.

51 James Chester Rockwell, "At the Grave of Lazarus," pp. 27-31, James Chester Rockwell Papers, WFU.

52 "Ordination to the Ministry," *The Biblical Recorder*, October 19, 1887, p. 3.

53 "The Editor's Desk," *The State Chronicle*, December 29, 1887, p. 1.

54 "James Chester Rockwell: A Memoir," p. 5, James Chester Rockwell Papers, WFU.

55 "The Marriage Bells A-Ringing," *The State Chronicle* (Raleigh, NC), March 9, 1888, p. 3. *See also* "Married," *The Biblical Recorder*, March 21, 1888, p. 3.

Chapter Four

1 The *Augusta Chronicle* printed two of his poems in March 1888, and both were written in Fair Bluff. Rebecca Louise Longstreet, "Beyond the Stars," *The Augusta Chronicle*, March 25, 1988, p. 4; and Rebecca Louise Longstreet, "Demon and Angel," *The Augusta Chronicle*, March 20, 1988, p. 4. Moreover, in September, he was still living in Fair Bluff. *See* "Personal and Other Items," *The Biblical Recorder*, September 5, 1888, p. 2. Rebecca Louise Longstreet was a *nom de plume* occasionally used by James Chester Rockwell. *See* Handwritten note on p. 22 of "An Idle Afternoon," KYR Papers, NCDNCR.

2 "Personal and Other Items," *The Biblical Recorder*, April 11, 1888, p. 2.

3 "Personal and Other Items," *The Biblical Recorder*, March 28, 1888, p. 2.

4 "Personal and Other Items," *The Biblical Recorder*, September 5, 1888, p. 2; *Three Centuries*, p. 59.

5 The first notes in his notebooks from his time in Louisville are dated October 2. *See* Notebooks, James Chester Rockwell Papers, WFU. Ads run at the time stated that classes started on October 1.

6 *Three Centuries*, p. 59.

7 Oldham, *North Carolina Poets, Past and Present*, p. 68. Mr. Hayne had apparently encouraged the young James Rockwell in his interests in writing and poetry. *See Three Centuries*, p. 58.

8 "Notes from the Mountains," *The Biblical Recorder*, July 31, 1889, p. 3. J.C. often referred to western North Carolina as the "land of the sky," a phrase increasingly used to describe the area following the 1876 publication of "*The Land of the Sky, or, adventures in mountain by-ways*," a novel by Mrs. Frances Tiernan (published under the pseudonym Christian Reid).

9   "Notes from the Mountains," *The Biblical Recorder*, July 31, 1889, p. 3.

10   "Personal and Other Items," *The Biblical Recorder*, May 29, 1889, p. 2.

11   *Id.*

12   "Personal and Social," *The State Chronicle*, (Raleigh, NC), May 31, 1889, p. 2.

13   "Notes from the Mountains," *The Biblical Recorder*, July 31, 1889, p. 3.

14   *See* "Amounts received from Waynesville Church," handwritten notes James Chester Rockwell Papers, WFU.

15   *The Waynesville Courier*, circa August 1889, as quoted in Mary Evelyn Underwood, *Faith of Our Fathers Living Still*, p. 229 (1981).

16   "Notes from the Mountains," *The Biblical Recorder*, July 31, 1889, p. 3.

17   "Western Baptists," *The Daily Citizen* (Asheville, NC), October 24, 1889, p. 1; "Baptist Convention," *The Daily Citizen* (Asheville, NC), October 25, 1889, p. 1.

18   *See* "Personal and Social," *The State Chronicle*, December 6, 1989; and "Items," *Baptist and Reflector*, December 5, 1889, p. 9.

19   "Personal and Other Items," *The Biblical Recorder*, December 4, 1889, p. 2.

20   "The Morristown Church," *The Baptist and Reflector*, November 28, 1889, p. 4.

21   For example, it was not until December 1889 that Loula was dismissed by letter from Bear Swamp "to join the 1st Baptist Church at Morristown." *See* Overturf, *The History of Bear Swamp Baptist Church*, p. 47.

22   "Personal and Other Items," *The Biblical Recorder*, December 25, 1889, p. 2.

23   *See* quote attributed to F.W. Robertson, handwritten notes, James Chester Rockwell Papers, WFU.

24   Handwritten notes James Chester Rockwell Papers, WFU.

25   "Go Forward," sermon preached in January 1890, James Chester Rockwell Papers, WFU.

26   "E.T. Sunday School Convention," *Baptist and Reflector*, August 3, 1893, p. 7.

27   "Personal and Other Items," *The Biblical Recorder*, July 2, 1890, p. 2.

28   "Items," *Baptist and Reflector*, July 17, 1890, p. 9; Untitled, *Baptist and Reflector*, July 10, 1890, p. 5.

29   "Items," *Baptist and Reflector*, July 17, 1890, p. 9.

30   *See* Sunday service schedules dated 1890, James Chester Rockwell Papers, WFU.

31   "Morristown, Tenn.," *Baptist and Reflector*, June 26, 1890, p. 5.

32   "James Chester Rockwell: A Memoir," p. 8, James Chester Rockwell Papers, WFU.

33   "Nollachucky Notes," *Baptist and Reflector*, August 21, 1890, p. 9.

34   *Proceedings of the Nolachucky Association of Baptists*, August 14, 15 and 16, 1890, p. 6, from the archives at Carson-Newman University, special thanks to Linda Gass.

35   "Personal and Other Items," *The Biblical Recorder*, January 7, 1891, p. 2.

36   "Tennessee Letter," *The Biblical Recorder*, April 22, 1891, p. 3; *The Morristown Record*, as quoted in "Rev. J.C. Rockwell," *The Biblical Recorder*, May 13, 1891, p. 3.

37   "Personal and Other Items," *The Biblical Recorder*, January 7, 1891, p. 2.

38   "Carsonville Dots," *Baptist and Reflector*, February 26, 1891, p. 4

39   "Carsonville Dots," *Baptist and Reflector*, March 26, 1891, p. 4.

40   "Personal and Other Items," *The Biblical Recorder*, April 8, 1891, p. 2; Untitled, *The Biblical Recorder*, April 29, 1891, p. 3; and "Rev. J.C. Rockwell," *The Biblical Recorder*, May 13, 1891, p. 3. *See also* "Items," *Baptist & Reflector*, April 9, 1891, p. 8 ("It gives us pain to learn that the brilliant young pastor at Morristown is under the necessity of resigning his charge on account of ill health.").

41   "Rev. J.C. Rockwell," *The Biblical Recorder*, May 13, 1891, p. 3. *See also* Untitled, *Baptist and Reflector*, June 4, 1891, p. 5 ("Bro. Rockwell is off on a tramp through the highlands of North Carolina. He expects the exercise to invigorate him."); and "Carsonville Dots," *Baptist and Reflector*, July 9, 1891, p. 1.

42   In August, he attended the Holston Baptist association convention in Tennessee, and in October was found preaching a sermon in Sevierville, Tennessee on "Canst thou by searching

find out God?" *See* "Two Associations," *Baptist and Reflector*, October 8, 1891, p. 8-9.

43   Untitled, *Baptist and Reflector*, February 25, 1892, p. 5 (noting that "our amiable brother ... is now pastor at Newport.").

44   "Personals and Other Items," *The Biblical Recorder*, August 10, 1892, p. 2 ("The Newport church has built a handsome pastorium since Bro. Rockwell became its pastor.").

45   "James Chester Rockwell: A Memoir," p. 6, James Chester Rockwell Papers, WFU. One correspondent stated it was an "elegant pastorium, overlooking the town." "This and That," *Baptist & Reflector*, January 19, 1893, p. 4. *See also* Ruth Webb O'Dell, *Over the Misty Blue Hills*, p. 289, 166 (there is a picture of the parsonage in between pages 288-289 in this book); and Marjorie McMahan, "The First Baptist Church, Newport, Tennessee," *Baptist and Reflector*, July 27, 1939, p. 8.

Chapter Five

1   *War Letters*, p. ix. While the 1890 census records were largely destroyed in a fire, the 1880 census shows a William Snoddy, druggist, living in Newport. Perhaps he was the "Dr. Snoddy" referred to.

2   Untitled, *Baptist and Reflector*, August 25, 1892, p. 15.

3   "Nolachucky Association," *Baptist and Reflector*, August 21, 1890, p. 4.

4   George Tayloe Winston, "Kiffin Yates Rockwell," typewritten notes in biographical files, KYR Papers, NCDNCR.

5   J.M. Cramp, *Baptist History: From the Foundation of the Christian Church to the Close of the Eighteenth Century*, p. 428 (1868).

6   William Kiffin, *Remarkable Passages in the Life of William Kiffin*, p. 71 (London, 1823).

7   "Yates Memorial Services," *The Biblical Recorder*, May 16, 1888, p. 2.

8   Charles E. Taylor, *Yates the Missionary*, p. 15 (1898).

9   "James Chester Rockwell: A Memoir," p. 6, James Chester Rockwell Papers, WFU.

10   *Id.*, p. 7; *Three Centuries*, p. 60-61.

11   "James Chester Rockwell: A Memoir," p. 7, James Chester Rockwell Papers, WFU.

12   Handwritten notes James Chester Rockwell Papers, WFU.

13   "Notes from the Mountains," *The Biblical Recorder*, July 31, 1889, p. 3.

14   "James Chester Rockwell: A Memoir," p. 7, James Chester Rockwell Papers, WFU.

15   *Id. See also* "First Baptist Church," pamphlet in the archives at Carson-Newman University (noting that "his private library was good and extensive.").

16   *Three Centuries*, p. 60.

17   "Items," *Baptist and Reflector*, December 15, 1892, p. 7.

18   For instance, at one convention he gave a talk titled "Influence of the Sunday School on Music." *See* "East Tennessee Baptist Sunday School Convention," *Baptist and Reflector*, June 30, 1892, p. 13.

19   "Carsonville Dots," *Baptist and Reflector*, May 26, 1892, p. 4.

20   *Id.*

21   "Thursday night Session," *Baptist and Reflector*, October 20, 1892, p. 4.

22   Handwritten notes James Chester Rockwell Papers, WFU.

23   "Items," *Baptist and Reflector*, December 15, 1892, p. 7.

24   *Id.*

25   Untitled, *Herald & Tribune*, March 16, 1893, p. 3 (noting Rockwell preached in the Baptist church in Jonesborough, Tennessee).

26   "If I Had A Dozen Sons I Should Want Them to Fight for France," *The Atlanta Constitution*, June 16, 1918, p. 12I.

27   "The Preacher and the Children," handwritten notes, James Chester Rockwell Papers, WFU.

28   *Three Centuries*, p. 59-60.

29   "The Preacher and the Children," handwritten notes, James Chester Rockwell Papers, WFU.

30 *Id.*

31 "This and That," *Baptist and Reflector*, January 19, 1893, p. 4.

32 "East Tennessee Notes," *Baptist and Reflector*, February 9, 1893, p. 4.

33 Untitled, *Herald and Tribune*, March 16, 1893, p. 3 (noting Rockwell preached in the Baptist church in Jonesborough, Tennessee). *See also* "Tennessee Delegates to Southern Baptist Convention," *Baptist and Reflector*, April 27, 1893, p. 13 (Rockwell was selected as the delegate from East Tennessee).

34 "Recent Events," *Baptist and Reflector*, July 13, 1893, p. 12.

35 "Programme," *Herald and Tribune* (Jonesborough, TN), June 22, 1893, supplement, p. 1.

36 "Wake Forest and Other Matters," *The Biblical Recorder*, August 23, 1893, p. 3.

37 Isabel Eastman Styll to Joseph R. Anderson, July 19, 1921, papers supplied by Mary Laura Kludy, Preston Library, archives of the Virginia Military Institute, Lexington, Virginia (hereafter "Rockwell Files, VMI.").

38 Ruth Webb O'Dell, *Over the Misty Blue Hills*, p. 166.

39 S.E. Jones, "Nay Question Not, God Knoweth Best," *Baptist & Reflector*, September 21, 1893, p. 4. Many of Reverend Rockwell's congregants from Newport attended the funeral. One of them recalled that, although there was no convenient passenger train between Newport and Morristown at that time, "a large group went anyhow." "Skill in Riding Bucking Pony Revealed Kiffin Rockwell's Will to Fly," undated clipping, Kiffin Rockwell file, Stokely Memorial Library, Newport, Tennessee.

40 A friend and member of his congregation built and owned the cemetery. *See* Marc Eric McClure, *Kiffin Rockwell: First American Hero of the Great War*, p. 1-2 (2017).

41 S.E. Jones, "Nay Question Not, God Knoweth Best," *Baptist & Reflector*, September 21, 1893, p. 4.

42 "Death of Rev. J.C. Rockwell," *The Biblical Recorder*, September 27, 1893, p. 3.

43 "Personal and Practical," *Baptist and Reflector*, September 21, 1893, p. 9.

44 "Editorial Notes," *The Henderson Gold Leaf*, October 12, 1893, p. 2.

45 "Rev. J.C. Rockwell Dead," *The Biblical Recorder*, September 27, 1893, p. 2; and "Death of Rev. J.C. Rockwell," *The Biblical Recorder*, September 27, 1893, p. 3.

Chapter Six

1 Loula A. Rockwell to the Ambassador to France, December 22, 1914, *National Archives*, Records of the Foreign Service Posts of the Department of State (Record Group 84). Census records from 1900 list Loula as a "school teacher" and note that she owned her home, with no mortgage.

2 *War Letters*, p. ix.

3 *War Letters*, p. x.

4 "Friends Honor Young Hero," undated clipping, circa September 1916, "Lest We Forget" memorial scrapbook, Rockwell Papers, WLU.

5 *War Letters*, p. x. *See also* Mattox, Henry E., *Chariots of Wrath: North Carolinians Who Flew for France in World War I*, p. 288 (1996) ("In the years following James Rockwell's untimely death from typhoid fever in 1893, the Rockwell children spent the summers in Newport and the winters on their maternal grandparents' plantation in eastern South Carolina."). In the 1900 census, Kiffin was in South Carolina on June 26, and in Tennessee on June 6, so he might have spent that summer with his grandmother.

6 "If I Had A Dozen Sons I Should Want Them to Fight for France," *The Atlanta Constitution*, June 16, 1918, p. 12I.

7 "Addenda to Rockwell Material," handwritten notes, biographical files, KYR Papers, NCDNCR (noting that Loula "would not teach in Carson-Newman College because she would have to give up personal care of her children[.]").

8 *See* Program from First Baptist Church in Newport Tennessee, August 2, 1959, Rockwell

Papers, WLU (noting that Loula "was well remembered for her teaching, both in the Sunday School and in the public schools.")

9   *Three Centuries*, p. 61. *See also* Transcribed Interview of Paul Rockwell by Dr. Louis D. Silveri, July 22, 1976, p. 6 (Southern Highlands Research Center, University of North Carolina at Asheville)

10   Paul Rockwell to Dr. James Patton, April 27, 1959, Loula Ayres Rockwell Recollections, #3119-z, Southern Historical Collection, The Wilson Library, University of North Carolina at Chapel Hill.

11   J.C. once called Washington "the great American patriot" who "won freedom for his native land[.]" James Chester Rockwell, "At the Grave of Lazarus," p. 15-16, James Chester Rockwell Papers, WFU.

12   Kate Lilly Blue, "2 Marion County Boys Found Adventure With French Army," *The Charleston News and Courier*, February 19, 1933, p. 4B.

13   "Kiffin Yates Rockwell," brief sketch prepared by Paul Rockwell, family records, courtesy of Sybil Rockwell Robb.

14   Transcribed Interview of Paul Rockwell by Dr. Louis D. Silveri, July 22, 1976, p. 4 (Southern Highlands Research Center, University of North Carolina at Asheville)

15   *Three Centuries*, p. 62. One long-time family friend remembered both Paul and Kiffin as "lovers of nature[.]" "Friends Honor Young Hero," undated clipping, *circa* September 1916, "Lest We Forget" memorial scrapbook, Rockwell Papers, WLU.

16   *War Letters*, p. xiii.

17   *Three Centuries*, p. 61. But many of those mountain men did not hold with the South's "peculiar institution" – as one historian has noted, "East Tennessee contained 46 percent of the white residents of Tennessee but only 17 percent of the slaves." Peter Wallenstein, "Which Side Are You On? The Social Origins of White Union Troops From Civil War Tennessee," *Journal of East Tennessee History*, No. 63 (1991), p. 75.

18   *Three Centuries*, p. 61.

19   "Skill in Riding Bucking Pony Revealed Kiffin Rockwell's Will to Fly," undated clipping, Kiffin Rockwell file, Stokely Memorial Library, Newport, Tennessee.

20   As his friend, Bill Jones, put it, "nary another boy in the ten, twelve, or even fourteen-year old class could stay with that bobbing mass of muscle in violent action." "Skill in Riding Bucking Pony Revealed Kiffin Rockwell's Will to Fly," undated clipping, Kiffin Rockwell file, Stokely Memorial Library, Newport, Tennessee.

21   "Skill in Riding Bucking Pony Revealed Kiffin Rockwell's Will to Fly," undated clipping, Kiffin Rockwell file, Stokely Memorial Library, Newport, Tennessee. While it is not clear if he was referring to the same animal, Paul mentioned that Kiffin "was especially fond of mounting a wild and unruly Puerto Rican pony we had at Newport." *War Letters*, p. xii. Another author tells how Kiffin, at only four years of age, repeatedly mounted and eventually subdued a Shetland pony given to him by his grandfather. *See* Dennis Gordon, *Lafayette Escadrille Pilot Biographies*, p. 47.

22   *War Letters*, p. xi.

23   "Paul Ayres Rockwell: War Correspondent, Author, Aviator, World Traveler," *The Sigma Phi Epsilon Journal*, p. 136 (November 1930).

24   *Three Centuries*, p. 62.

25   "Atlanta Boy, Now in France, Hasn't Glimpsed the War," *The Atlanta Journal*, March 21, 1915, Magazine, p. 2.

26   *War Letters*, p. xii.

27   *Three Centuries*, p. 62.

28   *War Letters*, p. xii; and *Three Centuries*, p. 83.

29   *See War Letters*, p. xii. *See also* "Maxton Happenings," *The Robesonian* (Lumberton, NC), July 7, 1897, p. 2 (mentions a two-foot alligator caught near a residence, the first reported of the year).

30 *War Letters*, p. xii.

31 *See* Michael R. Canfield, *Theodore Roosevelt in the Field,* p. 23 (2015).

32 Captain Mayne Reid, *The Boy Hunters, or Adventures in Search of a White Buffalo,* dedication page (1855).

33 "Kiffin Yates Rockwell," brief sketch prepared by Paul Rockwell, family records, courtesy of Sybil Rockwell Robb.

34 Loula Ayres Rockwell, "The Red Shirt Election," *The Atlantic,* November 1954, p. 60.

35 "The Rockwell Brothers," *The Charleston News and Courier,* January 26, 1917, p. 6.

36 Paul Rockwell to Robert House, September 29, 1920, KYR Papers, NCDNCR.

37 Transcribed Interview of Paul Rockwell by Dr. Louis D. Silveri, July 22, 1976, p. 3 (Southern Highlands Research Center, University of North Carolina at Asheville).

38 *Three Centuries*, p. 82.

39 *War Letters*, p. x.

40 Herbert Molloy Mason, Jr., *The Lafayette Escadrille*, p. 11 (1964). This is an excellent book.

41 Barnhill, *The Beatys of Kingston*, p. 118.

42 *Id. See also* "Some Military Ancestry of Kiffin Yates Rockwell," p. 2, typewritten notes in biographical files, KYR Papers, NCDNCR.

43 Barnhill, *The Beatys of Kingston*, p. 119.

44 Paul Ayres Rockwell, "The Reverend William Ayres," p. 1.

45 "Obituary," *The Biblical Recorder and Southern Watchman,* May 2, 1840, p. 3.

46 *Id.*

47 *Id.*

48 *Three Centuries*, p. 78.

49 Barnhill, *The Beatys of Kingston*, p. 122.

50 Paul Ayres Rockwell, "The Reverend William Ayres," p. 3.

51 *Three Centuries*, p. 80.

52 *Id.*

53 *Id.*

54 Paul Ayres Rockwell, "The Reverend William Ayres," p. 3.

55 Sellers, *A History of Marion County*, p. 166.

56 Paul Ayres Rockwell, "The Reverend William Ayres," p. 3.

57 "Notes – Kiffin Yates Rockwell," p. 6, typewritten notes in biographical files, KYR Papers, NCDNCR.

58 Paul Ayres Rockwell, "The Reverend William Ayres," p. 3.

59 *War Letters*, p. x-xi.

60 Loula Ayres Rockwell, "The Red Shirt Election," *The Atlantic,* November 1954, p. 61.

61 "The Rockwell Brothers," *The Charleston News and Courier,* January 26, 1917, p. 6.

62 Loula Ayres Rockwell, "The Red Shirt Election," *The Atlantic,* November 1954, p. 60.

63 *Id.* at p. 61.

64 *Three Centuries*, p. 82.

65 Loula Ayres Rockwell, "The Red Shirt Election," *The Atlantic,* November 1954, p. 61.

66 Murphy, *Kiffin Rockwell, The Lafayette Escadrille and the Birth of the United States Air Force*, p. 15.

67 *Id.*

68 Paul always said that Kiffin had a "youthful and impatient idea that the Southern people were old-fashioned and set in their ways," and while still young, Kiffin traveled west looking for place to settle. *War Letters*, p. xv-xvi. In France, Kiffin served alongside, and seemingly became friends with, black soldiers such as Bob Scanlon and at one point indicated he no longer wished to live in the South after the war. *See* Kiffin to Loula, May 2, 1915, *War Letters*, p. 43.

69 F.A. Thompson, "Color Goes to State Senate With Harry Kemper Cooke," *The Charleston News and Courier,* September 26, 1932, p. 7.

70 *Three Centuries*, p. 83.

71 "Friends Honor Young Hero," undated clipping, circa September 1916, "Lest We Forget" memorial scrapbook, Rockwell Papers, WLU.

Chapter Seven

1 Loula Rockwell, "Kiffin Yates Rockwell," p. 1, undated typewritten sketch in biographical files, KYR Papers, NCDNCR.

2 School History, Newport Grammar School, available at http://www.newportgrammar. org/?PageName=%27AboutTheSchool%27 (visited July 30, 2017).

3 Loula Rockwell, "Kiffin Yates Rockwell," p. 1, undated typewritten sketch in biographical files, KYR Papers, NCDNCR; and George Tayloe Winston, "Kiffin Yates Rockwell," typewritten notes in biographical files, KYR Papers, NCDNCR ("After supervising their early years in the schools of Newport, Tennessee, where she, herself, was principal...").

4 School History, Newport Grammar School website, available at http://www. newportgrammar.org/?PageName=%27AboutTheSchool%27 (visited July 30, 2017).

5 Paul noted he "read a great deal," and "collected Indian relics, bird eggs, tobacco tags, postage stamps, picture post cards, and various other things." *Three Centuries*, p. 62.

6 "Paul Ayres Rockwell: War Correspondent, Author, Aviator, World Traveler," *The Sigma Phi Epsilon Journal*, p. 136 (November 1930); and "A Most Unforgettable Character," *Charleston News and Courier*, December 16, 1979, p. 2F.

7 Loula A. Rockwell to the Ambassador to France, December 22, 1914, *National Archives*, Records of the Foreign Service Posts of the Department of State (Record Group 84) ("the oldest boy has had three attacks of pneumonia and one hemorrhage from the lungs.").

8 "A Most Unforgettable Character," *Charleston News and Courier*, December 16, 1979, p. 2F.

9 *Id.* Paul's health issues would dog him later in life as well.

10 "Osteopath Restores Sight," *The Charleston News and Courier*, March 31, 1903, p. 2.

11 It is interesting to note that Loula lived 92 years, and Paul 96.

12 Loula Rockwell, "Kiffin Yates Rockwell," p. 2, undated typewritten sketch in biographical files, KYR Papers, NCDNCR. *See also* Stephens, *The History of Medicine in Asheville*, p. 399.

13 *State v. McKnight*, 131 N.C. 717 (1902).

14 *State v. McKnight*, 131 N.C. at 722.

15 *See State v. Biggs*, 133 N.C. 729 (1903).

16 "Paul Ayres Rockwell: War Correspondent, Author, Aviator, World Traveler," *The Sigma Phi Epsilon Journal*, p. 136 (November 1930). I thank Mark H. Laughlin for verifying Paul's alumni status through several early Kirksville High School yearbooks in his possession.

17 *1904 Register Records*, p. 218, courtesy of Museum of Osteopathic Medicine, Kirksville, Missouri.

18 "An Open Letter," *The Journal of Osteopathy*, January 1906, p. 25.

19 *See* "How It Stands in North Carolina Today," *The Osteopathic Physician*, April 1904, p. 4.

20 *1904 Register Records*, p. 218, courtesy of Museum of Osteopathic Medicine, Kirksville, Missouri.

21 *Id.*

22 *See* Stephens, *The History of Medicine in Asheville*, p. 399.

23 The poem was apparently written by Margaret Johnston Graffin, the mother of General Douglas MacArthur, but I have been unable to establish when it was first published. It appeared in newspapers and periodicals throughout the early twentieth century but may not have been published until slightly after Loula's time in Missouri.

24 *1904 Register Records*, p. 218, courtesy of Museum of Osteopathic Medicine, Kirksville, Missouri. *See also* "Graduating Exercises," *The Journal of Osteopathy*, February 1906, p. 59-60.

25   *Id.* at p. 48. Loula is three rows down, third from the left.

26   *Id.* at p. 59.

27   Paul R. Davis, "Address of Class Representative," *The Journal of Osteopathy*, February 1906, p. 50.

28   "Notes from the Mountains," *The Biblical Recorder*, July 31, 1889, p. 3.

29   *See* "Dr. Meacham," *The Asheville Citizen*, February 2, 1906, p. 5. The move was pre-planned, as even her graduation program listed Loula as being from Asheville. "Graduating Exercises," *The Journal of Osteopathy*, February 1906, p. 60. Dr. Meacham was one of the few osteopaths in the state, and at the time the only one in Asheville. *See* Stephens, *The History of Medicine in Asheville*, p. 399. He would later serve as the President of the American Osteopathic Association and was a good connection in the community for Loula. Murphy, *Kiffin Rockwell, The Lafayette Escadrille and the Birth of the United States Air Force*, p. 18.

30   "Dr. Loula Rockwell to be Buried Today," *The Kingsport Times*, July 30, 1959, p. 12. *See also* "Dr. Loula Ayres Rockwell, 92, Marion Native, Dies in N.C.," *The Charleston News and Courier*, July 30, 1959, p. 8; and "Osteopathy Pioneer Dies," *The Charlotte Observer*, July 30, 1959, p. 4B. I thank Dr. Barbara Walker for providing me with the historical minutes from the North Carolina Osteopathic Society. The minutes show that Loula was elected a member of the N.C.O.S. in October 1906, along with Mrs. S.W. Tucker.

31   "North Carolina," *The Journal of Osteopathy*, November 1907, p. 405.

32   *A Pictorial History of Buncombe County*, p. 34.

33   Transcribed Interview of Paul Rockwell by Dr. Louis D. Silveri, July 22, 1976, p. 7 (Southern Highlands Research Center, University of North Carolina at Asheville)

34   "Paul Ayres Rockwell: War Correspondent, Author, Aviator, World Traveler," *The Sigma Phi Epsilon Journal*, p. 136 (November 1930).

35   1907 Asheville city directory, available at Ancestry.com. *U.S. City Directories, 1822-1995*

36   *Compilation of Senate Election Cases, from 1789 to 1913*, p. 952 (1913).

37   During the final debate before the vote seeking to oust him, one senator defended Smoot by asserting: "Reed Smoot has proved a better character than any other senator here has a right to claim. He is so good a man that I almost doubt him. He has no vices. He does not drink or smoke, or chew, or swear...." "Senate Refuses to Oust Smoot," *The New York Times*, February 21, 1907, p. 5.

38   Of course, others may have resented it, or viewed Kiffin as a "goody two-shoes."

39   *See* "Negro Runs Amuck on Asheville's Streets," *The Asheville Citizen*, November 14, 1906, p. 1.

40   "Bullets of Avengers End Negro Desperado's Career," *The Asheville Citizen*, November 16, 1906, p. 1.

41   *See* Thomas Wolfe, *The Child by Tiger* (1938).

42   Transcribed Interview of Paul Rockwell by Dr. Louis D. Silveri, July 22, 1976, p. 28 (Southern Highlands Research Center, University of North Carolina at Asheville). Wolfe mentioned Kiffin and Paul in his famous book, using the pseudonyms Paul and Clifton Wheeler. *See* Thomas Wolfe, *Look Homeward, Angel*, p. 301 (1929).

43   From February 1906 until the new school was purchased, Kiffin went to the same school as Tom Wolfe, who followed his older sister Mabel to school one day and stayed there. Paul knew and was friends with Mabel. *See* Transcribed Interview of Paul Rockwell by Dr. Louis D. Silveri, July 22, 1976, p. 28 (Southern Highlands Research Center, University of North Carolina at Asheville).

44   Loula Rockwell, "Kiffin Yates Rockwell," p. 2, undated typewritten sketch in biographical files, KYR Papers, NCDNCR.

45   "Orange Street Wins," *The Asheville Citizen*, November 28, 1907, p. 3.

46   Helen R. Blankenship, "She Remembers," *The State*, October 15, 1966, p. 7.

47   *Id.*

48 George Tayloe Winston, "Kiffin Yates Rockwell," p. 3, typewritten notes in biographical files, KYR Papers, NCDNCR.

49 Helen R. Blankenship, "She Remembers," *The State*, October 15, 1966, p. 7.

50 *Id.*

51 "Paul Ayres Rockwell: War Correspondent, Author, Aviator, World Traveler," *The Sigma Phi Epsilon Journal*, p. 136 (November 1930).

52 *Id.*

53 William Ray, "Wake Forester," *The Wake Forest Magazine*, p. 42 (Summer 1976).

54 *Id.*

55 *Id.* at 43.

56 "North Carolina's Annual," *The Osteopathic Physician*, November 1907, p. 16.

57 *Id. See also* "North Carolina," *The Journal of Osteopathy*, November 1907, p. 405-406.

58 "Loula Ayres Rockwell," *The Asheville Citizen*, July 31, 1959, p. 4.

59 Helen R. Blankenship, "She Remembers," *The State*, October 15, 1966, p. 7.

60 *Id.*

Chapter Eight

1   Isabel Eastman Styll to Joseph R. Anderson, July 19, 1921, Rockwell Files, VMI ("it was my dear husband who talked up the VMI to [Loula] so enthusiastically, as he always did, when occasion permitted, for he loved the memory of its associations."). *See also War Letters*, p. xii.

2   *VMI Official Register 1907-1908*, p. 47.

3   *Id.*

4   Loula Rockwell, "Kiffin Yates Rockwell," p. 2, undated typewritten sketch in biographical files, KYR Papers, NCDNCR.

5   Letter from Loula Rockwell to Hunter Pendleton, *circa* January 1909, Rockwell Files, VMI.

6   Copy in author's possession. *See also VMI Official Register 1908-1909*, p. 30.

7   The class historian later noted "the many valuable additions" to the Class of 1912 like Kiffin, who enrolled after Christmas, adding: "We feel assured that they will join us in teaching the ignorant Rat Class of 1913 respect for their betters." *The Bomb, 1909*, p. 93.

8   *War Letters*, p. xiii.

9   *VMI Official Register 1908-1909*, p. 20.

10 *VMI Official Register 1908-1909*, p. 23.

11 "V.M.I. to Attend Inauguration," *The Cadet*, February 2, 1909, p. 1.

12 *See* Camillus Christian, Jr. Account Book, Manuscript #0031, Virginia Military Institute Archives.

13 "Dance Given on the 22nd," *The Cadet*, March 2, 1909, p. 1.

14 Untitled, *The Cadet*, March 2, 1909, p. 2.

15 "Washington Trip a Great Success," *The Cadet*, March 9, 1909, p. 1.

16 *Id.*

17 The flag was a replica of the New Market battle flag, with a portrait of George Washington on one side and the coat of arms of Virginia on the other. "V.M.I. Flag," *The Free Lance* (Fredericksburg, VA), March 9, 1909, p. 1.

18 "Washington Trip a Great Success," *The Cadet*, March 9, 1909, p. 1.

19 *The Bomb, 1909*, p. 111.

20 "Washington Trip a Great Success," *The Cadet*, March 9, 1909, p. 1.

21 *Id.*

22 "President Views the Big Parade," *The Washington Herald*, March 5, 1909, p. 2.

23 "Washington Trip a Great Success," *The Cadet*, March 9, 1909, p. 4.

24 Years later, Loula donated the cap Kiffin wore during the inaugural parade to the North Carolina Hall of History. *See* Loula to Fred Olds, September 16, 1917, KYR Papers, NCDNCR.

25 "Hazing at Last Abolished," *The Cadet*, March 23, 1909, p. 1.

26 "Hazing at Last Abolished," *The Cadet*, March 23, 1909, p. 4. The *Richmond Times-Dispatch* editorialized in favor of the action, applauding the school for eliminating the "relic of barbarism" which, "far from being an indication of bravery or manliness" was only an "opportunity for the bully, the small tyrant and the coward" to inflict pain, annoyance and humiliation. *See* Untitled, *The Cadet*, March 30, 1909, p. 2.

27 "Camp Bell," *The Cadet*, June 1, 1909, p. 4.

28 *VMI Official Register 1908-1909*, p. 5.

29 *VMI Official Register 1909-1910*, p. 69.

30 *War Letters*, p. xiii.

31 *Three Centuries*, p. 62-63

32 Captain Donald I. Thomas, "Bobby Werntz's 'War College'" *Shipmate*, p. 18 (June 1992). *See also* Ann Jensen, "Maryland Avenue Schools Prepped Candidates for Naval Academy Exams," *Annapolitan*, p. 7, 50 (Dec. 1977).

33 *Three Centuries*, p. 63.

34 *Report of Superintendent J.M. Bowyer to the Secretary of the Navy*, p. 11 (July 1, 1910), U.S. Naval Academy Archives. Another source stated that at the academy, "[r]ules were at a minimum and discipline relaxed." Ann Jensen, "Maryland Avenue Schools Prepped Candidates for Naval Academy Exams," *Annapolitan*, p. 50 (Dec. 1977). There was also some ongoing North-South rivalry among the candidates – one local woman remembered that her aunt's piano was available for the use of the boys, "but under one strongly stipulated condition. Never, ever, under any circumstances, was 'Marching Through Georgia' to be played on it." *Id.* at p. 51.

35 *Report of Superintendent J.M. Bowyer to the Secretary of the Navy*, p. 11 (July 1, 1910), U.S. Naval Academy Archives.

36 Letter signed by R. L. Werntz, June 25, 1908, U.S. Naval Academy Archives.

37 In my research at the Naval Academy archives, I verified that Kiffin received an alternate appointment, and seems to have had another "alternate" in front of him.

38 Captain Donald I. Thomas, "Bobby Werntz's 'War College'" *Shipmate*, p. 18 (June 1992).

39 Paul A. Rockwell, "Virginia Epsilon," *The Sigma Phi Epsilon Journal*, p. 41 (October 1909). In the fraternity's journal, Paul noted Kiffin's initiation, stating he "has an appointment to Annapolis, and is preparing to take the April exams." *Id.*

40 Paul A. Rockwell, "Virginia Epsilon," *The Sigma Phi Epsilon Journal*, p. 126 (December 1909).

41 *War Letters*, p. xiii; *Three Centuries*, p. 63.

42 *War Letters*, p. xiii.

43 Washington and Lee Register of Matriculates, Session 1909-1910, p. 44.

44 William Howard Taft: "Proclamation 883—Thanksgiving Day, 1909," November 15, 1909. Available online, *The American Presidency Project*. (https://www.presidency.ucsb.edu/documents/proclamation-883-thanksgiving-day-1909) (visited April 28, 2019).

Chapter Nine

1 William A. MacDonough, "70 Years of SigEp Memories Relived ... Colonel Paul A. Rockwell," *The Sigma Phi Epsilon Journal*, p. 9 (June 1979). Before Paul was born, his father referred to Lee as "the grand old hero of the Lost Cause, around whose name clusters all the glory and fame of Southern manhood and chivalry[.]" James Chester Rockwell, "At the Grave of Lazarus," p. 16, James Chester Rockwell Papers, WFU.

2 "Paul Ayres Rockwell: War Correspondent, Author, Aviator, World Traveler," *The Sigma Phi Epsilon Journal*, p. 136-37 (November 1930).

3 *See* Parker S. Rouse, Jr., *George Washington: Patron of Learning and Father of Philanthropy at Washington and Lee University* (1996).

4   Gamaliel Bradford, *Lee the American*, p. 261 (1929).

5   *War Letters*, p. xv.

6   "Paul Ayres Rockwell: War Correspondent, Author, Aviator, World Traveler," *The Sigma Phi Epsilon Journal*, p. 137 (November 1930). *See also Three Centuries*, p. 63.

7   *The Calyx, 1909*, p. 277. The 1910 *Calyx* has a photo of Kiffin and Paul, with their fraternity brothers, about eleven pages from the end, at the top.

8   "Virginia Epsilon," *The Sigma Phi Epsilon Journal*, p. 298 (May 1, 1910).

9   *W&L Catalogue*, 1909, p. 208; *W&L Catalogue*, 1910, p. 198; and *War Letters*, p. xv.

10   *War Letters*, p. xiv.

11   "Virginia Epsilon," *The Sigma Phi Epsilon Journal*, p. 205 (March 10, 1910).

12   Untitled editorial, *Ring-Tum Phi*, September 27, 1910, p. 4.

13   *Id.*

14   "Virginia Epsilon," *The Sigma Phi Epsilon Journal*, p. 298 (May 1, 1910); "Virginia Epsilon," *The Sigma Phi Epsilon Journal*, p. 160 (December 25, 1910). During this time, Paul spent several months in Greenville, South Carolina. "Former Greenville Man, Member Foreign Legion, Writes Home," *The Greenville News*, February 10, 1916, p. 9.

15   Advertisement, *The Asheville Gazette-News*, July 27, 1910, p. 5.

16   P.A. Rockwell, "The Asheville Alumni Chapter," *The Sigma Phi Epsilon Journal*, p. 54 (October 20, 1911).

17   "Asheville Alumni Chapter of Sigma Phi Epsilon," *The Sigma Phi Epsilon Journal*, p. 324-25 (May 1, 1911).

18   "Drove His Car From New York in 6 Days," *The Asheville Citizen*, September 28, 1910, p. 3.

19   *See e.g.* "Society and Personal," *The Asheville Citizen*, June 30, 1910, p. 2; "Miss Oates Entertains," *The Asheville Gazette-News*, July 29, 1910, p. 5; "Miss McArthur Honored," *The Asheville Gazette-News*, August 27, 1910, p. 5; "Social Happenings," *The Asheville Gazette-News*, September 1, 1910, p. 5.

20   "Society and Personal," *The Asheville Citizen*, September 1, 1910, p. 2; "Social Happenings," *The Asheville Gazette-News*, September 1, 1910, p. 5. Fagg Malloy and Richard Loughran's brother Lawrence (also a close friend of Kiffin's) would later die in France. *War Letters*, p. xiv.

21   "Society and Personal," *The Asheville Citizen*, June 30, 1910, p. 2.

22   "Paul Ayres Rockwell: War Correspondent, Author, Aviator, World Traveler," *Sigma Phi Epsilon Journal*, p. 137 (November 1930); "District of Columbia Alpha," *The Sigma Phi Epsilon Journal*, p. 44 (October 20, 1911).

23   *Three Centuries*, p. 63.

24   *War Letters*, p. xv.

25   Loula Rockwell, "Kiffin Yates Rockwell," p. 2, undated typewritten sketch in biographical files, KYR Papers, NCDNCR.

26   *Id. See also* "German Machine Brought Down," *The Western Sentinel* (Winston-Salem), May 23, 1916, p. 2.

27   "The Asheville Alumni Chapter," *The Sigma Phi Epsilon Journal*, p. 56 (October 20, 1911).

28   Kiffin to the Vicomtesse du Peloux, March 7, 1915, *War Letters*, p. 30.

29   *War Letters*, p. xvi.

30   *See* photo in scrapbook, KYR Papers, NCDNCR.

31   *War Letters*, p. xv.

32   *Id.*

33   1913 San Francisco city directory, available at Ancestry.com. *U.S. City Directories, 1822-1995*. Paul believed that Kiffin started the agency and had at one time twenty people working for him, but there is no proof of that. *War Letters*, p. xv.

34   The Elm Hotel today serves as a sort of halfway house, providing subsidized housing for the homeless and formerly homeless.

35   "Society," *The Asheville Citizen*, December 21, 1913, p. 6.

Chapter Ten

1   "Bravery of Atlanta Boys In French Foreign Legion Is Told of by Evangelists," *The Atlanta Constitution*, February 17, 1915, p. 1. During his time in Atlanta, Kiffin often wore "a derby and a plain unassuming blue serge suit and gun metal shoes." Britt Craig, "The Fraternity of Fate," *The Atlanta Constitution*, August 19, 1917, p. 10H.

2   The 1914 Atlanta city directory, dated December 15, 1913, lists Paul A. Rockwell as a reporter for the Atlanta Georgian, living at 14 W. North Ave., available at Ancestry.com. *U.S. City Directories, 1822-1995*.

3   Loula tells of Mr. Agate, a former newspaper man from New York who knew Paul and Kiffin at the Majestic Hotel (which was on Peachtree Street) in Atlanta, and remembered Paul as working on the Frank case. Loula to Paul and Kiffin, July 1, 1916, in Rockwell Papers, WLU. Leo Frank, a 29-year old Jewish businessman, was convicted of the murder of 14-year old Mary Phagan, an employee at the pencil factory where Frank was the director. The murder trial drew national attention that only increased after Frank was (wrongfully) convicted. Two years later in 1915, after the governor commuted his capital sentence to life imprisonment, Frank was kidnapped by an armed mob and lynched in Phagan's hometown of Marietta. The case stirred up much anti-Semitism in the South.

4   Transcribed Interview of Paul Rockwell by Dr. Louis D. Silveri, July 22, 1976, p. 9 (Southern Highlands Research Center, University of North Carolina at Asheville).

5   *War Letters*, p. xvi.

6   *See* notations in check register, Rockwell Papers, WLU. The apartment was located at 136 West Peachtree Street. *See War Letters*, p. xviii.

7   *War Letters*, p. xvii.

8   The letter of introduction was written by Mrs. Louie K. Wells of Asheville. *See* St. Elmo Massengale, "Kiffin Rockwell," *War Letters of Kiffin Yates Rockwell, Supplement*, James Rogers McConnell Papers, 1915-1917, Accession #2104, James Rogers McConnell Memorial Collections, Albert and Shirley Small Special Collections Library, University of Virginia Library, Charlottesville, Va. (hereafter "McConnell Collection, UVA").

9   "Massengale Stresses Value of Advertising in Talk to Students," *The Atlanta Constitution*, November 7, 1914, p. 14.

10 Georgia Historical Society, Finding Aid to the St. Elmo and Alice May Massengale scrapbooks, 1901-1919, (available at http://ghs.galileo.usg.edu/ghs/view?docId=ead/MS%202367-ead.xml) (visited May 4, 2019). *See also* Dudley Glass, "Massengale Celebrates His 20th year of Advertising Success in the South," *The Twin-City Sentinel*, (Winston-Salem), May 20, 1916, p. 9; and St. Elmo Murray Massengale biographical sketch, in personality file at the Atlanta History Center. I thank Helen Matthews for providing me a copy of the file.

11 St. Elmo Murray Massengale biographical sketch, in personality file at the Atlanta History Center.

12 "Massengale Thanks Friends for Support," *The Atlanta Constitution*, Thursday, August 21, 1914, p. 7.

13 "Georgia Alpha," *The Sigma Phi Epsilon Journal*, p. 324 (March 1, 1914)(noting that Kiffin "has located in Atlanta with the Massengale Bulletin System."). Massengale also confirmed that Kiffin "impressed one as being older than he really was." St. Elmo Massengale, "Kiffin Rockwell," *War Letters of Kiffin Yates Rockwell, Supplement*, McConnell Collection, UVA.

14 St. Elmo Massengale, "Kiffin Rockwell," *War Letters of Kiffin Yates Rockwell, Supplement*, McConnell Collection, UVA.

15 *Id.*

16 In one of his letters to Kiffin, Massengale offered to send him anything he wanted, to which Kiffin wrote back: "you can buy me a drink in the M&M club the first day I am back in Atlanta." "Narrow Escapes from Death At Hands of German Soldiers Told By Kiffin Y. Rockwell," *The Atlanta Constitution*, February 28, 1915, p. 3. This must have been a reference to the

Mechanical & Manufacturer's Club, organized by the city's leading businessmen a few years earlier. The M&M club rooms were located on the top floor of the Candler Building, at the time the tallest building in Atlanta, at seventeen stories. The Massengale Advertising Agency offices were on the 16th floor.

17 "Fifty Fiddlers Enter for Fiddlers' Contest at the Auditorium," *The Atlanta Constitution*, February 8, 1914, p. 4B.

18 *See* "Crackers Win the Opener," *The Atlanta Constitution*, April 15, 1914, p. 8; and "9,687 Fans at First Game," *The Atlanta Constitution*, April 15, 1914, p. 8.

19 Britt Craig, "The Fraternity of Fate," *The Atlanta Constitution*, August 19, 1917, p. 10H.

20 Britt Craig, "The Fraternity of Fate," *The Atlanta Constitution*, August 19, 1917, p. 10H.

21 "Keith Vaudeville," *The Atlanta Constitution*, Thursday, April 16, 1914, p. 9.

22 "Keith Vaudeville," *The Atlanta Constitution*, Thursday, July 2, 1914, p. 12.

23 Britt Craig, "The Fraternity of Fate," *The Atlanta Constitution*, August 19, 1917, p. 10H.

24 *War Letters*, p. xvii.

25 Untitled, *Ring-Tum Phi*, May 16, 1914, p. 3.

26 *War Letters*, p. xvii.

27 "Society News of Asheville and the Surrounding Towns," *The Asheville Citizen*, July 5, 1914, p. 19; "Asheville Boys Become Members of Allies' Army," *The Asheville Citizen*, August 27, 1914, p. 1.

28 "For Fatherland They Committed Double Murder," *The Atlanta Constitution*, July 3, 1914, p. 1.

29 "Warning Not Heeded by the Royal Victim," *The Atlanta Constitution*, June 29, 1914, p. 2.

30 "Simple Services Attend Funeral of Slain Royalty," *The Asheville Citizen*, July 3, 1914, p. 1; "Bodies of Duke and Duchess Are Buried," *The Asheville Gazette News*, July 4, 1914, p. 1.

31 "Fourth of July Was Generally Observed," *The Asheville Citizen*, July 5, 1914, p. 17.

32 *War Letters*, p. xvii ("We were in Asheville with our mother for a few weeks in June and early July."). Paul's recollection was a bit off, however, as Kiffin came home only for the Fourth of July weekend. *See* "Asheville Boys Become Members of Allies' Army," *The Asheville Citizen*, August 27, 1914, p. 1 ("Both young men were at Asheville during the early part of July, Paul Rockwell spending several weeks here while his brother came here for a weekend visit on the fourth of July."). Paul was in Asheville before June 24, as he left to visit Knoxville around that time. "Society and Personals," *The Asheville Citizen*, June 24, 1914, p. 2.

33 "President Wilson Would Modernize Our Independence," *The Asheville Citizen*, July 5, 1914, p. 8.

34 Woodrow Wilson: Address at Independence Hall: "The Meaning of Liberty," July 4, 1914. Online by Gerhard Peters and John T. Woolley, *The American Presidency Project*. http://www.presidency.ucsb.edu/ws/?pid=65381. *See also* "President Wilson Would Modernize Our Independence," *The Asheville Citizen*, July 5, 1914, p. 8.

35 Woodrow Wilson: Address at Independence Hall: "The Meaning of Liberty," July 4, 1914. Online by Gerhard Peters and John T. Woolley, *The American Presidency Project*. http://www.presidency.ucsb.edu/ws/?pid=65381.

36 Kiffin never saw his sister Agnes again, either. One account asserts that the last time Kiffin and Loula saw one another was when Loula chased Kiffin from a pool hall with a horsewhip. Murphy, *Kiffin Rockwell, The Lafayette Escadrille and the Birth of the United States Air Force*, p. 22. But this is contradicted by a letter written by Loula on July 6, 1916, stating "I remember the last time I saw you, two years ago yesterday," describing Kiffin's question to her while waiting on a streetcar. Loula to Paul and Kiffin, July 6, 1916, Rockwell Papers, WLU. It is possible that the incident Murphy describes provided the impetus for Kiffin to leave Asheville and travel to Atlanta after his Christmas visit at the end of 1913, but there is no concrete proof of it.

37 "Asheville Boys Become Members of Allies' Army," *The Asheville Citizen*, August 27, 1914, p.1.

38   "Clews' Review," *The Asheville Citizen*, July 6, 1914, p. 10.

39   The Rockwell collection at Washington and Lee contains stubs from the Forsyth, dated July 13 and 29, 1914.

40   "Keith Vaudeville," *The Atlanta Constitution*, Sunday, July 12, 1914, p. 10M. Dickinson's monologue started a new trend – rather than being a stooge, his country farmer character turned the table on the city-slickers. Dickinson met an untimely death in Kansas City when the marquee of the Muelbach Hotel caved in on him. Joe Laurie, Jr., *Vaudeville: From the Honky-tonks to the Palace*, p. 178-79 (Holt and Company, NY, 1953).

41   *The Atlanta Journal*, July 20, 1914.

42   *Variety*, August 7, 1914, p. 23.

43   "Servia Threatened by Austria-Hungary," *The Atlanta Constitution*, July 24, 1914, p. 3.

44   *The Atlanta Constitution*, July 25, 1914, p. 1.

45   "Austria's Ultimatum to Servia Over Archduke's Assassination May Loosen War Dogs in Europe," *The Atlanta Constitution*, July 25, 1914, p. 1.

46   *The Atlanta Journal*, July 26, 1914, p. 1.

47   "Pages Mills," *The Dillon Herald*, August 6, 1914, p. 8.

48   Kiffin Rockwell to Loula Rockwell, September 25, 1914, KYR Papers, NCDNCR.

49   *The Atlanta Journal*, July 27, 1914, p. 1.

50   "All Nations of Europe Make Preparations for War," *The Atlanta Journal*, July 27, 1914, p. 1.

51   *The Atlanta Constitution*, July 29, 1914, p. 1.

52   Transcribed Interview of Paul Rockwell by Dr. Louis D. Silveri, July 22, 1976, p. 9 (Southern Highlands Research Center, University of North Carolina at Asheville).

53   "Keith Vaudeville," *The Atlanta Constitution*, July 29, 1914, p. 12.

54   *The Atlanta Journal*, July 27, 1914, p. 11.

55   "Governors Close Stock Exchange," *The New York Times*, August 1, 1914, p. 1.

56   Sean McMeekin, *July 1914*, p. 336 (Basic Books 2013). On August 2, 1914, Renè Viviani, French Minister for foreign Affairs, sent a diplomatic cable to the French ambassadors at London, St. Petersburg, Berlin, Vienna, Rome, Madrid and Constantinople explaining the decision to mobilize: "On her side France is taking all military measures required for protection against too great an advance in German military preparations. She considers that her attempts at solution will only have a chance of success so far as it is felt that she will be ready and resolute if the conflict is forced on her." *Collected Diplomatic Documents Relating to the Outbreak of the European War*, p. 229 (London, 1915).

57   "French Government Issues Proclamation to the Nation," *The New York Herald*, August 2, 1914, p. 1. The *Herald* said the proclamation "breathes the spirit of calm determination that inspires the entire French nation and places where it rightly belongs all the responsibility for the impending welter of blood and destruction." "The Eve of War," *The New York Herald*, August 2, 1914, p. 4.

58   "The Eve of War," *The New York Herald*, August 2, 1914, p. 4.

59   "Germany and France Mobilize," *The Atlanta Journal*, August 1, 1914, p. 3.

60   "Italy Tells Germany She Will Not Join in War of Nations," *The Atlanta Journal*, August 1, 1914, p. 1.

Chapter Eleven

1   "Three Young Atlantians Would Shoulder Arms in Defense of France," *The Atlanta Journal*, August 4, 1914, p. 5. The article stated that the boys made their decision to evidence "their gratitude to France for the noble part she played in the winning of American independence[.]" *Id.*

2   *War Letters*, p. xviii.

3   According to Paul, the boys had previously said to each other many times "If France fights Germany again, we shall fight with her." "American Boys Fighting for France to Repay Debt

Their Country Owes," *The New York Sun*, January 21, 1917, Sec. 5, p. 4.

4 "Three Young Atlantians Would Shoulder Arms in Defense of France," *The Atlanta Journal*, August 4, 1914, p. 5. The reporter for the *Atlanta Journal* was the other participant in the discussion. *See* Paul Rockwell to Dr. James Patton, April 27, 1959, in Loula Ayres Rockwell Recollections, #3119-z, Southern Historical Collection, The Wilson Library, University of North Carolina at Chapel Hill.

5 "War News!," *The Atlanta Journal*, August 3, 1914, p. 1.

6 Paul A. Rockwell to Consul Ferrand, August 3, 1914, MAE-CADN, La Nouvelle-Orleans, Consulate, 340PO/A/572. Thank you to Delphine Fourrez of the Centre des Archives diplomatiques de Nantes for sending me this letter, which proves that Paul – not Kiffin – signed the letter. When he published Kiffin's letters, Paul changed the signature on the letter to Kiffin, although the rest of the letter is nearly identical. *See War Letters*, p. xviii-xix. It is not clear whether Paul changed the letter to make Kiffin look better or to cover his fib that he had attended VMI.

7 "Three Young Atlantians Would Shoulder Arms in Defense of France," *The Atlanta Journal*, August 4, 1914, p. 5.

8 St. Elmo Massengale, "Kiffin Rockwell," *War Letters of Kiffin Yates Rockwell, Supplement*, McConnell Collection, UVA.

9 "Wilson Proclaims Neutrality of U.S. During Great War," *The Atlanta Journal*, August 4, 1914, p. 1. Another paper reported Kiffin and Paul had ancestors who had fought under Lafayette, and wished to enlist in the French army, but opined "they would probably be arrested if they made an attempt to leave the country on such a mission." "Young Atlantans Wish to Enlist," *The Greenville News*, August 6, 1914, p. 8.

10 American Neutrality: An Appeal by the President of the United States to the Citizens of the Republic, Requesting Their Assistance in Maintaining a State of Neutrality During the Present European War, 63d Congress, 2d Session, Senate Document No. 566, p. 3-4 (August 19, 1914).

11 The young man, R.L. Mock, was a friend of the boys. "Young Atlantans Wish to Enlist," *The Greenville News*, August 6, 1914, p. 8.

12 Paul Rockwell to Dr. James Patton, April 27, 1959, Loula Ayres Rockwell Recollections, #3119-z, Southern Historical Collection, The Wilson Library, University of North Carolina at Chapel Hill.

13 *Id.* The travel agent was J.T. North of North's Tours Co., an Atlanta travel agency located on Peachtree Street. *Id. See also War Letters*, p. xix.

14 *War Letters*, p. xix. "American Boys Fighting for France to Repay Debt Their Country Owes," *The New York Sun*, January 21, 1917, Sec. 5, p. 4.

15 Paul said everything happened between 10:00 a.m. and 2:45 p.m. "American Boys Fighting for France to Repay Debt Their Country Owes," *The New York Sun*, January 21, 1917, Sec. 5, p. 4. It took approximately twenty hours to get to Washington from Atlanta by train, and another six or eight to get to New York from Washington.

16 "American Boys Fighting for France to Repay Debt Their Country Owes," *The New York Sun*, January 21, 1917, Sec. 5, p. 4; and *War Letters*, p. xix.

17 "Constitution Men Fight for Liberty and Democracy," *The Atlanta Constitution*, March 17, 1918, magazine section, p. 1.

18 St. Elmo Massengale, "Kiffin Rockwell," *War Letters of Kiffin Yates Rockwell, Supplement*, McConnell Collection, UVA.

19 National Collection Agency to Loula, November 30, 1914, Rockwell Papers, WLU.

20 "American Boys Fighting for France to Repay Debt Their Country Owes," *The New York Sun*, January 21, 1917, Sec. 5, p. 4.

21 Kiffin Rockwell passport application, available at Ancestry.com, US Passport Applications, 1795-1925.

22 Kiffin's and Paul's August 6, 1914 passport applications are available on Ancestry.com.

Kiffin's application also lists him as a "short story writer," but it may be that Flournoy meant to add that to Paul's application, rather than Kiffin's.

23 The Expatriation Act of March 2, 1907, section 2. Interestingly, just a month before Kiffin and Paul presented themselves to him, Flournoy had published in a law journal an article discussing, among other things, that very Act, so he surely knew the law. *The American Journal of International Law*, Vol. 8, No. 3, p. 477, 481 (July 1914). Within the next few months, the United States added to its passport application form the following line: "and that I desire a passport for use in visiting the countries hereinafter named for the following purpose...."

24 Flournoy's physical description of the boys helps us picture the pair. Kiffin, 21 years old, stood 6 feet, 1½ inches, with a high broad forehead, blue-gray eyes, square chin, and fair complexion, while Paul was 25 years old, six feet tall, high forehead, blue-grey eyes, aquiline nose, with a firm chin and mouth and medium complexion.

25 "American Boys Fighting for France to Repay Debt Their Country Owes," *The New York Sun*, January 21, 1917, Sec. 5, p. 4.

26 Kiffin Rockwell to Loula Rockwell, August 6, 1914, KYR Papers, NCDNCR. One evening paper noted that "[o]wing to the disturbed conditions in Europe," the Cunard Line's steamships had been "indefinitely postponed," while the French Line had posted an ad stating: "Existing conditions abroad necessitate the deferring of our steamers until further notice." *See The New York Sun*, August 6, 1914, p. 11.

27 Kiffin Rockwell to Loula Rockwell, August 6, 1914, KYR Papers, NCDNCR.

28 *Id.*

29 *Id. Compare War Letters*, p. 2. This letter echoes one written by Lafayette to his father-in-law 138 years before upon his decision to strike for America. Lafayette wrote: "You will be surprised, dear father, at what I am about to tell you; it has cost me more than I can tell you to have not consulted you.... I have found a unique opportunity to distinguish myself and to learn my profession: I am a general officer in the army of the United States." As cited in Gonzague Saint Bris, *Lafayette: Hero of the American Revolution*, p. 80 (Pegasus Books, 2010). *See also* David A. Clary, *Adopted Son: Washington, Lafayette, and the Friendship That Saved the Revolution*, p. 81.

30 Kiffin Rockwell to Loula Rockwell, August 6, 1914, KYR Papers, NCDNCR.

31 *Id.*

32 The Hotel Imperial was at the corner of Broadway and 32nd, about a mile and a half from Pier 62.

33 "How Shall 'Miss Liberty's' Toilet Be Made?," *The New York Times*, July 29, 1906, p. 2.

Part Two

1 "The Great War," speech at Carnegie Hall, October 24, 1914, as printed in the pamphlet *America and the War*, p. 3 (1914).

2 Ford, Paul Leicester, ed. *The Writings of Thomas Jefferson*, Vol. 1:149 (New York: G.P. Putnam's Sons, 1892-99).

Chapter Twelve

3 Georges Clemenceau, *France Facing Germany*, p. 119 (1919).

4 Clemenceau, *France Facing Germany*, p. 123.

5 Bert Hall, *One Man's War*, p. 25 (New York, 1929).

6 Elov Nilson, a Swede who signed up with the Americans. This quote comes from his diary and is available at https://www.svd.se/21-8-han-ljuger-av-nagon-anledning-om-sitt-fodelsear (visited July 15, 2017) ("Överallt syns nu krigsfeber nertvingad. Här och där är en affär som stängts och en papperslapp på dörren förklarar orsaken – ägaren är vid fronten.").

7   One of the American enlistees later said he "had been given absolutely certain information that the war would not last nine months." F.W. Zinn, quoted in "Local Man Was One of the Few from U.S. Who 'Flew for France,'" *The Battle Creek Enquirer and News*, October 12, 1941, p. 26 (Frederick Zinn Files, Galesburg-Charleston Memorial District Library, Galesburg, Michigan). I thank Helena Hayes for tracking down this article.

8   *Journal Officiel de la Republique Francaise*, 8 Août, 1914, p. 7271.

9   *Id.*

10 Paul Rockwell, *American Fighters in the Foreign Legion, 1914-1918*, p. 6 (1930) (hereafter "American Fighters").

11 "American Students May Volunteer," *The New York Herald*, August 4, 1914, p. 2.

12 "Paris Calm and Certain of Victory," *The New York Sun*, August 7, 1914, p. 3.

13 "Extracts From the Diary of An American Artist in Paris," *Art and Progress*, December 1914, p. 41-42.

14 "Proposes American Corps," *The New York Herald*, August 3, 1914, p. 2.

15 Hall, *One Man's War*, p. 23. *See also* Bert Hall, "Fast Fighting and Narrow Escapes in the Air," *The American Magazine*, p. 44 (Sep. 1918). Paul Rockwell called Hall a "genial adventurer" when he published Kiffin's letters. *War Letters*, p. 189.

16 "Americans Enter the French Army," *The Brooklyn Daily Eagle*, September 20, 1914, p. 4.

17 Georges Casmeze, Certificate of Registration of American Citizen, available at Ancestry.com, *U.S., Consular Registration Certificates, 1907-1918*.

18 Proposes American Corps," *The New York Herald*, August 3, 1914, p. 2. An intriguing handwritten note in the World War I scrapbook of Charles Sweeny is dated Sunday, August 2, 1914, and reads: "For twenty-four hours France has been at war, and the Germans have already violated her borders. The French are recalling their regiments. Morale is high but the shadow of 1870 remains on all hearts. It is in these conditions that a young American George Casmeze, this sunny afternoon made a prolific, perhaps historic decision." Handwritten note in WWI scrapbook of Charles Sweeny, in possession of the author.

19 *See* William M. Emery, *The Howland Heirs*, p. 346 (1919).

20 Kenneth Weeks to Alice Weeks, August 12, 1914, in Rockwell Papers, WLU. Weeks was fully committed to France; near the end of September, he wrote his mother that he "would be glad to die in perhaps the most critical test that civilization has ever experienced." Kenneth Weeks to Alice Weeks, September 27, 1914, Rockwell Papers, WLU.

21 Pardoe, *Lost Eagles: One Man's Mission to Find Missing Airmen in Two World Wars*, p. 21-23 (2010). While at the University of Michigan, Zinn's I.Q. was tested at 168. *Id.* at p. 21.

22 "Local Man Was One of the Few from U.S. Who 'Flew for France,'" *The Battle Creek Enquirer and News*, October 12, 1941, p. 26.

23 *Id. See also* "Will Ask Detroiter to Take Son Out of Army," *The Detroit Free Press*, November 14, 1914, p. 12. It is understandable that Zinn went by his initials while in France – his given name was Frederick Wilhelm.

24 "With Casey at the Battle," *The Times* (Shreveport), November 7, 1915, magazine section, p. 6. *See also* John Joseph Casey, "The New 'Old Guard' of France," *The New York Times Current History*, vol. X, p. 855 (1917).

25 "Americans Enter the French Army," *The Brooklyn Daily Eagle*, September 20, 1914, p. 4; John Joseph Casey, "The New 'Old Guard' of France," *The New York Times Current History*, vol. X, p. 855 (1917).

26 "David King Survives Further Fighting in Verdun Inferno," *The Brooklyn Daily Eagle*, May 17, 1916, p. 2; "'2 Weeks of Hell,' American's Idea of Verdun Fight," *The Brooklyn Daily Eagle*, March 21, 1916, p. 1. *See also The Harvard Freshman Red Book*, Class of 1916, p. 114. King also served as the assistant manager for the freshman crew. *Id.* at 46. *See also* "Americans in Big Battle," *The New York Times*, November 10, 1915, p. 4.

27 Although an ocean apart when the war broke out, some of Seeger's cohorts were thinking the same thing as the Rockwells. The August 4, 1914 edition of *The New York Herald* contains

a brief article noting that the American students living in the Latin Quarter hastily planned a meeting in a local café the morning of August 5 to "discuss the question of volunteering, either to join the French army, or to become members of a separate corps to be placed at the disposal of the French commander-in-chief, should such a corps be formed." "American Students May Volunteer," *The New York Herald*, August 4, 1914, p. 2.

28   Alan Seeger, *Poems*, p. xxiv.

29   David Hanna, *Rendezvous With Death*, p. 43. As shown by an emergency passport application he filed that day with the embassy in London, Seeger was there through at least August 11, 1914. Available at Ancestry.com, US Passport Applications, 1795-1925.

30   "Many Americans Volunteer," *The New York Herald*, August 6, 1914, p. 2.

31   *Kenneth Weeks A Soldier of the Legion*, p. 23.

32   Hall, *One Man's War*, p. 24.

33   Although he resigned shortly after Wilson's election, Herrick's replacement was not confirmed until June 1914. One reporter there at the time called Herrick "a sort of guardian angel for Americans in Paris." Charles Inman Barnard, *Paris War Days: Diary of an American*, p. 106 (1914).

34   Colonel T. Bentley Mott, *Myron T. Herrick, Friend of France*, p. 144 (1929). At a speech dedicating a monument in Paris to these volunteers, Herrick himself said: "All I could find to transcribe my feelings, and yet keep within the limits of the duty imposed upon me, was to tell them that if I could change my place for theirs, or my age for their vigorous youth, my choice would be quickly made. This seemed to answer the predetermined question that I saw in their glowing eyes – there was no haste, no excitement, no foolish sentimentality, but sure determination and the courage of youth suddenly turned to manhood." Rockwell, *American Fighters*, p. 355.

35   "Les volontaires américains," *Le Temps*, 14 Août 1914, p. 2-3; Hall, *One Man's War*, p. 23.

36   Donald McCormick, *One Man's Wars*, p. 33 (1972). More recent and careful scholarship asserts that Sweeny was not expelled the second time, but resigned. Charley Roberts and Charles P. Hess, *Charles Sweeny, The Man Who Inspired Hemingway*, p. 48 (McFarland & Co., 2017).

37   "Many Americans Volunteer," *The New York Herald*, August 6, 1914, p. 2. *See also* "Two Flags of Deathless Glory," *Leslie's Weekly*, June 14, 1917, p. 730. Bach later stated: "I was abroad in 1914 at the outbreak of the war and joined the French Army. I was taken prisoner September 23, 1915 by the Germans and released December 6, 1918." Jules James Bach passport application dated February 14, 1919, available at Ancestry.com, US Passport Applications, 1795-1925. Bach also said that "when the war broke out, I joined a small group of Americans who had decided to enlist in the French Foreign Legion. We did so in August 1914, without having to take any oath of allegiance to France." Jules James Bach, Affidavit to Explain Protracted Foreign Residence and to Overcome Presumption of Expatriation, dated June 12, 1922. Available at Ancestry.com, US Passport Applications, 1795-1925.

38   "Two Flags of Deathless Glory," *Leslie's Weekly*, June 14, 1917, p. 730. *See also* "France Names First Victim," *The Boston Globe*, August 19, 1914, p. 11 ("Americans gather daily around the corps recruiting office, over the entrance of which hangs a large American flag."). One journalist recalled seeing the flag hanging over the headquarters under the arcade. *See* Herbert Adams Gibbons, *Paris Reborn*, p. 128 (1916). The flag had only 44 stars, although the admission of New Mexico and Arizona in 1912 had brought to 48 the number of states in the union. Moreover, the 44 stars were in an irregular pattern, with four rows of nine stars, two on top and two underneath one row of 8, aligned to the right, leaving a "blank" space on the far left of the middle row.

39   "American Volunteers in Paris," *The Times (London)*, August 7, 1914, p. 5. Other (slightly different) pleas were published in Paris dailies on August 6. *See* "Les étrangers te la France," *Le Temps*, 6 Août 1914, p. 4, and "Vibrant Appel Aux Americains," *La Petit Parisien*, 6 Août 1914, p. 2. I am not certain this is the appeal referenced by Paul Rockwell, supposedly signed

by Bill Thaw, James Carstairs, Rene Phelizot and J.J. Bach, but it perfectly fits the time frame. *See* Rockwell, *American Fighters*, p. 4. However, Paul seems to have gotten the committee members wrong. *The Times* listed the "temporary committee" as: George Casmeze, Paul Testard of Union University, Rene Phelizot, W.B. Hall, and Richard Macalister of the New Mexico Military Academy, while *La Petit Parisien* and *La Temps* both left Macalister out, listing only Casmeze, Hall, Testard and Phelizot.

40   "Les étrangers te la France," *Le Temps*, 6 Août 1914, p. 4.

41   "Les étrangers te la France," *Le Temps*, 6 Août 1914, p. 4. *See also* "Vibrant Appel Aux Americains," *La Petit Parisien*, 6 Août 1914, p. 2.

42   "Les étrangers te la France," *Le Temps*, 6 Août 1914, p. 4; "Vibrant Appel Aux Americains," *La Petit Parisien*, 6 Août 1914, p. 2.

43   "France Names First Victim," *The Boston Globe*, August 19, 1914, p. 11.

44   Hall, *One Man's War*, p. 24.

45   F.W. Zinn, "The Real Foreign Legion," *Leslie's Weekly*, June 29, 1916, p. 812.

46   Charles Sweeny, "Tells of Beginning of Foreign Legion," *The Evening Star*, June 29, 1917, p. 12. *See also* Rockwell, *American Fighters*, p. 7.

47   F.W. Zinn, "The Real Foreign Legion," *Leslie's Weekly*, June 29, 1916, p. 812.

48   "France Names First Victim," *The Boston Globe*, August 19, 1914, p. 11. Sidney B. Veit, an American businessman living in Paris, had earlier urged Americans to "Remember the lessons of Washington and Lafayette; we have obligations which should be redeemed." "Appeal to American Residents in Paris," *The New York Herald*, August 6, 1914, p. 3.

49   Charles Sweeny, "Tells of Beginning of Foreign Legion," *The Evening Star*, June 29, 1917, p. 12. To those "overcautious" few who protested that America should not allow its citizens to get involved, the volunteers responded "that the republic that owes a debt of gratitude to Lafayette should not place obstacles in the way of those of its citizens who, of their own free will, are risking life and limb in the cause of French democracy versus German imperialism." "Americans Enter the French Army," *The Brooklyn Daily Eagle*, September 20, 1914, p. 4.

50   McCormick, *One Man's Wars*, p. 76.

51   "William Thaw Leads an American Legion," *The Pittsburgh Post*, August 17, 1914, p. 7.

52   Mason, *The Lafayette Escadrille*, p. 6. Hall reported that after the recruits executed one particularly difficult movement, "a group of women broke into the Marseillaise." Hall, *One Man's War*, p. 24.

53   "Americans Volunteer to Fight for France," *The Washington Herald*, August 16, 1914, p. 2; "William Thaw Leads an American Legion," *The Pittsburgh Post*, August 17, 1914, p. 7. Upon his arrival in Paris from London, Chapman was less than impressed by what he found, and wrote his father that the "American Volunteer Corps is more like a corpse lying across the path than anything else." Chapman also stated he would not give the group any money, saying, "I am convinced it would be useless to give anything to the present band who squat at 11 rue de valois." Chapman then decided to become a chauffeur for the Red Cross, but that project came up short when in a limousine he failed to navigate a tough driveway corner for half an hour. Victor Chapman to John Jay Chapman, August 12, 1914, John Jay Chapman Papers, 1841-1940 (MS Am 1854)(339). Houghton Library, Harvard University (hereafter "John Jay Chapman Papers, Harvard."). Eventually, he enlisted in the Foreign Legion on August 29, 1914.

54   "William Thaw Leads an American Legion," *The Pittsburgh Post*, August 17, 1914, p. 7.

55   Edgar Bouligny, "Rendezvous," *Liberty Magazine*, March 17, 1934, p. 7.

56   "American Negroes Make Good in Foreign Legion," *The Akron Beacon Journal*, June 7, 1917, p. 10. *See also* Hall, *One Man's War*, p. 27. Scanlon later won the *Croix de Guerre* in an amusing way, accidentally uncovering an advanced post of German soldiers when he threw a grenade towards the German trenches in retaliation for being hit by a stone. *See* "French War Cross for Bob Scanlon," *The Brooklyn Daily Eagle*, December 13, 1915, p. 12.

57   "William Thaw Leads an American Legion," *The Pittsburgh Post*, August 17, 1914, p. 7.

58 "In the French Aero Corps," *The Yale Alumni Weekly*, December 29, 1916, p. 383. This may have occurred at the beginning of what would have been Thaw's junior year, as he later stated he had completed two years at Yale.

59 "William Thaw Ends Air Journey Here," *The New York Times*, October 6, 1913, p. 1. *See also* "Daring Aviator Flies Under Four Bridges," *The Telegraph* (Nashua), October 9, 1913, p. 1. The last article ran with a photo of Thaw flying under the Manhattan Bridge.

60 "At Palm Beach," *The Pittsburgh Gazette Times*, February 1, 1914, section 6, p. 4.

61 "Thaws in Plenty on Paris Bound Steamer," *The Evening World* (NY), February 11, 1914, p. 18.

62 "America to be Represented," *The Newport Daily News*, February 10, 1914, p. 7.

63 *Id. See also* "Thaw Makes Fine Flight," *The Pittsburgh Gazette Times*, April 20, 1914, p. 1. Thaw's scrapbook contains a letter from Les Commissaires Sportifs, assigning his machine No. 8 for the race.

64 "British Aviator is Victor," *The Pittsburgh Gazette Times*, April 21, 1914, p. 15; "British Aviator Wins," *The Pittsburgh Press*, April 21, 1914, p. 13; "Aviation – La Coupe Schneider," *La Presse*, 16 Avril 1914, p. 3; "Au meeting de Monaco – La Coupe Jacques Schneider," *Le Radical*, 20 Avril 1914, p. 4. *See also Aero Club of America 1915*, p. 77.

65 Garros was on the French team. *See* "Mr. William Thaw Makes Fine Flight," *The New York Herald*, April 17, 1914. In addition, the April 20, 1914 copy of *The New York Herald* has photographs of both Thaw and Garros. Both men would later win fame as pilots in the war.

66 Irving J. Newman, "A Biography of Colonel Thaw II," *Popular Aviation*, November 1934, p. 281.

67 Gordon, *Lafayette Escadrille Pilot Biographies*, p. 56.

68 "William Thaw is a Volunteer in the French Army," *The Pittsburg Press*, September 8, 1914, p. 9. *See also* "Joins French Army," *The Newport Daily News*, August 18, 1914, p. 5; "France Names First Victim," *The Boston Globe*, August 19, 1914, p. 11; and "Today's War Developments," *The Pittsburgh Post*, August 19, 1914, p. 1.

69 William Thaw Affidavit, January 3, 1916, National Archives, *General Records of the Department of State, 1763-2002*, Record Group 59, Central Decimal Files, 1910-1963, File Unit: 763.72111S04 – 763.72111z1. *The Brooklyn Daily Eagle* reported that Thaw was told "that it would be preferable for him to operate a French machine." "Americans Enter the French Army," *The Brooklyn Daily Eagle*, September 20, 1914, p. 4.

70 "Americans Enter the French Army," *The Brooklyn Daily Eagle*, September 20, 1914, p. 4.

71 Dowd graduated from Georgetown and went to law school at Columbia, where he rowed on the crew. *See* "Will Marry His Godmother," *The Chicago Daily News*, March 10, 1916, p. 2.

72 "Sea Cliff Mourns Death of Aviator Dennis Dowd, Jr.," *The Brooklyn Daily Eagle*, August 14, 1916, p. 2.

73 "Americans Enter the French Army," *The Brooklyn Daily Eagle*, September 20, 1914, p. 4. Dowd might have seen the call from Paris for an American Legion in the New York Sun. *See* "Paris Sees Short War; More British Volunteers," *The New York Sun*, August 7, 1914, p. 3.

74 "Comrade Genet Pays Tribute to Dennis Dowd, Killed in France," *The Brooklyn Daily Eagle*, September 17, 1916, Section 3, p. 4.

75 "Sea Cliff Man in the War," *The Brooklyn Daily Eagle*, February 1, 1915, p. 10.

76 "Americans Enter the French Army," *The Brooklyn Daily Eagle*, September 20, 1914, p. 4. *See also* "Brooklyn Lawyer Fights for Allies; Endures Hardships," *The Brooklyn Daily Eagle*, February 14, 1915, Sec. 3, p. 8; "Brooklyn Soldier Writes from Front," *The Brooklyn Daily Eagle*, January 6, 1915, p. 5.

77 *See* Passenger list for the ship *Rotterdam*, August 11, 1914, available in "Netherlands Passenger Lists Holland-America Line, 1900-1974," http://FamilySearch.org. Dowd was said to be the only American citizen on board the ship. "Dr. Riley in Paris; Sailing Uncertain," *The Brooklyn Daily Eagle*, August 24, 1914, p. 4.

78 "Police Clubs End Reservists' Riot," *The New York Tribune*, August 11, 1914, p. 4.

79 See Passenger list for the ship *Rotterdam*, August 11, 1914, available in "Netherlands Passenger Lists Holland-America Line, 1900-1974," http://FamilySearch.org.

80 "Americans Enter the French Army," *The Brooklyn Daily Eagle*, September 20, 1914, p. 4.

81 Hall, *One Man's War*, p. 25. While Casmeze did enlist, and went to initial training with the others, he eventually "took sick," and "had to be left behind." *Id*. at 27. *See also* "Only Three Days in 25 Off Firing Line," *The New York Sun*, January 24, 1915, Fifth Section, p. 4 (noting that Casmeze was "found unfit for service at Toulouse").

82 "L'enrolement des Volontaires Étrangers," *Le Figaro*, 22 Août 1914, p. 3.

83 *Id*.

84 "Americans Enter the French Army," *The Brooklyn Daily Eagle*, September 20, 1914, p. 4. *See also* "One American Killed, One Wounded by German Fire in First Battle in Which the Foreign Legion Fought," *The New York Sun*, November 8, 1914, p. 7.

85 Henry Farnsworth to his mother, January 5, 1915, *Letters of Henry Weston Farnsworth*, p. 92 (1916).

86 William Thaw Affidavit, January 3, 1916, National Archives, *General Records of the Department of State, 1763-2002*, Record Group 59, Central Decimal Files, 1910-1963, File Unit: 763.72111S04 – 763.72111Z1. One newspaper reported that the concluding paragraphs of the form were as follows: "Do you pledge absolute obedience to the French officers of the active army? Do you comply in advance with all the rigors of discipline and the exigencies of the war? Are you prepared to swear fidelity unto death, if that shall be necessary, to the French flag?" "Americans Enter the French Army," *The Brooklyn Daily Eagle*, September 20, 1914, p. 4.

87 "L'enrolement des Volontaires Étrangers," *Le Figaro*, 22 Août 1914, p. 3.

88 William J. Guard, *The Soul of Paris*, p. 42-43 (1914).

89 Alan Seeger, "A Soldier Thinks of War," *The New Republic*, p. 66-67 (May 22, 1915).

90 Charles Terrin, "Alan Seeger, Poète-Légionnaire," *La Légion Étrangére (revue bimestrielle illustrée militaire et coloniale)*, No. 21, p. 34, (1940). My thanks to Elodie Delcambre-Maillard at the *Bibliothèque de l'Institut de France, Paris* for providing this information.

91 M.A. DeWolfe Howe, *Memoirs of the Harvard Dead in the War Against Germany, Vol. 1*, p. 118 (Harvard University Press 1920). *See also* Alan Seeger to Miss Elsie A. Seeger, February 26, 1916, Alan Seeger Papers, Harvard.

92 David W. King, *L.M. 8046*, p. ix.

Chapter Thirteen

1 James Norman Hall to his mother, August 6, 1914, James Norman Hall Papers, 1906-1954, Collection MS 01.01, Burling Library Archives, Grinnell College, Grinnell, Iowa (hereafter "JNH Papers, Grinnell."). I thank Cindy Rutgers for permission to publish items from the James Norman Hall Papers at Grinnell College.

2 "London in War Time," *The Saturday Evening Post*, September 19, 1914, p. 7.

3 "What We Are Fighting For," *The Times (London)*, August 7, 1914, p. 8.

4 *The Trans-Atlantic American*, August 14, 1914, p. 1-2, printed onboard the *St. Paul*, Rockwell Papers, WLU.

5 Kiffin to Loula, August 14, 1914, KYR Papers, NCDNCR.

6 *Id*.

7 *Id*.

8 *Id*.

9 "Irvin S. Cobb Tells of War Suffering," *The New York Times*, December 2, 1914, p. 4 (noting Cobb worked for *The Saturday Evening Post*).

10 E.H. and F.B. Towle both appear on the *St. Paul* passenger list, Rockwell Papers, WLU.

11 "New York Boys Enlist to Fight in French Army," *The New York Evening World*, August 27, 1914, p. 12. A nice photo of the Towle brothers accompanies this article.

12   Kiffin to Loula, August 14, 1914, KYR Papers, NCDNCR. The passport of Lorenzo Speyer Count de Besa says he was a "lecturer" born in Topeka, Kansas.

13   Kiffin to Loula, August 14, 1914, KYR Papers, NCDNCR.

14   *Id.*

15   Kiffin to Loula, August 18, 1914, KYR Papers, NCDNCR.

16   *Id.*

17   *Id.*

18   "American Boys Fighting for France to Repay Debt Their Country Owes," *The New York Sun*, January 21, 1917, Sec. 5, p. 4.

19   Kiffin to Loula, August 24, 1914, *War Letters*, p. 4.

20   "The Stranded Americans," *The Times (London)*, August 14, 1914, p. 3 ("There are few busier places in London just now than the headquarters of the American Citizens' Committee in the Savoy Hotel, where, in the great ballroom of the hotel and the adjoining apartments, there surges a crowd of 300 or 400 'stranded' Americans at all hours of the day.").

21   Kiffin to Loula, August 18, 1914, KYR Papers, NCDNCR.

22   "American Boys Fighting for France to Repay Debt Their Country Owes," *The New York Sun*, January 21, 1917, Sec. 5, p. 4.

23   *Three Centuries*, p. 64.

24   Kiffin to Loula, August 24, 1914, *War Letters*, p. 4.

25   *Id. See also* "American Boys Fighting for France to Repay Debt Their Country Owes," *The New York Sun*, January 21, 1917, Sec. 5, p. 4.

26   Kiffin to Loula, August 18, 1914, KYR Papers, NCDNCR.

27   "German Machine Brought Down," *The Western Sentinel*, May 23, 1916, p. 2.

28   Kiffin to Loula, August 6, 1914, KYR Papers, NCDNCR. Interestingly, both ambassadors – Walter Hines Page (England) and Pleasant Alexander Stovall (Switzerland) – had served as editors of papers to which James Chester Rockwell had contributed, the *State Chronicle* and the *Augusta Chronicle*, respectively.

29   Kiffin to Loula, August 6, 1914, KYR Papers, NCDNCR.

30   "Asheville Boys Become Members of Allies' Army," *The Asheville Citizen*, August 27, 1914, p. 1. Not long after the events, Paul wrote "So remote did London seem from the actual fighting that, after a week or so, we decided to cross over to France to see if we couldn't get nearer the events." "Atlanta Boy, Now in France, Hasn't Glimpsed the War," *The Atlanta Journal*, March 21, 1915, Magazine, p. 1.

31   "Rockwell Boys Will Join Foreign Legion," *The Atlanta Constitution*, August 27, 1914, p. 12.

32   "Three Young Atlantians Would Shoulder Arms in Defense of France," *The Atlanta Journal*, August 4, 1914, p. 5.

33   *See* "New Yorker Leads U.S. French Corps; London Americans Seek Enlistment," *The Washington Post*, August 27, 1914, p. 3; "Americans Would Fight," *The Baltimore Sun*, August 27, 1914, p. 3; and "Many Americans Enlist for Service with Allies," *The Indianapolis Star*, August 27, 1914, p. 2.

34   "Asheville Boys Become Members of Allies' Army," *The Asheville Citizen*, August 27, 1914, p. 1. *See also* "Boys from Asheville to Volunteer in War," *The Asheville Gazette-News*, August 27, 1914, p. 6.

35   "Americans in the War," *The Asheville Citizen*, August 28, 1914, p. 4.

36   "Atlanta Boy, Now in France, Hasn't Glimpsed the War," *The Atlanta Journal*, March 21, 1915, Magazine, p. 1.

37   "Americans Enter the French Army," *The Brooklyn Daily Eagle*, September 20, 1914, p. 4.

38   *Id. See also* "One American Killed, One Wounded," *The New York Sun*, November 8, 1914, p. 7.

39   "Americans Enter the French Army," *The Brooklyn Daily Eagle*, September 20, 1914, p. 4.

40   *Id.*

41   "American Gets Baptism of Fire in Foreign Legion of France," *Morning Register* (Eugene,

Oregon), August 22, 1915, p. 14.

42   There were two American flags and one French one; it is unknown who carried the other flags. "Americans Enter the French Army," *The Brooklyn Daily Eagle*, September 20, 1914, p. 4.

43   "Hug American Recruits," *The New York Times*, August 26, 1914, p. 4.

44   "Americans Enter the French Army," *The Brooklyn Daily Eagle*, September 20, 1914, p. 4. *See also* Walter Adolphe Roberts, "The Alan Seeger I Knew," *The Bookman*, August 1918, p. 585.

45   "Parisians Cheer American Allies," *The Brooklyn Daily Eagle*, August 26, 1914, p. 4.

46   Guard, *The Soul of Paris*, p. 42. One Paris newspaper reported that crowds applauded them on their way, with passers-by saluting the American flag, "the folds of which were lost in the French tricolor." "Les volontaires étrangers," *Le Temps*, 28 Août 1914, p. 3. Paul Rockwell included a photo of the station from that day in his book *American Fighters in the Foreign Legion*, p. 14. Another reporter described the Americans as "a tall, stalwart lot, marching with a sort of cowboy swing." Barnard, *Paris War Days: Diary of an American*, p. 113.

47   "One American Killed, One Wounded," *The New York Sun*, November 8, 1914, p. 7.

48   B.F. Towle, "In the Foreign Legion and Royal Flying Corps," *The Seventh Regiment Gazette*, p. 185 (June 1915).

49   "One American Killed, One Wounded," *The New York Sun*, November 8, 1914, p. 7. A palmist on the train predicted the death of one of the Americans but would not tell them which one. The group was "rather impressed by this prediction," as in his readings the palmist "received the acknowledgement of his correctness both as to character and the past of the occupants of the compartment." *Id.*

50   "Parisians Accord Hearty Ovation to Departing American Volunteers," *The New York Herald*, August 26, 1914, p. 3.

51   *Id.*

52   *Id. See also* "Les volontaires étrangers," *Le Temps*, 28 Août 1914, p. 3.

53   Paul and Kiffin also "hunted up a friend" who had lived in Paris for several years, as neither of them spoke a word of French. "Atlanta Boy, Wounded on French Battlefield, Paints Graphic Pen Picture of European War," *The Atlanta Constitution*, May 2, 1915, p. 1.

54   Transcribed Interview of Paul Rockwell by Dr. Louis D. Silveri, July 22, 1976, p. 11 (Southern Highlands Research Center, University of North Carolina at Asheville).

55   "American Opposed to Impartiality," *The New York Herald*, August 26, 1914, p. 3.

56   *Id.*

57   "Let Americans Help France," *The New York Herald*, August 26, 1914, p. 3.

58   "Finds Impartiality Impossible," *The New York Herald*, August 26, 1914, p. 3. Several years after the war ended, Germany exacted its revenge on Professor Fagnani for his "enmity for Germany ever since 1914," expelling him and his wife from Germany shortly after they arrived for a visit. *See* "Rev. Dr. Fagnani and Wife Expelled from German Soil," *The New York Times*, September 21, 1921, p. 1.

59   "Well argued, Laddie!", *The New York Herald*, August 26, 1914, p. 3.

60   *Kelly of the Foreign Legion*, p. 5 (New York, Mitchell Kennerley, 1917).

61   Kiffin's and Paul's service record cards are available on the *Mémoire des Hommes* website (memoiredeshommes.sga.defense.gouv.fr/)

62   Transcribed Interview of Paul Rockwell by Dr. Louis D. Silveri, July 22, 1976, p. 11 (Southern Highlands Research Center, University of North Carolina at Asheville).

63   "Americans Enter the French Army," *The Brooklyn Daily Eagle*, September 20, 1914, p. 4.

64   "Atlanta Boy, Now in France, Hasn't Glimpsed the War," *The Atlanta Journal*, March 21, 1915, Magazine, p. 1.

1   *See* Thaw letter August 30, 1914, "The War Letters of Two Yale Undergraduates," *Yale Alumni Weekly*, January 22, 1915, p. 484; and King, *L.M. 8046*, p. 5.

2   "One American Killed, One Wounded," *The New York Sun*, November 8, 1914, p. 7.

3   *Id.*

4   "American Volunteers are 'Fresh and Fit as Paint,'" *The New York Herald*, September 2, 1914, p. 3.

5   Thaw letter August 30, 1914, "The War Letters of Two Yale Undergraduates," *Yale Alumni Weekly*, January 22, 1915, p. 484.

6   Charles Sweeny, "Tells of Beginning of Foreign Legion," *The Evening Star*, June 29, 1917, p. 12.

7   Thaw letter August 30, 1914, "The War Letters of Two Yale Undergraduates," *Yale Alumni Weekly*, January 22, 1915, p. 484.

8   Charles Sweeny, "Tells of Beginning of Foreign Legion," *The Evening Star*, June 29, 1917, p. 12.

9   *Id.*

10   Edgar Bouligny, "Rendezvous," *Liberty Magazine*, March 17, 1934, p. 9.

11   B.F. Towle, "In the Foreign Legion and Royal Flying Corps," *The Seventh Regiment Gazette*, p. 185 (June 1915).

12   Kiffin to Loula, August 31, 1914, KYR Papers, NCDNCR.

13   "Atlanta Boy, Now in France, Hasn't Glimpsed the War," *The Atlanta Journal*, March 21, 1915, Magazine, p. 1.

14   Thaw letter August 30, 1914, "The War Letters of Two Yale Undergraduates," *Yale Alumni Weekly*, January 22, 1915, p. 484.

15   King, *L.M. 8046*, p. 6.

16   "Atlanta Boy, Now in France, Hasn't Glimpsed the War," *The Atlanta Journal*, March 21, 1915, Magazine, p. 1.

17   Kiffin to Loula, August 31, 1914, KYR Papers, NCDNCR.

18   *Id.*

19   Paul Rockwell, "The Legionnaires of France," *Kenneth Weeks: A Soldier of the Legion*, p. 81-82 (1916).

20   Kiffin to Loula, August 31, 1914, KYR Papers, NCDNCR.

21   Georges Delpeuch to Dale Walker, July 31, 1967, Rockwell Papers, WLU. Delpeuch was a mechanic working on the repair of transatlantic ships.

22   Georges Delpeuch to Dale Walker, July 31, 1967, Rockwell Papers, WLU. *See also* "1,000 French Reservists Sail from Brooklyn," *The Brooklyn Daily Times*, August 8, 1914, p. 1.

23   "French Reservists Off, Show Fervor," *The Brooklyn Daily Eagle*, August 9, 1914, p. 7. A wonderful photo of the ship, with its many flag-waving reservists, accompanies this article.

24   *See* Rockwell, *American Fighters*, p. 10; and "Americans Win Promotion," *Greensboro Daily News*, October 24, 1914, p. 9.

25   *See* "Yankee Legion Man to Remain with Tri-Color," *The Pittsburg Press*, February 14, 1918, p. 11; "Notes of Life in the French Capital in Time of War," *The New York Sun*, January 2, 1918, p. 6.

26   Hall & Nordhoff, *The Lafayette Flying Corps*, Vol. 1, p. 464. Trinkard's declaration of intention from 1910 is available on Ancestry.com. At least initially, Alan Seeger was not as well-liked. Many of the men resented his habit of sitting apart and scribbling, refusing to show anyone what he had written. They felt the self-declared poet was a snob. *See* Walter Adolphe Roberts, "The Alan Seeger I Knew," *The Bookman*, August 1918, p. 589.

27   "South Boston Man Writes from Front," *The Boston Globe*, February 23, 1915, p. 5. Additional details are taken from Soubiran's August 14, 1914 passport application, available on ancestry.com. Soubiran's 1920 passport application contains a wonderful photo.

28   Rockwell, *American Fighters*, p. 58.

29   Thaw letter August 30, 1914, "The War Letters of Two Yale Undergraduates," *Yale Alumni Weekly*, January 22, 1915, p. 484. It seems likely that Thaw was referring to Kiffin when he wrote of meeting "a preacher from Georgia" at Rouen. This could have stemmed from Kiffin's bearing and perhaps from the boys' relating that their father had been a Baptist preacher. Interestingly, Thaw also mentioned "a pro gambler from Missouri," probably referring to Bert Hall.

30   Kiffin to Loula, August 31, 1914, KYR Papers, NCDNCR.

31   William Graves Sharp, *The War Memoirs of William Graves Sharp*, p. 9 (1931).

32   Sharp, *The War Memoirs of William Graves Sharp*, p. 10. One reporter noticed shortly after the start of the war an "extraordinary religious renaissance in France." Guard, *The Soul of Paris*, p. 136.

33   "One American Killed, One Wounded," *The New York Sun*, November 8, 1914, p. 7.

34   Thaw letter August 30, 1914, "The War Letters of Two Yale Undergraduates," *Yale Alumni Weekly*, January 22, 1915, p. 483.

35   Kiffin to Loula, August 31, 1914, KYR Papers, NCDNCR.

36   Thaw letter September 6, 1914, "The War Letters of Two Yale Undergraduates," *Yale Alumni Weekly*, January 22, 1915, p. 484.

37   Rockwell, *American Fighters*, p. 12.

38   "Atlanta Boy, Now in France, Hasn't Glimpsed the War," *The Atlanta Journal*, March 21, 1915, Magazine, p. 1.

39   "Wanderlust Lured Phelizot," *The Chicago Daily News*, October 23, 1915, p. 6.

40   Passenger List of S.S. *Cestrian*, Ancestry.com, *Massachusetts, Passenger and Crew Lists, 1820-1963*.

41   "Only Three Days in 25 Off Firing line," *The New York Sun*, January 24, 1915, p. 4.

42   "Chicagoan Slain by a Fellow Legionary," *The Chicago Daily News*, October 23, 1915, p. 6.

43   There has been a lack of clarity as to the precise date the Americans signed the flag. Paul Rockwell (who signed it) claimed the signing took place on "the last day of August, 1914," as they prepared to leave Rouen. Paul Rockwell, "Chicagoan Slain by a Fellow Legionary," *The Chicago Daily News*, October 23, 1915, p. 6. *See also* Paul Rockwell, "Americans Lose Heavily," *The Courier-Journal (Louisville)*, May 22, 1916, p. 3 (claiming Phelizot had each volunteer sign the flag during "[t]he last days of August..."). Others have claimed the date was October 17, 1914. (*See* http://www.monongahelabooks.com/flagvol.html) However, I have a photo of the flag, taken when the date was still legible, and the date of September 1, 1914 is clearly visible. WWI scrapbook of Charles Sweeny, in possession of the author.

44   "Chicagoan Slain by a Fellow Legionary," *The Chicago Daily News*, October 23, 1915, p. 6; and Martin Marshall, "Two Flags of Deathless Glory," *Leslie's Weekly*, June 14, 1917, p. 730.

45   Martin Marshall, "Two Flags of Deathless Glory," *Leslie's Weekly*, June 14, 1917, p. 730.

46   "Two Americans Leave Front," *The New York Sun*, December 9, 1914, p. 3. *See also* "Vincent Astor's Tutor in Trench," *The Washington Herald*, August 15, 1915, p. 4 (claiming Ganson was a "tutor to the children of the Astors, Harrimans, Vanderbilts and other millionaires.").

47   "American Legion Standard Enshrined with Napoleon's," *The New York Sun*, May 27, 1917, Sec. 3, p. 1.

48   Rockwell, *American Fighters*, p. 9. Chatkoff was a former student of Boys High School in Brooklyn. *See* "Making Aviators in France; Many Machines Are Used Up," *The Brooklyn Daily Eagle*, September 3, 1916, p. 20. The son of a Russian immigrant, Chatkoff later stated: "I was abroad at the outbreak of the war and joined the French Army." *See* Emergency Passport application, February 25, 1919, available at Ancestry.com.

49   One contemporary source discloses that after Phelizot's death the flag "had to be disinfected and the names inscribed upon it have thus become somewhat hard to decipher." "American Legion Standard Enshrined with Napoleon's," *The New York Sun*, May 27, 1917, Sec. 3, p. 1.

50   "One American Killed, One Wounded," *The New York Sun*, November 8, 1914, p. 7.

51   "200 Americans in French Army Ready to Fight," *The New York Sun*, October 13, 1914, p. 1.

52   *Id.*

53   "One American Killed, One Wounded," *The New York Sun*, November 8, 1914, p. 7.

54   King, *L.M. 8046*, p. 8-9.

55   Kiffin to Loula, *carte postale* September 7, 1914, KYR Papers, NCDNCR. *See also* Thaw letter September 6, 1914, "The War Letters of Two Yale Undergraduates," *Yale Alumni Weekly*, January 22, 1915, p. 484.

56   Bert Hall, "Three Months in the Trenches," *The New York Times*, February 14, 1915, magazine section, p. 1.

57   Thaw letter September 6, 1914, "The War Letters of Two Yale Undergraduates," *Yale Alumni Weekly*, January 22, 1915, p. 484.

58   *Id.*

59   "200 Americans in French Army Ready to Fight," *The New York Sun*, October 13, 1914, p. 1.

60   "One American Killed, One Wounded," *The New York Sun*, November 8, 1914, p. 7.

61   Irving Werstein, *Sound No Trumpet*, p. 65 (1967).

62   "American Gets Baptism of Fire in Foreign Legion of France," *Morning Register* (Eugene, Oregon), August 22, 1915, p. 14.

63   "One American Killed, One Wounded," *The New York Sun*, November 8, 1914, p. 7.

64   "Atlanta Boy, Now in France, Hasn't Glimpsed the War," *The Atlanta Journal*, March 21, 1915, Magazine, p. 1.

Chapter Fifteen

1   "*Bleu* is French military jargon for rookie, after the blue uniform that new recruits once wore." Jean-Vincent Blanchard, *At the Edge of the World: The Heroic Century of the French Foreign Legion*, p. 106 (2017). *See also* Edgar Bouligny, "Rendezvous," *Liberty Magazine*, March 17, 1934, p. 12 and "American Gets Baptism of Fire in Foreign Legion of France," *Morning Register* (Eugene, Oregon), August 22, 1915, p. 14.

2   "One American Killed, One Wounded," *The New York Sun*, November 8, 1914, p. 7.

3   Alan Seeger to Elsie Seeger, September 20, 1914, Alan Seeger Papers, 1907-1937, MS Am. 1578.2, Houghton Library, Harvard College Library (hereafter "Alan Seeger Papers, Harvard").

4   Entry dated September 27, 1914, Seeger, A. (1914). Diaries: Manuscript, 1914-1915, MS Am. 255.2, Houghton Library, Harvard University, Cambridge, Mass. (hereafter "Alan Seeger Diary, Harvard").

5   "One American Killed, One Wounded," *The New York Sun*, November 8, 1914, p. 7.

6   "Atlanta Boy, Now in France, Hasn't Glimpsed the War," *The Atlanta Journal*, March 21, 1915, Magazine, p. 1. Russell Kelly, who also attended VMI, stated after he joined the Foreign Legion that his training he had received there "comes in handy." *Kelly of the Foreign Legion*, p. 17.

7   B.F. Towle, "In the Foreign Legion and Royal Flying Corps," *The Seventh Regiment Gazette*, p. 185 (June 1915).

8   Paul Rockwell, "Soldiers of the Legion," *The Atlanta Constitution*, December 30, 1917, p. 4F.

9   John Joseph Casey, "The New 'Old Guard' of France," *The New York Times Current History*, vol. V, p. 856 (Jan. – Mar. 1917).

10   *See e.g.*, "Mrs. Thaw Shows Letters Murdered Man Wrote Her," *The Evening World*, (NY), June 26, 1906, p. 1.

11   Alan Seeger to Elsie Seeger, September 20, 1914, Alan Seeger Papers, Harvard.

12   Paul Rockwell, "Soldiers of the Legion," *The Atlanta Constitution*, December 30, 1917, p. 4F.

13   King, *L.M. 8046*, p. 14. VMI still has Kiffin's red *kepi*.

14   F.W. Zinn, "The Real Foreign Legion," *Leslie's Weekly*, June 29, 1916, p. 812.

15   "American Gets Baptism of Fire in Foreign Legion of France," *Morning Register* (Eugene,

Oregon), August 22, 1915, p. 14.

16   Edgar Bouligny, "Rendezvous," *Liberty Magazine*, March 17, 1934, p. 10.

17   "American Gets Baptism of Fire in Foreign Legion of France," *Morning Register* (Eugene, Oregon), August 22, 1915, p. 14.

18   Rockwell, *American Fighters*, p. 14; *Kelly of the Foreign Legion*, p. 10.

19   King, *L.M. 8046*, p. 11.

20   B.F. Towle, "In the Foreign Legion and Royal Flying Corps," *The Seventh Regiment Gazette*, p. 185 (June 1915).

21   "Find Mule Steaks a Battle Delicacy," *The Chicago Daily News*, January 25, 1916, p. 5.

22   *Id.*

23   Rockwell, *American Fighters*, p. 12. The bread had a thick crust and would keep for up to two or three weeks. *See* "Find Mule Steaks a Battle Delicacy," *The Chicago Daily News*, January 25, 1916, p. 5.

24   Rockwell, *American Fighters*, p. 12.

25   King, *L.M. 8046*, p. 13-14.

26   King, *L.M. 8046*, p. 15.

27   Rockwell, *American Fighters*, p. 13.

28   Werstein, *Sound No Trumpet*, p. 68.

29   Kiffin to Loula, *carte postale* September 7, 1914, KYR Papers, NCDNCR.

30   As quoted *in The New York Herald*, September 13, 1914. (also available at https://iht-retrospective.blogs.nytimes.com/2014/09/13/battle-of-the-marne-was-foreseen-as-decisive/)

31   Winston Churchill, *The World Crisis*, Volume I, p. 298-299 (New York, Scribner & Sons, 1923).

32   "Extracts from the Diary of An American Artist in Paris," *Art and Progress*, December 1914, p. 46.

33   Rockwell, *American Fighters*, p. 14. Ganson, for one, later said "I shall never forget the thrill that I had at the first sight of the Second Regiment *Etranger*." "American Gets Baptism of Fire in Foreign Legion of France," *Morning Register* (Eugene, Oregon), August 22, 1915, p. 14.

34   Edgar Bouligny, "Rendezvous," *Liberty Magazine*, March 17, 1934, p. 11.

35   "American Gets Baptism of Fire in Foreign Legion of France," *Morning Register* (Eugene, Oregon), August 22, 1915, p. 14.

36   Douglas Porch, *The French Foreign Legion*, p. 340 (1991).

37   David King made this funny and telling remark about the veterans' arrival: "By nightfall they had sold the eager recruits all their spare equipment, and two days later they had it all back again." King, *L.M. 8046*, p. 12.

38   B.F. Towle, "In the Foreign Legion and Royal Flying Corps," *The Seventh Regiment Gazette*, p. 185 (June 1915).

39   Alan Seeger to Elsie Seeger, September 20, 1914, Alan Seeger Papers, Harvard.

40   "American Boys Fighting for France to Repay Debt Their Country Owes," *The New York Sun*, January 21, 1917, Sec. 5, p. 4.

41   Rockwell, *American Fighters*, p. 19. Paul said he and Kiffin claimed eighteen months service in the Mexican army, while others "invented little Central American republics." "Atlanta Boy, Wounded on French Battlefield, Paints Graphic Pen Picture of European War," *The Atlanta Constitution*, May 2, 1915, p. 1.

42   "American Boys Fighting for France to Repay Debt Their Country Owes," *The New York Sun*, January 21, 1917, Sec. 5, p. 4. *See also* Mason, *The Lafayette Escadrille*, p. 18.

43   King, *L.M. 8046*, p. 22.

44   Edgar Bouligny, "Rendezvous," *Liberty Magazine*, March 17, 1934, p. 12.

45   Rockwell, *American Fighters*, p. 21.

46   For example, George Casmeze probably dropped out before the men left Toulouse. Hall

noted he "took sick after joining the Legion and had to be left behind." Hall, *One Man's War*, p. 27. Ellingwood Towle also remained in Toulouse. "American Fighters Handle Gun and Pick," *The New York Sun*, November 26, 1914, p. 1 ("we left Ellingwood Towle behind at Toulouse in the hospital with knee trouble, which we did not believe to be serious."). *See also* Rockwell, *American Fighters*, p. 21.

47   Thaw letter September 13, 1914, "The War Letters of Two Yale Undergraduates," *Yale Alumni Weekly*, January 22, 1915, p. 484.

48   Unknown to Kiffin and Paul, September 17, 1914, Rockwell Papers, WLU.

49   "How France Supplies Her Armies," *The Brooklyn Daily Eagle*, October 31, 1915, Junior Eagle Section, p. 3.

50   Garry James, "France's Great War Masterpiece," *American Rifleman*, Oct. 2014, p. 70.

51   Mason, *The Lafayette Escadrille*, p. 15.

52   "One American Killed, One Wounded," *The New York Sun*, November 8, 1914, p. 7.

53   Rockwell, *American Fighters*, p. 21.

54   King, *L.M. 8046*, p. 50-51.

55   "One American Killed, One Wounded," *The New York Sun*, November 8, 1914, p. 7.

56   Rockwell, *American Fighters*, p. 19.

57   "How France Supplies Her Armies," *The Brooklyn Daily Eagle*, November 7, 1915, Junior Eagle Section, p. 1.

58   "One American Killed by the German Fire," *The New York Sun*, November 8, 1914, p. 1.

59   *Kelly of the Foreign Legion*, p. 11-12.

60   Garry James, "France's Great War Masterpiece," *American Rifleman*, Oct. 2014, p. 71. *See also* David W. King October 12, 1915, *The Harvard Volunteers in Europe*, p. 139. Another French nickname for the bayonet was *La Dame Blanche* – the White Lady. *See* "Mixed Company: Some of my Friends in the Foreign Legion," *The Daily Mail*, January 14, 1915, p. 4. One source labels the assertion that the soldiers called their bayonets Rosalie a "resilient myth," and quotes a trench magazine of the time as saying, "The bayonet is called Rosalie only in a song by Théodore Botrel, which nobody sings, and in the *Bulletin des Armées de la République*, which nobody reads." Leonard V. Smith, Stéphane Audoin-Rouzeau, and Annette Becker, *France and the Great War 1914-1918*, p. 105 (Cambridge University Press, 2003).

61   Thaw letter September 25, 1914, "The War Letters of Two Yale Undergraduates," *Yale Alumni Weekly*, January 22, 1915, p. 485.

62   Kiffin to Loula, September 25, 1914, KYR Papers, NCDNCR.

63   Charles Sweeny, "Tells of Beginning of Foreign Legion," *The Evening Star*, June 29, 1917, p. 12.

64   King, *L.M. 8046*, p. 27.

65   "Cuffs and Leggings Costume at Front," *The New York Sun*, April 18, 1915, Fifth Section, p. 7.

66   King, *L.M. 8046*, p. 10.

67   "Atlanta Boy, Now in France, Hasn't Glimpsed the War," *The Atlanta Journal*, March 21, 1915, Magazine, p. 1.

68   "Germans Fight for Foe in Famed Legion," *The Chicago Daily News*, October 30, 1915, p. 6. The French author was apparently George d'Esparbès in his 1901 book, *The French Foreign Legion*.

69   King, *L.M. 8046*, p. 12.

70   Thaw letter September 6, 1914, "The War Letters of Two Yale Undergraduates," *Yale Alumni Weekly*, January 22, 1915, p. 484.

71   *Letters and Diary of Alan Seeger*, p. 2 (New York, 1917).

72   Thaw letter September 13, 1914, "The War Letters of Two Yale Undergraduates," *Yale Alumni Weekly*, January 22, 1915, p. 484.

73   King, *L.M. 8046*, p. 17.

74   "One American Killed, One Wounded," *The New York Sun*, November 8, 1914, p. 7.

75   "Paul Pavelka, A Soldier of Fortune," *The New York Sun*, December 30, 1917, Section 5, p. 1.

76   Alan Seeger to Mrs. Charles L. Seeger, September 28, 1914, Alan Seeger Papers, Harvard.

77   Kiffin to Loula, November 14, 1914, KYR Papers, NCDNCR. *See also* Gary Ward, "Engaged in Glory Alone: Yanks in The French Foreign Legion First to Fight," *VFW Magazine*, September 2014 ("Their enlistments were for the war's duration and their wages 30 cents per month.").

78   Rockwell, *American Fighters*, p. 19.

79   King, *L.M. 8046*, p. 16.

80   *Victor Chapman's Letters From France*, p. 90, (The MacMillan Company, 1917)

81   Rockwell, *American Fighters*, p. 20.

82   This is an important photograph, as it includes several of the men who could each be considered among the "founders" of the American volunteers: Casmeze, Sweeny, Casey, Hall, Carstairs, Thaw and Bach.

83   "Sees War and Hates It, But Says United States Must Arm," *The Asheville Citizen*, May 16, 1915, p. 24.

84   "One American Killed, One Wounded," *The New York Sun*, November 8, 1914, p. 7.

85   "200 American Volunteers Fight With Foreign Legion," *The New York Sun*, October 13, 1914, p. 5.

86   "Sees War and Hates It, But Says United States Must Arm," *The Asheville Citizen*, May 16, 1915, p. 24.

87   F.W. Zinn, "The Real Foreign Legion," *Leslie's Weekly*, June 29, 1916, p. 812.

88   Kiffin to Loula, *carte postale* September 17, 1914, KYR Papers, NCDNCR.

89   "Paul Rockwell Says He Enjoys War; Writes to a Friend in Atlanta," *The Atlanta Constitution*, October 11, 1914, p. 4A.

90   Thaw letter October 4, 1914, "The War Letters of Two Yale Undergraduates," *Yale Alumni Weekly*, January 22, 1915, p. 484.

91   Kiffin to Loula, September 25, 1914, KYR Papers, NCDNCR.

Chapter Sixteen

1   "If I Had A Dozen Sons I Should Want Them to Fight for France," *The Atlanta Constitution*, June 16, 1918, p. 12I.

2   Kiffin to Loula, September 25, 1914, KYR Papers, NCDNCR.

3   *Id.*

4   *Id.*

5   Alan Seeger to Mrs. Charles L. Seeger, September 28, 1914, Alan Seeger Papers, Harvard.

6   Alan Seeger to Elsie Seeger, September 20, 1914, Alan Seeger Papers, Harvard.

7   "U.S. Variety Actor Killed," *The Chicago Daily News*, July 29, 1916, p. 2.

8   Paul-Louis Hervier, *The American Volunteers with the Allies*, p. 290 (Paris, 1918). Another who knew Seeger suggested that he was "an intensely earnest youth," one who "posed without knowing that he was posing because he took himself with such intense seriousness." "From A Graduate's Window," *The Harvard Graduate's Magazine*, Vol. XXV, 1916-1917, p. 187 (Dec. 1916).

9   "Atlanta Boy, Now in France, Hasn't Glimpsed the War," *The Atlanta Journal*, March 21, 1915, Magazine, p. 2.

10   *Id.*

11   *Id.*

12   *Id.*

13   "American Boys Fighting for France to Repay Debt Their Country Owes," *The New York Sun*, January 21, 1917, Sec. 5, p. 4.

14   "In the Foreign Legion," *The Washington Post*, October 14, 1914, p. 3. Another in the unit would later state "Thaw has raised a beard that makes him the image of Henry VIII." "Life

of Americans in the French Army is Not Easy," *The Charlotte Observer*, December 28, 1914, p. 9.

15   "Vincent Astor's Tutor in Trench," *The Washington Herald*, August 15, 1915, p. 4.

16   "American Gets Baptism of Fire in Foreign Legion of France," *Morning Register* (Eugene, Oregon), August 22, 1915, p. 14.

17   "French Beards Are Doomed," *The Chicago Daily News*, June 21, 1916, p. 2.

18   François Cochet et Rémy Porte, *Dictionnaire de la Grand Guerre 1914-1918*, p. 825 (Paris 2008).

19   *See* Emily Brewer, *Tommy Doughboy Fritz: Soldier Slang of World War I*, p. 163 (2014).

20   "The Regiment That Never Retreats," *Goodwin's Weekly*, October 31, 1914, p. 6.

21   *See* Rockwell, *American Fighters*, p. 71.

22   "Life of Americans in the French Army is Not Easy," *The Charlotte Observer*, December 28, 1914, p. 9.

23   On their August 6, 1914, passport applications, Kiffin's height is listed as 6 ft. 1½ in., while Paul is listed at 6 feet even. Both available on Ancestry.com. *U.S. Passport Applications, 1795-1925*. Upon his enlistment in the Foreign Legion, Kiffin was listed at 1.85 meters. Legion enlistment book, p. 1, Rockwell Papers, WLU.

24   Bert Hall, *En L'Air!*, p. 149 (New York, 1918).

25   The average American soldier in World War I was five feet seven and a half inches. *See* Davenport and Love, *The Medical Department of the United States Army in the World War, Vol. XV, Statistics*, p. 124, Table 32 (1921). Interestingly, the study noted that the tallest men, by state, came from "the mountain section of North Carolina, with a mean stature of 68.67 inches, nearly 1.2 inches above the national average." *Id.* at p. 35. The average weight for an American soldier was 141.5 pounds. *Id.* at p. 36. Charles Trinkard was the shortest man in the American section. *See* "Life of Americans in the French Army is Not Easy," *The Charlotte Observer*, December 28, 1914, p. 9.

26   Known heights taken from passport applications available on Ancestry.com. *U.S. Passport Applications, 1795-1925*.

27   Rockwell, *American Fighters*, p. 31-32.

28   King, *L.M. 8046*, p. 18.

29   Available on the *Mémoire des Hommes* website.

30   Weidemann's service card notes he became a naturalized citizen of France in 1908.

31   "Wartime Sidelights," *The Indianapolis Star*, October 27, 1917, p. 6.

32   "Germans Fight for Foe in Famed Legion," *The Chicago Daily News*, October 30, 1915, p. 6.

33   "Michigan Boy, Fighting for France, Writes of Life In the Trenches," *The Detroit Free Press*, May 2, 1915, Feature Section, p. 7.

34   *War Letters*, p. 183. *See also* "Wartime Sidelights," *The Indianapolis Star*, October 27, 1917, p. 6.

35   *War Letters*, p. 183.

36   "Atlanta Boy, Now in France, Hasn't Glimpsed the War," *The Atlanta Journal*, March 21, 1915, Magazine, p. 2.

37   Entry dated October 4, 1914, Alan Seeger Diary, Harvard.

38   "American Boys Fighting for France to Repay Debt Their Country Owes," *The New York Sun*, January 21, 1917, Sec. 5, p. 4; and Edgar Bouligny, "Rendezvous," *Liberty Magazine*, March 17, 1934, p. 12. One source says that Seeger and Phelizot "tossed a coin to see who would carry the flag on the march through Toulouse; Phelizot won and strode proudly in the van of the American contingent." Werstein, *Sound No Trumpet*, p. 81.

39   Rockwell, *American Fighters*, p. 22.

40   "One American Killed, One Wounded," *The New York Sun*, November 8, 1914, p. 7.

41   Werstein, *Sound No Trumpet*, p. 82.

42   "Atlanta Boy, Now in France, Hasn't Glimpsed the War," *The Atlanta Journal*, March 21, 1915, Magazine, p. 2.

43 Thaw letter October 4, 1914, "The War Letters of Two Yale Undergraduates," *Yale Alumni Weekly*, January 22, 1915, p. 485.

44 "American Boys Fighting for France to Repay Debt Their Country Owes," *The New York Sun*, January 21, 1917, Sec. 5, p. 4.

45 "Atlanta Boy Wounded on French Battlefield," *The Atlanta Constitution*, May 2, 1915, p. 8A.

46 "Atlanta Boy, Now in France, Hasn't Glimpsed the War," *The Atlanta Journal*, March 21, 1915, Magazine, p. 2.

47 The photograph can be seen after p. 22 in Mason, *The Lafayette Escadrille.*

48 "Atlanta Boy, Now in France, Hasn't Glimpsed the War," *The Atlanta Journal*, March 21, 1915, Magazine, p. 2.

49 Rockwell, *American Fighters*, p. 24-25.

50 Thaw letter October 4, 1914, "The War Letters of Two Yale Undergraduates," *Yale Alumni Weekly*, January 22, 1915, p. 485.

Chapter Seventeen

1 "One American Killed, One Wounded," *The New York Sun*, November 8, 1914, p. 7.

2 "American Boys Fighting for France to Repay Debt Their Country Owes," *The New York Sun*, January 21, 1917, Sec. 5, p. 4.

3 Thaw letter October 4, 1914, "The War Letters of Two Yale Undergraduates," *Yale Alumni Weekly*, January 22, 1915, p. 485.

4 Letter from Edward Mandell Stone to Frederic M. Stone, October 9, 1914, quoted in Rockwell, *American Fighters*, p. 52.

5 "Atlanta Boy, Now in France, Hasn't Glimpsed the War," *The Atlanta Journal*, March 21, 1915, Magazine, p. 2.

6 *Id.* at p. 1.

7 Rockwell, *American Fighters*, p. 21. Thaw wrote that "although we'll probably just traipse along behind the advancing French army, still it's something to be in the war zone!" Thaw letter October 4, 1914, "The War Letters of Two Yale Undergraduates," *Yale Alumni Weekly*, January 22, 1915, p. 485.

8 Entry dated October 4, 1914, Alan Seeger Diary, Harvard.

9 Kiffin wrote Massengale from *Le Camp de Mailly*: "We can hear the big guns on the firing line, and will reach there tomorrow." "Atlanta Boy Fighting for Cause of France," *The Atlanta Constitution*, November 10, 1914, p. 4.

10 Rockwell, *American Fighters*, p. 23-24. *See also* Edgar Bouligny, Rendezvous," *Liberty Magazine*, March 17, 1934, p. 13.

11 Entry dated October 4, 1914, Alan Seeger Diary, Harvard.

12 "American Boys Fighting for France to Repay Debt Their Country Owes," *The New York Sun*, January 21, 1917, Sec. 5, p. 4.

13 King, *L.M. 8046*, p. 25.

14 Rockwell, *American Fighters*, p. 23.

15 Alan Seeger to Mrs. Charles L. Seeger, October 17, 1914, Alan Seeger Papers, Harvard.

16 B.F. Towle, "In the Foreign Legion and Royal Flying Corps," *The Seventh Regiment Gazette*, p. 186 (June 1915).

17 Kiffin to Loula, October 16, 1914, KYR Papers, NCDNCR.

18 Letter from Edward Mandell Stone to Frederic M. Stone, October 9, 1914, as quoted in Rockwell, *American Fighters*, p. 51.

19 Alan Seeger to Mrs. Charles L. Seeger, October 17, 1914, Alan Seeger Papers, Harvard.

20 Entry dated October 11, 1914, Alan Seeger Diary, Harvard.

21 Thaw letter October 12, 1914, "The War Letters of Two Yale Undergraduates," *Yale Alumni Weekly*, January 22, 1915, p. 485.

22 Entry dated October 11, 1914, Alan Seeger Diary, Harvard.

23 Alan Seeger to Mrs. Charles L. Seeger, October 17, 1914, Alan Seeger Papers, Harvard.

24 B.F. Towle, "In the Foreign Legion and Royal Flying Corps," *The Seventh Regiment Gazette*, p. 186 (June 1915). *See also* "One American Killed, One Wounded," *The New York Sun*, November 8, 1914, p. 7. Shooting at a kneeling figure four hundred meters distance, Bill Thaw said that he averaged four out of eight shots or better, and that his section averaged 47%. The next closest section hit 21%. Thaw letter October 12, 1914, "The War Letters of Two Yale Undergraduates," *Yale Alumni Weekly*, January 22, 1915, p. 485.

25 Rockwell, *American Fighters*, p. 24.

26 Thaw letter October 4, 1914, "The War Letters of Two Yale Undergraduates," *Yale Alumni Weekly*, January 22, 1915, p. 485. Paul also noted that at Camp de Mailly, the men "did very well on horse meat and potatoes for a few days[.]" "Atlanta Boy Wounded on French Battlefield," *The Atlanta Constitution*, May 2, 1915, p. 8A.

27 "Find Mule Steaks a Battle Delicacy," *The Chicago Daily News*, January 25, 1916, p. 5.

28 Kiffin to Loula, October 16, 1914, KYR Papers, NCDNCR.

29 Alan Seeger to Mrs. Charles L. Seeger, October 17, 1914, Alan Seeger Papers, Harvard.

30 Sweeney to his mother, postcard postmarked October 20, 1914, available at: https://monlegionnaire.wordpress.com/2015/06/04/post-card-from-legionnaire-charles-sweeny-to-mom/ (visited June 1, 2019).

31 *Id.*

32 Alan Seeger to Mrs. Charles L. Seeger, October 17, 1914, Alan Seeger Papers, Harvard.

33 "American Legion Standard Enshrined with Napoleon's," *The Asheville Citizen*, June 3, 1917, p. 14; and "Two Flags of Deathless Glory," *Leslie's Weekly*, June 14, 1917, p. 730.

34 "Chicagoan Slain by a Fellow Legionary," *The Chicago Daily News*, October 23, 1915, p. 6.

35 Alan Seeger to Miss. Elsie A. Seeger, October 20, 1914, Alan Seeger Papers, Harvard.

36 *See* Rockwell, *American Fighters*, p. 25. The quoted words were scratched on a scrap of paper in the Rockwell collection in WLU.

37 Entry dated October 20, 1914, Alan Seeger Diary, Harvard.

38 Alan Seeger to Miss. Elsie A. Seeger, October 20, 1914, Alan Seeger Papers, Harvard.

39 "Paul Rockwell Writes for Big European Daily Newspapers," *The Asheville Citizen*, January 15, 1915, p. 5.

40 Bert Hall, "Three Months in the Trenches," *The New York Times*, February 14, 1915, magazine section, p. 1.

41 "Paul Rockwell Writes for Big European Daily Newspapers," *The Asheville Citizen*, January 15, 1915, p. 5.

42 "The Peace of the Firing Line," *The Daily Mail*, September 17, 1914, p. 4.

43 King, *L.M. 8046*, p. 26. Paul Rockwell believed the two men were Bill Thaw and Carstairs. *See* Rockwell, *American Fighters*, p. 27.

44 B.F. Towle, "In the Foreign Legion and Royal Flying Corps," *The Seventh Regiment Gazette*, p. 186 (June 1915). G. H. Mumm & Cie is still one of the largest champagne producers in the world.

45 Entry dated October 21, 1914, Alan Seeger Diary, Harvard.

46 Entry dated October 22, 1914, Alan Seeger Diary, Harvard.

47 Rockwell, *American Fighters*, p. 27.

48 Entry dated October 23, 1914, Alan Seeger Diary, Harvard.

49 Rockwell, *American Fighters*, p. 28.

50 Rockwell, *American Fighters*, p. 59.

51 Entry dated October 23, 1914, Alan Seeger Diary, Harvard. *See also* Rockwell, *American Fighters*, p. 29.

52 Entry dated October 23, 1914, Alan Seeger Diary, Harvard. D.W. King mistakenly placed their quarters in Verzy, but it is clear he meant Verzenay. He described the "long sheds used by the grape gatherers" on which "we slept on concrete platforms, which sloped toward the middle of the room, divided by low partitions like stalls in a modern stable." King, *L.M.*

8046, p. 25.

53   Alan Seeger to Mrs. Charles L. Seeger, October 23, 1914, Alan Seeger Papers, Harvard.

54   Entry dated October 23, 1914, Alan Seeger Diary, Harvard.

55   Rockwell, *American Fighters*, p. 30.

56   "Paul Rockwell Writes for Big European Daily Newspapers," *The Asheville Citizen*, January 15, 1915, p. 5.

57   B.F. Towle, "In the Foreign Legion and Royal Flying Corps," *The Seventh Regiment Gazette*, p. 186 (June 1915).

58   Alan Seeger to Mrs. Charles L. Seeger, October 23, 1914, Alan Seeger Papers, Harvard.

59   Entry dated October 23, 1914, Alan Seeger Diary, Harvard. But the official reports the next day listed only one killed, and two wounded.

60   Entry dated October 24, 1914, Alan Seeger Diary, Harvard.

61   *Id.*

62   Entry dated October 23, 1914, Alan Seeger Diary, Harvard.

63   "American Boys Fighting for France to Repay Debt Their Country Owes," *The New York Sun*, January 21, 1917, Sec. 5, p. 4.

64   "American Fighters Handle Gun and Pick," *The New York Sun*, November 26, 1914, p. 1.

65   Entry dated October 25, 1914, Alan Seeger Diary, Harvard.

66   Granville Fortescue, *At the Front with Three Armies*, p. 175 (London, 1915). Another correspondent noted "the terrible truth that the temples of God – the beautiful churches of France and Belgium – have been picked in advance of all other edifices for destruction." "Churches of Ypres are Targets for German Guns," *The New York Herald*, November 24, 1914, available at https://iht-retrospective.blogs.nytimes.com/2014/11/23/1914-churches-of-ypres-are-targets-for-german-guns/ (visited June 1, 2019).

67   Entry dated October 25, 1914, Alan Seeger Diary, Harvard.

68   "Life of Americans in the French Army is Not Easy," *The Charlotte Observer*, December 28, 1914, p. 9. Dowd also noted that Sunday "is not necessarily a day of rest for us." "Brooklyn Soldier Writes from Front," *The Brooklyn Daily Eagle*, January 6, 1915, p. 5.

69   Rockwell, *American Fighters*, p. 32-33.

70   Entry dated October 27, 1914, Alan Seeger Diary, Harvard.

71   *Id.*

72   "Some Sidelights of the World War," *The Atlanta Constitution*, November 1, 1917, p. 8.

73   *Id.*

74   *Id.*

75   Entry dated October 27, 1914, Alan Seeger Diary, Harvard.

76   *War Letters*, p. 184.

77   *Id.*

78   Bert Hall, "Three Months in the Trenches," *The New York Times*, February 14, 1915, magazine section, p. 2.

79   Rockwell, *American Fighters*, p. 34.

80   Entry dated October 27, 1914, Alan Seeger Diary, Harvard.

81   "Paul Rockwell Writes for Big European Daily Newspapers," *The Asheville Citizen*, January 15, 1915, p. 5.

82   Entry dated October 27, 1914, Alan Seeger Diary, Harvard.

83   *Id.*

84   Rockwell, *American Fighters*, p. 352.

85   "Michigan Boy, Fighting for France, Writes of Life In the Trenches," *The Detroit Free Press*, May 2, 1915, Feature Section, p. 7.

86   Rockwell, *American Fighters*, p. 36.

87   Entry dated October 28, 1914, Alan Seeger Diary, Harvard.

Chapter Eighteen

1   "Atlanta Boy Wounded on French Battlefield," *The Atlanta Constitution*, May 2, 1915, p. 8A.
2   Vandevelde's service card is available on the *Mémoire des Hommes* website. *See also* Entry dated November 4, 1914, Alan Seeger Diary, Harvard.
3   Rockwell, *American Fighters*, p. 38.
4   *Id.*
5   Entry dated November 4, 1914, Alan Seeger Diary, Harvard.
6   "Paul Rockwell Writes for Big European Daily Newspapers," *The Asheville Citizen*, January 15, 1915, p. 5.
7   "One American Killed by the German Fire," *The New York Sun*, November 8, 1914, p. 1.
8   "Boxer in the Trenches," *The Winnipeg Tribune*, December 14, 1914, p. 4.
9   "Foreign Legion Works Prodigies," *The Charleston Evening Post*, December 15, 1916, p. 15.
10 Seeger letter December 8, 1914, as published in "University Man Tells Absorbing Tale," *The New York Sun*, January 10, 1915, p. 7.
11 "Där det regard, både vat ten ich granater," *VeckoJournalen 51*, 1914, p. 655. Henry Farnsworth, a classmate of Victor Chapman's at Groton, who enlisted and came to the front in early 1915, gave this polite description of the trenches: "there is a deal of mud and water and cold, and not overmuch room." Henry Farnsworth to his sister Ellen, about March 7, 1915, *Letters of Henry Weston Farnsworth*, p. 126.
12 In a single sentence written in 1915, David W. King may have summed up the experience of the Western Front for millions of soldiers: "We spent the night in the holes we dug." "With the Legion," *Harvard Alumni Bulletin*, March 22, 1916, p. 478.
13 Bowe, *Soldiers of the Legion*, p. 90.
14 *Id.* at p. 91.
15 "Chicagoan Slain by a Fellow Legionary," *The Chicago Daily News*, October 23, 1915, p. 6.
16 *Id.*
17 Entry dated November 4, 1914, Alan Seeger Diary, Harvard.
18 *Id.*
19 King, *L.M. 8046*, p. 38.
20 "South Boston Man Writes from Front," *The Boston Globe*, February 23, 1915, p. 5.
21 *Victor Chapman's Letters From France*, p. 79.
22 Kenneth Weeks, *A Soldier of the Legion*, p. 33 (London, 1916).
23 Weeks, *A Soldier of the Legion*, p. 31-32.
24 "Vincent Astor's Tutor in Trench," *The Washington Herald*, August 15, 1915, p. 4.
25 "American Boys Fighting for France to Repay Debt Their Country Owes," *The New York Sun*, January 21, 1917, Sec. 5, p. 4.
26 "One American Killed by the German Fire," *The New York Sun*, November 8, 1914, p. 1.
27 "'Change' in Trenches," *The New York Sun*, December 27, 1914, p. 3.
28 Entry dated November 10, 1914, Alan Seeger Diary, Harvard.
29 F.W. Zinn, "The Real Foreign Legion," *Leslie's Weekly*, June 29, 1916, p. 818.
30 "Där det regnar, både vatten och granater," *VeckoJournalen 51*, 1914, p. 655. *See also* Elow Nilson, *Svenska Hjalter vid Fronten*, p. 20 (Stockholm 1917).
31 Kiffin to Loula, November 14, 1914, KYR Papers, NCDNCR.
32 Entry dated November 10, 1914, Alan Seeger Diary, Harvard.
33 F.W. Zinn, "The Real Foreign Legion," *Leslie's Weekly*, June 29, 1916, p. 818.
34 "One American Killed by the German Fire," *The New York Sun*, November 8, 1914, p. 1.
35 Charles Sweeny, "Tells How It Feels to Face Battle Foe," *The Evening Star*, July 1, 1917, p. 5.
36 "Hot Lunch in the Trenches," *The Daily Mail*, October 22, 1914, p. 4.
37 Weeks, *A Soldier of the Legion*, p. 32.
38 "Americans Under fire Watch German Shells," *The New York Sun*, December 19, 1914, p. 3.
39 Alan Seeger to Mrs. Charles L. Seeger, November 6, 1914, Alan Seeger Papers, Harvard. This

letter is written in French.

40   Entry dated November 23, 1914, Alan Seeger Diary, Harvard. *See also* Rockwell, *American Fighters*, p. 39.

41   Entry dated November 23, 1914, Alan Seeger Diary, Harvard.

42   *Letters and Diary of Alan Seeger*, p. 33.

43   Alan Seeger to Mrs. Charles L. Seeger, November 17, 1914, Alan Seeger Papers, Harvard.

44   "Chicagoan Slain by a Fellow Legionary," *The Chicago Daily News*, October 23, 1915, p. 6.

45   *Victor Chapman's Letters From France*, p. 154.

46   *Letters and Diary of Alan Seeger*, p. 22.

47   Alan Seeger to Mrs. Charles L. Seeger, November 17, 1914, Alan Seeger Papers, Harvard.

48   *Letters and Diary of Alan Seeger*, p. 20-21. This letter is misdated as November 12, 1914. The actual letter in the Harvard collection bears a French postmark of 11-12-14, meaning December 11, 1914.

49   Seeger letter December 8, 1914, as published in "Harvard Man Describes Perils of Life in Trenches," *The New York Sun*, January 10, 1915, p. 6.

50   One source asserts Collins "suffered a nervous breakdown, left his post, and ran into the woods screaming, 'I've had enough!'" Werstein, *Sound No Trumpet*, p. 103.

51   Rockwell, *American Fighters*, p. 42. A source at the time noted that "The health of H.C. Collins of Boston has broken down and he has returned to headquarters." "New Yorker to be Aviator in France," *The New York Sun*, December 16, 1914, p. 2.

52   Rockwell, *American Fighters*, p. 43.

53   Rockwell, *American Fighters*, p. 134. Collins died during the Great Depression "after four years of unemployment and in very straitened circumstances," but some believed his claim to the end. "A War Hero Who Wasn't Drafted," *The Brooklyn Daily Eagle*, August 12, 1933, p. 4.

54   "26 Americans in His Company," *The Baltimore Sun*, December 24, 1914, p. 2.

55   "Galesburg Boy Tells War Aim in Last Letter," *The Detroit Free Press*, October 6, 1915, p. 3.

56   *The Daily Mail*, as reprinted in "Paul Rockwell Writes for Big European Daily Newspapers," *The Asheville Citizen*, January 15, 1915, p. 5.

57   One of Kiffin's later letters said that he had "made every trip to the trenches with my company except one, which was due to my feet being in very bad condition from the march here." Kiffin to Vicomtesse du Peloux, March 7, 1915, *War Letters*, p. 30. An entry in Kiffin's enlistment booklet shows that he passed through Paris on November 19, 1914. Legion enlistment book, p. 2, Rockwell Papers, WLU.

58   "Life of Americans in the French Army is Not Easy," *The Charlotte Observer*, December 28, 1914, p. 9. *See also* "Asheville Soldiers Sent to Hospital," *The Asheville Citizen*, December 18, 1914, p. 8.

59   Kiffin to Loula, *carte postale* December 1, 1914, KYR Papers, NCDNCR. On November 22, another soldier in his unit wrote that Kiffin had just gotten back from ten days layup and was "all right again." "Life of Americans in the French Army is Not Easy," *The Charlotte Observer*, December 28, 1914, p. 9. A letter from Kiffin's mother the next month confirms that Kiffin had spent some time in the hospital. *See* Loula A. Rockwell to the Ambassador to France, December 22, 1914, *National Archives*, Records of the Foreign Service Posts of the Department of State (Record Group 84). Further corroborating evidence comes from a letter written by Paul in April 1915 in which he asserted that Kiffin had not had any rest since enlisting "except nine days in October when he was out with a bum foot." "Atlanta Boy Wounded on French Battlefield," *The Atlanta Constitution*, May 2, 1915, p. 8A.

60   This quip is taken from an ambulance driver with the American Field Service. *See The American Field Service Bulletin*, No. 10, September 8, 1917, p. 10.

61   Werstein, *Sound No Trumpet*, p. 85. King said that at Verzenay the entire section had been "given a warm welcome by the Algerian Cooties' Rotary Club." King, *L.M. 8046*, p. 29. Paul remembered the same thing. *See* Rockwell, *American Fighters*, p. 29.

62   "American Boys Fighting for France to Repay Debt Their Country Owes," *The New York Sun*, January 21, 1917, Sec. 5, p. 4.

63   "Georgia Doctor in France Writes of Horrors of War," *The Atlanta Journal*, May 8, 1915, p. 2; Thaw letter August 30, 1914, "The War Letters of Two Yale Undergraduates," *Yale Alumni Weekly*, January 22, 1915, p. 484.

64   Hall, *One Man's War*, p. 46.

65   Rockwell, *American Fighters*, p. 24.

66   Isaac Rosenberg, *The Immortals*, 1918.

67   Hall, *One Man's War*, p. 54-55.

68   *Kelly of the Foreign Legion*, p. 62.

69   Photo is in the John Bowe and Family Papers, Minnesota Historical Society Library, P.1473, French Foreign Legion photography, Edgar Bouligny.

70   A photo of the sign appears in Mason, *The Lafayette Escadrille*, after page 22.

71   Rockwell, *American Fighters*, p. 59.

72   F.W. Zinn, "The Real Foreign Legion," *Leslie's Weekly*, June 29, 1916, p. 812.

73   It is notable that Zinn meant to defend the anciens when he averred that "[n]ot all these men had been criminals and at no time did they constitute more than 20 percent of the regiment." F.W. Zinn, "The Real Foreign Legion," *Leslie's Weekly*, June 29, 1916, p. 812.

74   "American Gets Baptism of Fire in Foreign Legion of France," *Morning Register* (Eugene, Oregon), August 22, 1915, p. 14.

75   Hall, *En L'Air!*, p. 8.

76   Hall, *One Man's War*, p. 39. *See also* King, *L.M. 8046*, p. 38; and Edward Morlae, *A Soldier of the Legion*, p. 7 (Boston, 1916).

77   "Brooklyn Lawyer Fights for Allies; Endures Hardships," *The Brooklyn Daily Eagle*, February 14, 1915, Sec. 3, p. 8.

78   "American Gets Baptism of Fire in Foreign Legion of France," *Morning Register* (Eugene, Oregon), August 22, 1915, p. 14. Later in the war, one former French soldier gave this explanation of "*Systeme D*," or what he called "the first aid to the wily *poilu*":
In full it is the "systeme débrouillard" – and a débrouillard *is a man who by ducking, dodging or devising can avoid work, trenches, danger, trouble or any other of the evil that harass a French soldier. When Petain saved Verdun by putting ten thousand auto trucks on a road that had previously been an occasional track for market carts – that was the* "Systeme D"; *when a* poilu *mends a hole in his boot with a piece of rubber he has hacked out from the tire of a headquarters staff car – that is* "Systeme D" *also. Anything that can evade a difficulty or handle an awkward situation is* "Systeme D"; *it is the base and the backbone of the French effort in this war. But of course, as far as the rank and file and the less important grades of our army are concerned, the* "Systeme D" *means chiefly an ingenious method of avoiding work or any other annoyance.* "Marius and the 'Systeme D,'" *The Franco-American Weekly*, December 22, 1917, p. 4.

79   "American Gets Baptism of Fire in Foreign Legion of France," *Morning Register* (Eugene, Oregon), August 22, 1915, p. 14. King also mentioned System D, defining it as "shift[ing] for yourself." King, *L.M. 8046*, p. 12.

80   Porch, *The French Foreign Legion*, p. 339-343.

81   "Germans Fight for Foe in Famed Legion," *The Chicago Daily News*, October 30, 1915, p. 6.

82   Werstein, *Sound No Trumpet*, p. 106-108.

83   Werstein, *Sound No Trumpet*, p. 108.

84   Entry for 15 Novembre, *Journal de Marche, 2e régiment de marche du 2e régiment étranger, 29 Août 1914 au 31 Decembre 1914*, available on the *Mémoire des Hommes* website. *See also* "Americans Under Fire Watch German Shells," *The New York Sun*, December 19, 1914, p. 3. It was a clean wound and after a month in the hospital, Bouligny returned to the front and was promoted to sergeant. He would be wounded three more times in the war, and died in 1931, of a gunshot wound inflicted by his wife. "Shot Her Hero Husband Because She Loved

Chapter Nineteen

1   Rockwell, *American Fighters*, p. 43. Paul Rockwell asserted that after seeing a plane fly overhead in October of 1914, Thaw remarked, "One day soon a squadron of American volunteers will be flying for France." Philip M. Flammer, *The Vivid Air*, p. 9 (University of Georgia Press, 1981). *See also* "Interview #550 of Colonel Paul Rockwell," *Northeastern Chapter, Cross & Cockade Society*, p. 2 (on file with the U.S. Air Force Oral History Program, Maxwell AFB); and Paul Rockwell to David King, March 1, 1976, Rockwell Papers, WLU ("I have been trying for years, without much success, to see that Bill Thaw is given the credit due him for helping organize the *Escadrille*."). Even if made, I discount Thaw's offhand statement as a valid basis for shifting credit to him for the idea of an American squadron.

2   Gordon, *Lafayette Escadrille Pilot Biographies*, p. 61.

3   "Local Briefs," *The Newport Daily News*, November 2, 1914, p. 6 (quoting a cable saying Thaw "went down for a trial in the aviation corps."). Thaw held the first hydro-aeroplane license issued by the French Aero Club. "Americans Study to Be French Officers," *The New York Sun*, December 24, 1914, p. 3.

4   Blaine L. Pardoe, *The Bad Boy, Bert Hall: Aviator and Mercenary of the Skies*, p. 55 (2012).

5   Thaw letter November 2, 1914, "The War Letters of Two Yale Undergraduates," *Yale Alumni Weekly*, January 22, 1915, p. 486 (noting his chance of "being shifted to another corps.").

6   Gordon, *Lafayette Escadrille Pilot Biographies*, p. 43.

7   "May Join French Aviation Corps," *The Boston Daily Globe*, February 9, 1915, p. 9.

8   "The Real Story of Norman Prince by Boston Friend," *The Boston Post*, October 22, 1916, p. 41.

9   *New England Aviators, 1914-1918*, Volume 1, p. 17 (Houghton Mifflin, 1919).

10   *Norman Prince, A Volunteer Who Died for the Cause He Loved*, p. 57 (1917).

11   "No Air Contests Today," *The Boston Evening Transcript*, August 29, 1911, p. 1. Prince was the 55th pilot licensed by the Aero Club of America. *See Aero Club of America 1912*, p. 55.

12   "Norman Prince Now A Recognized Aviator," *The Boston Daily Globe*, August 29, 1911, p. 1 (the front-page photograph of Prince accompanying this article captures him perfectly). *See also* "The Real Story of Norman Prince by Boston Friend," *The Boston Post*, October 22, 1916, p. 41.

13   *See* "News of Chicago Society," *The Chicago Tribune*, August 13, 1916, p. E4. *See also* "Prince Flies No More Now," *The Boston Evening Transcript*, August 31, 1911, p. 2 (noting that "In deference to the wishes of his family," Prince had "decided to quit aviation, for the present at least."). Prince was admitted to the Illinois bar on October 17, 1911. The firm is the oldest law firm in Chicago, and today is known as Winston & Strawn, with 16 offices and more than 900 lawyers globally.

14   "Norman Prince Chicago Flier, Dies in France," *The Chicago Daily Tribune*, October 16, 1916, p. 1. He was a member of Onwentsia Club, and starred for its polo team in 1913. *Id.*

15   "100 Mile An Hour Airplanes Fly For Cup Today," *The Chicago Tribune*, September 9, 1912, p. 1. According to one friend, "it took physical effort to keep Prince from flying" that day. "A Tribute to Norman Prince Written by a Boston Friend," *The Boston Post*, October 22, 1916, p. 44.

16   *See* "Norman Prince Is Dead," clipping *circa* October 1916, Frazier Curtis, *Lafayette Escadrille Scrapbook, 1914-1917*, Massachusetts Historical Society, Boston, MA (hereafter "Lafayette Escadrille Scrapbook, MHS."). *See also* "Pau," *L'Intransigent*, February 5, 1914, p. 4 (listing Prince as participant in steeple chase).

17   "Echos," *Le Journal de la Femme*, Nov. 1916, p. 8.

18   "From A Graduate's Window," *The Harvard Graduate's Magazine*, Vol. XXV, 1916-1917, p. 186 (Dec. 1916).

19   "A Tribute to Norman Prince Written by a Boston Friend," *The Boston Post*, October 22, 1916, p. 44.

20   T. Howard Kelly, "A Winged Knight Comes Home," *The Western Weekly Magazine*, July 7, 1929, in *Abilene Reporter-News*, July 7, 1929, p. 39.

21   "A Tribute to Norman Prince Written by a Boston Friend," *The Boston Post*, October 22, 1916, p. 44.

22   Air Department, Admiralty, London, to Frazier Curtis, September 19, 1914, Lafayette Escadrille Scrapbook, MHS.

23   M.A. DeWolfe Howe, *Memoirs of the Harvard Dead in the War Against Germany, Vol. 1*, p. 159-160 (quoting Curtis as saying: "The first time the idea of an American Escadrille came to Norman was probably at Marblehead in November, 1914, when he suggested it to me as we were flying together."); and *New England Aviators, 1914-1918*, Volume 1, p. 26 ("At Marblehead [Frazier] met Norman Prince and discussed with him the idea of creating an American Escadrille in the French Army."). *See also* Frazier Curtis to James Norman Hall, July 17, 1919, JNH Papers, Grinnell ("I talked over the idea of an Escadrille with Norman when I was back in Marblehead in November and December 1914.").

24   Frazier Curtis to James Norman Hall, July 17, 1919, JNH Papers, Grinnell.

25   "The Real Story of Norman Prince by Boston Friend," *The Boston Post*, October 22, 1916, p. 41.

26   Norman Prince passport application, December 8, 1914, available on Ancestry.com. *U.S. Passport Applications, 1795-1925*.

27   *Id.*

28   Loula to Paul and Kiffin, November 20, 1914, Rockwell Papers, WLU.

29   *Id.* Six months later, Kiffin told Loula he had "often laughed to myself about the letter of advice you wrote me as to what to do in case I was taken a prisoner. I never entertained the idea of being taken a prisoner, but if I had been and followed your advice, I would have been immediately put up against a tree and shot." Kiffin to Loula, May 21, 1915, KYR Papers, NCDNCR.

30   Loula to Paul and Kiffin, November 26, 1914, Rockwell Papers, WLU.

31   Thaw letter December 1, 1914, *Yale Alumni Weekly*, January 22, 1915 p. 486. In addition, the regimental journal notes there was a cannonade on the trenches from 3 to 5 pm. *See* Entry for 26 Novembre, *Journal de Marche, 2e régiment de marche du 2e régiment étranger, 29 Août 1914 au 31 Decembre 1914*, available on the *Mémoire des Hommes* website.

32   B.F. Towle, "In the Foreign Legion and Royal Flying Corps," *The Seventh Regiment Gazette*, p. 186 (June 1915) The quote actually says they sang the "old home things," but I imagine that is a misprint.

33   Thaw's family was active in the Episcopal Church, and his older brother served as a missionary in Syria and would later become a deacon. "Stephen Thaw Will Be Ordained Deacon," *The Pittsburg Press*, January 24, 1919, p. 16. *See also The Living Church*, Vol. LX, No. 15, p. 489 (February 8, 1919)(noting Stephen Dows Thaw was ordained to the diaconate).

34   *See* "Americans Win Promotion," *The New York Sun*, October 23, 1914, p. 1; and "American Boys Fighting for France to Repay Debt Their Country Owes," *The New York Sun*, January 21, 1917, Sec. 5, p. 4.

35   "William Thaw, Aviator, Killed, Is Paris Rumor," *The New York Sun*, April 22, 1915, p. 3.

36   Deuteronomy 20:1, 3-4, King James Version.

37   "Musicale in French Trench; Germans Only 45 Feet Away Quit Firing to Applaud," *The Evening World*, March 20, 1915, p. 4.

38   *See* Telegram from Secretary of State William Jennings Bryan to Myron T. Herrick, August 25, 1914. Copy from file 123 H 43, 1910-29 Central Decimal File, Record Group 59: General Records of the Department of State, National Archives, located at http://historyatstate. tumblr.com/post/95982933722/unusual-circumstances (last visited May 20, 2019)

39   *See* https://history.state.gov/departmenthistory/people/sharp-william-graves (visited on

October 27, 2017)

40   Mott, *Myron T. Herrick, Friend of France*, p. 220.

41   "American Fighters Handle Gun and Pick," *The New York Sun*, November 26, 1914, p. 1.

42   "From 26 Americans Fighting for France," *The New York Herald*, December 2, 1914, p. 2. The men quickly received a response, including twenty flannel jackets. "Response Made to 'Herald' Appeal on Behalf of American Volunteers," *The New York Herald*, December 4, 1914, clipping in William Thaw Scrapbooks, Papers of the Thaw Family, 1792-1981, MSS# 29, Historical Society of Western Pennsylvania, Senator John Heinz Pittsburgh Regional History Center, Pittsburgh, Pennsylvania (hereafter "William Thaw Scrapbooks, HSWP").

43   "Boxer in the Trenches," *The Winnipeg Tribune*, December 14, 1914, p. 4.

44   "Americans Under Fire Watch German Shells," *The New York Sun*, December 19, 1914, p. 3.

45   "Americans at Front Are Happy; 'Gunga Din' Found," *The New York Sun*, May 16, 1915, p. 4.

46   Alan Seeger to Mrs. Charles L. Seeger, November 17, 1914, Alan Seeger Papers, Harvard.

47   "Brooklyn Soldier Writes from Front," *The Brooklyn Daily Eagle*, January 6, 1915, p. 5.

48   "Americans Under Fire Watch German Shells," *The New York Sun*, December 19, 1914, p. 3.

49   "Seventh Men at the Front," *The Seventh Regiment Gazette*, p. 99 (February 1915).

50   "Only Three Days in 25 Off Firing line," *The New York Sun*, January 24, 1915, p. 4.

51   *Victor Chapman's Letters From France*, p. 79.

52   Weeks, *A Soldier of the Legion*, p. 26.

53   Thaw letter December 28, 1914, *Yale Alumni Weekly*, June 11, 1915 p. 1031.

54   "Cows Start Lively Battle," *The New York Sun*, December 12, 1914, p. 3.

55   Hall, *En L'Air!*, p. 30.

56   Bert Hall, "Three Months in the Trenches," *The New York Times*, February 14, 1915, magazine section, p. 2.

57   Rockwell, *American Fighters*, p. 41. *See also* King, *L.M. 8046*, p. 35.

58   Thaw letter December 28, 1914, *Yale Alumni Weekly*, June 11, 1915 p. 1031.

Chapter Twenty

1   "Two Americans Leave Front," *The New York Sun*, December 9, 1914, p. 3.

2   *See* "Americans Under Fire Watch German Shells," *The New York Sun*, December 19, 1914, p. 3; and "William Thaw, American, Now French Army Aviator," *The New York Sun*, December 27, 1914, p. 3. Olinger, a naturalized American citizen, was born in France. When the war began, he traveled from New York to "get a chance to use my bayonet on the Germans." "Americans Enter the French Army," *The Brooklyn Daily Eagle*, September 20, 1914, p. 4. Paul later noted that Olinger had been honorably discharged after his service in the trenches. Paul Ayres Rockwell, "American College Fraternity Men in Allied Armies," *Sigma Phi Epsilon Journal*, p. 176 (December 1916).

3   Rockwell, *American Fighters*, p. 58. *See also* "Auto Expert Threshes Wheat," *The New York Sun*, January 16, 1915, p. 2.

4   Rockwell, *American Fighters*, p. 41.

5   "Only Three Days in 25 Off Firing Line," *The New York Sun*, January 24, 1915, p. 4. *See also* Hall, *One Man's War*, p. 27; and Rockwell, *American Fighters*, p. 21.

6   "American Fighters Handle Gun and Pick," *The New York Sun*, November 26, 1914, p. 1. *See also* "Seventh Men at the Front," *The Seventh Regiment Gazette*, p. 99 (February 1915). Ellingwood Towle later served in the American Ambulance.

7   "American Fighters Handle Gun and Pick," *The New York Sun*, November 26, 1914, p. 1.

8   "Americans Under Fire Watch German Shells," *The New York Sun*, December 19, 1914, p. 3.

9   "American Evangelists Find Rockwell in French Hospital," *The Asheville Citizen*, April 12, 1915, p. 3.

10   *Id.*

11   Thaw letter December 1, 1914, *Yale Alumni Weekly*, January 22, 1915 p. 486.

12   Kiffin to Loula, December 1, 1914, KYR Papers, NCDNCR.

13   Matthew 26:41, King James Version.

14   A copy of the citation is in the Rockwell Papers, WLU. In a biographical note in the state archives of North Carolina, this statement was rendered in a slightly different way, as "severely wounded at Craonnelle in December 1914 during a patrol in front of the lines." Biographical note, KYR Papers, NCDNCR. Whatever the precise wording, the November 2, 1918, date of the citation – coming right at the end of the war, and almost four years after the supposed incident – erodes confidence in its accuracy. Kiffin's letter dated December 1 states that Paul was already "out of it," and that they were going back into the trenches that night. These statements further undermine the notion that Paul suffered a wound during a patrol in December 1914, as they make clear that Paul was not even in the frontline trenches that month. This unhelpful timeline forced Paul to move the sentences from Kiffin's December 1 letter to a letter written by Kiffin on December 26. See War Letters, p. 11.

15   See e.g. Gordon, Lafayette Escadrille Pilot Biographies, p. 255; Murphy, Kiffin Rockwell, The Lafayette Escadrille and the Birth of the United States Air Force, p. 55; Mason, The Lafayette Escadrille, p. 35; and McClure, Kiffin Rockwell: First American Hero of the Great War, p. 25-26. In his own book, Paul fails to ascribe a cause to his injury, saying only that he "was invalided out of the Legion." Rockwell, American Fighters, p. 58. However, a note in the archives at the Virginia Military Institute, which must have come from Paul, says he was "wounded in shoulder (collar bone broken) during night patrol near Craonnelle, (Chemin des Dames) December 1914." Note, Rockwell Files, VMI.

16   For example, one account from a local North Carolina paper noted that "Paul suffered a broken collar bone and two frozen toes, which kept him in the hospital for several weeks." "German Machine Brought Down," The Western Sentinel, May 23, 1916, p. 2. This comports with a personal interview of Paul by E.A. Marshall, noting that Paul had discomfort in a shoulder he had "dislocated for France." "American Boys Fighting for France to Repay Debt Their Country Owes," The New York Sun, January 21, 1917, Sec. 5, p. 4. But even that may have stretched things a bit – one new American recruit ran into Paul in the American Hospital in Paris. In a letter home not long after, the recruit (H.B. Willis) mentioned that Paul had told him during his time in the trenches he had "lost some 30 pounds and strained his left shoulder." "French Have Deadly Gases," The Boston Evening Globe, May 10, 1915, p. 9.

17   See Journal de Marche, 2e régiment de marche du 2e régiment étranger, 29 Août 1914 au 31 Decembre 1914, available on the Mémoire des Hommes website.

18   "Paul Rockwell Describes War as He Lies in Hospital," The Atlanta Constitution, December 30, 1914, p. 1. A similar letter failing to mention the origin of Paul's injury was received in Asheville on December 17. The following day, the Asheville Citizen reported that although Paul was in the hospital, "it is not thought that he is seriously hurt," and that he hoped to be "back in the trenches within the next few days." "Asheville Soldiers Sent to Hospital," The Asheville Citizen, December 18, 1914, p. 8.

19   "Paul Rockwell Describes War as He Lies in Hospital," The Atlanta Constitution, December 30, 1914, p. 1.

20   "Atlanta Boys Are No Longer in The Battles," The Atlanta Constitution, November 8, 1915, p. 6. This account was soon reprinted in at least one North Carolina paper. See "Tar Heel Boys Are No Longer In The Trenches," The Reidsville Review, November 12, 1915, p. 3

21   See "Dine at $750 a Plate at Banker's China Wedding," The New York Sun, January 10, 1915, p. 21.

22   "Bravery of Atlanta Boys in French Foreign Legion is Told of by Evangelists," The Atlanta Constitution, February 17, 1915, p. 1. The convent was the Couvent de Montléan, built in 1126 and occupied by the nuns of the Congrégation des dames de Nazareth since 1822.

23   Entry for 20 Novembre, Journal de Marche, 2e régiment de marche du 2e régiment étranger, 29 Août 1914 au 31 Decembre 1914, available on the Mémoire des Hommes

website. Hadley apparently vouched for Paul's courage, telling the Nortons that Paul was "as fearless a man as there was in his regiment." "Bravery of Atlanta Boys in French Foreign Legion is Told of by Evangelists," *The Atlanta Constitution*, February 17, 1915, p. 1.

24   I have slightly edited this account, taken from "Bravery of Atlanta Boys in French Foreign Legion is Told of by Evangelists," *The Atlanta Constitution*, February 17, 1915, p. 1, 3. *See also* "Narrow Escapes from Death at Hands of German Soldiers Told by Kiffin Y. Rockwell," *The Atlanta Constitution*, February 28, 1915, p. 3 (reporting that Paul was "now confined in a hospital from exposure.").

25   "Bravery of Atlanta Boys in French Foreign Legion is Told of by Evangelists," *The Atlanta Constitution*, February 17, 1915, p. 3.

26   *Id.*

27   *Id.* This account was reprinted in several newspapers. *See* "North Carolina Boys in the French Army," *The Farmer and Mechanic*, February 23, 1915, p. 11; and "North Carolina Boys in the French Army," *The News and Observer (Raleigh)*, February 21, 1915, p. 18. Paul's fraternity journal, which he surely would have corrected had it been inaccurate, also reprinted the account. "Sigma Phi Epsilons in French Army," *The Sigma Phi Epsilon Journal*, p. 36-38 (October 20, 1915). In addition, Mrs. Norton shared their story in several locations, including Asheville, where she stayed with Loula Rockwell. *See* "American Evangelists Find Rockwell in French Hospital," *The Asheville Citizen*, April 12, 1915, p. 3; and "Conducting Evangelistic Services In Trenches," *The Charlotte Observer*, April 13, 1915, p. 1. Had Paul been wounded in combat, it seems unlikely Loula would have allowed someone saying otherwise to stay in her home.

28   "Atlanta Boy, Wounded on French Battlefield, Paints Graphic Pen Picture of European War," *The Atlanta Constitution*, May 2, 1915, p. 1, 8A. A "marmite" is a piece of French crockery, a pan with a lid. During the war, the French used the term to describe incoming artillery shells, perhaps due to the whistling noise, or maybe because the holes left by the bombs looked like pans. *See* "Americans Under Fire Watch German Shells," *The New York Sun*, December 19, 1914, p. 3.

29   Evidently referring to Paul Rockwell, D.W. King later wrote that "Stuart [Carstairs], Paul, a long lanky Southerner, and two or three other Americans had been *reformès* (discharged physically unfit) mostly on account of inflammatory rheumatism." King, *L.M. 8046*, p. 59. *See also* Handwritten note "Rockwell" next to preceding Paul reference, in article: David King, "L.M. 8046," *Cavalier Magazine*, p. 70 (June 1961), Rockwell Papers, WLU.

30   "Brooklyn Soldier Writes from Front," *The Brooklyn Daily Eagle*, January 6, 1915, p. 5.

31   Kiffin to Loula, December 10, 1914, KYR Papers, NCDNCR.

32   "Only Three Days in 25 Off Firing Line," *The New York Sun*, January 24, 1915, p. 4.

33   *Id.*

34   Loula to Paul and Kiffin, December 1, 1914, Rockwell Papers, WLU.

35   "If I Had A Dozen Sons I Should Want Them to Fight for France," *The Atlanta Constitution*, June 16, 1918, p. 12I.

36   "Americans in the War," *The Asheville Citizen*, August 28, 1914, p. 4 ("we are not surprised; rather are we proud of them.").

37   As their mother, Loula paid little heed to those who were negative toward her sons' choice, viewed it in much more personal terms. As she later explained to Paul and Kiffin, she was not ashamed they had joined the French army but was instead "hurt that my boys had done a thing that looked like they did not love their mother and sister." Loula to Paul, January 11, 1915, in Rockwell Papers, WLU.

38   Loula to Paul and Kiffin, December 3, 1914; and Loula to Paul and Kiffin, December 1, 1914, both Rockwell Papers, WLU.

39   "National Collection Agency" to Loula, November 30, 1914, Rockwell Papers, WLU.

40   Loula to Paul and Kiffin, December 1, 1914, Rockwell Papers, WLU.

41   Kiffin to Loula, December 10, 1914, KYR Papers, NCDNCR.

42 Entry dated December18, 1914, Alan Seeger Diary, Harvard.

43 "Only Three Days In 25 Off Firing Line," *The New York Sun*, January 24, 1915, p. 4.

44 Rockwell, *American Fighters*, p. 59. The regimental journal notes that on November 29th a legionnaire disappeared from sentry duty after shots were heard, leaving behind only five shell casings. *See* Entry for 29 Novembre, *Journal de Marche, 2e régiment de marche du 2e régiment étranger, 29 Août 1914 au 31 Decembre 1914*, available on the *Mémoire des Hommes* website.

45 *See* "American to be Promoted," *The New York Sun*, December 18, 1914, p. 2; and "Americans Study to be French Officers," *The New York Sun*, December 24, 1914, p. 3.

46 "Only Three Days In 25 Off Firing Line," *The New York Sun*, January 24, 1915, p. 4.

47 Entry dated December 18, 1914, Alan Seeger Diary, Harvard.

48 "Only Three Days In 25 Off Firing Line," *The New York Sun*, January 24, 1915, p. 4.

49 Entry dated December18, 1914, Alan Seeger Diary, Harvard.

50 Thaw letter November 27, 1914, *Yale Alumni Weekly*, January 22, 1915 p. 486.

51 "New Yorker to be Aviator in France," *The New York Sun*, December 16, 1914, p. 2. *See also* Hall & Nordhoff, *The Lafayette Flying Corps*, Vol. 2, p. 324 (giving Bach's date of enlistment in aviation as December 10). Thaw held the first hydroaeroplane license issued by the French Aero Club. "Americans Study to be French Officers," *The New York Sun*, December 24, 1914, p. 3.

52 "New Yorker to be Aviator in France," *The New York Sun*, December 16, 1914, p. 2.

53 "Americans Study to be French Officers," *The New York Sun*, December 24, 1914, p. 3.

54 "William Thaw, American, Now French Army Aviator," *The New York Sun*, December 27, 1914, p. 3.

55 Thaw letter December 28, 1914, *Yale Alumni Weekly*, 1915 p. 1031 ("last Thursday morning I put all my worldly possessions on the back of my neck, got into a nice little Renault which they had sent for me, and motored a dozen kilometres southwest of here to Morval, and joined the *Escadrille D6* of the Aviation Corps, where I now hold a job as observer, while awaiting vacancy in one of the military flying schools to take a military license.").

56 "William Thaw, American, Now French Army Aviator," *The New York Sun*, December 27, 1914, p. 3.

57 Gordon, *Lafayette Escadrille Pilot Biographies*, p. 61.

58 Hall & Nordhoff, *The Lafayette Flying Corps*, Vol. 2, p. 324.

59 "Editorial Points," *The Boston Globe*, January 4, 1915, p. 10.

60 "Asheville Soldiers Sent to Hospital," *The Asheville Citizen*, December 18, 1914, p. 8.

61 Loula A. Rockwell to the Ambassador to France, December 22, 1914, *National Archives*, Records of the Foreign Service Posts of the Department of State (Record Group 84).

62 *Id.*

63 For example, Loula later said that she "made every possible effort to have my boys taken out of the army and returned to this country," including writing letters to the War Department at both Washington and Paris. "If I Had A Dozen Sons I Should Want Them to Fight for France," *The Atlanta Constitution*, June 16, 1918, p. 12I.

64 Loula A. Rockwell to the Ambassador to France, December 22, 1914, *National Archives*, Records of the Foreign Service Posts of the Department of State (Record Group 84).

65 Kiffin to Loula, January 11, 1915, KYR Papers, NCDNCR.

Chapter Twenty-one

1 Lionel K. Anderson to Paul, January 6 and February 4, 1915, Rockwell Papers, WLU.

2 *Id.*

3 *Id.*

4 *Id.* Loula confirmed that she had received letters from a couple of Paul's friends, including Lionel Anderson, who had written "just to tell me they are your friends and mine." Loula to

Paul, January 7, 1915, Rockwell Papers, WLU.

5   Thaw letter December 28, 1914, *Yale Alumni Weekly*, 1915 p. 1031.

6   *Id.*

7   "Coolness of Americans Saves Outpost in France," *The New York Sun*, February 2, 1915, p. 3.

8   Kiffin to Loula, December 26, 1914, KYR Papers, NCDNCR.

9   Kiffin to Paul, December 26, 1914, in Rockwell Papers, WLU.

10   The rum rations were very strong, the soldiers called it *la gnole* – the hooch. "Find Mule Steaks a Battle Delicacy," *The Chicago Daily News*, January 25, 1916, p. 5.

11   "Xmas Spirit Will Rule in the Trenches," *The New York Sun,* December 24, 1914, p. 3.

12   *Id.*

13   "Christmas in the Trenches," *The Daily Mail*, December 24, 1914, p. 5.

14   *Victor Chapman's Letters From France*, p. 74.

15   Adriannan Combry, "To an Unknown Soldier," *The Daily Mail*, December 23, 1914, p. 9.

16   A few days after Christmas, Kiffin received a gold piece from his sister Agnes, money she had earned by selling "fifty of my best tested recipes." Agnes to Kiffin, December 2, 1914, in Rockwell Papers, WLU.

17   Kiffin to Paul, December 26, 1914, Rockwell Papers, WLU. The article was reprinted in "Paul Rockwell Writes for Big European Daily Newspapers," *The Asheville Citizen*, January 15, 1915, p. 5. The *Citizen* noted that Paul was "not letting time hang heavily on his hands while confined in a French hospital as the result of injuries sustained in the trenches." *Id.*

18   Kiffin to Paul, December 26, 1914, Rockwell Papers, WLU. The doctor apparently walked 17 kilometers to the supply station at Fismes to secure the ham for the men. "William Thaw, American, Now French Army Aviator," *The New York Sun,* December 27, 1914, p. 3.

19   "Coolness of Americans Saves Outpost in France," *The New York Sun*, February 2, 1915, p. 3.

20   *Id.*

21   Kiffin to Paul, December 26, 1914, Rockwell Papers, WLU.

22   Alan Seeger to Miss Elsie A. Seeger, December 29, 1914, Alan Seeger Papers, Harvard.

23   Kiffin to Loula, December 29, 1914, KYR Papers, NCDNCR.

24   Kiffin to Agnes, January 7, 1915, KYR Papers, NCDNCR.

25   Entry dated January 5, 1915, Alan Seeger Diary, Harvard.

26   "Coolness of Americans Saves Outpost in France," *The New York Sun*, February 2, 1915, p. 3.

27   "With the Foreign Legion," *The Daily Mail*, January 13, 1915, p. 6.

28   Kiffin to Agnes, January 7, 1915, KYR Papers, NCDNCR.

29   A. Piatt Andrew to his parents, December 31, 1914, A. Piatt Andrew, *Letters Written Home From France in the First Half of 1915*, available at http://www.ourstory.info/library/2-ww1/APA/APATC.html (visited November 18, 2017).

30   Churchill, *The World Crisis*, Volume II, p. 1.

Chapter Twenty-two

1   Entry dated January 12, 1915, Alan Seeger Diary, Harvard.

2   "Michigan Boy, Fighting for France, Writes of Life In the Trenches," *The Detroit Free Press*, May 2, 1915, Feature Section, p. 7.

3   Seeger, *Letters and Diary*, p. 57-58. Seeger's letter was apparently begun on January 31 and finished on February 5, 1915. *See* "French Forced to Train Guns on French Towns to Rout Germans," *The New York Sun*, February 22, 1915, p. 3.

4   "Narrow Escapes from Death at Hands of German Soldiers Told by Kiffin Y. Rockwell," *The Atlanta Constitution*, February 28, 1915, p. 3.

5   "Brooklyn Lawyer Fights For Allies; Endures Hardships," *The Brooklyn Daily Eagle*, February 14, 1915, Section 3, p. 8.

6   "Michigan Boy, Fighting for France, Writes of Life In the Trenches," *The Detroit Free Press*, May 2, 1915, Feature Section, p. 7.

7   Kiffin to Paul, January 11, 1915, Rockwell Papers, WLU.

8   "Narrow Escapes from Death at Hands of German Soldiers Told by Kiffin Y. Rockwell," *The Atlanta Constitution*, February 28, 1915, p. 3. *See* John Bowe and Family Papers, Minnesota Historical Society Library, P.1473, French Foreign Legion photography, Edgar Bouligny.

9   "Narrow Escapes from Death at Hands of German Soldiers Told by Kiffin Y. Rockwell," *The Atlanta Constitution*, February 28, 1915, p. 3; Kiffin to Agnes, January 7, 1915, KYR Papers, NCDNCR.

10   Seeger, *Letters and Diary*, p. 59.

11   *The War Diary of Constant Vincent*, entry of September-October, 1914. The diary is available on the website of the soldier's great-grandson, Vincent Juillet. (vincent.juillet. free.fr/cahier-constant-vincent-1914-1.htm) (last visited May 21, 2019) Not long after they chased out the Germans, Vincent and some fellow soldiers spent all day in the *château*, after which he wrote the following poignant words: "Never has a day been so long and so sad. We have everything to eat and drink, but we cannot forget the absence of comrades whom we will never see again." *Id.*

12   King, *L.M. 8046*, p. 41. A great photo of the *château* was published in *The New York Sun* on March 21, 1915, and in Mason, *The Lafayette Escadrille*, after page 22.

13   Kiffin to Agnes, January 7, 1915, KYR Papers, NCDNCR.

14   "Coolness of Americans Saves Outpost in France," *The New York Sun*, February 2, 1915, p. 3.

15   Alan Seeger to Charles L. Seeger, January 11, 1915, Alan Seeger Papers, Harvard.

16   One paper published a neat photo of three of the men sitting in the bombed-out window of the smaller *château*. *See* "Michigan Soldier Boy Writes From the French Trenches," *The Detroit Free Press*, May 23, 1915, Feature Section, p. 3.

17   Handwritten caption to photo in John Bowe and Family Papers, Minnesota Historical Society Library, P.1473, French Foreign Legion photography, Edgar Bouligny.

18   Seeger, *Letters and Diary*, p. 60.

19   "Michigan Boy, Fighting for France, Writes of Life In the Trenches," *The Detroit Free Press*, May 2, 1915, Feature Section, p. 7; Seeger, *Letters and Diary*, p. 60.

20   Seeger, *Letters and Diary*, p. 61.

21   "Michigan Boy, Fighting for France, Writes of Life In the Trenches," *The Detroit Free Press*, May 2, 1915, Feature Section, p. 7. The Old Maid's Ball can be heard here: *Discography of American Historical Recordings*, s.v. "Victor matrix B-13111. The old maid's ball / Billy Murray," accessed November 4, 2017, http://adp.library.ucsb.edu/index.php/matrix/ detail/200013361/B-13111-The_old_maids_ball.

22   "Michigan Boy, Fighting for France, Writes of Life In the Trenches," *The Detroit Free Press*, May 2, 1915, Feature Section, p. 7. In the ruins one of the men found a photo postcard of the *château* before the war, which Zinn sent home along with a photo of how it looked when they lived in its cellar. The "before and after" contrast in the two photos is quite interesting. *See* "A French Chateau, Before and After German Occupation," *The Detroit Free Press*, June 27, 1915, p. 82.

23   Seeger, *Letters and Diary*, p. 59.

24   Seeger, *Letters and Diary*, p. 65-66.

25   Kiffin to Agnes, January 7, 1915, KYR Papers, NCDNCR.

26   "Michigan Boy, Fighting for France, Writes of Life In the Trenches," *The Detroit Free Press*, May 2, 1915, Feature Section, p. 7.

27   Seeger, *Letters and Diary*, p. 61.

28   "Brooklyn Lawyer Fights For Allies, Endures Hardships," *The Brooklyn Daily Eagle*, February 14, 1915, Sec. 3, p. 8.

29   Seeger, *Letters and Diary*, p. 63.

30   Kiffin to Paul, December 29, 1914, Rockwell Papers, WLU.

31   Henry Farnsworth to his sister Ellen, about March 7, 1915, *Letters of Henry Weston Farnsworth*, p. 127.

32   Seeger, *Letters and Diary*, p. vi.

33   Alan Seeger to Mrs. Charles L. Seeger, November 17, 1914, Alan Seeger Papers, Harvard.

34   "Brooklyn Lawyer Fights For Allies; Endures Hardships," *The Brooklyn Daily Eagle*, February 14, 1915, Section 3, p. 8.

Chapter Twenty-three

1   "Narrow Escapes from Death at Hands of German Soldiers Told by Kiffin Y. Rockwell," *The Atlanta Constitution*, February 28, 1915, p. 3.

2   Kiffin to Agnes, January 7, 1915, KYR Papers, NCDNCR.

3   Entry dated January 12, 1915, Alan Seeger Diary, Harvard.

4   Kiffin to Agnes, January 7, 1915, KYR Papers, NCDNCR.

5   Afterward, Dowd wrote that their location "constituted one of the worst death traps that I have seen or heard of." "Brooklyn Lawyer Fights For Allies; Endures Hardships," *The Brooklyn Daily Eagle*, February 14, 1915, Section 3, p. 8.

6   Entry dated January 12, 1915, Alan Seeger Diary, Harvard.

7   Kiffin to Paul, January 11, 1915, Rockwell Papers, WLU.

8   Kiffin to Agnes, January 7, 1915, KYR Papers, NCDNCR.

9   Entry dated January 12, 1915, Alan Seeger Diary, Harvard.

10   *Id.*

11   Seeger, *Letters and Diary*, p. 68.

12   Kiffin to Agnes, January 7, 1915, KYR Papers, NCDNCR.

13   Kiffin may have waited there by himself for ten minutes or more. *See* Alice Weeks to Allen Weeks, March 10, 1916, Weeks, *Greater Love*, p. 115.

14   Entry dated January 12, 1915, Alan Seeger Diary, Harvard.

15   Kiffin to Agnes, January 7, 1915, KYR Papers, NCDNCR.

16   Entry dated January 12, 1915, Alan Seeger Diary, Harvard.

17   *Id.*

18   Kiffin to Agnes, January 7, 1915, KYR Papers, NCDNCR.

19   *Id.* Kiffin told Paul he "lay in the woods, covering the path to the post, but afraid to move or be seen." Kiffin to Paul, January 11, 1915, in Rockwell Papers, WLU. When Paul published Kiffin's letters, he added in "My rifle had jammed, and I could not fire." *War Letters*, p. 19-20. Kiffin later told Mrs. Weeks he hid behind a tree "with his bayonet fixed and only one shot in his rifle." Alice Weeks to Allen Weeks, March 10, 1916, Weeks, *Greater Love*, p. 115.

20   Entry dated January 12, 1915, Alan Seeger Diary, Harvard.

21   "Michigan Boy, Fighting for France, Writes of Life In the Trenches," *The Detroit Free Press*, May 2, 1915, Feature Section, p. 7.

22   "New York Recruit Wounded In Battle," *The New York Sun*, January 14, 1915, p. 2.

23   "Michigan Boy, Fighting for France, Writes of Life In the Trenches," *The Detroit Free Press*, May 2, 1915, Feature Section, p. 7.

24   *Id.*

25   "New York Recruit Wounded In Battle," *The New York Sun*, January 14, 1915, p. 2

26   "Brooklyn Lawyer Fights For Allies; Endures Hardships," *The Brooklyn Daily Eagle*, February 14, 1915, Section 3, p. 8.

27   Entry dated January 12, 1915, Alan Seeger Diary, Harvard.

28   Kiffin to Paul, January 11, 1915, Rockwell Papers, WLU.

29   Kiffin to Agnes, January 7, 1915, KYR Papers, NCDNCR.

30   Entry dated January 12, 1915, Alan Seeger Diary, Harvard.

31   "Michigan Boy, Fighting for France, Writes of Life In the Trenches," *The Detroit Free Press*, May 2, 1915, Feature Section, p. 7.

32   Kiffin to Agnes, January 7, 1915, KYR Papers, NCDNCR.

33   *Id.*

34   "Michigan Boy, Fighting for France, Writes of Life In the Trenches," *The Detroit Free Press*, May 2, 1915, Feature Section, p. 7.

35   King, *L.M. 8046*, p. 44.

36   Seeger, *Letters and Diary*, p. 69.

37   King, *L.M. 8046*, p. 45.

38   Kiffin to Agnes, January 7, 1915, KYR Papers, NCDNCR.

39   "Michigan Boy, Fighting for France, Writes of Life In the Trenches," *The Detroit Free Press*, May 2, 1915, Feature Section, p. 7.

40   Kiffin to Paul, January 11, 1915, Rockwell Papers, WLU.

41   Kiffin to Agnes, January 7, 1915, KYR Papers, NCDNCR.

42   Kiffin to Paul, January 11, 1915, Rockwell Papers, WLU.

43   One soldier joked "Rockwell, standing between the grenade and the corporal, was so thin the charge missed him and lodged in the fat man." Bowe, *Soldiers of the Legion*, p. 116.

44   Kiffin to Agnes, January 7, 1915, KYR Papers, NCDNCR.

45   Entry dated January 12, 1915, Alan Seeger Diary, Harvard. Apparently, Seeger felt that Kiffin could have been called to answer for leaving his post when the Germans fired through the barricade.

46   Entry dated January 12, 1915, Alan Seeger Diary, Harvard.

47   *Id.*

48   "Brooklyn Lawyer Fights For Allies, Endures Hardships," *The Brooklyn Daily Eagle*, February 14, 1915, Section 3, p. 8.

49   "Michigan Boy, Fighting for France, Writes of Life In the Trenches," *The Detroit Free Press*, May 2, 1915, Feature Section, p. 7.

50   "Coolness of Americans Saves Outpost in France," *The New York Sun*, February 2, 1915, p. 3.

51   Alan Seeger to Charles L. Seeger, January 11, 1915, Alan Seeger Papers, Harvard.

52   Seeger, *Poems*, p. 144. Edgar Bouligny insisted that Seeger wrote the poem's opening lines at the *château* in Craonnelle around this time. *See* "Rendezvous," *Liberty Magazine*, March 24, 1934, p. 30. Maybe so, but the handwritten copy Seeger's mother later supplied to Harvard bore a date of February 9, 1916, more than a year after the incident. *See* Facsimile of "I Have a Rendezvous with Death," *Harvard Alumni Bulletin*, October 17, 1918, p. 75. A more recent biography suggests the poem may have been written in January 1916 in Crevècoeur. *See* Chris Dickon, *A Rendezvous With Death*, p. 170.

53   Seeger, *Letters and Diary*, p. 108-09.

54   "French Forced to Train Guns on French Towns to Rout Germans," *The New York Sun*, February 22, 1915, p. 3. Paul later said he would always have a soft spot in his heart for Corporal Weidemann (who "had more medals than he had room on his coat"), because "when he met his death he was saving the lives of my brother Kiffin Rockwell and Alan Seeger[.]" "American Boys Fighting for France to Repay Debt Their Country Owes," *The New York Sun*, January 21, 1917, Sec. 5, p. 4. Paul also reported that Weidemann told Capdeville on their march to Craonnelle that he felt this would be his last trip. "Some Sidelights of the World War," *The Atlanta Constitution*, November 1, 1917, p. 8. Bouligny took a photo of the gravesite and noted that within one square mile one hundred thousand French, German and English soldiers would lose their lives. *See* John Bowe and Family Papers, Minnesota Historical Society Library, P.1473, French Foreign Legion photography, Edgar Bouligny.

55   Kiffin to Agnes, January 7, 1915, KYR Papers, NCDNCR.

56   Loula to Fred Olds, August 18, 1917, KYR Papers, NCDNCR.

57   Loula to Paul and Kiffin, January 7, 1915, Rockwell Papers, WLU. When Loula received Kiffin's letter telling the story, she stated in a letter to Paul "how the Lord spared him encourages me." Loula to Paul, February 3, 1915, Rockwell Papers, WLU.

58   "Brooklyn Lawyer Fights for Allies; Endures Hardships," *The Brooklyn Daily Eagle*, February 14, 1915, Section 3, p. 8.

59   Kiffin to Loula, January 11, 1915, KYR Papers, NCDNCR.

Chapter Twenty-four

1   "Cuffs and Leggings Costume at Front," *The New York Sun*, April 18, 1915, Fifth Section, p. 7.

2   Kiffin to Paul, January 19, 1915, Rockwell Papers, WLU.

3   Entry dated January 24, 1915, Alan Seeger Diary, Harvard.

4   "Just Jottings," *The Atlanta Constitution*, February 28, 1915, p. 9M.

5   "Narrow Escapes from Death at Hands of German Soldiers Told by Kiffin Y. Rockwell," *The Atlanta Constitution*, February 28, 1915, p. 3.

6   Kiffin to Paul, January 19, 1915, Rockwell Papers, WLU.

7   *Id.*

8   Entry dated January 24, 1915, Alan Seeger Diary, Harvard.

9   *Id.*

10 *Id.*

11 "Michigan Soldier Boy Writes From the French Trenches," *The Detroit Free Press*, May 23, 1915, Feature Section, p. 3.

12 *Id.*

13 "Americans at the Front Long for a Real Battle," *The New York Sun*, February 28, 1915, p. 14.

14 "Coolness of Americans Saves Outpost in France," *The New York Sun*, February 2, 1915, p. 3.

15 "Michigan Soldier Boy Writes from the French Trenches," *The Detroit Free Press*, May 23, 1915, Feature Section, p. 3.

16 Seeger, *Letters and Diary*, p. 66.

17 "Narrow Escapes from Death at Hands of German Soldiers Told by Kiffin Y. Rockwell," *The Atlanta Constitution*, February 28, 1915, p. 3.

18 *Id.*

19 Kiffin was not known for his sense of humor. A friend from his Atlanta days once noted that "It also seemed that Kiffin said the funniest things – whenever he said them – by reason of the fact that you hardly expected Kiffin to say anything funny." "Paul Rockwell Tells Story of Kiffin's Last Air Fight and of His Drop to Death," *The Atlanta Constitution*, November 11, 1916, p. 5.

20 "Narrow Escapes from Death at Hands of German Soldiers Told by Kiffin Y. Rockwell," *The Atlanta Constitution*, February 28, 1915, p. 3.

21 You can listen to a great recording of it at the following site: *Discography of American Historical Recordings*, s.v. "Victor matrix B-11476. Nothing to do until to-morrow / Billy Murray," http://adp.library.ucsb.edu/index.php/matrix/detail/200011629/B-11476-Nothing_to_do_until_to-morrow (accessed November 4, 2017).

22 Kiffin to Paul, January 19, 1915, Rockwell Papers, WLU.

23 "Americans at the Front Long for a Real Battle," *The New York Sun*, February 28, 1915, p. 14.

24 Entry dated January 25, 1915, Alan Seeger Diary, Harvard.

25 "War Not Near End, Says U. of M. Man Now in Trenches," *The Detroit Free Press*, May 23, 1915, p. 12.

26 Kiffin to Paul, February 1, 1915, Rockwell Papers, WLU.

27 "Capture Germans With Hook and Line," *The New York Sun*, February 28, 1915, Fifth Section, p. 4.

28 "Americans at the Front Long for a Real Battle," *The New York Sun*, February 28, 1915, p. 14.

29 "French Forced to Train Guns on French Towns to Rout Germans," *The New York Sun*, February 22, 1915, p. 3.

30 Entry dated January 27, 1915, Alan Seeger Diary, Harvard.

31 Kiffin to Loula, January 31, 1915, Rockwell Papers, WLU.

32 "Capture Germans With Hook and Line," *The New York Sun*, February 28, 1915, Fifth Section, p. 4.

33 Letter from Edward Mandell Stone, January 20, 1915, quoted in Rockwell, *American*

Fighters, p. 52.

34 Kiffin to Paul, February 1, 1915, Rockwell Papers, WLU. One Englishman gave a good explanation for how men can thrive under the pressures of war. He said: "It may be the beast within one, but there is some long unused instinct that rises to the surface and makes you feel instantly at home carrying bread and water, digging trenches, marching, lying under fire – war is one of the natural functions of man, and the human being who has not experienced it is incomplete." "The Peace of the Firing Line," *The Daily Mail*, September 17, 1914, p. 4.

35 Kiffin to Paul, January 19, 1915, Rockwell Papers, WLU.

36 Kiffin to Paul, February 1, 1915, Rockwell Papers, WLU.

37 "Narrow Escapes from Death at Hands of German Soldiers Told by Kiffin Y. Rockwell," *The Atlanta Constitution*, February 28, 1915, p. 3.

38 Kiffin to Loula, February 8, 1915, Rockwell Papers, WLU.

39 Kiffin to Paul, January 19, 1915, Rockwell Papers, WLU.

40 Kiffin to Loula, February 8, 1915, Rockwell Papers, WLU.

41 Kiffin to Paul, January 21, 1915, Rockwell Papers, WLU.

42 Kiffin to Paul, January 31, 1915, Rockwell Papers, WLU. Note that this letter is misdated January 15, 1915, *War Letters*, p. 20.

43 "Americans at the Front Long for a Real Battle," *The New York Sun*, February 28, 1915, p. 14.

44 "Capture Germans With Hook and Line," *The New York Sun*, February 28, 1915, Fifth Section, p. 4.

45 *Id.*

46 Kiffin to Paul, February 1, 1915, Rockwell Papers, WLU.

47 "Narrow Escapes from Death at Hands of German Soldiers Told by Kiffin Y. Rockwell," *The Atlanta Constitution*, February 28, 1915, p. 32.

48 "Seventh Men at the Front," *The Seventh Regiment Gazette*, p. 99 (February 1915). There is a very small but interesting photo of Bartram and Ellingwood on the next page in this issue of the Gazette.

49 B.F. Towle, "In the Foreign Legion and Royal Flying Corps," *The Seventh Regiment Gazette*, p. 186 (June 1915).

50 *See* "Rescues American From War," *The New York Sun*, April 10, 1915, p. 7. One account from the time says Towle returned to America to take the entrance examinations at West Point. "141 On Board the Lapland," *The New York Sun*, April 25, 1915, p. 8.

51 Kiffin to Paul, February 1, 1915, Rockwell Papers, WLU.

52 "James Chester Rockwell: A Memoir," p. 3, James Chester Rockwell Papers, WFU.

53 Kiffin to Paul, January 21, 1915, Rockwell Papers, WLU.

54 Loula to Paul, January 14, 1915, Rockwell Papers, WLU.

55 Kiffin to Paul, February 1, 1915, Rockwell Papers, WLU.

56 *Id.*

57 *Id.*

58 "Alan Seeger Is Hit by German Sniper," *The New York Sun*, February 27, 1915, p. 1.

59 Alan Seeger to Charles L. Seeger, February 26, 1915, Alan Seeger Papers, Harvard.

60 "Alan Seeger Is Hit by German Sniper," *The New York Sun*, February 27, 1915, p. 1.

61 "American Wins Promotion," *The New York Sun*, February 3, 1915, p. 3.

62 Paul said Morlae "claimed to have been everywhere and to have done everything." Rockwell, *American Fighters*, p. 10.

63 "Americans Quit Legion Because of Drastic Rule," *The Minneapolis Star Tribune*, June 18, 1916, p. 5. Many years later, D.W. King said that Morlae was a "so-called soldier of fortune," who actually "was a loud speaking fourflusher and we all knew it." David W. King to Dale Walker, December 1, 1971, Rockwell Papers, WLU.

64 Zinn was transferred out on February 27, 1915. Kiffin wrote: "We had been trying to get him out for the last two or three months. He was a nice lad but a nuisance as a soldier. He was sick most of the time and would fall asleep on guard and snore loud as hell. They gave him

prison sentences and work but finally became convinced that he was really sick so now have sent him back." Kiffin to Paul, February 28, 1915, Rockwell Papers, WLU.

65 Alan Seeger to Mrs. Charles L. Seeger, April 13, 1916, Alan Seeger Papers, Harvard.

66 "Americans Quit Legion Because of Drastic Rule," *The Minneapolis Star Tribune*, June 18, 1916, p. 5.

67 In Paris on November 22, 1915, Morlae applied for an emergency passport for the stated purpose of "travelling to U.S. from France via Spain." Edward Morlae passport application, November 22, 1915, available on Ancestry.com. *U.S. Passport Applications, 1795-1925*.

68 F.W. Zinn, "The Real Foreign Legion," *Leslie's Weekly*, June 29, 1916, p. 818. *See also* Rockwell, *American Fighters*, p. 127-28.

69 Extract from letter of Benjamin Thaw dated February 28, 1916, William Thaw Scrapbooks, HSWP.

70 James Norman Hall to George Courtright Greener, October 2, 1916, JNH Papers, Grinnell. The men were still "very sore" at Mr. Ellery Sedgwick, the publisher of Morlae's piece, and did "not want any stories of the American Escadrille published in the Atlantic." *Id.*

71 Paul said that during his few months in the Legion, he never spoke more than fifty words to Morlae. And he knew right away to stay clear:
The first day he arrived at Toulouse, where the 2nd Regiment of the Legion was in training, he asked me to have a drink with him. In my newspaper career I have covered too many sessions of police court in Washington, Atlanta, and other cities, not to be able to recognize certain types at sight, so I refused Morlae's invitation. Then he asked me to have a cigarette, which also I refused. He demanded, "Well, what will you have?" I replied, "Nothing with you," so you can imagine that after that he made no other efforts to cultivate my acquaintance. Paul to Mr. Prince, May 16, 1916, Rockwell Papers, WLU.

72 Kiffin to Paul, February 16, 1915, Rockwell Papers, WLU.

73 *Id.*

74 Entry for 15 Février, *Journal de Marche, 2e régiment de marche du 2e régiment étranger, 1er Janvier au 11 Novembre 1915*, available on the *Mémoire des Hommes* website.

75 Howe, *Memoirs of the Harvard Dead in the War Against Germany, Vol. 1*, p. 10. *See also* "Baseball at Front, Cry of Americans," *The New York Sun*, March 7, 1915, Fifth Section, p. 4 (reporting that Stone was hit by two bullets).

76 "American Dies of Wounds at Front," *The New York Sun*, March 28, 1915, p. 2. Stone's service card states that he died for France on 27 Février 1915 and lists the nature of his death as "suites de blessures de guerre et pneumonie double." Available on the *Mémoire des Hommes* website.

77 Howe, *Memoirs of the Harvard Dead in the War Against Germany, Vol. 1*, p. 9.

78 "Chicagoan First U.S. Legionnaire to Fall," *The Chicago Daily News*, June 1, 1916, p. 2.

79 Letter to the editor by Rudolph Altrocchi, in "Communication," *The Harvard Crimson*, March 29, 1915.

80 Kiffin to Paul, April 10, 1915, Rockwell Papers, WLU.

81 *Id.*

82 Kiffin to Paul, March 11, 1915, Rockwell Papers, WLU.

83 "Chicagoan Slain by a Fellow Legionary," *The Chicago Daily News*, October 23, 1915, p. 6.

84 *Id.*

85 *Id.*

86 King, *L.M. 8046*, p. 61.

87 Edgar Bouligny, "Rendezvous," *Liberty Magazine*, March 31, 1934, p. 57.

88 "Chicagoan Slain by a Fellow Legionary," *The Chicago Daily News*, October 23, 1915, p. 6.

89 Kiffin to Paul, April 17, 1915, Rockwell Papers, WLU. Bouligny reported Phelizot's last words were: "I am an American, thank God." Edgar Bouligny, "Rendezvous," *Liberty Magazine*, March 31, 1934, p. 57.

90 Kiffin to Paul, March 11, 1915, Rockwell Papers, WLU.

91   "Chicagoan Slain by a Fellow Legionary," *The Chicago Daily News*, October 23, 1915, p. 6.

92   "Americans at Front Are Happy; 'Gunga Din' Found," *The New York Sun*, May 16, 1915, p. 4.

93   "Cuffs and Leggings Costume at Front," *The New York Sun*, April 18, 1915, Fifth Section, p. 7.

Chapter Twenty-five

1   Thaw letter February 14, 1915, "Letters of a French Army Aviator," *Yale Alumni Weekly*, June 11, 1915, p. 1032.

2   *Id.*

3   *Id.*

4   *Id.*

5   Gordon, *Lafayette Escadrille Pilot Biographies*, p. 7. In the same book, Gordon lists Thaw's license number as 714. *Id.* at p. 57. Gordon told me that 712 is correct. Another source says Thaw's license number was 714. *See* Irving J. Newman, "A Biography of Colonel Thaw II," *Popular Aviation*, November 1934, p. 282.

6   Thaw letter April 7, 1915, "Letters of a French Army Aviator," *Yale Alumni Weekly*, June 11, 1915, p. 1032.

7   Although I found no official record of his service, there is some evidence that an American exhibition flyer by the name of Frederick C. Hild may have gained acceptance into French aviation early in the war. *See* "Aviator Hild Off to Fly for France," *The Brooklyn Daily Eagle*, September 6, 1914, p. 4; "Aviator Hild in France," *Asbury Park Press*, November 17, 1914, p. 2; and "Aviator May Give Exhibition in City," *Lansing State Journal*, June 3, 1915, p. 10. Those who mention Hild's service say he trained with the French but deserted and then bad-mouthed their efforts from the other side of the Atlantic. *See* Flammer, *The Vivid Air*, p. 12; and Rockwell, *American Fighters*, p. 187. One source stated that after he deserted Hild was "seen in the company of German military attaches in Washington by French embassy personnel." H. Hugh Wynne, "Escadrille Lafayette," *Cross & Cockade Journal*, p. 5. (Spring 1961).

8   One account asserts that Norman borrowed $600 cash from a friend of his who was in charge of the Prince family stables. "A Winged Knight Comes Home," *The Western Weekly Magazine*, July 7, 1929, in *Abilene Reporter-News*, July 7, 1929, p. 37

9   "Norman Prince Has Gone to France," *The Boston Daily Globe*, February 8, 1915, p. 9.

10   Edmond Genet, diary entries of December 29 and 31, 1914, "Leaves from A War Diary," *The North American Review*, p. 271 (Jun.-Aug. 1927). Genet later told Paul Rockwell that "in fighting for France he [was] fighting also for the future safety of America from the German menace." "Young Genet Fights for Ancestor's Land," *The Chicago Daily News*, June 17, 1916, p. 2.

11   *War Letters of Edmond Genet*, p. 39. *See also* Edmond Genet, diary entry of January 20, 1915, "Leaves from A War Diary," *The North American Review*, p. 273 (Jun.-Aug. 1927).

12   Edmond Genet, diary entry of January 29, 1915, "Leaves from A War Diary," *The North American Review*, p. 273 (Jun.-Aug. 1927).

13   *War Letters of Edmond Genet*, p. 44-45.

14   Prince, *A Volunteer Who Died for the Cause He Loved*, p. 26.

15   Cowdin stated later that Prince asked him to fill in when another American aviator, Norman Read, was unable to secure his release from the Royal Flying Corps. Cowdin, "The Lafayette Escadrille," *Harvard Alumni Bulletin*, March 7, 1918, p. 434.

16   Elliott Christopher Cowdin, II, passport applications dated October 31, 1914, and January 18, 1917, available on Ancestry.com. *U.S. Passport Applications, 1795-1925*.

17   In one article, Prince called Cowdin "my pal, a classmate at college..." *See* "Boston Aviator in 10 Bombardments," *The Boston Globe*, October 16, 1915, p. 10.

18   Sergeant Marshall Peabody, "With the American Ambulance Corps in Belgium," *The Seventh*

Regiment Gazette, p. 124 (March 1915).

19   *Escroquerie* can be translated as swindle, fraud, gyp, ripoff, scam, trick, etc.

20   Hall & Nordhoff, *The Lafayette Flying Corps*, Vol. 1, pp. 4-6.

21   Curtis later wrote that he was "inclined to think that the Foreign Office looked on us favorably very largely because I was endorsed by Bliss." Frazier Curtis to James Norman Hall, July 15, 1919, JNH Papers, Grinnell. He also suggested that one could not "overstate what the Escadrille owes to Bob Bliss." According to Curtis, beyond the key introduction to de Sillac, Bliss was "always guide, counsellor & friend to the Escadrille," and "saw people & arranged things & got things done." *Id.*

22   Hall & Nordhoff, *The Lafayette Flying Corps*, Vol. 1, p. 65.

23   Hall & Nordhoff, *The Lafayette Flying Corps*, Vol. 1, p. 6.

24   "Dropping Bombs on the Boches," *The Boston Evening Transcript*, August 28, 1915, Part Two, p. 12.

25   *Id. See also* Hall & Nordhoff, *The Lafayette Flying Corps*, Vol. 1, p. 6.

26   Prince, *A Volunteer Who Died for the Cause He Loved*, p. 6.

27   Hall & Nordhoff, *The Lafayette Flying Corps*, Vol. 1, p. 459.

28   Thaw's personnel record shows that on March 6, he "left for Lyon for the *Escadrille Américaine*," but "returned to his division" on March 12. *See* Thaw personnel record, available on the *Mémoire des Hommes* website. He received his license on March 15 and was transferred to the front as part of *Escadrille C.42* on March 25. *Id.* Cowdin said Thaw "preferred not to go with us and instead went his own way, subsequently joining a French Squadron in Lorraine." Cowdin, "The Lafayette Escadrille," *Harvard Alumni Bulletin*, March 7, 1918, p. 434. *See also* Hall & Nordhoff, *The Lafayette Flying Corps*, Vol. 1, p. 459 (Thaw "received orders to join the other Americans at Pau but, instead, he went to the French Ministry of War and requested that he be sent to the Front at once."). Dr. Gros remembered: "In the spring of 1915, Prince, M. de Sillac, and myself met at M. de Sillac's office, Thaw being heartily in accord with us, but obliged to remain on duty at the front. The plans of the future American squadrilla were then drawn up." Edmund Gros, introduction to James Norman Hall, *High Adventure*, p. xiii, (1918).

29   "Neutrals," *The Times (London)*, August 24, 1914, p. 7.

30   "Regarding Our Neutrality," *The New York Times*, November 13, 1914, p. 10.

31   "Regarding Our Neutrality," *The New York Times*, November 13, 1914, p. 10.

32   *Victor Chapman's Letters From France*, p. 92, 93. William Astor Chanler apparently told his friend Theodore Roosevelt about Victor, as Teddy wrote William in January 1915: "I admire your nephew and the other young Americans who have gone to the front." Theodore Roosevelt to William Astor Chanler, January 13, 1915 (available at https://www.theodorerooseveltcenter.org/Research/Digital-Library/Record/ ImageViewer?libID=0211360&imageNo=1) (visited September 18, 2018) In the same letter, Roosevelt told his friend, "Willy":

I feel just as you do about neutrality, it means worse than nothing. We incur the contempt of both sides. If I had been President I should have taken such action that the United States would have been playing the proper part at this time. Nothing infuriates me more than the pacifistic prattling and prating, or all our people preening themselves upon being in safety while men are dying men's deaths and doing deeds worthy of men. Feeling the way I do, it has not been too easy for me to keep my head; but it is imperative, Willy, that I shall not contrive to live foolishly in the effort to live dangerously. As for my political future, it is like the snakes in Ireland. There is none.

33   Conrad Chapman to Victor Chapman, April 1, 1915, John Jay Chapman Papers. *See also* Jon Guttman, *SPA124 Lafayette Escadrille*, p. 13 (Osprey Publishing, 2004) (noting that Victor's uncles were "using their considerable financial and political influence to ensure Chapman would be one of [the squadron's] first members."); and *Victor Chapman's Letters From France*, p. 134 (Victor to stepmother, July 26, 1915, referring to his then-pending

transfer as "what you have crossed the ocean for and what you have been working on for months.").

34   Frazier Curtis to James Norman Hall, July 17, 1919, JNH Papers, Grinnell.

35   *Id.*

36   *Id.*

37   *See* "On Ecrit," *La Presse*, 13 Août 1914, p. 2; "American Volunteers," *The New York Herald*, August 23, 1914, p. 2.

38   Bert Hall, "Three Months in the Trenches," *The New York Times*, February 14, 1915, magazine section, p. 1.

39   King, *L.M. 8046*, p. 40; Thaw letter October 12, 1914, *Yale Alumni Weekly*, January 22, 1915 p. 485.

40   Indeed, not even Hall's biographer and defender believes he had prior flight experience. Pardoe, *The Bad Boy, Bert Hall: Aviator and Mercenary of the Skies*, p. 56. Although I incline towards this view, I am unwilling completely to discount the possibility that Hall had some basis for his claims. Hall once swore in an affidavit that he came to France in 1912 "in the business of racing automobiles and flying." Weston Bert Hall, affidavit in support of passport application, dated October 17, 1922, available on Ancestry.com. *U.S. Passport Applications, 1795-1925*. One author has a nice line: "If Hall really had any flying experience before he got to the *Escadrille*, then he concealed it well." Naraya Sengupta, *The Lafayette Escadrille*, p. 39.

41   King, *L.M. 8046*, p. 59-60. Hall's future captain, Georges Thénault, who surely had the story recounted to him, told it this way: "[Hall] pretended he was a pilot, though he had never seen an airplane in his life. He was given one at Buc, where, after having got some explanations from an instructor, he took his flight like a drunk duck and soon crashed into the wall of a neighbouring shed. As luck would have it, the machine was smashed but the pilot safe – he was sent to the training field." Thénault, "L'Escadrille La Fayette," *La Légion Étrangére (revue bimestrielle illustrée militaire et coloniale)*, No. 21, p. 28, (1940).

42   "The First American Flying Fighters," *Brooklyn Eagle Magazine*, July 5, 1931, p. 11.

43   King, *L.M. 8046*, p. 60.

44   1915 Pamphlet, *European War, The Franco-American Flying Corps*, p. 5. The Massachusetts Historical Society has a copy of this pamphlet.

45   "Petits Echos," *La Lanterne*, 14 Mars 1915, p. 2; and "Aviateurs Americains Au Service De La France," *Le Journal*," 12 Mars 1915, p. 3. Frazier Curtis took two photos of Norman Prince with Mayor de Lasenne, Lafayette Escadrille Scrapbook, MHS.

46   "American Aviators in the French Army," *The New York Sun*, May 16, 1915, Sec. 5, p. 4. The other person in the photograph is Robert Chanler, Victor Chapman's uncle.

47   Cowdin, "The Lafayette Escadrille," *Harvard Alumni Bulletin*, March 7, 1918, p. 434.

48   1915 Pamphlet, *European War, The Franco-American Flying Corps*, p. 5.

49   "American Airmen Praise Pau School," *The New York Sun*, March 24, 1915, p. 2.

50   Frazier Curtis to James Norman Hall, July 17, 1919, JNH Papers, Grinnell. Around this time Hall and Bach met a doctor from Georgia and told him life in the aviation corps was "pretty fine" in comparison to their former life in the trenches. "Georgia Doctor in France Writes of Horrors of War," *The Atlanta Journal*, May 8, 1915, p. 2.

51   Cowdin, "The Lafayette Escadrille," *Harvard Alumni Bulletin*, March 7, 1918, p. 434.

52   "William Thaw, Aviator, Killed, Is Paris Rumor," *The New York Sun*, April 22, 1915, p. 3.

53   Cowdin, "The Lafayette Escadrille," *Harvard Alumni Bulletin*, March 7, 1918, p. 434; and Frazier Curtis to James Norman Hall, July 17, 1919, JNH Papers, Grinnell. Paul Rockwell later reported that Ruel eventually left the hospital without permission, wore false decorations and was later sentenced to two years hard labor. "Flyer's Vanity His Undoing," *The Chicago Daily News*, March 10, 1916, p. 2.

54   Undated postcard from Frazier Curtis to his wife, Lafayette Escadrille Scrapbook, MHS.

55   Gordon, *Lafayette Escadrille Pilot Biographies*, p. 7; Frazier Curtis to James Norman Hall,

July 17, 1919, JNH Papers, Grinnell.

56 1915 Pamphlet, *European War, The Franco-American Flying Corps*, p. 9. Curtis denied being injured in the first accident, saying that his "motor caught fire in the air, but I landed safely and extinguished the blaze." "Frazier Curtis Not Hurt," *The New York Sun*, May 1, 1915, p. 2. Prince said that by the time Curtis landed, the flames had reached the back of the seat in which he was sitting, and that thereafter Curtis "could not sleep, worried a lot, and had to take a rest." "Boston Aviator in 10 Bombardments," *The Boston Globe*, October 16, 1915, p. 10.

57 Five days after his first incident, Curtis broke his axle while landing, "giving him a bad shaking." 1915 Pamphlet, *European War, The Franco-American Flying Corps*, p. 9.

58 Cowdin said "Curtis had two bad smash-ups, resulting in a nervous breakdown and his retirement to the hospital." Cowdin, "The Lafayette Escadrille," *Harvard Alumni Bulletin*, March 7, 1918, p. 434. *See also* Frazier Curtis to James Norman Hall, July 17, 1919, JNH Papers, Grinnell.

59 Cowdin, "The Lafayette Escadrille," *Harvard Alumni Bulletin*, March 7, 1918, p. 434.

Chapter Twenty-six

1 Kiffin to Vicomtesse du Peloux, March 7, 1915, *War Letters*, p. 30.

2 Kiffin to Loula, March 21, 1915, KYR Papers, NCDNCR.

3 *Id.*

4 Seeger, *Poems*, p. 132.

5 Kiffin to Paul, April 1, 1915, Rockwell Papers, WLU.

6 Kiffin to Loula, March 21, 1915, KYR Papers, NCDNCR.

7 Kiffin to Paul, April 10, 1915, Rockwell Papers, WLU.

8 *Kelly of the Foreign Legion*, p. 60-61.

9 *Kelly of the Foreign Legion*, p. 1.

10 *See Kelly of the Foreign Legion*, p. 124; and Rockwell, *American Fighters*, p. 90.

11 Kenneth Weeks, *Science, Sentiments and Senses*, publisher's note, (1914)

12 "Paul Pavelka, A Soldier of Fortune," *The New York Sun*, December 30, 1917, Section 5, p. 1.

13 *Kelly of the Foreign Legion*, p. 37-38.

14 "Paul Pavelka, A Soldier of Fortune," *The New York Sun*, December 30, 1917, Section 5, p. 1.

15 *Id.*

16 Rockwell, *American Fighters*, p. 67.

17 Kiffin to Paul, April 17, 1915, Rockwell Papers, WLU.

18 Kiffin to Paul, April 10, 1915, Rockwell Papers, WLU.

19 *Id.*

20 Kiffin to Paul, April 17, 1915, Rockwell Papers, WLU.

21 The ad ran in many major newspapers that summer. *See e.g.*, *The Los Angeles Times*, June 20, 1915, Part VI, p. 8; *The Boston Globe*, June 27, 1915, p. 45; and *The St. Louis Post-Dispatch*, July 11, 1915, p. 2S.

22 Kiffin to Paul, April 17, 1915, Rockwell Papers, WLU.

23 "Loses 3,300 of 4,00 Men In First Battle," *The Chicago Daily News*, March 6, 1916, p. 2.

24 Kiffin to Paul, April 17, 1915, Rockwell Papers, WLU.

25 *Id.*

26 "Narrow Escapes from Death at Hands of German Soldiers Told by Kiffin Y. Rockwell," *The Atlanta Constitution*, February 28, 1915, p. 3; and Kiffin to the Vicomte du Peloux, February 16, 1915, *War Letters*, p. 28.

27 Kiffin to Paul, April 17, 1915, Rockwell Papers, WLU. Obviously, the one who spoke French well was Kenneth Weeks.

28 Kiffin to Paul, April 17, 1915, Rockwell Papers, WLU.

29 *Id. See also* Alice Weeks to Allen Weeks, March 10, 1916, Weeks, *Greater Love*, p. 115

("Kenneth and Kiffin were on guard duty quite often together.").

30   Kenneth Weeks to Alice Weeks, April 16, 1915, Weeks, *Greater Love*, p. 29-30; Kiffin to Paul, April 17, 1915, Rockwell Papers, WLU. Shortly after his brush with death, Kiffin wrote on one of his envelopes in French a quote from the *Rubaiyat: paradis mais la vision de remplir Désir, Et enfer l'ombre de l'ame en feu* - Heaven but the vision of fulfill'd Desire, and Hell the shadow from a soul on fire. On envelope dated January, 1915, Rockwell Papers, WLU;

31   Kiffin to Paul, April 17, 1915, Rockwell Papers, WLU.

32   *Kelly of the Foreign Legion*, p. 65.

33   Paul must have been at Hospital 35, Chateau-Thierry in between, as both Loula and Kiffin wrote him there.

34   There is a nice photo of Paul with Mademoiselle Leygues outside the *château*. See Murphy, *Kiffin Rockwell, the Lafayette Escadrille and the Birth of the United States Air Force*, p. 71.

35   On his birthday, Loula wrote a letter to Paul that began, "This is your birthday. Twenty-six years ago you came to me to gladden my heart and brighten my life." Loula to Paul, February 3, 1915, Rockwell Papers, WLU.

36   "For the Cause of Liberty," *The Wilmington Morning Star*, August 19, 1917, p. 13 (says that Paul married "a noblewoman who was his nurse in a base hospital in France.").

37   Paul said he was invalided out of the Legion in the summer of 1915 and put into the information/propaganda section of the French army. *See* "Interview #550 of Colonel Paul Rockwell," *Northeastern Chapter, Cross & Cockade Society*, p. 12-13 (on file with the U.S. Air Force Oral History Program, Maxwell AFB).

38   A diplomatic note states that Paul had been sent to the hospital from April 6 to April 26, "not for wounds but suffering from bronchitis." Ambassador William G. Sharp to the Secretary of State, December 11, 1915, in National Archives, copy in possession of author.

39   The assertion that Jim McConnell drove Paul to the hospital is based on a statement from a movie filmed & edited by Colonel George B. Jarrett on which Paul Rockwell consulted as historian. *See The American Crusaders – The Story of the Escadrille La Fayette* (just before the 4:00 minute mark).

40   *The Bench and Bar of Illinois 1899*, Vol. 2, p. 1166.

41   James McConnell, *Flying for France*, p. xi (1917).

42   James McConnell to Lewis Crenshaw, April 21, 1915, McConnell Collection, UVA. A month later, however, McConnell told Guerin that Paul was going back to the front in three months, as "[h]e insists on another whack at the brutes." McConnell to Marcelle Guerin, May 21, 1915, McConnell Collection, UVA.

43   Kiffin to Paul, April 17, 1915, Rockwell Papers, WLU.

44   *Id.* It seems that Paul was given a three-month leave of absence "because of bad health," and at the end of that period was supposed to be reevaluated to determine whether he would return to the Legion. *See* "Kiffin Rockwell Wounded," *The New York Sun,* May 22, 1915, p. 2.

45   Kiffin to Paul, April 17, 1915, Rockwell Papers, WLU.

46   Given his stated willingness to die on France's behalf, it is probably true that Kiffin wrote to Paul around this time that "If France were to be defeated, I should prefer to die." *See* "L'Aviateur Kiffin Rockwell Mort Pour La France," *L'Illustration*, 7 Octobre 1916, p. 343. *See also* "French Journal Pays Tribute to Rockwell," *The Asheville Citizen*, November 12, 1916, p. 12 (translation of article).

47   "Baseball at Front, Cry of Americans," *The New York Sun*, March 7, 1915, Fifth Section, p. 4.

48   *Kelly of the Foreign Legion*, p. 63.

49   "Paul Pavelka, A Soldier of Fortune," *The New York Sun*, December 30, 1917, Section 5, p. 1.

50   Weeks, *A Soldier of the Legion*, p. 56.

51   Weeks, *A Soldier of the Legion*, p. 52.

52   "Loses 3,300 of 4,00 Men In First Battle," *The Chicago Daily News*, March 6, 1916, p. 2. Italy had in fact agreed in a secret treaty to enter the war on the side of the allies, but wouldn't declare war against Austria-Hungary until May 23, 1915.

53   *Kelly of the Foreign Legion*, p. 81-82.

54   *Kelly of the Foreign Legion*, p. 82.

55   Kiffin to the Vicomte du Peloux, May 2, 1915, *War Letters*, p. 42.

56   Weeks, *A Soldier of the Legion*, p. 60.

57   Kiffin to Loula, May 2, 1915, KYR Papers, NCDNCR.

58   Kiffin to Paul, May 5, 1915, Rockwell Papers, WLU.

Chapter Twenty-seven

1   Kiffin to Paul, May 5, 1915, Rockwell Papers, WLU.

2   Kiffin to Loula, May 2, 1915, KYR Papers, NCDNCR.

3   "Narrow Escapes from Death at Hands of German Soldiers Told by Kiffin Y. Rockwell,"
     The Atlanta Constitution, February 28, 1915, p. 3; and "Atlanta Boy With Legion Sees His
     Comrade Slain," *The Atlanta Journal*, April 4, 1915, p. 2.

4   Kiffin to Loula, May 2, 1915, KYR Papers, NCDNCR.

5   Kiffin to Paul, May 5, 1915, Rockwell Papers, WLU.

6   Alice Weeks to Allen Weeks, July 11, 1915, Weeks, *Greater Love*, p. 50.

7   Kiffin to Paul, May 5, 1915, Rockwell Papers, WLU.

8   Kiffin to Paul, May 13, 1915, Rockwell Papers, WLU.

9   *Id.*

10   *Id.*

11   *Kelly of the Foreign Legion*, p. 85; Kiffin to Paul, May 13, 1915, Rockwell Papers, WLU.

12   Kiffin to Paul, May 13, 1915, Rockwell Papers, WLU.

13   *Id.*

14   *Kelly of the Foreign Legion*, p. 86.

15   *Id.*, at p. 90.

16   Kiffin to Paul, May 13, 1915, Rockwell Papers, WLU.

17   "Loses 3,300 of 4,00 Men in First Battle," *The Chicago Daily News*, March 6, 1916, p. 2.

18   "Big Battle Raging in the North," *The New York Herald*, May 13, 1915, p. 1.

19   Kiffin to Paul, May 13, 1915, Rockwell Papers, WLU.

20   Recounting the battle in a letter to a friend, Pavelka wrote, "I lost my American side-partner
     by the name of Rockwell, he went down with the remark of 'I got it in the hip Paul; go on
     and give them hell.' That is the last I saw or heard of Rocky." "Paul Pavelka, A Soldier of
     Fortune," *The New York Sun*, December 30, 1917, Section 5, p. 1.

21   Kiffin to Paul, May 13, 1915, Rockwell Papers, WLU.

22   *Id.*

23   Kiffin to Paul, May 13, 1915, Rockwell Papers, WLU. See also *Victor Chapman's Letters
     From France*, p. 158 (Chapman relaying that Kiffin told him he "crawled back across the
     entire field in the afternoon.").

24   Kiffin to Paul, May 13, 1915, Rockwell Papers, WLU.

25   Kiffin to the Vicomte du Peloux, May 11, 1915, *War Letters*, p. 45.

26   Kiffin to Paul, May 13, 1915, Rockwell Papers, WLU.

27   *Id.*

28   "Big Battle Raging in the North," *The New York Herald*, May 13, 1915, p. 1.

29   *See* "Nos brillants succès au nord d'Arras," *Le Rappel*, 16 Mai 1915, p. 1; "French Official
     Communiquès," *The New York Herald*, May 12, 1915, p. 1; and "Nos succès du 9 Mai dans le
     secteur Carency-Neuville," *La Lanterne*, 14 Mai 1915, p. 2. Kiffin mentioned the capture of
     the German colonel on the outside of his envelope. *See* envelope for letter from Kiffin to Paul
     dated May 13, 1915, Rockwell Papers, WLU.

30   "Nos brillants succès au nord d'Arras," *Le Rappel*, 16 Mai 1915, p. 1.

31   "Big Battle Raging in the North," *The New York Herald*, May 13, 1915, p. 1.

32   "Loses 3,300 of 4,00 Men In First Battle," *The Chicago Daily News*, March 6, 1916, p. 2. *See*

also Paul Pavelka to Kiffin, June 28, 1915, Rockwell Papers, WLU (noting that only fifteen hundred men out of the four battalions answered roll-call after the battle).

33   Rockwell, *American Fighters*, p. 79; and *Kelly of the Foreign Legion*, p. 99. (The quote is a combination of the foregoing sources.)

34   Kiffin to the Vicomte du Peloux, May 18, 1915, *War Letters*, p. 51.

35   As quoted in *Victor Chapman's Letters From France*, p. 158.

36   Kiffin to the Vicomte du Peloux, May 18, 1915, *War Letters*, p. 50.

37   Henry Farnsworth to mother, August, 1915, *Letters of Henry Weston Farnsworth*, p. 194.

38   Kiffin to Loula, May 30, 1915, KYR Papers, NCDNCR.

39   *Kelly of the Foreign Legion*, p. 88.

40   Weeks, *A Soldier of the Legion*, p. 64.

41   "Paul Pavelka, A Soldier of Fortune," *The New York Sun*, December 30, 1917, Section 5, p. 1.

42   "Loses 3,300 of 4,00 Men In First Battle," *The Chicago Daily News*, March 6, 1916, p. 2. *See also* "Despite Loss of Arm He Would Aid Allies," *The Chicago Daily News*, June 20, 1916, p. 2.

43   Kiffin to the Vicomte du Peloux, May 26, 1915, *War Letters*, p. 54. Upon viewing the destruction left behind by battle, Chatkoff wrote that the talk of war being hell "is an insult to hell, for war is a thousand times worse. *See* "'Organized Butchery,' Says a Soldier of Foreign Legion in Speaking of Great Struggle," *The Greenville News*, July 6, 1915, p. 6.

44   Harry Butters, *An American Citizen*, p. 173 (1918).

45   Kiffin to the Vicomte du Peloux, May 18, 1915, *War Letters*, p. 51.

46   Paul Ayres Rockwell, "Our Pioneers in the Air," *The Franco-American Weekly*, March 2, 1918, p. 3.

47   "Kiffin Rockwell Wounded in Fight Against Germans," *The Atlanta Constitution*, May 25, 1915, p. 4.

48   "Kiffin Rockwell Wounded," *The New York Sun*, May 22, 1915, p. 2.

49   Kiffin to the Vicomte du Peloux, May 18, 1915, *War Letters*, p. 51.

50   James McConnell to Paul Rockwell May 18, 1915, McConnell Collection, UVA.

51   As Loula herself later explained, "Perhaps I was a silly mother, but I made every possible effort to have my boys taken out of the army and returned to this country." "If I Had A Dozen Sons I Should Want Them to Fight for France," *The Atlanta Constitution*, June 16, 1918, p. 12I.

52   Kiffin to Loula, May 21, 1915, KYR Papers, NCDNCR.

53   *Id.*

54   Unknown French woman to Loula, October 5, 1916, KYR Papers, NCDNCR.

Chapter Twenty-eight

1   *See* "Notice!", *The Evening Star*, May 1, 1915, Part 2, p. 8. *See also* "Germany Warns Against Travel in Allies' Ships," *The New York Tribune*, May 1, 1915, p. 3.

2   "More Than 3,000 Leave New York for Europe," *The Evening Star*, May 1, 1915, Part 2, p. 8.

3   Erik Larson, *Dead Wake: The Last Crossing of the Lusitania*, p. 93 (2016, first paperback edition).

4   "More Than 3,000 Leave New York for Europe," *The Evening Star*, May 1, 1915, Part 2, p. 8.

5   "The Lusitania Sunk Off the Irish Coast," *The New York Herald*, May 8, 1915, p. 1.

6   One American soldier wrote that the *Herald's* "vigorous American attitude in 1915 and 1916 gave the French people hope" and "the repatriated American comfort, for it strengthened his convictions." Bowe, *Soldiers of the Legion*, p. 91.

7   "It Is Inconceivable That We Should Refrain from Action Says Mr. Roosevelt," *The New York Herald*, May 9, 1915, p. 1.

8   Edmond Genet, diary entry of May 8, 1915, "Leaves from a War Diary," *The North American Review*, p. 278 (Jun.–Aug. 1927).

9   See Andrew Carroll, *My Fellow Soldiers: General John Pershing and the Americans Who Helped Win the Great War*, p. 41 (2017).

10 "Germany's Insult to America, Mourning; Dernburg's Threat to Torpedo American Ships," *The New York Herald*, May 12, 1915, p. 1.

11 "President Wilson Indicates That He Will Endeavor to Avoid War," *The New York Herald*, May 12, 1915, p. 1. Woodrow Wilson: "Address to Naturalized Citizens at Convention Hall, Philadelphia," May 10, 1915. Online by Gerhard Peters and John T. Woolley, *The American Presidency Project*. http://www.presidency.ucsb.edu/ws/?pid=65388 (enter Legacy PID number 65388 in search box and hit "submit").

12 "President Wilson Would Modernize Our Independence," *The Asheville Citizen*, July 5, 1914, p. 8.

13 Kiffin to Loula, May 21, 1915, KYR Papers, NCDNCR. In the published version, Paul changed this to "If the U.S. would do right, it would end sooner." *See War Letters*, p. 52.

14 *For France*, (Charles Hanson Towne, ed. 1917), introduction by Theodore Roosevelt.

15 Theodore Roosevelt, "Murder on the High Seas," *Metropolitan Magazine*, May 11, 1915.

16 "'Too Proud to Fight' Policy Would Make America Another China, Says Mr. Roosevelt," *The New York Herald*, May 13, 1915, p. 1.

17 Roy W. Lay, "Oh! for Roosevelt!", *The New York Herald*, May 13, 1915, p. 2.

18 Paul Rockwell to Robert House, September 29, 1920 KYR Papers, NCDNCR.

19 *Id.*

20 *War Letters of Edmond Genet*, p. 235.

21 *Id.* at p. 236.

22 "American Boys Fighting for France to Repay Debt Their Country Owes," *The New York Sun*, January 21, 1917, Sec. 5, p. 4.

23 Kiffin to Loula, June 8, 1915, KYR Papers, NCDNCR. In the published version, Paul removed the last sentence. *See War Letters*, p. 55.

24 "Bryan Pleads His Case Before the People," *The Atlanta Constitution*, June 11, 1915, p. 3.

25 Kiffin noted he "was always an ardent admirer of Bryan until he became Secretary of State." Kiffin to the Vicomte du Peloux, June 10, 1915, *War Letters*, p. 56.

26 Weeks, *A Soldier of the Legion*, p. 64.

27 *Id.* at p. 73.

28 Kiffin to the Vicomte du Peloux, June 10, 1915, *War Letters*, p. 56.

29 Edmond Genet, diary entry of June 11, 1915, "Leaves from a War Diary," *The North American Review*, p. 280 (Jun.–Aug. 1927).

30 "'Organized Butchery,' Says a Soldier of Foreign Legion in Speaking of Great Struggle," *The Greenville News*, July 6, 1915, p. 6 (letter dated June 7, probably written by Herman Chatkoff).

31 Kiffin to Loula, June 8, 1915, KYR Papers, NCDNCR.

32 Kiffin to Loula, June 27, 1915, *War Letters*, p. 63.

33 John Dunwoody to Kiffin, June 5, 1915, Rockwell Papers, WLU.

34 *Id.*

35 Kiffin to Loula, June 27, 1915, *War Letters*, p. 63; and Kiffin to Loula, June 8, 1915, KYR Papers, NCDNCR. Once again, Paul edited out the last quoted sentence when he published Kiffin's letters.

36 A. Piatt Andrew to his mother and father, July 5, 1915, A. Piatt Andrew, *Letters Written Home from France in the First Half of 1915*, available at http://www.ourstory.info/library/2-ww1/APA/APATC.html (visited November 18, 2017).

37 *Id.*

38 A. Piatt Andrew to his mother and father, August 5, 1915, A. Piatt Andrew, *Letters Written Home from France in the First Half of 1915*, available at http://www.ourstory.info/library/2-ww1/APA/APATC.html (visited November 18, 2017).

39 *Kelly of the Foreign Legion*, p. 98.

40 Kiffin to Loula, June 15, 1915, KYR Papers, NCDNCR.

41 *Id.* Earlier in the war, General Joffre himself had declared "France did not want the war. It has been forced upon her. She is waging it for humanity." "War for Humanity, Joffre Styles It," *The New York Times*, December 1, 1914.

42 "If I Had A Dozen Sons I Should Want Them to Fight for France," *The Atlanta Constitution*, June 16, 1918, p. 12I. I should note that I am taking some liberty in attributing Loula's reaction to this letter, for she herself said it was an earlier letter from Kiffin – the one in which he had rebuked her for writing the wild letters – that led to her change of heart. However, solid evidence supports the notion that she may have misremembered this point, as her recollection was three years after the fact. Moreover, it is easy to imagine that her mind was preoccupied with the fact of Kiffin's injury at the time she received his letter. The one solid memory Loula had was that Kiffin had written the letter that changed her mind and heart while he was in the hospital. She said:

    It was while Kiffin was in the hospital at Rennes recovering from his wounds that he wrote me the letter that brought me to my senses, and I am glad that he lived to know that I knew that he was right and I was wrong. "If I Had A Dozen Sons I Should Want Them to Fight for France," *The Atlanta Constitution*, June 16, 1918, p. 12I. I am not the first to reach this conclusion. *See* Murphy, *Kiffin Rockwell, the Lafayette Escadrille and the Birth of the United States Air Force*, p. 72.

43 Loula to Paul, February 3, 1915, Rockwell Papers, WLU.

44 "North Carolina Society Likes New Oregon Law," *The Osteopathic Physician*, July 1915, p. 13.

45 J.A. Susong to Kiffin, July 24, 1915, Rockwell Papers, WLU.

46 Kiffin to Kenneth Weeks, June 20, 1915, Rockwell Papers, WLU.

47 Kiffin to Paul, June 20, 1915, Rockwell Papers, WLU.

48 "Paul Pavelka, A Soldier of Fortune," *The New York Sun*, December 30, 1917, Section 5, p. 1. McConnell relayed the story this way: "An American friend of mine in the Foreign Legion was stuck by a German bayonet. When the German saw he hadn't killed [him] he yelled 'Kamrade, nicht kaput' (Comrade, don't kill me). The American said, "Nothing doing on the comrade business today," and shot him. *Tant mieux.*" McConnell to his mother, July 30, 1915, McConnell Collection, UVA.

49 Paul Pavelka to Kiffin, June 20, 1915, Rockwell Papers, WLU. Kiffin forwarded this letter to Paul, who apparently got it into the papers. *See* "Legioner Tells of Dash Into German Trenches," *The New York Sun*, July 11, 1915, Section 3, p. 3.

50 Kiffin to Kenneth Weeks, June 20, 1915, Rockwell Papers, WLU.

51 *Id.*

52 *Id.*

53 Barrett Wendell, "1915," Edith Wharton, *The Book of the Homeless*, p. 40 (1916).

Chapter Twenty-nine

1 Thaw's service card shows the date he left for *Escadrille C.42* as March 25, 1915, available on the *Mémoire des Hommes* website.

2 Thaw letter April 7, 1915, "Letters of a French Army Aviator," *Yale Alumni Weekly*, June 11, 1915, p. 1032.

3 Thaw letter April 11, 1915, "Letters of a French Army Aviator," *Yale Alumni Weekly*, June 11, 1915, p. 1032.

4 "William Thaw, Allies' Aviator, Meets 'Taube,'" *Pittsburgh Daily Post*, May 29, 1915, p. 1. "Taube" is German for dove or pigeon. It was also a type of aircraft, but the term was sometimes used broadly to refer to any German machine. *See* Stephen Pope & Elizabeth-Anne Wheal, *The MacMillan Dictionary of the First World War*, p. 465.

5 The original citation is contained in William Thaw Scrapbooks, HSWP.

6   *See e.g.* "Bill Thaw Is Awarded War Cross for Bravery," *The Gazette Times*, May 15, 1915, p. 1; "William Thaw Given French Military Cross," *The Atlanta Journal*, May 15, 1915, p. 2.

7   "Sees Thaw at Front; Honors Won by Flyer," *The Chicago Daily News*, May 28, 1915, p. 2, clipping William Thaw Scrapbooks, HSWP.

8   *Id.*

9   Hall & Nordhoff, *The Lafayette Flying Corps*, Vol. 1, p. 79.

10 "Sees Thaw at Front; Honors Won by Flyer," *The Chicago Daily News*, May 28, 1915, p. 2.

11 A fourth American, Didier Masson, earned his *brevet militaire* on May 10, 1915 (nine days after Prince), and soon went to the front to serve with *Escadrille C.18*. *See* Gordon, *Lafayette Escadrille Pilot Biographies*, p. 7, 106. However, although he had lived in America for a few years before the war, and would later fly with the *Escadrille Américaine*, Masson was born and raised in France by French parents. *See* Gordon, *Lafayette Escadrille Pilot Biographies*, p. 105.

12 "Billy Thaw Air Hero," *The Washington Post*, June 20, 1915, p. E3; "Miss McAdoo No Quitter; Was A Real Nurse, Not Scrubwoman, in France, and Is Going Back," *The New York Tribune*, June 16, 1915, p. 16; "William Thaw In Paris," *The New York Sun*, June 10, 1915, p. 3.

13 "American Aviators Dare German Fire," *The New York Sun*, June 13, 1915, p. 3.

14 Elliott Cowdin to John Jay Chapman, July 6, 1915, John Jay Chapman Papers, Harvard.

15 Hervier, *The American Volunteers with the Allies*, p. 86.

16 Elliott Cowdin to John Jay Chapman, July 6, 1915, John Jay Chapman Papers, Harvard.

17 "American Aviators Dare German Fire," *The New York Sun*, June 13, 1915, p. 3.

18 Prince, *A Volunteer Who Died for the Cause He Loved*, p. 26, 27.

19 Norman Prince, "Elliott Cowdin Wins Fame in Air Fight," *The New York Sun*, July 25, 1915, Section 3, p. 3.

20 "Dropping Bombs on the Boches," *The Boston Evening Transcript*, August 28, 1915, Part Two, p. 12. *See also* "To Fire the Four Corners of Berlin, Writes Aviator," *The New York Tribune*, August 29, 1915, p. 1.

21 Prince, *A Volunteer Who Died for the Cause He Loved*, p. 18. Prince told his family that his "first time out, while over the lines, my legs were shaking and I could not sit still." "Boston Aviator in Ten Bombardments," *The Boston Daily Globe*, October 16, 1915, p. 10.

22 "Boston Aviator in Ten Bombardments," *The Boston Daily Globe*, October 16, 1915, p. 10.

23 "Elliott Cowdin Wins Fame in Air Fight," *The New York Sun*, July 25, 1915, Section 3, p. 3.

24 "American Aviators Dare German Fire," *The New York Sun*, June 13, 1915, p. 3.

25 Elliott Cowdin to John Jay Chapman, July 6, 1915, John Jay Chapman Papers, Harvard.

26 *Id.* Prince wrote that "The *boche* fired first while a long way off before Elliott got in position, and then ducked with Elliott's mechanic firing the whole band of cartridges of the *mitrailleuse* full steam as the *boche* made off." Norman Prince, "Elliott Cowdin Wins Fame in Air Fight," *The New York Sun*, July 25, 1915, Section 3, p. 3.

27 *See* "Cowdin Wins Fame in Air," *The New York Sun*, July 17, 1915, p. 1. *See also* "Two American Fliers Win Honors with French Army," *The Chicago Tribune*, July 17, 1915, p. 3, and "American Aviator in France Brings Down a German," *The St. Louis Post-Dispatch*, July 17, 1915, p. 1.

28 Norman Prince, "Elliott Cowdin Wins Fame in Air Fight," *The New York Sun*, July 25, 1915, Section 3, p. 3.

29 *Id.*

30 "Dropping Bombs on the Boches," *The Boston Evening Transcript*, August 28, 1915, Part Two, p. 12.

31 Elliott Cowdin to John Jay Chapman, July 6, 1915, John Jay Chapman Papers, Harvard.

32 *Id.*

33 *Id.* A month earlier, Victor's friend Henry Farnsworth noted in a letter home that "Victor Chapman, at his family's suggestion, has put in application for transfer to the American

Flying Corps..." Henry Farnsworth to his mother, June 4, 1915, in *Letters of Henry Weston Farnsworth*, p. 157.

34   Elliott Cowdin to John Jay Chapman, July 6, 1915, John Jay Chapman Papers, Harvard.

35   Frazier Curtis to James Norman Hall, July 17, 1919, JNH Papers, Grinnell. *See also* Hall & Nordhoff, *The Lafayette Flying Corps*, Vol. 1, p. 66 ("Norman Prince was opposed to the plan for an enlarged corps.").

36   Frazier Curtis to James Norman Hall, July 17, 1919, JNH Papers, Grinnell.

37   *Id.*

38   "American Ambulance Offered to France," *The New York Herald*, August 4, 1914, p. 1.

39   Perley Poore Sheehan, "In Memory of Lafayette," *Munsey's Magazine*, November 1916, p. 196.

40   In France, any military hospital was known as an "ambulance." *See* Perley Poore Sheehan, "In Memory of Lafayette," *Munsey's Magazine*, November 1916, p. 196.

41   "Paris Americans Protest," *The New York Times*, May 13, 1915.

42   Edmund Gros, introduction to Hall, *High Adventure*, p. xiii.

43   Hall & Nordhoff, *The Lafayette Flying Corps*, Vol. 1, p. 10.

44   *Id.* at p. 69.

45   Frazier Curtis to James Norman Hall, July 17, 1919, JNH Papers, Grinnell.

46   *Id.*

47   *Id.*

48   Edmund Gros, introduction to Hall, *High Adventure*, p. xiv.

49   Hall & Nordhoff, *The Lafayette Flying Corps*, Vol. 1, p. 11.

50   Frazier Curtis to James Norman Hall, July 17, 1919, JNH Papers, Grinnell.

51   Edmund Gros, introduction to Hall, *High Adventure*, p. xv.

52   A few years later, Curtis said that Bacon had "agreed to find the men & money – with what success the world knows." Frazier Curtis to James Norman Hall, July 17, 1919, JNH Papers, Grinnell.

53   William's younger brother George Washington Vanderbilt II also built magnificent houses, such as the Biltmore Estate in Kiffin's adoptive hometown of Asheville, North Carolina.

54   Hall & Nordhoff, *The Lafayette Flying Corps*, Vol. 1, p. 66.

55   Edmund Gros, introduction to Hall, *High Adventure*, p. xv.

56   "Perfecting 100,000 American Aviators in France," *The Evening Star*, September 2, 1917, Part 4, p. 6.

57   "Lafayette Squadrilla and Flying Corps Founded By American Physician In Paris," *The New York Sun*, September 2, 1917, Sec. 5, p. 6.

58   Frazier Curtis to James Norman Hall, July 17, 1919, JNH Papers, Grinnell.

59   "1,000 Aviators to Aid France?" *The Chicago Tribune*, July 15, 1915, p. 2.

60   "1,000 Aviators to Aid France?" *The Chicago Tribune*, July 15, 1915, p. 2. *See also* "Americans to Offer an Aero Fleet to France," *St. Louis Post-Dispatch*, July 15, 1915, p. 1. I suspect Curtis as the source because of the inclusion of the line that the officers would probably be chosen "from Americans like William Thaw, Norman Prince and Frazier Curtis who have distinguished themselves as aviators with the French army." If it was Curtis who placed these stories, he must have been disappointed to see that both papers got his first name wrong – the *Tribune* called him Francis, while the *Post-Dispatch* got it down as Franzier.

61   1915 Pamphlet, *European War, The Franco-American Flying Corps*, p. 4.

Chapter Thirty

1   Kiffin to Paul, June 15, 1915, Rockwell Papers, WLU.

2   Charles Terrin, "Alan Seeger, Poète-Légionnaire," *La Légion Étrangére (revue bimestrielle illustrée militaire et coloniale)*, No. 21, p. 34, (1940).

3   M. René Besnard, *Speeches Delivered*, p. 13.

4 Alan Seeger, "A Soldier Thinks of War," *The New Republic*, p. 66 (May 22, 1915).

5 The hotel, located at 24 *Rue de Miromesnil* in Paris, is now a Holiday Inn.

6 Kiffin to Loula, July 8, 1915, KYR Papers, NCDNCR.

7 Henry Sheahan, *A Volunteer Poilu*, p. 27-28 (1916). Henry Sheehan was the pseudonym of Henry Beston.

8 Sheahan, *A Volunteer Poilu*, p. 29.

9 Kiffin to Loula, July 8, 1915, KYR Papers, NCDNCR.

10 *Id.*

11 *Id.*

12 "How Paris Defends Itself from Zeppelins," *St. Louis Post-Dispatch*, April 16, 1916, p. C5.

13 Edmond Genet, diary entry of July 6, 1915, "Leaves from A War Diary," *The North American Review*, p. 281-82 (Jun-Aug. 1927).

14 Alice Weeks to Fred Taber, July 17, 1915, Weeks, *Greater Love*, p. 52.

15 Kenneth Weeks to Alice Weeks, May 20, 1915, Weeks, *Greater Love*, p. 37.

16 Kiffin to Loula, July 20, 1915, KYR Papers, NCDNCR.

17 Alice Weeks to Fred Taber, May 29, 1915, Weeks, *Greater Love*, p. 38.

18 Weeks, *Greater Love*, p. xi. *Also see* "Mother of the Legion," *The New York Sun*, April 28, 1918, Sec. 5, p. 9; "Mme. Weeks Coming Here," *The New York Sun*, December 18, 1916, p. 2, and "Mother of the Regiment," *The New York Tribune*, March 17, 1918, Section 5, p. 6. Jim McConnell later dedicated his book to Weeks, noting how she "has given to a great number of us other Americans in the war the tender sympathy and help of a mother." McConnell, *Flying for France*, dedication page.

19 Weeks, *Greater Love*, p. xii.

20 "'Mother of the Regiment' Honor Title for Mrs. Weeks," *The Brooklyn Daily Eagle*, March 20, 1918, Sec.2, p. 5. Mrs. Weeks launched this work to memorialize her four favorite American soldiers, all fallen for France – her own son Kenneth, as well as Kiffin Rockwell, Jim McConnell and Victor Chapman. *See* "War Work Memorial to Kiffin Rockwell and James McConnell," *The Twin-City Sentinel* (Winston-Salem), January 15, 1918, p. 4.

21 Loula to Kiffin and Paul, June 22, 1916, Rockwell Papers, WLU.

22 Handwritten note in scrapbook album, KYR Papers, NCDNCR.

23 Kiffin to Alice Weeks, August 1, 1915, Weeks, *Greater Love*, p. 54. She once said, "I don't know the part that mothers played in other wars, but they play a big part in this." *Id.* at p. 142.

24 Alice Weeks to Allen Weeks, June 18, 1915, Weeks, *Greater Love*, p. 45. *See also* Alice Weeks to Allen Weeks, May 11, 1915, Weeks, *Greater Love*, p. 33.

25 Weeks, *A Soldier of the Legion*, p. 20.

26 Weeks, *A Soldier of the Legion*, p. 76.

27 "Interview #550 of Colonel Paul Rockwell," *Northeastern Chapter, Cross & Cockade Society*, p. 11-12 (on file with the U.S. Air Force Oral History Program).

28 Thaw's personnel record shows that Thaw came from *Escadrille C.42* on July 24 and did not return until August 4.

29 "To Become a Military Aviator," *The New York Herald*, September 11, 1915, p. 2.

30 *Id.*

31 In a letter to Paul shortly after entering aviation, Kiffin wrote that he would eventually need to go to "the camp at Paris" where they had seen Thaw and Hall. This suggests that Paul and Kiffin had seen Thaw and Hall at Le Bourget airfield in July, as that is the only time this could have happened. *See* Kiffin to Paul, September 10, 1915, *War Letters*, p. 81.

32 Alice Weeks to Allen Weeks, July 24, 1915, Weeks, *Greater Love*, p. 53.

33 Kiffin to Loula, July 31, 1915, KYR Papers, NCDNCR.

34 Kiffin to Alice Weeks, August 1, 1915, *War Letters*, p. 60.

35 Alice Weeks to Allen Weeks, August 1, 1915, Weeks, *Greater Love*, p. 54.

36 Kiffin to Paul, August 6, 1915, Rockwell Papers, WLU.

37   "Kiffin Rockwell to Join Air Fighters," *The Asheville Citizen*, August 17, 1915, p. 3. *See also* "Asheville Boy Shot in Battle," *The Asheville Gazette News*, October 6, 1915, p. 1) (noting that Loula received a letter from Mrs. Weeks "who aided the Asheville boy in securing an appointment to duty in the aeroplane department."). In a letter ten months later, Loula told Paul to treat Mrs. Weeks as he would want Loula treated and commented: "Had she not gotten Kiffin's transfer to the aviation, I feel sure the dear boy would now be dead." Loula to Kiffin and Paul, June 3, 1916, in Rockwell Papers, WLU.

38   Alice Weeks to Allen Weeks, August 1, 1915, Weeks, *Greater Love*, p. 54.

39   Kiffin Rockwell to Alice Weeks, August 1, 1915, Weeks, *Greater Love*, p. 54.

Part Three

1   "Fighting to settle the fate of the world," *The New York Herald*, December 23, 1914, p. 1.

2   Owen Oliver, "The Airman's Creed," *Munsey's Magazine*, August 1918, p. 593.

Chapter Thirty-one

3   Edmond Genet, diary entry of August 11, 1915, "Leaves from A War Diary," *The North American Review*, p. 283 (Jun-Aug. 1927).

4   Letter of Willis B. Haviland dated May 29, 1916, can be viewed at http://wbhaviland.net/ar021.html (visited on February 10, 2018).

5   Edwin W. Morse, *The Vanguard of American Volunteers,* p. 249 (1918).

6   Edmond Genet to his mother, June 5, 1916, in *War Letters of Edmond Genet*, p. 177. *See also* John Papic, "The Cult of the Ace: The Airman and His Role in the First World War," *The Wittenberg History Journal*, p. 7, Spring 2009; and Hall & Nordhoff, *The Lafayette Flying Corps*, Vol. 2, p. 7.

7   Edmond Genet to his mother, June 5, 1916, in *War Letters of Edmond Genet*, p. 177.

8   Bert Hall, "Three Months in the Trenches," *The New York Times*, February 14, 1915, magazine section, p. 1.

9   "Severely Wounded, The Story of a Wounded American in a French Hospital," *The Century Illustrated Monthly Magazine*, February 1919, p. 517.

10   James Norman Hall to Roy Cushman, July 23, 1915, JNH Papers, Grinnell.

11   Harry Butters, *An American Citizen*, p. 173.

12   1915 Pamphlet, *European War, The Franco-American Flying Corps*, p. 4. Curtis must have been quoting Prince, as Prince was likely Curtis' closest friend among the pilots at that time. They had trained together at Marblehead and worked together in Paris and at Pau. Additionally, Curtis did not know Cowdin, Thaw or Bach well, and apparently did not care much for Hall. Finally, the only aviators who had specifically "crossed the ocean" to volunteer were he and Prince.

13   Kiffin to Alice Weeks, August 1, 1915, Weeks, *Greater Love*, p. 55.

14   Kiffin to Zinovi Pechkoff, *circa* August 1, 1915, Rockwell Papers, WLU.

15   Kiffin to Paul, August 6, 1915, Rockwell Papers, WLU.

16   Paul Pavelka to Paul Rockwell, August 4, 1915, Rockwell Papers, WLU.

17   Kiffin to Alice Weeks, August 9, 1915, Weeks, *Greater Love*, p. 58.

18   Kiffin to Paul, August 8, 1915, Rockwell Papers, WLU.

19   Paul Pavelka to Paul Rockwell, August 4, 1915, Rockwell Papers, WLU.

20   "American Boys Fighting for France to Repay Debt Their Country Owes," *The New York Sun*, January 21, 1917, Sec. 5, p. 4. Paul described Thorin as a "true adventurer in the most picturesque as well as in the best sense of that much abused word." *Id.*

21   Kiffin to Paul, October 5, 1915, *War Letters*, p. 91.

22   Kiffin to Alice Weeks, August 6, 1915, Weeks, *Greater Love*, p. 57. The given date of this letter is probably wrong.

23   *Id.*

24   Kiffin to Alice Weeks, August 12, 1915, *War Letters*, p. 71-72.

25   Kiffin to Paul, August 15, 1915, Rockwell Papers, WLU.

26   Paul Pavelka to Alice Weeks, August 15, 1915, Weeks, *Greater Love*, p. 60.

27   Kiffin to Loula, August 22, 1915, KYR Papers, NCDNCR.

28   *Id.* Kiffin's use of the word "them" in referring to the U.S. is instructive of how far his feelings had hardened. Meanwhile, back in America, the incident further inflamed public opinion. The day after the sinking, one notable American paper ended its editorial stating, "By this act, Germany is insolently asking the United States: What are you going to do about it?" "Deliberately Unfriendly," *The Buffalo Express*, August 20, 1915, p. 4.

29   *The Story of the Great War*, Vol. VII, p. 2031.

30   Kiffin to Paul, August 26, 1915, Rockwell Papers, WLU.

31   *Id.*

32   *Id.*

33   Kiffin to Loula, August 22, 1915, KYR Papers, NCDNCR.

34   Paul Pavelka to Paul Rockwell, September 1, 1915, Rockwell Papers, WLU.

35   Kiffin to Paul, September 1, 1915, Rockwell Papers, WLU.

36   *Victor Chapman's Letters From France*, p. 144.

37   Cowdin, "The Lafayette Escadrille," *Harvard Alumni Bulletin*, March 7, 1918, p. 435.

38   *Victor Chapman's Letters From France*, p. 152.

39   Cowdin, "The Lafayette Escadrille," *Harvard Alumni Bulletin*, March 7, 1918, p. 435. Hall was breveted on August 19, 1915. Gordon, *Lafayette Escadrille Pilot Biographies*, p. 7. Bach received his license on July 4, 1915. Hall & Nordhoff, *The Lafayette Flying Corps*, Vol. 1, p. 100.

40   Cowdin, "The Lafayette Escadrille," *Harvard Alumni Bulletin*, March 7, 1918, p. 435.

41   The citation called Prince "an excellent military pilot, who has always shown the greatest audacity and presence of mind," and was "particularly happy in a region where the enemy artillery, through which his plane was repeatedly attacked, made the task difficult." *War Records of the Knickerbocker Club, 1914-1918*, p. 281 (privately printed 1922).

42   Letter dated 21 Août 1915, Lafayette Escadrille Memorial Association records, 1923-1928, Film MISC 611, Sterling Memorial Library, Yale University.

43   *Id.*

44   Prince, *A Volunteer Who Died for the Cause He Loved*, p. 29-30.

45   Kiffin to Alice Weeks, September 4, 1915, Weeks, *Greater Love*, p. 64.

46   Paul Pavelka to Alice Weeks, September 4, 1915, Weeks, *Greater Love*, p. 65.

47   *Id.*

48   Kiffin to Paul, September 6, 1915, Rockwell Papers, WLU.

49   *Id.*

50   Kiffin to Loula, September 8, 1915, KYR Papers, NCDNCR.

Chapter Thirty-two

1   Morse, *The Vanguard of American Volunteers*, p. 206.

2   James Hamilton-Paterson, *Marked for Death: The First War in the Air*, p. 84-85 (2016).

3   *The Fokker Monoplanes*, Profile Publications No. 38, p. 5.

4   *A History of French Military Aviation*, p. 92 (translated by Francis Kianka), originally published as *Histoire de l'Aviation Militaire Francaise*, by Charles-Lavauzelle, (Paris, 1980) (hereafter "A History of French Military Aviation").

5   *Victor Chapman's Letters From France*, p. 157.

6   Gordon, *Lafayette Escadrille Pilot Biographies*, p. 87.

7   *See* Gordon, *Lafayette Escadrille Pilot Biographies*, p. 93, 97. After school at UVA, McConnell had briefly been in business with Johnson in New York. *See* Paul Ayres Rockwell,

"Jim McConnell for France," *The State*, February 1979, p. 9.

8   Gordon, *Lafayette Escadrille Pilot Biographies*, p. 40.

9   J.R. McConnell, "With the American Ambulance in France," *The Outlook*, September 15, 1915, p. 125.

10 *Id.*, introduction by Theodore Roosevelt.

11 "Roosevelt Would Back President Only if Right," *The New York Times*, August 26, 1915, p. 4.

12 Introduction by Theodore Roosevelt to J.R. McConnell, "With the American Ambulance in France," *The Outlook*, September 15, 1915, p. 125-26.

13 McConnell to Paul Rockwell, October 8, 1915, Rockwell Papers, WLU.

14 "New York Pulpits Sound Note of War," *The New York Times*, August 23, 1915, p. 4.

15 *Id.*

16 Alan Clark, *Aces High*, p. 1 (1973).

17 In fact, later Americans took to calling the trainers "grass cutters," because the tail and rudders drug along in the grass. "Making Aviators in France; Many Machines Are Used Up," *The Brooklyn Daily Eagle*, September 3, 1916, Magazine section, p. 2.

18 Laurence Rumsey, "Training an American Aviator in France," *National Service*, May 1917, p. 261.

19 "The Diary of H. Clyde Balsley," *Cross & Cockade*, Vol. 18, No. 2, p. 104 (Summer 1977).

20 *Victor Chapman's Letters From France*, p. 169.

21 "The Diary of H. Clyde Balsley," *Cross & Cockade*, Vol. 18, No. 2, p. 104 (Summer 1977).

22 Granville Fortescue, *France Bears the Burden*, p. 130 (The MacMillan Co., 1917).

23 "Making Aviators in France; Many Machines Are Used Up," *The Brooklyn Daily Eagle*, September 3, 1916, p. 20.

24 Kiffin to Paul, September 6, 1915, Rockwell Papers, WLU.

25 Kiffin to Alice Weeks, October 11, 1915, *War Letters*, p. 94.

26 Kiffin to the Vicomte du Peloux, September 8, 1915, *War Letters*, p. 81, 80.

27 Kiffin to Paul, September 10, 1915, *War Letters*, p. 82.

28 Cowdin was the son of John Cowdin, a wealthy New York silk ribbon manufacturer and sportsman (one of America's finest polo players for many years). Apparently, the younger Cowdin was also a jockey. *See* "Gentleman Riders Return from War," *The New York Tribune*, March 30, 1915, p. 11 (noting Cowdin was a jockey who was "still at the front, serving in a French aviation corps.").

29 As quoted in Mason, *The Lafayette Escadrille*, p. 47.

30 Bert Hall used the same type of uniform. *See* Pardoe, *The Bad Boy, Bert Hall: Aviator and Mercenary of the Skies*, p. 58.

31 Kiffin to Paul, September 19, 1915, Rockwell Papers, WLU.

32 Kiffin to Loula, September 15, 1915, KYR Papers, NCDNCR.

33 Kiffin to Paul, September 10, 1915, *War Letters*, p. 81.

Chapter Thirty-three

1   Kiffin to Alice Weeks, September 22, 1915, *War Letters*, p. 86.

2   *Id.* at p. 87.

3   *Carnet d'emploi du temps de M. Rockwell*, Rockwell Papers, WLU.

4   Hall & Nordhoff, *The Lafayette Flying Corps*, Vol. 1, p. 101.

5   Kiffin to Paul, September 27, 1915, Rockwell Papers, WLU. Victor Chapman, who arrived at the camp the day Kiffin wrote this letter, told his uncle that there had been "so many machines here smashed up lately, that there is quite a dearth in some of the makes." Victor Chapman to William Chanler, September 28, 1915, John Jay Chapman Additional Papers, Harvard.

6   *Victor Chapman's Letters From France*, p. 157.

7   Victor Chapman to William Chanler, September 28, 1915, John Jay Chapman Additional

Papers, Harvard.

8   Kiffin to Paul, September 27, 1915, Rockwell Papers, WLU. Note that Paul changed this statement in the published version to "and seems to be a very fine fellow indeed." Kiffin to Paul, September 27, 1915, *War Letters*, p. 88. Within two weeks Kiffin would refer to Chapman as "a very nice fellow[.]" Kiffin to the Vicomte and Vicomtesse du Peloux, October 7, 1915, *War Letters*, p. 90. Shortly after meeting him, Genet wrote in his diary that Chapman was "mighty clean and straight." Edmond Genet, diary entry of April 2, 1915, "Leaves from a War Diary," *The North American Review*, p. 278 (Jun.–Aug. 1927).

9   *Victor Chapman's Letters From France*, p. 8. Victor's godfather was Phillips Brooks, the Rector of Boston's Trinity Church and the lyricist of the Christmas carol, "O Little Town of Bethlehem."

10   *Victor Chapman's Letters From France*, p. 17.

11   Victor Chapman to John Jay Chapman, October 31, 1915, John Jay Chapman Additional Papers, Harvard.

12   M.A. DeWolfe Howe, *Memoirs of the Harvard Dead in the War Against Germany, Vol. 1*, p. 93.

13   "An Appeal to Americans," *The Times (London)*, August 5, 1914, p. 7.

14   *Id.* A mere three months later, he would write that "[t]he great neutral public feels that there is in Germany an element of unreason, and instinctively opposes her as one would oppose any mad creature." John Jay Chapman, *Deutschland Über Alles*, p. 6 (1914).

15   "An Appeal to Americans," *The Times (London)*, August 5, 1914, p. 7.

16   "American Volunteers in Paris," *The Times (London)*, August 7, 1914, p. 5.

17   *Victor Chapman's Letters From France*, p. 22.

18   *Id.* at p. 62.

19   "Musicale in French Trench; Germans Only 45 Feet Away Quit Firing to Applaud," *The Evening World*, March 20, 1915, p. 4.

20   "Ten Thousand Americans Fighting in French Army," *The Evening Star*, August 13, 1916, Part 4, p. 6.

21   *Id. See also* "Chapman's Heroism Wins High Tribute," *The New York Sun*, July 2, 1916, p. 2. Chapman was definitely rich. When he died, he left a personal estate worth more than half a million dollars. *See* "Chapman Left $500,000 Estate," *The New York Times*, October 25, 1916, p. 3.

22   M.A. DeWolfe Howe, *Memoirs of the Harvard Dead in the War Against Germany, Vol. 1*, p. 95.

23   *Victor Chapman's Letters From France*, p. 159.

24   Victor Chapman to Elizabeth Chapman, November 15, 1915, John Jay Chapman Additional Papers, Harvard.

25   *Victor Chapman's Letters From France*, p. 160. Victor switched schools and began training on the dual command Maurice Farman on October 8. *Id.*

26   Victor Chapman to Elizabeth Chapman, October 23, 1915, John Jay Chapman Additional Papers, Harvard.

27   Victor Chapman to Elizabeth Chapman, October 16, 1915, John Jay Chapman Additional Papers, Harvard.

28   Kiffin to the Vicomte and Vicomtesse du Peloux, October 7, 1915, *War Letters*, p. 90.

29   Kiffin to Paul, October 5, 1915, *War Letters*, p. 91.

30   Kiffin to Paul, October 12, 1915, Rockwell Papers, WLU.

31   Kiffin to Alice Weeks, October 11, 1915, *War Letters*, p. 93. The date of this letter may be October 7, as at least one paragraph is published under that date by Mrs. Weeks. *Compare War Letters*, p. 93 with *Greater Love*, p. 78.

32   Kiffin to Paul, October 16, 1915, Rockwell Papers, WLU.

33   *Id.* In his flight log, Kiffin recorded: *manqué pour cause le Brouillard* – missed because of the fog. *See* Entry of October 15, *Carnet d'emploi du temps de M. Rockwell*, Rockwell

Papers, WLU.

34   Kiffin to Paul, October 16, 1915, Rockwell Papers, WLU.

35   Kiffin to Loula, October 18, 1915, KYR Papers, NCDNCR.

36   Kiffin to Paul, October 16, 1915, Rockwell Papers, WLU.

37   *Id.*

38   Kiffin to Loula, October 18, 1915, KYR Papers, NCDNCR.

39   Helene Girard to Kiffin Rockwell, *circa* November 28, 1915, Rockwell Papers, WLU. I found a Helene Cecile Girard, born on February 8, 1893 in France, but she might not be the author of the letter.

40   KYR, October 14, 1915, p. 84. The letter appears in a slightly different form in Mrs. Weeks' book. *See* Weeks, *Greater Love*, p. 80.

41   Kiffin to Loula, October 18, 1915, KYR Papers, NCDNCR.

42   Kiffin to Alice Weeks, October 20, 1915, *War Letters*, p. 100.

43   *Id.*

44   Kiffin to Agnes Rockwell, October 21, 1915, KYR Papers, NCDNCR.

45   *See* Entry of October 22, *Carnet d'emploi du temps de M. Rockwell*, Rockwell Papers, WLU. *See also* Gordon, *Lafayette Escadrille Pilot Biographies*, p. 7.

46   *See* "Chicagoan Slain by a Fellow Legionary," *The Chicago Daily News*, October 23, 1915, p. 6; and "Germans Fight for Foe in Famed Legion," *The Chicago Daily News*, October 30, 1915, p. 6.

47   "Americans Among Legionnaires," *The Chicago Daily News*, October 30, 1915, p. 6.

48   *See* Kiffin to Loula, October 31, 1915, *War Letters*, p. 103 ("Mrs. Weeks has made this like home to me and is now sitting near me, doing some work on my uniform."). *See also* Alice Weeks to Fred Taber, October 24, 1915, Weeks, *Greater Love*, p. 74 ("Kiffin has come for six days' leave, and looks very handsome in his new uniform.").

49   Alice Weeks to Fred Taber, October 24, 1915, Weeks, *Greater Love*, p. 75.

50   Alice Weeks to Allen Weeks, October 30, 1915, Weeks, *Greater Love*, p. 84. Mrs. Weeks likened Thorin to "Mulvaney," a character in Rudyard Kipling's novels. Mulvaney was a rough Irishman serving as a soldier in the British army, regularly confined to barracks and stripped of all his good conduct pay and badges for drinking and other misdemeanors. *Id.* at p. 83.

51   D.W. Thorin to Kiffin, November 22, 1915, Rockwell Papers, WLU.

52   "Atlanta Boys Are No Longer in the Battles," *The Atlanta Constitution*, November 8, 1915, p. 6. The news soon made it to North Carolina, as well. *See* "Tar Heel Boys Are No Longer in the Trenches," *The Reidsville Review (Reidsville, N.C.)*, November 12, 1915, p. 3.

53   "Atlanta Boys Are No Longer in the Battles," *The Atlanta Constitution*, November 8, 1915, p. 6.

54   Kiffin to Loula, October 31, 1915, *War Letters*, p. 103.

Chapter Thirty-four

1   Kiffin to Alice Weeks, November 2, 1915, *War Letters*, p. 104.

2   Victor Chapman to John Jay Chapman, November 6, 1915, John Jay Chapman Additional Papers, Harvard.

3   Kiffin to Alice Weeks, November 2, 1915, *War Letters*, p. 104.

4   Kiffin to Loula, November 9, 1915, KYR Papers, NCDNCR.

5   Kiffin to Paul, November 6, 1915, Rockwell Papers, WLU.

6   Victor Chapman to John Jay Chapman, November 14, 1915, John Jay Chapman Additional Papers, Harvard.

7   Kiffin to the Vicomte du Peloux, November 10, 1915, *War Letters*, p. 107.

8   Victor Chapman to John Jay Chapman, October 31, 1915, John Jay Chapman Additional Papers, Harvard.

9   Victor Chapman to Elizabeth Chapman, November 15, 1915, John Jay Chapman Additional Papers, Harvard.

10   *See* Entries of November 12-14, *Carnet d'emploi du temps de M. Rockwell*, Rockwell Papers, WLU.

11   Kiffin to Paul, October 29, 1915, Rockwell Papers, WLU. The date, taken from *War Letters*, p. 101, is incorrect. Judging from context and other letters, the correct date must be November 14, 1915.

12   Victor Chapman to Elizabeth Chapman, November 15, 1915, John Jay Chapman Additional Papers, Harvard.

13   Victor Chapman to William Chanler, November, 1915, John Jay Chapman Additional Papers, Harvard.

14   Victor Chapman to William Chanler, November, 1915, John Jay Chapman Additional Papers, Harvard. This letter is different from the letter in the prior footnote, but neither has a specific date. My guess is that the letter cited in this footnote was written not long before the one cited in the prior footnote.

15   Victor Chapman to Elizabeth Chapman, November 15, 1915, John Jay Chapman Additional Papers, Harvard.

16   Victor Chapman to William Chanler, November 18, 1915, John Jay Chapman Additional Papers, Harvard.

17   Victor Chapman to Elizabeth Chapman, November 15, 1915, John Jay Chapman Additional Papers, Harvard.

18   Kiffin to Paul, October 29, 1915, Rockwell Papers, WLU. Again, the correct date must be November 14, 1915.

19   *Carnet d'emploi du temps de M. Rockwell*, Rockwell Papers, WLU.

20   Kiffin to Alice Weeks, November 22, 1915, *War Letters*, p. 111. *See also Carnet d'emploi du temps de M. Rockwell*, Rockwell Papers, WLU.

21   Kiffin to Alice Weeks, November 20, 1915, Weeks, *Greater Love*, p. 91.

22   Kiffin to the Vicomte du Peloux, November 22, 1915, *War Letters*, p. 109.

23   Kiffin to Paul, November 22, 1915, Rockwell Papers, WLU.

24   Kiffin to Alice Weeks, November 22, 1915, *War Letters*, p. 111.

25   Kiffin to Loula, November 26, 1915, KYR Papers, NCDNCR. When Paul published Kiffin's letters, he added the following words to this one: "I am giving the best that is in me in this war and will not stop at anything as long as it helps toward the final victory. This is a war of the world and means as much to the people of America as it does to anyone else. There is not one human being who is not being affected by the war. So no one has the right to forget about it or lose interest in it." *See War Letters*, p. 112. This language does not appear in the original letter written by Kiffin.

26   Victor Chapman to Elizabeth Chapman, November 30, 1915, John Jay Chapman Additional Papers, Harvard.

27   Kiffin to Alice Weeks, September 28, 1915, Weeks, *Greater Love*, p. 75. This letter is misdated, the actual date is around November 28. *See also Carnet d'emploi du temps de M. Rockwell*, Rockwell Papers, WLU.

28   *Id.*

Chapter Thirty-five

1   Kiffin to Paul, November 22, 1915, Rockwell Papers, WLU.

2   Alice Weeks to Fred Taber, December 7, 1915, Weeks, *Greater Love*, p. 96.

3   *Id.* I found a neat Prunier poster on Vintage European Posters (available at https://vepca. wordpress.com/2012/08/07/the-world-is-my-oyster/) In addition, a cool ad on the front page of the *New York Herald* in May stated, "When in Paris, Go to Prunier." *See The New York Herald*, May 12, 1915, p. 1.

4   Alice Weeks to Fred Taber, December 11, 1915, Weeks, *Greater Love*, p. 97.

5   James McConnell to Lewis Crenshaw, December 27, 1915, McConnell Collection, UVA.

6   McConnell to A. Piatt Andrew, November 28, 1915. I thank Ronald Poteat for sharing this letter with me.

7   As told by Clyde Balsley to Paul Adams, "The Story of the Lafayette Escadrille," *The Bellman*, July 20, 1918, p. 68.

8   "Message: 'Mother, I am All Right' Answers Prayers for San Antonio Air Hero Reported Killed in Battle," *San Antonio Evening News*, July 17, 1919, p. 7.

9   "More Americans at Front," *The New York Times*, December 24, 1915, p. 2.

10   "German Machine Brought Down," *The Western Sentinel*, May 23, 1916, p. 2. *See also*, Biographical note, KYR Papers, NCDNCR ("During the winter of 1915-1916, he was on duty at Le Bourget Field, as a member of the Paris Air Guard."). In a letter dated January 4, 1916, Paul said that "at present" Kiffin was "part of the air-guard of Paris, but returns to the front next week." "Brothers in the War," *The Sigma Phi Epsilon Journal*, p. 129 (December 25, 1915 – March 1, 1916).

11   Alice Weeks to Fred Taber, January 2, 1916, Weeks, *Greater Love*, p. 102.

12   The photo is in Weeks, *Greater Love*, immediately following p. 78.

13   "Kiffin Rockwell Now Serving As Aviator," *The Atlanta Constitution*, December 19, 1915, p. 14.

14   Kiffin to Loula, January 7, 1916, *War Letters*, p. 114.

15   Alice Weeks to Fred Taber, December 19, 1915, Weeks, *Greater Love*, p. 100.

16   Victor Chapman to Elizabeth Chapman, December 19, 1915, John Jay Chapman Additional Papers, Harvard. Of course, Victor's note may simply reflect nothing more than the hope that Kiffin would prove more careful in the future.

17   Bill Thorin to Alice Weeks, December 13, 1915, Weeks, *Greater Love*, p. 98.

18   Paul later wrote a good article about Thorin, in which he quoted from another letter Thorin wrote about the incident:

        The other night we went to a café called "The Universe." Two Spaniards told us the U.S.A. was no good and that the Americans could not fight. So just to show them that there was no ill feeling and that none of us American guys was afraid to fight, I cracked one between the eyes. That started it. We were four and they were five, but it didn't make no odds to us. We went through them in good style; they got assistance from two civilians, but they were no good with their dukes, so we laid them low as well. They sent for patrols, but we had just warmed up then, and as the gendarmes said, "Nothing but a '75' could have stopped those four Americans." We smashed up a few things, like chairs and windows, etc. Well, they got too many for us at last but the gendarmes were good sports and told us they would help us right as much as they possibly could. Their word was good. When we were taken up in front of the four-striper (commandant) the gendarmes told him that the other fellows started the trouble, and that if we each paid 15 francs, the café would let it go at that. The finish of it was that we got fifteen days' cell. We have paid ten francs each already, but, believe me, I wouldn't have missed that fight for a $50 bill. I will be sitting in a cell over Christmas, but what of it? "War One More Thrill of Dakota Wanderer," *The Chicago Daily News*, May 23, 1916, p. 16.

19   Rockwell, *American Fighters*, p. 152-53.

20   Marion Fiedler to Kiffin, postmarked December 16, 1915, Rockwell Papers, WLU.

21   *Id.*

22   Helen Gwynne to Kiffin, December 2, 1915, Rockwell Papers, WLU. Perhaps Ms. Gwynne was some relation to Alfred Gwynne Vanderbilt, who had died on the *Lusitania*.

23   Several nice color photos of the actual uniform can be seen at https://airandspace.si.edu/collection-objects/coat-service-french-air-service-kiffin-rockwell-lafayette-escadrille (visited March 31, 2018).

24   D.W. Thorin to Kiffin, December 24, 1915, Rockwell Papers, WLU.

25   D.W. Thorin to Kiffin, February 22, 1916, Rockwell Papers, WLU.

26   D.W. Thorin to Kiffin, December 24, 1915, Rockwell Papers, WLU.

27   "Paris, In Quiet Hope, Passes Second Christmas Eve of War," *The New York Herald*, December 25, 1915, p. 1.

28   *Id.*

29   A. Piatt Andrew to Mme. René Puaux, January 1, 1916, Hoover Institution Archives, A. Piatt Andrew, Box No. 25, Accession No. 2006C26-16.55/56. Folder 25.7, Correspondence 1916. René Puaux was a French journalist for the Paris paper *Le Temps*.

Chapter Thirty-six

1   "American Aviators Flying in France," *The Brooklyn Daily Eagle*, October 31, 1915, Magazine section, p. 4.

2   1915 Pamphlet, *European War, The Franco-American Flying Corps*, p. 12.

3   *See e.g.* "American Airmen Defiant," *The New York Times*, October 30, 1915, p. 3. "American Aviators Win Honors in France," *The New York Times*, October 9, 1915, p. 3.

4   "French-American Air Corps Planned," *The New York Times*, December 16, 1915, p. 3.

5   Cowdin, "The Lafayette Escadrille," *Harvard Alumni Bulletin*, March 7, 1918, p. 435.

6   "Three Airmen Homebound," *The New York Times*, December 11, 1915, p. 5. See also Passenger list for S.S. *Rotterdam*, Ancestry.com. *New York, Passenger and Crew Lists (including Castle Garden and Ellis Island), 1820-1957;* and "The Seagoers," *The New York Sun*, December 24, 1915, p. 7.

7   "Thaw is a Frenchman," *The New York Times*, December 12, 1915, p. 4. The passports apparently described the three men as "French citizens on military leave." *See* "Air Fighters Get Holiday," *The New York Sun*, circa December 13, 1915, clipping, William Thaw Scrapbooks, HSWP.

8   Victor Chapman to Elizabeth Chapman, December 19, 1915, John Jay Chapman Additional Papers, Harvard.

9   Cowdin, "The Lafayette Escadrille," *Harvard Alumni Bulletin*, March 7, 1918, p. 436.

10   *See The Chicago Tribune*, December 27, 1915, p. 3; *The New York Tribune*, December 24, 1915, p. 2; and *The Boston Evening Transcript*, December 24, 1915, p. 4. Another good one was "Daring American Aviators Home From France," *The York Daily*, December 28, 1915, p. 1.

11   "American Aviators Back from Western Front," *The Chicago Tribune*, December 27, 1915, p. 3.

12   "American Heroes of Air Battles in France Are Home," *The Evening World* (NY), December 23, 1915, p. 3.

13   "American Aviators Home," *The New York Herald*, December 24, 1915, clipping, William Thaw Scrapbooks, HSWP.

14   *Id.*

15   "Norman Prince Home, Wearing War Cross," *The Boston Globe*, December 24, 1915, p. 1, 3.

16   "American War Eagles Flying for France," *The Boston Evening Transcript*, December 24, 1915, p. 4.

17   "Three Oft-Killed American Flyers Home from France for Christmas," *The New York World*, December 24, 1915, clipping, William Thaw Scrapbooks, HSWP. *See also* "American War Fliers Here," *The New York Tribune*, December 24, 1915, p. 2; and "American Heroes of Air Battles in France are Home," *The Evening World* (NY), December 23, 1915, p. 3.

18   "Intern American Flyers, His Cry," *The New York Tribune*, December 25, 1915, p. 4.

19   Edwin C. Parsons, *I Flew With the Lafayette Escadrille*, p. 15 (1963).

20   "Soldier Airman is Here," *The Pittsburg Press*, December 27, 1915, p. 1.

21   "American War Eagles Flying for France," *The Boston Evening Transcript*, December 24, 1915, p. 4. One later pilot said that on these nameplates (worn by all the French aviators) was

nearly always found a figure of St. Elijah, because his chariot of fire was the first authentic flying machine. "How the Lafayette Escadrille Chose Its Leader," *San Francisco Chronicle*, August 11, 1918 p. 52. I have never been able to corroborate it, but several sources assert that Kiffin once said, "Elijah was reputed to be the patron saint of aviators, but as he went to heaven in a chariot of fire, this was something we weren't too keen about."

22   "Permits Wrist Watch," *The Washington Post*, March 5, 1916, p. 8.

23   *Id.* Of note, the objects on their wrists may not have been watches at all, but rather compasses. *See* "American War Eagles Flying for France," *The Boston Evening Transcript*, December 24, 1915, p. 4.

24   "French Believe U.S. Should Aid Allies," *Pittsburgh Post-Gazette*, December 24, 1915, p. 3.

25   "Norman Prince, Daring Aviator, Killed by Fall," *The Boston Post*, October 16, 1916, p. 6.

26   "American War Eagles Flying for France," *The Boston Evening Transcript*, December 24, 1915, p. 4.

27   "Norman Prince Home Wearing War Cross," *The Boston Globe*, December 24, 1915, p. 3.

28   "Three Violaters of the Law," *The Fatherland*, January 5, 1916, p. 381. *See also* "Seeks Arrest of Aviators," *The New York Times*, December 25, 1915, p. 3.

29   "Three Violaters of the Law," *The Fatherland*, January 5, 1916, p. 381.

30   Stamp on telegram from George Viereck to Robert Lansing dated December 24, 1915, National Archives, *General Records of the Department of State, 1763-2002*, Record Group 59, Central Decimal Files, 1910-1963, File Unit: 763.72111S04 – 763.72111Z1.

31   Handwritten notes on telegram from George Viereck to Robert Lansing dated December 24, 1915, National Archives, *General Records of the Department of State, 1763-2002*, Record Group 59, Central Decimal Files, 1910-1963, File Unit: 763.72111S04 – 763.72111Z1. Lansing did not care for Viereck or his publication. Many years after the war he would write: "Of all the pro-German publications in this country none was so contemptible as a New York weekly named *The Fatherland....*" Of its editor Viereck, Lansing stated: "That many of his assertions were untrue did not appear to trouble him in the least. Possibly of course he believed them, for no one can be sure of the mental processes of such a man." *War Memoirs of Robert Lansing*, p. 77 (1935).

32   Robert Lansing to George S. Vierick, December 28, 1915, National Archives, *General Records of the Department of State, 1763-2002*, Record Group 59, Central Decimal Files, 1910-1963, File Unit: 763.72111S04 – 763.72111Z1.

33   Robert Lansing to J.J. Jusserand, December 28, 1915, National Archives, *General Records of the Department of State, 1763-2002*, Record Group 59, Central Decimal Files, 1910-1963, File Unit: 763.72111S04 – 763.72111Z1.

34   "War Aviators Here Cannot Be Interned," *The New York Sun*, December 26, 1915, p. 8.

35   *See* "Asks the Internment of French Army Flyers," *The Evening Star*, December 27, 1915, p. 9; and "Aviator Won't Be Interned," *The New York Sun*, December 28, 1915, p. 2.

36   "Thaw Cannot Be Interned in America," *Pittsburgh Gazette Times*, December 26, 1916, p. 7.

37   *Id.*

38   *Id.*

39   "Soldier Airman is Here," *The Pittsburg Press*, December 27, 1915, p. 1.

40   "Here as a Civilian, Says Mr. W. Thaw, To Stop 8 Days," undated clipping probably from *The New York Herald*, December 27, 1915, William Thaw Scrapbooks, HSWP. *See also* "Lieut. Thaw, French Aviator, Home; Does Not Fear Internment," *The Sun (Pittsburgh)*, December 27, 1915, p. 1-2.

41   "Norman Prince at Home," *The Boston Globe*, December 26, 1915, p. 10; and "Norman Prince Departs," *The Boston Globe*, December 30, 1915, p. 8.

42   "Will Fight Internment," *The New York Times*, December 26, 1915, p. 1.

43   "Aviation in War," *The Boston Globe*, December 29, 1915, p. 14. This speech took place at the Lombardy Inn in Boston.

44   "American War Eagles Flying for France," *The Boston Evening Transcript*, December 24,

1915, p. 4.

45 "Boston Needs Big Navy, Prince Says," undated clipping, Lafayette Escadrille Scrapbook, MHS. Prince's father later recalled some more personal words spoken by his son: *When the Germans begin firing at me I get scared to death. Sometimes my knees crack together when the shells start bursting. I know that sometime I shall be killed. Every aviator gets it sooner or later, flying even in peace times. In war a flyer doesn't stand a chance.* "True Story of American Millionaire's Son Who Died in European War," *St. Louis Post-Dispatch*, November 5, 1916, p. B1.

46 George Viereck to Robert Lansing, telegram dated December 28, 1915, National Archives, *General Records of the Department of State, 1763-2002*, Record Group 59, Central Decimal Files, 1910-1963, File Unit: 763.72111S04 – 763.72111z1. *See also* "U.S. Again Asked to Intern Fliers," *The Washington Times*, December 29, 1915, p. 6; and "New Demand Made for the Internment of Lieut. William Thaw," *The Evening World* (NY), December 29, 1915, p. 2. Viereck responded immediately to Lansing's letter, and forcefully suggested it was "incumbent upon this Government" to hold the men "until it has been definitely decided that our refusal to do so does not constitute a violation of neutrality." George S. Viereck to Robert Lansing, December 29, 1915, National Archives, *General Records of the Department of State, 1763-2002*, Record Group 59, Central Decimal Files, 1910-1963, File Unit: 763.72111S04 – 763.72111z1.

47 "Aviator Won't Be Interned," *The New York Sun*, December 28, 1915, p. 2.

48 "U.S. Again Asked to Intern Fliers," *The Washington Times*, December 29, 1915. *See also* "Deaf to Men in Alien Army," *The Washington Post*, December 28, 1915, p. 14.

49 Handwritten note on telegram from George Viereck to Robert Lansing, December 24, 1915, National Archives, *General Records of the Department of State, 1763-2002*, Record Group 59, Central Decimal Files, 1910-1963, File Unit: 763.72111S04 – 763.72111z1, and Undersecretary Frank L. Polk to the Attorney General, December 29, 1915, National Archives, *General Records of the Department of State, 1763-2002*, Record Group 59, Central Decimal Files, 1910-1963, File Unit: 763.72111S04 – 763.72111z1.

50 Undersecretary Frank L. Polk to the Attorney General, December 29, 1915, National Archives, *General Records of the Department of State, 1763-2002*, Record Group 59, Central Decimal Files, 1910-1963, File Unit: 763.72111S04 – 763.72111z1.

51 James Brown Scott, "The Neutrality Board," *The American Journal of International Law*, Vol. 13, No. 2, p. 308 (Apr. 1919).

52 Robert Lansing to James Brown Scott, December 29, 1915, National Archives, *General Records of the Department of State, 1763-2002*, Record Group 59, Central Decimal Files, 1910-1963, File Unit: 763.72111S04 – 763.72111z1.

53 Memorandum from Joint State and Navy Neutrality Board to the Secretary of State dated December 30, 1915, National Archives, *General Records of the Department of State, 1763-2002*, Record Group 59, Central Decimal Files, 1910-1963, File Unit: 763.72111S04 – 763.72111z1.

54 "New Protest on Aviators," *The New York Sun*, December 30, 1915, p. 4. The Board was merely advisory, so its opinion was not binding on Lansing.

55 "New Demand Made for the Internment of Lieut. William Thaw," *The Evening World* (NY), December 29, 1915, p. 2.

56 "Norman Prince Is Dead," undated newsclipping, Lafayette Escadrille Scrapbook, MHS.

57 I have not been able to locate the story in the *New York American*, but it was reprinted. *See* "How Love Made a War Hero of Pittsburg's Wealthy Scapegrace," *Richmond Times-Dispatch*, June 13, 1915, Part 6, p. 2.

58 "'Can't Drink and Fly,' Says W. Thaw in Court," *The Evening World* (NY), December 30, 1915, p. 1.

59 *The Harrisburg Telegraph*, January 8, 1916, p. 10. About his citizenship status, Thaw was later quoted as saying: "I am for France until the war is over; but I am not a Frenchman. My

allegiance to France will continue during the war, and while this lasts I am not an American. I have not applied to France to become a citizen, and when the war is over I will again be an American." *The Pittsburgh Gazette Times*, November 21, 1916, p. 1. Given his status, Thaw said, "I might be called a man from No Man's Land..." "William Thaw Back from No Man's Land," *The Boston Globe*, November 21, 1916, p. 2.

60   "Thaw Gives Love of France as Reason for Enlistment," *The Pittsburgh Gazette Times*, December 31, 1915, p. 5. *See also* "Fliers Can't Drink, Says Lieut. Thaw," clipping dated December 31, 1915, William Thaw Scrapbooks, HSWP.

61   William Thaw Affidavit, January 3, 1916, National Archives, *General Records of the Department of State, 1763-2002*, Record Group 59, Central Decimal Files, 1910-1963, File Unit: 763.72111S04 – 763.72111z1.

62   *Id.*

63   J.J. Jusserand to Robert Lansing, December 30, 1915, National Archives, *General Records of the Department of State, 1763-2002*, Record Group 59, Central Decimal Files, 1910-1963, File Unit: 763.72111S04 – 763.72111z1. These documents can be viewed by on history.state. gov office of the historian. Look under historical documents, foreign relations of the united states, Woodrow Wilson Administration, 1916, Supplement, The World War. Document 912, 913 File No. 763.72111S04/71.

64   "Will Fight Internment," *The New York Times*, December 26, 1915, p. 1; "Norman Prince Leaves," *The Boston Evening Transcript*, December 29, 1915, p. 1.

65   "Vive la France!" *The New York Tribune*, December 27, 1915, p. 6. One of the many letters to the editor that followed the editorial came from Charles F. Kingsley, who wrote: "Let us begin the new year with the solemn resolution to eliminate all poltroons from national counsels and substitute for them vigorous and virile Americans who will never doubt that a two-handed job requires two-handed methods." "Our Humiliation," *The New York Tribune*, December 29, 1915, p. 8.

66   *See* "A Tribute to Norman Prince, Written by a Boston Friend," *The Boston Post*, October 22, 1916, p. 44; and "Norman Prince, Daring Aviator, Killed by Fall," *The Boston Post*, October 16, 1916, p. 6.

67   "Notable Birthdays Today," *The Buffalo Enquirer*, March 24, 1917, p. 4. The finished portrait can be seen after page 18 in Prince, *A Volunteer Who Died for the Cause He Loved*. Benson was an American impressionist painter, quite famous even then. In fact, throughout the month of December 1915, he had an exhibition at Kennedy & Co, on Fifth Avenue in New York. In 1995, one of Benson's paintings sold for 4.1 million dollars.

68   John Jay Chapman to Victor Chapman, January 4, 1916, John Jay Chapman Papers, Harvard.

69   Prince, *A Volunteer Who Died for the Cause He Loved*, p. 31.

70   "From A Graduate's Window," *The Harvard Graduate's Magazine*, Vol. XXV, 1916-1917, p. 187 (Dec. 1916).

Chapter Thirty-seven

1   Hall & Nordhoff, *The Lafayette Flying Corps*, Vol. 1, p. 198. Hall also stated that "the motive which actuated France in permitting the establishment of the Lafayette Flying Corps was largely political." *Id.* at p. 3.

2   *Id.* at p. 198.

3   "Laud American Airmen," *The New York Times*, January 19, 1916, p. 3.

4   Thénault, *The Lafayette Escadrille*, p. 14.

5   Thénault, *The Lafayette Escadrille*, p. 14-15. The Americans were also to have "far greater liberty of action" than typical French pilots. *See* "American Flying Corps," *The Washington Post*, January 22, 1916, p. 2.

6   "Lips of American Aviators Sealed on Daring Air Feats for France," *The New York Herald*, January 13, 1916, p. 2.

7   "Laud American Airmen," *The New York Times*, January 19, 1916, p. 3. This lunch may have taken place at Maxim's in the *Rue Royale*.

8   *"The Diary of H. Clyde Balsley," Cross & Cockade* Journal, Vol. 18(2), Summer 1977, p. 108; *Victor Chapman's Letters From France*, p. 165.

9   *Victor Chapman's Letters From France*, p. 166.

10   *Id.*

11   *Id.*

12   Victor Chapman to John Jay Chapman, January 23, 1916, John Jay Chapman Additional Papers, Harvard.

13   "'Snap' Vote on Besnard," *The New York Times,* January 4, 1916, p. 2.

14   Victor Chapman to John Jay Chapman, January 23, 1916, John Jay Chapman Additional Papers, Harvard.

15   Hall & Nordhoff, *The Lafayette Escadrille*, Vol. 1, p. 13-14.

16   "7 Killed, Including 1 Child, and 20 Wounded by Bombs of Second Zeppelin on Paris," *The New York Herald*, January 30, 1916, p. 1.

17   One website has photos of the two holes left by the bombs. (http://albindenis.free.fr/Site_ escadrille/RGA.htm) (visited April 21, 2018)

18   Still, one of Paul's colleagues credited the aviators with driving off the zeppelin on both nights. *See* "Zeppelin Was Routed by Thirty Air Pilots," *The Chicago Daily News*, February 1, 1916, p. 2.

19   "Paris Aviators Are Constantly Ready to Give Chase to Hostile Raiders," *The New York Herald*, January 31, 1916, p. 1.

20   "French Newspapers Demand Reprisals for Night Murders," *The New York Herald*, January 31, 1916, p. 1.

21   "Un depart demission de M. René Besnard Sous-secrétaire d'État à aeronaùtique," *Le Journal*, 9 Février 1916, p. 1.

22   Irene Susong to Paul, January 11, 1916, Rockwell Papers, WLU.

23   Loula to Paul, February 2, 1916, Rockwell Papers, WLU.

24   Kiffin to Loula, January 17, 1916, Rockwell Papers, WLU.

25   "Five Americans in the Legion Die for France," *The New York Herald*, January 16, 1916, p. 2.

26   Kiffin to Loula, January 17, 1916, Rockwell Papers, WLU.

27   1 Corinthians 13:4, 7, 11, King James Version.

28   Alice Weeks to Fred Taber, February 6, 1916, Weeks, *Greater Love*, p. 108.

29   "Deuil," *Le Figaro*, 9 Février 1916, p. 4.

30   Alice Weeks to Fred Taber, February 6, 1916, Weeks, *Greater Love*, p. 108.

31   Victor Chapman to Elizabeth Chapman, February 16, 1916, John Jay Chapman Additional Papers, Harvard.

32   Kiffin to Alice Weeks, February 8, 1916, *War Letters*, p. 115. Although undated, this letter must have been written on February 8, 1916, as Kiffin's service card shows that he left to Plessis-Belleville on February 7. The hotel must have been the *Hôtel de la Bonne Rencontre*.

33   Paul to Kiffin, April 25, 1916, Rockwell Papers, WLU.

34   In an interview later in life, Paul said that when he arrived in France, although he had taken three or four years of French, he needed practice in speaking. *See* Transcribed Interview of Paul Rockwell by Dr. Louis D. Silveri, July 22, 1976, p. 12 (Southern Highlands Research Center, University of North Carolina at Asheville).

35   "Rockwell Sure Allies Will Triumph," *The Atlanta Georgian*, February 8, 1916, p. 2.

36   *Id.*

37   Loula to Paul, February 10, 1916, Rockwell Papers, WLU.

38   Kiffin to Loula, February 17, 1916, KYR Papers, NCDNCR. Paul added perhaps Kiffin's most famous quote to this letter when he published it: "If I die, I want you to know that I have died as every man ought to die fighting for what is right. I do not feel that I am fighting for France alone, but for the cause of all humanity, the greatest of all causes." *See War Letters*, p. 116.

While Kiffin probably said this or something like it, it is not in this letter.

39   *Victor Chapman's Letters From France*, p. 167.

40   Prince, *A Volunteer Who Died for the Cause He Loved*, p. 32.

41   *Victor Chapman's Letters From France*, p. 171.

42   Frank W. Bailey & Christophe Cony, *The French Air Service War Chronology, 1914-1918*, p. 36 (2002).

43   "Americans at Work Under Verdun Shells," *The New York Times*, June 1, 1916, p. 2.

44   Kiffin to Loula, February 28, 1916, KYR Papers, NCDNCR.

45   Gordon, *Lafayette Escadrille Pilot Biographies*, p. 7.

46   James McConnell to Marcelle Guerin, January 9, 1916, McConnell Collection, UVA.

47   James McConnell to Paul Rockwell, February 18, 1916, Rockwell Papers, WLU.

48   Marcelle Guerin to Paul Rockwell, February 21, 1916, Rockwell Papers, WLU.

49   Hall, *En L'Air!*, p. 151.

50   Id. at p. 62-63.

51   Victor Chapman to Elizabeth Chapman, January 6, 1916, John Jay Chapman Additional Papers, Harvard.

52   "*The Diary of H. Clyde Balsley*," Cross & Cockade Journal, Vol. 18(2), Summer 1977, p. 113.

53   Victor Chapman to Elizabeth Chapman, undated, John Jay Chapman Additional Papers, Harvard. The likely date for this letter is late February or early March, 1916.

54   "Elliott Cowdin Now Flying Over Verdun," *The Boston Globe*, March 20, 1916, p. 8. *See also* "Thaw to Command All American Fliers," *Pittsburgh Chronicle Telegraph*, April 7, 1916, clipping, William Thaw Scrapbooks, HSWP.

55   James McConnell, "Flying for France," *The World's Work*, November 1916, p. 43.

56   Hall & Nordhoff, *The Lafayette Flying Corps*, Vol. 1, p. 14.

57   *Id.* at p. 15.

Chapter Thirty-eight

1   *See* Entry of 4 Avril 1916, Escadrille N.65, *Journal de Marche, commence le 2 Août 1915 fin le 29 Juillet 1916*, available on the *Mémoire des Hommes* website. *See also* Bailey & Cony, *The French Air Service War Chronology*, p. 44; and "American, Flying for Allies, Wings Second Taube at Verdun," *The New York Tribune*, April 24, 1916, p. 1. For this victory, Cowdin was awarded the *croix de guerre* on April 12. *See* Entry of 12 Avril 1916, Escadrille N.65, *Journal de Marche, commence le 2 Août 1915 fin le 29 Juillet 1916*.

2   James McConnell, "Flying for France," *The World's Work*, November 1916, p. 44 (noting that "Before the *American Escadrille* became an established fact, one of its members, Elliot Cowdin, succeeded in bringing down a German machine....").

3   "Air Honors for an American," *The Chicago Daily News*, April 7, 1916, p. 2.

4   Entry of 27 Mars 1916, Escadrille N.65, *Journal de Marche, commence le 2 Août 1915 fin le 29 Juillet 1916*, available on the *Mémoire des Hommes* website.

5   *See* "Thaw Fells a German Flyer," *The Chicago Daily News*, April 10, 1916, p. 2 (reporting that Thaw "felled a German machine, which, however, dropped behind the German lines.").

6   "Thaw Enjoys Sport of Chasing Flyers," *The Chicago Daily News*, April 11, 1916, p. 2.

7   *Id.*

8   Paul Stanley Bond and M.J. McDonough, *Technique of Modern Tactics*, p. 381 (3d ed., 1916).

9   *Victor Chapman's Letters From France*, p. 172.

10   Laurence Rumsey, "Training an American Aviator in France," *National Service*, May 1917, p. 265-66.

11   "The Diary of H. Clyde Balsley," *Cross & Cockade*, Vol. 18, No. 2, p. 113 (Summer 1977).

12   Hamilton-Paterson, *Marked for Death: The First War in the Air*, p. 49. *See also The Nieuport 17*, Profile Publications No. 49, p. 4 (noting the Nieuport 11 "tend[ed] to break up

in the air.").

13   Walter A. Musciano, *Capt. Georges Guynemer*, p. 49 (1963).

14   Laurence Rumsey, "Training an American Aviator in France," *National Service*, May 1917, p. 265.

15   *See Carnet d'emploi du temps de M. Rockwell*, Rockwell Papers, WLU.

16   Kiffin to Loula, March 11, 1916, KYR Papers, NCDNCR.

17   Bill Thorin to Alice Weeks, March 16, 1916, Weeks, *Greater Love*, p. 116.

18   Alice Weeks to Allen Weeks, March 26, 1916, Weeks, *Greater Love*, p. 119.

19   James McConnell to Ward McClanahan, April 13, 1916, McConnell Collection, UVA.

20   "Prof. Baldwin Cables to President Wilson, Demanding Reparation for Daughter's Injury," *The New York Times*, April 3, 1916, p. 1.

21   President Wilson, Address to a Joint Session of Congress on German Violations of International Law, April 19, 1916, available at http://www.presidency.ucsb.edu/ws/index.php?pid=65390 (visited May 27, 2019).

22   "Prof. Baldwin Thinks Germany Won't Relinquish Her Submarine Warfare," *The New York Herald*, April 25, 1916, p. 3.

23   On May 4, 1916, the German government informed the United States of the following order given to its naval forces: "In accordance with the general principles of visit and search and destruction of merchant vessels recognized by international law, such vessels, both within and without the area declared as naval war zone, shall not be sunk without warning and without saving human lives, unless these ships attempt to escape or offer resistance." Ambassador James Gerard to Secretary Robert Lansing, telegram dated May 4, 1916, *Papers Relating to the Foreign Relations of the United States, 1916, Supplement, The World War*, File No. 763.72/2654.(available online at https://history.state.gov/historicaldocuments/frus1916Supp/d337) (last visited on February 23, 2019)

24   Alice Weeks to Fred Taber, April 2, 1916, Weeks, *Greater Love*, p. 122.

25   Kiffin to the Vicomte du Peloux, April 6, 1916, *War Letters*, p. 117-118. Less than a week later, Captain de Saint-Sauveur of N.67 responded: "I should be very pleased to have in my *escadrille* for some time my personal friend Norman Prince, Chapman and you, but I am afraid it is impossible to obtain.... The only thing I could do is to translate your letter to the Colonel Barès, as he is here for some days, informing him you are in a hurry to say goodbye to Plessis-Belleville." Capt. De Saint-Sauveur to Kiffin, April 12, 1916, Rockwell Papers, WLU.

26   Kiffin to Loula, April 7, 1916, KYR Papers, NCDNCR.

27   Alice Weeks to Allen Weeks, April 8, 1916, Weeks, *Greater Love*, p. 124.

28   The Vicomte du Peloux told Kiffin that McConnell's presence would "no doubt improve the morale status of the American set, as he is so congenial." Vicomte Peloux to Kiffin Rockwell, April 16, 1916, Rockwell Papers, WLU.

29   James McConnell to Marcelle Guerin, April 10, 1916, McConnell Collection, UVA.

30   *Id.*

31   McConnell reported in March that Rumsey was serving fifteen days in the infantry prison at Pau for going to Paris. James McConnell to Paul Rockwell, March 9, 1916, Rockwell Papers, WLU.

32   "Americans Learn to be War Fliers in French School of Aviation at Pau," *The New York Sun*, March 26, 1916, p. 2.

33   An American passport agent rendered perhaps the most accurate description of Hall a few years after the war ended. The man suspected Hall of lying during their interview, and in a memo to the file concluded the American flyer was "an exceptionally smooth talker giving one the impression of his being of the adventurer type." *See* William A. Newcome, note to the file, Weston Bert Hall passport application dated October 17, 1922, available on Ancestry. com. *U.S. Passport Applications, 1795-1925*.

34   Thaw and Cowdin left *Escadrille N.65* on April 17 to be assigned to N.124. *See* Entry of 17

Avril 1916, Escadrille N.65, *Journal de Marche, commence le 2 Août 1915 fin le 29 Juillet 1916* ("*quittent l'Esc[adrille] pour être affecté á la Escadrille N.124 (á Luxeuil).*"), available on the *Mémoire des Hommes* website. The two pilots first went back to Paris for ten days, however, so did not join N.124 until April 28.

35   "American Air Fleet Formed in France," *The New York World*, April 19, 1916, p. 3. *See also* "U.S. Air Squadron Complete," *The New York Sun*, April 19, 1916, p. 3.

36   "American Air Fleet Formed in France," *The New York World*, April 19, 1916, p. 3; Hall, *One Man's War*, p. 123. Chapman called it "a kind of wind-up dinner of Americans." *Victor Chapman's Letters From France*, p. 172.

37   Thaw once remarked that *Ciro's* was "always full of Americans[.]" Thaw letter April 7, 1915, "Letters of a French Army Aviator," *Yale Alumni Weekly*, June 11, 1915, p. 1032.

38   Chapman's stepmother wrote to her "Darling Victor" when she read about the dinner in a New York paper:
Two days ago, William appeared at breakfast with a clipping from the World *of the day before, describing your banquet on the 17th - & stating that the* Escadrille Américaine *was at last off to the front. Imagine our mingled feelings – uppermost, rejoicings that the wish of your heart was now fulfilled. What a birthday feast that was for you! I wonder if, in the hurly-burly you remembered that it was your birthday.* Elizabeth Chapman to Victor Chapman, April 21, 1916, John Jay Chapman Additional Papers, Harvard.

39   Hall, *One Man's War*, p. 124. *See also* Laurence Driggs, *Heroes of Aviation*, p. 8 (1919).

40   But one article, likely written by McConnell, indicates that Thaw and Cowdin were there. *See* "Americans Grouped in Air Squad at Front," *The Chicago Daily News*, June 24, 1916, p. 4 ("Two of the men had just come in from the work above Verdun, and they were the center of interest."). It could be that Thaw and Cowdin arrived from N.65 in time for the dinner but then stayed in Paris before officially joining the new squadron.

41   "Chicago Flyer Died for Love of France," *The Chicago Daily News*, March 28, 1917, p. 2. *See also* Paul Rockwell, "Kiffin Rockwell's Letters to His Brother," *Every Week*, December 3, 1917, p. 3.

42   "Chicago Flyer Died for Love of France," *The Chicago Daily News*, March 28, 1917, p. 2.

43   *See* Paul Rockwell, "Kiffin Rockwell's Letters to His Brother," *Every Week*, December 3, 1917, p. 3.

44   McConnell, *Flying for France*, p. 21.

Chapter Thirty-nine

1   Kiffin to Alice Weeks, April 20, 1916, Weeks, *Greater Love*, p. 128.

2   *Id.*

3   Victor Chapman to William Astor Chanler, April 20, 1916, John Jay Chapman Additional Papers, Harvard. *Escadrille MF.24* was stationed in Rosnay around April 1916.

4   *Victor Chapman's Letters From France*, p. 173.

5   Kiffin to Paul, April 20, 1916, Rockwell Papers, WLU.

6   James McConnell to Marcelle Guerin, April 20, 1916, McConnell Collection, UVA.

7   Kiffin to Loula, April 20, 1916, KYR Papers, NCDNCR.

8   Kiffin to Alice Weeks, April 20, 1916, Weeks, *Greater Love*, p. 128.

9   Victor Chapman to William Astor Chanler, April 20, 1916, John Jay Chapman Additional Papers, Harvard.

10   Kiffin to Alice Weeks, April 20, 1916, Weeks, *Greater Love*, p. 128.

11   Thénault, *The Lafayette Escadrille*, p. 18.

12   Henry Farré, *Sky Fighters of France*, p. 101.

13   Bailey & Cony, *The French Air Service War Chronology*, caption to photo insert of Captain Happe following p. 152.

14   Mason, *The Lafayette Escadrille*, p. 57.

15   *See A History of French Military Aviation*, p. 89; Flammer, *The Vivid Air*, p. 54-55; and Thénault, *The Lafayette Escadrille*, p. 18.

16   Kiffin to Alice Weeks, April 20, 1916, Weeks, *Greater Love*, p. 128.

17   *Id.* at p. 128-29.

18   *Victor Chapman's Letters From France*, p. 173.

19   Victor Chapman to William Astor Chanler, April 20, 1916, John Jay Chapman Additional Papers, Harvard.

20   *Id.*

21   *Id.*

22   *Victor Chapman's Letters From France*, p. 173. *See also* James McConnell to Marcelle Guerin, April 20, 1916, McConnell Collection, UVA. Of course, McConnell had delivered his own crosses as part of the American Ambulance. *See* James McConnell to Paul Rockwell, May 18, 1915, McConnell Collection, UVA ("Today we took up a box of little crosses. You probably know what that indicates."). One authoritative source indicates that MF.29 lost four planes on March 18, each with two men. Amazingly, two of the French pilots took out German planes by intentionally colliding into them during combat. Bailey & Cony, *The French Air Service War Chronology*, p. 41.

23   Victor Chapman to William Astor Chanler, April 20, 1916, John Jay Chapman Additional Papers, Harvard.

24   Thénault, *The Lafayette Escadrille*, p. 21.

25   Kiffin to Alice Weeks, April 20, 1916, Weeks, *Greater Love*, p. 128.

26   James McConnell to Lewis Crenshaw, May 1, 1916, McConnell Collection, UVA.

27   Thénault, *The Lafayette Escadrille*, p. 21.

28   Thénault, "L'Escadrille La Fayette," *La Légion Étrangére (revue bimestrielle illustrée militaire et coloniale)*, No. 21, p. 28, (1940). Most people give the date of the formation of the *escadrille* as April 20, 1916. However, the first four pilots arrived with Thénault on April 19.

29   Victor Chapman to William Astor Chanler, April 20, 1916, John Jay Chapman Additional Papers, Harvard.

30   Thénault, *The Lafayette Escadrille*, p. 22.

31   James McConnell to Paul Rockwell, April 21, 1916, Rockwell Papers, WLU.

32   Victor Chapman to William Astor Chanler, April 20, 1916, John Jay Chapman Additional Papers, Harvard.

33   *Id.*

34   "Americans Grouped in Air Squad at Front," *The Chicago Daily News*, June 24, 1916, p. 4.

35   Thénault, *The Lafayette Escadrille*, p. 43.

36   Kiffin to Alice Weeks, April 20, 1916, Weeks, *Greater Love*, p. 129. *See also* "France Fetes Daring Americans in Flying Corps," *St. Louis Post-Dispatch*, July 9, 1916, p. 3B ("each man contributes a fixed percentage of his pay to the mess bill.").

37   Entry of 20 Avril 1916, Groupe de Bombardement No. 4, *Journal du Marches et Operations*, available on the *Mémoire des Hommes* website.

38   One article even speculated that Thaw would be in full command, with Cowdin and Prince serving as his under officers. *See* "Thaw to Command All American Flyers," *The Pittsburgh Chronicle Telegraph*, April 7, 1916, clipping in William Thaw Scrapbooks, HSWP. Another article reported that Thaw actually was second in command. "U.S. Air Squadron Complete," *The New York Sun*, April 19, 1916, p. 3.

39   Thénault, *The Lafayette Escadrille*, p. 16.

40   Victor Chapman to William Astor Chanler, April 20, 1916, John Jay Chapman Additional Papers, Harvard. It is a safe bet that Prince was a bit disappointed, as well.

41   Kiffin to Alice Weeks, April 20, 1916, Weeks, *Greater Love*, p. 129.

42   Gordon, *Lafayette Escadrille Pilot Biographies*, p. 243.

43   Kiffin to Loula, April 20, 1916, KYR Papers, NCDNCR.

44　*Id.*

45　James McConnell to Marcelle Guerin, April 20, 1916, McConnell Collection, UVA. *See also* "Americans Grouped in Air Squad at Front," *The Chicago Daily News*, June 24, 1916, p. 4.

46　James McConnell to Lewis Crenshaw, May 1, 1916, McConnell Collection, UVA.

47　*Id.*

48　James McConnell to Marcelle Guerin, April 20, 1916, McConnell Collection, UVA.

49　*Id.*

Chapter Forty

1　James McConnell to Lewis Crenshaw, May 1, 1916, McConnell Collection, UVA.

2　James McConnell to Alice Weeks, April 29, 1916, Weeks, *Greater Love*, p. 132.

3　Kiffin to Paul, undated postcard *circa* April 25, 1916, Rockwell Papers, WLU.

4　Kiffin to Alice Weeks, April 20, 1916, Weeks, *Greater Love*, p. 129.

5　Alice Weeks to Kiffin, April 27, 1916, Rockwell Papers, WLU.

6　Loula to Kiffin, April 13, 1916, Rockwell Papers, WLU.

7　Victor Chapman to William Astor Chanler, April 20, 1916, John Jay Chapman Additional Papers, Harvard.

8　James McConnell to Paul Rockwell, April 25, 1916, Rockwell Papers, WLU.

9　James McConnell to Marcelle Guerin, April 26, 1916, McConnell Collection, UVA.

10　Victor Chapman to William Astor Chanler, undated letter *circa* April 28, 1916, John Jay Chapman Additional Papers, Harvard.

11　James McConnell to Paul Rockwell, April 25, 1916, Rockwell Papers, WLU.

12　James McConnell to Lewis Crenshaw, May 1, 1916, McConnell Collection, UVA.

13　Kiffin to Loula, April 20, 1916, KYR Papers, NCDNCR. The fishing was pretty good in Luxeuil - when the crew returned that fall, Thaw would land a trout well over 6 pounds. Paul Pavelka to Paul Rockwell, October 1, 1916, Rockwell Papers, WLU.

14　Victor Chapman to Conrad Chapman, May 3, 1916, *The Harvard Volunteers in Europe*, p. 230 (Correct date of letter is probably May 12).

15　Victor Chapman to William Astor Chanler, undated letter *circa* April 28, 1916, John Jay Chapman Additional Papers, Harvard.

16　Paul Ayres Rockwell, "Jim McConnell for France," *The State*, February 1979, p. 8.

17　Thénault, *The Story of the Lafayette Escadrille*, p. 29.

18　Whitehouse, *Legion of the Lafayette*, p. 31.

19　*Victor Chapman's Letters From France*, p. 175.

20　Thénault, *The Story of the Lafayette Escadrille*, p. 31.

21　*Id.*

22　Kiffin to Loula, April 28, 1916, KYR Papers, NCDNCR.

23　James McConnell to Marcelle Guerin, April 26, 1916, McConnell Collection, UVA.

24　*Victor Chapman's Letters From France*, p. 176-77.

25　James McConnell to unknown (Mother?), February 23, 1915, McConnell Collection, UVA.

26　"Atlanta Boy Wounded on French Battlefield," *The Atlanta Constitution*, May 2, 1915, p. 8A.

27　James McConnell to Marcelle Guerin, April 26, 1916, McConnell Collection, UVA. *See also Journal Officiel de la Republique Française*, 21 Mai 1922, p. 1974. Masse is buried in the cemetery at Luxeuil.

28　Entry of 26 Avril 1916, Groupe de Bombardement No. 4, *Journal du Marches et Operations*, available on the *Mémoire des Hommes* website.

29　Victor Chapman to [] Kisling, April 28, 1916, John Jay Chapman Additional Papers, Harvard. Kisling was a Polish painter, and a "great friend" of Victor's from his days in the Legion. *Victor Chapman's Letters From France*, p. 23.

30　Victor Chapman to William Astor Chanler, undated letter *circa* April 28, 1916, John Jay Chapman Additional Papers, Harvard.

31   Kiffin to Paul, April 29, 1916, Rockwell Papers, WLU.

32   Entry of 28 Avril 1916, Groupe de Bombardement No. 4, *Journal du Marches et Operations*, available on the *Mémoire des Hommes* website.

33   Entry of 30 Avril 1916, Groupe de Bombardement No. 4, *Journal du Marches et Operations*, available on the *Mémoire des Hommes* website. See also *Victor Chapman's Letters From France*, p. 177.

34   James McConnell to Paul Rockwell, April 30, 1916, Rockwell Papers, WLU.

35   Bailey & Cony, *The French Air Service War Chronology*, p. 51.

36   "Lieut. Navarre Victor in Nine Aerial Duels," *The New York Herald*, April 27, 1916, p. 1. Chapman, for one, felt Navarre was "in a class by himself." "France Fetes Daring Americans in Flying Corps," *St. Louis Post-Dispatch*, July 9, 1916, p. 2B, 4B.

37   Kiffin to Paul, April 29, 1916, Rockwell Papers, WLU.

38   James McConnell to Paul Rockwell, April 30, 1916, Rockwell Papers, WLU.

39   James McConnell to Sarah Rogers McConnell, May 3, 1916, McConnell Collection, UVA.

40   When they first arrived, Chapman noted that Prince was "contemplating having his *poule* come up." Victor Chapman to William Astor Chanler, April 20, 1916, John Jay Chapman Additional Papers, Harvard. A few weeks later Chapman said of his friend Prince: "I begin to think he is a little insane about copulation – he gets so he only has waking periods now and then when he stops thinking about it." Victor Chapman to William Astor Chanler, undated postcard *circa* May 14, 1916, John Jay Chapman Additional Papers, Harvard.

41   Hall, *One Man's War*, p. 124.

42   Mason, *The Lafayette Escadrille*, p. 56.

43   "Americans Grouped in Air Squad at Front," *The Chicago Daily News*, June 24, 1916, p. 4. This article was written by McConnell.

44   James McConnell to Lewis Crenshaw, May 1, 1916, McConnell Collection, UVA.

45   James McConnell to Marcelle Guerin, April 26, 1916, McConnell Collection, UVA.

46   James McConnell to Paul Rockwell, April 30, 1916, Rockwell Papers, WLU.

47   James McConnell to Marcelle Guerin, May 6, 1916, McConnell Collection, UVA.

48   "Titine" to Kiffin, June 6, 1916, Rockwell Papers, WLU.

49   "Titine" to Kiffin, undated letter, Rockwell Papers, WLU.

Chapter Forty-one

1   Entry of 5 Mai 1916, Groupe de Bombardement No. 4, *Journal du Marches et Operations*, available on the *Mémoire des Hommes* website.

2   Victor Chapman to Elizabeth Chapman, May 6, 1916, John Jay Chapman Additional Papers, Harvard.

3   Victor Chapman to Elizabeth Chapman, May 10, 1916, John Jay Chapman Additional Papers, Harvard.

4   James McConnell to Marcelle Guerin, May 6, 1916, McConnell Collection, UVA

5   Kiffin to Paul, May 6, 1916, Rockwell Papers, WLU.

6   Thénault, *The Lafayette Escadrille*, p. 33. Thénault gets the date wrong – it was May 5, not May 10.

7   In addition to the American squadron, which flew Nieuports (N.124), there were two Maurice Farman squadrons (MF.29 and MF.123) located at Luxeuil. Entry of 5 Mai 1916, Groupe de Bombardement No. 4, *Journal du Marches et Operations*, available on the *Mémoire des Hommes* website.

8   Thénault, *The Lafayette Escadrille*, p. 34.

9   Kiffin to Paul, May 6, 1916, Rockwell Papers, WLU.

10   Thénault, *The Lafayette Escadrille*, p. 34.

11   Kiffin to Paul, May 6, 1916, Rockwell Papers, WLU.

12   Entry of 5 Mai 1916, Groupe de Bombardement No. 4, *Journal du Marches et Operations*,

available on the *Mémoire des Hommes* website.

13   Bailey & Cony, *The French Air Service War Chronology*, p. 48.

14   *A History of French Military Aviation*, p. 75.

15   "American Aviators with French Army Receive Thorough Training; Are Only Foreigners in Service," *The Washington Post*, June 11, 1916, p. ES3.

16   Kiffin to Paul, May 6, 1916, Rockwell Papers, WLU.

17   Kiffin to Paul, May 10, 1916, Rockwell Papers, WLU.

18   Victor Chapman to Elizabeth Chapman, May 6, 1916, John Jay Chapman Additional Papers, Harvard (Victor described the plane as "an old Nieuport we are bored to fly on."). It is unclear if the photo was taken before Prince wrecked the first machine; it might have been a second old *bébé* sent for the Maurice Farman pilots to practice on. *See* Victor Chapman to Conrad Chapman, May 3, 1916, *The Harvard Volunteers in Europe*, p. 230 (Correct date of letter is probably May 12).

19   *Victor Chapman's Letters From France*, p. 178.

20   *Id.* at 179.

21   Victor Chapman to William Astor Chanler, undated postcard *circa* May 14, 1916, John Jay Chapman Additional Papers, Harvard.

22   James McConnell to Paul Rockwell, May 9, 1916, McConnell Collection, UVA.

23   *Victor Chapman's Letters From France*, p. 178.

24   Hall later had "BERT" stenciled on one side, and "TREB" on the other – so passing planes could read it either way, or so he said. McConnell, *Flying for France*, p. 51.

25   Gordon, *Lafayette Escadrille Pilot Biographies*, p. 39. McConnell had nearly been expelled from Virginia when he sabotaged an unveiling of a statue of Thomas Jefferson by placing a chamber pot on its head. *Id.*

26   Kiffin to Loula, May 8, 1916, KYR Papers, NCDNCR.

27   Kiffin to Alice Weeks, May 15, 1916, Weeks, *Greater Love*, p. 135. The dates of the two letters on this page have been switched; the letter dated May 15 should be May 10 and vice versa.

28   *Victor Chapman's Letters From France*, p. 179. A *pompier* is a fireman, so the *pompier* horns must have been fire alarm horns.

29   Victor Chapman to Conrad Chapman, May 3, 1916, *The Harvard Volunteers in Europe*, p. 231 (correct date of letter is May 12). This letter must have been written on May 12, 1916, as it references "my machine," and describes "my little cockpit," phrases which show that Chapman's machine had arrived by the time this letter was written. In addition, on May 14, Chapman told his stepmother he had "made my first two trips over the enemy yesterday and the day before (wrote Conrad at length)." Victor Chapman to Elizabeth Chapman, May 14, 1916, John Jay Chapman Additional Papers, Harvard.

30   Victor Chapman to Conrad Chapman, May 3, 1916, *The Harvard Volunteers in Europe*, p. 232 (correct date of letter is May 12).

31   *Id.* at p. 233.

32   *Id.* at p. 234.

33   James McConnell to Marcelle Guerin, May 13, 1916, McConnell Collection, UVA. *See also* "Bill Thaw's Airplane Hit by Shell in German Raid," *Pittsburgh Post-Gazette*, May 18, 1916, p. 1; and "Thaw's Airplane is Hit by Shell," *Pittsburgh Chronicle-Telegraph*, *circa* May 18, 1916, clipping in William Thaw Scrapbooks, HSWP.

34   C.F. Bertelli, "Americans in Verdun Fly in Post of Honor," *The New York American*, May 18, 1916, clipping in William Thaw Scrapbooks, HSWP.

35   "American Airmen Make Daring Dash Over German Lines," *The New York World*, May 18, 1916, p. 1.

36   Elizabeth Chapman to Victor Chapman, May 18, 1916, John Jay Chapman Additional Papers, Harvard.

37   *Victor Chapman's Letters From France*, p. 186. Left out of the published letter was the culprit responsible for the exaggerated report: Jarousse de Sillac, the president of the

Franco-American Committee, who visited the *escadrille* the day after Chapman's flight. The original letter includes the line, "we made the mistake of letting de Sillac do a little publicity and he has very bad taste." Victor Chapman to Elizabeth Chapman, June 5, 1916, John Jay Chapman Additional Papers, Harvard.

38   Thénault, *The Lafayette Escadrille*, p. 33.

39   Victor Chapman to Elizabeth Chapman, May 14, 1916, Chapman, John Jay Chapman Additional Papers, Harvard. This sentence was removed when the letter was published. *See Victor Chapman's Letters From France*, p. 179.

40   Victor Chapman to William Astor Chanler, April 20, 1916, John Jay Chapman Additional Papers, Harvard ("Thénault and his Lieutenant … have to learn to ride the Nieuport, being both Caudron pilots[.]").

41   Cowdin, "The Lafayette Escadrille," *Harvard Alumni Bulletin*, March 7, 1918, p. 436.

42   Theodore Roosevelt, "Lafayettes of the Air," *Collier's*, July 29, 1916, p. 16.

43   "Six Americans Flying for France," *The New York Sun*, August 22, 1915, Section 3, p. 3 (noting that along with Jimmie Bach, Hall was "training at le Bourget on 80-horsepower Nieuport biplanes, the smallest and fastest machines used in the French army."). Gordon asserts that at Le Bourget, "Hall and Bach smashed up so many training machines that the school's authorities began to wonder if they were German spies." Gordon, *Lafayette Escadrille Pilot Biographies*, p. 73.

44   James McConnell to Paul Rockwell, May 9, 1916, McConnell Collection, UVA.

45   James McConnell to Marcelle Guerin, March 17, 1916, McConnell Collection, UVA.

46   James McConnell to Marcelle Guerin, January 28, 1916, McConnell Collection, UVA.

47   Thénault, *The Lafayette Escadrille*, p. 25, xii.

48   McConnell, *Flying for France*, p. 13.

49   James McConnell to Marcelle Guerin, May 13, 1916, McConnell Collection, UVA.

50   Victor Chapman to Conrad Chapman, May 13, 1916, *The Harvard Volunteers in Europe*, p. 235.

51   James McConnell to Marcelle Guerin, May 13, 1916, McConnell Collection, UVA.

52   Thénault, *The Lafayette Escadrille*, p. 36. Henri Farre painted a good picture of this scene in one of his famous paintings. *See* Eric W. Wood, "The Lafayette Escadrille," *Think*, p. 8 (Aug. 1957).

53   James McConnell to Marcelle Guerin, May 13, 1916, McConnell Collection, UVA.

54   *Id.*

55   Victor Chapman to Conrad Chapman, May 13, 1916, *The Harvard Volunteers in Europe*, p. 236.

56   James McConnell to Marcelle Guerin, May 13, 1916, McConnell Collection, UVA.

57   Thénault, *The Lafayette Escadrille*, p. 39.

58   *Id.* at p. 41.

59   James McConnell to Marcelle Guerin, May 13, 1916, McConnell Collection, UVA.

60   Kiffin to Paul, May 10, 1916, Rockwell Papers, WLU.

61   Hall & Nordhoff, *The Lafayette Flying Corps*, Vol. 1, p. 66.

62   James McConnell to Marcelle Guerin, May 13, 1916, McConnell Collection, UVA.

63   Conrad Chapman to Victor Chapman, April 28, 1916, John Jay Chapman Additional Papers, Harvard.

64   *Victor Chapman's Letters From France*, p. 180.

65   James McConnell to Paul Rockwell, May 28, 1916, McConnell Collection, UVA.

66   *Victor Chapman's Letters From France*, p. 180.

67   "Ambulance Corps in France Filmed," *The New York Times*, July 6, 1916, p. 11.

68   "Ambulance Film a Monument to Brave Aviator," *The Triangle*, p. 8 (October 7, 1916).

Chapter Forty-two

1   Victor Chapman to Chanler Chapman, May 17, 1916, John Jay Chapman Additional Papers, Harvard.

2   *Id.*

3   *Id.* That's 100 miles per hour. A few days earlier, Chapman had calculated his speed at almost 104 miles per hour.

4   Victor Chapman to Chanler Chapman, May 17, 1916, John Jay Chapman Additional Papers, Harvard.

5   *Id.*

6   Victor Chapman to M. de Sillac, introduction to Hall, *High Adventure*, p. xviii.

7   *See* Kiffin to Paul, May 18, 1916, Rockwell Papers, WLU.

8   McConnell to Marcelle Guerin, May 19, 1916, McConnell Collection, UVA. Chapman appended a "PS" to his letter said "The artillery report having seen Bill's *boche* fall. He got him after all." Victor Chapman to Chanler Chapman, May 17, 1916, John Jay Chapman Additional Papers, Harvard. The observers reported they saw the "appareil ennemi regagnant ses lignes en paraissant bien touché. Il est piqué á mort." ("enemy aircraft returning to its lines appearing damaged. It took a fatal nosedive." Reprinted in introduction to Hall, *High Adventure*, p. xviii.

9   "Thaw Drops Fifth Flyer," *The Chicago Daily News*, May 23, 1916, p. 1.

10 Kiffin to Paul, May 18, 1916, Rockwell Papers, WLU.

11 "American Destroys German Aeroplane," *The Chicago Daily News*, May 20, 1916, p. 2.

12 Kiffin to Paul, May 18, 1916, Rockwell Papers, WLU.

13 Without noting him by name, the journal of operations recorded Kiffin's victory on May 18: *Avion allemand abattu ce matin près de l'Hartmannswillerkopf* – German plane brought down this morning near the Hartmannswillerkopf. *See* Entry of 18 Mai 1916, Groupe de Bombardement No. 4, *Journal du Marches et Operations*, available on the *Mémoire des Hommes* website.

14 Hall, *One Man's War*, p. 132.

15 Victor Chapman to Chanler Chapman, May 17, 1916, John Jay Chapman Additional Papers, Harvard. Although this letter is dated May 17, it is clear that the postscript was written on May 18, as that is the date Kiffin shot down his first German.

16 James McConnell to Paul Rockwell, telegram dated May 18, 1916, Rockwell Papers, WLU.

17 Paul to Kiffin, May 20, 1916, Rockwell Papers, WLU.

18 Kiffin to Paul, May 18, 1916, Rockwell Papers, WLU.

19 "American Destroys German Aeroplane," *The Chicago Daily News*, May 20, 1916, p. 2.

20 "American Aviators Win French Honors," *The New York Times*, May 22, 1916, p. 2.

21 Kiffin to Alice Weeks, May 19, 1916, Weeks, *Greater Love*, p. 136-37. When Mrs. Weeks responded to her "Dear Kiffin" a few days later, she wrote:
    I wonder if I can make you understand. I want you to feel nothing about me but courage, that I am here cheering you on and helping you when I can. It is sweet of you to have felt a care of me as you have and I loved it but this is not the time for that for either you or I. I know this is war alone until we finish the Boche *and hope you will be able to think of me sometimes as an inspiration and also a home to come to when you wish one.* Alice Weeks to Kiffin, May 22, 1916, Rockwell Papers, WLU.

22 "Nouvelles bréves," *Le Rappel*, 20 Mai 1916, p. 2; "Avion Allemand Descendu," *Le Figaro*, 20 Mai 1916, p. 1; "Exploit d'un Américain," *La Lanterne*, 21 Mai 1916, p. 2; and "L'exploit du caporal aviateur Kiffin Rockwell," *Le Matin*, 22 Mai 1916, p. 1.

23 "Avion Allemand Descendu," *Le Temps*, 20 Mai 1916, p. 4; "L'aviateur américain Rockwell," *Le Temps*, 22 Mai 1916, p. 2.

24 "American Aviator Brings Down Hun," *The New York Herald*, May 20, 1916, p. 1.

25 "Relatives in Confederate Army," *The New York Herald*, May 21, 1916, p. 1.

26 "American Downs First Aeroplane He Encounters," *The New York Herald*, May 21, 1916, p. 1.

27 Hall, *One Man's War*, p. 132.

28 F.A. McKenzie, *Americans at the Front*, p. 7. *See also* "Death of Rockwell Ends Daring Career," *The Chicago Daily News*, September 25, 1916, p. 2 ("Why should we be written up for doing what our French comrades do as well every day?"). Paul later wrote that "Kiffin detested being written about, he used to request me time and again to do what I could to keep his name out of the newspapers. He often stated that his French comrades did daily, without one word of praise, much more than he did, and that it was not just that the exploits of the American aviators be given such prominence." Paul Ayres Rockwell, "Our Pioneers in the Air," *The Franco-American Weekly*, March 2, 1918, p. 3.

29 Herman Chatkoff to Kiffin, postcard dated May 21, 1916, Rockwell Papers, WLU.

30 W. Playort to Kiffin, 23 May 1916, Rockwell Papers, WLU.

31 Adjutant Daujard(?) to Kiffin, undated letter *circa* May 1916, Rockwell Papers, WLU.

32 Norman Prince to Kiffin, telegram dated May 20, 1916, Rockwell Papers, WLU.

33 Paul Pavelka to Paul Rockwell, May 21, 1916, Rockwell Papers, WLU.

34 Paul Pavelka to Paul Rockwell, May 23, 1916, Rockwell Papers, WLU.

35 Robert M. Knott to Kiffin, May 22, 1916, Rockwell Papers, WLU.

36 St. Elmo Massengale to Kiffin, May 23, 1916, Rockwell Papers, WLU.

37 "German Machine Brought Down," *The Western Sentinel*, May 23, 1916, p. 2. Loula wrote Kiffin on May 22, "I am glad for all your good work for France and very proud of you.... I am praying for and loving you." Loula to Kiffin, May 22, 1916, Rockwell Papers, WLU.

38 Loula to Paul & Kiffin, June 3, 1916, Rockwell Papers, WLU. A few weeks earlier, Agnes had written Paul a letter which sheds some light on the relationship between she and her brothers. Like Paul, Agnes was engaged to be married, and wrote: "Since I shall probably not be married until this fall or winter, let us hope that things will be so that you and Kiffin can be home at that time. I feel at times about as if I had lost my family, but I hope that we will all be together again sometime, and that before so very long. I suppose none of us have ever shown very much how we felt towards each other, but I have always loved my brothers sincerely, and have been proud of them nearly all the time, and wanted to very much all the time. I hope that there won't be any qualification of 'nearly' in the future." Agnes Rockwell to Paul Rockwell, May 9, 1916, Rockwell Papers, WLU.

39 *See* Steven A. Ruffin, *The Lafayette Escadrille*, p. 38 (2016); Murphy, *Kiffin Rockwell, the Lafayette Escadrille and the Birth of the United States Air Force*, p. 7-8; Flammer, *The Vivid Air*, p. 59; Pardoe, *The Bad Boy, Bert Hall: Aviator and Mercenary of the Skies*, p. 77; and Gordon, *Lafayette Escadrille Pilot Biographies*, p. 51. *See also* "The Story of the Bottle of Death," *The Pittsburgh Press*, September 28, 1930, World of Today Section, p. 2.

40 Gordon, *Lafayette Escadrille Pilot Biographies*, p. 51. Gordon seems to have gotten his account from Edwin Parsons' book, *I Flew With the Lafayette Escadrille* (see pages 6-7 of that book). Murphy also followed Parsons' account, as did Flammer and Pardoe. *See* Murphy, *Kiffin Rockwell, the Lafayette Escadrille and the Birth of the United States Air Force*, prologue, footnote 1; Flammer, *The Vivid Air*, p. 211-212, footnotes 19-20; and Pardoe, *The Bad Boy, Bert Hall: Aviator and Mercenary of the Skies*, p. 77, footnote 22. But Parsons did not join the unit until January 1917, four months after Kiffin died, so his story is second-hand, at best.

41 James McConnell to Paul Rockwell, May 20, 1916, McConnell Collection, UVA.

42 Any bottle sent to Luxeuil after May 20 would have missed Kiffin. As McConnell noted in his letter to Paul, he was the sole member of the unit remaining there: "We received orders to go to Bar-le-Duc and the *escadrille* flew off ... this a.m. and left me to hold down Luxeuil." James McConnell to Paul Rockwell, May 20, 1916, McConnell Collection, UVA.

43 Paul to Kiffin, May 20, 1916, Rockwell Papers, WLU.

44 *Id.*

45 *See* "Money Prizes for Airmen," *The Washington Post*, July 9, 1916, p. ES5; Hall, *High Adventure*, p. xx; and Hall, *One Man's War*, p. 133.

46   James McConnell to Paul Rockwell, May 20, 1916, McConnell Collection, UVA.

47   "Thaw Chases Flyer Over German Lines," *The Chicago Daily News*, May 22, 1916, p. 2.

48   Victor Chapman to William Chanler, May 19, 1916, John Jay Chapman Additional Papers, Harvard.

49   "American Aviators Win French Honors," *The New York Times*, May 22, 1916, p. 2.

50   "Thaw Chases Flyer Over German Lines," *The Chicago Daily News*, May 22, 1916, p. 2.

51   James McConnell to Marcelle Guerin, May 19, 1916, McConnell Collection, UVA.

52   Hall, *High Adventure*, p. xix.

53   "American Airmen Chase Two Germans to Cover," *The New York Globe*, May 22, 1916, clipping, William Thaw Scrapbooks, HSWP.

54   Thénault, "L'Escadrille La Fayette," *La Légion Étrangére (revue bimestrielle illustrée militaire et coloniale)*, No. 21, p. 28, (1940).

55   James McConnell to Paul Rockwell, May 20, 1916, McConnell Collection, UVA.

56   Thénault, *The Story of the Lafayette Escadrille*, p. 46. Thénault says no one was wounded, but the unit's journal of operations lists five wounded and five killed, all from *escadrilles* 123 and 29. Entry of 20 Mai 1916, Groupe de Bombardement No. 4, *Journal du Marches et Operations*, available on the *Mémoire des Hommes* website.

57   Service cards for each of the men are available on the *Mémoire des Hommes* website. *See also* Entry of 20 Mai 1916, Groupe de Bombardement No. 4, *Journal du Marches et Operations*, available on the *Mémoire des Hommes* website. Guillang is buried in the cemetery in Luxeuil. *Journal Officiel de la Republique Française*, 21 Mai 1922, p. 1974.

Chapter Forty-three

1   James McConnell to Paul Rockwell, May 20, 1916, McConnell Collection, UVA.

2   "American Flyer is in Luck," *The Chicago Daily News*, May 25, 1916, p. 2.

3   Edward Jablonski, *Warriors with Wings*, p. 77 (1966).

4   Thénault, *The Story of the Lafayette Escadrille*, p. 55.

5   Captain B.H. Liddell Hart, *The Real War 1914-1918*, p. 215 (1930).

6   Paul Jankowski, *Verdun: The Longest Battle of the Great War*, p. 114 (2014).

7   *A History of French Military Aviation*, p. 95.

8   Guttman, *Nieuport 11/16 Bébé vs. Fokker Eindecker, Western Front 1916*, p. 54.

9   *A History of French Military Aviation*, p. 95-96.

10   Jankowski, *Verdun: The Longest Battle of the Great War*, p. 114.

11   "Depicts Verdun Air Battles," *The Chicago Daily News*, March 22, 1916, p. 2.

12   It appears that de Rose knew Kiffin personally and had signed off on his flight log the prior November at Avord. Unfortunately, de Rose was killed on May 11 demonstrating the Nieuport *bébe* shortly before the *Escadrille Américaine* arrived.

13   Kiffin to Loula, May 23, 1916, KYR Papers, NCDNCR.

14   *See* Carroll Dana Winslow, *With the French Flying Corps*, p. 143 (1917).

15   Hall & Nordhoff, *The Lafayette Flying Corps*, Vol. 1, p. 74-76.

16   Bailey & Cony, *The French Air Service War Chronology*, p. 50.

17   *Id.*

18   "The Diary of H. Clyde Balsley," *Cross & Cockade*, Vol. 18, No. 2, p. 116 (Summer 1977).

19   *See* Laurence Rumsey, "Training an American Aviator in France," *National Service*, May 1917, p. 266; and "France Fetes Daring Americans in Flying Corps," *St. Louis Post-Dispatch*, July 9, 1916, p. 3B.

20   James McConnell to Sarah Rogers McConnell, June 13, 1916, McConnell Collection, UVA. McConnell's joke was a reference to General William Tecumseh Sherman's famous statement that "war is hell." In this same letter, McConnell suggested the war would end in three or four months, "and then I'll be a regular grocery store orator with the 'And Joffre says to me, says he' line of talk." *Id.*

21   "Bold Feats By Yankee Flyers," *The Boston Globe*, June 6, 1916, p. 4.

22   *See* Kiffin to Loula, May 23, 1916, KYR Papers, NCDNCR; and "France Fetes Daring Americans in Flying Corps," *St. Louis Post-Dispatch*, July 9, 1916, p. 3B.

23   Thénault, "L'Escadrille La Fayette," *La Légion Étrangére (revue bimestrielle illustrée militaire et coloniale)*, No. 21, p. 29, (1940). *See also* "France Fetes Daring Americans in Flying Corps," *St. Louis Post-Dispatch*, July 9, 1916, p. 3B.

24   "France Fetes Daring Americans in Flying Corps," *St. Louis Post-Dispatch*, July 9, 1916, p. 3B.

25   Thénault, *The Story of the Escadrille*, p. 48.

26   Carroll Dana Winslow, *With the French Flying Corps*, p. 145 (1917).

27   Kiffin to Loula, May 23, 1916, KYR Papers, NCDNCR.

28   Thénault, *The Story of the Lafayette Escadrille*, p. 50.

29   Parsons, *I Flew With the Lafayette Escadrille*, p. 72.

30   Kiffin to Paul, May 22, 1916, Rockwell Papers, WLU.

31   Hall, *En L'Air!*, p. 68. *See also* Bailey & Cony, *The French Air Service War Chronology*, p. 51.

32   Although he sought to avoid the limelight himself, Kiffin told Paul to "give Bertie Hall some publicity." Kiffin to Paul, May 22 and May 23, 1916, Rockwell Papers, WLU. Within days, the *New York World* and *Washington Post* each carried stories proclaiming Hall's win. "American Routs Four Germans in Air Fight," *The New York World*, May 25, 1916, p. 3; "Fights Three Aeros, Then Fells Fourth," *The Washington Post*, May 25, 1916, p. 2.

33   *The Story of the Great War*, Vol. X, p. 2964.

34   Gordon, *Lafayette Escadrille Pilot Biographies*, p. 20.

35   "Thaw Enjoys Sport of Chasing Flyers," *The Chicago Daily News*, April 11, 1916, p. 2.

36   Victor Chapman to Elizabeth Chapman, undated, *circa* late February or early March, 1916, John Jay Chapman Additional Papers, Harvard.

37   *Victor Chapman's Letters From France*, p. 181.

38   *Id.*

39   *Relevé des vols effectués pendant mois de mai – aout 1916; le chef d'escadron commandant l'aeonautique de la II armee; Hoover Institute at Stanford University, Microfilm collection 91053, Box 4, 19N 491. Ordres d'operations de l'aeronautique, execution des missions, reconnaissances aeriennes, avions d'artilleries, releves des vols executes 1914 September – 1918 October* (hereafter "*Relevé des vols effectués* [month], records of the 2nd Armée); *and Victor Chapman's Letters From France*, p. 182.

40   Hall, *En L'Air!*, p. 68.

41   "Americans Win Aerial Battle with Germans," *The New York Sun*, May 27, 1916, p. 3.

42   "Thaw Tells of Fight with Three Flyers," *The Chicago Daily News*, May 29, 1916, p. 2.

43   Thénault, *The Story of the Lafayette Escadrille*, p. 50.

44   *Id.* at p. 51. Paul wrote the pair hastily refilled their reservoirs, then joined the other men. "Kiffin Rockwell's Letters to His Brother," *Every Week*, December 3, 1917, p. 3.

45   Cowdin letter quoted in Theodore Roosevelt, "Lafayettes of the Air," *Collier's*, July 29, 1916, p. 16.

46   Thénault, *The Story of the Lafayette Escadrille*, p. 52.

47   *Id.*

48   Thénault graciously disclaimed knowledge of the culprit. "Who rushed down the first, I never knew, but everybody followed..." Thénault, "L'Escadrille La Fayette," *La Légion Étrangére (revue bimestrielle illustrée militaire et coloniale)*, No. 21, p. 28, (1940).

49   Cowdin letter quoted in Theodore Roosevelt, "Lafayettes of the Air," *Collier's*, July 29, 1916, p. 16.

50   *Id.*

51   "Americans Win Aerial Battle with Germans," *The New York Sun*, May 27, 1916, p. 3.

52   Thénault, "L'Escadrille La Fayette," *La Légion Étrangére (revue bimestrielle illustrée*

militaire et coloniale), No. 21, p. 28, (1940).

53   "Verdun Fight in Air and in Trench," *The New York Sun*, July 30, 1916, Sec. 6, p. 2. In a letter to John Jay Chapman, Allen spoke of the "extraordinary coincidence" of his being there and witnessing Victor's fight, and told John Jay "You can imagine with what interest we watched the struggle." Frederick H. Allen letter to John Jay Chapman, June 11, 1916, John Jay Chapman Additional Papers, Harvard.

54   Cowdin letter quoted in Theodore Roosevelt, "Lafayettes of the Air," *Collier's*, July 29, 1916, p. 16.

55   The most reliable source credits these to the patrol, rather than any individuals. *See* Bailey & Cony, *The French Air Service War Chronology*, p. 51.

56   *See* "Americans Bring Down Three German Planes," *The New York Times*, May 27, 1916, p. 2; "Americans Wounded," *The New York Evening Journal*, May 27, 1916, clipping, William Thaw Scrapbooks, HSWP; and "American Airmen Rout Fokkers in 8-Hour Fight," *The New York Tribune*, May 27, 1916, p. 1 (all three crediting Rockwell and Cowdin); and Guttman, *SPA124 Lafayette Escadrille*, p. 19 (Chapman and Rockwell). Perhaps each of the men deserve credit – Thénault remembered "at least three" enemy planes being seriously hit and landing one after the other. Thénault, *The Story of the Lafayette Escadrille*, p. 53. But it seems likely that one of these planes was properly assignable to Kiffin. To begin with, Kiffin told his mother that while he "couldn't tell how much damage I did," he had assisted in bringing down one plane. *See* Kiffin to Loula, May 30, 1916, KYR Papers, NCDNCR. Mrs. Weeks also suggested that Kiffin claimed credit for the victory, which was also confirmed by Bert Hall. *See* Weeks, *Greater Love*, p. 139 ("We found that Kiffin had brought down one of the three machines he was fighting and will be quite covered in decorations soon."); Hall, *One Man's War*, p. 142. A Paris paper also gave Kiffin credit for shooting down his second enemy plane that day. *See* "Dans les Airs, L'escadrille américain à Verdun," *Le Gaulois*, 31 Mai 1916, p. 2.

57   Cowdin letter quoted in Theodore Roosevelt, "Lafayettes of the Air," *Collier's*, July 29, 1916, p. 16.

58   Victor Chapman to William Astor Chanler, May 24, 1916, John Jay Chapman Additional Papers, Harvard.

59   Cowdin letter quoted in Theodore Roosevelt, "Lafayettes of the Air," *Collier's*, July 29, 1916, p. 16. Apparently, it was quite a close call – Chapman's mechanic reported that the bullet passed through his sleeve "grazing the flesh and slightly burning the skin." *Victor Chapman's Letters From France*, p. 33-34. Reading of his nephew's exploits in the *New York Herald*, Uncle Willie wrote Chapman "You must be having a hot time & I hope you are all right." William Astor Chanler to Victor Chapman, May 30, 1916, John Jay Chapman Additional Papers, Harvard.

60   Victor Chapman to William Astor Chanler, May 24, 1916, John Jay Chapman Additional Papers, Harvard.

61   *Id.*

62   Kiffin to Loula, May 30, 1916, KYR Papers, NCDNCR.

63   *Certificat d'origine de blessure de guerre*, dated 24 Mai 1916, Rockwell Papers, WLU.

64   Kiffin to Loula, May 30, 1916, KYR Papers, NCDNCR.

65   "William Thaw Back From No Man's Land," *The Boston Globe*, November 21, 1916, p. 2. A later member of the squadron stated that Thaw's "arm never straightened out completely, and he always carried it in first drinking position." Parsons, *I Flew With the Lafayette Escadrille*, p. 100.

66   "William Thaw Back from No Man's Land," *The Boston Globe*, November 21, 1916, p. 2.

67   "Thaw Tells of Fight With Three Flyers," *The Chicago Daily News*, May 29, 1916, p. 2.

68   "Americans Bring Down Three German Planes," *The New York Times*, May 27, 1916, p. 2.

69   "Thaw Tells of Fight With Three Flyers," *The Chicago Daily News*, May 29, 1916, p. 2.

70   James McConnell to Paul Rockwell, May 28, 1916, McConnell Collection, UVA.

71   Thénault's May 25 order is in the Rockwell Papers, WLU.

72   Alice Weeks to Fred Taber, May 28, 1916, Weeks, *Greater Love*, p. 138-39.

73   *Id.* at p. 139.

74   *Id.* Back in Thaw's hometown of Pittsburgh, a French pilot was telling the press that Lieutenant Thaw was known as "the American Eagle" among the French aviators. "'American Eagle' is Name French Give Airman Thaw," *The New York World*, June 1, 1916, p. 3.

75   "Les exploits de l'escadrille américaine d'aviation," *Le Matin*, 28 Mai 1916, p. 2.

76   "Les exploits des aviateurs américains," *Le Gaulois*, 28 Mai 1916, p. 3 ; and "Les aviateurs américains font merveille sur notre front," *Le Gaulois*, 29 Mai 1916, p. 4.

77   "American Airmen Rout Fokkers in 8-Hour Fight," *The New York Tribune*, May 27, 1916, p. 1; "U.S. Flyers Wounded," *The Baltimore Evening Sun*, May 27, 1916, p. 1; "Lieut. Thaw Wounded in Desperate Battle With German Aviators," *The Pittsburgh Gazette Times*, May 27, 1916, p. 1; "Thrilling Air Battle Won by Americans in France, *The Indianapolis Star*, May 27, 1916, p. 1; "Air Fight Won by Americans Aiding French, *The Chicago Daily Tribune*, May 27, 1916, p. 1; and "Americans Win 8-Hour Air Battle For France," *The San Francisco Chronicle*, May 27, 1916, p. 1.

78   "Titine" to Kiffin, May 31, 1916, Rockwell Papers, WLU.

79   "American Airmen Rout Fokkers in 8-Hour Fight," *The New York Tribune*, May 27, 1916, p. 1.

80   *Id.*

81   Loula to Kiffin and Paul, May 31, 1916, Rockwell Papers, WLU.

82   "Thaw for Legion of Honor," *The New York Sun*, May 31, 1916, p. 4.

83   Kiffin to Loula, May 30, 1916, KYR Papers, NCDNCR.

Chapter Forty-four

1   The order is available on the Department of Veterans Affairs website. *See* https://www.cem.va.gov/cem/history/memdayorder.asp (visited on March 30, 2019)

2   "Americans Observe Decoration Day in Church and at Statue in Paris," *The New York Herald*, May 31, 1916, p. 2.

3   "Aux Américains morts pour la France," *Le Figaro*, 31 Mai 1916, p. 2.

4   "Americans Observe Decoration Day in Church and at Statue in Paris," *The New York Herald*, May 31, 1916, p. 2.

5   "Paris Honors to Americans," *The Chicago Daily News*, May 31, 1916, p. 2.

6   "Americans Observe Decoration Day in Church and at Statue in Paris," *The New York Herald*, May 31, 1916, p. 2. *See also* "Service in Paris for Americans Fallen in France," *The St. Louis Post-Dispatch*, May 31, 1916, p. 17. The name of the street has since changed, and the address of what is now called the American Cathedral in Paris is *23 Avenue George V.*

7   "Americans Observe Decoration Day in Church and at Statue in Paris," *The New York Herald*, May 31, 1916, p. 2. Incredibly, over one minute of video footage of this ceremony survives, and it shows a snippet of the speech by Georges Leygues, as well as the statue covered in flowers and wreaths and what I believe to be Paul Rockwell in a few shots. In one brief shot, Bill Thaw can be seen with his arm in a sling, standing near what might be Mrs. Weeks and his sister, Henrietta Slade. *See* Our Friend France, https://www.youtube.com/watch?v=lJzq8IcGGSA (visited on July 28, 2018). I also located a photo of the crowd and the flower-covered statue from that day. *See* "Paris Honored American Heroes on Memorial Day," *The New York Sun*, July 9, 1916, Sec. 6, p. 1.

8   "Aux Américains morts pour la France," *Le Figaro*, 31 Mai 1916, p. 2.

9   *Id. See also* "En l'honneur des Américains morts pour la Patrie," *Le Gaulois*, 31 Mai 1916, p. 1.

10   "Paris Honors to Americans," *The Chicago Daily News*, May 31, 1916, p. 2.

11   "Aux Américains morts pour la France," *Le Figaro*, 31 Mai 1916, p. 2.

12   "Paris Honors to Americans," *The Chicago Daily News*, May 31, 1916, p. 2.

13   *Deeds of Heroism and Daring*, p. 143 (Elwyn A Barron, ed., 1920); Rockwell, *American Fighters*, p. 137-38.

14   Seeger, *Letters and Diary*, p. 203.

Chapter Forty-five

1   Lufbery was eight months older than Bert Hall.

2   Farré, *Sky Fighters of France*, p. 103.

3   Ed Lufbery to James Norman Hall, August 23, 1919, JNH Papers, Grinnell.

4   Dale L. Walker, "Raoul Lufbery: The Enigmatic Ace," *Aviation Quarterly*, April 1984, p. 287; Farré, *Sky Fighters of France*, p. 103.

5   Jacques Mortane, "The Lafayette Squadron," *L'Opinion*, 28 December 1918, clipping in scrapbook, Rockwell Papers, WLU.

6   "Personal Glimpses," *The Literary Digest*, p. 44, 42 (June 8, 1918).

7   Lufbery's conduct appears to have been "textbook." In fact, later one French ace who literally wrote the textbook on tactics said "the pursuit pilot ought to be an armorer. He should know his gun to the bottom, and he should take care of it equally with his motor, look each day into its condition and upkeep, assist in loading the belts, understand all possible jams and train himself in avoiding them as well as in repairing them quickly in the air. Many have neglected this essential principle. They have always regretted it." Albert Deullin, *Fighter Tactics*, as translated by Charles J. Biddle, in *Fighting Airman: The Way of the Eagle*, p. 263 (1968). In contrast, Kiffin kept himself somewhat intentionally ignorant of the workings of his machine. As he would later tell a reporter after many months of fighting at the front: "Aviators who know too much about their craft are usually nervous. They understand what it means when the motor makes a funny noise. We others go on flying blissfully ignorant and hoping for the best." "Death of Rockwell Ends Daring Career," *The Chicago Daily News*, September 25, 1916, p. 2.

8   Dale L. Walker, "Raoul Lufbery: The Enigmatic Ace," *Aviation Quarterly*, April 1984, p. 290.

9   One article noted that "Lufbery was born in France and did not see America until he was well grown. Further than that he had spent but about two of his thirty years in America when the war broke out." "Connecticut's Famous 'Ace,' Major Raoul Gervais Lufbery," *The Hartford Courant*, April 28, 1918, Part Three, p. 1.

10   "Aerial Hero Made Coffin Trimmings Before Great War," *The Bridgeport Times*, January 1, 1918, p. 3.

11   Following Lufbery's death, Simpson, Hall, Miller & Co. would give its latest silver-plated flatware pattern the name of Lufbery. *See* "Major Raoul Lufbery," pamphlet available at U.S. Army War College Library in Carlisle, Pennsylvania.

12   Marc Pourpe, "Comment Je Connus Lufbery," *La Guerre Aerienne*, 20 Decembre 1917, p. 100. *See also* Philip M. Flammer, "Lufbery: Ace of the Lafayette Escadrille," *The Air Power Historian*, January 1961, p. 14-15.

13   Philip M. Flammer, "Lufbery: Ace of the Lafayette Escadrille," *The Air Power Historian*, January 1961, p. 14-15. *See also* Paul Ayres Rockwell, "The American Ace: Lufbery," *The New France*, July 1918, p. 136.

14   Parsons, *I Flew With the Lafayette Escadrille*, p. 73.

15   Of course, "[n]othing much was said to him as he is an American." "The Diary of H. Clyde Balsley," *Cross & Cockade*, Vol. 18, No. 2, p. 115 (Summer 1977).

16   Thénault, *The Story of the Lafayette Escadrille*, p. 56.

17   "The Diary of H. Clyde Balsley," *Cross & Cockade*, Vol. 18, No. 2, p. 115 (Summer 1977). Thénault later said Balsley had "all the shyness and gentleness of a girl," but his "soul was that of a man." Thénault, *The Story of the Lafayette Escadrille*, p. 57.

18   James McConnell to Paul Rockwell May 28, 1916, McConnell Collection, UVA.

19   *Id.* A *brancard* is a stretcher.

20   James McConnell to Paul Rockwell, June 3, 1916, McConnell Collection, UVA.

21   Kiffin to Alice Weeks, June 1, 1916, Weeks, *Greater Love*, p. 131. This letter is incorrectly dated April 29, 1916.

22   *Victor Chapman's Letters From France*, p. 184.

23   Thénault, *The Story of the Lafayette Escadrille*, p. 63.

24   Kiffin to Paul, June 2, 1916, Rockwell Papers, WLU.

25   "The Diary of H. Clyde Balsley," *Cross & Cockade*, Vol. 18, No. 2, p. 116 (Summer 1977).

26   "American Fliers in Furious Flight," *The New York Tribune*, June 6, 1916, p. 6. *See also* "Americans Chased Bar-le-Duc Raiders," *The New York Times*, June 6, 1916, p. 5.

27   Kiffin to Paul, June 2, 1916, Rockwell Papers, WLU.

28   *Id.*

29   *Victor Chapman's Letters From France*, p. 185.

30   One of the American aviators reported that the approach of the fourteen German planes had been a "complete surprise," and that "before any machines could get up after them, they had completed their bombardment and returned." *See* Major James A. Logan, Jr., "Aeronautical Notes," Paris, France 20 September 1916. Office of the Military Observers with the French Army, Report 5770-142, National Archives, Record Group 165.

31   "Bold Feats by Yankee Flyers," *The Boston Globe*, June 6, 1916, p. 4.

32   "American Airmen Beat Back A Big Flock of Germans," *The St. Louis Post-Dispatch*, June 9, 1916, p. 19.

33   There is some evidence that one of the German raiding planes was forced to land behind French lines. *See* "German Aviators Murder Innocents at Bar-le-Duc," *The New York Herald*, June 2, 1916, p. 1 (noting that an Aviatik was forced to land and its two crewmembers were made prisoner).

34   "The Diary of H. Clyde Balsley," *Cross & Cockade*, Vol. 18, No. 2, p. 117 (Summer 1977); "American Fliers in Furious Flight," *The New York Tribune*, June 6, 1916, p. 6.

35   James McConnell to Paul Rockwell, June 3, 1916, McConnell Collection, UVA.

36   *Id.* Just five weeks before, McConnell had told Marcelle Guerin that he had his "first chance to practice with a mitrailleuse," and that he would not "have an opportunity of shooting one from a machine until we actually get into a fight." James McConnell to Marcelle Guerin, April 26, 1916, McConnell Collection, UVA.

37   James McConnell to Paul Rockwell, June 3, 1916, McConnell Collection, UVA; and James McConnell to Sarah Rogers McConnell, June 4, 1916, McConnell Collection, UVA.

38   James McConnell to Paul Rockwell, June 3, 1916, McConnell Collection, UVA.

39   *Id. See also* "American Fliers in Furious Flight," *The New York Tribune*, June 6, 1916, p. 6.

40   James McConnell to Paul Rockwell, June 3, 1916, McConnell Collection, UVA.

41   *Id.*

42   James McConnell to Sarah Rogers McConnell, June 4, 1916, McConnell Collection, UVA.

43   *Id.*

44   James McConnell to Paul Rockwell, June 3, 1916, McConnell Collection, UVA.

45   *Id.*

46   "German Aviators Murder Innocents at Bar-le-Duc," *The New York Herald*, June 2, 1916, p. 1. *See also* "German Aeros Kill 18 in French Town," *The New York World*, June 2, 1916, p. 4.

47   "American Fliers in Furious Flight," *The New York Tribune*, June 6, 1916, p. 6.

48   "American Airmen Beat Back A Big Flock of Germans," *The St. Louis Post-Dispatch*, June 9, 1916, p. 19.

49   Bert Hall later wrote that he always thought that the raid was "the result of a lot of ill-advised publicity we received after our first victories." Hall, *One Man's War*, p. 143.

50   *Victor Chapman's Letters From France*, p. 185. The squadron was getting plenty of publicity back home, too – Victor's father wrote him that "Your doings [and] the Am. Aviation are on everybody's lips...." John Jay Chapman to Victor Chapman, June 4, 1916, John Jay Chapman

Additional Papers, Harvard.

51 Kiffin to Paul, June 2, 1916, Rockwell Papers, WLU.

52 *Victor Chapman's Letters From France*, p. 186.

53 James McConnell to Paul Rockwell, June 15, 1916, McConnell Collection, UVA.

54 Paul Rockwell to James McConnell, June 20, 1916, Rockwell Papers, WLU.

55 Guttman, *Nieuport 11/16 Bébé vs. Fokker Eindecker, Western Front 1916*, p. 22. *See also* Thénault, *The Story of the Lafayette Escadrille*, p. 24.

56 *The Fokker Monoplanes*, Profile Publications No. 38, p. 5. The foregoing pamphlet states: "The likelihood that Fokker personally had anything to do with the design of the mechanical interrupter gear ... can be dismissed, and there is little doubt that the mechanism that Fokker proudly took back ... was designed by Heinrich Luebbe, Fritz Heber and Leimberger." *Id.*

57 "Thaw Enjoys Sport of Chasing Flyers," *The Chicago Daily News*, April 11, 1916, p. 2.

58 Mason, *The Lafayette Escadrille*, p. 60.

59 "Leading a Battle Charge in an Aeroplane," *The Pittsburgh Dispatch*, August 18, 1918, clipping, William Thaw Scrapbooks, HSWP.

60 Bert Hall, "Fast Fighting and Narrow Escapes in the Air," *The American Magazine*, p. 45 (Sep. 1918).

61 Christopher T. Carey, *A Brief History of US Military Aviation Oxygen Breathing Systems*, p. 2.

62 Kiffin to Paul, June 17, 1916, Rockwell Papers, WLU.

63 "France Fetes Daring Americans in Flying Corps," *The St. Louis Post-Dispatch*, July 9, 1916, p. 3B-4B.

64 *Id.*

Chapter Forty-six

1 "The Diary of H. Clyde Balsley," *Cross & Cockade*, Vol. 18, No. 2, p. 117-18 (Summer 1977). Rumsey gave a similar description. *See* Lawrence Rumsey, "Training an American Aviator in France," *National Service*, May 1917, p. 266 ("From high up the country beyond Verdun looks just like a plowed field. It is all brown, and all the trees have been swept away by shells and fire."). McConnell probably gave the most vivid account: "Peaceful fields and farms and villages adorned that landscape a few months ago – when there was no Battle of Verdun. Now there is only that sinister brown belt, a strip of murdered Nature. It seems to belong to another world. Every sign of humanity has been swept away. The woods and roads have vanished like chalk wiped from the blackboard; of the villages nothing remains but gray smears where stone walls have tumbled together." McConnell, *Flying for France*, p. 33.

2 "The Diary of H. Clyde Balsley," *Cross & Cockade*, Vol. 18, No. 2, p. 117 (Summer 1977).

3 "Thaw Describes Work Done by American Airmen," *The Pittsburg Press*, November 21, 1916, p. 4.

4 "The Story of the Lafayette Escadrille," *The Bellman*, July 20, 1918, p. 68.

5 *Victor Chapman's Letters From France*, p. 182.

6 Gordon, *Lafayette Escadrille Pilot Biographies*, p. 99.

7 "The Diary of H. Clyde Balsley," *Cross & Cockade*, Vol. 18, No. 2, p. 107 (Summer 1977).

8 Paul to Kiffin, June 5, 1916, Rockwell Papers, WLU.

9 James McConnell to Paul Rockwell, June 15, 1916, McConnell Collection, UVA. McConnell didn't exclude himself from his own high standard, acknowledging that he "felt that way about myself at times." *Id.* McConnell knew Rumsey in flight school, where Rumsey had apparently snuck off to Paris at least twice and may have been briefly jailed for desertion. *See* James McConnell to Marcelle Guerin, March 2, 1916, McConnell Collection, UVA; James McConnell to Marcelle Guerin, April 10, 1916, McConnell Collection, UVA; and James McConnell to Lewis Crenshaw, May 1, 1916, McConnell Collection, UVA

10   Bert Hall, "Fast Fighting and Narrow Escapes in the Air," *The American Magazine*, p. 43 (Sep. 1918) ("I never have drunk liquor.").

11   Victor Chapman to Elizabeth Chapman, May 14, 1916, John Jay Chapman Additional Papers, Harvard. Paul Rockwell told one man that Hall "had a mouth like a sewer." E.R. Van Gorder, "Bert Hall – Soldier or Scoundrel?", *Cross & Cockade*, Vol. 4, No. 3, p. 275 (Autumn 1963).

12   Hall, *En L'Air!*, p. 149.

13   *Victor Chapman's Letters From France*, p. 189.

14   "The Story of the Lafayette Escadrille," *The Bellman*, July 20, 1918, p. 70; Hall, *One Man's War*, p. 139.

15   Thénault, "L'Escadrille La Fayette," *La Légion Étrangére (revue bimestrielle illustrée militaire et coloniale)*, No. 21, p. 29, (1940).

16   Kiffin to Alice Weeks, June 5, 1916, Weeks, *Greater Love*, p. 140. See also *War Letters*, p. 196.

17   "American Aviators in One Escadrille," *The New York Sun*, August 6, 1916, p. 2. They probably also had a recording of "The Saucy Little Bird on Nellie's Hat," and another Al Jolson song, "You Made Me Love You." *See* Ruth Dunbar, *The Swallow*, p. 149, and "Severely Wounded," *The Century Magazine*, February 1919, p. 519.

18   Performed by Frederick Wheeler, with lyrics by George Graff and music by Jack Glogau. The Library of Congress has a copy you can listen to at this website: (https://www.loc.gov/item/jukebox.4342/)

19   The Republican convention was held in the Coliseum at 15th Street and Wabash Avenue while the Progressive convention met in the Auditorium building at Michigan Avenue and Congress Parkway.

20   "Hughes Accepts Republican Nomination for President; Declares for Upholding American Rights on Land and Sea; Roosevelt, Named by Moose, Declines; He's 'Out of Politics,'" *The New York Times*, June 11, 1916, p. 1.

21   "Text of Hughes's Message, Accepting the Nomination, and Attacking the Wilson Administration," *The New York Times*, June 11, 1916, p. 1.

22   *Official Report of the Proceedings of the Democratic National Convention, Held in St. Louis, Missouri, June 14, 15 and 16th, 1916*, p. 84.

23   Theodore Roosevelt, "Lafayettes of the Air," *Collier's*, July 29, 1916, p. 16.

24   "Roosevelt Declines Progressive Nomination," *The Commoner*, July 1916, p. 25.

25   Gordon, *Lafayette Escadrille Pilot Biographies*, p. 101.

26   *Id.* at p. 103.

27   James McConnell to Paul Rockwell, June 21, 1916, McConnell Collection, UVA.

28   Gordon, *Lafayette Escadrille Pilot Biographies*, p. 105-106.

29   *Relevé des vols effectués pendant le mois de mai 1916*, records of the 2nd Armée.

30   Paul to Kiffin, June 5, 1916, Rockwell Papers, WLU.

31   James McConnell to Marcelle Guerin, June 13, 1916, McConnell Collection, UVA.

32   "American Flyers Attacked," *The Chicago Daily News*, June 7, 1916, p. 4.

33   Kiffin to Paul, June 11, 1916, Rockwell Papers, WLU.

34   "Lion is U.S. Flyer's Mascot," *The Chicago Daily News*, September 14, 1916, p. 2. Several of the dogs and the little fox can be seen in the video of the crew in the movie *Our Friend France*, at about the 48:45 mark.

35   Bert Hall, "Fast Fighting and Narrow Escapes in the Air," *The American Magazine*, September 1918, p. 45.

36   "Lion is U.S. Flyer's Mascot," *The Chicago Daily News*, September 14, 1916, p. 2.

37   "War Aviator in Flight with Goat," *The Chicago Daily News*, November 11, 1915, p. 6. The article has a good photo of Hall, and the goat.

38   Bert Hall, "Fast Fighting and Narrow Escapes in the Air," *The American Magazine*, September 1918, p. 45.

39   Kiffin to Alice Weeks, June 23, 1916, Weeks, *Greater Love*, p. 148. Paul told a friend back

home that while at the front, Kiffin and Victor "roomed together and flew together much." "'Actual Fighting Will be Over by Fall of 1917,' Says Paul Rockwell in Letter to Atlanta Friend," *The Atlanta Constitution*, July 30, 1916, p. A11.

40   *Relevé des vols effectués pendant le mois de mai / juin 1916*, records of the 2nd Armée.

41   Lt. Col. Philippe D. Rogers, *L'Escadrille Lafayette: Unité Volontaire de Combat Oubliée de l'Amérique*, Chapter 6 (available at http://www.institut-strategie.fr/Arogers_6.htm) (visited September 1, 2018)

42   This excludes only Raoul Lufbery and Didier Masson, both of whom were born and raised in France.

43   Hall, *One Man's War*, 132. One Hall biographer pegs Thaw as Hall's closest friend in the squadron. *See* Pardoe, *The Bad Boy, Bert Hall: Aviator and Mercenary of the Skies*, p. 96.

44   Hall, *One Man's War*, p. 126. Hall seems to indicate this was in May, but McConnell got lost on June 1.

45   James McConnell to Paul Rockwell, May 28, 1916, McConnell Collection, UVA.

46   Paul to Kiffin, June 5, 1916, Rockwell Papers, WLU.

47   Cowdin letter quoted in Theodore Roosevelt, "Lafayettes of the Air," *Collier's*, July 29, 1916, p. 16.

48   Paul to Kiffin, June 12, 1916, Rockwell Papers, WLU.

49   Kiffin to Paul, June 5, 1916, Rockwell Papers, WLU.

50   Paul told Kiffin he "ought to have two," and that "if your citations are not coming along to your liking, let me know and I will have the matter looked into at once." Paul to Kiffin, June 12, 1916, Rockwell Papers, WLU.

51   Hall & Nordhoff, *The Lafayette Flying Corps*, Vol. 1, p. 408.

52   James McConnell to Paul Rockwell, June 8, 1916, McConnell Collection, UVA.

53   James McConnell to Paul Rockwell, June 15, 1916, McConnell Collection, UVA.

54   Of course, Thaw was still on leave in Paris and had no official flights in either June or July.

55   *Relevé des vols effectués pendant le mois de juin 1916*, records of the 2nd Armée.

56   Robert L. Cavanagh, "U.S. Army Intelligence Report on L'Escadrille Americaine," *Cross & Cockade*, Vol. 20, No. 1, p. 39 (Spring 1979).

57   Major James A. Logan, Jr., "American Aviators Serving in French Army," Paris, France 30 June 1916. War Department, Office Chief of Staff, War College Division Report WCD-5770-127, National Archives, Record Group 165.

58   *See* Alan D. Toelle, "A White-Faced Cow and the Operational History of the Escadrille Américaine N.124 to September 1916," *Over the Front*, Vol. 24, No. 4, p. 335 (Winter 2009). Kiffin totaled 141.2 hours during those same three months.

59   James McConnell to Paul Rockwell, June 26, 1916, McConnell Collection, UVA.

60   *See, e.g.*, Lt. Col. Philippe D. Rogers, *L'Escadrille Lafayette: Unité Volontaire de Combat Oubliée de l'Amérique*, Chapter 6 (available at http://www.institut-strategie.fr/Arogers_6.htm) (visited September 1, 2018); and Gordon, Lafayette Escadrille Pilot Biographies, p. 45 (referring to "a seething hostility which had existed for some time between Prince and Kiffin Rockwell.").

61   Thénault, *The Story of the Lafayette Escadrille*, p. 72.

Chapter Forty-seven

1   Elizabeth Chapman to Victor Chapman, June 8, 1916, John Jay Chapman Additional Papers, Harvard.

2   *Id.*

3   John Jay Chapman to Victor Chapman, June 4, 1916, John Jay Chapman Additional Papers, Harvard.

4   Elizabeth Chapman to Victor Chapman, June 8, 1916, John Jay Chapman Additional Papers, Harvard.

5 Kiffin to Paul, June 5, 1916, Rockwell Papers, WLU. The dead pilot was Caporal Rodolphe Filaines and the injured mechanic was Soldat Gabriel Chaux. *See* Bailey & Cony, *The French Air Service War Chronology*, p. 53.

6 "The Diary of H. Clyde Balsley," *Cross & Cockade*, Vol. 18, No. 2, p. 118 (Summer 1977). As one sharp-eyed historian has noted, Balsley's diary entry is misdated June 16; the proper date should be June 11. Alan D. Toelle, "A White-Faced Cow and the Operational History of the Escadrille Américaine N.124 to September 1916," *Over the Front*, Vol. 24, No. 4, p. 301 (Winter 2009).

7 Bailey & Cony, *The French Air Service War Chronology*, p. 53.

8 Kiffin to Loula, June 14, 1916, KYR Papers, NCDNCR.

9 *See* Thénault, *The Story of the Lafayette Escadrille*, p. 48 (noting that the villa "soon became the rendezvous at lunch hour for all the French pilots passing through Bar-le-Duc.").

10 Bailey & Cony, *The French Air Service War Chronology*, p. 53-54; Don Hollway, *The Eagle of Lille*, (available at www.donhollway.com/immelmann/) (visited on September 7, 2018); and "Immelmann Killed by Airship's Fall, Is Report," *The New York World*, June 22, 1916, p. 4.

11 Manfred von Richtofen, *The Red Air Fighter*, p. 79 (London, 1918).

12 "France Fetes Daring Americans in Flying Corps," *The St. Louis Post-Dispatch*, July 9, 1916, p. 4B.

13 Kiffin to Paul, June 17, 1916, Rockwell Papers, WLU.

14 "Boelke Still Fighting, American Airmen Say," *The New York Times*, June 21, 1916, p. 6.

15 Kiffin to Elizabeth Chapman, June 30, 1916, *War Letters*, p. 140. (The actual date of this letter is August 10, 1916. *See* Kiffin to Elizabeth Chapman, August 10, 1916, KYR Papers, NCDNCR; and *Victor Chapman's Letters From France*, p. 38). *See also* Bailey & Cony, *The French Air Service War Chronology*, p. 53 (crediting Chapman with a FTL – forced to land).

16 Thénault, *The Story of the Lafayette Escadrille*, p. 57. *See also* Kiffin to Paul, June 17, 1916, Rockwell Papers, WLU.

17 Kiffin to Paul, June 17, 1916, Rockwell Papers, WLU.

18 However, one knowledgeable source says that Chapman and his fellow pilots "were convinced he had tangled with Boelcke, but [Walter] Höhndorf is a far more likely candidate." Greg Van Wyngarden, *Early German Aces of World War I*, p. 57.

19 Kiffin told Paul that in one of his flights that day he had "dropped straight down from 4,050 meters to 1,800 meters on top of a *boche*, but he got away." Kiffin to Paul, June 17, 1916, Rockwell Papers, WLU.

20 Boelcke, *An Aviator's Field Book*, p. 134. One serious scholar hypothesizes that the plane that alerted Boelcke was forced down by Chapman, and maybe that's so. *See* Alan D. Toelle, "A White-Faced Cow and the Operational History of the Escadrille Américaine N.124 to September 1916," *Over the Front*, Vol. 24, No. 4, p. 306 (Winter 2009). But the enemy aircraft Chapman was credited with forcing down that day landed in Béthincourt, not Sivry. Bailey & Cony, *The French Air Service War Chronology*, p. 53. Perhaps the German plane that landed and alerted Boelcke was the one which Kiffin "dropped straight down from 4,050 to 1,800 meters on top of..." Kiffin to Paul, June 17, 1916, Rockwell Papers, WLU. After forcing down that plane, Kiffin and the others went home, while Chapman landed at Vadelaincourt and refueled. When Chapman went back up, he met Boelcke, who had risen in the meantime. According to his "*certificat d'origine de blessure*," signed by Thénault, Bert Hall and Prince, Chapman was wounded at 12:45 p.m. above Belleville, which lies about midway between Vadelaincourt and Sivry. *See* "*Certificat d'origine de blessure*," dated 21 Juin 1916, John Jay Chapman Additional Papers, Harvard. After Chapman was wounded, he landed at either Froidos or Vadelaincourt (although Vadelaincourt is closer to Belleville, Kiffin stated Chapman landed at Froidos) and, after being treated and bandaged, and having his plane patched up, he flew back to Bar-le-Duc, arriving at 3:30 p.m. Alan D. Toelle, "A White-Faced Cow and the Operational History of the Escadrille Américaine N.124

to September 1916," *Over the Front*, Vol. 24, No. 4, p. 303 (Winter 2009).

21   The hypotheses in the foregoing endnote also accounts for the six planes the German pilot claimed to have seen.

22   Boelcke, *An Aviator's Field Book*, p. 134.

23   Professor Johannes Werner, *Knight of Germany: Oswald Boelcke, German Ace*, p. 176-77.

24   *Id.* at p. 177. The planes chasing Boelcke must have been from a French *escadrille*.

25   "Boelke Still Fighting, American Airmen Say," *The New York Times*, June 21, 1916, p. 6; "Chapman's Opponent," *The New York Times*, June 30, 1916, p. 5 (confirms that Boelcke was piloting an all-black plane).

26   "Boelke Still Fighting, American Airmen Say," *The New York Times*, June 21, 1916, p. 6. This letter was likely the last letter Chapman ever wrote; at least there are none dated later in his posthumously-published book.

27   *See* "Certificat d'origine de blessure," dated 21 Juin 1916, John Jay Chapman Additional Papers, Harvard. Medical assistant Georges Becus treated Chapman's wound.

28   *See e.g.*, Thénault, *The Story of the Lafayette Escadrille*, opposite p. 52; *The Story of the Great War*, Vol. X, following p. 2698; *Le Monde Illustre*, 29 Juillet 1916, p. 66. The last source shows Victor, head bandaged, speaking to personnel surrounded by planes. Interestingly, Bill Thaw is in the same picture, which shows that he must have come back to visit the *escadrille* at this time. The same photo appears to show Lufbery with his back to the camera. Thaw's visit is corroborated in a letter McConnell wrote to a friend on June 18, thanking her for the box of candy Thaw had brought out. *See* James McConnell to Marcelle Guerin, June 18, 1916, McConnell Collection, UVA.

29   "N.Y. Aviator Wounded in Fight with Six Germans," *The New York Sun*, June 20, 1916, p. 5.

30   "N.Y. Aviator Wounded in Fight with Six Germans," *The New York Sun*, June 20, 1916, p. 5; and "Chapman, Shot in Air, Barely Escapes Death," *The New York World*, June 21, 1916, p. 5.

31   Elizabeth Chapman to Victor Chapman, June 22, 1916, John Jay Chapman Additional Papers, Harvard.

32   "Chapman, Shot in Air, Barely Escapes Death," *The New York World*, June 21, 1916, p. 5.

33   "Yankee Flyers as Skillful as Allies or Foes," *The Chicago Tribune*, November 12, 1916, Part 2, p. 2.

34   *Victor Chapman's Letters From France*, p. 39. One of his superiors stated that Chapman paid "more attention to attacking the enemy than to watching whether the enemy is attacking him." "New York Flier Dies in Battle," *The New York Evening Sun*, June 24, 1916, p. 1.

35   *See also Victor Chapman's Letters From France*, p. 40.

36   *Victor Chapman's Letters From France*, p. 33.

37   James McConnell to Marcelle Guerin, June 18, 1916, McConnell Collection, UVA.

38   The next week, Chanler sent Kiffin the huge sum of one thousand francs as a contribution to the common "*popote*," telling him "you must have no hesitancy in accepting this because it comes from Uncle Willie." William Astor Chanler to Kiffin, June 26, 1916, Rockwell Papers, WLU.

39   *Victor Chapman's Letters From France*, p. 40.

40   *Id.* at p. 188.

41   "Boelke Still Fighting, American Airmen Say," *The New York Times*, June 21, 1916, p. 6.

42   "Immelmann Killed by Airship's Fall, Is Report," *The New York World*, June 22, 1916, p. 4.

43   "U.S. Airmen Rout German Fliers," *The New York Tribune*, July 13, 1916, p. 4. It is not likely that Lufbery's opponent was Boelcke. *See* Greg Van Wyngarden, *Early German Aces of World War I*, p. 57.

44   Loula to Kiffin, July 13, 1916, Rockwell Papers, WLU.

45   James McConnell to Marcelle Guerin, June 18, 1916, McConnell Collection, UVA.

46   "3 American Aeros Fight 40 Germans; One Badly Injured," *The New York World*, June 22, 1916, p. 4.

47 James McConnell to Marcelle Guerin, June 18, 1916, McConnell Collection, UVA.
48 Kiffin to Paul, June 19, 1916, Rockwell Papers, WLU. Kiffin's account as given in this letter was clearly the basis for the report in the *New York World* a few days later. *See* "3 American Aeros Fight 40 Germans; One Badly Injured," *The New York World*, June 22, 1916, p. 4.
49 "The Story of the Lafayette Escadrille," *The Bellman*, July 20, 1918, p. 70.
50 Kiffin to Paul, June 19, 1916, Rockwell Papers, WLU.
51 "3 U.S. Airmen Fight 40 of Foe," *The New York Tribune*, June 22, 1916, p. 6.
52 Kiffin to Paul, June 19, 1916, Rockwell Papers, WLU.
53 "The Story of the Lafayette Escadrille," *The Bellman*, July 20, 1918, p. 70.
54 "Severely Wounded," *The Century Magazine*, February 1919, p. 517.
55 "Wounded U.S. Flyer Proves He Is A Stoic," *The Chicago Daily News*, August 14, 1916, p. 2.
56 "The Story of the Lafayette Escadrille," *The Bellman*, July 20, 1918, p. 71.
57 *Id.*
58 "San Antonio Aviator Wounded; Wins Medals in European War," *The San Antonio Express*, June 23, 1916, clipping in Horace Clyde Balsley Personal Papers, SC.10013, San Diego Air & Space Museum Archives.
59 The cablegram, with a handwritten note from Balsley's mother describing the circumstances under which it arrived, are in the Horace Clyde Balsley Personal Papers, SC.10013, San Diego Air & Space Museum Archives.
60 Balsley later reported that just before his last ill-fated flight, Chapman had referenced the star painted on Balsley's fuselage in honor of Texas, the Lone Star State, and told him "Prove yourself the star." "Brave Deeds of Young Texas Aviator Bring Honors in France," *The Asheville Citizen*, October 22, 1916, p. 33.
61 Kiffin to Paul, June 19, 1916, Rockwell Papers, WLU. Paul responded that he was "indeed sorry to hear about poor Balsley. I hope the lad is not seriously touched and that his wound is clean. All of you seem to be having close shaves. I will be glad when the war is over, for it is telling on my nerves." Paul to Kiffin, June 20, 1916, Rockwell Papers, WLU.
62 James McConnell to Paul Rockwell, June 21, 1916, McConnell Collection, UVA.
63 Paul to Kiffin, June 22, 1916, Rockwell Papers, WLU.
64 "Severely Wounded," *The Century Magazine*, February 1919, p. 522-23.
65 James McConnell to Marcelle Guerin, June 23, 1916, McConnell Collection, UVA.
66 *Victor Chapman's Letters From France*, p. 32-33.

Chapter Forty-eight

1 Hall, *One Man's War*, p. 146.
2 James McConnell, "Flying for France," *The World's Work*, November 1916, p. 48.
3 James McConnell to Marcelle Guerin, June 23, 1916, McConnell Collection, UVA.
4 Most of the boys believed he had been shot in the head before falling forward on his stick. *See* "Chapman's Machine Riddled," *The Chicago Daily News*, June 26, 1916, p. 2.
5 Kiffin to Alice Weeks, June 23, 1916, Weeks, *Greater Love*, p. 148.
6 James McConnell to Marcelle Guerin, June 23, 1916, McConnell Collection, UVA.
7 "Severely Wounded," *The Century Magazine*, February 1919, p. 524.
8 *Id. See also* "La Guerre Airienne - Mort d'un pilote américain," *Le Figaro*, 25 Juin 1916, p. 2; and "Mr. Victor Chapman Died Fighting on the Verdun Front," *The New York Herald*, June 25, 1916, p. 2.
9 James McConnell to Paul Rockwell, June 25, 1916, McConnell Collection, UVA. McConnell missed Chapman as much as anyone. He felt Chapman's "heart was as big as a house," and wrote several friends expressing the esteem in which he held Victor. *See* Hervier, *The American Volunteers with the Allies*, p. 103. For instance, he told one friend that Chapman "was one of the finest men I have ever known," and another that Chapman "was the best – and as a man he was one of those rare types who, broadened by the world, had not been

disillusioned." James McConnell to Lewis Crenshaw, July 2, 1916, McConnell Collection, UVA; and James McConnell to Henry Suckley, June 28, 1916, McConnell Collection, UVA. To still another he wrote: "We are all terribly grieved over the death of poor, old Victor. He was the best and bravest of us all and I admired him more than any man I knew. He was a wonderful character and a great loss to the world as well as the French Army. As a soldier he was the most conscientious I've ever known." James McConnell to Henry Suckley, June 29, 1916, John Jay Chapman Additional Papers, Harvard.

10   Georges Thénault to John Jay Chapman, 24 Juin 1916, John Jay Chapman Additional Papers, Harvard. Even many years later, Thénault still felt the loss. "Glory to Chapman," he wrote. "Men like him are the pride of a Nation, their names should ever be spoken with respect." Thénault, *The Story of the Lafayette Escadrille*, p. 61.

11   Thénault called Thaw as soon as they learned of Chapman's fate. Paul Rockwell happened to be having dinner with Thaw in Paris that Friday night, and so learned the news as well, and could not sleep that night. "Somehow the loss is a personal one to me," Paul told Kiffin. "From seeing Victor the few times I did, I formed a higher regard for him than for any of the other boys and he was very sympathetic to me in many ways. It is the good ones that go first." Paul to Kiffin, June 25, 1916, Rockwell Papers, WLU. The next month, Paul was quoted as saying "He had a charming personality and was absolutely without fear." "'Actual Fighting Will Be Over by Fall of 1917,' Says Paul Rockwell in Letter to Atlanta Friend," *The Atlanta Constitution*, July 30, 1916, p. A11.

12   "American Aviator Killed at Verdun 8000 Feet in Air," *The St. Louis Post-Dispatch*, June 25, 1916, p. A1; "Chapman, Daring American Flyer, Slain in the Air," *The New York World*, June 25, 1916, p. 5.

13   Hall, *En L'Air!*, p. 153.

14   Prince, *A Volunteer Who Died for the Cause He Loved*, p. 34. *See also* Norman Prince to his family, *circa* June 26, 1916, *The Harvard Volunteers in Europe*, p. 237.

15   Kiffin told Loula that Victor was his "best friend in the *escadrille*," and that he "was one of the finest boys I ever knew, the most courageous and the strongest character." Kiffin to Loula, June 30, 1916, Rockwell Papers, WLU. John Jay Chapman later wrote that "Of all the men that Victor met in the aviation corps Kiffin Rockwell was the dearest to him," and that Victor "worshipped Rockwell's courage and romantic spirit." Chapman, *Victor Chapman's Letters From France*, p. 38.

16   Kiffin to Paul, June 23, 1916, Rockwell Papers, WLU. *See also* "Chapman Hailed as Hero by French," *The New York Sun*, June 26, 1916, p. 5.

17   *Victor Chapman's Letters From France*, p. 39.

18   Kiffin to Alice Weeks, June 23, 1916, Weeks, *Greater Love*, p. 148. As this letter speaks of "last night" being the date of Chapman's death, it must have been written on June 24.

19   Alice Weeks to Allen Weeks, June 25, 1916, Weeks, *Greater Love*, p. 149.

20   *See* "L'escadrille américaine," *Le Temps*, 1 Juillet 1916, p. 4; "Mr. Victor Chapman Died Fighting on the Verdun Front," *The New York Herald*, June 25, 1916, p. 2; "U.S. Flyer Dies in Fight," *The Chicago Daily News*, June 24, 1916, p. 1; "Victor Chapman, American Airman, Killed at Verdun," *The Brooklyn Daily Eagle*, June 24, 1916, p. 1; "American Flyer Dies in Air Battle After Bagging Two Germans," *The Pittsburg Press*, June 24, 1916, p. 1; and "Chapman is Killed in Aeroplane Fight," *The New York Times*, June 25, 1916, p. 8. *See also* "Chapman Hailed as Hero by French," *The New York Sun*, June 26, 1916, p. 5.

21   "Un Roi de l'Air," *L'Opinion*, 1 Juillet 1916, p. 16. *See also* "Chapman's Heroism Wins High Tribute," *The New York Sun*, July 2, 1916, p. 2.

22   "Victor Chapman, N.Y. Flier, Killed in Verdun Airfight; Wrecked Three Aeroplanes," *The New York Evening World*, June 24, 1916, p. 1. The *New York Sun* also ran a nice photo, and noted that Chapman was killed while aiding his comrades. "American Flier Chapman Killed in Verdun Fight," *The New York Sun*, June 25, 1916, p. 7.

23   "Chapman Died While Fetching Orange for Friend," *The New York Evening World*, June

30, 1916, p. 13. *See also* "Chapman Slain on Errand of Mercy," *The New York Sun*, July 1, 1916, p. 5; and "Victor Chapman Died While on an Errand of Mercy," *The Syracuse Herald*, June 30, 1916, p. 4.

24   "American Flier Dead," *The Washington Post*, June 25, 1916, p. 3; "Victor Chapman, N.Y. Flier, Killed in Verdun Airfight; Wrecked Three Aeroplanes," *The New York Evening World*, June 24, 1916, p. 1; "Chapman, Daring American Flyer, Slain in the Air," *The New York World*, June 25, 1916, p. 5; and "Died In Good Cause, Says Father," *The Chicago Daily News*, June 24, 1916, p. 1.

25   Letter from John Jay Chapman to Jusserand dated June 27, 1916, *Extrait du Bulletin de la Societe autour du monde*, Juillet-October 1916, p. 7

26   John Jay Chapman to Henry Howell van Cleef, August 3, 1916, copy in Brown University Library.

27   *Victor Chapman's Letters From France*, p. 38.

28   *Id.* at 42-43.

29   Elizabeth Chapman to Kiffin, September 5, 1916, Rockwell Papers, WLU.

30   Thénault, "L'Escadrille La Fayette," *La Légion Étrangére (revue bimestrielle illustrée militaire et coloniale)*, No. 21, p. 28-29, (1940).

31   Undated Thénault letter, as quoted in clipping included in June 4, 1917 letter from S.P. McConnell to John Jay Chapman, John Jay Chapman Additional Papers, Harvard.

32   James McConnell to Paul Rockwell, June 25, 1916, McConnell Collection, UVA.

33   James McConnell to Paul Rockwell, June 21, 1916, McConnell Collection, UVA.

34   *Relevé des vols effectués pendant le mois de juin 1916*, records of the 2nd Armée.

35   Paul to Kiffin, June 30, 1916, Rockwell Papers, WLU. Despite any issues he may have had at Bar-le-Duc, Cowdin's overall record in France was strong. Not only was he the first American to shoot down an enemy airplane in combat, but he flew with distinction over various parts of the front for more than one year.

36   Pardoe, *The Bad Boy, Bert Hall: Aviator and Mercenary of the Skies*, p. 87. This reason may not have been entirely false, for Elliott apparently spent some time in August at V.R.75, an auxiliary aviation hospital in Viry-Châtillon. One record available on the *Mémoire des Hommes* website notes that Cowdin came to a Versailles hospital on August 10 and transferred to Viry on August 13. After this, Cowdin secured a posting with the British Military Aviation Section in Paris, but there is no indication that he did any flying for the Royal Flying Corps, and he was released from this assignment in late December. Elliott Cowdin returned to America in January 1917. *See* letter from Robert Innes Ker dated 23 Decembre 1916, in Cowdin's emergency passport application dated January 18, 1917, available on Ancestry.com.

37   *See* "Americans Decorated for French Air Feats," *The New York Sun*, June 30, 1916, p. 1.

38   Mason, *The Lafayette Escadrille*, p. 83.

39   James McConnell to Paul Rockwell, June 26, 1916, McConnell Collection, UVA. Chapman had been named for the military medal prior to his death. *See* "Aviator Thaw, Wounded, Wins Legion of Honor," *The Pittsburgh Gazette Times*, June 23, 1916, p. 1.

40   Kiffin to Alice Weeks, June 26, 1916, Weeks, *Greater Love*, p. 149.

41   Major James A. Logan, Jr., "American Aviators Serving in French Army," Paris, France, 30 June 1916. War Department, Office Chief of Staff, War College Division Report WCD-5770-127, National Archives, Record Group 165.

42   Lieutenant Colonel Spencer Cosby, "Americans Serving in French Army," Paris, France, 30 June 1916. American Embassy, Office of the Military Attache, 5770-129, National Archives, Record Group 165. As of the end of June, no such application had been submitted.

43   "American Aviators Abroad," *The Chicago Daily Tribune*, June 20, 1916, p. 8.

44   James McConnell to Paul Rockwell, June 26, 1916, McConnell Collection, UVA.

45   One scholarly article notes that "[o]nly one out of several hundred Harvard men [who volunteered before America entered the war] decided to join the German army." Axel

Jansen, "Heroes or Citizens? The 1916 Debate on Harvard Volunteers in the 'European War,'" chapter 9 in *War Volunteering in Modern Times* (Krüger & Levsen, ed. 2011), p. 155.

46 "Asks American Airmen to Return From France," *The New York Times*, June 21, 1916, p. 5. *See also* "U.S. Fliers in French Army Invited Back," *The New York Sun*, June 21, 1916, p. 2. At the same time, the *Washington Post* joined in the action, editorializing that the "aviation clubs and individual aviators owe it to the country to come forward at this time and volunteer their services...." "Volunteer Aviators," *The Washington Post*, June 23, 1916, p. 6.

47 However, almost immediately an article appeared in the *New York Times* declaring that the volunteers were "prevented from replying by the fact that they have enlisted in the French Army for the duration of the war and are subject to army discipline." "American Aviators Must Stay in France," *The New York Times*, June 23, 1916, p. 4.

48 James McConnell to Lewis Crenshaw, July 2, 1916, McConnell Collection, UVA.

49 "War Flier Plans to Try for the Pulitzer Trophy," *The St. Louis Post-Dispatch*, June 10, 1916, p. 3.

50 In June and July, Hall totaled only 23 flights and just over 37 hours. *Relevé des vols effectués pendant le mois de juin et juillet 1916*, records of the 2nd Armée.

51 An American military observer was also told that Winslow "was not much good and would hardly be worthy of consideration" for use in America. *See* Major James A. Logan, Jr., "Aeronautical Notes," Paris, France 20 September 1916. Office of the Military Observers with the French Army, Report 5770-142, National Archives, Record Group 165.

52 James McConnell to Paul Rockwell, July 1, 1915, McConnell Collection, UVA. This letter is misdated 1915, the correct date is 1916. One author asserted that Hall had "more than a normal quota of raw nerve," an assessment with which I tend to agree. *See* E.R. Van Gorder, "Bert Hall – Soldier or Scoundrel?", *Cross & Cockade*, Vol. 4, No. 3, p. 274 (Autumn 1963).

53 Later in July, Paul wrote Kiffin the following: "Hear Cowdin is trying to go to America. Winslow loafing about Paris, boasting and lying." Paul to Kiffin, July 18, 1916, Rockwell Papers, WLU. Hall eventually did leave the squadron, but not until November 1916. *See* Gordon, *Lafayette Escadrille Pilot Biographies*, p. 74-75.

54 Typewritten notes related to members of *escadrille*, circa 1917, Rockwell Papers, WLU.

55 The purported picture of Prince was actually Lieutenant de Laage. "Their Country Needs Them," *The Chicago Tribune*, July 9, 1916, p. 21.

56 "The Need of an Air Patrol," *The Chicago Tribune*, July 15, 1916, p. 6.

57 "Resent 'Bring Back Our Aviators' Talk," *The Chicago Daily News*, August 2, 1916, p. 2. Pavelka expressed this sentiment more bluntly when he stated in a letter to a friend back home that hostilities with Mexico would "only be child's play compared to this conflict.... If you could only see this little game of war you'd realize what a slim chance the greasers have against Uncle Sam." "Paul Pavelka, A Soldier of Fortune," *The New York Sun*, December 30, 1917, Section 5, p. 1.

58 "Resent 'Bring Back Our Aviators' Talk," *The Chicago Daily News*, August 2, 1916, p. 2.

59 *Id.* In his article, Paul did not include by name Hall, Cowdin, or (surprisingly) Thaw, among those who had told him frankly they would "flatly refuse" to go back.

60 "Resent 'Bring Back Our Aviators' Talk," *The Chicago Daily News*, August 2, 1916, p. 2.

61 *Id.*

62 James McConnell to Henry A. Johnston, September 9, 1916, McConnell Collection, UVA.

63 Rumsey, "Training an American Aviator in France," *National Service,* May 1917, p. 266.

64 "Chapman's Opponent," *The New York Times*, June 30, 1916, p. 5.

65 James McConnell to Paul Rockwell, letter misdated July 1, 1915, should be 1916, McConnell Collection, UVA.

66 *Id. Vrille* means tailspin, and "Nach Berlin" is German for "to Berlin."

67 Loula to Kiffin, July 1, 1916, Rockwell Papers, WLU.

68 James McConnell to Alice Weeks, July 2, 1916, Weeks, *Greater Love*, p. 151.

69 The French *pilote* was Sergent Marcel Louis Garet, of *Escadrille N.23. See* Bailey & Cony,

The French Air Service War Chronology, p. 57.

70   James McConnell to Lewis Crenshaw, July 2, 1916, McConnell Collection, UVA.

Chapter Forty-nine

1   Interestingly, Elliott's father John E. Cowdin shared a pew with Norman Prince's parents at a similar service held at Trinity Church in New York a few days earlier. *See* "Victor Chapman, American Hero, Who Died For France, Is Honored," *The New York Herald*, July 1, 1916, p. 1.

2   "Americans in the French Army Get Fourth of July Leave," *The New York World*, July 5, 1916, p. 3.

3   "Americans Honor Chapman," *The Chicago Daily News*, July 5, 1916, p. 2; "Briand Pays Honor to Victor Chapman," *The New York Sun*, July 5, 1916, p. 7. Chapman's forlorn mechanic Louis Bley had also come from Bar-le-Duc for the service. "Americans Honor Chapman," *The Chicago Daily News*, July 5, 1916, p. 2.

4   *Victor Chapman's Letters From France*, p. 27.

5   "A la mémoire de l'aviateur Chapman," *Le Temps*, 5 Juillet 1916, p. 4. *See also* "Un héros américain, Victor Chapman," *Le Temps*, 5 Juillet 1916, p. 2.

6   *Sermon of Reverend Ashman at the American Church in Paris*, July 4, 1916, John Jay Chapman Additional Papers, Harvard. Reverend Ashman was the associate of the Reverend Dr. Samuel N. Watson. *See* "Names of General Lafayette and Sergeant Chapman Linked at Independence Day Gatherings in Paris," *The New York Herald*, July 5, 1916, p. 3.

7   Edmond Genet to his mother, July 8, 1916, *War Letters of Edmond Genet*, p. 189. Genet noted that the speeches at the cemetery were "excellent," and that "Chapman's name was linked with that of Lafayette and the bond of good feeling between the sister republics was very strongly and excellently expressed." *Id.*

8   "Americans Glorify Lafayette; M. Briand Honors Americans Who Are Fighting for France," *The New York Herald*, July 5, 1916, p. 1. The paper ran a nice photo of the ceremony on page three.

9   "Paris Pays Tribute to Washington and Lafayette," *The Salt Lake Telegram*, July 9, 1916, p. 13.

10   *See* "Manifestation Franco-Américaine," *Le Temps*, 5 Juillet 1916, p. 4.

11   "Names of General Lafayette and Sergeant Chapman Linked at Independence Day Gatherings in Paris," *The New York Herald*, July 5, 1916, p. 3. *See also* "Manifestation Franco-Américaine," *Le Temps*, 5 Juillet 1916, p. 4.

12   "Americans Glorify Lafayette; M. Briand Honors Americans Who Are Fighting for France," *The New York Herald*, July 5, 1916, p. 1. *See also* "Americans in the French Army Get Fourth of July Leave," *The New York World*, July 5, 1916, p. 3.

13   Chapman, *Letters From France*, p. 28.

14   *Id.* at p. 27-28.

15   Theodore Roosevelt, "Lafayettes of the Air," *Collier's*, July 29, 1916, p. 16.

16   John Jay Chapman to Victor Chapman, May 26, 1916, John Jay Chapman Papers, Harvard.

17   Chapman, *Letters From France*, p. 189.

18   Aerial combat combined man's oldest game with his newest and was viewed in romantic terms from the start. *See e.g.* "War Aviators More Than Ever in the Limelight," *The New York Times Magazine*, March 26, 1916, p. 2.

19   "News of Chicago Society," *The Chicago Tribune*, August 13, 1916, p. E4.

20   Fortescue, *France Bears the Burden*, p. 123.

21   Papic, John, *The Cult of the Ace: The Airman and His Role in the First World War*, The Wittenberg History Journal, Vol. XXXVIII, p. 8 (Spring 2009).

22   *Our Friend France*, which came out the next year, included the same footage, and can be viewed here. (https://www.youtube.com/watch?v=lJzq8IcGGSA) (the aviation footage begins around the 45:24 mark)

23   James McConnell to Marcelle Guerin, May 30, 1916, McConnell Collection, UVA.

24   "Triangle Gets Official War Pictures – Big Scoop Scored," *The Triangle*, June 10, 1916, p. 1.

25   I cannot confirm the Joffre quote appeared on the program for this precise event, but it did appear on at least one program for a showing in Paris. *See* "Our American Boys in Paris," *The Triangle*, August 5, 1916, p. 7. The quote was also copied on later invitations for showings in America. *See* for example, the invitation to the December 8, 1916 showing at The Strand in New York City. (available at https://hrvh.org/cdm/compoundobject/collection/wilderstein/id/101/show/41/rec/38) (visited October 27, 2018)

26   Paul to Kiffin, June 12, 1916, Rockwell Papers, WLU.

27   Alice Weeks to Fred Taber, May 28, 1916, Weeks, *Greater Love*, p. 139. The movie may have been playing elsewhere in Paris as late as September; McConnell wrote Paul on September 12, "Hope those pictures are running when I get in." James McConnell to Paul Rockwell, September 12, 1916, McConnell Collection, UVA.

28   "Triangle Gets Official War Pictures – Big Scoop Scored," *The Triangle*, June 10, 1916, p. 1. Of course, showing the movie in America was planned all along.

29   "Triangle Gets Official War Pictures – Big Scoop Scored," *The Triangle*, June 10, 1916, p. 1.

30   "Ambulance Field Corps Film Arousing Interest," *The Triangle*, June 17, 1916, p. 1.

31   "Mrs. Vanderbilt Talks of the American Ambulance Corps Film," *The Triangle*, July 8, 1916, p. 8.

32   "Ambulance Corps in France Filmed," *The New York Times*, July 6, 1916, p. 11. *See also* Ed Klekowski and Libby Klekowski, *Eyewitnesses to the Great War: American Writers, Reporters, Volunteers, and Soldiers in France, 1914-1918*, p. 38. (2012).

33   "Ambulance Corps in France Filmed," *The New York Times*, July 6, 1916, p. 11.

34   *See* Klekowski & Klekowski, *Eyewitnesses to the Great War*, p. 38. The *Moving Picture World* declared the film "four reels of absorbing realism," and the "most remarkable war picture yet offered to the public." Ad printed in *The Moving Picture World*, July 29, 1916, p. 840.

35   "Ambulance Corps in France Filmed," *The New York Times*, July 6, 1916, p. 11.

36   Klekowski & Klekowski, *Eyewitnesses to the Great War*, p. 38.

37   "Our American Boys in the European War," *The Moving Picture World*, July 22, 1916, p. 648; "'Our American Boys in the European War' – Thriller," *The Triangle*, July 22, 1916, p. 4.

38   "America Preparing," *The New York Times*, July 11, 1916, p. 9.

39   Michael T. Isenberg, *War on Film: The American Cinema and World War I, 1914-1941*, p. 70.

40   "War Film at Newport," *The Triangle*, July 29, 1916, p. 7. *See also* "For the American Ambulance Service," *The American Club Woman*, September 1916, pp. 41-42.

41   "American Ambulance Films Screened in Newport Villa," *The New York Herald*, September 9, 1916, p. 2.

42   "Our American Boys, on the Screen, Thrill Newport," *The Triangle*, August 26, 1916, p. 1; "Handsome Program for War Film at Newport," *The Triangle*, August 19, 1916, p. 3.

43   "American Boys in France Filmed," *The Moving Picture World*, September 9, 1916, p. 1721.

44   The alumnus was a chap named Leslie Buswell. "Our American Boys, on the Screen, Thrill Newport," *The Triangle*, August 26, 1916, p. 1. *See also* Klekowski & Klekowski, *Eyewitnesses to the Great War*, p. 39. The Thaw family once owned Beach Mound, a beautiful summer cottage in Newport, and likely had many friends there. *See* "Two Funds Get Aid From Newport Colony," *The New York Tribune*, August 20, 1916, p. 13.

45   "'Our American Boys' Proves Startling Film," *The Triangle*, September 9, 1916, p. 1. This included exhibitions at "The Orchard" in York Harbor, Maine, on August 25; and at "Gallery on the Moors" in Gloucester, Massachusetts, on August 29. The invitations for each of these showings can be viewed at the website for Hudson River Valley Heritage by searching "Our American Boys in the European War." (https://www.hrvh.org) (visited October 27, 2018)

The film was also shown at the Bohemian Club and the Burlingame Club in San Francisco. *See* "War Pictures on the Coast," *The Triangle*, August 12, 1916, p. 1; and "'Our American Boys in the European War' Shown on Both the Atlantic and Pacific Coasts," *The Triangle*, September 23, 1916, p. 3.

46   "'Our American Boys in the European War' Shown on Both the Atlantic and Pacific Coasts," *The Triangle*, September 23, 1916, p. 3. At the same place, pro-Allies sentiment ran so strong that no young woman wanted to play the part of the German maid in a so-called "neutrality ballet." Miss Suzette Sturgis, who finally accepted the role, stated "I want it plainly understood that I am not German or pro-German. I am taking the part to be accommodating." "Neutrality at Bar Harbor Becomes a Social Issue," *The New York Herald*, September 3, 1916, p. 3.

47   "War Film Expected to Break All Moving Picture Records," *The Triangle*, August 26, 1916, p. 7; and "'American Boys' Film Now Society Diversion," *The Triangle*, September 16, 1916, p. 1. One scholar notes that between August 1916 and April 1917, the film raised the huge amount of $174,255.00 for the American Ambulance Field Service. *See* Axel Jansen, "The Incorporation of Sacrifice: The American Ambulance Field Service and the American Volunteer Motor-Ambulance Corps, 1914-1917," p. 37 (Univ. of Oregon, 1995).

48   "Roosevelt at Film of American Valor," *The New York Times*, September 24, 1916, p. 20.

Chapter Fifty

1   Paul Ayres Rockwell, "Our Pioneers in the Air," *The Franco-American Weekly*, February 23, 1918, p. 5.

2   "'Actual Fighting Will Be Over by Fall of 1917' Says Paul Rockwell in Letter to Atlanta Friend," *The Atlanta Constitution*, July 30, 1916, p. A11.

3   *Id.*

4   Paul to Kiffin, July 3, 1916, Rockwell Papers, WLU. *See also* "'Actual Fighting Will Be Over by Fall of 1917' Says Paul Rockwell in Letter to Atlanta Friend," *The Atlanta Constitution*, July 30, 1916, p. A11. The actual pass was good for rail travel to and from Bar-le-Duc and valid from July 3 to July 10. *See Safe-Conduit*, Rockwell Papers, WLU.

5   Paul Ayres Rockwell, "Our Pioneers in the Air," *The Franco-American Weekly*, February 23, 1918, p. 5.

6   The photos can be seen, along with many others, in the Flickr stream for the North Carolina Department of Natural and Cultural Resources. (available at https://www.flickr.com/photos/north-carolina-state-archives/albums/72157670120706717/) (visited June 2, 2019).

7   William Astor Chanler to Kiffin, June 26, 1916, Rockwell Papers, WLU.

8   Kiffin to Paul, July 27, 1916, Rockwell Papers, WLU.

9   Kiffin to Loula, July 9, 1916, KYR Papers, NCDNCR.

10   *See* "American Chases Aeroplane Thought to be Capt. Boelke's," *The St. Louis Post-Dispatch*, July 13, 1916, p. 2; "American Fliers in Raid," *The New York Sun*, July 13, 1916, p. 2.

11   "American Aviators Win Fierce Battle," *The San Francisco Chronicle*, July 13, 1916, p. 1. *See also* Paul Ayres Rockwell, "Our Pioneers in the Air," *The Franco-American Weekly*, February 23, 1918, p. 5.

12   Thénault allowed Thaw to take a short flight in his Nieuport, but did not allow him to fly over the lines, as his wounded arm was still not entirely healed. "American Fliers in Raid," *The New York Sun*, July 13, 1916, p. 2; "U.S. Airmen Rout German Fliers," *The New York Tribune*, July 13, 1916, p. 4. The squadron's official flight records for the month of July show no flights or hours for Thaw. *See Relevé des vols effectués pendant le mois de juillet 1916*, records of the 2nd Armée.

13   James McConnell to Marcelle Guerin, July 12, 1916, McConnell Collection, UVA.

14   Steve Ruffin has a cool picture of Thaw and Nungesser – who had previously served together in N.65 – together at the Behonne airfield that must have been taken around this time,

before Thaw went back to Paris. Thaw's arm is no longer in a sling, but he does look to be holding it funny. *See* Ruffin, *The Lafayette Escadrille*, photos after p. 74.

15   *See* Bailey & Cony, *The French Air Service War Chronology*, p. 55.

16   Nungesser was seconded from N.65 to N.124 from July 12 to August 15. *See* Jablonski, *Warriors with Wings*, p. 101.

17   Guttman, *SPA124 Lafayette Escadrille*, p. 27; Bailey & Cony, *The French Air Service War Chronology*, p. 60.

18   Ruffin, *The Lafayette Escadrille*, p. 65. McConnell may have authored an article about Nungesser which appeared in the *New York Sun* around this time. *See* "'Prince of Pilots' Once Cavalryman, *The New York Sun*, July 30, 1916, Sec. 6, p. 2. In a more personal communication, however, he wrote Marcelle Guerin that Nungesser "[s]eems a nice chap but draws the long bow." James McConnell to Marcelle Guerin, July 25, 1916, McConnell Collection, UVA. To "draw the long bow" means to exaggerate or overstate things.

19   Laurence Rumsey, "Training an American Aviator in France," *National Service*, May 1917, p. 266.

20   *See Relevé des vols effectués pendant le mois de juillet 1916*, records of the 2nd Armée. And yet Rumsey put in 15 patrols and almost 28 hours in July which, although at the lower end of the American squadron, was actually better than most of the rest of the pilots in the French service that month.

21   James McConnell to Paul Rockwell, July 16, 1916, McConnell Collection, UVA. *See also* Pardoe, *The Bad Boy, Bert Hall: Aviator and Mercenary of the Skies*, p. 88.

22   *See Relevé des vols effectués pendant le mois de juillet 1916*, records of the 2nd Armée.

23   "Lieut. Nungesser Destroys Tenth German Aeroplane," *The New York Herald*, July 26, 1916, p. 1. *See also* Guttman, *SPA124 Lafayette Escadrille*, p. 27; Bailey & Cony, *The French Air Service War Chronology*, p. 60.

24   Kiffin to Paul, July 23, 1916, Rockwell Papers, WLU.

25   *Id.*

26   "American Aviators Battle in the Clouds," *The New York Sun*, July 23, 1916, p. 2.

27   "Yankee Fliers Fool Enemy by Diving into Cloud Bank," *The New York Tribune*, July 25, 1916, p. 1. I was unable to locate a direct source, but one author asserts that after the fight Kiffin wrote: "Hall saved my skin, no doubt about it. When we returned, both our ships were more hole than whole." Pardoe, *The Bad Boy, Bert Hall: Aviator and Mercenary of the Skies*, p. 90.

28   "American Aviators Battle in the Clouds," *The New York Sun*, July 23, 1916, p. 2.

29   Kiffin to Paul, July 23, 1916, Rockwell Papers, WLU.

30   McConnell to Alice Weeks, July 22, 1916, Weeks, *Greater Love*, p. 153.

31   Kiffin to Paul, July 23, 1916, Rockwell Papers, WLU. Kiffin even made the front page of the *New York Times*. *See* "American Aviator Rockwell Downs Third German," *The New York Times*, July 25, 1916, p. 1.

32   Kiffin to Paul, July 23, 1916, Rockwell Papers, WLU. *See also* "New Yorker Drives German to Ground," *The Chicago Daily News*, July 27, 1916, p. 2.

33   James McConnell to Paul Rockwell, July 25, 1916, McConnell Collection, UVA.

34   Bailey & Cony, *The French Air Service War Chronology*, p. 61. *See also* "New Yorker Drives German to Ground," *The Chicago Daily News*, July 27, 1916, p. 2.

35   Guttman, *SPA124 Lafayette Escadrille*, p. 29.

36   "Hides in Cloud to Trap German Flier," *The New York Sun*, July 27, 1916, p. 1.

37   James McConnell to Marcelle Guerin, July 25, 1916, McConnell Collection, UVA.

38   James McConnell to Paul Rockwell, July 19, 1916, McConnell Collection, UVA.

39   *Id.*

40   "American Aviators in One Escadrille," *The New York Sun*, August 6, 1916, p. 2. This article was written by Jim McConnell.

41   Major James A. Logan, Jr., "Aeronautical Notes," Paris, France 20 September 1916. Office of

the Military Observers with the French Army, Report 5770-142, National Archives, Record Group 165.

42   Fortescue, *France Bears the Burden*, p. 128.

43   As one British editor later wrote: "The policy of the American aviators serving with the French Army is that of the British and French – to attack. They have played a goodly part in the invention of the constantly changing tactics of air fighting." "The American Soldiers in France," *The Daily Mail*, February 2, 1917, p. 4.

44   Hall, *One Man's War*, p. 167.

45   Bert Hall, "Fast Fighting and Narrow Escapes in the Air," *The American Magazine*, p. 45 (Sep. 1918).

46   "New French Aeros Swiftest Known, Says Rockwell," *The New York Tribune*, January 26, 1917, p. 4.

47   Hall, *One Man's War*, p. 167.

48   "American Aviators in One Escadrille," *The New York Sun*, August 6, 1916, p. 2.

49   Deullin, *Fighter Tactics*, as translated by Charles J. Biddle, *Fighting Airman: The Way of the Eagle*, p. 248.

50   "France Fetes Daring Americans in Flying Corps," *The St. Louis Post-Dispatch*, July 9, 1916, p. 2B, 4B.

51   *See* "Death of Rockwell Ends Daring Career," *The Chicago Daily News*, Sep. 25, 1916, p. 2.

52   "Thaw Describes Work Done by American Airmen," *The Pittsburg Press*, November 21, 1916, p. 4.

53   "Thaw, 'Dead Man' in France, Livest Thing in New York," *The Evening World*, November 21, 1916, p. 12.

54   "Thaw Enjoys Sport of Chasing Flyers," *The Chicago Daily News*, April 11, 1916, p. 2.

55   "Thaw, 'Dead Man' in France, Livest Thing in New York," *The Evening World*, November 21, 1916, p. 12.

56   Edmond Genet, diary entry of February 15, 1917, "Leaves from a War Diary," *The North American Review*, p. 410 (Sep. – Oct. 1927).

57   James McConnell, "Flying for France," *The World's Work*, November 1916, p. 51.

58   Hall, *One Man's War*, p. 132.

59   Kiffin to Paul Rockwell, date unknown, Hall & Nordhoff, *The Lafayette Flying Corps*, Vol. 1, p. 83.

60   James McConnell to Sarah Rogers McConnell, July 23, 1916, McConnell Collection, UVA.

61   Kiffin to Paul, August 4, 1916, Rockwell Papers, WLU.

62   Kiffin to Loula, August 4, 1916, KYR Papers, NCDNCR.

63   *Id.*

Chapter Fifty-one

1   Bailey & Cony, *The French Air Service War Chronology*, p. 61; James McConnell to Paul Rockwell, July 25, 1916, McConnell Collection, UVA.

2   Laurence Rumsey, "Training an American Aviator in France," *National Service*, May 1917, p. 266; Bailey & Cony, *The French Air Service War Chronology*, p. 62.

3   "French Aviator Rams Antagonist in Air and Falls to Earth with Two Germans," *The New York Times*, July 30, 1916, p. 1. *See also* Bailey & Cony, *The French Air Service War Chronology*, p. 61.

4   James McConnell to Paul Rockwell, July 25, 1916, McConnell Collection, UVA.

5   "Hides in Cloud to Trap German Flier," *The New York Sun*, July 27, 1916, p. 1.

6   Quoted in Flammer, *The Vivid Air*, p. 75.

7   "Hides in Cloud to Trap German Flier," *The New York Sun*, July 27, 1916, p. 1.

8   James McConnell to Paul Rockwell, July 25, 1916, McConnell Collection, UVA.

9   *See* James McConnell to Paul Rockwell, July 25, 1916, McConnell Collection, UVA; and

"Battles with Dead Aviator," *The New York Sun*, July 28, 1916, p. 1.

10 "Battles with Dead Aviator," *The New York Sun*, July 28, 1916, p. 1.

11 Kiffin to Paul, July 27, 1916, Rockwell Papers, WLU. Paul changed this quote to the less Southern "I almost ran into" a German. *War Letters*, p. 146.

12 James McConnell to Paul Rockwell, July 25, 1916, McConnell Collection, UVA.

13 Kiffin to Loula, July 26, 1916, KYR Papers, NCDNCR.

14 Kiffin to Paul, July 27, 1916, Rockwell Papers, WLU.

15 *Id.* See also Bailey & Cony, *The French Air Service War Chronology*, p. 61.

16 While it is probably not the same fight, Bailey and Cony give Kiffin credit for a FTL (forced to land) on July 28, rather than July 27. *See* Bailey & Cony, *The French Air Service War Chronology*, p. 62. *See also Aviation militaire cahiers manuscrits de comptes-rendus des activités et opérations aériennes des unites*, entry for 28 Juillet 1916, available on the *Mémoire des Hommes* website.

17 While not an official victory, forcing down an enemy aircraft usually meant a citation.

18 Kiffin to Paul, July 27, 1916, Rockwell Papers, WLU. When Paul published this letter, he removed Kiffin's derogatory references to the Captain. *See War Letters*, p. 145-46.

19 Paul to Kiffin, July 29, 1916, Rockwell Papers, WLU.

20 Kiffin to Paul, July 31, 1916, Rockwell Papers, WLU. Paul removed the derogatory references to Thénault from this letter. *See War Letters*, p. 147. Paul also changed to "X" the reference to the person who attempted to prevent Hall from receiving a citation. Other authors have speculated that the culprit was Norman Prince. *See* Pardoe, *The Bad Boy, Bert Hall: Aviator and Mercenary of the Skies*, p. 90. However, Kiffin's original letter states clearly that it was Captain Thénault.

21 Hall, *En L'Air!*, p. 148.

22 Paul to Kiffin, August 1, 1916, Rockwell Papers, WLU.

23 *See War Letters*, p. 198.

24 Chapman, *Letters From France*, p. 177.

25 Paul to Kiffin, August 4, 1916, Rockwell Papers, WLU.

26 *Id.*

27 Pavelka joined the *escadrille* on August 11, 1916. Hall & Nordhoff, *The Lafayette Flying Corps*, Vol. 1, p. 379. That day, while waiting for his train in a station in Paris, Pavelka sent a message to Mrs. Weeks, letting her and Paul know "that Skipper is at last on his way to the big noise." Paul Pavelka to Alice Weeks, August 11, 1916, Weeks, *Greater Love*, p. 158.

28 Phillip C. Brown, "Pavelka of the Lafayette," *Cross & Cockade* (Vol. 19, No. 2 (Summer 1978), p. 102.

29 Most of the pilots put in less hours in August, so even while taking it easy, Kiffin ranked fourth in flight hours, behind Prince, Lufbery and de Laage. *See Relevé des vols effectués pendant le mois de août 1916*, records of the 2nd Armée.

30 Kiffin to Loula, August 13, 1916, KYR Papers, NCDNCR.

31 Loula to Paul and Kiffin, July 1, 1916, Rockwell Papers, WLU.

32 St. Elmo Massengale to Kiffin, August 14, 1916, Rockwell Papers, WLU.

33 Loula to Paul and Kiffin, July 1, 1916, Rockwell Papers, WLU.

34 Loula to Paul and Kiffin, July 20, 1916, Rockwell Papers, WLU. Loula's point about prosperity echoed a popular Wilson campaign song, "Stonewall Wilson." A portion of the song's lyrics went like this:
Under Wilson peace and plenty,
Reign supreme from shore to shore,
Under Wilson we have prospered,
Could another give us more?
"Stonewall Wilson," Mortimer, Robert, National Music Publishing Co.: New York, 1916.

35 Loula to Paul and Kiffin, July 6, 1916, Rockwell Papers, WLU.

36 Loula to Paul and Kiffin, July 20, 1916, Rockwell Papers, WLU.

37 "Kiffen Rockwell Still Harassing Germans," *The Charlotte Observer*, August 28, 1916, p. 3.

38 Mark Wilkins, "The Dark Side of Glory," *Air & Space Magazine*, February 2018 (available at https://www.airspacemag.com/military-aviation/world-war-i-pilot-ptsd-180967710/) (last visited on November 21, 2018)

39 *Id.* The pilot was John MacGavrock Grider.

40 Kiffin Rockwell to Elizabeth Chapman, August 10, 1916, KYR Papers, NCDNCR.

41 Bailey & Cony, *The French Air Service War Chronology*, p. 65.

42 "Den," as his father called him, descended from Robert Morris, who fought in the War of 1812. "Sea Cliff Mourns Death of Aviator Dennis Dowd, Jr.," *The Brooklyn Daily Eagle*, August 14, 1916, p. 2.

43 Edmond Genet told his mother "Dowd was our star man here, and one of the best liked." Edmond Genet to his mother, August 14, 1916, in *War Letters of Edmond Genet*, p. 194. Dowd had narrowly escaped death a few days earlier when his plane fell. *See* "Death Misses Aviator," *The Chicago Daily News*, August 8, 1916, p. 1. The day before, Dowd had written his fiancée – a beautiful French girl named Paulette Parent de St. Glin – of being extremely tired. "Comrade Genet Pays Tribute to Dennis Dowd, Killed in France," *The Brooklyn Daily Eagle*, September 17, 1916, Sec. 3, p. 4. *See also* "Will Marry His Godmother," *The Chicago Daily News*, March 10, 1916, p. 2. Because of this, Dowd's friends theorized he must have lost consciousness before the plane crashed. *See* "Young Dowd's Body Now at Versailles; Funeral Tomorrow," *The Brooklyn Daily Eagle*, August 14, 1916, p. 2; and "Comrade Genet Pays Tribute to Dennis Dowd, Killed in France," *The Brooklyn Daily Eagle*, September 17, 1916, Sec. 3, p. 4.

44 Paul Pavelka to Paul Rockwell, August 18, 1916, Rockwell Papers, WLU.

45 "Funeral Honors for Dowd," *The New York Sun*, August 16, 1916, p. 3.

46 "Comrade Genet Pays Tribute to Dennis Dowd, Killed in France," *The Brooklyn Daily Eagle*, September 17, 1916, Sec. 3, p. 4.

Chapter Fifty-two

1 *See* Major James A. Logan, Jr., "Aeronautical Notes," Paris, France 20 September 1916. Office of the Military Observers with the French Army, Report 5770-142, National Archives, Record Group 165.

2 Paul Pavelka to Paul Rockwell, August 18, 1916, Rockwell Papers, WLU.

3 "American aviators highly praised for many daring deeds," undated clipping, Lafayette Escadrille Scrapbook, MHS.

4 *See* "Lufbery to Get Medal," *The New York Sun*, August 3, 1916, p. 2 (noting Lufbery was to receive medal for victory near Etain). On July 31, Kiffin noted that immediately after Lufbery's victory, Thénault proposed him for the *médaille*, which further supports the idea that this victory was Lufbery's first. *See* Kiffin Rockwell to Paul Rockwell, July 31, 1916, Rockwell Papers, WLU. If, as some suggest, Lufbery had scored an earlier win on July 30, Thénault surely would have proposed Lufbery for the *médaille* then.

5 "American Airman Brings Down a German," *The New York Times*, August 3, 1916, p. 1. Two other New York papers also reported Lufbery's victory as his first. *See* "American Flier Smashes Fokker," *The New York Tribune*, August 3, 1916, p. 1; and "American Airmen Busy," *The New York Sun*, August 2, 1916, p. 1.

6 Mason, *The Lafayette Escadrille*, p. 103. *See also* Fortescue, *France Bears the Burden*, p. 124-25.

7 R. Conrad Stein, *The Story of the Lafayette Escadrille*, p. 15.

8 "Personal Glimpses – Lufbery Vanquished in a Battle With Huge German Plane," *The Literary Digest*, p. 41, 44 (June 8, 1918). As predicted, Lufbery did not survive the war.

9 "American Wins Air Battle," *The New York Sun*, August 6, 1916, p. 5.

10 Bailey & Cony, *The French Air Service War Chronology*, p. 63.

11 "American Wins Air Battle," *The New York Sun*, August 6, 1916, p. 5.

12 Mrs. Weeks published Kiffin's letter under the incorrect date of June 30. *See* Weeks, *Greater Love*, p. 149. As the letter matches a report in the *New York Sun* in all particulars, it was almost certainly written on August 4. *See* "American Wins Air Battle," *The New York Sun*, August 6, 1916, p. 5.

13 Hall & Nordhoff, *The Lafayette Flying Corps*, Vol. 1, p. 36. *See also* Flammer, *The Vivid Air*, p. 75.

14 Two solid authorities assert that one of Lufbery's August 4th victories must have occurred on July 30, as Lufbery's first citation credits him with attacking four enemy aircraft during his first victory on July 31, while by his own account, the first machine he brought down was alone. *See* Dennis Connell and Frank W. Bailey, "Victory Logs, Lafayette Escadrille and Lafayette Flying Corps," *Cross & Cockade*, Vol. 21, No. 4, p. 357 (Winter 1980). *See also* "Connecticut's Famous 'Ace,' Major Raoul Gervais Lufbery," *The Hartford Courant*, April 28, 1918, Part Three, p. 1 (quoting citation). However, two contemporary sources note that after attacking and bringing down the Fokker on July 31, three additional machines attacked Lufbery, for a total of four. *See* "American Airman Brings Down a German," *The New York Times*, August 3, 1916, p. 1; and "American Flier Smashes Fokker," *The New York Tribune,* August 3, 1916, p. 1. Thus, Lufbery's first citation (which asserts a first victory date of July 31) is not incompatible with the evidence, and there is no need to assume an earlier victory date. Finally, at least according to Kiffin, Thénault treated Lufbery more favorably than the others, and he might have counted the unofficial victory with Mac on August 4.

15 Kiffin to Paul, August 8, 1916, Rockwell Papers, WLU.

16 James McConnell, "Flying for France," *The World's Work*, November 1916, p. 51.

17 "Lufberry Wins Again in Air," *The New York Sun*, August 10, 1916, p. 1. *See also* "American a Double Hero," *The New York Tribune*, August 13, 1916, p. 2 ("It was his second exploit of the kind in a week.").

18 Paul wrote that "by a clever maneuver, Lufbery succeeded in getting alongside the German aeroplane, fatally wounding the pilot." *See* "American Wounded by German Mortar," *The Chicago Daily News*, August 11, 1916, p. 2.

19 Whitehouse, *Legion of the Lafayette*, p. 104. This appears to be translated from an article titled "Un Boche Abattu," by Lufbery himself in *La Guerre Aerienne*, January 3, 1918, p. 139.

20 James McConnell, "Flying for France," *The World's Work*, November 1916, p. 51. One account quotes the French communiqué as saying the plane "fell in flames within our lines, to the south of Douaumont." "American Aviator Brings Down Hun Machine Ablaze," *The New York Herald*, August 12, 1916, p. 1.

21 "Lufberry Wins Again in Air," *The New York Sun*, August 10, 1916, p. 1.

22 James McConnell, "Flying for France," *The World's Work*, November 1916, p. 52. Lufbery once told Bert Hall it would be "awful to burn up in the air," and swore he would jump first. *See* Hall, *One Man's War,* p. 177.

23 McConnell, *Flying for France*, p. 67. McConnell misspelled Pain's, an ancient English fireworks company, famous for (among other things) putting on the fireworks show at the dedication of the Statue of Liberty in 1886.

24 James McConnell to Paul Rockwell, July 25, 1916, McConnell Collection, UVA.

25 Jon Guttman, *Nieuport 11/16 Bebe vs. Fokker Eindecker*, p. 27.

26 *Id.*

27 McConnell, *Flying for France*, p. 68. The *New York Sun* reported Prince's accomplishment, calling it "a particularly hazardous feat." It said that Prince "fired at the gas bag at about 100 yards range and the 'sausage' immediately disappeared in a cloud of smoke." "Prince Explodes 'Sausage,'" *The New York Sun*, August 4, 1916, p. 3.

28 "Missing U.S. Aviator Returns," *The Chicago Daily News*, August 8, 1916, p. 1.

29 "Norman Prince Not Killed," *The New York Sun*, August 16, 1916, p. 3.

30 Paul Rockwell later confirmed the August 4 victory, writing: "On August 4, Lufbery and

McConnell riddled a *Boche* machine with bullets, its fall being officially confirmed, and half the credit for the victory was given Jim." *See* Paul A. Rockwell, "Our Pioneers in the Air," *The Franco-American Weekly*, February 23, 1918, p. 5.

31 James McConnell, "Flying for France," *The World's Work*, November 1916, p. 52, fn. 1.

32 *Id.*

33 Hall, *One Man's War*, p. 171.

34 "U.S. Flyer Hurt in Smash," *The Chicago Daily News*, August 30, 1916, p. 1. This article includes a nice picture of McConnell in his uniform.

35 Paul Pavelka to Alice Weeks, August 14, 1916, Weeks, *Greater Love*, p. 158-59.

36 *Id.*

37 Kiffin to Loula, August 13, 1916, KYR Papers, NCDNCR.

38 *See* "American Athlete is Killed," *The Chicago Daily News*, August 12, 1916, p. 2.

39 Alice Weeks to Kiffin Rockwell, August 12, 1916, Rockwell Papers, WLU.

40 Kiffin to Loula, August 22, 1916, KYR Papers, NCDNCR.

41 "Atlanta Youth With Allies Lays to Luck Success as Aviator," *The Atlanta Journal*, September 17, 1916, p. 1.

42 *See* Paul Ayres Rockwell, "Our Pioneers in the Air," *The Franco-American Weekly*, March 2, 1918, p. 2.

43 "Thrills for Aviator Fighting at Verdun," *The Chicago Daily News*, August 25, 1916, p. 2.

44 James McConnell, "Flying for France," *The World's Work*, November 1916, p. 41.

45 James McConnell to unknown, August 28, 1916, McConnell Collection, UVA.

46 "'Actual Fighting Will Be Over by Fall of 1917,' Says Paul Rockwell in Letter to Atlanta Friend," *The Atlanta Constitution*, July 30, 1916, p. A11.

47 "Paul Rockwell Tells Story of Kiffin's Last Air Fight and of His Drop to Death," *The Atlanta Constitution*, November 11, 1916, p. 5.

48 James McConnell to Paul Rockwell, August 25, 1916, McConnell Collection, UVA. Mac also reported that Prince "denied the 'Cowdin to be shot' rumor." *Id.*

49 Paul Pavelka to Alice Weeks, August 26, 1916, Weeks, *Greater Love*, p. 162.

50 James McConnell to Paul Rockwell, August 25, 1916, McConnell Collection, UVA.

51 *See* Mason, *The Lafayette Escadrille*, p. 98; Parsons, *I Flew with the Lafayette Escadrille*, p. 168-69 and Jablonski, *Warriors with Wings*, p. 107. These sources are supported by a citation stating that Prince forced an aircraft to land on that date. *See* Hall & Nordhoff, *The Lafayette Flying Corps*, Vol. 1, p. 391. Another author suggests this occurred a month later in Luxeuil. *See* Whitehouse, *Legion of the Lafayette*, p. 121

52 Prince, *A Volunteer Who Died for the Cause He Loved*, p. 38-39.

53 Also noted in *Aviation militaire cahiers manuscrits de comptes-rendus des activités et opérations aériennes des unites*, entry for 25 Août 1916, available on the *Mémoire des Hommes* website.

54 Of course, it may be the case that Mac's letter served as the basis for the report in the *Sun*. "Norman Prince Scores Again," *The New York Sun*, August 27, 1916, p. 1. The squadron's journal of operations noted that at 8:42 a.m. on August 25, Prince brought down an enemy plane after seriously hitting it. *Escadrille N.124, Journal des marches et operations pendant la compagne du 14/8/16 au 9/9/17*, entry of 25 Août 1916 (available online by the Smithsonian Libraries) (https://library.si.edu/digital-library/book/journaldesmarch00). Interestingly, one source credits Prince with one victory and with forcing a plane to land that day. Bailey & Cony, *The French Air Service War Chronology*, p. 68. *See also* Dennis Connell and Frank W. Bailey, "Victory Logs Lafayette Escadrille and Lafayette Flying Corps," *Cross & Cockade*, Vol. 21, No. 4, p. 358 (Winter 1980).

55 Kiffin to Paul, September 1, 1916, Rockwell Papers, WLU.

56 *Id.*

57 Prince, *A Volunteer Who Died for the Cause He Loved*, p. 38. Prince did not mention it, but he turned 29 years old on August 31 while on *permission*.

58   "Raid Brings Lufbery Honor, Prince Death," *The Chicago Daily News*, October 18, 1916, p. 2.

59   "Full Text of Mr. Hughes's Speech of Acceptance," *The New York Times*, August 1, 1916, p. 6.

60   "Colonel Assails Wilson in Maine," *The New York Times*, September 1, 1916, p. 6.

61   "Victor Chapman's Father Thanks M. Leroy-Beaulieu," *The New York Herald*, August 30, 1916, p. 2. The *Union of the Fathers and Mothers Whose Sons Have Died for France* had written Mr. Chapman to express reverence and admiration for "all those who are fighting on the soil of France for the cause of civilization and justice," and asked him to "accept the sympathy of the fathers and mothers of France who are bowed with the same grief that has come to you." "Those Who Die for France," *The New York Times*, August 17, 1916, p. 10.

62   *Escadrille N.124, Journal des marches et operations pendant la compagne du 14/8/16 au 9/9/17*, entry of 31 Août 1916. *See also* Alan D. Toelle, "A White-Faced Cow and the Operational History of the Escadrille Américaine N.124 to September 1916," *Over the Front*, Vol. 24, No. 4, p. 335 (Winter 2009).

63   Kiffin to Paul, September 1, 1916, Rockwell Papers, WLU.

64   *Escadrille N.124, Journal des marches et operations pendant la compagne du 14/8/16 au 9/9/17*, entry of 2 Septembre 1916.

65   *See* translation of citation, *War Letters*, p. 175. *See also* "Joffre Praises Rockwell," *The Chicago Daily News*, February 12, 1917, p. 2.

66   Kiffin to Loula, September 2, 1916, KYR Papers, NCDNCR.

67   "Kiffin Rockwell Killed in Air Fight," *The New York Times*, September 24, 1916, p. 4. As it was quoting the letter's recipient, the actual quote from the *Times* reads "unless the Germans *got him*."

Chapter Fifty-three

1   *See* Bailey & Cony, *The French Air Service War Chronology*, p. 68. *See also* Dennis Connell and Frank W. Bailey, "Victory Logs Lafayette Escadrille and Lafayette Flying Corps," *Cross & Cockade*, Vol. 21, No. 4, p. 358 (Winter 1980).

2   This list gives full credit to Lufbery (and none to McConnell) for his first victory on August 4. The patrol's two victories on May 24 are awarded to Kiffin and either Chapman or Cowdin. *See* Bailey & Cony, *The French Air Service War Chronology*, p. 51. Kiffin is given credit for his presumed victory in late July and Prince is given credit for his claimed victory of August 25. None of the other pilots – Thénault, Balsley, Johnson, Masson, Rumsey, Hill and Pavelka – had yet scored a confirmed victory as part of the squadron.

3   *Escadrille N.124, Journal des marches et operations pendant la compagne du 14/8/16 au 9/9/17*, entry of 3 Septembre 1916.

4   Paul Pavelka to James McConnell, August 31, 1916, Rockwell Papers, WLU.

5   The original telegram is pasted in the squadron's journal of operations. *See Escadrille N.124, Journal des marches et operations pendant la compagne du 14/8/16 au 9/9/17*, entry of 3 Septembre 1916.

6   Thénault, *The Lafayette Escadrille*, p. 67.

7   *Id.*

8   *Escadrille N.124, Journal des marches et operations pendant la compagne du 14/8/16 au 9/9/17*, entry of 6 Septembre 1916.

9   *See* Bailey & Cony, *The French Air Service War Chronology*, p. 71.

10   "Rockwell Downs His Fourth Aeroplane," *The New York Times*, September 12, 1916, p. 4.

11   *Escadrille N.124, Journal des marches et operations pendant la compagne du 14/8/16 au 9/9/17*, entry of 9 Septembre 1916. *See also Aviation militaire cahiers manuscrits de comptes-rendus des activités et opérations aériennes des unites*, entry for 9 Septembre 1916, available on the *Mémoire des Hommes* website.

12   "American Aviator Who Has Bested Four German Fliers in France," *The St. Louis Post-Dispatch*, September 12, 1916, p. 1.

13   "Rockwell Gets His 4th German Aviator," *The New York Sun*, September 12, 1916, p. 1. "American Drops His Fourth German Aero," *The New York Tribune*, September 12, 1916, p. 1; "U.S. Airman Defeats Foe," *The Washington Post*, September 12, 1916, p. 1; "American Airman Brings Down His Fourth German," *The New York World*, September 12, 1916, p. 3; "Rockwell Downs His Fourth Aeroplane," *The New York Times*, September 12, 1916, p. 4; and "Brings Down 4th Aircraft," *The Chicago Daily News*, September 12, 1916, p. 2.

14   "American Beats Air Enemy," *The Chicago Tribune*, September 12, 1916, p. 5.

15   This count comes from my own rough tally of French victories between May 18 and September 9, 1916, as listed in the best source for such information. *See* Bailey & Cony, *The French Air Service War Chronology*, p. 49-71.

16   Thénault, *The Lafayette Escadrille*, p. 65.

17   "Navarre Lionized by Night Crowd in a Paris Café," *The New York World*, September 17, 1916, Second News Section, p. 2.

18   *Id.*

19   "Three Young Atlantians Would Shoulder Arms in Defense of France," *The Atlanta Journal*, August 4, 1914, p. 5.

20   Many people recalled Kiffin expressing the sentiment. For example, McConnell remembered Kiffin saying, "I pay my part for Lafayette and Rochambeau," while Thénault quoted Kiffin this way: "I am paying my part of our debt to Lafayette and Rochambeau." McConnell, *Flying for France*, p. 97; and *War Letters*, p. 160. Others also remembered Kiffin saying these lines. *See* Gaston Riou, *Lafayette, nous voila!*, p. 14 (Librairie Hatchette et Cie, 1917).

21   "French Confident of German Defeat, Asserts Rockwell," *The Atlanta Constitution*, October 5, 1916, p. 3.

22   "Homage Accorded Lafayette's Name," *The New York Sun*, September 7, 1916, p. 3.

23   "Jusserand Lauds Our 'Lafayettes,'" *The New York Times*, September 7, 1916, p. 7.

24   "Homage Accorded Lafayette's Name," *The New York Sun*, September 7, 1916, p. 3.

25   Combined account taken from "Jusserand Lauds Our 'Lafayettes,'" *The New York Times*, September 7, 1916, p. 7, and "Homage Accorded Lafayette's Name," *The New York Sun*, September 7, 1916, p. 3. *See also* "Americans Repay Lafayette Debt," *The Charleston Evening Post*, September 7, 1916, p. 10.

26   "Lafayette's Birthday Celebrated in Paris," *The New York Herald*, September 7, 1916, p. 2.

Chapter Fifty-four

1   Hall, *One Man's War*, p. 179.

2   Thénault, *The Story of the Lafayette Escadrille*, p. 68-69.

3   *Id.* at p. 68.

4   "French Confident of German Defeat, Asserts Rockwell," *The Atlanta Constitution*, October 5, 1916, p. 3.

5   "Promotion for K.Y. Rockwell," *The Chicago Daily News*, September 13, 1916, p. 2.

6   Kiffin to Loula, September 14, 1916, KYR Papers, NCDNCR.

7   The lion was advertised in the *Herald* on September 10 and 12. *See* "Announcements, Lion, 4 mois, a vendre," *The New York Herald*, September 10, 1916, p. 4, and "Lion, 4 mois, a vendre," *The New York Herald*, September 12, 1916, p. 3. Both ads included a photo of the lion and referenced the address 11 Boulevard Voltaire.

8   "Lion is U.S. Flyer's Mascot," *The Chicago Daily News*, September 14, 1916, p. 2. Thénault reports that the lion cost five hundred francs. Thénault, *The Story of the Lafayette Escadrille*, p. 73.

9   Alice Weeks to Allen Weeks, September 16, 1916, Weeks, *Greater Love*, p. 166.

10   "Lion is U.S. Flyer's Mascot," *The Chicago Daily News*, September 14, 1916, p. 2.

11   *See* Klekowski, *Eyewitnesses to the Great War*, p. 38; Thénault, *The Story of the Lafayette Escadrille*, p. 73; Granville Fortescue, *Front Line and Deadline*, p. 272 (G.A. Putnam's Sons,

1937); and Hall & Nordhoff, *The Lafayette Flying Corps*, Vol. 1, p. 286. Most people called the New York Bar "Harry's," after the name of its bartender.

12 Paul A. Rockwell, "Our Pioneers in the Air," *The Franco-American Weekly*, March 2, 1918, p. 2.

13 "That Lion Has Now Become an Aviation Corps' Mascot," *The New York Herald*, September 16, 1916, p. 2. After the war, Thénault visited Whiskey, by then kept in the Paris Zoo. At the sound of Thénault's voice Whiskey, who had been lying in a corner, jumped up and began "licking his hand like a dog." Thénault embraced his old friend through the bars of the cage, drawing a crowd of 500 people. "Lion Mascot Knew Him," *The New York Times*, July 12, 1919, p. 3.

14 "Death of Rockwell Ends Daring Career," *The Chicago Daily News*, September 25, 1916, p. 2.

15 Kiffin to Loula, September 14, 1916, KYR Papers, NCDNCR.

16 On September 20, Rumsey noted: "We did not go to the Somme after all, and all are disappointed." Laurence Rumsey, "Training an American Aviator in France," *National Service*, May 1917, p. 267.

17 Alice Weeks to Allen Weeks, September 17, 1916, Weeks, *Greater Love*, p. 166.

18 Mason, *The Lafayette Escadrille*, p. 108.

19 Alice Weeks to Allen Weeks, September 17, 1916, Weeks, *Greater Love*, p. 166-67.

20 Paul Rockwell, "Our Pioneers in the Air," *The Franco-American Weekly*, March 2, 1918, p. 2.

21 Gordon, *Lafayette Escadrille Pilot Biographies*, p. 115; Mason, *The Lafayette Escadrille*, p. 109.

22 Paul Rockwell, "Our Pioneers in the Air," *The Franco-American Weekly*, March 2, 1918, p. 2.

23 *See* Thénault, *The Story of the Lafayette Escadrille*, p. 74.

24 *Id.* at p. 75-76.

25 Paul Pavelka to James McConnell, September 27, 1916, Rockwell Papers, WLU.

26 Hall & Nordhoff, *The Lafayette Flying Corps*, Vol. 2, p. 147.

27 Kiffin to James McConnell, September 21, 1916, Rockwell Papers, WLU.

28 A photo of this event may be in iCare, *L'Escadrille La Fayette*, Tome II, p. 51.

29 *Escadrille N.124, Journal des marches et operations pendant la compagne du 14/8/16 au 9/9/17*, entry of 19 Septembre 1916.

30 Kiffin Rockwell to Paul Rockwell, September 20, 1916, Rockwell Papers, WLU.

31 Thénault, *The Story of the Lafayette Escadrille*, p. 76.

32 *Escadrille N.124, Journal des marches et operations pendant la compagne du 14/8/16 au 9/9/17*, entry of 22 Septembre 1916.

33 Paul Rockwell to John Jay Chapman, October 5, 1916, John Jay Chapman Additional Papers, Harvard. *See also* "Kiffin Rockwell to Rest at Place Where Life Ebbed," *The Atlanta Constitution*, October 1, 1916, p. 1; "Paul Rockwell Tells Story of Kiffin's Last Air Fight and of His Drop to Death," *The Atlanta Constitution*, November 11, 1916, p. 5; and "Vow to Avenge Rockwell," *The Chicago Daily News*, September 30, 1916, p. 2.

34 "Mates of Rockwell in Vow of Vengeance," *The Chicago Daily News*, September 30, 1916, p. 1. *See also* Thénault, "L'Escadrille La Fayette," *La Légion Étrangére (revue bimestrielle illustrée militaire et coloniale)*, No. 21, p. 30, (1940).

35 Fred A. Olds, "For the Cause of Liberty," *The Wilmington Morning Star*, August 19, 1917, p. 13. The day before, Michel took a photo of Kiffin standing by his plane in his flight gear. It was the last photograph ever taken of Kiffin.

36 Thénault, *The Story of the Lafayette Escadrille*, p. 78. *See also Escadrille N.124, Journal des marches et operations pendant la compagne du 14/8/16 au 9/9/17*, entry of 23 Septembre 1916.

37 Paul Pavelka to James McConnell, September 26, 1916, Rockwell Papers, WLU; "Paul Rockwell Writes of Brother," *The Greenville News*, December 5, 1916, p. 5.

38 "Mates of Rockwell in Vow of Vengeance," *The Chicago Daily News*, September 30, 1916, p. 1.

39   Hall & Nordhoff, *The Lafayette Flying Corps*, Vol. 2, p. 148. Pavelka, who saw Kiffin's body, told McConnell the explosive bullet had made "a hole as big as your fist in his breast." Paul Pavelka to James McConnell, September 26, 1916, Rockwell Papers, WLU.

40   "Brave Awful Fire to Get Rockwell's Body," *The New York Sun*, September 27, 1916, p. 2.

41   Hall, *One Man's War*, p. 191. In his funeral oration, Thénault stated that he had told the men that "The best and bravest of us all is no longer here." *See* "Kiffin Yates Rockwell," *The Sigma Phi Epsilon Journal*, Vol. 14, No. 2, December 1916, p. 203.

42   Alice Weeks to Fred Taber, September 25, 1916, Weeks, *Greater Love*, p. 167.

43   "Paul Rockwell Writes of Brother," *The Greenville News*, December 5, 1916, p. 5.

44   Paul Rockwell to William "Uncle Billy" Phillips, November 12, 1916, "Kiffin Yates Rockwell," *The Sigma Phi Epsilon Journal*, Vol. 14, No. 2, December 1916, p. 194.

45   "Paul Rockwell Writes of Brother," *The Greenville News*, December 5, 1916, p. 5.

46   "Paul Pavelka, a Soldier of Fortune," *The New York Sun*, December 30, 1917, Fifth Section, p. 4.

47   Bill Thorin to Alice Weeks, September 27, 1916, Weeks, *Greater Love*, p. 171.

48   Bill Thorin to Alice Weeks, September 25, 1916, Weeks, *Greater Love*, p. 170.

Chapter Fifty-five

1   Hall & Nordhoff, *The Lafayette Flying Corps*, Vol. 2, p. 147-48.

2   Paul Pavelka to Alice Weeks, September 24, 1916, Weeks, *Greater Love*, p. 168; Paul Pavelka to James McConnell, September 26, 1916, Rockwell Papers, WLU.

3   McConnell, *Flying for France*, p. 54.

4   Paul Pavelka to James McConnell, September 26, 1916, Rockwell Papers, WLU.

5   Many sources state that Thaw and Paul returned to Luxeuil together. *See* Alice Weeks to Fred Taber, September 25, 1916, Weeks, *Greater Love*, p. 167-68 ("Paul went to Luxeuil yesterday with Thaw."); "Kiffin Y. Rockwell, Slain in Air Battle," *The New York Sun*, September 24, 1916, p. 1; and "U.S. Airman Shot Dead," *The Washington Post*, September 24, 1916, p. A1. Pardoe asserts that Bert Hall was with Thaw in Paris and did not return to Luxeuil for Kiffin's funeral. *See* Pardoe, *The Bad Boy*, p. 96.

6   *Escadrille N.124, Journal des marches et operations pendant la compagne du 14/8/16 au 9/9/17*, entries of 23 and 24 Septembre 1916.

7   *See* "Rockwell's Body Eventually Will Rest Where He Fell," *St. Louis Post-Dispatch*, October 1, 1916, p. A1.

8   "Kiffin Yates Rockwell," *The Sigma Phi Epsilon Journal*, Vol. 14, No. 2, December 1916, p. 202-203.

9   *Id*. p. 203. There must have been a later memorial service in Paris; in November, the *New York Times* ran a photo of Thaw talking to what appears to be Mrs. Weeks. *See The New York Times*, November 5, 1916, Photo section, Part 4, p. 3.

10 Thénault, *The Story of the Lafayette Escadrille*, p. 80.

11 "French Journal Pays Tribute to Rockwell," *The Asheville Citizen*, November 12, 1916, p. 12. *See also* "American Boys in France," *The New York Times*, November 21, 1916, p. 10.

12 The Paris edition of the *New York Herald* carried the news on its front page the day before, along with a photograph of Kiffin in uniform. *See* "Corporal Rockwell, American Aviator, Killed in France," *The New York Herald*, September 24, 1916, p. 1. *Le Petit Parisien* also carried Kiffin's picture, and many other Paris papers reported the news of his death. *See* "L'aviateur américain Rockwell mort pour la France," *Le Petit Parisien*, 25 Septembre, 1916, p. 2; "Un aviateur américain tué au service de la France," *La Lanterne*, 25 Septembre, 1916, p. 2; "Nos Echos," *L'Intransigent*, 24 Septembre, 1916, p. 2; and "Aviateur américain tué au service de la France," *L'Homme Libre*, 25 Septembre, 1916, p. 2.

13 McConnell to Alice Weeks, September 25, 1916, Weeks, *Greater Love*, p. 169. Mac still felt ashamed of his country, too – not long after, he wrote "I cannot reconcile America's attitude

with her much vaunted ideals and am ashamed of the part she has played." McConnell to Bessie Alderman, October 30, 1916, Papers of Edwin A. Alderman, Accession #1001, Special Collections, University of Virginia Library, Charlottesville, Va.

14   James McConnell to Alice Weeks, two letters dated September 25, 1916, Weeks, *Greater Love*, p. 169 and 170. *See also* Paul A. Rockwell, "Our Pioneers in the Air," *The Franco-American Weekly*, March 2, 1918, p. 2.

15   "Dixie Flyers Fall Before Grim Adversary," *The Atlanta Constitution*, May 27, 1917, p. 5.

16   Paul Pavelka to James McConnell, September 27, 1916, Rockwell Papers, WLU.

17   Norman Prince to Alice Weeks, September 25, 1916, Weeks, *Greater Love*, p. 169.

18   "Mates of Rockwell in Vow of Vengeance," *The Chicago Daily News*, September 30, 1916, p. 1. Thus, the "bottle of death" came about only after Kiffin's death, and was meant as a remembrance of his life and sacrifice. An earlier account by Thénault supports this: "I remember a few days later [after Kiffin's funeral, Paul] sent us a bottle of old Bourbon whiskey, which is true nectar for every genuine American. It was an old family liqueur, which had been preserved for over a century. For each victory, the victor was entitled to a thimbleful of the divine drink. Lufbery alone drank more than half the bottle." Thénault, "L'Escadrille La Fayette," *La Légion Étrangére (revue bimestrielle illustrée militaire et coloniale)*, No. 21, p. 30, (1940). The bottle currently on display in Blerancourt provides further support for this version of events – it is labeled "The Famous Escadrille Lafayette Brand," but the name "Lafayette Escadrille" was not in use until more than two months after Kiffin's death. Thus, the front label (which appears much newer than the rear label with signatures) must have been placed on the bottle later. In addition, the first signatures on the bottle appear to be on October 12, 1916, which fits with the idea that the tradition came about after Kiffin's death and was not the result of Kiffin's first victory in May.

19   Paul Pavelka to James McConnell, September 26, 1916, Rockwell Papers, WLU.

20   Paul Rockwell to John Jay Chapman, October 5, 1916, John Jay Chapman Additional Papers, Harvard.

21   "Vow to Avenge Rockwell," *The Chicago Daily News*, September 30, 1916, p. 2.

22   Thénault, *The Story of the Lafayette Escadrille*, p. 80.

23   John Casey, Charles Trinkard and Edgar Bouligny to Paul Rockwell, September 25, 1916, Rockwell Papers, WLU.

24   Charles Trinkard to Paul Rockwell, October 3, 1916, Rockwell Papers, WLU.

25   Laurence Scanlan to Paul Rockwell, September 25, 1916, Rockwell Papers, WLU.

26   Harold Willis to Paul Rockwell, undated *circa* September 25, 1916, Rockwell Papers, WLU.

27   *An American for Lafayette: The Diaries of E.C.C. Genet, Lafayette Escadrille*, p. 97. Genet wrote his mother:
"As you perhaps already know from accounts which already must be in the papers in the States, another one of our brave aviators has been killed at the front. One of the very best of them, too. Paul Rockwell's brother, Kiffin, has gone this time – brought down in an aerial duel. Thus it is and will be right along with all the best ones – those who really do the biggest amount of the fighting. We can't help but predict which ones will be killed. This game is only that of *get* or be *gotten* and those who go right into the fray to *get* are almost sure to be killed sooner or later." Edmond Genet to his mother, September 26, 1916, *War Letters of Edmond Genet*, p. 209.

28   *War Letters of Edmond Genet*, p. 324-325.

29   "Paul Rockwell Tells Story of Kiffin's Last Air Fight and of His Drop to Death," *The Atlanta Constitution*, November 11, 1916, p. 5.

30   John Jay Chapman to Paul Rockwell, telegram dated September 25, 1916, actual telegram is in Rockwell Papers, WLU. Unsure of Paul's current address, John Jay Chapman had sent the telegram to Robert Bliss at the American embassy on September 25, but Paul did not get it until ten days later.

31   Paul Rockwell to John Jay Chapman, October 5, 1916, John Jay Chapman Additional

Papers, Harvard.

Part Four

1   M. René Besnard, *Speeches Delivered*, p. 12.
2   *Manuscript of Col. C. E. Stanton's Speech at Lafayette's Tomb, July 4, 1917*, Albert Hatton Gilmer Collection, MS 062, Skillman Library, Lafayette College (hereafter "Albert Hatton Gilmer Collection"). Thank you to Diane Shaw, the Director of Special Collections & College Archives at the Skillman Library for sending the materials from this collection.

Chapter Fifty-six

3   "Kiffin Rockwell Gets Aeroplane," *The Winston-Salem Journal*, September 14, 1916, p. 3.
4   "Fresh Laurels For Aviator Kiffin Rockwell," *The Winston-Salem Journal*, September 19, 1916, p. 6.
5   "Kiffin Rockwell Killed During Aerial Battle," *The Twin-City Sentinel*, September 25, 1916, p. 7. *See also* "Kiffin Yates Rockwell," *The Sigma Phi Epsilon Journal*, Vol. 14, No. 1, October 1916, p. 16.
6   Kiffin to Loula, September 2, 1916, KYR Papers, NCDNCR.
7   The words are taken verbatim from the actual telegram sent by Lieutenant Thaw to J.A. Susong in Newport, Tennessee. *See* Lieutenant Thaw to J.A. Susong, telegram dated September 23, 1916, Rockwell Papers, WLU. *See also* "Kiffin Rockwell, Famous Atlanta Flyer, Is Killed," *The Atlanta Constitution*, September 24, 1916, p. 1 (quoting telegram as saying "Kiffin killed this morning in aerial battle in Alsace."); and "Kiffin Rockwell Killed During Aerial Battle," *The Twin-City Sentinel*, September 25, 1916, p. 7 (same).
8   Alice Weeks to Loula Rockwell, cablegram dated September 24, 1916, Rockwell Papers, WLU.
9   "A very young French nurse" to Loula Rockwell, October 4, 1916, KYR Papers, NCDNCR.
10   Leila J. Waddell to Loula Rockwell, September 24, 1916, KYR Papers, NCDNCR.
11   Unknown to Loula Rockwell, September 24, 1916, KYR Papers, NCDNCR.
12   James Chester Rockwell, "At the Grave of Lazarus," p. 38, James Chester Rockwell Papers, WFU.
13   "Shall We Meet Again?" by James Chester Rockwell, "An Idle Afternoon," KYR Papers, NCDNCR.
14   "Seabrook Overcome by Cloud of Gas in Verdun Sector," *The Atlanta Constitution*, October 12, 1916, p. 1.
15   J. Cambon, Ministry of Foreign Affairs to Ambassador Sharp, dispatch dated September 29, 1916, reproduced from the unclassified holdings of the National Archives, copy in possession of the author. Cambon begged Ambassador Sharp to accept for himself "and for the family of this brave aviator who came voluntarily to serve France, the expression of condolences of the Government of the Republic."
16   "If I Had A Dozen Sons I Should Want Them to Fight for France," *The Atlanta Constitution*, June 16, 1918, p. 12I.
17   Marjorie Paget to Loula Rockwell, card dated Paris 1916, KYR Papers, NCDNCR.
18   "Requiem for Rockwell," *The New York Sun*, October 13, 1916, p. 3.
19   A few weeks later, the *New York Times* ran a photo of Bill Thaw (with Bert Hall and Dudley Hill) speaking with Mrs. Weeks outside the service. *The New York Times*, November 5, 1916, Picture section, p. 3. That Bert Hall is in the photo is interesting, as Paul Rockwell apparently later accused Hall of never expressing any feelings over Kiffin's death. *See* Pardoe, *The Bad Boy*, p. 98. But although Hall may not have attended the funeral in Luxeuil, he apparently did attend the memorial service in Paris. Still, Paul carried a grudge against Hall for the rest of his life, and many decades later wrote that Hall was "the most perfect specimen of a scoundrel I ever have met ... yet I do not dislike him and wish I could see him again and

try to find out what actuated him." Paul Rockwell to Lawrence C. Newcomb, January 22, 1973, Rockwell Papers, WLU. Whatever Paul felt about him, Hall and Kiffin were usually on the same wavelength, and Hall later asserted that he and Kiffin had an agreement: "If I was killed first, Kiffin would tell certain members of the outfit to go to hell and ... [i]f he was killed first, I would do the same thing for him." Hall, *One Man's War*, p. 126.

20   Alice Weeks to Allen Weeks, October 22, 1916, Weeks, *Greater Love*, p. 175.

21   "Paul Rockwell Writes of Brother," *The Greenville News*, December 5, 1916, p. 5.

22   Clara Young to Loula Rockwell, September 24, 1916, KYR Papers, NCDNCR.

23   John Jay Chapman to Loula Rockwell, telegram dated September 25, 1916, KYR Papers, NCDNCR. After the earlier death of his own son, on August 3, 1916, John Jay had written a similar sentiment to Van Cleef, telling him that "[t]hose Americans who are working and fighting abroad in this war are saving the name of the country – in deed they have saved it." John Jay Chapman to Henry Howell van Cleef, August 3, 1916, copy in Brown University Library.

24   John Jay Chapman to Loula Rockwell, September 26, 1916, KYR Papers, NCDNCR.

25   "For Lafayette," *The Greensboro (NC) News*, September 25, 1916, p. 4.

26   Zinovi Pechkoff to Loula Rockwell, September 24, 1916, KYR Papers, NCDNCR.

27   "Kiffin Rockwell's Death," *The New York Tribune*, October 9, 1916, p. 6. Perhaps it's not a coincidence that Kiffin's words, quoted by Loula, echoed those of Benjamin Franklin who, *while in Paris* in 1777, wrote a friend in America that it was "a common observation here that our cause is the cause of all mankind, and that we are fighting for their liberty in defending our own." *See* Letter from Benjamin Franklin to Samuel Cooper, May 1, 1777 (available at http://franklinpapers.org)

28   Fred A. Olds, "For the Cause of Liberty," *The Wilmington Morning Star*, August 19, 1917, p. 13. Loula reiterated this point the next year, telling an Atlanta reporter that when Kiffin died, "I could thank God that he died facing the enemy of civilization.... And while I am proud of the record he made as a soldier and the standard he set for those who shall fight after him, I am proudest of the character that I have seen develop, through their letters, in both my boys. I would not change it if I could, and if I had a dozen sons I should want them, too, to fight for France." "If I Had A Dozen Sons, I Should Want Them to Fight for France," *The Atlanta Constitution*, June 16, 1918, p. 12I. Loula's statements echo those made by Volumnia in Shakespeare's *Coriolanus*. *See* Shakespeare, *The Tragedy of Coriolanus*, Act. 1, Scene 3 ("Hear me profess sincerely: had I a dozen sons ... I had rather had eleven die nobly for their country than one voluptuously surfeit out of action.").

Chapter Fifty-seven

1   *See* Richard Striner, *Woodrow Wilson and World War I: A Burden Too Great to Bear*, p. 77 (2014). Gerard himself said that Germany's foreign minister "insistently urged me to go ... in order to make every effort to induce the President to do something towards peace[.]" James W. Gerard, *My Four Years in Germany*, p. 250 (1917).

2   Joseph C. Grew to Secretary Robert Lansing, confidential cable dated October 16, 1916, National Archives, Record Group 59, General Records of the Department of State, 1763-2002, Central Decimal Files, 1910-1963, Microcopy 367, Roll 141, File Unit: 763.72/354-13348A.

3   Joseph C. Grew, *Turbulent Era: A Diplomatic Record of Forty Years*, Vol. I, p. 244 (Houghton Mifflin Co. Boston, 1952)

4   *Id.* at p. 243.

5   *Id.*

6   "U.S. Aviators Anger Germans," *The Chicago Tribune*, September 30, 1916, p. 1.

7   As quoted in "German Attack on Our Neutrality Based on American Aviators' Exploits," *The New York Times*, September 30, 1916, p. 1.

8   "German Attack on Our Neutrality Based on American Aviators' Exploits," *The New York Times*, September 30, 1916, p. 1; and "Rockwell Death Stirs Berlin," *The Chicago Daily News*, September 30, 1916, p. 2.

9   As quoted in "German Attack on Our Neutrality Based on American Aviators' Exploits," *The New York Times*, September 30, 1916, p. 1.

10   Joseph C. Grew to Secretary Robert Lansing, confidential cable dated October 16, 1916, National Archives, Record Group 59, General Records of the Department of State, 1763-2002, Central Decimal Files, 1910-1963, Microcopy 367, Roll 141, File Unit: 763.72/354-13348A.

11   Joseph C. Grew, *Turbulent Era: A Diplomatic Record of Forty Years*, Vol. I, p. 244.

12   Joseph C. Grew to Secretary Robert Lansing, confidential cable dated October 16, 1916, National Archives, Record Group 59, General Records of the Department of State, 1763-2002, Central Decimal Files, 1910-1963, Microcopy 367, Roll 141, File Unit: 763.72/354-13348A.

13   Joseph C. Grew to Secretary Robert Lansing, telegram dated October 1, 1916, *Papers Relating to the Foreign Relations of the United States, 1916, Supplement, The World War*, File No. 763.72/2894. (available online at https://history.state.gov/historicaldocuments/frus1916Supp/d386) (accessed February 23, 2019)

14   Joseph C. Grew to Secretary Robert Lansing, confidential cable dated October 16, 1916, National Archives, Record Group 59, General Records of the Department of State, 1763-2002, Central Decimal Files, 1910-1963, Microcopy 367, Roll 141, File Unit: 763.72/354-13348A.

15   Paul Pavelka to Paul Rockwell, October 7, 1916, Rockwell Papers, WLU. The mystery woman was not Mrs. Weeks; she had written Pavelka to place roses on Kiffin's grave. *See* Paul Pavelka to Alice Weeks, October 1, 1916, Weeks, *Greater Love*, p. 171.

16   Paul Pavelka to Alice Weeks, October 6, 1916, Weeks, *Greater Love*, p. 173.

17   "Narrow Escape for Prince in Air Duel," *The Boston Post*, October 10, 1916, p. 20.

18   Paul Pavelka to Paul Rockwell, October 7, 1916, Rockwell Papers, WLU.

19   Paul Pavelka to Paul Rockwell, October 14, 1916, Rockwell Papers, WLU.

20   "Air Battles in Raid Biggest Ever Fought," *The Chicago Daily News*, October 21, 1916, p. 1.

21   *See* John Guttman, "The October 1916 Oberndorf Raid in Germany produced the first American ace," *Air Force Times*, October 12, 1916 (available at https://www.airforcetimes.com/2016/10/12/the-october-1916-oberdorf-raid-in-germany-produced-the-first-american-ace/) (last visited on February 4, 2019)

22   *Id.* Thaw stated that on Prince's return, "it grew hazy and as he neared the landing area he failed to notice a string of telegraph wires. His machine crashed into those, turning over and plunging to the ground. He suffered injuries from which he died." "Thaw Describes Work of American Airmen in France," *The St. Louis Post-Dispatch*, November 21, 1916, p. 7. Paul Rockwell reported that even with his legs broken, Norman ordered that lights be put out on the field so others would not smash and was singing the *Marseillaise* as he was carried off on a stretcher. "Air Battles in Raid Biggest Ever Fought," *The Chicago Daily News*, October 21, 1916, p. 1.

23   "Norman Prince Dies for France," *The Boston Post*, October 16, 1916, p. 1; "Norman Prince Dead," *The New York Sun*, October 16, 1916, p. 1; and "Foreign News," *Aerial Age Weekly*, October 23, 1916.

24   "Debutantes Hold Centre of Hub Society Stage Throughout Merry Week," *The Boston Post*, November 19, 1916, p. 39.

25   Frederick H. Prince to Roscoe Thayer, January 16, 1917, William Roscoe Thayer Papers, (MS Am 1081), Houghton Library, Harvard University. A sad Edmond Genet wrote his mother: "We've lost, as you must already know, the originator of the American *escadrille* – Norman Prince. He died from having had both legs broken in an aerial flight on Oct. 15th. He was in a hospital near the front when he died and very near the end he was decorated with the Legion

of Honor. He certainly deserved it. He was on the *Rochambeau* with me when I came over."
War Letters of Edmond Genet, p. 219.

26   Indeed, a memorandum from Ambassador Bernstorff dated October 18, 1916 stated that "the constellation of war has taken such a form that the German Government foresees the time at which it will be forced to regain the freedom of action that it has reserved to itself in the note of May 4th last." As quoted in Richard Striner, *Woodrow Wilson and World War I: A Burden Too Great to Bear,* p. 78.

27   One reporter for the *Chicago Daily News* reported that "one of the biggest men in Paris" had recently told him: "We seldom have out of our minds what we fear are the pacifist dreams of President Wilson." "British Supporting No Meddling Policy," *The Chicago Daily News,* September 29, 1916, p. 2.

28   "U.S. in Next War, Wilson Declares," *The New York Tribune,* October 27, 1916, p. 10.

29   *Id.*

30   A few years after the war, Paul wrote that it was "a pity Kiffin could not live to see America wake up to war, but I suppose and hope he saw the awakening from another world." Paul Rockwell to Robert House, September 29, 1920, KYR Papers, NCDNCR.

Chapter Fifty-eight

1   "American Fliers to Change Title," *The New York Tribune,* November 3, 1916, p. 1; "American Corps in War to Lose Name," *The New York Sun,* November 3, 1916, p. 1. By way of background, the same sources reported that "When Kiffin Rockwell was killed in September, German newspapers printed violent attacks upon the United States, declaring that the presence of Americans in the French army was proof that this country's neutrality was vanishing."

2   "In the Name of 'Neutrality,'" *The New York Tribune,* November 6, 1916, p. 8. The letter was signed by C. I. Claflin.

3   "Defends American Aviators in France," *The Washington Times,* November 4, 1916, p. 1.

4   *See* Order dated 13 Novembre 1916, *Escadrille N.124, Journal des marches et operations pendant la compagne du 14/8/16 au 9/9/17. See also* Paul Pavelka to Paul Rockwell, November 16, 1916, Rockwell Papers, WLU (says name was changed "for diplomatic reasons.").

5   "Thaw Describes Work of American Airmen in France," *The St. Louis Post-Dispatch,* November 21, 1916, p. 7.

6   James McConnell, "The Day's Work of an American Airman on the Somme," *National Service,* p. 107, Mar. 1917.

7   Dr. Gros took credit for suggesting the change from the "colorless name" of *Escadrille des Volontaires* to the *Lafayette Escadrille. See* Hall, *High Adventure,* p. xxii. However, a letter from the French Minister of Foreign Affairs communicating the decision states that it was suggested by the American ambassador, which must have been referring to Mr. Sharp. *See* Letter dated 2 Decembre 1916, Lafayette Escadrille Memorial Association records, 1923-1928, Film MISC 611, Sterling Memorial Library, Yale University.

8   Loula Rockwell to John Jay Chapman, November 10, 1916, John Jay Chapman Additional Papers, Harvard.

9   "American Boys in France," *The New York Times,* November 21, 1916, p. 10. The writer of the letter mistakenly called him *Henry* Butters.

10   As quoted in Richard Striner, *Woodrow Wilson and World War I: A Burden Too Great to Bear,* p. 82.

11   Richard Striner, *Woodrow Wilson and World War I: A Burden Too Great to Bear,* p. 84.

12   As quoted in William G. Sharp to Secretary Robert Lansing, telegram dated January 10, 1917, in *Papers Relating to the Foreign Relations of the United States, 1917, Supplement, The World War,* File No. 763.72119/370½ (available online at https://history.state.gov/

historicaldocuments/frus1917Supp01v01/d8) (accessed February 23, 2019)

13   *Information Quarterly*, April 1917, p. 116. The foremost Wilson scholar states that "[r]eceipt of the German announcement of unrestricted submarine war on January 31 was a grievous blow to Wilson." Arthur S. Link, "That Cobb Interview," *The Journal of American History*, Vol. 72, No. 1, (Jun. 1985), p. 9.

14   *Information Quarterly*, April 1917, p. 116.

15   Arthur S. Link, "That Cobb Interview," *The Journal of American History*, Vol. 72, No. 1, (Jun. 1985), p. 9.

16   Robert W. Tucker, *Woodrow Wilson and the Great War: Reconsidering America's Neutrality, 1914-1917*, p. 189 (University of Virginia Press, 2007).

17   Hohler to Hardinge, March 23, 1917, as quoted in Thomas Boghardt, *The Zimmermann Telegram: Intelligence, Diplomacy, and America's Entry Into World War I*, p. 183 (Naval Institute Press, 2012).

18   "Over the period from February 3 through April 4, 1917, the Germans sank a total of nine American ships." Rodney Carlisle, *Sovereignty at Sea: U.S. Merchant Ships and American Entry into World War 1*, p. xiii (University Press of Florida, 2009).

19   "State of War Now Exists; Wilson Waits on Congress," *The Evening World*, March 19, 1917, p. 1. *See* Carlisle, *Sovereignty at Sea: U.S. Merchant Ships and American Entry into World War 1*, p. 106.

20   "Vigilancia's Captain Talks," *The New York Sun*, March 21, 1917, p. 2; Carlisle, *Sovereignty at Sea: U.S. Merchant Ships and American Entry into World War 1*, p. 9.

21   "Does Mr. Wilson's Incredulity Still Persist?", *The New York Sun*, March 19, 1917, p. 12.

22   As quoted in "Comment of Today's Newspapers on Sinkings of American Ships," *The New York Times*, March 19, 1917, p. 2.

23   "Virtually a State of War," *The Brooklyn Daily Eagle*, March 19, 1917, p. 6.

24   Arthur S. Link, "That Cobb Interview," *The Journal of American History*, Vol. 72, No. 1, (Jun. 1985), p. 8.

25   One interesting book labels the *Vigilancia, City of Memphis*, and *Illinois* the "tipping point ships," and convincingly asserts that "the three events together constituted the long-awaited set of overt acts, and constituted the tipping point in the decision for war." Carlisle, *Sovereignty at Sea: U.S. Merchant Ships and American Entry into World War 1*, p. 106.

26   "Declaration of War Against Germany Expected at Session," *The Buffalo Evening Times*, March 21, 1917, p. 1.

27   "The Madison Square Garden Meeting," *The New York Tribune*, March 23, 1917, p. 6.

28   National Archives, Records of the Adjutant General's Office (Record Group 94), Record Cards, 1890-1917 (entry 26), letters dated February 24 and 26, 1917, between George Squier and H.P. McCain. McCain's nephew was the grandfather of John McCain, the future U.S. Senator and presidential candidate.

29   National Archives, Records of the Adjutant General's Office (Record Group 94), Record Cards, 1890-1917 (entry 26), letters dated February 24 and 26, 1917, between George Squier and H.P. McCain.

Chapter Fifty-nine

1   "Chicagoan is Back at Front," *The Chicago Daily News*, November 13, 1916, p. 2.

2   McConnell to Alice Weeks, November 15, 1916, Weeks, *Greater Love*, p. 181-82. Paul Pavelka had earlier voiced a similar sentiment, telling Paul: "I miss Kiffin and am getting lower in courage each day." Paul Pavelka to Paul Rockwell, October 1, 1916, Rockwell Papers, WLU.

3   "Yankee Flyers as Skillful as Allies or Foes," *The Chicago Tribune*, November 12, 1916, Part 2, p. 2.

4   One account noted that Jeanne was "heiress to one of the largest fortunes in France." "Paul Rockwell Weds Mlle. Jeanne Leygues," *The Atlanta Constitution*, December 22, 1916, p. 7.

5 "American Weds in Paris," *The Washington Post*, December 3, 1916, p. 14. *See also* "Mariages," *Le Gaulois*, 20 Decembre 1916, p. 3.

6 "Paul Rockwell, Flier, Weds French Heiress," *The New York Tribune*, December 22, 1916, p. 9.

7 James McConnell to Paul Rockwell, December 17, 1916, McConnell Collection, UVA. The cigarette case, held by the university of Virginia as part of the James Rogers McConnell collection, was engraved "J. R. McC. en Souvenir du 4 December 1916."

8 Paul later called *Flying for France* "by far the best of all the written accounts" of the squadron. *See* "James R. McConnell," biographical sketch likely written by Paul Rockwell, in the James Rogers McConnell Collection [Truitt] NASM.XXXX.0232, National Air and Space Museum Archives.

9 *See* Bailey & Cony, *The French Air Service War Chronology*, p. 83, 87, 90.

10 James R. McConnell, "The Day's Work of an American Airman on the Somme," *National Service*, March 1917, p. 115.

11 "Americans Who Died for France Honored," *The Boston Globe*, January 22, 1917, p. 3.

12 Herman Chatkoff to Alice Weeks, January 22, 1917, Weeks, *Greater Love*, p. 193.

13 M. René Besnard, *Speeches Delivered*, p. 16.

14 "Tribute Paid Americans Who Have Been Killed Fighting for France," *The Atlanta Constitution*, January 22, 1917, p. 2; and Herman Chatkoff to Alice Weeks, January 22, 1917, Weeks, *Greater Love*, p. 193.

15 Alan Seeger, "Champagne, 1914-15."

16 Paul Rockwell to Alice Weeks, February 2, 1917, Weeks, *Greater Love*, p. 196.

17 McConnell wrote his publisher that the big check "enabled me to have the time of my life..." "M'Connell Hoped to Serve America," *The New York Times*, March 30, 1917, p. 12. February 3 was also Paul's 28th birthday.

18 "M'Connell Hoped to Serve America," *The New York Times*, March 30, 1917, p. 12.

19 Quote in memoir by Marcelle Guerin, McConnell Collection, UVA.

20 Paul Ayres Rockwell, "Our Pioneers in the Air," *The Franco-American Weekly*, March 2, 1918, p. 2-3.

21 Willis Haviland to Alice Weeks, May 23, 1917, Weeks, *Greater Love*, p. 212.

22 "Chicago Flyer Died for Love of France," *The Chicago Daily News*, March 28, 1917, p. 2.

23 Paul Ayres Rockwell, "Our Pioneers in the Air," *The Franco-American Weekly*, March 2, 1918, p. 2-3. McConnell's words bring to mind a quote that appeared in the *The Harvard Graduate's Magazine* around that time: "War is an enormously serious matter, a tragically sad matter in its maiming and killing of the body, and sometimes very beautiful and glorious in its remaking of the soul." "From A Graduate's Window," *The Harvard Graduate's Magazine*, Vol. XXV, 1916-1917, p. 315 (Mar. 1917).

24 Gordon, *Lafayette Escadrille Pilot Biographies*, p. 42.

25 *See* "Bishop Brent Conducts Memorial Service for James R. McConnell and Henry Suckley," typewritten article likely written by Paul Rockwell and published in the *Chicago Daily News*, circa April 1917, in the James Rogers McConnell Collection [Truitt] NASM.XXXX.0232, National Air and Space Museum Archives.

26 "Féridah" to Alice Weeks, April 2, 1917, Weeks, *Greater Love*, p. 204.

27 Polly Root to Julia Hollansbee (McConnell's sister), April 4, 1917, in the James Rogers McConnell Collection [Truitt] NASM.XXXX.0232, National Air and Space Museum Archives.

28 Paul Rockwell to Alice Weeks, April 14, 1917, Weeks, *Greater Love*, p. 206.

29 "Americans in France," *The Asheville Citizen*, April 10, 1917, p. 4.

30 Edmond Genet to his mother, April 15, 1916, *War Letters of Edmond Genet*, p. 318.

31 "U.S. Scion of Envoy Genet Killed in Air," *The Chicago Daily News*, April 19, 1917, p. 1; and "First to Die Under U.S. Flag," *The Chicago Daily News*, April 19, 1917, p. 1.

Chapter Sixty

1   "U.S. Flag Presented to the French Army," *The Chicago Daily News*, July 6, 1917, p. 2.
2   "Paris acclame l'armee américaine," *La Lanterne*, 5 Juillet 1917, p. 1.
3   "A la gloire de nos allies d'amerique," *Le Matin*, 5 Juillet 1917, p. 1.
4   "Paris acclame l'armee américaine," *La Lanterne*, 5 Juillet 1917, p. 1. Here is a portion of the words spoken by the marquis of Dampierre to General Pershing: "In the name and in the glorious memory of the French officers who 140 years ago had the honor to fight on sea or land in the new world to defend rising American liberty we, the descendants of those combatants, feel ourselves greatly honored in offering to you, the strenuous and already glorious head of the American forces in France, these two guidons, as the double symbol of a precious memorial and a victorious omen. Those stars and stripes are the same our people formerly cheered as the first emblem of democracy. French gentlemen have fought for this emblem. French blood was spilt. French lives and loves were broken to make it living and strong. It ought to fly at the zenith of the new world as the victorious flag of justice and liberty. And now that flag we welcome to the soil of our old France as the valiant comrade of our colors in defending the rights of all humanity, for while all our allies are now our friends only the American and French armies are such old comrades – nay, more – comrades who have never fallen out." "U.S. Flag Presented to the French Army," *The Chicago Daily News*, July 6, 1917, p. 2.
5   "U.S. Flag Presented to the French Army," *The Chicago Daily News*, July 6, 1917, p. 2.
6   Samuel N. Watson, *Those Paris Years*, p. 280-81 (1936). Paul Rockwell, who was surely there, rendered a slightly different account of Watson's words. *See* "U.S. Flag Presented to the French Army," *The Chicago Daily News*, July 6, 1917, p. 2.
7   Samuel N. Watson, *Those Paris Years*, p. 281.
8   "La République francaise a célébré hier la féte nationale américaine," *Le Radical*, 5 Juillet 1917, p. 1.
9   "Paris a fait aux soldats americains un accueil inoubliable, triumphal," *Le Petit Journal*, 5 Juillet 1917, p. 1.
10 John J. Pershing, *My Experiences in the World War*, Volume 1, p. 92.
11 "La République francaise a célébré hier la féte nationale américaine," *Le Radical*, 5 Juillet 1917, p. 1.
12 "Paris Goes Wild Over Our Troops in July 4 Parade," *The New York Times*, July 5, 1917, p. 1.
13 "Ovation to U.S. Army at Parade in Paris," *The Chicago Daily News*, July 5, 1917, p. 4.
14 "A la gloire de nos allies d'amerique," *Le Matin*, 5 Juillet 1917, p. 1.
15 "Paris a fait aux soldats americains un accueil inoubliable, triumphal," *Le Petit Journal*, 5 Juillet 1917, p. 1. *See also* Heywood Broun, *The A.E.F. - With General Pershing and the American Forces*, p. 33 (1919); and "Ovation to U.S. Army at Parade in Paris," *The Chicago Daily News*, July 5, 1917, p. 4 ("The name Teddy became suddenly popular as an expression of good will, perhaps because it is easily pronounced by the French.").
16 John J. Pershing, *My Experiences in the World War*, Volume 1, p. 92.
17 Hall & Nordhoff, *The Lafayette Flying Corps*, Vol. 2, p. 17.
18 Stanton's words are quoted directly from his own manuscript. *Colonel C.E. Stanton's Speech at Lafayette's Tomb, July 4, 1917*, Albert Hatton Gilmer Collection. Video of the event, and the parade that preceded it can be viewed at the following link. http://archives.ecpad.fr/le-4-juillet-1917-a-paris-et-le-serment-sur-la-tombe-du-marquis-de-la-fayette/) (visited on March 16, 2019) Some wonderful pictures of the days' events can be found in *Le Monde Illustré*, 14 Juillet 1917, p. 18-22.
19 "Ovation to U.S. Army at Parade in Paris," *The Chicago Daily News*, July 5, 1917, p. 4. This article quotes Pershing as saying: "I had intended to say nothing, but I feel so deeply the significance of this occasion that I do not desire it to pass without some expression on my part."

20 *Transcribed copy of remarks made by General Pershing at the Tomb of Lafayette, Picpus Cemetery, Paris, France, July 4, 1917*, Albert Hatton Gilmer Collection.

21 Clark Hill, "Lafayette We Are Here," sheet music published by Delmar Music Co., Chicago, Illinois (March 13, 1919).

Afterword

1 "Ambulance Film a Monument to Brave Aviator," *The Triangle*, p. 8 (October 7, 1916).

2 As quoted in Rockwell, *American Fighters*, p. 352.

3 Loula Rockwell to Robert House, September 2, 1920, KYR Papers, NCDNCR.

4 Kiffin to Loula, June 15, 1915, Rockwell Papers, WLU.

5 Loula to Joseph R. Anderson, September 10, 1921, Rockwell Files, VMI.

6 Loula Rockwell to Robert House, September 2, 1920, KYR Papers, NCDNCR.

7 Paul Rockwell, "Our Pioneers in the Air," *The Franco-American Weekly*, March 2, 1918, p. 3.

8 Thénault, *The Lafayette Escadrille*, p. xiv.

9 Kiffin to Vicomte du Peloux, May 18, 1915, *War Letters*, p. 51.

10 Transcribed Interview of Paul Rockwell by Dr. Louis D. Silveri, July 22, 1976, p. 8 (Southern Highlands Research Center, University of North Carolina at Asheville).

11 "From A Graduate's Window," *The Harvard Graduate's Magazine*, Vol. XXV, 1916-1917, p. 185 (Dec. 1916).

12 Whitehouse, *Legion of the Lafayette*, p. xiv

13 "Lafayette Escadrille – Lafayette Flying Corps," a catalogue of books created by The Colophon Book Shop, in possession of the author.

14 Edmund Gros, introduction to Hall, *High Adventure*, p. xxiii.

The Boys Who Remembered Lafayette

1 I am not entirely convinced the translation is accurate, but the following article says something similar. "Americans Fighting for France," *The Detroit Free Press*, August 13, 1916, p. 74.

2 Edmund Gros to John Jay Chapman, July 5, 1919, John Jay Chapman Additional Papers, Harvard.

3 "Drifting and dreaming," *The Belles Lettres*, August 1, 1885, p. 1.

Author's Note

4 "Troops Have Forms for Letter Writing," *The New York Sun*, May 16, 1915, Sec. 5, p. 4.